BOOKS BY
DOUGLAS SOUTHALL FREEMAN

———

LEE'S LIEUTENANTS

THE SOUTH TO POSTERITY

R. E. LEE

———

CHARLES SCRIBNER'S SONS

LEE'S LIEUTENANTS

VOLUME TWO

Cedar Mountain to Chancellorsville

LEE'S LIEUTENANTS

A Study in Command

BY DOUGLAS SOUTHALL FREEMAN

◆❯ VOLUME TWO ❮◆

CEDAR MOUNTAIN TO CHANCELLORSVILLE

A CHARLES SCRIBNER'S SONS BOOK

MACMILLAN PUBLISHING COMPANY

NEW YORK

Charles Scribner's Sons
Macmillan Publishing Company
866 Third Avenue, New York, NY 10022
Collier Macmillan Canada, Inc.

Library of Congress Catalog Card Number 77-82742
ISBN 0-684-15487-0

Macmillan books are available at special discounts for bulk
purchases for sales promotions, premiums, fund-raising, or
educational use.

For details, contact:
Special Sales Director
Macmillan Publishing Company
866 Third Avenue
New York, NY 10022

10 9 8 7

Printed in the United States of America

CONTENTS

vii

APPENDIX

ILLUSTRATIONS

MAPS

INTRODUCTION

INTRODUCTION

Would the Army of Northern Virginia be more successful under R. E. Lee than it had been under Joseph E. Johnston; had a wise choice of leaders been made after the Seven Days? Those were questions that might have been asked after Malvern Hill. A succession of battles among the most celebrated in the history of nineteenth-century warfare gave the answer. Lee quickly showed that he could simplify strategy to fit the limited experience of staff and line, and with inferior forces could continue to defeat changing adversaries. Within three months "Stonewall" Jackson dissipated whatever doubts may have been raised regarding his ability to co-operate as a subordinate after he had won success as an independent commander. He became of all Lee's executive officers the most understanding and the most co-operative. James Longstreet proved himself the possessor of the solid qualities with which Gustavus Smith mistakenly had been credited six months previously. Ewell remained as picturesque and as chivalrous as he had been during the Valley Campaign. A. P. Hill displayed under Jackson the same fiery sensitiveness that had provoked trouble with Longstreet. Other men who had shown promise in June, 1862, continued to develop and to justify their higher commissions. Most of the promoted officers who failed or disappointed expectations did so because they would not accept on the striking hour or at the dangerous post the responsibility of full and instant action. Not rashness but irresolution, not the fury of the field but the fear of failure dragged them down.

Under this command, steadily improving, the Army of Northern Virginia won resounding victories in 1862–63, but seldom easily or at light cost. The Army faced a foe strong, well-equipped and determined. A venerable Confederate, with judgment time-sharpened and humor not dulled, spoke in remembrance of many a close action when he said: "My son, never disparage the Army of the Potomac; it was the greatest army of the age, with the exception of one that modesty forbids me to mention." That Union army developed a personality of its own. It no longer was a vague adversary with which the Confederates wrestled in the dark. The Army of Northern Virginia came to know something of the tactical methods of different Union commanders and something even of the distinctive qualities of the various Corps. Foes were identified and respected, mocked or despised.

The rifles and the artillery of these Federals took greedy toll of officers. Death was on the heels of fame. Never was there any certitude of command, any guarantee that a fighting-machine which was rolling faultlessly forward might not break down overnight and require roadside repair under fire. Always some Division was without a commander; daily the search for new leaders went on; the roster of the army changed ceaselessly. Every campaign had to be followed by a reorganization.

From August, 1862, through May, 1863, the period covered by these chapters, a new type of officer was rising. He usually commanded already a Brigade, but in the absence of an invalided chief, he may have shown himself capable of leading a Division. Before the long roll was beaten on the Rappahannock for the second offensive beyond the Potomac, one or more of this type of officer was a Major General. He was not yet qualified to counsel on strategy. Good administration was his continuing credit. His firm, intelligent discipline was the explanation of the steadiness, the fire power, the élan of those magnificent troops of his who always were anonymous and, in the reports, were inarticulate save when their volleys spoke. Their commander was rapid on the march. In the camp he could not afford to be negligent. He was learning, he was rounding to the full stature of a leader, but it was at the front of battle that he shone. Combat was his glory. At Second Manassas, he was John Hood; at South Mountain he was Robert Rodes; at Sharpsburg he was John Cooke, and at Chancellorsville he was a goodly fellowship, Rodes and Ramseur and Pender and Wilcox. The average age of these young leaders in 1862 was 31. Most of them received professional training in arms and for that reason had early opportunity, but they rose by performance that none could dispute or disparage. What they had, they earned.

When one has read enough about these men to distinguish them as individuals, it is as pleasant to see them advance in service and in fame as it is to hear of the good fortune of friends. The tragic element in the changing drama appears to be relieved by the readiness with which new men of capacity take the place and equal the exploits of their instructors and models. One thinks the picture is that of an endless file of eager young Generals on horse-back—until the reorganization after Chancellorsville is reached.

Then came what was mentioned in the Foreword as a major surprise of this study: The rear of the file was reached; qualified men to take the place of those who failed or fell were not to be found in sufficient number. A few were emerging. Doubtless some Colonels and perhaps some Captains possessed qualities of higher command as yet undisclosed; but in several Brigades that had the names of many battles stencilled on their banners, no Colonel possessed the full equipment for brigade leadership. The school of combat did not graduate men enough to make good the casualties of instruction. Command, which always had been an adventure, became after Chancellorsville a gamble against length-ening odds.

This crisis in command was deepened by the mortal wound-ing of Jackson. He is the central figure of this volume. The his-tory of the Army from Cedar Mountain to Sharpsburg and back again to the Rappahannock is, in its finest lines, his military biog-raphy. By the spring of 1863 he personified the mobility, the reso-lution and the offensive daring of the army. His death was admit-ted to be a defeat that cancelled all the gains of Chancellorsville. Lee was paying no exaggerated funerary tribute when he said of Jackson, "I know not how to replace him." In writing Hood, "we must all do more than formerly," Lee meant precisely that. If Southern independence was to be won, an Army in which Jack-son no longer led a Corps was one to which every officer had to contribute more of effort and of military wisdom. The answering pledge of the army was given in those high words of Dorsey Pender's with which this volume closes; but deepest anxiety was mingled with submissive faith in Lee's lament: "God's will be done! I trust He will raise up some one in his place." Fate could not have shaped a nobler contrast for the military fame of Jack·

son. After the Seven Days had shown that Jackson the victoriou: independent commander was an awkward and embarrassed subordinate, it might have been asked, Could the Army win victories with him? As the men fall in for the march to Pennsylvania on the last page of this volume, the question is, Can the Army continue to achieve success without Jackson?

Such, in outline, is the story these pages tell. The development of the leaders and not the strategy of the campaigns is the theme. This does not imply that the battles have lost their appeal. Pulse beats up after eighty years at the sight of Maxcy Gregg with his grandfather's scimitar in his hand as he cries at Groveton, "Let us die here, my men; let us die here." Blood surges still as Powell Hill in his red shirt rides on the field of Sharpsburg. Americans of every racial stock must feel pride in soldiers who could sweep around the flank of an enemy and rush forward as the Second Corps did, when Jackson put his watch back in his pocket and said to Rodes, "You can go forward, then." Over and over, these tales will be told and adorned, but the historians have done their work. Little will be added to the narrative of Confederate military operations in Virginia during 1862–63. The story is apt to stand substantially as it has been since Lee's confidential dispatches to Davis were made public in 1915, unless, improbably, some cache of the wartime letters of Longstreet or of Powell Hill be discovered. Certainly these chapters, while they supply some new details of Cedar Mountain and of Suffolk, and resolve a few doubts, change in no material way the accepted version of any of the operations. Further study of Lee's army may prove both more profitable and more interesting where it deals with men and morale than where it merely describes in new terms the familiar strategy and the battles.

In the development of these sketches against the background of the army command, a continuing difficulty has been that of portraying accurately without overpainting. The picture of Powell Hill presents singular temptation to a writer. Because the outline is obscure, there is risk of attempting to draw too many inferences from the new material on his controversy with Jackson. In the absence of adequate records, it has been necessary to present Hill solely as he raged and fought or wrote and spoke remembered words. Restraint may sacrifice drama but it preserves truth. Although Hill is a clear figure only in the lightning flash of his wrath, it is the man one sees then and not the writer's theory of what the man might have been. Longstreet presents the same problem in this volume as in the last. His was not a nature to flash or to flame. He talked little, but his silence should not be assumed to cover some deep mystery. Essentially a solid, unimaginative, workaday soldier who did not pretend to brilliance, he would be caricatured in this part of the history of the army command were he painted in high color. A day was coming when the flash of the guns in the Peach Orchard made every line of his face stand out.

In contrast to Longstreet and to Hill, this volume presents Jackson at the tragic climax of his career when the taste of our generation would tone down the pigments his contemporaries used. As stated in the Foreword, he does not lend himself to portraiture. His features, his peculiarities and his subtler characteristics must be developed slowly, shade after shade, by verbal color printing. The winter of 1862–63 at Moss Neck manifestly offered opportunity of adding the final impression. There it was that he said of the Federals, "We must do more than defeat their armies; we must destroy them." At a time when he was preparing his officers for this war to the death, he was ripping the braid from his cap to make a fillet for five-year Janie Corbin. For her, too, he was cutting out long, long lines of paper dolls which, being joined elbow to elbow, he characteristically styled the Stonewall Brigade. That was one of many contrasts difficult to present otherwise than in the spirit of the sentimental age in which Jackson lived.

Even more of perplexity was presented in the treatment of his death. That event was regarded in the South, after 1865, as equal in fate with secession or the repulse at Gettysburg or the loss of Vicksburg. Sentimentality half blinded itself in weeping over him. How were those last days to be described? Mrs. Jackson fortunately was realistic and at the same time measurably restrained in her narrative. Jed. Hotchkiss' love of nature led him to note in his diary what flowers were blooming then and what trees were in blossom. Most of the needed "properties" were at hand. All the incidents could be authenticated. Historically there was no trouble except for a few conflicts of date and a most exasperating rounded eloquence to the remarks Jackson's ministerial biographer insisted on putting in the dying man's mouth. The literary task was to reflect the sentiment of Jackson's day, an historical state of mind, without seeming to overwrite and to sentimentalize. It is not probable that the treatment given the two passages that called for the most delicate handling—Jackson's farewell to his wife on April 29 and the moment of his death —will satisfy readers unfamiliar with the contemporary accounts. Most certainly, on the other hand, Jackson's chaplain and Maj. R. L. Dabney would have insisted that the account in these pages failed to stress the moral lesson and the spiritual grandeur of Jackson's death.

If this difficulty of presentation has been greater than was apprehended, that of dealing with General Lee's proper place in this narrative proves in this second volume to have settled itself. An earlier book had been written entirely from his point of view. The lamp had been held on him. It was through his field glasses that every battlefield was examined. In these sketches, where General Lee appeared, he was to be observed, not the observer. That seemed a logical difference of method. The one question was whether the historical facts would justify literary logic. It now appears that established historical realities probably would have forced the abandonment of any other plan of treatment. In letters of brigadiers and of some division commanders, General Lee was mentioned with surprising infrequency. Most soldiers saw the nearer, lesser leaders. This was not because Lee hid himself behind clouds of tentage. Unostentatiously, he moved among his troops as duty required, but when army business did not compel him to be afield, his modesty kept him in the background. There he remained to counsel and to correct. He dominated a scene in which he never was deliberately conspicuous. His were the decisions, his the moral influence that restrained the violent and strengthened the discouraged; his equally was the wisdom that trusted competence, encouraged initiative and did not hamper ability by needless direction. He respected the individuality of his lieutenants and trusted their direction so long as it was intelligent. When this became plain, as the research progressed, there remained no appreciable risk that the historical verities would be distorted by saying little of Lee himself in this study of his lieutenants.

Writers on military history present one test of their trustworthiness in the limits they recommend for the application of the facts they establish. Doomed would be the army that fought its battles "out of books." Hopeless would be the strategy that disdained tactical changes wrought by new weapons, increased mobility, higher fire power, quicker communication and aerial observation. No less certainly, the strategy that ignores history because of tactical changes deprives itself of light that may relieve some of the darkness of a night of decision. In war as in much besides, the great maxim of George Adam Smith is vindicated: "History never repeats itself without interpreting itself." The writer consequently is grateful that this volume of a work undertaken in 1936, when war seemed remote, should have become ready for publication in a year that may parallel events described here. Ours it may be in 1943 to duplicate the experience of the Army of Northern Virginia from the Seven Days to Chancellorsville. In the next phase of this Second World War, the period from our Gettysburg to Appomattox, may the fortunes of our men be not those of the Army of Northern Virginia but those of its gallant adversary, the Army of the Potomac.

DOUGLAS SOUTHALL FREEMAN

Westbourne,
Richmond, Va.
Feb. 21, 1943.

Dramatis Personæ"

Officers sketched in this volume are here listed substantially in the chronological order in which they attained new distinction, died, rendered their most conspicuous service, or lost their prominence in the Army.

Principal lieutenants, some of whom have established per-
manently their position. Others are waning in fame
or owe their distinction more to their position than
to their service.

THOMAS JONATHAN JACKSON

He has a brief period of semi-independent command, during which he does not excel. After Lee joins him again he develops incredibly and gives by his brilliant obedience to orders the unqualified answer to the ugly questions asked after the Seven Days. His are the most shining of the Army's achievements during the period of its greatest prowess. First place professionally among Lee's Lieutenants and popular reputation exceeding his chief's he wins; but in army administration he is not uniformly successful. Perhaps because of his stern conceptions of duty, he is exacting of his subordinates. The result is a continuing bitter quarrel with A. P. Hill and inability to find men who fulfill his standards of command. In consequence, some of the units of Jackson's Corps suffer excessively from attrition. Although he always is marching or winning a battle or preparing for another, he cannot forget the home he has not visited in two years or the baby he never has seen. He is not homesick—that would be unsoldierly weakness—but, in the spring of 1863, he does not attempt to conceal his satisfaction at having his family visit him. After that comes what the Greeks would have termed apotheosis.

JAMES LONGSTREET

"Old Pete" is the senior Lieutenant General and the commander of the First Corps of the Army of Northern Virginia. He improves his already high rating as an army administrator and, as yet, he has little trouble with organization. His opportunities are not so numerous nor so dazzling as Jackson's. During this period of ten months, except for one afternoon near Manassas, he does not have to fight an offensive battle. This experience may be spoiling him, may be leading him to think that if he chooses a good position and remains there, an impatient enemy will attack and will give him all the advantage of the defensive. Nobody seems aware of this at the time. He has a curious experience in separate command of Southside Virginia, and there he carries on a correspondence in a tone that a sensitive partisan of General Lee's might have disliked. Lee took no offense. In his eyes, Longstreet remains what he called his stout lieutenant after Sharpsburg—my "war horse." Longstreet is dependable, solid, an excellent tactician, not a great strategist: Will he be content to be what he admirably is?

JAMES EWELL BROWN STUART

The chief of cavalry, now thirty years of age, has only one large opportunity between Malvern Hill and the end of April, 1863. He makes the most of that in a fast, horse-killing raid. Spectacular raids, in fact, are becoming his specialty, but he continues to learn the arts of reconnaissance, observation and military intelligence. Unexpectedly, at midnight, he is called to the largest command he ever has exercised, and over infantry, not cavalry. While he fulfills the expectations of his friends, somehow he does not get quite the measure of praise he seems to have expected. That is one of his peculiarities—that love of praise, and it does not diminish as his solid fame increases. He seeks all the credit to which he possibly can shape a title. "Jeb" is at his best where he is liked. He is not happy with those who do not admire him. That is why he is distinctly a "Jackson man," and that the reason, also, for growing friction with "Grumble" Jones and perhaps with others. Good taste Stuart does not always display. His headquarters music, for instance, is furnished by a fiddle, a banjo and a pair of bones. At heart, this noisy, ostenta-

"JEB" STUART

tious young man fears God and loves country. He may
be a courtier; his most depreciative critic never denies he
is a fighter.

AMBROSE POWELL HILL

Unequal fortune is his during the ten months covered by
this volume. He begins by displeasing Jackson and until
the end he is at odds with his chief. Hill is proud and
sensitive. Insistent on all his rights, he is intent on his
duties. He harbors his feeling of injustice at the hands of
Jackson, but he is as quick to demand fair play for his
subordinates as for himself. Perhaps there is something
of the army politician in him; there certainly is no dis-
taste on his part for the praise which John M. Daniel
voices in the carping *Richmond Examiner*. None of this
affects Hill's Division, which probably is the best in the
Army. It remains the largest not only because it contains six Brigades, but also because it has intelligent administration at his hands. He has three great days in
these chapters. Then, at the close of the third of them, a
trivial injury cheats him of his rightful part in the glory
of the Army's high noon.

RICHARD STODDERT EWELL

The character *sui generis* of Lee's Army is in this part of
the narrative for no more than three weeks of brilliant
performance. Then he loses a leg. For months he is an
impatient invalid, but unlike some invalids he does not
try to manage and to order. He *is* the same amusing,
chirping dyspeptic, but he is as gallantly generous as ever.
His career has a curious sequence—wound, promotion,
marriage. When he, as notorious a bachelor as "Jube"
Early, returns to the Army with a wife, he is cheered and
she is welcomed. Soon there is a suspicion that "Old Bald
Head" is changed and not altogether for the better. It
may be difficult for even a Lieutenant General to have
two commanders.

A. P. HILL

JUBAL ANDERSON EARLY

On occasion, "Jube" snarls so raspingly that he seems to raise a question whether he is acting division commander or still at heart the Commonwealth's Attorney of Franklin County, Virginia. In this period he shows rapid development as a soldier. Stubbornness in combat takes the place of impetuosity. If he knew or cared a little more about the art of ingratiation, he would be something of a hero. Certainly, as an executive officer, his fighting record from Cedar Mountain to Salem Church is second only to that of Jackson himself.

DANIEL HARVEY HILL

Much of the strength of Harvey Hill is shown in these pages and, with it, the weakness of which he was suspected in the days after Malvern Hill. It is not so much a lack of control of his critical and sometimes gloomy temperament as it is a disgust for routine administrative duty and a singular unwillingness to make important decisions off the field. He increases his reputation as a combat officer but he barely escapes disaster in a certain mountain battle in Maryland where the full responsibility rests on him. It is his fate—not unusual in war—to be denied the service he magnificently performed and to be assigned unwelcome duty for which he has no aptitude. Before this part of the tragedy ends, he leaves the scene of his Virginia successes to return once and briefly in 1864.

JOHN BELL HOOD

This magnificent young Kentuckian, by choice a Texan, becomes in these pages a major figure. He now is a division commander whose soldiers are, man for man, perhaps the best combat troops in the Army, though in numbers they never approach and in fame do not equal, as yet, Powell Hill's "Light Division." Hood is conspicuous in three of the battles described here. If, in one, he fails to win the commendation of Longstreet, it may be evidence

JUBAL A. EARLY

of Hood's rising fame that the Chief of the First Corps does not press a complaint. Later, on a quiet front, Hood has one ambition only—to get back to the fight. In the spring of 1863, he is 32 years of age. As the fighting quality of his troops is, in a measure, of his making, he appears to have a brilliant future. He is loyal to his corps commander, Longstreet, but it is to the General-in-chief that he looks.

RICHARD HERON ANDERSON

Promoted Major General after the Seven Days, "Dick" Anderson receives at Sharpsburg a wound which is not altogether misfortune because it demonstrates how much of the efficiency of his Division is due to his personal influence and leadership. He has no subsequent opportunity till Chancellorsville. Then he shows himself willing that Stuart shall have the glory and he the sense of duty done; but the commanding General has seen what has happened and, in the list of those who may lead a Corps, if need be, the name of Anderson is entered. He now is a distinguished figure in the Army.

WILLIAM NELSON PENDLETON

Small comfort and no promotion come to the Chief of Artillery. Instead, during September, some ridicule and contempt are visited on him for mishandling an operation that might have had disastrous consequences. Then he earns solid credit for sound reasoning, hard work and the tactful adjustment of posts and personalities in an admirable reorganization of the artillery. Before he can expand in the satisfaction he deserves, doubtful disposition of his guns on a difficult day brings new humiliation. His is a curious fate: while young professional artillerists and infantrymen laugh at him, most of them have high admiration and proudly admitted affection for his magnificent son.

JOHN B. HOOD

Lesser leaders who, in some instances, fail and deserve to disappear and, in other cases, evidently are the rising "new men" of the Army.

CHARLES S. WINDER

Somewhat belatedly, this Marylander and professional soldier, age 33, is beginning in August, 1862, to be credited with the abilities he had demonstrated in the Valley Campaign the previous spring; but Fate outruns Fame. At Cedar Mountain, before he wins formal command of Jackson's old Division, he fights his last battle. Like Robert Garnett, he seemed to have the mould and the hall mark of the true soldier.

ISAAC RIDGEWAY TRIMBLE

In the comradeship of the Army's command, this senior fulfills his ambition and heads for the enemy's country, where he had built and had operated railroads and had quarreled over them. A bad leg wound, erysipelas and osteomyelitis in turn assail but cannot subdue him. He contests wrathfully the delay in his promotion and then, as this part of the story ends, gets a surprising honor which it seems doubtful he will be strong enough to accept.

SAMUEL GARLAND

A rise in fame comes to this well-read young lawyer of Lynchburg, Virginia. There is a whisper, too, that he is forgetting in a new love the affliction that had darkened the winter of 1861–62. He goes on a difficult mission down the ridge of South Mountain, where he lacks adequate support, and he does not come back.

RICHARD H. ANDERSON

JOHN ROGERS COOKE

Army born and Harvard-schooled, this 29-year-old son of General P. St. George Cooke, U.S.A., is a brother-in-law of "Jeb" Stuart. Like Stuart, young Cooke has been in the "old army." When he resigned, he was a First Lieutenant. He has been an excellent, careful Colonel and, at Sharpsburg, almost before his panting men have caught their breath, he has the entire Army talking of him. Promotion comes quickly and, after that, a ball that hits him in the forehead but, happily, does not kill him.

MAXCY GREGG

A glorious day on Groveton Heights is allotted the South Carolina lawyer and savant, one of the politest gentlemen of the Army. Then he has a narrow escape at Sharpsburg, and after that a wound, an affecting interview with "Stonewall" Jackson, and the long, long silence. The command loses a certain measure of gentility when he dies.

LAFAYETTE McLAWS

This Georgian, square morally and physically, encounters bad luck on Maryland Heights and drags slowly along on the road to Sharpsburg when he should be demanding the last energies of weary men. At Fredericksburg he easily holds a strong position with ample force, but in the spring, when he has a chance to deliver a hammerstroke, he hesitates. McLaws is not progressing.

ROBERT TOOMBS

The most vocal and violent of the "political generals" no sooner is out of a row with Harvey Hill than he is in another with Longstreet. Momentarily the thunderous Georgian is silenced but soon, by an ironical twist, he is

WILLIAM N. PENDLETON

presented with such an opportunity as he coveted. He does well enough but he somewhat overpraises himself. The promotion he feels he deserves but does not expect to get from Davis he fails to receive. He resigns with a roar and subsequently shouts in the shadows.

JOHN BROWN GORDON

A notable collection of wounds is accumulated by the ramrod Georgian who leads a fine regiment in Rodes's Brigade. After a succession of legislative mishaps, he receives his deserved commission as Brigadier General. His men adore him, but they wish he would not loose his eloquence on them just before they go into a battle: he makes them feel as if they can charge hell itself!

JOHN PELHAM

The magnificent young commander of Stuart's Horse Artillery, the blond idol of many of the soldier-loving girls, goes on from splendor to splendor, makes peculiarly his own the title "gallant," and on a March day, shouting "Forward" and smiling at troopers in a charge, he falls from his horse. Three girls in nearby towns put on mourning for him.

GUSTAVUS WOODSON SMITH

Recovery from his collapse in June, 1862, has been rapid if not complete. He has returned now to duty, but it soon is apparent that the administration, having lost faith in the ability of the former Street Commissioner of New York, intends to assign him to quiet sectors. He resents this. Although he does not meet the requirements of even a minor mission in North Carolina, he raises a storm because he is not made a Lieutenant General. When he is

From an original negative in the Meserve Collection

JOHN PELHAM

put off with assuaging words, he is provoked to tender his resignation, which President Davis gratefully and caustically accepts. Smith is to be seen no more in the Army of Northern Virginia. Travellers returning from Georgia, months later, are to report him in the service of Governor Joe Brown, who hates the administration as much as he does. Smith is an embittered man.

ROBERT EMMETT RODES

As if he stepped out from the pages of Beowulf, the tall Rodes stalks through the camps and fights always as if his battle were to decide a great cause. He has alternating fortune, now good, now bad, in the Maryland expedition, but when the spring of 1863 comes, he wins in an afternoon fame that brings him the closest approach the Army can offer to promotion for valor on the field. Rodes is the personification of the new type of Confederate leader.

WADE HAMPTON

About the time that Pelham dies, this millionaire planter and exemplar of much of South Carolina's best observes his forty-fifth birthday. By standards of the youthful cavalry, Hampton is mature, almost old. He shares in most of Stuart's raids and proudly conducts two of his own without the help, thank you, of any of those Virginians who act as if they discovered horsemanship. Outwardly all is well between Stuart and Fitz Lee on one side and Hampton on the other, but perhaps feeling is developing. A certain uneasiness is in the air: Hampton does not seem to be having much of a chance, though the truth simply may be that the season is inactive.

GEORGE EDWARD PICKETT

Slow recuperation from the wound received at Gaines' Mill is the fate of Longstreet's younger brother in spirit.

From an original negative in the Meserve Collection

ROBERT RODES

Longstreet looks after his interests and sees that, when the Major Generals are named in the reorganization of the autumn of 1862, Pickett is one of them. Pickett returns to the Army in time for the Battle of Fredericksburg, but he has little to do that December day. In the spring of 1863, when Pickett goes to Southside Virginia, he is 38 years old but has the good fortune of being near the home of a vivacious young girl, not half his age, who thinks him the greatest of cavaliers. She sees nothing but romance in those long ringlets of his that his brother officers consider odd.

THOMAS REED ROOTES COBB

A Brigade is entrusted to this hard-working Colonel of 39 years, who is a younger brother of Howell Cobb. By his management of his men, Tom Cobb soon restores the family prestige, which had been impaired by Howell Cobb's mishandling of his troops at Crampton's Gap. As fine a fortune in the field as at the bar seems to await Tom Cobb, but in his first battle as a general officer, he is killed.

ROBERT FREDERICK HOKE

A dependable line officer since Bethel, Hoke is 26 in 1863. At Fredericksburg, in the absence of Trimble, he leads an excellent Brigade with so much fury that men who did not know him begin to ask, Who is Hoke? His father had been a North Carolina politician of station who had died when the boy was seven. Robert Hoke had not attended West Point but he had received some professional training at the Kentucky Military Institute. After that, he had some experience in the family's manufacturing business. Manifestly, he has the true-born soldier's sense of combat. In appearance he is handsome, tall, strong, with a long face and deepset eyes.

WILLIAM DORSEY PENDER

Seasoned and much scarred is now this hard-hitting, realistic North Carolinian, who becomes 29 in the winter of 1862–63. More than ever he hates a war that keeps him from his family, but if he must fight, he wants to be at the front in rank and in service. He is distinctly the partisan of Hill in the controversy with Jackson, and occasionally he has bitter thoughts for those who dispute the pre-eminence of the "Light Division." These matters are diversions or emotional outlets. He is efficient in campaign and is responsible for the good behavior of what he regards as the best Brigade of the best Division. In battle he forgets all else in persistent, flaming combat. He retains that habit of getting wounded in almost every fight.

STEPHEN DODSON RAMSEUR

Always Dodson to his intimates, Ramseur was graduated at West Point in 1860 and, at 25, was a Colonel of a fine North Carolina regiment. Now, in his 26th year, he is a Brigadier General. He does not behave as if he can get enough of fighting. Although he bristles with a brigand's beard, he is small, slight of frame, alert. His speech is direct and brisk, his dark prominent eyes do not flicker. He is ambitious and is sensitive alike to success and to failure, almost in adolescent degree.

CADMUS MARCELLUS WILCOX

No happy career in the Army is Wilcox's from August, 1862, to May, 1863. In his 39th year, he is older than most of the other professional soldiers who command Brigades. At West Point, he was in the class with T. J. Jackson, with David Jones, and with George Pickett. In the next class was Powell Hill. All these now outrank him. He is restless, sore, and disposed to go to another Confederate Army where he will have a chance. Then, at an unwanted post, while a battle that will bring fame to others is raging a few miles away, his great hour comes. He meets it in a manner to make Banks' Ford and Salem Church a model of what an observant commander of a detached Brigade sometimes can accomplish.

JAMES J. ARCHER

Experience in Mexico and long service as a Captain in the United States Army are part of the background of this Maryland Brigadier General. He is 45 years old and may be resentful that he does not seem in the line of promotion. By lucky chance, on a May morning when the troops are groping in the woods, he advances his Brigade from a refused flank position. Before he knows it, he has captured a dominating ridge.

FITZ LEE

For the loud-laughing, hard-riding nephew of the commanding General, there are some dazzling adventures. In the serious business of covering the rear of a retreating army, he wins many plaudits. He is of the mature age of 27 in the winter of 1862–63, but not too old to expect more thanks than he gets after a singular experience with "Stonewall" Jackson.

MICAH JENKINS

After displaying at Seven Pines the fighting spirit of South Carolina, Jenkins is a Brigadier before he is 27 and is distinguished at Second Manassas, but he is wounded there and for most of the months after his recovery, during this period of the war, he is on the unexciting line of the Blackwater. Longstreet appreciates him; fortune does not smile. Soon there is to arise a vindictive rivalry with Evander Law, another young South Carolinian-

THOMAS LAFAYETTE ROSSER

Giant of the younger cavalrymen, Rosser is a Colonel and one of the best. Stuart and the commanding General are trying to make a Brigade for him but, as yet, they cannot find the troops.

EDWARD PORTER ALEXANDER

By the spring of 1863, Alexander has a part of the recognition his consistent service since First Manassas has deserved. He is approaching 28, is erect and thin, and has more the look of the scholar than of the soldier. Those who know the artillery officers say this Georgian is among the most scientific and resourceful of them all. He is a man of the sort on whom a busy commander safely may rely.

WILLIAM JOHNSON PEGRAM

Incredibly, after all his exposure in battle, this young artillerist is still alive, and behind his spectacles he looks scarcely any older. He ends this period of the war a Major and in command of an artillery battalion that is marked, by the fact of his leadership, for hard fighting and for fame.

SAMUEL G. FRENCH

In the active rôle of a commander who is cognizant of all his rights and is resolved to maintain them, Sam French, age 44, appears briefly. Punctilious, precise and imperturbable, he certainly puzzles and perhaps provokes Longstreet.

HENRY HETH

Of Virginia stock, long distinguished in war and in fortune, Harry Heth, age 37, is himself a West Pointer and a former Captain in the "old army." He has a high reputation, personally and professionally, and he is as devoted a soldier as he is an attractive individual. In Western Virginia, his small command once was seized with panic through no dereliction on his part. Now that he is a Brigadier in the Army of Northern Virginia, he is called within two months to lead a famous Division on a field of victory and, in less than three, he is promoted Major General. This seems good fortune, but it is to prove a continuance of the ill fortune experienced in Western Virginia. As yet, nobody realizes that Harry Heth, as he is called by his friends, is doomed to be one of those good soldiers, unhappily numerous in military history, who consistently have bad luck.

RALEIGH EDWARD COLSTON

An unusual, puzzling person is Raleigh Colston. He was born in France of wealthy Virginia parents long resident there, and in youth he was sent to Lexington, Virginia, where he was entered and duly was graduated at the Virginia Military Institute. He remained there, became Professor of French and bore himself as became a faculty-colleague of T. J. Jackson and of R. E. Rodes. Because of Jackson's high opinion of him, Colston is called to brigade command in the Second Corps at a time when attrition has worn the corps of officers. War is not kind to "Old Parlez," as his former cadets nicknamed him, but precisely why and wherein he fails on his day of great opportunity, is a mystery not easily resolved. His age is thirty-seven.

EDWARD JOHNSON

By the wound received at McDowell, May 8, 1862, "Old Allegheny" was invalided for almost a year in Richmond. As he had means as well as station, he enjoyed the best company in the Confederate capital, though his proclivity for making love at the top of his voice caused young ladies to be a bit cautious in his presence. Now, in the spring of 1863, too late for the great battle, he is placed in command of a Division of the Second Corps. He comes with a roar and with a limp which he eases with a long staff; wherefore the boys sometimes call him "Old Club" or "Old Clubby." He is a powerful, bulky man of 47, a soundly schooled professional soldier, but as yet he does not know the quality and limitations of his subordinates.

LEE'S LIEUTENANTS

CHAPTER I

New Troubles for "Old Jack"

Was it a major change of Federal strategy with which "Stone wall" Jackson had to deal in mid-July, 1862? Had the enemy opened a "second front"? At the time of Jackson's departure from the Richmond line, after the Seven Days' Battles, the new Federal Army of Virginia appeared to be making ready for an advance to the "Gordonsville Loop" of the Virginia Central Railroad. The commander of this Army, Maj. Gen. John Pope, was intent on assuming and holding the offensive. Another Federal force of unknown strength[1] was at Fredericksburg. This column, uniting with Pope, might overwhelm Jackson. Either one of the Union armies might push forward, cut the railway and sever communications between Richmond and the Shenandoah Valley.

Against the possibility of such a drive, Jackson had, first of all, to protect the long stretch of rail from Hanover Junction to Charlottesville. He had, also, to watch for an opening and, if he found it, to strike at once. The Southern cause could not wait on the leisured convergence of superior force. In this spirit, Jackson's first counter-move was to place his Army at Beaver Dam, whence he marched a little westward to Frederickshall. When Jackson had satisfied himself that the greater part of the Union troops under Pope were North and West of Culpeper, the Confederate Army of the Valley advanced on the 19th of July to Gordonsville.[2]

Upon the arrival of Jackson at the town where he had halted a month previously it was observed that both he and his troops looked the worse for their adventures in the defense of the capital.[3] Jackson may not have been aware of this, but he was con-

---

[1] Actually, this force comprised Rufus King's Division and Abner Doubleday's Brigade, approximately 11,000 infantry, with thirty guns and about 500 cavalry. Cf. *O. R.*, 12, pt. 2, p. 103; *ibid.*, pt. 3, p. 523.

[2] *Hotchkiss' MS Diary*, 59. Notes inserted in the diary by "Sandie" Pendleton state that Jackson's Headquarters were at Beaver Dam on the 17th and at Frederickshall on the 18th. At the second of these stops, Jackson lodged with Mr. and Mrs. Nat M. Harris, from whose home he had started his ride to Richmond on June 23. *Ibid.*

[3] *Hotchkiss' MS Diary*, 61.

scious that his men needed a renewal of stiff discipline. Before he had left the scene of the battles around Richmond, he had prescribed for his troops the tonic of three drills a day and the prophylaxis of abstention from visits to the Confederate capital.[4] Now, as Jackson awaited developments, he sought vigorously to restore whatever might have been lost in soldierly qualities. It was an exacting task. Nine days after he reached Gordonsville, the General wrote Mrs. Jackson briskly: "My darling wife, I am just overburdened with work, and I hope you will not think hard at receiving only very short letters from your loving husband. A number of officers are with me, but people keep coming to my tent—though let me say no more. A Christian should never complain. The apostle Paul says, 'I glory in tribulations!' What a bright example for others!"[5] Among the "tribulations" he may have counted that of having no time to read a copy that Jeb Stuart had sent him of a new, Confederate edition of the strategist's bible, Napoleon's *Maxims of War*. Jackson put the volume carefully with his personal baggage, but neither then nor thereafter, so far as the pages indicate, did he ever read it.[6] If he had time for Holy Writ, that was all. Newspapers he still declined to peruse lest they destroy his Christian humility. They spoke too well of him.

For a few days, the General's personal hard work meant ease for his subordinates. Maj. Franklin Paxton, who was then acting as a voluntary aide to Jackson, wrote cheerfully home: "Everything here seems so quiet. The troops are drilling, and there is every indication that [they] will rest here for sometime. Considering the severe hardships through which they have passed since the war began, it is very much needed. Everything has a happy, quiet appearance, such as I have not seen in the army since we were in camp this time last year after the battle of Manassas."[7]

[4] General Order of July 10, 1862. No soldier could go to Richmond otherwise than on a pass signed by a divisional commander or issued at Jackson's own headquarters.
[5] *Mrs. Jackson*, 310.
[6] For Stuart's reference to sending the book, see *O. R.*, 51, pt. 2, p. 594. The volume itself, now in the Confederate Museum, Richmond, was the West & Johnson edition of 1862. See D. S. Freeman, ed., *Calendar Confederate Papers*, 519. When the writer examined the copy for the first time in 1907, he could not see that it ever had been opened, much less read.
[7] P. G. P[axton], ed. *Elisha Franklin Paxton, Memoir and Memorials* (cited hereafter as *Paxton*), 59.

The arrival of A. P. Hill's Division did not disturb this calm or add to Jackson's troubles. Quietly and in good order, though perhaps with more transportation than regulations allowed, the Light Division reached Jackson on July 29 and the days immediately following.[8] In dispatching Hill from Richmond Lee had written the commander of the Army of the Valley: "A. P. Hill you will, I think, find a good officer with whom you can consult, and by advising with your division commanders as to their movements much trouble can be saved you in arranging details, as they can act more intelligently. I wish to save you trouble from increasing your command." [9] This was as pointed as it was tactful and it would be particularly apropos of the projected movement, which involved a large force for one man to handle unless he was willing to trust his subordinates and to reveal to them enough of his plans to assure swift, co-ordinated action. The event was to show that Lee's counsel was lost on Jackson. If "Stonewall" was willing, as he had told Boteler, to follow Lee blindfolded, he required no less of his subordinates. Hill said nothing and asked nothing. Doubtless he was glad enough to be away from Longstreet.

If Hill kept the peace that Paxton had praised, others did not. Col. John F. Neff of the Thirty-third Virginia was involved in some unexplained clash with General Winder and was placed under arrest.[10] Some of Winder's privates of the Stonewall Brigade had straggled badly on the march to Gordonsville and had wandered far in search of food at private homes. Winder decided that the one way of stopping this was to punish it severely. Thirty offenders were marched into the woods and were "bucked" for a day. Their resentment was worse than their straggling. About half of them deserted that night. Others were so embittered that their officers went to Jackson and acquainted him with the incident. He thought it politic to direct that men be not bucked again. This ended that humiliating form of punishment, but it did not cool the wrath of the sufferers. John Casler reported: "[General Winder] was a good general and a brave man, and knew how to handle troops in battle; but he was very severe, and

[8] Hotchkiss recorded in his MS Diary, July 29, p. 63, that he found some of Hill's Division at Gordonsville that day: ". . . it has not all arrived as yet." The diary does not state when the rear Brigade reached the concentration area.

[9] O. R., 12, pt. 3, p. 919.

[10] C. D. Walker, Memorial, Virginia Military Institute, 403, said of this incident only that it arose from "a misunderstanding."

very tyrannical, so much so that he was 'spotted' by some of the Brigade; and we could hear it remarked by some one nearly every day that the next fight we got into would be the last for Winder."[11] That in the Southern Cromwell's own Brigade of the Model Army!

Simultaneously with this unhappy affair in the Stonewall Brigade, Jackson's cavalry was in the turmoil of reorganization. Following the death of Ashby, the Secretary of War had asked Lee, not Jackson, to suggest a possible successor, who would have the rank of Brigadier General. Lee had not been able to recommend a competent, available cavalryman. He had thought of Robert Ransom, but he did not feel he could spare that officer, nor did he believe the North Carolinian would care to exchange command of a strong infantry Brigade for the direction of Jackson's horse. The name of Fitz Lee, which was urged by Stuart, was rejected by Lee on the ground that he did not know whether his nephew could win the support of Ashby's men. Col. T. T. Munford had been mentioned by Lee as a possibility, as had been George H. Steuart.[12] Instead of Munford, who had shown much promise, and of "Maryland" Steuart, who had failed definitely in cavalry command, the President chose Col. Beverley H. Robertson and promoted him to the grade of Brigadier General.[13]

Colonel Robertson was a Midland Virginian, 36 years of age, a graduate of West Point in the Class of 1849,[14] a veteran of much Indian service and in person the embodiment of the fashionable French cavalry officer of the time. Somewhat bald, with unsmiling eyes, Robertson wore long, flowing mustaches and whiskers in the mode of Louis Napoleon. The month before the outbreak of war, while he was on duty in Utah, Robertson was promoted Captain of the Second Dragoons. After the attack on Sumter, he sent word to his friends that he would be in Virginia and ready to serve in her behalf as soon as he could get home; but he was not able to reach Richmond until Aug. 18, 1861. Ten days before his arrival there, he had been dismissed officially from the United States Army on the ground that he had "given proof of his dis-

---

[11] *Casler*, 112–13. The reason for saying that Jackson considered it "politic" to suspend bucking is that he subsequently went much further than ever Winder did in ordering punishment for stragglers. See *infra*, pp. 81, 149.

[12] *O. R.*, 11, pt. 3, p. 580.

[13] As of June 9, 1862; *Wright*, 84.

[14] *Cullum*, No. 1431; twenty-fifth in his class.

loyalty."[15] By the time the order to this effect was published, he was a Captain in Confederate service[16] and soon he was Colonel of the Fourth Virginia Cavalry.[17] In command of that regiment he had gone with Stuart to the Peninsula, but because of sickness he had been denied any part in the skirmishing at Williamsburg.[18] His only engagement had been a brisk exchange at New Bridge on May 23-24.[19]

Because Robertson adhered sternly to the rigorous discipline of the regular Army, he was defeated for election as Colonel in the reorganization of his command.[20] That cancelled his commission, but it made him available for other service. The President's hope, in promoting him in June, was that Robertson's admitted abilities as a drill master could be well employed in the training of Ashby's men. Col. William E. ("Grumble") Jones, of the First Virginia, had shared Robertson's fate in the election and had lost both his troops and his rank. For him, too, the War Department at length found a place. The loose, cumbersome organization of the cavalry in the Shenandoah area was conformed to army regulations. Ashby's troopers were regimented as the Seventh and Twelfth Virginia, and the Seventeenth Virginia Battalion. With Munford's Second and Flournoy's Sixth, they constituted Robertson's "Laurel Brigade," in which Jones was given the Seventh Virginia.

These regiments from the Valley, moving via Mechum River and Charlottesville,[21] joined Jackson at Gordonsville. Upon Munford's arrival from the Richmond front with the Second, he was ordered to report to Robertson.[22] The organization thus was completed but it was not popular. Boys who had been accustomed to the easy-going, if adventuresome life under Ashby could not be reconciled overnight to "old army" Colonels and methods. The Valley troopers, moreover, had held an unofficial election of their own for the choice of officers and felt much resentment because their action had been disregarded.[23]

Had this been all, Jackson readily could have dealt with it. He who had made teamsters of the Dunkards and had laid an iron

15 *Cullum, loc. cit.*; *Richmond Dispatch*, Aug. 19, p. 2, col. 6; Aug. 29, 1861, p. 2, col. 3.
16 *Richmond Dispatch*, Aug. 29, 1861, p. 2, col. 3.
17 *Cf.* IV *O. R.*, 1, 631; 3 *C. M. H.*, 657.
18 *O. R.*, 11, pt. 1, pp. 445, 572.
19 *Ibid.*, 663.   20 *Laurel Brigade*, 76.
21 Hotchkiss met the command at Charlottesville on July 17. *MS Diary*, 59.
22 *O. R.*, 12, pt. 3, p. 921.   23 *Laurel Brigade*, 75-76.

hand on mutineers and hiding conscripts would not have hesitated to curb the cavalry. Now that Ashby's influence no longer could have been exerted against him, Jackson could have assured support for Robertson had he himself had faith in that officer. There was the barrier. Despite the devotion of Robertson to Jackson's ideals of endless drill, "Stonewall" seems from an early date to have disliked his new chief of cavalry. It is impossible to say whether this was because Jackson may not have been consulted about the appointment or because he did not believe Robertson was qualified for the command. In either event, Jackson quickly concluded that Robertson lacked vigor in reconnaissance and outpost duty. On the 2nd of August, "Grumble" Jones had a brush with Federal cavalry in the streets of the town of Orange. Ten men were wounded, fifty were captured.[24] Jackson seemed to think the fault was Robertson's, rather than Jones's,[25] and, on August 7, he forwarded a request that he be rid of Robertson and that Jones be put in command. "That subject," answered Lee, "is not so easily arranged, and without knowing any of the circumstances attending it except as related by you, I fear the judgment passed upon [Robertson] may be hasty." With the frankness he always displayed in dealing with Jackson, the commanding General continued: "Neither am I sufficiently informed of the qualifications of Col. W. E. Jones, though having for him high esteem, to say whether he is better qualified." [26] To Mr. Davis, prior to this episode, Lee had written: "Probably Jackson may expect too much, and Robertson may be preparing his men for service, which I have understood they much needed. With uninstructed officers, an undisciplined brigade of cavalry is no trifling undertaking and requires time to regulate." [27] There, uncertainly and unpleasantly, the matter had to rest.

If Jackson could not have his way with the cavalry, he could do his full duty, as he saw it, in disciplining his infantry. Now

[24] O. R., 12, pt. 2, pp. 112–14.
[25] In his report, O. R., 12, pt. 2, pp. 181–82, Jackson noted that Jones "by direction of Brigadier-General Robertson was moving with the Seventh Virginia Cavalry to take charge of picket posts on the Rapidan" when Jones "received intelligence before he reached Orange Court House that the enemy was in possession of the town." Jackson commended Jones for charging "boldly" at the head of the Federal column. There may be in this language an implication that Robertson should have supported Jones.
[26] O. R., 12, pt. 3, p. 926; Aug. 8, 1862. Jackson's letter to Lee is not in O. R., but can be reconstructed from Lee's reply.
[27] July 31, 1862; Lee's Dispatches, 43.

that he had a respite from battles he could take up again the always unfinished business of courts martial. The case of Col. Z. T. Conner, who had fled from Front Royal on May 30,[28] had never been decided. Jackson was determined that it should be. Before leaving Richmond, he had sent G. H. Q. the charges and specifications[29] and, when no attention was paid them, he dispatched another copy.[30] This he followed with a list of officers for the court. Forthrightly he observed that he had so many courts martial under way that he had been compelled to assign all his general officers to that duty, though it was desirable that only one General at a time be detailed.[31]

Of all the courts martial, the one that involved the largest issue of justice was that of Brig. Gen. Richard B. Garnett for withdrawing the Stonewall Brigade from the front of action at Kernstown.[32] The accused officer had seen the letter in which Jackson had expressed the opinion that "General Garnett is incompetent to command a Brigade, and if he is given charge of a good Brigade, it would become a bad one."[33] Intimation also had reached Garnett that during the winter of 1861–62 Jackson, without apprising him, had filed with Lee some complaint of his conduct.[34] As Garnett was satisfied that his action at Kernstown was proper, he was determined to have vindication and, no less, to renew in some capacity his military service in defense of the South. On May 6, Garnett had written the Adjutant General that he would waive all consideration of rank in the composition of a court to try him. If, said he, it was impracticable to organize a court even of officers of subordinate grade, he appealed to the War Department to defer a hearing of the charges and to give him active duty anywhere.[35]

General Lee had regretfully to endorse this request with the statement that he saw no possibility at that time of hearing the charges. He explained: "If General Jackson had closed his letter with the expression of his wish not to press the matter further I

28 See *supra*, Vol. I, pp. 416–7.
29 *Jackson's MS Letter Book*, p. 39, July 11, 1862.
30 *Ibid.*, p. 40; July 23, 1862.
31 *Ibid.*, p. 40; July 31, 1862. Conner ultimately resigned.
32 See *supra*, Vol. I, p. 312 ff.
33 See *supra*, Vol. I, p. 318. This letter was quoted substantially, but not literally, by General Garnett in his answer of June 30 to Jackson's charges and specifications—*R. B. Garnett MSS*, Confederate Museum, Richmond.
34 *Ibid.*
35 Garnett to Samuel Cooper, MS, May 6, 1862—*R. B. Garnett MSS*.

should recommend it be dropped. But his closing remarks[36] make it necessary as an act of justice to General Garnett and the service to bring it to trial." [37] On the eve of the Battle of Mechanicsville, when Lee had needed every officer of experience, he had suspended the arrest of Garnett and had ordered that officer to join D. H. Hill for temporary duty,[38] but by the time Garnett had reported, the Seven Days' Campaign had closed. The decision then had been reached to proceed with the court martial and to dispose of the charges.[39] "In [that] decision," Garnett subsequently wrote, "I most heartily concurred." [40] At length a court was named. On the very day it was to convene, Jackson was ordered to the Rapidan.[41] Lee arranged that another court, one that could move with Jackson's troops, was named promptly.[42]

About August 6, this court assembled at Ewell's headquarters near Liberty Mills and began to take testimony. Jackson had drawn with much care broad charges of neglect of duty under seven specifications, and he had covered virtually all Garnett's disputable movements on March 23. The allegation was that Garnett had divided his command at Kernstown, had separated himself from his troops, had permitted them to become confused, and had "given the order to fall back, when he should have encouraged his command to hold its ground." [43] To all of this, Garnett had prepared a detailed answer.[44]

On the stand, Jackson gave coldly his story of what he had sought to do at Kernstown and of what he believed to be Garnett's derelictions. Garnett himself cross-examined his former chief.

"What," said the defendant, "was your plan of the battle fought near Kernstown . . . ?"

"First," Jackson answered, "to defeat the enemy by gaining heights on his right, which commanded his position, pressing on towards Winchester, then turning his right and getting in his rear."

"Did you," said Garnett, "communicate this plan to me before or during the action?"

---

[36] Presumably those that challenged Garnett's competency for command.
[37] Lee to Cooper, MS, May 6, 1862, *loc. cit.*   [38] *S. O.*, 146, June 25, 1862.
[39] Garnett to Cooper, MS, July 26, 1862—*R. B. Garnett MSS.*
[40] *Ibid.*
[41] R. H. Chilton to R. B. Garnett, MS, July 18, 1862, *loc. cit.* Chilton said "left for the Valley" rather than for the Rapidan, but his meaning seems to be clear.
[42] *Ibid.*   [43] April 1, 1862—*R. B. Garnett MSS.*
[44] As of June 30, 1862—*R. B. Garnett MSS.*

Jackson's reply was uncompromising: "I did not to my recollection."

The examination then turned to the tactical details of the advance. Jackson's memory of the circumstances was completely at variance with that of Garnett. So far were they apart that at three points on his transcript of the testimony, Garnett wrote opposite Jackson's answer, "*Lie.*" [45]

When Garnett opened his defense, he prefaced it with the assertion that, at Kernstown, "Gen'l Jackson did not communicate to me any plan of battle, if he had decided on one" and that consequently, when entering action, "I was . . . entirely ignorant of his schemes and intentions . . . Had he conferred freely with me on that occasion, I am confident all cause of complaint, as far as this specification [of not advancing the regiments in proper order] is concerned, would have been avoided." [46] More in detail, Garnett entered denial of each of the specifications and asserted that his various movements had been demanded by proper management of the field. He supplemented his own statement by reports, personal letters and affidavits from several of his Colonels and from other officers who had fought at Kernstown. In his summing-up he said: "General Jackson not content with arresting me and depriving me of my command, was determined that I should not be restored to active duty as far as it was in his power to prevent it." Garnett cited Jackson's letter alleging unfitness for command and also referred to the complaint that he understood Jackson earlier had made against him. "Such covert attacks," said he, "are inconsistent with honor and justice, and should arouse grave doubts as to the motives and truthfulness of these secret allegations."

He went on: "It is bare justice to the First Brigade to say that they were the most orderly and best behaved troops in General Jackson's army whilst I served with it, and it is a well known fact that fewer complaints were made of depredations committed by it than by any body of men who served in the Valley of Virginia. I have every reason to believe when I was with my command, and after I left it, that I enjoyed its confidence, affection and respect; which could scarcely be the case with an incompetent officer."

Garnett recalled the duration of his service with Jackson, from

[45] *R. B. Garnett MSS.*   [46] *R. B. Garnett MSS.*

December, 1861, to April 1, 1862, and he proceeded: " . . . Much the greater portion of this time I was second in command, yet General Jackson never conferred or advised with me in any important matter, except on a single occasion, when he called me to a council with the regimental commanders of my Brigade. I was thus kept in [as] profound ignorance of his plans, instructions, and intentions as the humblest private in his army. It is almost unnecessary to say that it was extremely embarrassing and dis-spiriting for my superior officer thus to withhold from me his confidence, and the requisite information to guide and direct me in the intelligent discharge of my duties, and whose position even, I might by many accidents of service have been called on suddenly to fill."

This defense probably was being presented when the spies who had been sent to ascertain the position of Pope's forces arrived and made their report. Jackson had been convinced that Pope was preparing to concentrate at Culpeper. The spies had established the interesting fact that a part only of the new Army of Virginia actually had reached the town. Stirred by this intelligence, which he considered accurate, Jackson believed that precisely such an opportunity as he had hoped to find now was offered him. Pope apparently had made a mistake. By a swift march, Jackson might destroy the Federal van ere the whole army could be concentrated.

If full advantage was to be taken of Pope's incautious exposure of his advanced units, no time must be lost. Jackson must move at once. The court was suspended.[47] Orders were snapped. On August 7, the columns were in motion [48] from the camps around Gordonsville.[49] Their route was over plantation roads where Jackson hoped they would not be observed by the enemy. The day's objective was Orange Court House. Thence Jackson intended to drive straight on Culpeper, which was twenty miles up the wagon road that paralleled the Orange and Alexandria Railroad.

[47] The *Garnett MSS* contain a section only of the testimony, which covers parts of Jackson's and of "Sandie" Pendleton's testimony. Nothing in the *Official Records* indicates that the court submitted findings.

[48] *O. R.*, 12, pt. 2, p. 182.

[49] Apparently, in the case of Winder's (Jackson's) Division, orders for the march were not received until afternoon. Jackson in his report, *O. R.*, 12, pt. 2, p. 182, said the troops "were moved on the 7th" but he specified no hour.

To reach Orange was an easy matter, because Jed Hotchkiss had gone over the roads and had chosen those that scarcely would be under the observation of the enemy.[50] The one immediate trouble, a minor one, concerned Charles Winder. When he received his orders on the torrid afternoon of August 7, he had been sick for several days. His surgeon insisted that he should not attempt to assume active field command. Winder was willing to obey the surgeon if the march did not involve a battle, but if there was to be a fight, he was determined to have a hand in it. To that end, he told Lt. McHenry Howard to ride to Jackson's headquarters, to report him sick, and to inquire confidentially whither the army was moving and whether Jackson expected an action. Howard was to explain that Winder made the unusual request for information because, if a battle was in prospect, he wished to be at any point designated by Jackson and in time to assume command. The Lieutenant did not like the idea of putting such questions to the taciturn Jackson and he said so. Winder answered sharply, "Go to General Jackson and ask him what I told you." Obediently, Howard rode to headquarters. There he found Jackson on his knees and busily packing a carpet-bag.

"General," began Howard, "General Winder sent me to say that he is too sick to go with the command."

"General Winder sick? I am sorry for that."

"Yes, sir, and the medical director has told him he must not go with the Brigade. But he sent me to ask you if there will be a battle, and if so, when and he would be up, and which way the army is going."

Howard spoke it all in a mouthful and expected to be met with a sharp retort. Instead, Jackson remained on his knees, turned his head away for a few minutes, reflected and then indulged in a diffident smile at the manifest confusion of the young man. "Say to General Winder I am truly sorry he is sick"—a pause and then: "that there will be a battle, but not tomorrow, and I hope he will be up; tell him the army will march to Barnett's Ford, and he can learn its further direction there." It was an exhibition of considerate candor for which Howard was grateful. Without

---

[50] Brig. Gen. George D. Bayard reported to General Pope from ten miles below Culpeper on the 7th that his pickets were being driven in, but apparently the Federals were not aware of the advance of the Confederate infantry. Cf. *O. R.*, 12, pt. 2, pp. 88, 129–30; pt. 3, p. 544.

more ado he hurried away and reported to Winder, who resolved to follow the column.[51]

The troops started promptly. Arriving at the Court House, part of the Army bivouacked around the village. Jackson himself went to sleep on the stile in the street, but when his presence became known, he was asked to the Willis home.[52] There, some time during the night, Jackson issued written orders for the three Divisions to march at dawn. Ewell was to lead; Hill was to follow; Jackson's own Division under Winder was to close the rear.[53] These orders duly were delivered to Hill, but before he started, perhaps even before orders reached him, the plan was changed. Jackson decided to send Ewell's Division by roads to the left of the main line of march. The route of Ewell was to be via Liberty Mills, which were located on the Rapidan, where the road to Madison Court House crosses the river. Thence, Ewell's men were to move down roads on both sides of the Rapidan to the Orange-Culpeper highway[54] and were to reunite with the other Divisions in the vicinity of Barnett's Ford. This modification of plan was made for one or more of three reasons: Jackson may have hoped to deceive the enemy into thinking Ewell was heading for Madison Court House, where part of Pope's forces was supposed to be; a second reason for the new orders to Ewell may have been a belief that the wagon train needed protection against possible attack from the West; the third explanation would be the natural desire to spread the march and not to crowd three Divisions and all the trains on one road.

Of this change in plan, whatever the reason, A. P. Hill was not informed.[55] At the appointed hour, on the morning of the 8th, he had his leading Brigade near the street in Orange up which he expected Ewell to move. Shortly after sunrise, troops began to pass. Not unnaturally, Hill assumed that they were Ewell's men.

[51] *McHenry Howard*, 162–63.

[52] *Hotchkiss' MS Diary*, Aug. 7, 1862, p. 65.

[53] *O. R.*, 12, pt. 2, p. 214. For assertion that the orders were in writing, see A. P. Hill to A. S. Pendleton, MS, Mch. 13, 1863—*Jackson MSS*.

[54] The doubt concerning the time at which these orders were issued to Ewell arises from the fact that Hotchkiss in his *MS Diary* stated that Ewell crossed at—and did not merely reach—Liberty Mills on the 7th, which necessarily would mean a start early in the evening. Hill wrote only: "That night orders were received," etc. If Ewell's Division already was concentrated around Liberty Mills, where his headquarters are known to have been on the 6th, then, obviously, a crossing of part of the Division at that point could have been effected easily during the evening of August 7.

[55] So Hill, *O. R.*, 12, pt. 215. Jackson in his endorsement of Hill's report, *ibid.*, 216–17, made no denial of this.

A Brigade or more had tramped northward before Hill learned that the troops were of Jackson's Division. Upon inquiry, he heard for the first time that Ewell had marched via Liberty Mills.

What was Hill to do? Was he to halt Jackson's Division and place his own troops between two of the commanding General's own Brigades? That would mix the units in a most unsoldierly manner. Should he attempt to get ahead of the troops who already had passed? That would be difficult. Would it not be better to keep the Light Division where it was until all of Jackson's men had passed? Hill so concluded.

After a time, up rode Jackson. From the Willis House, "Stonewall" had seen loitering men of A. P. Hill's command. Why, he asked, were not they on the march? Hill explained, perhaps too briefly, that he was waiting for Jackson's Division to pass. Jackson looked down the street, saw the head of a halted column of his men and apparently assumed that it was the leading Brigade of his Division. Tersely he told a staff officer to ride to the Division and to order it to move on. Then he turned his horse and rode off.[56]

Hill remained where he was and presently saw a wagon train come up the street. It was following Jackson's Division, and apparently was under orders to do so. Should Hill wait on it, too? His written instructions had contained no reference to the trains; but if Jackson had placed the wagons where they were, in rear of the Division to which they belonged, it was proper to let them pass and to fall in behind them. This Hill did, and, later,

[56] The time-element seems to offer the only means of reconciling the statements of Hill on one side and of Jackson and Maj. E. F. Paxton on the other. As noted in the text, Hill wrote subsequently that a Division, which he took to be Ewell's, began to pass "a little after sunrise" and that "one or two brigades" moved northward before he identified them as belonging to Jackson's Division (O. R., 12, pt. 2, pp. 214–15). Jackson affirmed that, when he met Hill at Orange Court House, he "understood Hill to say" that the Light Division was "waiting for Jackson's Division to pass." At that time, Jackson added: "The sun was . . . probably over an hour high. The advance of Jackson's Division had reached the town and halted" (ibid., 217). Major Paxton wrote seven months later, in answer to an inquiry from Jackson: "Finding that Maj. Genl. A. P. Hill had not moved, and that the head of your division had reached the town, where it was then resting, waiting I think for Ewell's Division to pass, you directed me to order your division to take the road which I did. This I think was about an hour after sunrise" (Paxton to Jackson, MS, Mch. 11, 1863; Jackson MSS). The conflict of testimony thus may be limited to the question whether the troops seen by Jackson and by Paxton formed the head of Jackson's Division or the head of a Brigade which one or more Brigades of the same Division had preceded. The fact that the troops seen by Jackson were at a halt might mean either that they were waiting for another Brigade to clear the town or that the Division expected Hill to file in ahead of it. If an hour, or even half an hour elapsed between the time Hill took his station and the time Jackson arrived, the misunderstanding is explicable.

when he found the progress of the column almost stopped on the Culpeper Road, he went up to Barnett's Ford to ascertain the reason. At the ford he saw part of Jackson's Division waiting on some of Ewell's troops whose route converged at that point. Thereupon, Hill sent word to Jackson that the march was delayed and he inquired whether Jackson intended that each train should follow its Division. No answer came, according to Hill, until between 4 and 5 P.M. At that time, he subsequently reported, Jackson sent him a verbal order to return to Orange Court House and to encamp there.[57] Jackson denied that any such order had been dispatched. On the contrary, he maintained, he twice urged Hill to press on.[58]

A feeble, a farcical performance the advance had been! On a day when sound strategy demanded maximum speed, "Jackson's foot cavalry" had crawled. Instead of reaching Culpeper, Jackson had been able to do no more than eight miles with Ewell's Division, which was renowned for its swift, long marches. Hill had carried his Division only one mile North of Orange Court House.[59]

What had gone awry? Why had the fast moving Army of the Valley dragged along at a rate that would have humiliated a Quartermaster in charge of a reserve wagon train? Excessively hot weather on the 8th was in a measure responsible, but the prime reason was a combination of poor planning, bad staff work and unnecessary reticence on Jackson's part. Barnett's Ford was a bottleneck. The crossing itself was not particularly difficult, but when part of Ewell's Division filed into the road at that point, where wagons were entangled with troops, delay was inevitable.[60]

---

[57] O. R., 12, pt. 2, p. 215.

[58] O. R., 12, pt. 2, p. 217; S. Crutchfield to Jackson, MS, Mch. 13, 1863; E. F. Paxton to Jackson, MS, Mch. 11, 1863; A. P. Hill to A. S. Pendleton, MS, Mch. 13, 1863; Jackson MSS. Jackson did not make the events of the evening of Aug. 8, 1862, as distinguished from those of the morning, the basis of any specification in his subsequent court martial charges against Hill. For that reason, the various points of dispute do not seem to justify review.

[59] O. R., 12, pt. 2, p. 215. Jackson stated, ibid., 181, that Hill had started a mile "on the other side" of Orange and had made two miles.

[60] Jackson stated that Ewell "did not cross at Barnett's Ford [but] he passed near that point in coming into the road upon which the troops were to move." This obscure statement may mean that those of Ewell's troops who were on the eastern bank of the Rapidan approached Barnett's Ford from the direction of Poplar Run Ford to the Southwest and crossed the river just above Barnett's. There certainly would have been no point in having Ewell cross the Orange-Culpeper Road and pass the Rapidan at any of the fords East of Barnett's. On the other hand, had Ewell negotiated the Rapidan at Poplar Run or at Bankhead's Ford, he would not have "passed near" Barnett's Ford "in coming into" the Culpeper Road.

Sound logistics would have brought none of Ewell's troops back to the Culpeper Road South of the ford. Neither Jackson nor any of his staff seems to have realized that A. P. Hill's Division was much larger and therefore required more road space than did any Division that Jackson had commanded in the Valley.[61] In addition, during the day the enemy's cavalry repeatedly threatened the trains and probably unnerved the teamsters. Worst of all was Jackson's failure to notify A. P. Hill of the change of orders on the night of August 7–8, or to acquaint him with even the essentials of the general plan. Lee's admonition to Jackson to advise with Hill had violated something deep, something almost instinctive in "Stonewall." Caution, distrust, jealousy, inborn reticence —whatever it was, it cost Jackson a day's march by his largest Division.

For the failure of the day's advance, Jackson blamed himself, but he blamed Hill for not preceding Jackson's Division from Orange Court House.[62] He did not arrest the commander of the Light Division, but he became doubtful of Hill's ability to conduct a march. Seeds were sown that August day for animosities that might have a grim harvest.

[61] Cf. *O. R.* 12, pt. 2, p. 181.   [62] *Ibid.*

CHAPTER II

JACKSON FUMBLES AT CEDAR MOUNTAIN

AFTER THE wretched march of August 8, Jackson began the next morning a movement that was related almost as vitally to the grand strategy of the changing campaign in Virginia as his advance on Front Royal had been to a somewhat analogous situation that had prevailed in May. Then, as now, McClellan was in front of Richmond; a column was waiting at Fredericksburg; in Northern Virginia, a third force was afield. The first difference was in the balance among these hostile armies. At the beginning of the second phase of the Valley campaign, McClellan was threatening Richmond; in August, he was passive at Harrison's Landing. The force at Fredericksburg under McDowell was powerful, when Jackson moved on Front Royal; as Jackson proceeded northward in August, the strength of King's troops on the Rappahannock was not believed to be large. In contrast, Pope was known to have many more troops around Culpeper than had been credited to Banks at Strasburg fifteen weeks previously.

Another and a confusing strategic difference there was. Maj. Gen. A. E. Burnside, who had commanded a small army on the coast of North Carolina, had left that area and had taken transport for Fort Monroe. What did the War Department plan to do with his troops? Was it to use them to reinforce McClellan, or to strengthen Pope still further? No ship movement up James River had been observed: Did this indicate that Burnside was to join Pope? If so, what would be his line of advance? Suppose he ascended the Rappahannock and debarked at Fredericksburg: Would he move thence southward and deliver more vigorously against the Virginia Central Railroad the attack that had been anticipated when Jackson first reached Beaver Dam? Did the Federals now hope by such a movement to force Jackson to retreat so that Pope would have a clear road to Gordonsville? Was that, in turn, to be preliminary to a junction by Pope with McClellan in front of Richmond? If Burnside did not move against the Virginia Central, would he march westward from Fredericksburg —the distance was only some thirty-five miles—and join Pope on the Rapidan in an effort to overwhelm Jackson?

All these possibilities had been debated anxiously in Richmond, but without sufficient information to shape an answer. On August 5, "Jeb" Stuart, who had been sent to make a reconnaissance in force toward Fredericksburg, reported that he had located two Brigades of Federal infantry. His prisoners stated that Burnside with 16,000 troops was to the rear. The enemy, Stuart thought, was preparing for an advance to the railroad that linked Jackson with Richmond.[1] That day or the next, John S. Mosby, who was returning from Fort Monroe as an exchanged prisoner of war, reported to Lee's headquarters that Burnside, according to gossip at the post, had been ordered to Fredericksburg.[2]

This information had been suggestive but not conclusive. Lee had been able to do no more than to forward it to Jackson and to leave to that officer's discretion the choice of maneuver. At the moment, Lee could not send further reinforcements to Jackson because McClellan had become active and had tramped thousands of his men from Harrison's Landing to the blood stained crest of Malvern Hill. While this, in Lee's judgment, probably was done in order to cover a move by Burnside, the strength of McClellan still was so superior that Lee could not weaken the force that defended Richmond.[3] Jackson therefore had started his march northward from Gordonsville in the hope that he could engage Pope before the full Army of Virginia could concentrate; but he did not know what flanking operation he might encounter, or whether his advance would be the signal for a drive southward from Fredericksburg toward the railway on which he depended.

The underlying strategy and the tactical dispositions of the Federals were being influenced by circumstances which no opposing General could have divined. Pope's mission had been outlined on June 26. He was to cover Washington, to control the Shenandoah Valley, "and at the same time so [to] operate upon the enemy's lines of communication in the direction of Gordonsville and Charlottesville as to draw off, if possible, a considerable

[1] O. R., 12, pt. 3, p. 924.   [2] 2 R. E. Lee, 269 and n. 65.
[3] O. R., 12, pt. 3, pp. 625–26.

force of the enemy from Richmond, and thus relieve the opera-tions against that city of the Army of the Potomac."[4] Before Pope could undertake this, McClellan's retreat to the James had been made. Pope thereupon had suggested, through correspond-ence with McClellan, that a plan of joint operations be devised.[5] McClellan in his answer [6] merely urged the rapid concentration of Pope's Army and hinted vaguely that the Army of the Potomac might advance on Richmond in the event that Lee moved against Pope.

By that date, July 7, Mr. Lincoln had begun to doubt whether the two Generals could work together, and four days later he had decided that some officer must be named to coordinate operations in Virginia. For this difficult task he had chosen Maj. Gen. Henry W. Halleck, to whom he gave the title of General-in-Chief and the command of "the whole land forces of the United States." [7] While General Halleck had been preparing to come eastward from Corinth to enter upon his new duties,[8] General Pope had undertaken a succession of cavalry raids against the Virginia Cen-tral Railroad. One of these, well directed from Fredericksburg, had done some minor damage. The principal thrust, twice launched under Brig. Gen. John P. Hatch, had failed because of the slowness of the officer in charge.[9] Pope had displaced Hatch, but before he had been able to start another advance, Jackson had reached Gordonsville and had secured the railway against any-thing short of a general offensive.

Almost a fortnight of hesitation had followed. Then, after General Halleck had held many conferences,[10] orders had been sent McClellan on August 3 to abandon operations on James River and to move his entire army by water to Aquia Creek, near Fred-ericksburg. Thence, it was reasoned, he could defend Washington and, later, could participate in a new, overland campaign.[11] To

---

[4] Pope's report of Jan. 27, 1863; *O. R.*, 12, pt. 2, p. 21.

[5] *Ibid.*, 22; *O. R.*, 11, pt. 3, p. 295.

[6] *O. R.*, 11, pt. 3, p. 295. Subsequent communication between McClellan and Pope was by telegraph and was concerned solely with day-by-day operations.

[7] *O. R.*, 11, pt. 3, p. 314. For a statement of the growing distrust by the Administra-tion of General McClellan at this time see J. C. Ropes, *The Army under Pope*, 12 ff.

[8] *O. R.*, 11, pt. 3, p. 321.   [9] *O. R.*, 12, pt. 2, pp. 21–22.

[10] He had assumed command in Washington on July 23. *O. R.*, 11, pt. 3, p. 371.

[11] For a statement of the controlling reason for this move, see Halleck's report, *O. R.*, 12, pt. 2, p. 5. The Administration did not feel that it could supply McClellan promptly with the 35,000 reinforcements he considered necessary for active operations against Richmond. Rather than permit the larger of the Federal armies in Virginia to remain

cover the projected landing at Aquia and to strengthen the consolidated Army, General Burnside had been ordered on August 1
to move by transports from Fort Monroe to the same advanced
base. He had proceeded with admirable dispatch,[12] and by the
night of the 3rd had debarked.[13]

This change of underlying strategy had not modified greatly
the mission of General Pope. He had to discharge his original
duty of protecting Washington and of guarding the Shenandoah
Valley. As previously, he had to demonstrate against the Confederate lines of communication with the Valley in the hope of
compelling Lee to make heavy detachments to guard those lines.
If this were done, McClellan's prospects of an untroubled departure from James River manifestly would be increased.[14] For the
moment, Pope specifically was required to hold the line of the
Rappahannock and to maintain contact with Burnside on his left
at Fredericksburg.[15] On the 5th of August, while in the first stages
of a concentration on Culpeper, Pope was planning to advance
toward the Rapidan and to launch from his extreme right a demonstration against Charlottesville. This operation, he believed,
would force Jackson to do one of three things: to fall back from
Gordonsville to Charlottesville, to send heavy detachments thither,
or to start northward and give battle in circumstances adverse to
the Southern Army.[16] General Halleck, on the 8th, urged Pope to

passive, while the smaller of the two faced the possibility of a Confederate offensive
against Washington, the Administration decided on a concentration of all the forces.
In determining to withdraw an army that was within easy striking distance of Richmond, Halleck was misled by his incredible overestimate of Lee's strength. The Federal General assumed the Army of Northern Virginia to have more than 200,000 men
(O. R., 12, pt. 2, p. 10) at a time when its effectives probably did not exceed 70,000.
This error is a classic example of the manner in which an intelligence service, if lacking
in competence, may mislead disastrously the high command. Again, the ability of Lee
to influence the withdrawal of McClellan shows how boldness in maneuver, when
wisely reasoned, may create on an adversary the impression of superior strength. For
Halleck's justification of his course, see his letter of Aug. 6, 1862, O. R., 12, pt. 2, pp.
9–11. McClellan's objections were set forth in his dispatch of August 4 to Halleck,
ibid., 8–9, and were elaborated in his final report, O. R., 11, pt. 1, p. 77. General Pope's
views, which conformed substantially to those of General Halleck, are given in O. R.,
12, pt. 2, pp. 22–23.

[12] McClellan did not fail to point out, when the relative speed of his own and of
Burnside's movement was compared, that the troops from the coast of North Carolina
were not encumbered with wounded, wagons or artillery. O. R., 11, pt. 1, p. 88.

[13] O. R., 12, pt. 2, p. 5.

[14] O. R., 12, pt. 2, p. 23. It should be noted that in his report, which was not written
until January 1863, General Pope confused the sequence of events and attributed his
movements after July 14 to the decision of the Administration to withdraw McClellan
from the Peninsula. That decision was not reached until July 29 or 30. See Halleck's
report, O. R., 12, pt. 2, p. 5.

[15] O. R., 12, pt. 2, p. 25; ibid., pt. 3, p. 532.   [16] O. R., 12, pt. 3, p. 536.

display caution until the line of the Rappahannock was more strongly defended, but General Pope continued to prepare for an advance. Besides ordering his immediate command to converge on Culpeper, he directed King's Division of McDowell's III Corps to march westward from Fredericksburg, to establish contact with him and thereby to extend protectively the left flank of the main army.[17] Although the news of Jackson's forward movement on the 8th led Pope to canvass the possibility that his adversary had seized the initiative, he decided that Jackson more probably was undertaking a reconnaissance in force.[18] As the hot day of Jackson's slow march burned on, Pope's principal doubt was whether the main advance of the Confederates would be on Madison Court House or on Culpeper.[19]

At dawn on the 9th, Pope was satisfied only that the attack, if delivered, would be on his right.[20] His dispositions were made accordingly. Close to the Confederate outposts, and on a wide front, was the greater part of Bayard's cavalry, of the III Corps. This mounted force had shown a strength of 2904 on the morning report of July 31,[21] but as it faced Robertson, it probably did not exceed 1200 sabres.[22] In support of the cavalry, and waiting on Cedar Run, was Crawford's Brigade of Banks's II Corps, about 1700 effectives.[23] The remainder of Banks's Corps, probably not more than 7000 infantry, were five miles South of Culpeper, or about three miles in rear of Crawford.[24] Rickett's Division of McDowell's III Corps, 9200 infantry,[25] was three miles behind Banks on the road.[26] Sigel's I Corps, formerly the command of John C. Frémont, should have been as near the front as were the

---

[17] O. R., 12, pt. 3, pp. 548–49, 550.
[18] O. R., 12, pt. 3, p. 548.   [19] O. R., 12, pt. 2, p. 25.
[20] O. R., 12, pt. 3, p. 553.   [21] O. R., 12, pt. 2, p. 53.
[22] Andrews in 2 *Papers of the Military Historical Society of Massachusetts* (cited hereafter as *M. H. S. M.*), 417. *Cf.* Pope's comment, O. R., 12, pt. 2, p. 20: "The cavalry numbered about 5000 men for duty, but most of it was badly mounted and armed and in poor condition for service." In the report cited in the preceding note, the total cavalry was given as 8738, less 3000 "unfit for service."
[23] O. R., 12, pt. 2, p. 153.
[24] O. R., 12, pt. 2, p. 133. The effective strength of Banks's Corps on August 9 is one of the unsettled questions of this campaign. The morning report of July 31, *loc. cit.*, credited Banks with 13,343 infantry; but Pope insisted, O. R., 12, pt. 2, p. 25, that Banks's effectives "did not exceed 8000 men." Ropes, *op. cit.*, 4, though accepting these figures, noted that Pope was credited with 10,000 on August 29. William Allan, in his *Army*, pp. 167–68 n, computed Banks's infantry at 11,000 and attributed to "sickness and heat" the fact that only 8000 were in action at Cedar Mountain. General Andrews, in 2 *M. H. S. M.*, 417, put the infantry at 6800.
[25] O. R., 12, pt. 3, p. 555.   [26] O. R., 12, pt. 3, p. 133.

units of the II Corps, but Sigel had halted on a plain road to ask for instructions concerning his route, had then made an all-night march under peremptory orders, and had not yet reached Culpeper.[27] King's Division of McDowell's III Corps presumably was on the march from Fredericksburg. Buford's cavalry of the II Corps, five regiments,[28] which had been at Madison Court House, were retreating toward Sperryville in the belief that they might be cut off.[29]

In spite of the instructions from General Halleck that he should be "very cautious" until more troops reached the line of the Rappahannock,[30] Pope decided to advance the remainder of Banks's II Corps to the position occupied by Crawford's Brigade. Verbal orders to this effect were sent at 9.45 A.M. by Col. Louis Marshall, a nephew of Gen. R. E. Lee. When Banks found that the order was verbal and was somewhat complicated, he had it written down by one of his staff officers at Marshall's dictation as follows:

"General Banks to move to the front immediately, assume command of all forces in the front, deploy his skirmishers if the enemy advances, and attack him immediately as he approaches, and be reenforced from here." [31]

Of so much of this as occurred in the early morning of August 9, Jackson knew only that the Federal cavalry were in his front and that infantry of unknown strength were behind the horsemen. Gloomily, ere he took horse, Jackson wrote Lee: "I am not

[27] O. R., 12, pt. 2, pp. 26, 133. See also Pope to Sigel, Aug. 8, 1862, ibid., 54.
[28] O. R., 12, pt. 2, p. 24.
[29] Ibid., 55.   [30] O. R., 12, pt. 3, p. 547.
[31] 3 Com. Con. War, 1865, supplement, p. 45. The form and interpretation of this order were disputed violently in 1865. General Pope, Colonel Marshall and Gen. B. S. Roberts denied that the order contemplated any advance other than that of the skirmishers. Colonel Marshall, on Dec. 26, 1864 (ibid., 54) gave from memory a version of the order at variance with that presented by General Banks, but as the text presented by Banks was that of the original, copied down on the day of the battle, naturally it is preferred. The version given by Col. D. H. Strother in Harper's Magazine, August 1867, p. 295, also is later than that cited by Banks. The contention of Banks, General Pope and his staff officers was that General Banks was sent forward with the clear understanding that. if attacked, he was to hold a designated, strong position until other troops arrived. While there could have been no misunderstanding of Pope's intentions, the equivocal language of the order given Banks by Colonel Marshall was discreditable to Pope's staff and confusing to Banks. The case was another in the long familiar list of disasters due in the War between the States to the habit many commanders had of transmitting verbal, instead of written orders. An echo of the controversy was heard in the McDowell Court of Inquiry, O. R., 12, pt. 1, pp. 184–90. 200–2.

making much progress. The enemy's cavalry yesterday and last night also threatened my train . . ."[32] Today I do not expect much more than to close up and [to] clear the country around the train of the enemy's cavalry. I fear that the expedition will, in consequence of my tardy movements, be productive of but little good. My plan was to have been at Culpeper Court-House this forenoon. Should I learn that Burnside has gone in the direction of Richmond J will try to cut him off. Scouts were sent out yesterday to ascertain . . . The enemy's infantry, from reports brought in last night, is about 5 miles in front; his cavalry near ours." [33] Still in the belief that no more than the advanced units of Pope's Army had reached Culpeper, he determined to press on toward that town. With Robertson's cavalry in advance,[34] though less active than Jackson desired it to be, Ewell moved northward from Barnett's Ford on the Rapidan.

The leading Confederate Brigade was that of Jubal A. Early, "Old Jube." It was the first time Early had shared in a new operation since that bloody charge of May 5, near Fort Magruder, outside Williamsburg.[35] Even now, because of his crippled shoulder, he required help in mounting his horse; [36] but he was full of fight and was to show, ere the day was done, that he had disciplined well the old Brigade of the invalided Arnold Elzey, a Brigade that included some of the best troops of "Allegheny" Johnson.

As Early advanced, he picketed both sides of the road, in accordance with instructions, to guard against a cavalry attack.[37] Behind him tramped the rest of Ewell's Division. Trimble was with his men, but in the absence of Harry Hays, the Louisianians followed Col. Henry Forno of the Fifth [38] regiment. Next came three Brigades of Jackson's old Division,[39] which formally, at 4 A.M., had been placed under Winder. That officer was little better than on the 7th and was urged by the Medical Director not to return to duty, but he insisted on taking the field. Pale and manifestly

---

[32] For the demonstration against the train on the night of August 8, see *O. R.*, 12, nt. 2, pp. 180, 210, 211.

[33] *O. R.*, 12, pt. 2, p. 181.   [34] *O. R.*, 12, pt. 2, p. 226.

[35] Early, it will be remembered, had shared briefly in the action at Malvern Hill, *see supra*, Vol. I, p. 588, but that was in no sense a new operation.

[36] *O. R.*, 12, pt. 2, p. 227.

[37] *O. R.*, 12, pt. 2, p. 228.   [38] *O. R.*, 12, pt. 2, p. 237.

[39] For Lawton's detached service see *infra*, n. 45.

weak though he was, he soon abandoned his ambulance and rode to the head of his column.[40] His second in command was Brig. Gen. William B. Taliaferro, in charge of the Third Brigade. The other Brigades of the Division, with the exception of Lawton's Georgians, were under field officers. Colonel Ronald of the Fourth Virginia headed the "Stonewall" Brigade; Lt. Col. Thomas S. Garnett of the Forty-eighth Virginia had the Second Brigade.[41]

Powell Hill, smarting under the black look that "Old Jack" had given him the previous day, had begun his march before daylight on the 9th and had closed the leading Brigade of his Division on Lawton and Taliaferro while they were leaving their bivouacs.[42] Whatever the price, Hill was determined that the Division which had fired the first shots in the Battle of Gaines' Mill should not be backward in any action the Army of the Valley might undertake. All his Brigadiers were at their posts.

Twenty-four thousand men [43] crossed the Robertson River in the sunshine of what promised to be a blistering day. Of the heat Jackson scarcely seemed conscious, but to the vulnerability of his train of 1200 wagons he was sensitive.[44] A force of Federal cavalry was hovering near. His own troopers seemed too inactive under Robertson, for Jackson to feel easy. North of the river he ordered the trains halted. Gregg of Hill's Division and Lawton of Jackson's were left to guard them.[45] This arranged, the column pressed its march, but still not to Jackson's satisfaction. Persistently he urged Robertson to locate the enemy; as persistently Robertson complained that his men were straggling.[46] "Grumble"

<hr>

[40] *O. R.*, 12, pt. 2, p. 183; *Hotchkiss' MS Diary*, 67; *McHenry Howard*, 165. Douglas, *op cit.*, 125, gave a different and more dramatic version of Winder's assignment to command on August 9; but as McHenry Howard quoted the order, timed 4 A.M., Douglas must have confused the incident with some other, or else he dated on the 9th a conversation that may have occurred on the 8th.

[41] *O. R.*, 12, pt. 2, pp. 190, 191, 199, 206.   [42] *Ibid.*, 215.

[43] The estimate is William Allan's, *op. cit.*, 165, and probably is not in error by more than 1000 or 2000.

[44] For the undue size of the wagon train, see *O. R.*, 12, pt. 2, p. 223. A part of the train may have represented the excess transportation that Hill, through some misunderstanding, had brought with him from Richmond. Cf. *O. R.*, 12, pt. 3, pp. 919, 923. See *supra*, p. 3.

[45] *O. R.*, 12, pt. 2, pp. 188, 215. It is quite probable that Jackson assigned Lawton to this duty in order that Winder might handle the Division in the impending battle. Lawton ranked Winder and, had he been on the field, would have commanded the Division.

[46] *Hotchkiss' MS Diary*, 67.

Jones, for all his name, was missed that morning. He might be rendering good service to the left, in the direction of Madison Court House, whither he had been sent, but he or some other good outpost officer was needed on the Culpeper Road. In a situation that called for the eyes of an Ashby, the Army was half-blinded.

The debouch of the cavalry, soon after crossing the river, was into the southern end of a rolling valley. Ahead, the roads con-stituted a capital "Y." To the Northwest, from the angle, the route led to Madison Court House. Northeastward ran the highway to Culpeper. The main features of the terrain—all that anyone took pains to observe on approach—were woods in the angle of the "Y," low ridges and cleared land to the right of the easterly prong, the low shoulders of Cedar Mountain [47] to the East and Southeast, and forests to the westward. Small watercourses among the ridges presented no material obstacle, but they gave to most of the field a slope from Northwest to Southeast. Beyond them, not yet within the vision of the Southern advance guard, was a wooded position of good, though not of forbidding defensive strength.

About midmorning, when Early's leading regiment reached a point three-quarters of a mile South of the angle of the "Y," the infantry came upon the Confederate cavalry at a stand. Some 800 yards to the Northeast, on a long, cleared ridge, the Union mounted troops could be seen. Soon Ewell rode up and ordered Early to reconnoiter to the right. Part of Early's artillery moved out, also, and opened on the cavalry. The blue coated horsemen withdrew. As they did so, an answering salvo came across the ridge from their rear.

Enemy guns in support! Was there infantry behind the ridge also? Neither Ewell nor Early could be sure as yet, but word was sent back to the commanding General. Then Early was with-drawn from reconnaissance and, with skirmishers deployed, was moved up the road to the angle of the "Y," where he arrived and

---

[47] This was known also as Slaughter's Mountain. Richmond newspapers, after the battle, recorded that the ground of the action was the farm of the late Capt. Philip Slaughter, of the Revolutionary Army, who died in 1849. He had predicted a sectional war and had named one of his farms "Brandywine" because of a supposed resemblance to the scene of that action, in which he had participated. *Richmond Dispatch*, Aug. 20, 1862, p. 2, col. 1. See also *Richmond Enquirer*, Aug. 14, p. 1, col. 2; *Richmond Whig*, Aug. 21, 1862, p. 2, col. 1.

halted about 11.30.[48] He perceived at once that the Federals did
not intend to give ground. The Union cavalry, who had disappeared in the face of the first artillery fire, were back again on
the ridge to the Confederate right.[49]

Jackson by this time reached the front and rode to the house
where "Dick" Ewell was waiting for orders and meantime was

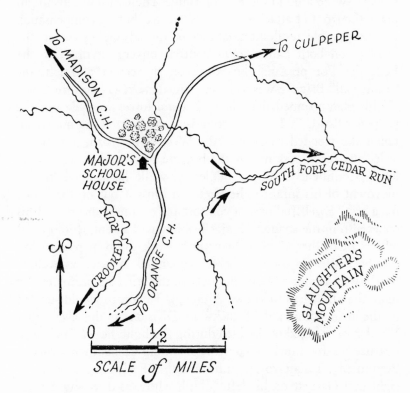

The "Y" in the Roads at Major's School House, South of the Battlefield of Cedar
Mountain, Aug. 9, 1862—after Jed. Hotchkiss

enjoying himself with some little children he had coaxed into
coming on the porch. Jackson laid out his map; he and Ewell
bent over it.[50] The topographical fact which fairly smote them
in the face was that the ridges of Cedar Mountain covered the

[48] Early stated in his report, O. R., 12, pt. 2, pp. 228–29, that he was at this intersection less than an hour when ordered forward by Ewell, who reported, ibid., 227,
that he issued shortly after noon the instructions for the advance.

[49] O. R., 12, pt. 2, p. 182; Early, 94.

[50] F. M. Myers, The Comanches (cited hereafter as F. M. Myers), 88.

Confederate right and commanded the Union left. On that feature of the ground Jackson based this plan of action: Ewell was
to take two of his Brigades [51] over the shoulder of the mountain
and was to turn the Federal left flank; Early was to advance up
the Culpeper Road; Winder was to support Early and was to
extend the Confederate left in such a fashion that, from the West,
it could sweep around the Federal right. These dispositions might
make the front of attack somewhat concave, but, in compensation
for the possible resultant weakness of the advancing center, the
artillery on both flanks could pour a converging fire into the
Federals. For pressing the attack on the center and left, the
"Stonewall" Brigade was to be in immediate reserve on the left.[52]

This plan assumed that all the Federal forces were East of the
Culpeper Road. So far as the records show, Jackson did not reconnoiter the wooded country to the West of the road, nor did he
order any reconnaissance by the brigade commanders sent to the
left.[53] Confidently, almost indolently, while he awaited the deployment of his infantry, he stretched himself out on the porch
for a rest. Ewell followed a comfortable example and spread his
bones also in the shade.[54] Major Dabney was absent. Junior staff
officers of neither General had much work to do in preparation
for the battle. Jackson probably acquainted Winder, as well as
Ewell, with his plan but he did not tell the other subordinates any
more than they had to know. Although Taliaferro would succeed
to the field command of Jackson's Division in the event that
Winder were killed or disabled during the fight, he was not given
instructions for much besides the handling of his own Brigade.
Presumably, Taliaferro was informed that Early would be on his
right and Garnett on his left.[55] Hill, who was directing a large

[51] Trimble's and Hays's under Forno.
[52] Early in *O. R.*, 12, pt. 2, p. 229. The whole of Hill's Division, less the Brigade
guarding the trains, apparently was to constitute the general reserve, though, on this
point, the reports are silent.
[53] Reservation has to be made on this score because the details of Jackson's instructions to Winder are not known; but the reports of Taliaferro, *O. R.*, 12, pt. 2, p. 188,
Ronald, *ibid.*, 183, and T. S. Garnett, *ibid.*, 200, do not mention any orders for reconnaissance. The inference from all the reports is that the brigade commanders took
specified positions which designated lines of advance, which conditions, needless to say,
would have led them to conclude that previous reconnaissance had been made by divisional or army headquarters.
[54] *F. M. Myers*, 88.
[55] "Presumably" has to be inserted in the text because Taliaferro reported, *O. R.*, 12,
pt. 2, p. 189: "[I was] ignorant of the plans of the general, except so far as I could
form an opinion from my observation of the dispositions made."

part of the entire force, subsequently reported as if he had been in the dark concerning the plans of the commanding General.[56] Ewell was not quite so reserved with Early. "Old Jube" was acquainted with all that Ewell's Division was to undertake, and he was advised, also, that he would be supported by three Brigades of Winder, who would notify him when the troops were at hand.[57]

Winder required time in which to advance his batteries and to bring up his troops. While he was doing so, Early had opportunity of making reconnaissance. He found to the left of the Culpeper Road a meadow in which he thought he could form his troops unseen by the Federal cavalry. If this could be accomplished, he reasoned that he could move eastward, assail the mounted force of the enemy, and then swing around and advance parallel to the northeasterly course of the road.[58] This maneuver Early decided to make, and he rode back to the angle of the "Y" to prepare for it. When he arrived there, he found awaiting him a courier with a message that Winder was less than three-quarters of a mile in rear and was ready to advance. This was about 2 P.M.[59]

Quietly and unobserved, Early moved his troops through the woods in the angle of the "Y," crossed a branch,[60] entered the meadow he had visited, formed his regiments there, and led them

[56] Hill stated in his report: "Arriving within about 6 miles of Culpeper Court-House, the heavy firing in front gave notice that the battle had commenced. I was directed by General Jackson to send a brigade to the support of Taliaferro, who was in line of battle on the right of the main road." (O. R., 12, pt. 2, p. 215). As the orders actually were for Hill to reinforce Early, not Taliaferro, and as Taliaferro was on the left, not on the right of the road, this language would seem to be prima facie evidence that Hill did not know Jackson's plan of action. At the same time, it should be remembered that Hill's report was written eight months after the battle and during a period of controversy with Jackson. While Hill would not have misrepresented facts wittingly, he was not in a mood, when he wrote, to concede anything to his superior.

[57] O. R., 12, pt. 2, p. 229; Early, 94.

[58] Early, 94–95. The student of this battle will find interest in retracing the route of Early, who on occasion was confused somewhat readily by strange ground. An admirable example this move was of the manner in which even a soldier who lacks a developed sense of direction may, by careful reconnaissance, find cover for a small command. In this instance, Early concealed 1500 men or more. Ibid., 93.

[59] McHenry Howard, 167; O. R., 12, pt. 2, p. 229. Early did not state that he learned the exact position of Winder from the courier, but as he noted in a later paragraph, ibid., 230, that Winder was three-fourths of a mile behind his advanced position, he must have ascertained that fact before he went forward.

[60] This branch flows southward and then turns eastward and crosses the Culpeper Road about a quarter of a mile above the entrance to the farm road that leads to the Major House. Later, the small stream enters the South Fork of Cedar Run midway between the Major and the Crittenden houses as shown on Hotchkiss' map of the battlefield.

into the open ground to the East of the road. As the Federal cavalry on the nearer ridge scampered off at the sight of advancing infantry, Early wheeled his Brigade to the Northeast. With his skirmishers admirably deployed, he climbed the ridge.[61]

The moment Early's troops showed themselves over the crest, three Union batteries opened from his left front. They were well served batteries, too, and they were able to find the range quickly. Men began to fall. Early, feeling they were needlessly exposed, quickly recalled his regiments to the south slope. There, sheltered,

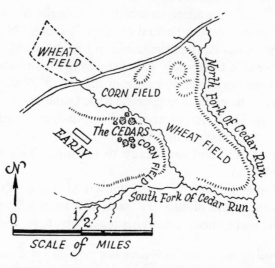

Early's Position at Cedar Mountain, Aug. 9, 1862—after Jed. Hotchkiss

they formed a long line of battle that extended on the left as far as the Culpeper Road. Early was ready now for the attack he had been told he was to deliver. He sent back a request for Winder to move up promptly, and, as he waited, he studied the terrain again.

Many features of it that had not been visible from a distance were clear now. For half a mile southward from his right, open ground sloped down to a fork of Cedar Run. Early's left was separated only by the road from the woods to the westward. In his front, over the crest, the undulating ridge fell away to a little branch. On the farther side of this branch, almost directly North

[61] O. R., 12, pt. 2, pp. 182, 229–30; Early, 95–96.

of Early's left was a wheat field on rising ground. North of this wheat, and running as far as the Culpeper Road, was tall, growing corn. Opposite Early's right, and on his side of the branch, was another corn field. Between his right and this corn field, was a clump of cedar trees on an advanced knoll that dominated the little valley to the southeast. That clump of trees, Early decided at a glance, was an excellent artillery position. Immediately a staff officer was dispatched to bring up a battery.

As Early continued to examine the ground, two things troubled him. One was the distance between his right flank and the Brigades that Ewell was advancing over the shoulder of Slaughter's Mountain. The interval was a mile, a dangerously long mile. It must be protected by something more than the battery that Early intended to place among the cedars. A Brigade should be there: Early sent Jackson a request for that reinforcement.[62]

The second condition that disturbed Early was uncertainty of what might be going on beyond the little watercourse in his front. He could see, when he peered over the ridge, that the grain fields, or at least the visible parts of them, were not occupied by the enemy; but above the fields, on the Federal side, was a crest similar to the one that covered Early's line of battle. Were Union infantry waiting behind that farther ridge? The Federal cavalry had halted on the second crest as if they had ample support at hand. Those batteries near the cavalry were barking confidently. It might be an easy matter for Federal infantry, if present, to slip to the Confederate left, under shelter of that northern ridge, and to enter the thick woods that spread far to the West of the corn field. All in all, it was ground that might lend itself to surprises, ground that should be watched. Early did his best to ascertain what he could not see. He counted the Federal guns by the smoke from their fire, and he kept a vigilant eye for any sign of the presence of infantry.

"Old Jube" had not been long on the lookout when, from the Culpeper Road opposite his left, there galloped horses with three Confederate field pieces. Evidently his appeal for artillery had been anticipated by Maj. A. R. Courtney, Ewell's Chief of Artillery. Capt. W. D. Brown, with one rifle of the Chesapeake Artillery, and Capt. W. F. Dement, with two Napoleons of the

[62] O. R., 12, pt. 2, p. 230.

Maryland Battery that bore his name, were at the General's command.[63]

Well enough! Put them in the grove of cedars. A few minutes more, and the three pieces were blazing away.[64] To support these guns, and to give some protection to his exposed right, until reinforcements could arrive, Early detached the veteran Twelfth Georgia and moved it to the right of the batteries. Its Colonel was absent, and it had no other field officers, but its senior Captain, William F. Brown, was the man who had brought the Twelfth safely from Front Royal after Colonel Conner had fled and Major Hawkins had wished to surrender. About 60 years of age, with a son as one of his Lieutenants,[65] Captain Brown was to be trusted. He had the vigor and the determination his new position demanded.

After these dispositions had been made, the immediate prospect on Early's front was for nothing more than an artillery duel. Was a different adventure ahead of Winder's men? Apparently, as he brought them up about 3 o'clock, the sick but careful General did not think infantry action was imminent. He took his time in making his dispositions and did not complete them until 4 P.M.[66] His orders indicate that he expected, East of the Culpeper Road, an artillery action in which opportunity might be offered for the capture of Federal guns. By his direction, part of the Second Brigade, under Lt. Col. T. S. Garnett, was filed to the Northeast through the woods until the troops approached the wheat field. There, Garnett was to protect the left of the Division and, at the same time, was to prepare for a flank movement against the nearest Union battery.[67] On the right of Garnett, Taliaferro had orders to form and to face East virtually at right angles to Early's left.[68] In short, with his extreme left refused, to cover a possible attack from the North, Winder prepared for an attack across the front of Early to capture the Federal guns.

These tactics were reminiscent of those employed at Win-

[63] O. R., 12, pt. 2, pp. 237-38.   [64] O. R., 12, pt. 2, p. 230; Early, 96-97.
[65] Early, 99.   [66] McHenry Howard, 169.
[67] Garnett's report, O. R., 12, pt. 2, p. 200; Daniel A. Grimsley, Battles in Culpeper County, 28-29.
[68] It should be noted here, as well as in the legend of the sketch, that Hotchkiss' map in O. R. Atlas Plate LXXXV, which Henderson reproduced (op. cit., 2, 96) without any explanation, shows the situation after the Federal attack. For an experienced soldier to have exposed his left in the manner indicated by that map would have been inconceivable.

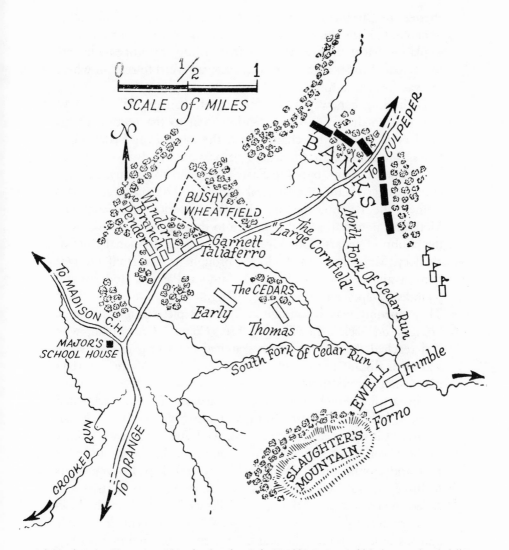

Battlefield of Cedar Mountain. This sketch, after Jed. Hotchkiss' map, which is reproduced fully in O. R. *Atlas*, Plate LXXXV-4, is the best of several in existence, but it is not satisfactory. It shows the Federals before they charged, and Garnett and Taliaferro on the Confederate left after their position had been turned by the Union assault. Winder, Branch and Pender are shown coming up to the relief of Taliaferro. The position of Early is the one he occupied before the assault had shaken his left

chester; but, unfortunately, Garnett realized, as soon as he reconnoitered, that the guns and the infantry on the Federal right were
so placed that the movement expected of him was impossible. He
so advised Winder and, in answer, received word to remain where
he was for a few moments.[69]

To finding a new position for his left Brigade, Winder gave
less of immediate personal attention than to the posting of his
artillery to support his charge from the left on the Federal batteries. He decided that it would be possible to advance guns on
the Culpeper Road, opposite Early's left, and to occupy, perhaps
even to overwhelm, the Federal batteries. The prospect of this
seemed the brighter because Ewell's batteries on Slaughter's
Mountain now had added their fire to that of the three pieces in
the clump of cedars. Quickly Winder and his divisional chief of
artillery, Maj. Snowden Andrews, brought to the front the best
guns available—two of Poague's famous Parrotts and his 12-
pounder Napoleon, Carpenter's Parrott and Caskie's rifles.[70]
Their opening was discouraging. The first piece to test the range
brought on itself a bewildering fire. Colonel Crutchfield, who
had reached the front, at once searched out rising ground some
250 yards distant to the right and front and had Major Andrews
place the batteries there.

The artillery duel now began in earnest. To those who had
witnessed the Federal fire from Malvern Hill, this was a small
affair, but it was spectacular enough. Andrews's men went grimly
to their work, but shell from the opposite ridge began to break
over and around them. Winder, his coat off, kept his binoculars
to his eyes, watched the fall of the Confederate projectiles and
called the correction of the range.[71] Presently, struck in the head
by a fragment of shell, Capt. Joseph Carpenter went down. He
and his brother John, who was a Lieutenant of the same battery,
had made it a rule always to go out together when they sent even
one of their guns into action; consequently John now took direction of the Parrott.[72]

[69] O. R., 12, pt. 2, p. 200.   [70] O. R., 12, pt. 2, pp. 186, 213–14.
[71] E. A. Moore, 98.

[72] Of the wound received here, Capt. Joe Carpenter died. His brother John, who
succeeded to the battery command, was wounded at Sharpsburg. Again at Fredericksburg he was hit and was removed from the field, but he was so intent on his duty that
he made his way back to his battery. Carried off again, he repeated the performance.
During Early's operations in 1864, he lost his right arm. Although he had not recovered when Lee surrendered, John Carpenter started southward to join General John-

Winder kept his post, cool, intent. To him, in a few minutes, a courier delivered an interesting message General Early had sent: From what he could see in his advanced position, said Early, he believed infantry could take the Federal batteries in flank by moving around the wheat field.[73] As Winder already had projected a less elaborate flank movement by his Second Brigade, he remained with the artillery.

The Confederate fire was beginning to have effect now; the Federal batteries were changing position; Winder could not pull himself away at a moment so thrilling.[74] He turned to give new directions to the boys who were serving Poague's nearest Parrott. In the din, his words were inaudible. One of the gunners started to him to ask what he said. Winder put his hand to his mouth to repeat the order. At that instant, a shell passed through his left arm and side and mangled him frightfully. With his frame in a spasmodic quiver, he fell straight back, full length.[75] As he lay on

ston. With him rode his brother Ben, Lieutenant of the battery, who was suffering from a wound through the lungs. A fourth brother lost his leg during the closing operations of the war (E. A. Moore, 155-56).

[73] Early, 97.

[74] Gen. Geo. L. Andrews, U. S. A., then a Colonel, remembered (1895) that the Federals appeared to have "the greater number of pieces and the better service," but, said he, "the enemy replied vigorously, and some of his pieces had a heavier sound as if of a larger calibre" (2 M. H. S. M., 422). Actually the Confederates used only the guns mentioned in the text—3-inch rifles and 12-pounder Napoleons.

[75] E. A. Moore, 98. It was noted after the battle that casualties in the artillery had been of an unusual character. Besides General Winder and Captain Carpenter, mortally wounded, Captain Caskie was hurled eight or ten feet when a ricocheting shell struck his seat. Fortunately, he sustained no serious hurt. Maj. Snowden Andrews, divisional Chief of Artillery, was wounded desperately in attempting to advance some smooth-bore guns farther to the front. In addition to these four, Lieutenant Graham of the Rockbridge Artillery was wounded, but in that battery not one private soldier was touched during the battle (E. A. Moore, 99). Total casualties in the artillery of Jackson's Division numbered six only (O. R., 12, pt. 2, pp. 179-80). Snowden Andrews's wound was the talk of the army. He had received during the Seven Days a wound that still was requiring surgical care in August, but he went boldly into the fight at Cedar Mountain, where a fragment of shell tore his abdominal wall and eviscerated him. The Richmond Enquirer (August 14, p. 1, col. 2), reported him among the killed, the victim of a "shell bursting inside him." In reality he was carried to the rear but scarcely was given attention by surgeons who felt that peritonitis would be certain. Finally, a country surgeon, moved by his courage, agreed to sew him up. Andrews himself aided in pulling over the skin of his abdomen to cover the wound. Fortunately for him, his wife and a skilled physician came through the lines promptly and gave him exquisite attention. To the amazement of everyone, peritonitis did not develop. He soon recovered sufficiently to give the Federals some amusing misinformation while he was within their lines (New York Herald, Aug. 20, 1862). For months he walked with a stoop, and for the remainder of his life he had to wear a silver shield over his abdomen, but he recovered sufficiently to resume his duties and to get another wound in the battle of Winchester, en route to Gettysburg. (See infra, Vol. III). Subsequently he was sent to Europe on ordnance duty. (McHenry Howard, 62, 171; Tunstall Smith, ed. Richard Snowden Andrews, a Memoir, 45, 65 ff, 102 ff; C. A. Fonerden, History of Carpen-'er's Battery, 31.)

the ground,[76] not quite unconscious, there spurred to him through the smoke and roar, one of Early's staff officers. An ominous warning the rider brought: General Early had caught the glint of the bayonets of a Federal column moving toward the Confederate left through the woods North of the wheat field. An attack might be launched at any time against that exposed wing of the Army.[77]

Taliaferro may not have been informed of this threat, but he was notified at once that the command had devolved on him— on him who knew nothing of Jackson's plan of action beyond what he could see for himself from the position where Winder had posted him. At once Taliaferro rode into the woods to ascertain the situation on his left. He did not meet Garnett but fortunately he reached the position of some of that officer's troops and he went on to the flank element, the First Virginia battalion,[78] which was in woods so dense that it could not see the regiment on its right.[79] No enemy was visible on Taliaferro's reconnaissance in front of the battalion, but to the right, half hidden in the corn field opposite Early, a blue line was visible to Taliaferro.[80]

Jackson did not see that much. When informed of Winder's mortal wound, he made his way to Garnett's post of command and, in stern, terse words, told the Colonel to "look well" to the left flank and to send at once to Taliaferro for re-enforcements.[81] Garnett immediately dispatched his two aides to find the acting division commander.[82] They searched in vain for him on the flank, but at length one aide found Taliaferro on the Culpeper Road, whither he had [83] returned in order to direct those of his troops nearest the corn field on the right where he had seen the Federals.

As soon as Taliaferro was informed that the bluecoats were beginning to show themselves on the left, he directed the Tenth Virginia to start to the support of the First Virginia Battalion, and he ordered up the Stonewall Brigade, then under Ronald, from the reserve. Garnett's line, as finally formed by Taliaferro,

[76] Grimsley, *op. cit.*, 29, quoted local tradition that Winder fell "in the main road, a short distance South of the Crittenden gate, and about where the fence of the Throgmorton land now comes to the road."

[77] *Early*, 97.
[79] *Ibid.*, 265.
[81] *O. R.*, 12, pt. 2, p. 200.
[88] *O. R.*, 12, pt. 2, p. 189

[78] *O. R.*, 12, pt. 2, p. 189.
[80] *Ibid.*, 189.
[82] *Ibid.*

retained the First Virginia battalion on the extreme left; adjoining it on the right was the Forty-second Virginia, parallel to a fence that ran on the south side of the wheat field.[84] The Forty-eighth Virginia, next to the right, formed an angle. Its left faced almost North, its right East.[85] Looking East, also,[86] was the right unit of the Brigade, the Twenty-first Virginia.

Thus far—it was about 4.30 P.M.—no Federal attack had developed in the quarter where Early had seen the moving Federal infantry. The action continued to be one of artillery, and was shifting somewhat toward the right. There, Trimble and Forno, of Ewell's Division, had skirted a mill pond and had reached an advantageous position, from which they might have turned the Federal left had their front been clear. As it was, the field ahead of them still was swept by shell from Southern guns on the center.[87]

More guns were added now on the center, and rashly added. Hill, hearing the fire ahead, ordered his Chief of Artillery, Lt. Col. R. Lindsay Walker, to send forward all the long-range guns of the Division. Walker made the effort but found the Culpeper Road so badly blocked with ambulances and wagons that he could get to the front only the most persistent, hardest riding battery commanders. One of them, as might have been expected, was young Capt. "Willie" Pegram. The other was Lieut. W. B. Hardy, who that day had charge of Fleet's Battery.[88] Led by Colonel Walker, who did not take time to reconnoitre, these two batteries dashed past an exposed point where the enemy seemed to be converging his fire. Out into the open field on Early's left the teams galloped and down the grade to a point only 150 yards [89] from the unseen skirmishers of the enemy. There, quickly and defiantly, without any infantry support, the guns were unlimbered.

Horrified, Early saw the Federals begin to creep forward to capture so recklessly exposed and easy a prize. Unless Hill's guns were protected instantly, they would be lost. "Old Jube" did not hesitate. Doubtless he swiftly shifted his quid of tobacco from one jaw to the other, as was his habit in moments of great excitement. Then, in his high penetrating voice he ordered his Brigade to advance at the double quick to the batteries. With a yell his men

[84] O. R., 12, pt. 2, pp. 203, 205.
[86] Ibid., 202.
[88] Ibid., 226.
[85] Ibid., 204.
[87] O. R., 12, pt. 2, p. 227.
[89] Ibid.

sprang over the crest and dashed for Walker's guns. The surprised enemy halted and wavered. Early's troops rushed on. They
fired, they raised a yell, they won the race. Pegram's and Fleet's
boys, who were as surprised by their deliverance as they had been
by their danger, joined their fire with Ewell's, with that of the
battery in the clump of cedars, and with that of Winder's gunners. The Southern fieldpieces roared; those of the Federals answered. Then slowly, like the fury of dogs that could bark at each
other but could not get close enough to fight, the firing grew
slower. After 5 o'clock it lost all its wrath.[90]

At 5.45 [91] from the left there came the tearing sound of infantry volleys, a terrific, rolling din. Those Federals, the glint of
whose bayonets Early had seen on the edge of the wheat field,
were attacking. Already, it was reported, they had turned the
left of Garnett's Brigade and were closing in on its rear. In front
of Early, too, and of Taliaferro's own Brigade, the enemy was
advancing.[92] An assault evidently was being made against the
center and the left. The infantry battle was on. Every commander must look to his own command, and Jackson to the
whole!

Early hurried to his right to straighten his line; Taliaferro
counter-attacked immediately with his Brigade and the right of
Garnett's. Across Early's rear and toward his right—as if timed
for that dramatic moment—there moved the reinforcements Jackson had promised. They were of Thomas's Brigade which, under
J. R. Anderson at Frayser's Farm, had delivered the final attack
of A. P. Hill's Division.[93] Welcome they were! They would
lengthen the line, support the guns in the clump of cedars, and
add their missiles to the fire of Early's regiments. There might
be difficulty in extricating the advanced batteries, but the right
and the center of Jackson's line now could be maintained, probably—if the left held.

The left did not hold. First reports that its flank had been
turned by the enemy's attack were confirmed by the sound of
irregular, retreating fire and by loud Federal cheers. Soon, through
the woods, panting and begrimed Confederates began to appear.
Some were bloody, many were without arms. All had the same

90 2 M. H. S. M., 423.
92 O. R., 12, pt. 2, pp. 189, 231.
91 O. R., 12, pt. 2, p. 205.
93 O. R., 12, pt. 2, p. 219; 2 R. E. Lee, 191.

tale to tell: The Federals, advancing boldly, had reached the woods beyond the left of the Virginia battalion; that command and the Forty-second Virginia had broken. No organization existed on the left.

Now the firing was nearer. The enemy was taking Taliaferro in the rear while his right regiments were beating off the assault on their front. Again, over the heads of their infantry, the Federal artillerists were firing fast. Pegram and Hardy, sorely battered, withdrew swiftly.[94] Officers shouted and exhorted their men to stand firm. Riderless horses charged and turned and galloped madly. Back went the Forty-eighth Virginia. The valiant Twenty-first, under Lt. Col. R. H. Cunningham, found itself under a cross fire. Two green Alabama regiments of Taliaferro's Brigade, fighting their first battle, caught the contagion of panic. The other regiments of Taliaferro's Brigade kept some semblance of order but they had to fall back.[95] Taliaferro's retreat exposed the left of Early. Riding back from the right, "Old Jube" found his left regiments gone from the ridge. Here, a dozen men or so were disputing the enemy's advance; yonder a short, irregular line had halted and was firing. A few companies remained, with their left reversed and their flank in the air.[96]

Was it a second Kernstown—or worse? Far to the right, Ewell heard and quickened the fire of his guns, but he could not hope to advance as yet. Thomas's Brigade, the Twelfth Georgia and fragments of two Virginia regiments[97] kept their ground. The remainder of the Army of the Valley appeared to be close to rout. Jackson realized it. Always an artillerist, he thought first of his exposed batteries. Order the rifled guns to the rear before the enemy took them;[98] rally Taliaferro and Garnett! Where was Ronald with the Stonewall Brigade? How close at hand was Hill? Could not Ewell attack?

Into the confusion on the eastern fringe of the wood, Jackson spurred his horse. For the first time in the war he was seen to draw his saber. In the spirit of Joshua but with the fervor and the phrases of the pulpit he cried: "Rally, brave men, and press forward! Your general will lead you. Jackson will lead you. Fol-

[94] *Ibid*, 187, 231.   [95] *O. R.*, 12, pt. 2, p. 206.
[96] *Early*, 99.
[97] Four companies of the Fifty-second and part of the Fifty-eighth, *Early*, 99.
[98] *O. R.*, 12, pt. 2, pp. 187, 234.

low me!" [99] Bullets were flying in three directions. No man was safe, nowhere was shelter. Taliaferro hastened to Jackson's side and insisted that the commanding General should not expose himself. For a moment Jackson hesitated and then with his habitual, "Good, good!" he turned to the rear.[100]

Some fugitives by this time had stopped at Jackson's word and had turned to face the foe. Colonel Walker's Thirteenth Virginia of Early's Brigade, still a compact body, halted under fire and made ready to go forward again. Little by little the center began to mend, though Lt. Col. R. H. Cunningham of the Twenty-first Virginia fell as he was bringing his regiment together.[101]

Early had seen that the line could not be restored unless his right kept its formation and maintained its fire. He sent his A. A. G. to rally the broken regiments, and he galloped over to the Twelfth Georgia. It was holding magnificently. Thomas had not fallen back a yard. The battery in the clump of cedars continued its furious fire. No man on that part of the line seemed to have a thought of running. The enemy was being beaten off: he might be pursued.

"General," said old Captain Brown of the Twelfth, as Early rode up, "my ammunition is nearly out; don't you think we had better charge them?" Early shook his head, but his sharp eyes burned the brighter in admiration of the stout-hearted Captain.[102]

After six o'clock it was now, the sun blood red in the West,[103] and a situation still at touch-and-go, but the din that came from the left was beginning to change in pitch. The infantry fire was heavier again; through the wood there rolled the sound of a volley and snatches of a rebel yell. Ronald was up at last. The Stonewall Brigade already had attacked and was driving the Federals. Its ranks were thin, its commander did not know what had happened; both flanks of the Brigade were in the air.[104] Could it

[99] Dabney, *op. cit.*, 501, insisted that these were Jackson's "own words, as repeated by a member of his staff, who was present."

[100] 2 *Henderson*, 95.   [101] *Worsham*, 113.

[102] *Early*, 99.

[103] D. H. Strother in *Harper's Magazine*, August, 1867, p. 284.

[104] Ronald's report, *O. R.*, 12, pt. 2, p. 192, which is much confused, seems to have been ignored by some who have written of Cedar Mountain, but the document makes plain (1) that Ronald advanced with little opposition to the edge of the wheat field, and (2) that he did not know until after he arrived there that his right did not rest on the left of the Second Brigade, or even that the left of the Second had been turned. On the basis of those facts, it is almost impossible to escape the conclusion that the advance of Ronald was earlier than has been assumed and that, by reason of the gradual turn of

press on? For a few minutes, the answer seemed to be hopeful. The Federals retreated into the wheat field and to the woods North and Northeast of it, but they still were firing heavily. They might return to the attack and drive Ronald back. He had learned, by this time, that the Second Brigade had retreated and he began at once to change front so that he could rake the enemy's line of advance.[105]

Of Ronald's progress and of his danger, the commanding General was unaware. After Taliaferro had protested his presence so near the front, Jackson had ridden in search of the leading Brigade of Hill's Division, the general reserve. Soon he found it— Branch's North Carolinians, veterans of Hanover Court House and of the Seven Days. Already these excellent troops had their line of battle West of the road and with their faces to the enemy. General Branch, a renowned orator, was making them a speech. Past the men Jackson rode to their commander. Few words he had for Branch: The left wing was beaten and broken, Jackson said; the enemy had turned the flank. "Push forward, General, push forward."[106]

The Carolinian waited only long enough to be sure he understood the orders. Then he cried: "Forward, march!" As if the drum had tapped on the parade ground, the whole front of the Brigade moved on the instant. Ere Branch had gone 100 yards through the woods, he met fugitives—fugitives of the Stonewall Brigade itself! The Twenty-seventh Virginia, finding its right exposed and assailed by the enemy, had broken incontinently and had run. Ranks were opened to permit the fleeing men to pass and to re-form. Branch's alignment was maintained. His regi-

the Culpeper Road to the Northeast, his advance had the same effect, in relation to the general line, as if it had been a left oblique. A gap of increasing width must have been created as he moved forward. Jackson noted in his report, *O. R.,* 12, pt. 2, p. 183, that Winder (i.e., Ronald) was farther to the left than was Branch.

[105] His deployment was approximately Northwest to Southeast across the western corner of the wheat field and in the stubble. This is made plain not only by Ronald's own account (*O. R.,* 12, pt. 2, p. 192), but also by the regimental reports of the Stonewall Brigade. On the right was the Twenty-seventh Virginia (*O. R.,* 12, pt. 2, p. 197); next on the left, partly in the wood and partly in the field, was the famous Thirty-third (*ibid.*). The Fifth was on the left of the Thirty-third and was the center regiment. To the left of the Fifth was the Second, across the farther fence line (*ibid.,* 195), and, on the extreme left, the Fourth. The only question in doubt is the exact orientation of the line. It may have been more nearly North and South than Northwest and Southeast, because Ronald observed in his report that his line was parallel to the road (*O. R.,* 12, pt. 2, p. 192), but this he could have meant in a general sense only.

[106] *Douglas,* 124. It is probable that Douglas confused the incidents that preceded and those that followed Branch's first advance.

ments crashed onward in the forest. Soon blue forms were visible among the trees. Branch gave them a volley,[107] and pressed them hard. Once he threw the weight of his fresh Brigade against the now exhausted Federals, he cleared them speedily from the gap between Winder's right and the shattered left of Garnett's and Taliaferro's Brigades.

Taliaferro's men and the Twenty-first Virginia of Garnett's command were rallied by this time. Early had reorganized his left. The Thirteenth Virginia was in line again. Slowly these troops began to fight their way northeastward along the Culpepei Road and to the right of it. Their panic ended, they seemed to be determined to redeem swiftly their disgrace. As they advanced, there came down the highway and across the front a roaring Federal cavalry charge. It was courageous but foolhardy. One volley from Early and Taliaferro, and a flanking fire by Branch's men disposed of it.[108]

That was the last thrust of the enemy. Now was Jackson's turn. He himself rode admiringly behind Branch's line, which scarcely paused in its advance, and later, when the Carolinians halted, he rode along their line again and doffed his cap in tribute to them. On the Confederate left, Archer's and Pender's Brigades soon extended the flank to the Northwest.[109] Ewell on the right, free at last of the Confederate cross fire, advanced *en échelon*.[110] While he pressed forward, Taliaferro's men recovered the western side of the corn field. A general attack by the Confederate left, none too well directed, swept back in the twilight of the sultry day the last reserve units of the Federal right.[111]

Jackson was determined to make the most of the advantage he narrowly had won. In an effort to drive the enemy back to Culpeper that night, he ordered A. P. Hill to take the lead and to press steadily forward.[112] Hill was willing. His stout column pushed on, but before it had covered a mile and a half of road,

---

[107] *O. R.,* 12, pt. 2, pp. 222–23.

[108] *O. R.,* 12, pt. 2, pp. 184, 189. This reckless charge, ordered by General Bayard and led by Col. R. I. Falls of the 1st Pennsylvania, was made to cover the withdrawal of the infantry. In the charge rode no more than 164 men, of whom only seventy-one returned unhurt (*ibid.,* 141).

[109] 2 *N. C. Regis.,* 551; *O. R.,* 12, pt. 2, pp. 215, 218–19, 225.

[110] *Ibid.,* 184, 236.

[111] Archer's and Pender's Brigades overlapped. In the advance, Archer lost nineteen killed and 116 wounded. *O. R.,* 12, pt. 2, p. 219.

[112] *Ibid.,* 184.

darkness fell. Jackson's most trusted scout reported that the enemy was just beyond a wood which Hill's vanguard was approaching. Cautiously if reluctantly, "Stonewall" called a halt for Crutchfield to shell the woods.[113] The advance batteries unlimbered quickly. With their target the camp fires that Union gunners carelessly had lighted,[114] the Confederate artillerists created a momentary stampede and drove the enemy from the wood.[115] Through it, after the Federals, Hill advanced, but Jackson stopped him on the farther side and directed that Pegram's battery go forward, with a Brigade in support, and feel out the front. Pegram obediently proceeded to a little knoll [116] and opened gallantly. Three batteries answered him at once and pounded him hard. He held on for an hour and then had to withdraw.[117]

By this time, it was past 11 o'clock. The moon was bright and full in mid-heaven, but foreboding was in the air. Rumor was stalking in every shadow. "Grumble" Jones had clattered over from Madison Court House with his regiment, had scouted to the right and had captured a Federal officer's servant. The Negro had news, important news. A second Federal Corps, he said, had arrived on the ground.[118]

Correct or false, this information was enough to stop even Jackson. He ordered the troops to bivouac, and himself, weary to exhaustion, sought shelter for the night. At every farmhouse where he inquired, the answer was the same: the General of course was welcome, but the place was full of wounded. Presently in the moonlight he observed by the roadside a grass plot that seemed to invite sleep. He drew rein and announced that he would go no farther. A long coat was spread for him. He threw himself down on his stomach, and when someone offered him food, he muttered: "No, I want rest, nothing but rest." In a moment, he was slumbering.[119] Two miles to the rear lay Winder, forever asleep.

The 10th of August dawned with clear sky and every promise of a day insufferably hot. To the awakened Jackson, not the weather but the news that Jones had forwarded the previous

113 O. R., 12, pt. 2, pp. 187, 226.   114 O. R., 12, pt. 2, p. 142.

115 An amusing account of this stampede, written by Col. D. H. Strother of Pope's staff, appears in *Harper's Magazine*, August, 1867, p. 285 ff.

116 O. R., 12, pt. 2, p. 216.   117 *Ibid.*, 187, 216, 218, 226.

118 *Ibid.*, 184, 239.   119 *Dabney*, 503; *Mrs. Jackson*, 312.

night was the disturbing reality. Two Federal Corps in front, one of them fresh! The remainder of Pope's Army might be near at hand. If it were, the outlook for a swift march on Culpeper was unpromising. It would be prudent to wait, to bury the dead, to get the wounded safely to the rear, and, of course, to collect all arms and booty left on the field. Jackson's wagon hunting instinct demanded that.[120]

While the burial details [121] went about their sad work and the ordnance officers were directing the salvage of hundreds of arms, there was a jingle-jingle outside headquarters.[122] A loud, friendly voice was inquiring for the General. It was "Jeb" Stuart, who arrived, as Jackson later explained, on a tour of inspection. Had the act been seemly, Jackson might have embraced him, because "Stonewall" had felt himself badly served by Robertson. On the 9th, little or nothing had been done by the Confederate cavalry with the Army. Jones, not Robertson, had learned of the arrival of Federal reinforcements, whose approach should have been dis-covered much earlier.[123] Now Stuart would use his discerning eyes, his restless energies, to find how many Federals had joined Banks. Readily "Jeb" undertook the task at Jackson's request and, after reconnaissance, brought information which led Jackson to conclude that the enemy was too strong to be attacked.[124]

What, then, should be done? Fortunately, on the 11th, before a decision was forced, the enemy sent in a flag and asked for a truce during which the wounded and the unburied could be removed.[125] By consent, as the labor proved long, the truce was

[120] Cf. *O. R.*, 12, pt. 2, p. 184.

[121] This word "detail," used to describe a detachment of men assigned special duty, still is in military dictionaries but is used much less widely now than in the eighteen-sixties.

[122] Jackson, *O. R.*, 12, pt. 2, p. 184, gave this sequence of events; but McHenry Howard, *op. cit.*, 173, recorded that "about midnight" he met Stuart coming forward while he was going to the rear with the body of General Winder.

[123] For Jackson's reference to Stuart's arrival, see *O. R.*, 12, pt. 2, p. 184. A question arises concerning the nature of Stuart's "inspection." He was in command of the Cavalry of the Army of Northern Virginia, but it is not certain that this included Jackson's forces. As will appear *infra*, p. 56, Lee soon gave Stuart that authority by formal order, either because Stuart did not have it before that time or else because it was dis-puted. Despite the subsequent official extension of authority, the fact may have been that Stuart considered his command to embrace Jackson's Army and that he came, as Jackson's report stated, on inspection. There remains a possibility that Jackson, whose relations with Stuart already were close, may have asked him to come and to ascertain what was amiss with the cavalry. A possibility exists, also, that the inspection was made by direction of Lee, who knew of Jackson's dissatisfaction with Robertson.

[124] *O. R.*, 12, pt. 2, p. 184.   [125] *Ibid.*, 184.

extended to 5 P.M., after which hour neither side renewed the fighting. That night Jackson had campfires lighted all along the front and, while they burned, he led his troops back across the Rapidan. This, he explained later, he did "in order to avoid being attacked by the vastly superior force in front of me, and with the hope that by thus falling back General Pope would be induced to follow me until I should be reenforced." [126] Jackson's hope was not realized. High water delayed immediate pursuit. [127] Beyond the Rapidan, Pope did not venture. [128]

Jackson considered that he had won a success and, in a characteristic dispatch of August 11 to Lee he so asserted. "On the evening of the 9th," he said, "God blessed our arms with victory." [129] Privately, Jackson regarded the battle, according to Dabney, as "the most successful of his exploits." [130] He had 400 prisoners, one gun, three colors and a goodly store of small arms to justify his assertion. [131] Possession of the field for two days after the battle was his also. As for casualties, his dead numbered 229 and his wounded 1047. This total of 1276 [132] was not high in terms of the number of troops engaged, but it mounted to 611 in two Brigades, Garnett's and Taliaferro's. [133] The Federal losses, in comparison, were 2381, among whom were the 400 prisoners. [134] Not less than 20,000 Confederate troops had been within easy striking distance

126 *Ibid.,* 185.

127 *Ibid.,* 143. This reference by General Milroy to "a narrow and deep creek" 800 yards below and emptying into Robertson River identifies this obstructing stream as Beaver Dam Creek.

128 *O. R.,* 12, pt. 2, p. 12.

129 *Dabney,* 505-06.

130 *Ibid.,* 505. Douglas, *op. cit.,* 50, quoted an amusing exchange between Jackson and "Jeb" Stuart after the battle. Jackson: "General, I cannot agree with you. I think General Banks a better officer than his people think he is. I always found he fought well." Stuart: "Well, General, you at least have no cause to complain; indeed it would be ungrateful if you did, for he has been the best commissary and quartermaster you ever had!"

131 Jackson, in his final report, *O. R.,* 12, pt. 2, p. 184, gave the number of captured small arms as 5302, and in the dispatch of August 11 to Lee, quoted by Dabney, he stated that the number collected by the morning of that day was about 1500. The larger figure was disputed by Ropes, *op. cit.,* 29-30, "as there were not many more muskets in all Banks' corps." William Allan, in his *Army,* 176, n. 2, concluded that the total of 5302 included those, estimated by him at 1000, of Confederate dead and wounded. To these recovered Southern arms are properly to be added those thrown away in the rout of the Confederate left.

132 *O. R.,* 12, pt. 2, p. 180. These are the figures of the Medical Director of the Army. Jackson, in his report (*ibid.,* 185), gave his loss as 223 killed, 1060 wounded and thirty-one missing; total, 1314.

133 Garnett, 301; Taliaferro, 310. Of these, 136 were killed. *O. R.,* 12, pt. 2, p. 179.

134 *Ibid.,* 139.

44 LEE'S LIEUTENANTS

on the day of battle;[135] Banks had on the ground less than half that number. Jackson, therefore, lost about 6 per cent of his force, Banks close to 30 per cent.

Viewed tactically, rather than in terms of casualties, the battle should have added nothing to Jackson's reputation. On the contrary, had all the facts been known and appraised critically, they might have raised doubts concerning Jackson's leadership. Misgiving would have been aggravated by the reflection that with his superior numbers he should have taken larger advantage of Banks's gross recklessness.

However vague the terms of the orders Banks had received,[136] he had with him on the field Pope's staff representative, Brig. Gen. B. S. Roberts, who knew that the commanding General intended that Banks, if attacked, should do no more than skirmish and defend a strong position until reinforcements arrived. Banks had not been content to do merely this. He had been convinced, without adequate reconnaissance, that a small force confronted him, and probably he had been goaded by General Roberts's tactless hints that the Corps must not hold back that day. An opportunity was offered, Banks apparently thought, of winning the field and of effacing the discredit of defeat by Jackson in the Shenandoah Valley. Against the Confederates, he had hurled three of his four Brigades in an assault for which he had not prepared. The initial attack on the Confederate left had been made by no more than three regiments and six companies of a fourth.[137]

Why, in these circumstances, had not the assault been crushed at once? How were the two left Brigades of Jackson's Army thrown into wild confusion and one of them and part of the other routed? There is one answer only: The Confederate left was not protected with the measure of precaution that should have been expected of a soldier of competence. That flank had been in the air. Although the wood had been so thick that surprise might

135 As noted, *supra*, p. 23, William Allan in his *Army*, 159–60, 165 n., computed Jackson's total to be 24,000, from which number should be deducted Jones's Seventh Virginia Cavalry, on the left, and also Lawton's and Gregg's Brigades, which two, it will be remembered, were guarding the trains.
136 See *supra*, p. 21.
137 5th Conn., 28th N. Y., 46th Penn. and part of the 3rd Wisconsin. *O. R.*, 12, pt. 2, pp. 146–47. For a blistering Federal criticism of these tactics, see G. H. Gordon, *Brook Farm to Cedar Mountain*, 290. At the outset, it would appear, Banks ordered the attack on the left to be delivered by a single regiment. *Ibid.*, 291.

have been expected, no reconnaissance had been made to the left. No scouts, even, appear to have been sent out there.

Was this the fault of Jackson, or was it due to the wounding of the divisional commander before the Brigades on the left had been deployed fully? Winder's previous management of action and his final message to Garnett to remain in position for a few minutes, make it reasonable to conclude that if Winder had not been wounded when he was, he would have deployed his left anew and, doubtless, more carefully. After Winder's fall, Jackson saw quickly the danger to the left, but his instructions to Garnett on his brief call at that officer's post of command seem to have been inadequate. Could Jackson be said to have taken proper precaution when a Lieutenant Colonel, called to direct brigade operations for the first time on confusing terrain, simply was told to "look well" to his flank and to call on his divisional chief for reinforcements? [138] Should not Jackson personally have acquainted himself with conditions on a flank that was threatened and in the air? As for Taliaferro's share of responsibility, the change made by that officer in Garnett's line was ordered hurriedly under marked disadvantage. When a senior Brigadier is kept in ignorance of the part the Division is to play in action, how can he be blamed if, on sudden call, he does not follow a plan he does not know? Jackson's reticence—not to say secretiveness—was responsible in part for the rout of his left wing.

Criticism of Jackson or of Ewell for the failure of the two Brigades on the Confederate right to share in the battle until the last hour must be more reserved. It often is difficult to say when fire that protects one part of a line should be stopped in order that another part of the line may be advanced. A sound decision depends on the particular circumstances of the field. In this instance, until the time Thomas's Brigade extended Early's right and perhaps even then, the gap between Ewell and Early was so wide that less risk was run by keeping Ewell's two Brigades inactive than by exposing Early's right to a possible flanking movement. There is reason to believe, also, that the artillery fire on the Confederate right checked the enemy there and, further, that the

138 None of this, not even the rout of his men, implies discredit of Lt. Col. Garnett. In reporting on Cedar Mountain, General Taliaferro said of Garnett: "[He] exhibited a rare skill and courage, refusing to leave the field, although severely [wounded] until the close of the fight . . ." *O. R.*, 12. pt. 2, p. 190.

cross fire did not delay Ewell for a time much longer than he required to prepare for his advance.[139]

A third criticism, and one of definite validity, is that Jackson's general management of the action was lacking in grasp and control. The battle was marked by some of the elements of a meeting engagement and for that reason should not be judged inexorably by the standards of balance of force; but the picture one gets is wholly at variance with that of Jackson at Winchester. On May 25, Jackson seemed to have his hand on all his Brigades, on all his regiments even. At Cedar Mountain, though he outnumbered his adversary two to one, he did not utilize anything like his entire force. Nor did he dominate the field. Except for a hand in rallying the center after it broke, Jackson had small part in the critical operations of the day. Early fought his battle undirected; Taliaferro received too little counsel from the commanding General. As far as the records show, the sole order to Hill was for the dispatch of a Brigade to reinforce the center.[140] The advance and deployment of the other units of the general reserve seem to have been on Hill's initiative.[141] Is this to be explained on the ground that Jackson was unable personally to direct as many as three Divisions, and had not learned, as yet, to share his plans and his responsibility with any of his subordinates except Ewell? Had Lee's advice to him, when Hill was sent to Gordonsville, been based on the belief that Jackson's handling of his enlarged command during the Seven Days had shown that same deficiency?

None of these questions was asked in Richmond. When Jackson announced that "God blessed our arms with another victory," Lee sent his congratulations and assured Jackson "the country owes you and your brave officers and soldiers a deep debt of gratitude." [142] Jackson himself ordered a day of thanksgiving in the Army,[143] and in writing Mrs. Jackson preached a private sermon

---

139 On the one point, see General Augur's report, *O. R.,* 12, pt. 2, p. 158. General Williams stated (*ibid.,* 146) that the attack by his Division, on the Federal right, was undertaken to "relieve the left wing, severely pressed by the enemy, especially by a heavy cross-fire of artillery . . ." Concerning the length of the delay in bringing the Confederate right into action, Ewell (*ibid.,* 227), reported: "a mill-pond stopped the farther progress of our right and for a short time the only approach against the enemy was swept by our batteries in the valley."

140 See *supra,* p. 27.

141 Here again reservation has to be made for the reasons given *supra,* p. 27, n. 56.

142 *O. R.,* 12. pt. 2, p. 185.   143 *Ibid*

on faith. Said he: "All glory be to God for his unnumbered blessings . . . Let us all unite more earnestly in imploring God's aid in fighting our battles for us. The thought that there are so many of God's people praying for His blessing upon the army, which in His providence, is with me, greatly strengthens me. If God be for us, who can be against us? That he will still be with us, and give us victory after victory, until our independence shall be established, and that He will make our nation that people whose God is the Lord, is my earnest and oft-repeated prayer. Whilst we attach so much importance to being free from temporal bondage, we must attach far more to being free from the bondage of sin." [144]

Neither Jackson's thanksgiving nor the satisfaction of the Confederate government was marred by the withdrawal behind the Rapidan. Pope's assertion of a victory and his publication of General Halleck's congratulations on his "hard earned but brilliant success against vastly superior numbers" [145] were received with ridicule by the Southern people and were denounced as "effrontery." [146] The Battle of Cedar Mountain, rightly or not, confirmed the faith of the Southern press in the military prowess of Jackson. If the contest with Pope elicited less praise than did the Valley campaign, that may have been because public attention was centered in August on the reports of McClellan's impending withdrawal from James River.[147]

The incident of the Battle of Cedar Mountain that most often was mentioned, and always with sorrow, was the death of General Winder. McHenry Howard reached him not long after he had been placed on a stretcher. "General," said the young staff officer, "do you know me?" Winder answered, "Oh, yes," but his mind had left the battlefield and had gone back home. He spoke vaguely a few words about his wife and children and then he

---

[144] *Dabney,* 507.   [145] *O. R.,* 12, pt. 2, p. 135.
[146] Cf. *Dabney,* 507.

[147] For comment on Cedar Mountain and for reprint of Northern reports, see *Richmond Enquirer,* Aug. 13, p. 1, col. 1, and p. 2, col. 5; Aug. 14, p. 1, col. 2; Aug. 19, p. 1, cols. 3–5; Aug. 20, p. 1, cols. 7–8; Aug. 21, p. 1, col. 6; *Richmond Examiner,* Aug. 13, p. 1, col. 1; Aug. 19, p. 1, cols. 2–3; *Richmond Whig,* Aug. 13, p. 2, col. 2; Aug. 16, p. 1, col. 1; *ibid.,* p. 1, col. 3 (quoting *Savannah Republican*), Aug. 20, p. 1, col. 4; *Richmond Dispatch,* Aug. 13, p. 1, col. 1; Aug. 18, p. 1, col. 2; Aug. 20, 1862, p. 1, cols. 2–3. In the *Richmond Enquirer,* Aug. 16, p. 1, col. 1, was reprinted an exceptionally good article from the *Savannah News* on the "magnificent plainness" of Jackson.

relapsed into the silence of shock. "General," a Chaplain exhorted, "lift up your head to God." "I do," said Winder calmly,
"I do lift it up to him."

He was taken to the rear, past the advancing Stonewall Brigade, whose veterans sorrowfully took their last look at him.
McHenry Howard recorded: "Perhaps prompted by this, he asked
me how the battle was going, and seemed gratified at my reply.
He became quieter presently, and as I walked beside him with his
hand in mine, I could feel it growing colder . . . We stopped in
a grove surrounding a church or school house on the west side of
the road. By this time—I suppose it was after 6 o'clock—he had
become totally unconscious and at sundown, with my arm around
his neck and supporting his head, he expired, so quietly that I
could scarcely mark the exact time of his death."

On behalf of the men who had been "bucked" by Winder for
straggling, Private Casler recorded: "[General Winder's] death
was not much lamented by the Brigade, for it probably saved
some of them the trouble of carrying out their threats to kill him.
I would not have done it had I the chance; but I firmly believe it
would have been done by some one in that battle." [148] Far different were the reflections on Winder's death by those best qualified to gauge his finer qualities. Said Jackson: "I can hardly think
of the fall of Brigadier General C. S. Winder, without tearful
eyes." In his account of the battle Jackson wrote: "It is difficult
within the proper reserve of an official report to do justice to the
merits of this accomplished officer . . . Richly endowed with
those qualities of mind and person which fit an officer for command and which attract the admiration and excite the enthusiasm
of troops, he was rapidly rising to the front rank of his profession." [149] In similar spirit Lee spoke of the "courage, capacity and
conspicuous merit" of Winder. [150] The body of the gallant Mary-

[148] *Casler*, 148.
[149] *O. R.*, 12, pt. 2, p. 183. Second only to the death of Winder as a source of general regret in Jackson's Division was the loss of Lt. Col. R. H. Cunningham, Jr., of
the Twenty-first Virginia. He led his regiment, Taliaferro reported, with "most heroic
gallantry" (*O. R.*, 12, pt. 2, p. 190. Cf. *ibid.*, 201, 202). Cunningham, like Winder,
had been sick on the day of the battle, but at the sound of action, had left his ambulance, had mounted and had taken charge of his regiment. Had he lived, promotion
would have been certain (*Worsham*, 115).
[150] *O. R.*, 12, pt. 2, p. 178.

lander was buried first at Orange Court House but soon was brought to Richmond and was placed temporarily in one of the vaults of Hollywood Cemetery.[151]

If the loss of Winder deprived Jackson of the best lieutenant he had, Ewell alone excepted, the Battle of Cedar Mountain set a star opposite Early's name. "Old Jube" had been the most conspicuous figure on the field. His dispositions, which were as careful as those at Williamsburg had been the reverse, stood flawlessly the tension of the struggle. Had not his right held firmly with Thomas when the Confederate left was turned, the day probably would have been lost. That was not stated by Jackson in his report, but even he, loath though he was to compliment living men, stated that Early's right had stood "with great firmness." [152] Ewell, who always was more generous in praise than was Jackson, singled out Early for special mention, and urged his promotion. In Early's own recommendation that Col. J. A. Walker of the Thirteenth Virginia be made a Brigadier General, Ewell concurred warmly. Nothing was done at the time, but Walker, who had been on Jackson's black books at V. M. I., was a marked man from that day. Although another vigorous fighter, Isaac R. Trimble, had no opportunity at Cedar Mountain, he rejoiced in the northward advance of the army. "Comrades," he said to his men after the action, "I feel that I am on my way to my home in Maryland!" [153]

Ewell's part in the battle, though wholly creditable, had been limited, as already indicated, by the difficulties of ground. Nothing did the modest Ewell claim for himself. Generously he said: "Where the printed accounts speak of Ewell, Jackson ought to be substituted. My Division being in advance, movements were

---

[151] The Richmond funeral was August 18. Cf. *Richmond Examiner,* Aug. 13, p. 1, col. 1; *Richmond Dispatch,* Aug. 19, p. 1, col. 7; *Richmond Whig,* Aug. 18, 1862, p. 1, col. 2; *McHenry Howard,* 176–77 n, stated that the body was removed again in the autumn of 1865 to the "old Lloyd graveyard at Wye House," Talbot County. Kyd Douglas, *op. cit.,* 126, observed "[Winder] was the most brilliant of the many valuable officers Maryland gave to the Confederacy, and I have no doubt that had he lived he would have been the commander of a corps before the war ended. But he was one of the victims to the position of commander of the Stonewall Brigade. After General Jackson's promotion, no general of that Brigade ever lived long enough to secure further promotion: none ever escaped wounds or death long enough to be made a Major General."

[152] *O. R.,* 12, pt. 2, p. 183. For the next part of the sketch of Early, see *infra,* p. 73
[153] 2 *N. C. Regts.,* 133.

attributed to me that, in effect, were Jackson's." [154] To a kinswoman he wrote soon after the battle: "I fully condole with you
over the gloomy prospect in regard to the war. Some 100,000
human beings have been massacred in every conceivable form of
horror, with three times as many wounded, all because of a set of
fanatical abolitionists and unprincipled politicians backed by
women in petticoats and pants and children." [155]

Not all of Ewell's explosive power was employed in his letter-
writing. Hundreds must have chuckled over the story of his indignation with a Lieutenant who had not supplied a detail of ten
couriers at a point where Ewell had expected the men. After
finding and abusing the young officer roundly, Ewell asked why
the couriers had not appeared. The Lieutenant began: "I supposed, General—" but he got no further. Ewell pounced upon
him: "You 'supposed,' you 'supposed' you say! What right have
you to suppose anything about it, sir? Do as I tell you, sir; do as
I tell you!" With that he went off, nor did he ever give the Lieutenant a chance of getting beyond the "I supposed—" [156]

A. P. Hill had not been permitted to throw into the action the
full weight of his Division, but into the rout of Taliaferro's men
he had ridden, coat off and sword bared, and had rallied some of
those who were fleeing. When a captured Federal Brigadier,
Henry Prince, came up and started in the midst of a heavy fire
to speak of the "fortunes of war" that "have thrown me into your
hands," Hill interrupted: "Damn the fortunes of war, General;
get to the rear; you are in danger here!" [157] Zealous though Hill
had been in all of this he received scant mention in reports. Jackson recorded the part played by Thomas on the right, and when
he came to describe the counter-stroke on the left, he said: "At
this critical moment Branch's brigade, of Hill's division, with
Winder's brigade farther to the left, met the Federal forces, flushed
with temporary triumph, and drove them back with terrible
slaughter through the wood." There was a word, also, of what
Archer and Pender had done in the final charge, but with that,

---

154 P. G. Hamlin, *Old Bald Head* (cited hereafter as *Old Bald Head*), 121. This
work must be distinguished from Dr. Hamlin's earlier *The Making of a Soldier: Letters
of General R. S. Ewell*, which is cited as *Hamlin's Ewell*.
155 *Hamlin's Ewell*, 114.
156 *Myers*, 94–95. For the continuance of the sketch of Ewell, see *infra*, pp. 84, 102
157 10 *S. H. S. P.*, 89; 19 *ibid.*, 182.

the references to the Light Division's part in the immediate battle ended.[158]

If Hill and his men thought these scant tributes an under-appraisal of their service, they had their secret satisfaction. Branch doubtless spoke for the entire Division when he wrote in his diary with grim pleasure of Jackson's call for him to save the day, and of the instant advance of his Brigade. "I had not gone 100 yards through the woods," wrote Branch, "before we met the celebrated Stonewall Brigade, utterly routed and fleeing as fast as they could run." [159] Actually, as noted already, it was not the entire Brigade but only the Twenty-seventh Virginia [160] to which Branch's North Carolinians had opened their ranks while they pressed to the front. That did not lessen the contrast which Ham Chamber-layne, young artillerist, shaped in a proud sentence: "[The Fed-erals] fought miserably and but for a wavering on the part of two Brigades of Jackson's Division, they would have given us no trouble whatever; as it was, as soon as the men found our Brigades coming up to their support, the whole thing became a mere pur-suit." He added: "We chased them upwards of three miles. Com-pared with the battles around Richmond this whole affair was a skirmish. Several of Jackson's regiments behaved very badly, yielding to a mere panic." [161]

What more could A. P. Hill have wished? Had Jackson counted him tardy in his march toward the battle? There could be no complaint of him after he had reached the field of action and had found some of Jackson's own men running from it.

---

[158] *O. R.*, 12, pt. 2, pp. 183–84, though there was a sentence or two on the abor-tive pursuit under Hill after dark.

[159] *O. R.*, 12, pt. 2, p. 223.

[160] *Ibid.*, 197. On Apr. 17, 1863, Jed. Hotchkiss (*MS Diary*, 163) noted that he had reviewed Jackson's report of Cedar Mountain. Jackson, said Hotchkiss, wrote that Win-der and Branch had gone into the fight at the same time. Actually, Hotchkiss asserted, Winder had charged through the "bushy field" and had taken several stands of colors before Branch had passed Major's School House.

[161] *Ham Chamberlayne*, 90. The sketch of Hill is resumed, *infra*, pp. 84, 104.

CHAPTER III

JEB STUART LOSES HIS PLUME

THE BATTLE OF Cedar Mountain exposed much and decided nothing. Mr. Lincoln's advisers were not to be shaken from their belief that they must deprive the Confederates of the advantage of strategic interception. Halleck stated the case explicitly, as he saw it, in a dispatch to McClellan three days before the action: "You are thirty miles from Richmond and General Pope eighty or ninety, with the enemy directly between you, ready to fall with his superior numbers upon one or the other as he may elect. Neither can re-enforce the other in case of such an attack." [1] It had been for this reason that Halleck had decided McClellan must abandon James River and take shipping to some point whence the Army of the Potomac could march easily to form an early junction with Pope. The Fredericksburg area seemed the most convenient point for the debarkation of McClellan. If Pope could hold the upper Rappahannock while McClellan mustered farther downstream, Halleck hoped "to prevent any farther advance of Lee, and eventually with the combined armies to drive him back upon Richmond." [2] This reasoning was not changed by the battle. McClellan must move, Pope must stand, the two must unite.

To the Confederates, after Jackson's withdrawal from Cedar Mountain, the danger on the Rappahannock seemed more imminent than that on the James. Pope manifestly was too strong to be attacked by Jackson. The Army of Virginia might resume its advance on Gordonsville; rumor persisted that McClellan was preparing to evacuate.[3] The wisest course, in the judgment of Lee, was to concentrate against Pope and, if possible, to dispose of him

---

[1] *O. R.*, 12, pt. 2, p. 10. [2] *Ibid.*

[3] *Richmond Whig*, Aug. 12, p. 2, col. 1; *Richmond Examiner*, Aug. 12, p. 1, col. 1, ibid., Aug. 14, p. 1, col. 1; *Richmond Enquirer*, Aug. 13, p. 1, col. 3 and p. 2, col. 2; *Richmond Dispatch*, Aug. 14, p. 1, col. 1. Numerous accounts of the actual evacuation were published. The most informative were those of the *Richmond Examiner*, Aug. 21, p. 1, col. 1, and of the *New York Herald* of Aug. 20, reprinted in the *Richmond Dispatch* of Aug. 27, 1862, p. 1, cols. 3-4.

before McClellan could join him.[4] Already, it was feared, Pope might have been reinforced because, on August 13, it was apparent that Burnside either had left or was ready to leave Fredericksburg.[5] His objective, as previously considered, might be either Pope's Army or an attack on Jackson's line of supply, the Virginia Central Railroad. To protect that line, Lee decided to post two Brigades at Hanover Junction.[6] In order that the blow against Pope might be heavy, reinforcements sent directly to Jackson, August 13, were formidable—ten Brigades under Longstreet. Upon reaching Gordonsville, Longstreet by seniority took command; but before "Old Pete" had learned more than the first bare facts of the situation, Lee himself arrived and opened Army Headquarters.

All of this entailed some changes in the high command and, in the developing new crisis, involved four unpleasant incidents. For the general supervision of the Richmond front, there returned to duty a one-time celebrity who already was being forgotten—Maj. Gen. Gustavus W. Smith. That officer had recovered slowly from his collapse of June 1,[7] and during his convalescence had about persuaded himself that Lee had cheated him of the army command in succession to Johnston;[8] but by August 10, Smith was well enough to undertake divisional command again. To him were assigned D. H. Hill's old troops, some of whom were as good as the best.[9] In addition, Lee requested Smith as "senior officer of this wing of the Army" to "direct its operations," which included those of "Dick" Anderson's Division at Drewry's Bluff and those in D. H. Hill's Department of North Carolina.[10] As Hill's Department had been extended to James River, and his troops were regarded as a part of Lee's Army, Smith now exercised as conspicuous a command as ever had been his under Johnston. If there was any hesitation about entrusting so large a field to Smith, it does not appear in surviving records. Nor was there any discussion of the willingness and ability of Smith and of Harvey Hill

---

[4] For the detailed outworking of this plan, see 2 *R. E. Lee*, 265 ff.

[5] *Ibid.*, p. 272, n. 79; *Richmond Enquirer*, Aug. 13, p. 2, col. 2; *Richmond Dispatch*, Aug. 14, p. 1, col. 1; Aug. 20, p. 1, col. 4.

[6] 2 *R. E. Lee, loc. cit.*

[7] "I do not get straight in brains and nerves as fast as I hoped."—Smith to Joseph E. Johnston, July 18, 1862; *O. R.*, 51, pt. 2, pp. 593–94.

[8] *Ibid.*: ". . . If provoked much further I will tear the mask off some who think themselves wonderfully successful in covering up their tracks."

[9] *O. R.*, 11, pt. 3, p. 671.   [10] *O. R.*, 12, pt. 3, pp. 930–31.

to work together. At the award of so shining a station, Smith was mollified, pleased perhaps, though his surgeons doubted whether his physical condition would permit him to discharge any other than post command in a healthful climate.[11]

Before Smith had undertaken his new duties, the rumors of McClellan's evacuation of his base on James River were verified. By transport and by march, the Army of the Potomac moved to join Pope. This could not have been prevented by Lee, even had he not been anxious to get the Federals away from the vicinity of Richmond. The humiliation was that McClellan escaped without casualties. In the whole operation, August 7–20, he lost scarcely a wagon wheel. For this, Lee blamed himself only; but the failure of D. H. Hill to make any move against McClellan somewhat shocked Lee and, no doubt, the President. This was the first unpleasantness of mid-August. It arose because Hill commanded directly across James River from McClellan's base and must have observed the activity of the Federals, but he neither harassed them on the river nor organized any pursuit of the rearguard.

Such negligence would have been surprising at any time. It was worse than surprising in the light of what had happened earlier in August. On the 1st, Hill had been directed to bombard the Federal camps at Harrison's Landing and the shipping in James River. From the Southside, Hill had good approaches to the river and he received ample artillery, but he had gone about his mission without the display of any driving spirit or administrative skill. Because General Lee had suggested that the services of Gen. S. G. French be employed, Hill had turned the expedition over to that officer and had ridden back to Petersburg the night before that on which the attack was delivered.[12] The bombardment, which caused no more than twenty-two Federal casualties,[13] had been in every respect a fiasco and had been the occasion of painful concern on Lee's part regarding Hill's fitness for departmental command.

Now that Hill did nothing to interfere with McClellan's withdrawal, Lee had regretfully to write the President: "This induces

---

[11] Cf. Davis to Gov. F. W. Pickens: 5 Rowland, 319.
[12] O. R., 11, pt. 2, pp. 939 ff, 941; 3 N. C. Regts., 167; S. G. French, Two Wars, 148.
[13] Ibid., 935—ten killed and twelve wounded.

me to say what I have had on my mind for some time. I fear
General Hill is not entirely equal to his present position. An excellent executive officer, he does not appear to have much administrative ability. Left to himself, he seems embarrassed and backward to act." [14] These were not pleasant phrases to couple with
the name of the soldier who had shone through the battle-smoke
of Seven Pines and of Gaines' Mill, but the facts could not be
blinked.

Unhappily, too, if there was a lack of vigor in Hill's administration of his department, there was no lack of venom. Within a
few days after the assumption of departmental command, Hill
had recommended the "raising of guerrilla companies, and the
arming of them by the Government, to operate in the counties of
Nansemond [Va.] and Gates [N.C.], or wherever the infernal
Yankees and their rascally Dutch allies can be found." Hill had
explained: "The special duty of these guerrillas is to kill the
murderers and plunderers wherever they show their villainous
faces." [15]

With the author of this remarkable statement, what should be
done? Was it better to leave him in departmental command or
to return him to his old place as a chief of Division in the Army
of Northern Virginia? Lee's decision was to recall Hill to field
service when opportunity offered. [16]

Personalities as marked as those that concerned D. H. Hill and
Gustavus Smith provoked some of Jackson's subordinates. Between "Stonewall" and A. P. Hill, ill-feeling was brewing. Unpleasantness threatened, for a time, even between Jackson and
Ewell because of Jackson's first report on Cedar Mountain. The
modest Ewell cared nothing for public recognition of his own
services, but he was jealous of the reputation of his lieutenants
and was insistent that they receive the credit due them. He interpreted Jackson's reference to Winder, in the dispatch of August
11, as an intimation that Winder had led the advance. [17] Early
had challenged this as inaccurate; Ewell supported Early and took

14 O. R., 51, pt. 2, p. 1075.
15 O. R., 51, pt. 2, p. 601. Secretary Randolph authorized the enlistment.
16 The next detailed reference to Harvey Hill is *infra*, pp. 154, 166 ff.
17 The language of Jackson was "Brigadier-General Charles S. Winder was mortally
wounded whilst ably discharging his duty at the head of his command, which was the
advance of the left wing of the army." *Dabney*, 506.

up the question with the commanding General. Fortunately.
Jackson saw the point of the inquiry and answered it reasonably.
He quoted his dispatch, of which he enclosed Ewell a full copy,
and he added: "Had I spoken of Gen. Early's position it would
have been the centre of the advance of the army. It was not my
design at the time of writing the dispatch to speak of the individual services of our surviving officers."[18] That satisfied Early and
Ewell. In Jackson's final report, which was not written until
almost eight months later, full justice was done Early.[19]

The remaining difficulty of a personal sort, the one involving
Beverley Robertson of the cavalry, continued to cause friction but
it presented no new difficulty after Lee's arrival at Gordonsville.
Jackson persisted in his belief that Robertson had rendered less
service than he had a right to expect, but Lee, it would seem, continued to think that Jackson might have been too exacting. The
simplest and most efficacious remedy was applied: On August 17,
Robertson's Brigade and the other cavalry of Jackson's command
were put under Stuart who, by private order or on his own judgment, personally supervised, for a time, the movements of Robertson.[20]

Little time was spent on these personal controversies, because
of a new Federal blunder that offered an opening for swift, decisive action. When Lee reached Gordonsville on August 15, the
Federal commander remained in an exposed position North of the
Rapidan. Behind him was the Rappahannock, into which, at a
point about twelve miles West of Fredericksburg, the Rapidan
flowed. With the angle to the East, the Union Army thus was in a
"V". If the Confederates could throw their cavalry in rear of Pope
and burn the main railroad bridge across the Rappahannock, he
would be cut off from his base. That done, his army might be
attacked furiously and captured or slaughtered in detail.

To effect this, promptness and secrecy were essential: any dis-
cernible preparations for a Confederate offensive would send the
troops of Pope streaming back across the Rappahannock to wider
fields of maneuver. Lee believed that speed was the muzzle of
secrecy. Accordingly, to reduce the chance that his adversary

---

[18] *Jackson's MS Letter Book*, Aug. 19, 1862, p. 41.
[19] *O. R.*, 12, pt. 2, p. 181 ff.
[20] *O. R.*, 12, pt. 2, p. 726 ff; the orders appear in *O. R.*, 12, pt. 3, p. 934.

might discover his plan by loss of a single hour beyond the time required for essential preparation, Lee decided to ford the Rapidan on the night of August 17 and to assail Pope on the 18th.[21]

A great opportunity this presented the cavalry, which, unfortunately, was not concentrated. Hampton was on the Richmond front and could not be used. Fitz Lee, commanding the other Brigade of cavalry, was at Hanover Court House with Stuart. On the 16th, Stuart moved with Fitz Lee's men to Davenport's Bridge on the North Anna.[22] There, on the morning of the 17th, Stuart left Fitz Lee and proceeded by train to Army Headquarters. Stuart's understanding was that Fitz Lee was to proceed that day across country to the vicinity of Raccoon Ford on the Rapidan, a march of approximately thirty-two miles.[23]

After Stuart had completed his railroad journey and had reported to the commanding General, he sent two of his staff ahead and, with the others, rode on to Verdiersville, a hamlet by which Fitz Lee would be compelled to pass en route to Raccoon Ford. Around Verdiersville lived several branches of the Rhodes family, which already had felt the heavy hand of war. A Federal cavalry column on a reconnaissance from Fredericksburg had stopped at Verdiersville, had stolen all of Catlett Rhodes's corn and bacon and had broken open and had looted the dwelling and store of Postmaster T. J. Hatch.[24]

Among these suffering people, Stuart's advance officers were welcome but from the residents they did not get the expected answer to their question concerning the arrival of the cavalry. No Confederates had been seen, nor was there any news of an encampment nearby. When Stuart arrived, late in the evening of August 17, he was puzzled but not alarmed: doubtless Fitz Lee would come up shortly. To hasten his march, Major Norman Fitzhugh could ride out to meet him. For the others, meantime, there could be relaxation and perhaps sleep.

In the garden and on the porch of the Rhodes house, some 400

---

[21] *O. R.,* 12, pt. 2, p. 552.

[22] About five miles Northwest of Beaver Dam Station on the Virginia Central Railroad, and near the boundary of Spotsylvania and Caroline Counties.

[23] The route would have been via Waller's Tavern, St. John's Church, the Lawyers Road and Verdiersville.

[24] *Richmond Dispatch,* Aug. 8, 1862, p. 1, col. 1.

yards East of the crossroads, the officers prepared to bivouac.[25] Stuart divested himself of his haversack and carefully laid to one side his plumed hat—a new hat of which, if tradition be correct, he had particular reason to be proud. On the day of the truce for burying the dead at Cedar Mountain, Stuart had met on the field Brig. Gen. Samuel W. Crawford and Brig. Gen. Geo. D. Bayard, both of whom he had known in the "old army." They had made their jesting claims concerning the battle, whereupon Stuart had bet Crawford a hat that the Federals would assert that Cedar Mountain had been a victory for the Union. In due time, under a flag of truce, a hat had arrived at the outpost for Stuart and with it a copy of a New York paper that proclaimed a triumph for Pope in the action of August 9. This was the hat Stuart now doffed and put in a safe place beside him on the porch where he spread out his cloak for a bed.[26]

The short summer night yielded scant sleep. At dawn, the mist of August lay so heavily over the fields that the crossroads a quarter of a mile distant scarcely were visible. As the men stirred, they heard from the East the clatter of a column of cavalry and the rumble of wagons in motion. Stuart got up and walked down to the fence that fronted the highway. Through the mist, he could see troopers moving at right angles across the main road and down the one that led to the fords of the Rapidan.

The column came from the direction of Fitz Lee's delayed advance; the men must be his. Stuart directed two of his companions to go up the road, to halt the column, and to direct its commanding officer to report immediately. A fine if jovial rebuke there would be for Fitz Lee, twelve hours late on a march of thirty-two miles! Off trotted the messengers. Stuart made ready his verbal barbs. A minute more and then pistol shots, the

[25] Von Borcke's account, *op. cit.*, 1, 105, placed the bivouac "in the little garden of the first farmhouse on the right of the village," and later he noted that this was "about 400 yards" from "the road which led through the village."
[26] Douglas, *op. cit.*, 128, is authority for the statement that Bayard and Stuart met. The story of the origin of Stuart's hat is from a MS note of Charles M. Blackford in the *MS Memoirs of W. W. Blackford*, 138. Charles M. Blackford stated that he was in charge of the flag of truce for the burial of the dead and that he witnessed the scene between Stuart and the Federals. Neither of the Union officers was, as Mr. Blackford thought, a classmate of Stuart's at West Point. General Bayard was two years behind Stuart at the Military Academy. That institution General Crawford had never attended. He had been graduated from the University of Pennsylvania and had been an officer of the Medical Corps prior to the outbreak of hostilities. Von Borcke stated, *op. cit.*, 1, 108, that Stuart's "beautiful hat" was "the present of a lady in Baltimore." For Stuart's account of his resting place on the porch, etc., see *O. R.*, 12, pt. 2, p. 726.

challenge of voices, the scamper of returning horsemen—the column was not Fitz Lee's but the enemy's!

Every man for himself! Stuart did not wait for hat and cloak. He turned; he ran to his horse; he vaulted into the saddle; he

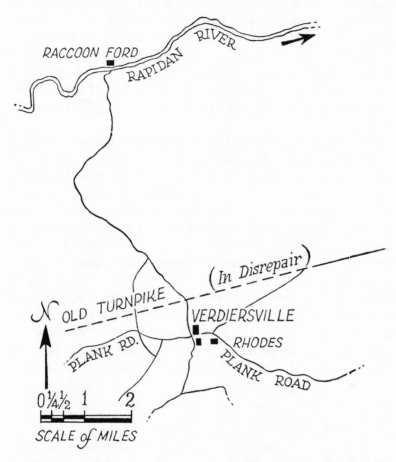

The Vicinity of Verdiersville. Many farm roads crossed and recrossed between the Old Turnpike and the Rapidan. The one figured here seems to have been the most direct from Verdiersville to Raccoon Ford

struck with his spurs. Over the garden fence, at one bold jump, went horse and rider. Von Borcke galloped through the gate which a resident had the presence of mind to open for him. The other officers scattered. Vigorously they were pursued. The gigantic von Borcke, a large target, kept to the road and brought on his heels a number of bluecoats. Hard pressed, he outrode them. His companions, too, escaped. When they assembled again, after the blue column had clattered off to the river, they were chagrined, humiliated and amused all at the same time. Stuart had lost not only his cloak, his hat, his sash and his plumage but also something much more serious, the haversack that contained his maps and some recent correspondence that would be informative to the enemy. When the sun mounted hotly, Stuart had to make of his handkerchief a cover for his reddish locks. Thus adorned with what seemed to be a capillose flag of truce, he was greeted everywhere with the same jibing question, "Where's your hat?" [27]

Fitz Lee did not feel that he was to blame for the embarrassment of his chief. His explanation was the simple one that he never had understood his presence was required on the Rapidan at a particular time. He knew that Stuart expected him to march to the vicinity of Raccoon Ford, but when Stuart had left him in the early morning of the 17th, Fitz's impression was that the advance could be leisurely. Besides, he was short both of ammunition and of rations; and as his loaded wagons were at Louisa Court House, he decided to move via that town. This made his march fifty-two instead of thirty-two miles and it prevented his joining Stuart until the night of the 18th. [28] Before he did arrive, he notified Gen. R. E. Lee that his horses were in bad condition and would not be fit for hard service on the 19th. [29] The commanding General, accordingly, deferred the advance of the Army

<hr/>

[27] I von Borcke, 105 ff; W. W. Blackford's MS Memoirs, 138; Stuart's account in O. R., 12, pt. 2, p. 726. The variations between Stuart's narrative and that of von Borcke relate to minor details only, but where the two differ, Stuart's account, earlier and official, is followed in the text. Cooke's account in Wearing of the Gray, 204 ff, is accurate, though its author was not present. The finder of Stuart's belongings was Adjutant Ford H. Rogers of the 1st Mich. Cav. He described the headgear as a "broadbrimmed, light brown soft hat with a long feather on it." This hat, said Lieutenant Rogers, he "immediately donned" and after he learned its owner, he preserved it for years with care. Its fate he thus recorded: "The hat I took to California with me packed in a trunk, and being smashed very flat, I took it to a hat store in San Francisco to be put in order, where I allowed it to remain for a long time, and when I called for it, it could not be found, having been cleared out with a lot of old second-hand hats."—Jeb Stuart's Hat, by Ford H. Rogers, War Paper No. 22, Michigan Commandery, Loyal Legion (Detroit, 1893).

[28] O. R., 12, pt. 2, p. 726. Fitz Lee filed no report, but in his General Lee (1895) he said, p. 183, that he "did not understand from any instructions he had received that it was necessary to be at this point on that particular afternoon."

[29] O. R., 12, pt. 3, p. 934.

until the 20th.[30] By that time, Pope had taken alarm, had crossed the Rappahannock and had escaped from the "V".[31]

Stuart was outraged that the tardiness of one of his officers should have been responsible, even in part, for the escape of the Federals. He wrote in his report: "By this failure to comply with instructions not only the movement of the cavalry across the Rapidan was postponed a day, but a fine opportunity lost to overhaul a body of the enemy's cavalry on a predatory excursion far beyond their lines."[32] This criticism was in a measure justified, but in a measure only. Although Fitz Lee manifestly should not have carried his Brigade twenty miles off its march without authority for doing so, he was not solely responsible for delaying the offensive. Even had he arrived on schedule, during the evening of the 17th, the Army would not have been able to carry out its original plan of advancing on the 18th. The commissary was unready; Anderson's Division was not at hand. At the earliest, had Fitz Lee reached Raccoon Ford on the 17th, the crossing would have been on the night of the 18th–19th. Pope would not then have been caught between the rivers, but his rearguard might have been assailed. Loss of that opportunity was the extent of the damage done by Fitz Lee's delay. If he was culpable, Stuart himself was not free of blame. Apparently his orders to Fitz Lee were verbal and they may have been vague when, needless to say, they should have been written and unmistakable in terms. This seems to have been overlooked at the time. Stuart blamed Fitz Lee; nobody blamed Stuart.

The incident was a concern to Longstreet as well as to Stuart, because when Fitz Lee had not appeared on the 17th "Old Pete," with his usual vigilance, had sent infantry to watch the roads that led up from the crossings of the river. How had the Federals passed that guard? Why were they able to reach Verdiersville and so nearly to catch Stuart?

---

[30] *Ibid., loc. cit.*, and 940.

[31] In *ibid.*, 13, Pope stated that he began his withdrawal on the night of the 17th and completed it on the 18th; but in his correspondence with General Halleck, *ibid.*, pt. 3, pp. 591, 601, he put the movements twenty-four hours later. His retirement was not observed until the late afternoon of the 19th (*ibid.*, pt. 2, p. 728) because of low visibility from the Confederate signal station on Clark's Mountain (*ibid.*, pt. 3, p. 940).

[32] *O. R.*, 12, pt. 2, p. 726. For the next detailed references to Stuart, see *infra*, p. 69.

Inquiry showed that Longstreet's order to cover the road from Raccoon Ford had been sent to Brig. Gen. Robert Toombs, whose Brigade chanced to be near. Toombs himself was absent, making a call on a long time political friend who resided nearby, but the senior Colonel duly detached two regiments in accordance with instructions.

On his return, Toombs found that word had been sent for all the troops to cook three days' rations in preparation for the advance. He later explained that he did not wish to have any of his men denied their cooked rations when they started after the enemy; and as he heard that a Brigade of A. P. Hill's Division was between his troops and the ford, he sent request to Longstreet for permission to withdraw his regiments. Longstreet, unfortunately, was not to be found. Thereupon Toombs on his own account ordered the men back to their Brigade. It was over the road the Georgians thus left open that the Federal cavalry passed.

Toombs was put under arrest on the 18th,[33] but ignorantly or defiantly, the next day he strapped on his sword when he went to ride, an act contrary to regulations. Further, he was reported to have delivered a violent speech to his men, who cheered him. For these new offences he was ordered back to Gordonsville and was told to stay there.

He did, but he prepared forthwith to make a political issue of his treatment. In a long letter to his confidant, Vice President Stephens, he explained the arrangement he had in mind for feeding his men. Curiously enough, in describing the affair, he postdated it twenty-four hours and made no reference to Stuart or to the fact that the enemy had penetrated the position he had vacated. In his eyes, the entire affair was persecution. Said he to Stephens: "My zeal for the public service and desire to prepare my starving regt. for battle is my sole and only fault. I must think it a pretext. You shall have all the papers so soon as I have them copied."[34]

---

[33] *O. R.,* 12, pt. 2, p. 580.

[34] *Toombs, etc. Letters,* 603–04. The letter to Stephens was dated August 22. See also *Sorrel,* 100–02; *Longstreet,* 161; *Alexander,* 188. For the continuance of the sketch of Toombs, see *infra,* p. 218.

CHAPTER IV

Rappahannock: Act One of a New Drama

THE INFANTRY that crossed the Rapidan on the 20th of August, 1862, were divided, without formal order, into Longstreet's Right and Jackson's Left Wings. This of itself was historic because it meant that the Army of the Valley ceased to exist as a separate force. Jackson continued to command the Valley District and, on many occasions, dated his communications "Headquarters Valley District";[1] but he considered that his forces definitely became a part of the Army of Northern Virginia after the Battle of Cedar Mountain.[2]

To this unified army, two new Brigades had come. At the head of one, returned "Shanks" Evans who had won fame at Manassas. "Shanks" was full of fight and sure of the valor of his four South Carolina regiments,[3] which, for some reason, were left as an "Independent Brigade," unattached to any Division. The other new Brigade had been brought, as had Evans's, from South Carolina, and was under the command of Thomas F. Drayton, a former classmate of President Davis's at West Point, and a member of one of the leading families of the Palmetto State. In that family, the tragedy of the divided nation was exemplified: While Thomas Drayton had been defending the coast of South Carolina, his brother had been in charge of the U. S. S. *Pocahontas,* one of the vessels engaged in the operations against Port Royal. General Drayton was in spirit a gentleman and in bearing a soldier. Whether he had the qualities of command had been put in some doubt.[4] He was brigaded now with Toombs and with G. T. Anderson in D. R. Jones's Division, a connection which was

---

[1] Cf. *O. R.,* 12, pt. 3, p. 939.

[2] *Cf.* Jackson to R. E. Lee, Dec. 2, 1863 ". . . I hope none of the guns which belonged to the Army of the Valley, before it became part of the Army of Northern Virginia—after the Battle of Cedar Run—will be taken from it" (*Jackson's MS Letter Book,* p. 45).

[3] Seventeenth, Eighteenth, Twenty-second and Twenty-third. Cf. *O. R.,* 12, pt. 2, p. 548.

[4] *O. R.,* 6, 13–14, 110, 312. The first and second of these references are from J. H. Easterby's article on Drayton in 5 *D. A. B.*

not ideal. Jones was both a gentleman and a soldier, but his health was getting progressively worse. He could not be expected to direct closely the administration of his command.

This Division was one of four to undergo change at the beginning of the campaign. A second was Ewell's, to which was transferred Lawton's Brigade from Jackson's Division.[5] The third change was in the command of Whiting's Division. On August 4, before Lee had left Richmond for Gordonsville, Whiting had sent the commanding General a file of papers which showed that he had been cherishing grievances for months. Precisely what his complaints were, the record does not show. Most probably he felt, as well he might, that merited promotion had been denied him. Lee had read the documents and had returned then with this counsel: ". . . forget them, General; do not let us recollect unpleasant things; life is very short. We have so much to do. We can do so much good, too, if we are not turned aside. Everything will come right in the end."[6] Whiting, it would appear, was on sick leave at the time [7] and did not attempt to share in the new campaign. His old Brigade, now under Col. E. M. Law, continued to serve with Hood's in a half Division that Hood commanded.[8] Soon it became known as Hood's.

The fourth change presented a problem of administration and, still more, of command. Longstreet's old Division, it may be remembered, counted six Brigades, two of which were under general officers whose ability in the field was subject to question. George Pickett, who was reckoned among the best leaders in the Division, had not yet recovered from the wound he had received at Gaines' Mill. Longstreet himself was charged with duties so numerous that he could not undertake to handle the Division in action. What should be done with it? Should it be divided, and if so, under whom? No decision had been reached when the "Right Wing" started northward; but the necessities of war soon dictated the informal assignment of three of them to Cadmus Wilcox, and of the other three to James Kemper. Both arrangements were known to be temporary and both seem to have been devised by Longstreet himself. He was beginning to show excel-

[5] O. R., 12, pt. 2, p. 550.
[6] Letter of Aug. 9, 1862; 26 S. H. S. P., 149.
[7] Cf. Ibid., "I am glad to hear you are doing well."
[8] O. R., 12, pt. 2, p. 547

lent judgment of his subordinates, whose admiring support he was winning rapidly.

The "Left Wing," Jackson's, had to undergo less reorganization. No successor to Winder had been named. William B. Taliaferro, as senior Brigadier, was acting head of the Division as, indeed, Winder had been; but the Virginian lacked the reputation the Marylander had earned. Although Winder had died a Brigadier, and not a Major General, his ability to handle four Brigades had been established. Taliaferro's had not been. He was young enough—not yet 40—and he had abundantly the social station and the acquaintance with public life that counted for much in easing the way. Did he possess, besides, the essential qualities of command? Evidently, in the mind of Jackson, the Battle of Cedar Mountain had not answered that question one way or the other. Some of "Stonewall's" misgivings of the spring [9] must have been relieved. Otherwise he would have found a way, however difficult, of keeping the command out of Taliaferro's hands.

In Jackson's Division, for the first time as a Brigadier General, William E. Starke now was serving at the head of one of the two Louisiana Brigades. He was 48 and by birth a Virginian, but he had lived for years in Mobile and in New Orleans,[10] where he had prospered as a large dealer in cotton and had interested himself in politics,[11] though he never held office.[12] To him early in the war had been assigned the Sixtieth Virginia,[13] which he had disciplined well without losing the goodwill of the men.[14] When the Louisiana troops in Virginia were brigaded separately, in accordance with Mr. Davis's cherished policy of organization by States, Colonel Starke's associations with the Gulf seemed to warrant appointment as a Louisiana Brigadier.[15] He was new to the Louisiana troops, but in Field's Brigade of A. P. Hill's Division he was known as a hard fighter. At Mechanicsville he had been wounded painfully in the hand and had been compelled to relinquish command. On June 30, at Frayser's Farm, he had insisted

[9] See *supra*, Vol. I, p. 327.
[10] *Richmond Enquirer*, Oct. 2, 1862. Starke was a native of Brunswick County.
[11] Monier's Diary, in *Military Annals of Louisiana* (cited hereafter as *Mil. An. La.*), 30; *Cf.* 4 *Rowland*, 474.
[12] *Richmond Enquirer, loc. cit.*
[13] *O. R.*, 51, pt. 2, pp. 345, 370, 375, 407; *Richmond Examiner*, Nov. 14, 1862, p. 3, col. 1.
[14] Cf. *Richmond Examiner*, Dec. 12, p. 2, col. 4; Dec. 23, 1862 p. 3, col. 1.
[15] *Wright*, 87; appointed as of Aug. 6, 1862.

on leading his regiment.[16] Now a surprising climb awaited him.

The qualifications of Starke and of Taliaferro probably were studied by Jackson more closely than his letters and his reported conversation indicated. He never was indifferent to brigade or regimental command, though he never balked at battle because his subordinates were inexperienced. His reliance primarily was upon discipline, upon himself, and upon God, not upon the eminence of officers.

Because of this demand for the letter and the spirit of discipline, Jackson had a new encounter with A. P. Hill. In making preparations for the passage of the Rapidan, "Stonewall" remembered what had happened at the start of the advance to Cedar Mountain. In the fear that Hill again might be tardy, the commander of the "Left Wing" particularly admonished him to march on August 20 at moonrise and, with his Division, to take the lead in crossing Somerville Ford. No time was to be lost after reveille: Three days' rations were to have been cooked overnight.[17]

So Jackson specified. Early on the designated morning he rode forward to see whether Hill was on the move. He found to his annoyance that none of the troops of the Light Division had left their camps. One of Hill's Brigadiers, when questioned, said that he had received no marching orders. It was then, Jackson computed, two hours beyond the time at which the start should have been made. Indignantly he ordered forward the first of Hill's Brigades that he found ready for the road. He was much "put out," Hotchkiss wrote, at the slow start,[18] and he no doubt was convinced that whatever the military virtues of A. P. Hill, promptness was not among them.

Of the reasons for Hill's delay, no explanation appears in the records. Hill may have been misled by the orders sent from Army headquarters on the 19th. Lee then had stipulated that the march should begin at "dawn of day." [19] Subsequently,[20] he had stated his intention of marching at the rise of the moon.[21] Hill may not have been sure which orders prevailed or, again, he may have

---

[16] O. R., 11, pt. 2, pp. 836, 839, 841, 842, 846, 848 ff.

[17] Hotchkiss' MS Diary, 71; Rough draft of Jackson's charges and specifications against A. P. Hill; Jackson MSS, Confederate Memorial Institute.

[18] Hotchkiss' MS Diary, Aug. 20, 1862, p. 71.

[19] O. R., 12, pt. 2, p. 729.

[20] So said Stuart, ibid., 726.   [21] Ibid., 729.

been misinformed concerning the time of the moonrise.[22] Whatever Hill's excuse, it did not acquit him in Jackson's mind:
"Moonrise" was established by the almanac, not determined by
the differing judgment of individuals. No wonder the soldiers
said that when Jackson ordered a march at "early dawn," he actually started the night before.

In the earliest light of what gave promise of being a hot, dry
20th of August,[23] the infantry clambered up the banks of the
Rapidan and began a drama in three acts. The first was shaped
by the country in which the rival armies were operating. On its
upper stretches, the Rappahannock comes down from the Bull
Run Mountains to the Orange and Alexandria Railway almost on
the meridian. Below the railroad crossing at Rappahannock Station, the river bends to the Southeast until it receives the waters
of the Rapidan. For the greater part of this distance, the left
bank of the Rappahannock commands the lower right bank.
Consequently, if Pope showed diligence and had good fortune,
he could hope to move up or down the river and to dispute Lee's
attempts to cross at any point. By guarding the fords, Pope could
protect his swift and convenient line of supply via the railroad, or,
at the least, should receive early warning of a threat to that line.
Most of the advantage seemed to be on the side of the defensive.
Pope, by every applicable test, should be able to stand off Lee till
McClellan arrived.

Lee, for his part, scarcely could afford to lose time or men in
forcing the Rappahannock. An attempt to do so East of the railroad was ruled out completely. Such a move would expose the
right of the Confederate army to an attack from the direction of
Fredericksburg and would shorten the distance that Federal
troops would cover in marching from the lower Rappahannock to
form a junction with Pope. Lee could not think of placing his
army between Pope and McClellan. A speedy crossing of the
Rappahannock, West of the railroad, in order to lengthen the
distance between Pope and reinforcements from Fredericksburg,
was the strategy imposed on Lee. That is to say, Lee had to make

[22] The moon, past its last quarter, rose at 12.42 A.M. Sunrise was at 5.21. Stuart,
in his report of Feb. 5, 1863, stated that the cavalry crossed the Rapidan "at moonrise
on the 20th, about 4 A.M." (ibid., 726). He either had forgotten the hour or else
"moonrise" meant the time at which the orb was high enough in the heavens to afford
same light in a broken country.
[23] Hotchkiss' MS Diary, 73.

an effort to outflank Pope by marching up the river. In doing this Lee had, of course, to protect the lower crossings of the river so that his adversary could not get on his flank or in his rear.[24]

The first actors in this part of the drama, which covered the 20th–25th of August, were the cavalry. On the day the Rapidan

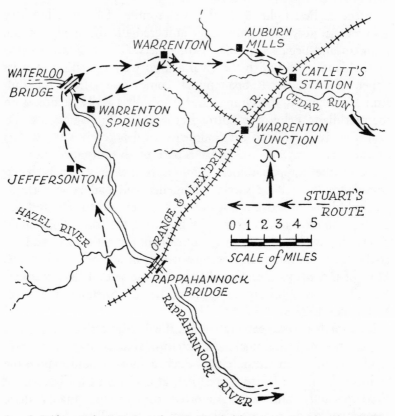

Stuart's Raid on Catlett's Station, after W. W. Blackford in *O. R. Atlas*, Plate XXIII-5

was passed, Robertson's Brigade got into a lively action between the village of Stevensburg and Brandy Station, which is about five miles South and West of the point where the railway crosses the Rappahannock. Stuart rode with Robertson for some hours that morning and gave general directions for the conduct of the action, but most of the fighting was done by "Grumble" Jones of the

[24] The strategics of this operation and the tactical details, which are of unusual interest, are described in 2 *R. E. Lee.* 280 ff.

Seventh Virginia. When the affair ended in a Federal withdrawal across the Rappahannock, Stuart had praise for Jones's "courage and determination." Stuart could say of Robertson that he had "cause to be proud of the command which his superior discipline, organization, and drill have brought to the stability of veterans." [25]

This, needless to say, was gratifying to Lee and perhaps reassuring to Jackson, who had been skeptical about Robertson's handling of Ashby's men; but to Stuart, the brush of August 20 was far from satisfying. He wanted to do more than merely to drive Bayard's cavalry across the river. [26] By Fitz Lee's failure to arrive on the 17th, Stuart felt that he had lost his opportunity of burning Rappahannock Bridge and had been robbed, besides, of hat and cloak. He could not recover his apparel, but he could get revenge.

In studying the map to get the answer to the soldier's eternal question, "Where?" Stuart's eye settled on the point where the Orange and Alexandria Railroad crossed Cedar Run near Catlett's Station. To be sure, Cedar Run was not reckoned among the mighty rivers of the Old Dominion; but it was on Pope's main line of supply. If the bridge across the Run were destroyed, Pope would be inconvenienced and perhaps would be compelled to retire. In any event, there would be adventure in a raid against the railroad.

The proposal was made to Lee, was pondered, and on the second day after the passage of the Rapidan, was approved by Army Headquarters. Stuart hastened to select his stoutest lieutenants and boldest blades—Fitz and "Rooney" Lee, Williams C. Wickham and Tom Rosser among them—and with these and 1500 troopers, he started up the Rappahannock. Far in advance of the sweating, slow-tramping infantry, he found unguarded fords, through which his cheerful boys splashed their way. Warrenton was reached without contest. The enemy, said the residents, had not been there for days. No bluecoats were known to be close at hand.

So far, all gain and good prospects! Stuart turned the column toward Auburn Mills, whence a descent upon Cedar Run bridge would be simple. Unfortunately, as the troopers jingled on, black

<hr/>

25 *O. R.*, 12, pt. 2, p. 727. Cf. *Laurel Brigade*, 74.
26 For Bayard's account of the action of August 20, see *O. R.*, 12, pt. 2, pp. 88–90.

clouds gathered and, ere evening, emptied themselves in a typical
Virginia thunderstorm, which never is more violent than in
August. The horse artillery fell behind. Stuart began to wonder
whether he would be able, if the streams rose, to get out as easily
as he was getting into the enemy's country, but he had Rosser in
command of the advance. That youngster had a sixth sense of
direction and, along with it, incredible luck. While the thunderstorm continued in all its fury, Rosser captured the Union pickets
before they could give the alarm, and soon he conducted Stuart
within the Federal lines. At intervals the lightning gave a
glimpse of the surroundings. Then, when the flash passed, the
heavy, low-hanging clouds made the night drip blackness.[27] It
was, Stuart wrote, "the darkest night I ever knew." [28]

Was it prudent to venture on? Would not the regiments become confused? Might they not fire one into another? The
drenched young Generals and Colonels asked and hesitated, but
the goddess of chance, who had deserted "Jeb" Stuart at Verdiersville, favored him now. Out of the rain and the pitch, someone
brought in a Negro who had been captured nearby. He had lived
in Berkeley County, where Stuart had served in the early summer
of 1861, and he promptly recognized the cavalryman. More than
that, he explained that he had been 'pressed to wait on a Federal
staff officer, though his heart was with his "own folks." The
Negro professed to know where General Pope's tent, staff and
horses were to be found, and he offered to lead the Confederates
to the place. To accept his tender was to gamble heavily on the
Negro's fidelity; to go on without a guide was to play against
odds that might be heavier.[29]

Quickly Stuart decided to trust the Negro and to act with
utmost speed. Those swollen streams to the westward might be
impassable soon! "Rooney" Lee must take the Ninth Virginia
and try to capture whatever and whoever was at the headquarters
to which the Negro would conduct him; the First and the Fifth
were to attack another camp nearby and were to obstruct the rail-

   [27] Cf. G. M. Neese, Three Years in the Confederate Horse Artillery (cited hereafter
as Neese), 100.
   [28] O. R., 12, pt. 2, p. 731.
   [29] Stuart, O. R., 12, pt. 2, p. 731, is authority for the statement that the Negro had
known him in Berkeley. Von Borcke, op. cit., 1, 124, gave the facts about the man's
impressment. Blackford must have been in error when he stated inferentially, in his
MS Memoirs, 143, that the Negro did not know Stuart.

road; a picked contingent under Colonel Wickham and Capt. W. W. Blackford was to set the Cedar Run bridge afire; Robertson was to constitute the reserve and was to be on the lookout for the arrival of his Twelfth Regiment, which was escorting the belated and half-bogged horse artillery.

Through the violence of the downpour, the regiments stumbled to their posts. Soon they were ready. A dash was made for Pope's tent; shouts were raised; firing broke out; frightened teamsters extinguished lights and sought shelter behind or in their wagons; nobody seemed to know who was attacking what. Guided by the lightning, the Confederate cavalrymen seized prisoners by the score and picked up much booty; but against the bridge, their comrades could do nothing. It was too wet to burn and too heavy to cut down. Said Stuart in his report: "The commanding general will, I am sure, appreciate how hard it was to desist from the undertaking, but to one on the spot there could be but one opinion—its impossibility. I gave it up"—which he seldom said of anything he undertook to do.[30]

If the span over Cedar Run could not be destroyed, nothing was to be gained by lingering. Before morning, Stuart withdrew all his men and started back to the Confederate position. When the prisoners could be counted and the loot examined in daylight Stuart was satisfied. The captured Federals were more than three hundred in number. Among them were many officers. Some of the horses being led by Confederates manifestly were animals of blood and style, and doubtless were from the stable of Army Headquarters. Troopers who had picked the choice mounts in the darkness were as proud as they were lucky. Many other prizes and souvenirs of the raid were brought to Stuart's attention during the day. Of manifest importance were Pope's dispatch-book and the originals of numerous letters sent him. These were collected now—perhaps with less promptness than their military value should have dictated—and were sent to Lee's headquarters.[31]

Chief of all the treasures were General Pope's hat, his military cloak, and one of his uniform frock coats, which some of the troopers had taken from the General's headquarters tent and had

---

[30] O. R., 12, pt. 2, p. 731.
[31] For the delay in forwarding the papers, see 2 R. E. Lee, 297, n. 26.

given Fitz Lee. Later in the day, when Fitz met General Field and staff, he called to them to stop and dismount because he had something to show them. Maj. Roy Mason must tell what followed: "[Fitz] then slipped behind a big oak-tree, and, in a moment or two, emerged . . . in the long blue cloak of a Federal general that reached nearly to his feet, and wearing a Federal general's hat with its big plume. This masquerade was accompanied by a burst of jolly laughter that might have been heard for a hundred yards." [32]

The uniform coat was given to Stuart, as partial payment for the hat he had lost at Verdiersville. After showing the garment to Jackson and proposing to trade it to Pope for his hat,[33] Stuart sent it to Richmond as a present to Governor Letcher. His Excellency, much pleased, had the coat hung with other trophies in the gallery of the State Library, which then occupied the loft of the Capitol. Newspapers did not fail to report that the coat was of fine, black broadcloth, that the velvet collar bore the insignia of a Major General, and that the front and sleeves were resplendent with brass buttons.[34]

Before Richmond knew that it was to feast its eyes on General Pope's coat, the wet but jubilant Confederate troopers rode back to Warrenton, where occurred an incident that amused Stuart's staff almost as much as did the capture of Pope's habiliments. The field quartermaster of the Federal forces, Maj. Charles N. Goulding, had been captured in the raid and had been brought along to the town. Previously he had maintained his office at Warrenton and, being a somewhat loquacious gentleman, he had boasted to one of the young ladies that he would get to Richmond within a month. The high-spirited girl who was a daughter of the gentleman at whose house the Major was quartered mockingly bet him a bottle of champagne that he would not reach that destination so soon. When she learned now that Major Goulding was among the prisoners and that he undoubtedly would be sent promptly to Richmond, she considered that her bet was due, and she asked Stuart if she might pay it. As

---

[32] 2 B. & L., 528.   [33] Douglas, 133–34.
[34] Richmond Enquirer, Aug. 27, p. 1, col. 3, Aug. 28, p. 1, col. 2 and p. 2, col. 5; Richmond Examiner, Aug. 28, 1862, p. 1, cols. 1 and 2. The Enquirer noted, Aug. 28, p. 1, col. 2, that the coat was brought to Richmond by W. Keith Armistead of the Sixth Virginia Cavalry. If usage was followed, this delivery would indicate that Armistead had been the man who took the coat from General Pope's tent.

the General was wholly agreeable, she presented the Major with the champagne, which, von Borcke records, the Federal accepted "very willingly, declaring that he should always be happy to drink the health of so charming a person." [35]

Thus, in the clinking of glasses, ended the raid on Catlett's Station. The affair created talk of the kind most pleasing to Stuart's ears, but of military value it had little. It was dismissed with few words in Lee's next dispatch. Stuart, he told the President, "accomplished some minor advantages, destroyed some wagons, and captured some prisoners." [36] The violence of the storm, Lee explained, had made impossible the burning of the bridge.

That same storm of August 22 supplied something more than the stage-effects for the second scene in the first act of the new drama, a scene in which General Early played a central and a singular role. Jackson's advance up the Rappahannock, in search of an uncontested crossing, brought Ewell's Division on the afternoon of August 22 to a point opposite Warrenton Springs,[37] about seven miles Southwest of Warrenton.

Here the bridge had been destroyed, but, as no enemy was on guard,[38] Jackson decided to throw troops across the Rappahannock and, if they found a favorable situation, to follow with the entire force. Lawton's Brigade, with two batteries, started the passage of the river directly opposite the Springs; Early used an old dam about a mile down the stream, which already was rising from the inflow of a hard shower. As Early's regiments moved over the unstable crossing, the rain started afresh. Before the last of "Old Jube's" men were on the left bank, night was settling. It was too dark for the next Brigade, Forno's, to attempt to use the treacherous dam. Ewell went over, gave Early his instructions, and then returned to the right bank to await daylight and falling water for the passage of the other troops.

In a dripping wood, Early took an uncomfortable position that Ewell had indicated, and then he sent Maj. A. L. Pitzer, one of his aides, to ride up stream and to locate the Brigade of Lawton, with whom Early had been ordered to establish communication.

35 *Von Borcke*, 1, 128.

36 *O. R.*, 12, pt. 3, p. 941. For the next treatment of Stuart, see *infra*, pp. 89, 93, 139.

37 Sometimes called Fauquier White Sulphur Springs or merely Sulphur Springs. For a description of the resort, see G. H. Gordon, *History of the Campaign of the Army of Virginia under John Pope* . . . p. 103.

38 *O. R.*, 12, pt. 2, p. 642

The rain continued to pour down; the black darkness of which Stuart was then complaining at Catlett's Station engulfed the woods where Early's half-drowned soldiers waited. Before long there was the sound of horsemen, the challenge by the guard, the countersign . . . and Major Pitzer was back with six bewildered Federal cavalry, all of them fully armed. The Major explained that he had run into the troopers on the road, where they had halted. They had taken him prisoner, but had been told by him that they were within the Confederate lines, completely surrounded, and that they were certain to be shot by the first picketpost they encountered. Only by following him, the Major had said, could they escape with their lives. They would be captives, but was not that preferable to being killed? The cavalrymen, completely outtalked, had agreed to go with Pitzer. Here they were, at the order of the Provost Marshal.

It was boldly done, and much to the credit of Pitzer; but the incident disturbed Early no little. The presence of those Federals on the road showed that the enemy was near, perhaps in force. An attempt to establish contact with Lawton that night certainly would involve risks and perhaps would disclose to the enemy the presence of the Southern troops. Early concluded that however wet and hungry his men might be, they must remain in the woods and hug the ground till daylight.

Morning brought as much of new concern as of relief. The rain was over; woods and fields were a lustrous green; the men might hope to dry themselves when they could emerge from the forest. They were cheerful despite empty stomachs. What now troubled their commander was the stage of the river between him and the remainder of Jackson's force. Angrily the Rappahannock rushed southward, full-banked and impassable for troops. The dilapidated dam, over which Early's Brigade had passed the previous afternoon, was awash and roaring. Early was cut off. Nor could he count on material aid from Lawton at Sulphur Springs. A messenger, sent there soon after daylight, reported that the two batteries were on the ground. One regiment only of infantry, the Thirteenth Georgia, and not the whole of Lawton's command, had crossed. Early's thinned Brigade, plus those Georgians, might have to face overwhelming Federal attack.

The prospect that the alternatives might be reduced to capture or annihilation did not appeal to "Old Jube," but he could see no way of escape other than that of ascending the river four miles to Waterloo Bridge, where he could recross. Even that depended upon good fortune in passing up the left bank unobserved or before the enemy could organize a strong attack.

While Early was pondering what he should do, Jackson busily was examining from the other side of the river all the ground between Early's position and the Springs. Behind a bending creek that flowed into the river, "Stonewall" observed a good defensive position which he directed Early to occupy until the bridge could be repaired. Early sent back word of his plight and, for his pains, merely received confirmation of previous orders. If, Jackson added, Early ascertained that the Federals in their front were too numerous to assail, the Confederate column should proceed up the river to Waterloo Bridge. Should that march become necessary, Jackson explained, he would advance simultaneously, along the opposite side, and would cover Early's movement. Doubtless "Old Jack" reasoned that if Early were hard beset, enough artillery could be massed on the right bank to keep the enemy from closing in.

No time was lost by Early in slipping into the position Jackson designated behind the bend of the creek. The shift was made without opposition, but ere the morning was far advanced, scouting Federal cavalrymen were seen. They hovered around Early's right in a manner to provoke and to alarm him. The swollen creek was his only barrier against attack whenever these Federals were ready, and now the creek began to fall steadily, though the river itself remained past fording.

Anxious hours crawled around the clock-face. In the afternoon, Federal infantry in large numbers began to arrive in support of the cavalry opposite the Confederate right. "Old Jube" observed and doubtless swore and prudently changed his defensive front. His infantry he kept in the woods; his field guns he placed where they could open on an advancing force, but he hid them carefully from the enemy's view. The one consolation Early found, as he viewed what he styled a "critical condition," [39] was that the

[39] O. R. 13. pt. 2, p. 706.

bluecoats proceeded with great caution. They evidently did not know his numerical weakness and had as much fear of him as he had of them.

While the afternoon dragged along,[40] who should clatter into sight but Beverley Robertson with the greater part of a Brigade of cavalry and two guns, a part of Chew's famous battery. Robertson's troopers were returning from the raid on Catlett's Station. As they had been in reserve the previous night and thereby had been denied all hand in looting Pope's camp, they probably were not in the mood of a happy holiday, but they were a most welcome reinforcement.

Robertson had seen at a distance what he took to be a Federal ordnance train, a tempting target always, and he felt that he must have a shot at it. After consultation with Early, he moved his guns up to a position near the Springs hotel and began to give the distant teamsters a taste of Confederate metal. The train proved to be well guarded. A six-gun battery, which was part of the escort, replied to Robertson with vigor if not with expertness. "They scattered their shell," said a contemptuous Southern gunner, "all over the adjacent fields, ranging in altitude from the earth to the moon." [41] To discomfit the Federals the more, General Early sent up two Parrott guns from Brown's Battery, which had defended the right of Early's Brigade at Cedar Mountain.[42]

A noisy, banging affair it was, with little hurt to either side; but in the end it raised Early's apprehension. He could not see the situation otherwise than that one Brigade plus one Regiment of Infantry, with Robertson's troopers and ten guns, were exposed to attack by as many thousand troops as Pope chose to hurl at them. The river still was too high to be forded. Jackson was at work on a temporary bridge, but there was no ascertaining when—or even whether—it could be completed. Scarcely a man in Early's regiments had tasted food for thirty hours or more. As if that were not a full measure of misery, the Federal infantry seemed to be moving around to the Confederate left as if to surround the force.

Night approached; a baffling mist obscured everything.[43] Through it, ominously, Union infantry began to advance. When

---

40 Neese, op. cit., 102, put the time as 4 o'clock.   41 Neese, 102.
42 O. R., 12, pt. 2, p. 707.   43 O. R., 12, pt. 2, p. 707.

Early heard the bluecoats crashing into the woods, he thought that the end had come and that his men would have to fight to the death. Presently there roared among the trees a volley from the Federals, a volley to which Early did not permit his men to reply, because they must not waste ammunition on an enemy they could not see. They waited for the nearer approach of the blue-coats and for another volley. Neither came. Instead, there were three cheers and a "tiger." These were given as if the men were obeying orders to shout in unison, but why they cheered, or whom, the Confederates did not know. Early waited a few moments for some further move and. when the Federals did not attack, he ran out two Napoleons and had them open with canister. The Federals fell back in silence and made no further demonstration.[44]

Early was relieved, but only to the extent that he no longer feared an attack that night. All the concern of a pessimistic nature was aggravated by the startling news that Jackson was sending the remainder of Lawton's Brigade to Early's side of the river. Instead of permitting the hungry troops on the left bank to return to safety, that strange man Jackson was exposing more troops by resuming the movement of Ewell's Division which had been interrupted the previous evening by the rise of the river! To Early it seemed incomprehensibly rash. He was satisfied that he faced very heavy opposition, against which two Brigades or the whole of Ewell's Division could not stand.

In this belief, "Old Jube" began to think more than ever of the slaughter or imprisonment of his fine regiments. About 1 A.M. on the 24th, General Lawton crossed the river and visited the bivouac. He had seen orders, he said, for Ewell to come to the left bank at daylight, but he understood that if Ewell found the Federals very strong, Early's Brigade and the Georgians were to be recalled to the right bank. The army command did not desire to bring on a general engagement at Warrenton Springs.

This news seemed to Early a veritable promise of deliverance from death. "I immediately dispatched a messenger to General Ewell," said Early, all in a breath, "to inform him that there was no doubt of the enemy's being in heavy force, and if I was to

<hr/>

[44] *Wingfield*, 15. Gen. Geo. H. Gordon, *op. cit.*, p. 65, said of this performance by the Federals: "Sigel's infantry again were at it. They were evidently enjoying the purest delirium of New York militia achievement."

be recrossed it had better be at once without waiting for daylight, as the enemy by moving to the left could place artillery so as to command the bridge and ford at the Springs, and from the sounds of carriages moving in that direction I was satisfied such was his purpose, and that it would be accomplished before I could recross if it was postponed until daylight." [45] In answer, Ewell crossed in person about 3 o'clock, listened to report of the enemy's movements, and promptly ordered the whole force back to the other bank.

Hungry men lost no time in getting the guns to safety and in following, regiment by regiment, as fast as the feeble bridge would take them. Soon after daylight, they were safe on Jackson's side of the stream. "My command," Early concluded, "was thus rescued from almost certain capture, as it has since appeared from General Pope's report that he had brought up his whole force to attack what he supposed to be General Jackson's whole force." [46]

Early was as pleased as he was relieved, and particularly was he proud that in his exposed position he had not lost a man, killed or wounded.[47] Praise came to him widely and even from "Stonewall," who usually saved his encomia for the dead that might not disappoint him thereafter or make embarrassing appeals for promotion. "In this critical situation," said Jackson as he reviewed the rise of the river and the isolation of the troops on the left bank, "the skill and presence of mind of General Early was favorably displayed." [48]

One other there was, besides Early and Stuart, to have his moment in the center of the stage during this first act of the new drama. The day that "Jeb" rode to Catlett's and "Jube" found himself cut off near Warrenton Springs, August 22, General Trimble was left by Ewell to guard the crossing of Hazel River, near Welford's Mill, while the Confederate wagon train was laboring northward. All of Jackson's other troops had passed; Trimble was to remain until the vanguard of Longstreet's command should reach the ford.

[45] O. R., 12, pt. 2, p. 707.
[46] Ibid., loc. cit. Pope's reference to this incident will be found in ibid., 31. All the infantry of the Army of Virginia, except McDowell's Corps, had been ordered directly to Sulphur Springs on the 23rd. McDowell was directed to move on Warrenton, whence he could advance either to Sulphur Springs or to Waterloo Bridge (ibid., 31).
[47] Ibid., 707.
[48] O. R., 12, pt. 2, p. 642. The sketch of Early is continued infra, p. 140.

To the pugnacious Trimble, a duty that normally was boresome proved welcome. Soon after he had taken position, he received word that a Federal force had crossed the Rappahannock and had captured some mules and ambulances from the train. Immediately Trimble detached one of his regiments in pursuit. It quickly overtook the marauders and recaptured the property which Jackson, the wagon hunter, never would have forgiven him for losing.

Next, a prisoner told Trimble that one, and perhaps two Brigades of Federal infantry were on the south side of the river and were intent on mischief. Trimble reasoned, regretfully but coolly, that the bluecoats might be too numerous for him to assail without help, and as no other Confederates were within five miles, either ahead or to the rear, he had to emulate the rabbit and "lay low." He watched the passing trains, ascertained the enemy's position, and awaited the coming of Hood, who was in the lead for Longstreet.

To most men, the prospect of having the hard biting Texans as companions in adventure would not have been displeasing; but to Trimble, the matter appeared in a different light. When Hood came up, about 4 o'clock, Trimble, as the senior, directed the reinforcements to form on his flanks and in reserve, and then, with little more ado, he went straight for the Federals.

He was proud of what followed, and he described it later with gusto: "After a sharp conflict . . . the enemy were driven back to the hills on the river, where they made another stand. At this point, supported by their artillery on the north side of the river, they made an effort by the blowing of trumpets, beating of drums, and cheers, to encourage their men to charge. The command was given to drive them at the point of the bayonet. Our men boldly advanced with enthusiastic cheers and drove the opposing forces into the river and across it in great disorder, to seek protection in General Sigel's camp and under his guns, which opened a furious discharge against us without serious injury. Our men pursued them closely and slaughtered great numbers as they waded the river or climbed up the opposite bank. The water was literally covered with dead and wounded. Over 100 prisoners were captured, and among the dead was found one colonel. Deeming it useless in the absence of my artillery to continue the contest longer, after half-an-hour's occupation of the battle ground

I retired unmolested and camped one and a half miles distant, leaving General Hood, who had taken no part in the contest, to look after the enemy." [49]

This exploit was soldierly and creditable, though, as it developed, one Federal Brigade, and not two, was in front of Trimble. The dead Colonel found on the field was the Brigade commander, Henry Bohlen, who apparently had never changed the insignia of rank after his promotion about four months previously. [50] From across the Rappahannock, Federal officers had watched with horror the Confederate fire "on the unhappy wretches struggling to regain the shore." [51] It was war, it was well managed from the Southern point of view, and it was written down to Trimble's credit in the book of Jackson's long memory.

The one unpleasant aspect of the affair was Trimble's casual, not to say slurring, remark that Hood "had taken no part in the contest." That was not like Hood. Nor did Hood's report conform to Trimble's on that score. Said Hood: "The Texas Brigade being placed on the right and Colonel Law's on the left, the attack was made at once, General Trimble leading off in the center. The enemy was driven precipitately over the Rappahannock with considerable loss." Moreover, Hood reported the death of one of his Majors in the engagement. [52] What did this conflict of testimony indicate? Would Hood have sought credit for an action he had not fought? Was Trimble disposed to ignore what others had done in the battle? [53]

[49] O. R., 12, pt. 2, p. 719. Hotchkiss in his MS Diary, 73, stated that Trimble's battle was between St. James's Church and Beverly Ford.

[50] Bohlen was a German, commissioned Colonel of the 75th Pennsylvania Sept. 30, 1861, and promoted Brigadier General April 28, 1862; Heitman, 1, 228. G. H. Gordon, writing of the affair, Army of Virginia, 30, apparently had forgotten that Bohlen had been promoted.

[51] G. H. Gordon, op. cit., 31.

[52] O. R., 12, pt. 2, p. 605.

[53] For continuance of the sketch of Trimble, see infra, p. 121, and of the sketch of Hood, infra, pp. 118, 138.

CHAPTER V

JACKSON IS HIMSELF AGAIN

IT WAS a Sunday morning that Trimble was receiving congratulations and Early was returning from his marooned post, but "Old Jack," for all his love of the Lord's Day, was not in a Sabbath mood. His quartermaster's and commissary services were not working well. The troops were ill fed.[1] Officers were not uniformly setting the example they should in discipline. To discourage the straggling that might weaken the army in an hour when every bullet counted, Jackson already had staged a dramatic warning. Three deserters who had been caught, court-martialled and condemned, had been prepared for execution. Blindfolded, they had been placed by the side of open graves. The whole of Jackson's Division had been marched through somber woods to see the trio fall before a firing squad, and then the Division had been filed past the dead bodies to observe how they had been riddled.[2] Not content with this lesson, Jackson perhaps was pondering the wisdom of an order under which stragglers would be shot down without ceremony or delay.[3] He insisted that officers bestir themselves to enforce the discipline without which there could be no army. One dragging Georgia Colonel was told tartly, if in a figure not of particular originality, that field-officers were "intended to be useful as well as ornamental." [4] Five other regimental commanders—all those in Gregg's Brigade—Jackson already had placed under arrest on the 22nd because their men, contrary to orders, had burned some fence palings.[5]

Despite all this disciplinary action, which ordinarily would have

---

[1] *Hotchkiss' MS Diary*, 74–75.

[2] *E. A. Moore*, 99–100. These may have been the executions that Casler, *op. cit.* 164–65, placed earlier in the vicinity of Pisgah Church. Casler noted: "In the battle of Manassas, which soon came off, all three of the officers who composed the court-martial were killed or mortally wounded (my colonel, A. J. [John F.] Neff, being one of the number), and most of the soldiers looked upon it as a judgment." Casler himself did not believe this applied to Neff, who, said he, was a "splendid officer, a gallant man, who always treated us with respect and kindness." *Ibid.*

[3] See *infra*, p. 149.   [4] *Hotchkiss' MS Diary*, 74–75.

[5] 14 *S. H. S. P.*, 209–10. Col. Edward McCrady, Jr., who recorded these arrests, was of opinion that General Gregg, too, had been arrested.

stimulated him, "Old Blue Light" remained so ill-humored that
even a vigorous cannonade at 10 o'clock, between A. P. Hill's
batteries and the enemy across the Rappahannock, failed to raise
his spirits.[6] He moved back the camps to the vicinity of Jeffersonton,[7] in order to save the infantry from exposure to the bursting
shells; and in losing the presence of battle, he did not have the
compensation of attendance on religious services.[8]

Early afternoon brought a change, a thrilling change. Lee rode
over to Jeffersonton, found Jackson, and in a brief conversation [9]
presented him such an opportunity as never had come to him, not
even on that May day when he had been told he could advance
on Banks.[10] An end was to be put to watching fords, to side slipping on the Rappahannock, and to futile artillery exchanges.
Larger maneuver was necessary. Jackson was to move secretly
up the river, was to cross at some convenient place and was to
strike in Pope's rear the Orange and Alexandria Railroad, which
was the Federal line of supply. The remainder of the Army was
to occupy the enemy long enough for Jackson to get a good start.
Then the troops left on the Rappahannock would march to rejoin
him. On this bold move Lee had decided because he believed a

---

[6] For the details of this cannonade, which continued until late afternoon, see *O. R.,*
12, pt. 2, pp. 650, 670, 673.

[7] The Federals usually called this village Jefferson.

[8] That is to say, Hotchkiss does not mention Jackson's participation in public worship on the 24th, though he seldom failed to record Jackson's presence at church. The
known events of the day, moreover, do not seem to allow time for preaching to the
Division.

[9] Douglas, *op. cit.,* 132–33, stated that the council which decided on the renowned
movement to the rear of Pope's army was attended by Longstreet and by Stuart as well
as by Jackson and by Lee, and was held at "a table . . . placed almost in the middle
of a field, with not even a tree within hearing." The rest of the incident Douglas thus
described: "General Lee sat at the table on which was spread a map. Longstreet sat on
his right, General Stuart on his left, and General Jackson stood opposite him: these four
and no more. A group of staff officers were lounging on the grass of an adjacent knoll.
The conversation was a very brief one. As it closed I was called by General Jackson and
I heard the only sentence of that consultation that I ever heard reported. It was uttered
by the secretive Jackson and it was—'I will be moving within an hour.' I was sent by
the General to put his divisions in motion and to concentrate them upon Jefferson, and
during that afternoon there was quick cooking of rations and getting the corps in
readiness to cross the river." There is no confirmation of this from any source. Hotchkiss, in his *Diary,* did not even mention the conference between Lee and Jackson that
impressed itself upon the memory of Dr. McGuire in the manner explained in note 12,
infra. Longstreet in none of his writings mentioned a council of war attended by him.
Stuart did not refer in his report to his presence at such a council as Douglas described.
So far as concerns Jackson's alleged purpose to "be moving within an hour," evidence
that contradicts that statement follows in the text. Probability is that Douglas confused
the memory of some other council with the one held briefly between Longstreet and
Jackson later in the afternoon of the 22nd.

[10] See *supra,* Vol. I, p. 371.

threat to the Federal rear would force Pope to retreat quickly and thereby would lengthen the distance between Pope and the reinforcements that soon would be arriving from Alexandria or Fredericksburg.[11] Jackson was to take with him all three of his Divisions and was to start as soon as arrangements could be made.

The mission fired "Old Jack." [12] As soon as Lee rode off, Jackson set about his preparations for the march. He had travelled several times on the railroad that ran by way of Thoroughfare Gap to Manassas Junction, and he knew in detail the country immediately around Manassas; but with the routes East of the Blue Ridge that led to the Orange and Alexandria, he was unacquainted. J. K. Boswell, his Topographical Engineer, came from that section of Virginia. He was ordered to report immediately and, upon arrival, was instructed to ascertain the best, most covered route around Pope's right and to the Federal rear.[13] No immediate decision concerning a precise objective was attempted at the moment. The imperative task was to reach the railroad. Where it was to be struck by the Confederates would depend upon circumstance and convenience. From the very nature of the terrain and the course of the roads, the vicinity of Manassas Junction was the indicated general objective.

Arrangements had to be made, next, for the issuance and cooking of rations that evening and for the driving of beef-cattle with the column. Then, later in the afternoon, when Longstreet rode up for conference, agreement had to be reached with him concerning the time and manner of relieving A. P. Hill's batteries with guns from Longstreet's command, so that the Brigades of Hill would be free to start with Jackson's other Divisions. Longstreet did his part admirably in all of this and amusingly helped to create military deception. He blustered about, as if examining

---

[11] For a detailed discussion of the strategical considerations that prompted this course, see 2 *R. E. Lee*, 297 ff.

[12] In a letter quoted in 2 *Henderson*, 123–24, Dr. Hunter McGuire stated that Jackson traced with his boot some lines on the ground and made swift, earnest comments that Lee approved with a nod of the head. Jackson's gestures and his manifest excitement led his Medical Director to believe that Jackson himself had proposed the movement, but of this there is no positive evidence of any sort. The language of Lee's report was: "In pursuance of the plan of operations determined upon, Jackson was directed" etc. (*O. R.*, 12, pt. 2, pp. 553–54). This was phrasing of a sort the modest Lee often employed to avoid the use of the personal pronoun. He always was careful to see that full credit was given officers who originated plans or initiated movements. Had Jackson proposed the march to the rear of Pope's Army, it is almost certain that Lee would *not* have said, "Jackson was directed."

[13] *O. R.*, 12, pt. 2, p. 650.

the country, and announced openly that he was going to force a crossing at Warrenton Springs and drive the enemy off.[14] All the preliminaries were smooth and encouraging, in fact, except for the fear that the commissary could not supply sufficient rations. Should meat and bread be lacking, the men would have to subsist on the corn that was nearing maturity in the fields along the roads Jackson would follow.[15]

After nightfall, Hill's guns quietly were replaced by some of Longstreet's batteries. Marching orders for Jackson's troops were issued. All baggage and the wagons used for hauling it were to be left behind. With the columns were to move only the cattle, the ordnance train, and the ambulances. The order of march was to be Ewell, A. P. Hill, Taliaferro. Doubtless this was arranged deliberately: Ewell was a fast, sure man on the road. If Hill followed him and kept Ewell's pace, there could be none of the tardiness that Jackson charged against the Light Division. Should Hill fall behind, despite Ewell, then the Stonewall Division, under Taliaferro, could close on Hill. The start was to be at early dawn, "with the utmost promptitude, without knapsacks." [16] The last detail provided, Jackson sought to sleep, but there was so much activity among the camps that he got little rest.[17]

When "Fall in" was shouted in the half-dawn of August 25, fears of a breakdown of the commissary were realized. Either because rations were issued late, or else because the men loitered too long, some of the commands had not finished the cooking of three days' food. Not a few of the men had regretfully to throw away their dough or their half-baked bread.[18] As for the beef, there was little salt to rub on what had not been well cooked.[19] Jackson was irritated by this but, as always, he was careful to set a soldierly example. He arose early, breakfasted frugally, and ere he started wrote a few lines to his wife. "The enemy," he said, "has taken a position, or rather several positions, on the Fauquier side of the Rappahannock." That was all he related of military movements, and that was meaningless. Not a hint was there of great adventure or of his pulse-raising new opportunity. The only reference to preoccupation and unusual duty was a line he scrawled to excuse the brevity of his greetings. "I have," he con-

[14] *Hotchkiss' MS Diary*, 74–75.   [15] *Allan's Army*, 203.
[16] *O. R.*, 12, pt. 2, p. 678.   [17] *Hotchkiss' MS Diary*, 74–75.
[18] *Worsham*, 118.   [19] 2 *B. & L.*, 532.

cluded, "only time to tell you how much I love my little pet dove."[20] He signed the note and sealed it, and soon he was in the saddle. Act Two of the drama had begun.

The day was bright, but as the night had been cool, the morning air was invigorating.[21] Quietly and swiftly, the column moved northwestward about five and a half miles, past the hamlet of Amissville, and then turned Northeast another two miles to Hedgeman's River at Henson's Mill. Hedgeman's, in reality, was the larger of the two streams the united flow of which, meeting at Waterloo Bridge, made the Rappahannock. As the other stream, Carter's Run, had a course almost North and South, Jackson now had no river of any consequence to bar his way. Unhindered and unopposed, he was "across the Rappahannock" and headed for the rear of Pope's Army. In the van of Ewell's Division rode Captain Boswell to guide the column. Well in advance, after Henson's Mill was passed, the Second Virginia Cavalry scouted to make sure no enemy troopers lay in wait.[22]

The order was the familiar one, "Close up, men, close up." [23] No straggling and no delays were permitted. Those infantrymen who had cooked rations devoured them soon on the soldiers' principle that food is safer in th stomach than in the haversack. The men who had not been able to salt their meat soon had to throw it away. Corn from the fields and apples from nearby trees were snatched and eaten as the men pushed on. To the toiling column Captain Boswell gave the benefit of all the short-cuts. Where the road curved around a field, he had the fence removed for a direct march.[24] Progress was excellent.

Orlean was passed; Salem, which was eleven miles farther North,[25] and on the Manassas Gap Railroad, must have been set by Jackson as his objective for the day. Intent on reaching it, he rode from one unit to another or sent his staff officers to see that the brigade commanders kept the column closed.

Late in the afternoon, as he approached Salem, Jackson halted, got off his horse, and stood for a time on a large stone by the

20 *Mrs. Jackson,* 317.
21 Although William Allan, *op. cit.,* 203, remembered the day as fresh and cool, Hotchkiss, *loc. cit.,* and W. W. Blackford, *MS Memoirs,* 155, stated that the afternoon of the 25th was very warm.
22 *O. R.,* 12, pt. 2, p. 747.   23 *Cf.* 2 *B. & L.,* 533.
24 *Worsham,* 118; J. E. Cooke, *Stonewall Jackson* (cited hereafter as *Cooke's Jackson*), 275.
25 As the road then ran.

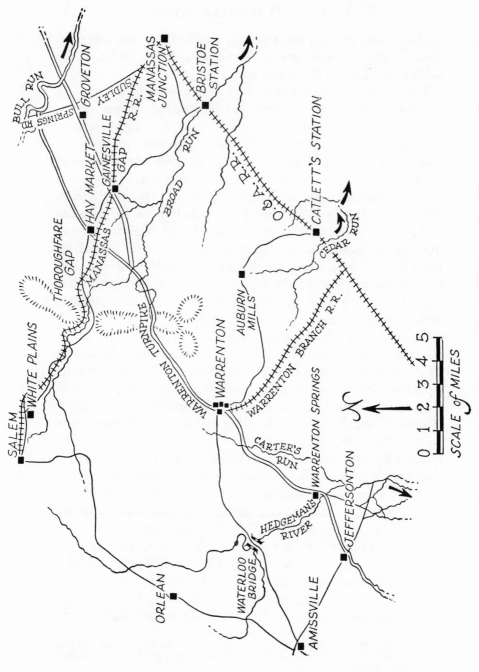

Sketch of the Terrain of Jackson's March to Cut Pope's Line of Supply, August, 1862

roadside. Even he was warm, for once, or else his old cap had pressed his brow. Bareheaded, he paused to look at the sun as it disappeared behind the mountains. In that dramatic posture, Jackson was seen by a regiment that came up the road from the direction of Orlean. Immediately, the men forgot their own weariness and began to cheer him. He made a swift, friendly gesture to silence them and then he sent an officer to explain that they must be careful not to make any noise lest the enemy hear. The word was passed down the column—"No cheering." Obediently, the men passed in silence. Their look, their smiles, their uplifted caps and their raised arms were more eloquent than their shouts, more thrilling, even, than their rebel yell could have been. Jackson was proud and pleased, and actually admitted it. "Who could not conquer," he said to his staff, "with such troops as these?" [26]

About one mile South of Salem, where the cavalry kept guard, the column halted for the night. Ewell's Division arrived in time for reasonable slumber. The rearguard, Jackson's own, did not reach the bivouac until late in the evening.[27] Some of the men had been given food by the generous people of Salem Valley.[28] Thousands of the soldiers had to stretch themselves out hungry. Jackson regretted, of course, that these men had not been fed; but otherwise he was at ease and gratified. The Army had marched twenty-five miles.[29]

Ahead, on the morning of August 26, was a march equally as long as that for the advanced units and a few miles longer for Hill and Taliaferro than the march of the 25th.[30] One material obstacle, one only, had to be faced. About halfway between Salem and the Orange and Alexandria Railroad was Thoroughfare Gap in the Bull Run Mountains. This was a weak pass compared with some of those in the main Appalachian range; but if it was de-

26 *Dabney*, 517. As Dabney was present, his account may be accepted. The theatrical narrative of Cooke in his *Jackson*, 275, is an amusing example of the manner in which the imagination of the novelist hampered that splendid gentleman in writing history.

27 *O. R.*, 12, pt. 2, p. 650.   28 *Ibid.*, 679.

29 *Ibid.*, 650.

30 On the morning of the 26th, when Jackson was doing everything within his power to keep his operation secret, a Richmond newspaper announced that his Division was advancing toward Manassas. This was typical of the lack of intelligent co-operation between press and government; but, fortunately, as the report stated that Jackson's headquarters were at Warrenton Junction, Union authorities, if acquainted with the item by spies, may have assumed that all of it was as inaccurate as this (*Richmond Enquirer*, Aug. 26, 1862, p. 1, col. 2).

fended by a Federal force of any size, it might be held long
enough for the alarm to be sounded and for Jackson to be cheated
of a surprise attack on the railway. The military question was not
one of what he could do to storm the pass but one of what the
enemy already had done to protect it. Jackson had to face that
uncertainty, but he made the best of the unescapable gamble: In
the hope of catching off guard any foe who might be occupying
the high ground, he sent his cavalry forward as soon as there was
a touch of gray in the eastern sky. When the Second Viriginia
climbed to the pass and scrutinized all the approaches, it found—
not one Federal. The gap was unguarded. By this good news the
long column was cheered, but the men were less talkative than
they had been on the 25th.[31] The more intelligent of them could
reason from the direction of their march that they were bound for
the enemy's line of supply. What they would encounter there,
they did not know. They would save their breath for the grinding
march and for the grapple with the bluecoats.

Upward by White Plains and through the gap the column
moved and then over the rolling hills that led toward Hay Market.
The order of march was the same as that of the previous day—
Ewell, Hill and Taliaferro.[32] In front moved the Second Virginia. Cautiously it approached the road intersections; vigilantly
it examined all the lookouts. Not until the troopers reached Hay
Market did they encounter any Federals. The dozen or fifteen
horsemen picked up there and at Gainesville seemed more like
stragglers than videttes and seemed, moreover, in Colonel Munford's words, "entirely ignorant of any movement of our Army." [33]
Everything, so far, gave promise that the ideal military situation
would be created—that the enemy would be surprised in his own
rear. Excitement was higher for every mile covered, hunger
pinched more deeply. When officers were absent or considerately
blind, the men plundered corn fields and orchards, but the soldier who slipped out of the road to find an apple or a "roasting
ear" caught up again. The speed of the march was not slackened.
Always Jackson's exhortation was, "Close up, men, close up; push
on, push on!"

[31] 2 B. & L., 533.
[32] O. R., 12, pt. 2, p. 650. The name Hay Market, instead of the more recent Hay-
market, was used generally during the War between the States.
[33] O. R., 12. pt. 2, p. 747.

"Old Jack" himself was dust-covered and alert, but not tense. He spoke seldom and then briefly. Of his thoughts and of his reasoning on the choice of a route for the last stage of his march to the railroad, he said not a word. In midafternoon, to the high satisfaction of Jackson, the main body of Stuart's cavalry overtook the laboring column. "Jeb" had broken camp on the Rappahannock at 2 A.M. and had overtaken Jackson's wagons and artillery before they had left Salem. By using farm roads and a gap impassable for infantry, Stuart then had paralleled the route Jackson was following, and now he was at hand and ready to cover the van and the flanks.[34]

Screened in this manner, "Old Jack" was able to relax somewhat the rigor of his march and to allow a longer interval between units. Said Col. W. W. Blackford: "The men were given plenty of room to march rapidly and regularly at the paces which suited them best, without wearing them out by the fatiguing and vexatious alternations of halts and double quicks usually so frequent on marches. It was like every man was walking the distance alone, stopping to rest a moment or drink, within certain wide limits." [35]

The direction as well as the style of the march changed. At Gainesville, where Stuart had ridden up, Jackson reached the main road from Warrenton to Alexandria. This highway crossed Bull Run at Stone Bridge on the battlefield of Manassas, but it did not lead directly to the railway bridge over the Run. To reach the railroad, which was Jackson's assigned objective, the shorter, easier route was from Gainesville to Bristoe Station, four miles below Manassas Junction. Besides, near Bristoe Station, the railway bridged Broad Run. Destruction of that crossing would make the quick repair and reopening of the railway impossible. Whether Jackson decided on the line of march before he met Stuart, or whether he conferred with Stuart and made his final choice at Gainesville, there is no record.[36]

Obediently toward Bristoe Station, now, the soldiers turned

---

[34] *O. R.*, 12, pt. 2, p. 734.   [35] *W. W. Blackford's MS Memoirs*, 155.

[36] Captain Boswell, in his report, stated that Jackson on August 24 directed him to "select the most direct and covered route to Manassas" (*O. R.*, 12, pt. 2, p. 650); but neither Lee (*ibid.*, 554), nor Jackson (*ibid.*, 642–43), gave that town as the original objective. Jackson's language would indicate that the advance to Manassas Junction was undertaken solely because he learned that the enemy there had "collected . . . stores of great value." See 2 *R. E. Lee*, 300, n. 36.

their faces. As Colonel Blackford remembered it: "The spirit of the men, their unbounded confidence in their leader, and their perfect faith in the success of the expedition, whatever that might be, was abundantly evinced by their talk on the march. The feeling seemed to be a dread with each one that he would give out and not be there to see the fun. Toward the latter part of the day, the troops began to show the effects of the hard labor and of the heat to which they were exposed. Many fainted, and great numbers became foot-sore." [37] Limping and weary, they were encouraged by the absence of any Federal outposts and by the assurance of natives that only one company of Union infantry and one of cavalry were stationed at Bristoe.[38] A dash on the village would result, no doubt, in the capture of this guard. Then would come the work of destroying the railroad and the bridge.

So sure was success that when evening approached, Jackson drew out of road from his place with the van and stopped at a house near Bristoe to wait for the column to close. He sat down in a cane-bottomed armchair, which he tilted back against the wall. As nearly always happened when he relaxed after a ride, he quickly fell asleep. Soon "Sandie" Pendleton came into the room and shouted his chief back into the land of consciousness. "General Jackson," he said, "General Blank failed to put a picket at the crossroads and the following Brigade took the wrong road." Without moving, Jackson opened his eyes, listened attentively and snapped at once: "Put him under arrest and prefer charges." Then he shut his eyes and, almost on the instant, resumed his nap.[39]

It was not for long. The curtain was about to rise on Act Three of the drama. Munford, by previous orders, had made ready his Second Virginia Cavalry for a dash to Bristoe Station. His infantry support was now coming up. It was Harry Hays' Brigade, commanded temporarily by Col. Henry Forno, and it included some of "Dick" Taylor's Louisiana troops. A fine tribute Ewell had paid them and their former chief in selecting those regiments as pacemakers for the long, long march. Although they scarcely would be needed for the petty work immediately in hand, they probably scented booty from afar. For that reason, when they came within hearing distance of Bristoe, they must have groaned

37 *W. W. Blackford's MS Memoirs*, 155.   38 *O. R.*, 12, pt. 2, p. 747.
39 *W. W. Blackford's MS Memoirs*, 159.

at the diminishing rattle of a train of freight cars northward bound. It was empty, but a train was a prize they coveted.

As the infantry waited in the sunset, Munford quietly advanced his regiment and got within 100 yards of the station before he was seen.[40] Then, as his troopers rushed forward with a shout, the few Union cavalrymen who had been loitering at the station made off in frenzied haste. Most of the blue infantry, having no alternative, ran to the hotel and to the other buildings and from that shelter opened a weak, nervous fire.[41]

While Munford's troopers were dealing with these Federals, the Louisianians and the Twenty-first North Carolina of Trimble's Brigade moved in—to the accompaniment of another engine-whistle. Like the previous one, the locomotive was coming north-ward from the direction of Warrenton. Had it been the approach-ing wagon of an unsuspecting Federal sutler, the train could not have excited the troops more. Some of them snatched up a few wooden sills, which they threw across the track. Other men sought frantically to unbolt a rail. On roared the cars. Before the men even could loosen the track, the engine was upon them. It passed, it struck the sills, it scattered them without injury to itself and, in a shower of bullets, it proceeded up the road, where its crew, of course, quickly would spread the alarm.

Disappointed Confederates learned that they had arrived at the hour when Federal supply trains were run, one after another back to Manassas or to Alexandria from Pope's front. Stuart's men de-cided they would try again. Another train would "be along" soon. The boys found a derailing switch which they opened, and then, to make assurance double sure, some infantrymen of the Twenty-first North Carolina lined up alongside the right of way to give the next train crew a deliberate volley. The soldiers had not long to wait. Again from "down the line" came the sound of a locomotive. It swept confidently nearer with no reduction of speed. The next moment it came under the fire of the North Carolinians, and the next it hit the switch. Hundreds of soldiers had the novel expe-rience of witnessing a wreck they had been privileged to prepare. With a crash the engine and half the train plunged down the embankment. Around it, almost as it crumpled, the Confederates gathered. Loud were the guffaws and many the jests when the

[40] O. R., 12, pt. 2. p. 748.   [41] Ibid., 747.

men saw that the locomotive was named the "President" and that its steam dome bore a picture of Mr. Lincoln. Through this a Confederate rifle ball had passed.

Obligingly, a third train, composed of twenty "empties," soon followed. It ran into the cars left on the track, and created a jungle of shattered wood and twisted iron. The one regret of the Confederates, on examining the wreck, was to discover that the cars had been fitted with wooden benches and evidently had been used to move troops to Pope. If only the Federals had been caught en route!

While Ewell's men rued and searched, they heard another train coming from the same direction, but by this time the drama was played out. The engineer saw the wreckage ahead of him, put on his brakes, sensed the cause of the trouble and quickly backed out of range. He would give warning to the southward as surely as the crew of the train which had passed the obstructions had, ere this, doubtless put the garrison of Manassas Junction on notice. There would be no more trains to wreck that evening! [42]

Jackson, duly grateful to God, was as diligent a train retriever as he was a wagon hunter, and he promptly directed Captain Boswell to get the captured locomotives and cars across Broad Run; but Boswell, for once, could not carry out his orders. He had to report that the equipment was wrecked beyond repair. Thereupon, regretful that no more could be done, Jackson told his engineer to burn the bridge over the run. [43]

"Old Jack" had not then heard and perhaps never knew of the incident that made the most exhausted infantryman laugh and slap an aching thigh. On one of the wrecked trains was found a Federal civilian, probably a politician, whose ankle was broken. Now Capt. William C. Oates of the Twelfth Alabama takes up: "He was laid upon the ground near a fire. He inquired who we were, and when informed he expressed a desire to see Stonewall Jackson. I pointed out Jackson to him, who just then stood on the opposite side of the fire closely engaged in interrogating the engineer. He requested to be raised, which was done. He surveyed the great Confederate general in his dingy gray uniform,

---

[42] *W. W. Blackford's MS Memoirs*, 160 ff; *O. R.*, 12, pt. 2, pp. 650–51, 708; 2 *N. C. Regts.*, 151. Various accounts state differently the number of trains, but Jackson and Lee officially reported that two were wrecked.

[43] *O. R.*, 12, pt. 2, p. 651.

with his cap pulled down on his nose, for half a minute, and then in a tone of disappointment and disgust exclaimed, 'O my God! Lay me down!' " [44]

All who heard this roared, but they could not forget in laughter the lamentable fact that no booty was to be had from all the smashed freight cars. To relieve disappointments, rewarding prospects were held out by residents of Bristoe. Seven miles up the railroad,[45] said the natives, at the old Confederate base of Manassas Junction, General Pope had accumulated enormous supplies of every sort. Rations by the hundreds of thousand were in storage or on freight cars. Quartermasters' stores in equal quantity awaited call. Swarming sutlers offered at Manassas all that could tempt the palate and empty the pocket of the soldier. Jackson listened, calculated, and concluded that he could not afford to wait till morning to start after these treasures. Lest they be spoiled or burned, they must be seized forthwith for the Confederacy, but by whom?

That was the question. Many of the infantry, far back in the column, had lain down where they had halted and already they had fallen into exhausted sleep.[46] They had earned that rest and as much besides as could be allowed them. Hill computed that on the two days' march his men had covered fifty-four miles.[47] Jackson's own Division, which might be expected to respond to an emergency call, was the rear unit and too far away for immediate service. Who, then, would march in the darkness four long miles up the railroad, to secure those supplies?

Trimble was the man. As soon as he heard that troops were wanted for the extra march, he offered his. Had he not been urging, ever since he joined Jackson, that all advantage be pushed to the ultimate? Was it not he who had been reluctant to halt at Cross Keys and on the advance of June 26 to Beaver Dam Creek? On the evening after Malvern Hill, had he not advocated a night attack? Now he was to have his opportunity. Jackson gratefully accepted the offer to march on Manassas.

With the Twenty-first North Carolina and the Twenty-first Georgia, less than 800 muskets all told, Trimble set out about 9 o'clock.[48] A little later, Jackson decided that Trimble's success would be more probable if he had cavalry with him. Conse-

[44] *Oates*, 134.
[46] *Worsham*, 119.
[48] *O. R.*, 12, pt. 2, p. 720.
[45] *O. R.*, 12, pt. 2, pp. 554, 643.
[47] *O. R.*, 12, pt. 2, p. 670.

quently, Stuart was ordered to move on Manassas and, as senior, to take command.[49] Of this, Trimble was not informed, nor was Stuart told that when Trimble had started, the Marylander had understood that the expedition was to be his own.

The result was a lack of understanding which subsequently led to a dispute; but at the moment, Stuart pushed ahead in the darkness until he came under the fire of the Federal guard. There he waited for Trimble who, on arrival, disposed a regiment on either side of the railroad and advanced. The Twenty-first North Carolina was lucky enough to reach some box cars, behind which the men made so much noise that the enemy thought the Confederates were charging. In the darkness the Union battery fired its salvo wildly, whereupon the North Carolinians rushed forward and took the battery before the guns could be reloaded.[50] Shifts of position and the confusion of the night left in doubt the progress of the Georgians on the north side of the railway. When an officer of the Carolina regiment crossed the track and failed to find the other force, he called out:

"Halloo, Georgia, where are you?"

"Here," came the answer, "all right! We have taken a battery!"

"So have we," the Carolinian shouted.

Proud of themselves, both regiments cheered and, as soon as they might, examined their capture. Wrote General Trimble: ". . . each of the two batteries contained four field pieces, horses, equipments, and ammunition complete."[51]

These were no more than the first fruits. The base itself was incredibly rich, even to a train that had arrived from the North not long before with all the promiscuous supplies that Pope particularly had ordered forward. What loot there would be when daylight came . . . provided "Old Jack" would allow the soldiers a free hand.

Would Jackson do that? At Winchester, he sternly had admonished his men that all captured supplies were the property of the Confederate government. Some of his veterans had not forgotten how he had made them take off the Union overcoats they had found so comfortable. Was he to be more moderate now? Of course he would take into account the fact that his soldiers had

[49] *Ibid.*, 643.
[50] 2 *N. C. Regts.*, 153.
[51] *O. R.*, 12, pt. 2, pp. 720–21.

received no rations since the evening of the 24th, but beyond the formal issue of bread and bacon, would he throw open the stores?

After the manner of man when hungry, that question bulked larger in the dawn of August 27 than did the fact that one of the great marches of history had been made.

CHAPTER VI

JACKSON DEFIES POPE AND THANKS GOD

BEFORE EVEN HIS usual insomnious "early dawn," Jackson advanced in support of Trimble the Stonewall Brigade and Poague's Battery. After them, toward the treasure house at Manassas, moved Hill's Division, and then the remainder of Taliaferro's troops. At Bristoe, Ewell was left with three Brigades.[1] His orders were to resist any Federal advance and, if hard pressed, to fall back on the main force, which would have been revictualed ere that.

Jackson himself rode early to the Junction, where he found fully as much Federal property as the residents of Bristoe had told him to expect. Two tracks for a distance of half a mile each[2] were covered with freight cars. More than 100 they were, all new, all loaded with supplies of a variety that outscaled imagination.[3] Flour and like staples crowded warehouses. As for the goods that had been offered by the vanished sutlers who followed the Union Army, Col. W. W. Blackford had seen those on the Pamunkey, but now he had to admit "the display of luxuries among the sutlers' stores was even more extensive than at the White House, for none had been destroyed before we got possession."[4]

To this loot, without asking leave of any officer, the cavalrymen helped themselves liberally upon their arrival; but General Trimble held a stern hand on the actions of his two regiments of the vanguard: Instead of being allowed to plunder, they were ordered to guard the captured stores. The Stonewall Brigade, which reached Manassas soon after daylight, likewise was restrained and was ordered to advance over familiar ground to positions where it could meet attack.[5]

Before the Brigade left the vicinity of the sutlers' stores, some

---

[1] *Allan's Army*, 215.
[2] E. A. Moore, 103. A. P. Hill, *O. R.*, 12, pt. 2, p. 670, stated that there were two miles of cars.
[3] E. A. Moore, *loc cit.*; *O. R.*, 12, pt. 2, p. 656.
[4] *W. W. Blackford's MS Memoirs*, 165.   [5] *O. R.*, 12, pt. 2, p. 721.

of the soldiers pushed forward those in front of them and broke the circle of guards. Then the men of the Model Brigade grabbed as they chose until the guard was strengthened. Driven off, the most persistent went to a commissary depot. Comrade Casler is adequate witness of what followed: "I soon found, in one corner of the second story, a room filled with officers' rations and several soldiers supplying themselves with coffee, sugar, molasses, etc. When we had appropriated all we could carry, we found a barrel of whiskey, which we soon tapped; but as we had our canteens full of molasses, and our tin cups full of sugar, we had nothing to drink out of. We soon found an old funnel, however, and while one would hold his hand over the bottom of it, another would draw it full. In this way it was passed around. But the officers soon found us out and broke up that game." [6]

A. P. Hill's men, following the Stonewall Brigade, were of irrepressible appetite. Nor, after two days of hunger, were their officers disposed to make them wait for the regular issue of rations. Stiffly General Trimble had to report: "It was with extreme mortification that, in reporting to General A. P. Hill for orders about 10 o'clock, I witnessed an indiscriminate plunder of the public stores, cars and sutlers' houses by the army which had just arrived, in which General Hill's division was conspicuous, setting at defiance the guards I had placed over the stores." [7]

This did not last long. From a considerable distance, a solitary Federal battery had been firing protestingly at the plunderers and soon had made itself so obnoxious that Poague was sent out to silence it. First Branch's Brigade and then the remainder of Hill's Division, except for Gregg, were called from their holiday in the warehouses to support Poague and to ascertain what force of infantry might be in rear of the battery.

Before the Light Division started, Jackson himself had gone with Poague and now he was far in advance. Ere long, as he followed the road along the railroad from Manassas toward Bull Run, he saw about a mile ahead the glint of the sunlight on a line of bayonets. Whose bayonets were they, Confederate or Union? He halted and looked again and exchanged observations with his staff. Suspicions aroused by the direction of the advance were confirmed by field glasses as soon as the color of the uni-

---

[6] *Casler,* 151–52.   [7] *O. R.,* 12, pt. 2, p. 721. Cf. *Douglas,* 136.

forms could be ascertained. Federal the troops were, a Brigade of them, and they were marching straight toward a strong, veteran Confederate Division.

A quarter of a mile North of the Bull Run railroad bridge, as it later developed, the train carrying this New Jersey Brigade had been halted by the debris of a collision.[8] The men were detrained by their General, George W. Taylor, and were marched to the bridge. Their orders were to hold this structure and to prevent demolition by the Confederates,[9] but in his ardor General Taylor decided to press on to Manassas and to drive off a Confederate force he evidently thought small. When his four regiments had reached the ridge that overlooks the plain of Manassas from the North, he had halted them, had ordered them to leave their tents, their blankets and their haversacks, and then he had started them straight for Manassas,[10] though they had no artillery.[11] By 10 o'clock or about that hour,[12] they had formed line of battle and were advancing to their death.

Poague's old colleague Carpenter brought up his battery; together they opened fire—prematurely it seemed to the infantrymen. Had the gunners waited, the critical infantrymen asserted, the whole Federal Brigade would have marched on until it was surrounded.[13] As the inexperienced Jerseymen came on, in the face of the shells, Jackson watched them with admiration and felt that he should save them, if he could, from the slaughter that was beginning. Poague and Carpenter were sweeping the front and the right. Shifting soon to better ground and shorter range, they changed to canister. Hill's men commanded the Federal left.

It was enough, Jackson thought. He halted the artillery fire, rode out in front of Poague's guns, waved his handkerchief and shouted to the enemy to surrender. In response, a Federal infantryman raised his gun, took careful aim, and fired at Jackson. The missile came close enough for a cannoneer near the General's side to hear the spiteful whistle.[14] With such men there could be no other argument than the one they were using. Confederate fire

[8] O. R., 12, pt. 2, p. 541. The troops consisted of the 1st, 2nd, 3rd and 4th New Jersey, and formed the 1st Brigade of Slocum's 1st Division of the VI Corps. O. R., 12, pt. 2, p. 536.

[9] Ibid., 540.   [10] Ibid.

[11] Ibid., 401.   [12] Ibid., 541–42, 543.

[13] 2 N. C. Regts., 551; Hotchkiss' MS Diary, 161. Oates, op. cit., 136, blamed this fire on the horse artillery.

[14] E. A. Moore, 104.

was reopened; the Federals stumbled on for a few minutes, and then they broke. They were pursued over the railroad bridge, which was destroyed, and back to their train, which was burned;[15] but at least one observer believed that no serious effort was made to annihilate the Brigade.[16] Although approximately 300 prisoners were taken, the killed and wounded did not exceed 135.[17]

The unequal fight was over by 11 o'clock.[18] Most of Hill's hungry men then returned to Manassas Junction in the hope of resuming the plunder. They found that Taliaferro had arrived from Bristoe and, by order, had assumed command and had taken charge of the supplies.[19] He was loading the ambulances and the ordnance wagons with all they would hold of the stores the Southern Army most lacked; and, at the same time, he was issuing to the men in a haphazard, if liberal fashion. Whenever new commissary stores were found, no matter what their nature, some of them were given the soldiers. Boylike, the members of numerous messes would stop the preparation of plain, familiar food when a member of the mess triumphantly brought in a delicacy. For better or for worse they would try their hand at cooking the rare viand.

Jackson had seen to it early that all discoverable liquor was dumped from barrels and that every displayed bottle not requisitioned by the surgeons was remorselessly smashed. So grievous a waste this was, in the eyes of some soldiers, that they sought to recover even from pools and from ditches the fluid that Jackson threw away.[20] Men dared not do this where they could be seen by their General. He, observing their wasteful cooking and quick casting away of one edible for a rarer, was torn between indulgence and dismay. His hope was—at least the men so thought—that Lee would arrive in time to haul off or to distribute the bulk of the supplies.[21]

---

15 O. R., 12, pt. 2, p. 670.

16 E. A. Moore, 104–05. That artillerist made the curious mistake of calling Hill's Division "Rhodes." The other details of his narrative of this affair seem authentic. Most of them are verifiable.

17 O. R., 12, pt. 2, p. 260. Unfortunately, General Taylor was among those mortally wounded. As he was being carried from the field, he appealed to an officer to rally the men "and for God's sake to prevent another Bull Run." Ibid., 408.

18 Ibid., 543.   19 O. R., 12, pt. 2, p. 656.

20 23 S. H. S. P., 333. This reference covers a somewhat theatrical account of the steps Jackson took to keep his men from getting liquor; but as the narrative is late and anonymous, with its author distinctly the hero of the occurrence, it has to be classified as unconfirmable.

21 Worsham, 121.

Later in the day, as word came that the Federals were beginning to press Ewell South of Bristoe, Jackson decided that the
men might as well enjoy what their government could not salvage. The soldiers were told that they must put four days' rations
in their haversacks,[22] that they must not dress in any of the abundant blue uniforms they found,[23] and that they must not interfere
with the large Federal bakery, which prisoners were to operate
continuously in order that an issue of fresh bread might be made.[24]
With these reservations, every man might take whatever he
pleased. Truth was, nearly all who could do so had been plundering on the sly ever since their arrival. Now they could go about it
openly and with discrimination.

The hours that followed never were to be rivalled in the Army
of Northern Virginia and never forgotten. To the end of his life,
almost every survivor of Jackson's command could remember
some of the articles he had chosen, though he could not always
recall why. Said John H. Worsham: "It was hard to decide what
to take. Some filled their haversacks with cakes, some with
candy, others oranges, lemons, canned goods, etc. I know one who
took nothing but French mustard, filled his haversack and was so
greedy that he put one more bottle in his pocket. This was his
four days' rations, and it turned out to be the best thing taken,
because he traded it for meat and bread, and it lasted him until
we reached Frederick," [Maryland].[25]

Gregg's men, who were not sent after Taylor's New Jersey Brigade, had happy fortune which their historian thus jubilantly
described: ". . . before we reached the stores, we passed a sutler's
establishment which was speedily stripped. Fine whiskey and
segars circulated freely, elegant lawn and linen handkerchiefs
were applied to noses hitherto blown by the thumb and forefinger,
and sumptuous underclothing was fitted over limbs sunburnt, sore
and vermin-splotched. Many a foot more worn and more weary
than those of the olden time pilgrims here received its grateful
protection from the rocky soil. At the Junction there was a general jubilee. Hard-tack and bacon, coffee and sugar, soap even,
was distributed to us, and we were invited to help ourselves to

22 *Worsham*, 121.   23 *E. A. Moore*, 107.
24 *Allan's Army*, 216.   25 *Op. cit.*, 121; Cf. *Douglas*. 136.

anything in the storehouses, from a dose of calomel to a McClellan saddle." [26]

The first lament was that certain of the troops did not get their share. Poague's men, for example, and probably some of the other artillerists did not return from hunting Taylor's troops and the vanished Union battery until the choicest viands had been devoured. "What we got was . . . disappointing," Ned Moore wrote with a grumble, "and not of a kind to invigorate, consisting, as it did, of hard-tack, pickled oysters, and canned stuff generally." [27]

Worse still, in the view of infantrymen, was the advantage enjoyed by the mounted men. The boy on foot had his haversack and his pockets—no more; the trooper had an animal that could bear much loot. Not cavalry alone, but horse artillery could carry off far more than a foot soldier could. The advantage enjoyed by an officer who had two horses was scandalous. "For my part," wrote a gallant artillery lieutenant, "I got a tooth brush, a box of candles, a quantity of lobster salad, a barrel of coffee and other things which I forget." [28] Mention of lobster, alien to soldiers' diet, introduces the final personality of this unique scene in the drama of Lee's lieutenants. He was a private, in tatters, barefooted and well-nigh starved; but he must have had the memory of earlier days of amplitude and luxury. Through the stock of a sutler he had searched until he had found what he craved; and now, in the full heat of the August afternoon, with his fingers as his fork, he was eating canned lobster salad and was washing it down with Rhine wine.[29]

The whole plundering was more than a feast and a frolic. It proved to be a subtle if unintentional challenge to the hungry troops of a blockaded land, and a promise of what might await them at the end of other daring marches. Long the boys were to talk of that day. More than a year later, through bleak and biting weather, their march was to be incredibly rapid because it again was directed toward Manassas Junction. Times uncounted the route step was quickened by a rumor that a sutler's shack was ahead. In the beginning of the bitter campaign of 1864, as will in

26 J. F. G. Caldwell, Gregg's South Carolina Brigade (cited hereafter as *Caldwell*), 31. *Cf.* Monier Diary, *Mil. Annals La.*, 30–31.

27 *E. A. Moore*, 107.   28 *Ham Chamberlayne*, 99.

29 *Ibid.*, 100.

due place appear, nothing so aroused the Confederates against General Grant as the report that he had forbidden sutlers to move with the Army of the Potomac. To the Southerners, that seemed an unfair, an illegal method of waging war.

Delightful plundering, like affrighting battles, had to end. The pressure on Ewell at Bristoe rapidly was becoming heavier. Long Federal columns by midafternoon were threatening the flank of his three Brigades. It was manifest that Pope's Army was coming up and that the possession of the road to Washington was to be disputed. For a time, Ewell scattered the blue cloud with his artillery fire; but when he found that his infantry were close to a general action, he decided to retire, as Jackson had authorized, to Manassas.

The tactical arrangements for a withdrawal, while engaged, he left in part to General Early, whose Brigade he designated as rearguard. "Old Jube" was easily equal to the task. After the other troops had slipped back unscathed, he adroitly pulled out his regiments one by one until the Thirteenth Virginia alone was left on the farther side of Broad Run, in front of the new position. Soon that regiment disengaged itself and crossed with trifling losses. Ewell thereupon posted Early in line of battle on a hill over which passed the road to Manassas. As if they were reinforcements, troops conspicuously displayed their flags for the enemy's observation, and ostentatiously moved to right and to left by Ewell's orders. The enemy halted; Ewell moved off the other Brigades; Early held his ground till dusk and then he followed his chief. Not unreasonably he was proud of his men, and especially of James A. Walker's Thirteenth Virginia, originally A. P. Hill's Regiment, which had rallied magnificently at Cedar Mountain.[30] With equal pride, Ewell combined deliberate, ostentatious defiance. Every time a horse was killed in the action, the General had the harness removed and carried to the rear in order to show the Federals, when they came up, that he had not been hurried in his retreat.[31]

So admirably was all this done that when Ewell's veterans arrived at Manassas and drew rations, they had earned a full share of the luxuries, but they probably got prosaic meat and bread and

30 O. R., 12, pt. 2, p. 710.
31 Memo. of Gen. T. T. Munford—*Munford MSS.*

perhaps some coffee. The delicacies doubtless were gone. Already Jackson was prepared to evacuate the place and regretfully to give to the flames what he could not consume or transport and would not leave to the enemy.[32]

The first part of Jackson's mission now was performed: he had cut off the supplies of the Federal Army and thereby had assured the speedy withdrawal of a part, perhaps of the whole of it, from the Rappahannock. Ahead of him was the second part of his mission, the task of preserving his force until the two wings of the Army were reunited.

A swift withdrawal toward the mountains, there to await Lee, would have represented a permissible, a not-unsoldierly aftermath of the fine performance of August 25–27. Jackson was not content to take that course. Realistically he determined to stay close to the line of Lee's advance from Thoroughfare Gap, so that he would be ready to co-operate on Lee's arrival, to retreat if Lee were delayed and, meantime, to strike a blow should the Federals give him an opening.

For this bold maintenance of his advanced position Jackson would need strong, readily defensible ground. Reconnaissance and inquiry based on his own knowledge of the terrain—the result of three and a half months' observation the previous year— led him to select a low ridge North of and roughly parallel to a stretch of the road from Warrenton to Alexandria. This ridge, which subsequently was elevated by the Federals to the loftiness of "heights," was styled Groveton after a nearby settlement of that name, on the south side of the Warrenton road.[33] As if in good augury, the ground was slightly more than one mile West of the site of the Henry House, around which, in the First Battle of Manassas, Jackson had fought.[34] Groveton was not a perfect position, as soon will appear, but it probably was the best the nearby countryside offered for the mission Jackson had assigned himself.

That advantage of position Jackson might never have real-

[32] O. R., 12, pt. 2, pp. 644, 656, 670.

[33] "This Groveton was simply a place of cross-roads where the Groveton and Sudley road crossed the Warrenton turnpike, and might have had a post office and a petty grocery. We remember but two or three buildings and some stacks, as we saw the place through clouds of dust." Frederick Denison, The Battle of Groveton (Providence, R. I., 1885).

[34] The clearest of the many maps of the area are those in Allan's Army.

ized, had his adversaries been alert, because he got into a tangle on
the 27th–28th as a result of an excess of the reticence which, in
form more moderate, ranked high among his military virtues.
Upon evacuating Manassas Junction, Jackson dispatched Taliaferro on the road from Manassas to Sudley Springs Ford, and he
probably instructed A. P. Hill to move to the same point under
the direction of a guide he furnished. Ewell was told only that a
guide would be sent him. When the man reached Ewell's headquarters, Trimble and his Brigade had disappeared—literally.
Nobody knew where they had marched or when or why. Ewell
had his aides go in search of the missing regiments, and finally
he concluded that Trimble, having no orders, had assumed that
he should fall in behind the rear Brigade of A. P. Hill.

The remainder of Ewell's Division then started northward; but,
as Campbell Brown subsequently explained with much disgust.
the guide "had not been told where to take us or, if told, it had
been in some very general terms, as that he was to follow A. P.
Hill." [35] Uncertainly, Ewell tramped toward Bull Run and at
length came upon Trimble who, as suspected, had followed Hill
and already had gone into camp. At a time when Jackson should
have had the three Divisions preparing to take position at Groveton, Taliaferro alone was on the ground. Hill had marched to
Centreville. Ewell was South of Blackburn's Ford. There was, in
short, worse confusion than had prevailed on any of Jackson's
marches save that of August 8 en route to meet Pope at Cedar
Mountain. Trimble was boiling with wrath; Ewell may have
taken philosophically the reticence of his chief; Powell Hill
scarcely would have been human had he not reflected that the
General who held him so sternly to the letter of marching orders
was not himself immune to error.[36]

Ewell was close to Blackburn's Ford and most readily could get
to Groveton with his van by crossing Bull Run and then swinging westward over the fields and through the woods to Stone
Bridge. Thence he could return to the right bank and could

[35] Brown in Hamlin's *Old Bald Head*, 126.

[36] This curious incident was mentioned vaguely in reports or was avoided altogether. Jackson merely said: ". . . Taliaferro moved his Division that night across to
the Warrenton and Alexandria turnpike, pursuing the road to Sudley's Mill . . . Ewell's
and Hill's Divisions joined Jackson's on the 28th" (*O. R.*, 12, pt. 2, p. 644). Hill (*ibid.*,
670) simply recounted his movements. Early (*ibid.*, 710) is authority for the march of
his and of Trimble's Brigades. Publication of Campbell Brown's statement in Hamlin's
Old Bald Head, 125–26, explained for the first time the confused details.

follow the Warrenton Road to Groveton. Seven extra miles this exacted of the front units of Ewell's Division. The rear Brigade [37] lost four miles.

Before the scattered Divisions could be concentrated on the morning of the 28th, Jackson got word at 8 o'clock that a Federal force was in full retreat northward in the direction of Bull Run. Immediately Jackson sent word to A. P. Hill to move down to the fords of Bull Run and to intercept the enemy. This message reached Hill about 10 A.M., while he was on the march from Centreville to Stone Bridge. A dilemma was presented. Jackson's orders were not to be disregarded, as many an officer already had learned; but in this instance, Hill was satisfied that he had more information than Jackson possessed concerning the enemy's plans. Two orders from Pope to McDowell had been captured and brought to Hill. From these documents it appeared that instead of starting a precipitate retreat on Alexandria, Pope was concentrating around Manassas in the belief that he could destroy Jackson before Lee could arrive.[38]

Should Hill act on this information, which apparently had not reached Jackson, or should he blindly obey orders and let the blame rest on Jackson for not knowing what the enemy was doing? Hill resolved his dilemma manfully and at once. "I deemed it best," said he, "to push on and join General Jackson"—that and no more. If he were making a mistake, he would take the consequences.

Jackson, by 10 o'clock, was beginning to get somewhat different information from that which had shaped his early message to Hill. The commander of an advanced Brigade sent under guard to field headquarters a Federal courier who had been captured while carrying an order from General McDowell to his subordinates.[39] This paper showed that McDowell was in command of Sigel's Corps as well as of his own. Sigel was directed by the order to march on Manassas Junction; the units of McDowell's Corps were to follow. In other words, Jackson most considerately was warned that two Corps were to advance along the Warrenton

---

[37] This was Forno's. Apparently it did not cross the Run. It must have moved by the road that parallels the south bank. Cf. *O. R.*, 12, pt. 2, p. 710.

[38] *O. R.*, 12, pt. 2, p. 670. One of the dispatches from Pope to McDowell, as mentioned by Hill, almost certainly is that of Aug. 27, 9 P.M., *O. R.*, 12, pt. 1, p. 304. The other cannot now be identified with certainty.

[39] *O. R.*, 12, pt. 2, p. 664.

Turnpike and were to concentrate on Manassas,[40] presumably for an attack on him. He probably learned also that Maj. Gen. Phil Kearny, who had been with the Army of the Potomac, had joined Pope and was commanding a Division which presumably had been part of McClellan's Army. Information may have reached Jackson, in addition, that Maj. Gen. Jesse L. Reno, who was known to have commanded part of the force Burnside had brought to Fredericksburg, now was serving with Pope.[41]

All this evidence of gathering opposition did not lead Jackson to modify his plan of remaining where he was until Lee arrived. Jackson was not convinced, even, that the enemy intended to make a stand. There remained a distinct possibility, he thought, that Pope might be retreating in order to unite with McClellan and to resume the offensive. On this theory, the retreat might continue all the way to Washington. The concentration on Manassas, mentioned in McDowell's orders, might be for the reorganization of the Federal right. Reported demonstrations on the Warrenton turnpike led Jackson to suspect that Pope might be planning to move part of the Federal Army across Bull Run at Stone Bridge and at Sudley's Ford.[42]

As soon, therefore, as Jackson could assume that his three scattered Divisions would be reunited in the course of a few hours, he began to seek an opportunity of striking a blow. By noon, his outposts sent word that a Federal column was advancing from Gainesville toward Sudley's Ford. Instantly Jackson decided to assail it on the march. Taliaferro with Jackson's Division was moved by the left in the direction of Gainesville. Ewell followed.[43]

---

[40] McDowell's order, which is described in detail by Bradley Johnson, *O. R.*, 12, pt. 2, p. 664, probably was an elaboration of G.O. No. 10, printed in *O. R.*, 12, pt. 1, p. 304, and delivered to Sigel in the manner noted in *ibid.*, 138 ff.

[41] Cf. *O. R.*, 12, pt. 1, p. 304. Qualification is made because there is no direct proof that the dispatch containing the references to Kearny and Reno was one of the two delivered to A. P. Hill; nor, for that matter, is there any positive record of the transmission to Jackson of the captured papers. The circumstantial evidence is convincing.

[42] *O. R.*, 12, pt. 2, p. 656.

[43] *O. R.*, 12, pt. 2, p. 656. It is to be regretted that the stirring account of the start of this march, given by Taliaferro in 2 *B. & L.*, 507–08, and used effectively in 2 *Henderson*, 143, has to be discarded because of its obvious inaccuracies of time. General Taliaferro stated that the advance, which his report timed about noon (*O. R.*, 12, pt. 2, p. 656), was ordered immediately after the receipt of the captured order of McDowell; but Bradley Johnson's report, *O. R.*, 12, pt. 2, p. 664, shows that the order was taken from the Federal courier early in the morning and was sent at once to Jackson. It is unnecessary to add that the mistake of General Taliaferro was unintentional. The incident may have occurred later in the day, precisely as he relates it, in connection with some other message received by Jackson.

After a march of about two miles and a half, they were halted by Jackson [44] because reports from the outposts convinced him that he had been mistaken in his estimate of the Federal plan. The main force of the enemy was not moving toward Bull Run.[45] On the contrary, the Federals were doing exactly what the captured order provided. They were, in Jackson's own words, "leaving the turnpike to their left and apparently making for the railroad about Manassas Junction." [46] Instead of running away from Jackson, the enemy might be preparing to give him battle. For the time, he could do nothing except to watch the Federals. Once he rode out to a private road whence Col. Thomas L. Rosser had driven with two borrowed guns a strong Union column; [47] but he saw no opportunity there.

Jackson returned and waited—and not in vain. Toward sunset, another blue column came up the Warrenton Turnpike, but it did not follow the route of those that had turned southeastward toward Manassas. It was marching straight for the Stone Bridge. The flankers were out heavily; the column itself was compact and well closed.

What immediately followed the appearance of these troops has been told perfectly by Stuart's engineer, W. W. Blackford, who witnessed the whole affair: "Jackson rode out to examine the approaching foe, trotting backwards and forwards along the line of the handsome parade marching by, and in easy musket range of their skirmish, but they did not seem to think that a single horseman was worthy of their attention—how little they thought that this single, plainly dressed horseman was the great Stonewall himself, who was then deliberating in his own mind the question of hurling his eager troops upon their devoted heads. Many of our Generals and Colonels . . . were on the ridge across which the enemy were now crossing, and these were watching Jackson's every movement with intense interest, for we could almost tell his thoughts by his movements. Sometimes he would halt, then trot on briskly, halt again, wheel his horse and pass again along the

[44] The position was near the Browner House, which is seven-eighths of a mile West of the intersection of the Groveton-Sudley Springs Road with the Warrenton Road. Browner's thus is North of the main road and about a quarter of a mile Southwest of the end of the cut of the "unfinished railroad."

[45] O. R., 12, pt. 2, pp. 644-45, 656-57.

[46] Ibid., 656.

[47] O. R., 12, pt. 2, p. 750; Cf. Ibid., 336, 665.

front of the marching column, or rather along its flank. About a quarter of a mile off, troops were now opposite us. All felt sure Jackson could never resist that temptation, and that the order to attack would come soon, even if Longstreet was beyond the mountain. Presently General Jackson pulled up suddenly, wheeled and galloped toward us. 'Here he comes, by God,' said several, and Jackson rode up to the assembled group as calm as a May morning and touching his hat in military salute, said in as soft a voice as if he had been talking to a friend in ordinary conversation, 'Bring up your men, gentlemen.' Every officer whirled around and scurried back to the woods at full gallop. The men had been watching their officers with much interest and when they wheeled and dashed toward them they knew what it meant, and from the woods arose a hoarse roar like that from cages of wild animals at the scent of blood." [48]

Almost at once, Taliaferro sent his cheering men forward. Ewell followed with two of his Brigades. Trimble was in his glory. Said one participant: "Trimble gave the loudest command I ever heard, to 'Forward, guide center, march!' I could hear the echo in Bull Run Swamp for miles." [49] Almost simultaneously, three batteries found a position whence they could fire over the heads of the Confederate skirmishers. Into the open the infantry on the right plunged and advanced to an orchard and a farmhouse enclosure.

There the advance abruptly was halted; there at close quarters was begun a bitter standup fight. [50] The Federals, as the Southerners later discovered, belonged to King's Division of Burnside's Corps. Gibbon's Brigade, of one Indiana and three Wisconsin regiments, was the tough bone Jackson attempted to crack. Quickly to the support of Gibbon came a part of Doubleday's Brigade. These six regiments stood off Jackson's Division and half of Ewell's, [51] and forced the Confederate artillery to shift its ground. [52] Jackson promptly sent for additional guns, but John Pelham only, and he with no more than three of his pieces, got to the front. [53] For two hours and a half, [54] until 9 o'clock, artillery

---

[48] W. W. Blackford's MS Memoirs, 172–73.
[49] Oates, 138.   [50] O. R., 12, pt. 2, p. 657.
[51] Trimble's and Lawton's Brigades. It is plain that Early's and Hays's men were not called up until too late to share in the action. O. R., 12, pt. 2, pp. 710–11
[52] Ibid., 645, 657.   [53] Ibid., 645, 652, 735, 754.
[54] Ibid., 657.

and infantry banged furiously away. Then the Federals, with-drawing slowly, broke off the fight.

Tactically, the action taught nothing, and it demonstrated noth-ing save the stubbornness of both forces. In casualties, for the numbers engaged, it was one of the costliest battles Jackson ever had fought.[55] The Stonewall Brigade had been reduced before the action to about 635 rank and file [56] and should have been spared that day, but it was thrust where the fire was heaviest. Some 200 of its men were killed or wounded,[57] with the result that it was left with about the personnel of a regiment of moderate strength. Its command was hard hit. Col. John F. Neff of the Thirty-third Virginia was killed. The picturesque A. J. Grigsby of the Twenty-seventh Virginia was wounded slightly, and Lawson Botts, Lieu-tenant Colonel in command of the Second Virginia, mortally.[58]

All these were definite losses not only to the Stonewall Brigade but to the Division also. Botts had been a lawyer of distinction before the war, and had been named by the court to defend John Brown, a duty he had discharged as ably as his grandfather had defended Aaron Burr.[59] In command of the Second Virginia after the death of Colonel Allen at Gaines' Mill, Botts had won good opinions. John Neff, it will be recalled, had been elevated to the colonelcy from the rank of regimental Adjutant when A. C. Cummings declined to be a candidate for election. An admirable fighter and a most attractive man, 28 years of age, Neff had been released by Jackson after a hearing on the charges Winder had made during the period of encampment at Gordonsville. Although Neff's father was a Dunkard minister and he himself was of that pacifist faith, he was calm and relentless in action [60] and one of the best of Jackson's Colonels.

More serious losses there were. General Taliaferro was wounded painfully, though he was able to keep the field till the action closed.[61] Worse, far, was the case of "Dick" Ewell. That incor-

---

[55] Federal losses were at least 898. Cf. O. R., 12, pt. 2, pp. 372, 373, 378.

[56] O. R., 12, pt. 2, pp. 661, 663, 663–64.

[57] Ibid. Regimental losses of all save the Thirty-third Virginia were reported. If that regiment lost the average of the others, brigade casualties would be 216.

[58] O. R., 12, pt. 2, p. 667. For Botts's correct rank, elsewhere loosely given as Colonel, see ibid., 661.

[59] C. D. Walker, Memorial, V. M. I., 55.

[60] Ibid., 396 ff. See Casler's tribute, supra, p. 81, n. 2. Casler added, op. cit., 165: "He was greatly beloved by the whole regiment, and his death was much lamented."

[61] O. R., 12, pt. 2, pp. 645, 658. He was shot in the foot, in the neck and in the arm. The last was the worst of the three wounds. 3 Moore's Rebellion Record, 404.

rigible had yielded once too often to his love of being in the middle
of a fight. Personally he had led a regiment forward to drive
from a gully some Federals who had been particularly obnoxious.
As he knelt for a moment to ascertain the direction of the enemy's
fire, a few of the Georgia troops proudly announced his arrival,
"Here's General Ewell, boys." As if the words had been an order,
the enemy swept the front. Ewell went down; the regiment scattered. For a time, the brigade commanders did not know whether
he was killed or wounded. Not until the fight was over and the
litter bearers were searching the front of Early's command did
they find Ewell on the ground with a bad leg wound. A minié
ball had struck him on the knee and had shattered the bones. A
severe hemorrhage had followed. When the consulting surgeons
examined him, they could say one thing only—*amputate*. That
might be at worst the end of "Dick" Ewell; at best it would involve the absence for long months of the most generous, the best
disciplined and, in many soldierly qualities, the ablest of Jackson's
subordinates.[62]

To lose, within less than three weeks, Winder, Taliaferro and
the irreplaceable Ewell must have seemed, even to the believing
heart of Jackson, a stern "dispensation of Providence." When
Taliaferro fell, the new Brigadier, William E. Starke, who had
received his appointment August 6 and never had handled a Brigade in action until Groveton, suddenly found himself in command of the most famous Division of the Army.[63] Ewell's troops
passed, by seniority, not to Early but to the devoted Alexander R.
Lawton.[64]

The effect of these changes in command Jackson could not
ponder. Once he had offended a Colonel deeply by answering a
friendly observation with the brusque remark that he had *no time*

[62] Oates, 141; *Old Bald Head*, 129; *O. R.*, 12, pt. 2, p. 711; *Southern Generals*, 350.
According to the last of these references, Ewell was removed to a hospital near Aldie,
where the operation was performed, and later he was transported to the home of Capt.
T. L. Farish in Charlottesville. Dr. Hamlin states, *op. cit.*, 130, that Ewell was sent
from the hospital to Dunblane, the home of his cousin, Dr. Jesse Ewell, near Bull Run
Mountains. Thence, in the autumn, he was brought to Richmond and was nursed back
to strength at the home of Dr. F. W. Hancock, 306 E. Main St. For the next detailed
reference to Ewell, see *infra*, p. 240 and Chap. XXVI.

[63] For the transfer of command to Starke, see *O. R.*, 12, pt. 2, p. 658.

[64] Lawton was accustomed to refer to himself as the "oldest Brigadier in the army."
After the promotion of Beauregard and of Braxton Bragg, he was precisely that, and
that he remained because his abilities, though high, were those of army administration
rather than of field command. His appointment was made Apr. 13, 1861. *Wright*,
48–49. Cf. *McHenry Howard*, 144.

to talk of anything but military business.[65] This now was true to the letter. "Although the enemy moved off under cover of the night and left us in quiet possession of the field," said Jackson, "he did not long permit us to remain inactive or in doubt as to his intention to renew the conflict." [66] Daylight of the 29th showed the enemy farther to the East and interposed deliberately, as Jackson thought, between the Confederates and Washington.[67] Actually, the Federal commander was striving, though with information far from complete, to concentrate 25,000 men East of Jackson and a like number West of him, in order, as Pope wrote, "to crush Jackson before Longstreet could by any possibility reach the scene of action." [68]

If "Stonewall" misjudged the purpose of this concentration, he sensed its magnitude. Carefully he drew back his tired men to take full advantage of the higher ground and of the right of way of an unfinished railroad cut North of the Warrenton Road. A compact front it was of not more than 3000 yards, on which could be put as many of his forty guns as could be brought to bear. For this front, three Divisions should have been adequate, but casualties had reduced the infantry to not more than 18,000. Some regiments in number scarcely equalled a small company. The Twenty-seventh Virginia of the Stonewall Brigade, for example, mustered twenty-five men only, rank and file.[69] Several regiments virtually were without officers [70] and should not have been put in line even where the front was strongest.

The chief weakness of the position was the cover it offered an adversary who attacked the left center or the left, where thick green forest extended at some points into the Confederate line.[71] For that reason, upon assignment to this part of the front, Hill put his Division in two lines. Lawton, on the center with two Brigades, had far less density. The depleted Division of Jackson held the right, where a better field of protective fire was offered. Stuart ranged widely and covered the flanks; but with his own and Hays's (Forno's) Brigade, Early was put on the right of Jackson to guard against a turning movement that seemed to be in preparation.[72]

[65] McHenry Howard, 81.   [66] O. R., 12, pt. 2, p. 645.
[67] Ibid.   [68] Ibid., 38.   [69] Ibid., 663.
[70] The Second Virginia had only one Captain and a Lieutenant, ibid., 659.
[71] Cf. 2 Henderson, 153–54.
[72] O. R., 12, pt. 2, p. 711. Cf. ibid., 645. The order of battle of Hill's Division is incorrectly given in ibid., 652, but is stated aright in ibid., 670.

This movement did not materialize. Instead there were demonstrations on the right, easily repulsed, and some vigorous artillery exchanges.[73] The Union batteries continued to shell the woods, as the morning of the 29th wore on, but the eyes of the opposing Confederates were less on the Federal flank than on the Warrenton Road beyond it and on the distant blue silhouette of Bull Run Mountain. Thence Lee was to come.

From that direction there rose a long cloud of dust, ominously red.[74] Was that cloud raised by the hurrying feet of Longstreet's regiments? To the officers and men on the right no immediate answer was given. They were both hopeful and apprehensive. About 10.30 or a little later, they saw a Brigade boldly filing into position almost at right angles to their line. Were these confident newcomers Federals who disdained the proximity of Jackson's guns; or were the regiments Confederate and were they extending Jackson's flank along the high ground to the South of the Warrenton Turnpike?

General Starke, who was discharging his new duties admirably, was not sure whether the arriving force was gray or blue. Quickly he sent off a courier to ascertain. Anxiously, though the Federal fire already was bringing down the boughs around them, the men of Jackson's Division rose from the ground where they had been ordered to remain. Earnestly they looked after the horseman; warmly they argued the nature of the force that was forming line of battle with speed and easy precision. Soon the courier came flying back. "It is Longstreet!" he cried even before he reached his General. A great cry that Longstreet had come was taken up by the men all down the line.[75]

---

[73] O. R., 12, pt. 2, pp. 645, 652. General McDowell is authority for describing this phase of the battle as one of "demonstrations" (O. R., 12, pt. 2, p. 337). Geo. H. Gordon (Army of Virginia, 258 n.), stated: "It is remarkable that the most patient research among Confederate reports reveals no account of any heavy or prolonged struggle up to this time, with either General Schurz or Milroy." The reason for this silence in Confederate reports was, in part, the death of General Starke before he could prepare an official account of Second Manassas. Reports of Col. B. T. Johnson for Jackson's Second Brigade and those of regimental commanders of the Stonewall Brigade refer to action later in the day (O. R., 12, pt. 2, 658 ff., 665–66). Early Federal attacks on the Confederate left seem to have been regarded by Hill and his brigade commanders as part of the continuing mêlée there. It perhaps should be added that Gen. G. H. Gordon's singular admiration of Gen. Robert Milroy, whom he regarded as a paladin of the Federal Army, may have disposed him to attach undue importance to a brush in which Milroy had a part. For Milroy's report, see O. R., 12, pt. 2, p. 319.
[74] E. A. Moore, 114.
[75] This sentence is a direct quotation from Worsham, 130–31.

The news was true. After a march that rivalled Jackson's and a succession of maneuvers that had cleared Thoroughfare Gap of Federals,[76] some of Longstreet's men on the night of the 28th–29th had bivouacked triumphantly East of the pass. Hood's Division had been the van during the early morning of the 29th and had raised the red dust that Jackson's Division had seen. The advance guard of Hood, in fact, had driven the Federal outposts so fast on the roads to Gainesville that the proud commander subsequently could write, "General Longstreet sent me orders, two or three times, to halt, since the Army was unable to keep within supporting distance of my forces." [77] Hood, scarcely moderating his pace, was among the first to greet Stuart, who had gone out to welcome and to guide Lee.[78] The Texan had continued his advance until he was in contact with Early's outposts and then he had formed the line of battle that Jackson's men admiringly had observed. Under Lee's eyes, other Brigades now were spreading a long front that hinged on the right of Jackson.

For the time, General Pope gave no evidence that he intended to attack on that flank, or even that he was aware of Longstreet's arrival. A brief foray was undertaken against Jackson's wagon train and was repelled by the cavalry and the horse artillery.[79] Next came on Ewell's front two attacks of no great vigor. At one point in the second of these, a Union Major on horseback led his troops straight at the Confederates. He was shot down, but after the action an Alabama captain rebuked his company for slaying the Federal. So brave a man, he insisted, should have been captured, not killed. Jackson happened to hear this and he repeated substantially what he had told Ewell after Port Republic.[80] "No, Captain," he said, "the men are right; kill the brave ones, they lead on the others." [81]

Ere this, the heavy pressure of the enemy seemed to be shifting to the left, A. P. Hill's part of the line. To strengthen Hill, the two Brigades under Early, which no longer were needed as a flank

[76] For a description of Longstreet's advance, see 2 *R. E. Lee*, 304–18. In 1 *N. C Regts.*, 206, the statement is made that the troops in Thoroughfare Gap could see the smoke from Jackson's guns at Groveton but could not hear any sound of the battle.
[77] *Hood*, 33.   [78] 2 *R. E. Lee*, 318.
[79] *O. R.*, 12, pt. 2, pp. 646, 735–36, 755. For a critical review of all the evidence concerning the hour of Longstreet's arrival on the right of Jackson, the author gratefully is indebted to the late Thomas Kearny of New York City.
[80] See *supra*, Vol. I, p. 464.   [81] *Oates*, 144.

guard on the right, were moved eastward and were placed in rear of the Light Division.[82]

Jackson ordered this, but he did not himself visit that flank early

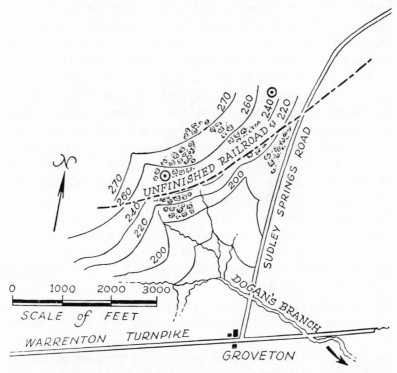

Jackson's Position at Groveton, after the Map made by Gen. G. K. Warren for the hearing in the case of Fitz-John Porter. Jackson's position was in the interval between contours 240 and 260, but it cannot be determined precisely. The right was to the East of the head of Dogan's Branch and approximately at the point surrounded by a circle. Gregg's left was in the position correspondingly marked above the Sudley Springs Road

in the day. Had he done so he would have been proud of the spirit of the men who awaited calmly the Federal attack, but the position of Hill's force he would have condemned and, where possible, would have corrected. Nothing had been done, apparently, during the forenoon, to clear the ground where the front passed through the woods. Part of Hill's line remained in a tangle of trees and bushes; much of it was drawn where undergrowth

[82] Early in O. R., 12, pt. 2, pp. 711-12.

concealed all movement.[83]   Almost no artillery could be used.[84]
On the extreme left, Maxcy Gregg and his South Carolinians held
a wooded knoll that overlooked the Sudley Springs Road and
Ford. The flank of this Brigade was refused until the front represented an obtuse angle.[85] To the Brigade had been assigned no
more ground than it could occupy,[86] but between the right of
Gregg and the left of the next Brigade, which was Thomas's, there
was an interval of 125 to 175 yards.[87] Nobody ever explained why
this gap was left, or how Hill failed to observe that immediately
in front of it the railroad cut was deep enough to shelter a considerable force. Had Jackson known of this he of course would
have occupied the cut or would have cleared ground and placed
guns where they could command it.[88]

On first contact during the morning, Gregg and Thomas advanced and drove the enemy without difficulty, but the assailed
Federals soon became the aggressors. As fast as successive lines
could be formed, they were directed against Hill's left. If their
attack was not vigorous, it was persistent. Beaten off, they renewed
the assault or gave place to fresh troops who appeared to be of a
number inexhaustible.

As morning passed meridian, the Federals seemed more than
ever determined to destroy Hill. Their attacks were heavier and
were centered on Thomas and on Gregg, who met them with
volleys as furious as their own. Ere long, from the railroad cut in
front of the interval in the line, a cloud of bluecoats swept forward. Quietly these men had crept into the cut; from it they now
interposed swiftly between the two Brigades.

The Federals did not catch Gregg wholly off his guard. He had
in reserve Colonel McGowan's Fourteenth South Carolina, the

---

[83] *Ibid.*, 687.   [84] *Ibid.*, 652.
[85] *O. R.*, 12, pt. 2, p. 679.
[86] G. H. Gordon, in his *Army of Virginia*, 252, palpably was in error when he stated
that Gregg occupied a fourth of Jackson's front. Could Gordon have meant a fourth
of Hill's? Colonel McGowan particularly noted that the "spot" was "barely large enough
to hold the Brigade," and that "the space covered by the Brigade was so small and the
distance between the regiments so inconsiderable" that he could not distinguish all the
movements (*O. R.*, 12, pt. 2, p. 680).
[87] *O. R.*, 12, pt. 2, pp. 646, 680.
[88] Hotchkiss noted in his *MS Diary*, Apr. 15, 1863: "[Jackson in private conversa-
tion] was comparing our Engineers with the enemy's and thought they had the best—
instancing that they found a gap in our lines at Fredericksburg and there massed their
troops, and that they did the same at Groveton, and their Engineers must have found
that out."

regiment that had made a rapid march and had arrived in the hour of need at Gaines' Mill.[89] Promptly Gregg called for McGowan; quickly the regiment came up; the Forty-ninth Georgia of Thomas's Brigade united with it; in a short time their thunderous counterattack restored the line.[90]

To achieve this, the Carolinians had to give and take fire at ten paces,[91] and even then, they won only the briefest of respites. Back came the Federals to the assault. Their fire seemed more blasting than ever. Could Gregg hold out? Anxiously Hill sent to inquire; Gregg answered "modestly he thought he could, adding, as if casually, that his ammunition was about expended, but he still had the bayonet." [92]

About that time, Hill felt that he must warn Jackson of the danger to the Confederate left. By one of Jackson's staff officers, who arrived opportunely,[93] he sent word that if he were attacked again, he would do his best but scarcely could hope for success. "Old Jack" heard this grimly, and started the staff officer back to Hill with the sharp message, "Tell him if they attack him again he must beat them!" An instant later, he decided to go in person to the threatened left. On the way he met Hill, who was spurring to consult him. In a few words, Hill repeated the message he had sent. Jackson replied calmly, though perhaps with a greater struggle for self-mastery than was apparent: "General, your men have done nobly; if you are attacked again, you will beat the enemy back."

At that moment, a rattle of musketry swept the left. "Here it comes," Hill said and, without another word, he galloped back toward his command.

"I'll expect you to beat them," Jackson called after him.

In the face of this assault, Gregg's South Carolinians gave ground, but so slowly that they scarcely realized they were falling back. Soon they were atop the hill whence, if they were driven, they would be routed. Their commander was determined to retire no farther. From one end of the line to the other strode Gregg.

[89] See *supra*, Vol. I, p. 529.

[90] *O. R.*, 1::, pt. 2, pp. 646, 687. For the shift in the reserve of Gregg's Brigade, see *ibid.*, 680–81.

[91] *Ibid.*, 681.

[92] McGowan, in *ibid.* Hill, *ibid.*, 671, dramatized the answer: "Tell General Hill that my ammunition is exhausted, but that I will hold my position with the bayonet."

[93] This was Kyd Douglas. He stated, *op. cit.*, 138, that the incident occurred "late in the afternoon" but the circumstances place it earlier.

His old revolutionary scimitar was bare; his words were inflexible: "Let us die here, my men, let us die here!" [94]

About 3.30,[95] Hill had to draw on his reserves. Forno was sent to relieve the pressure on the left. Half an hour later, Early was thrown in. As "Old Jube" advanced, uncertain where to interpose, he was joined by the Eighth Louisiana and the Thirteenth Georgia, which also were marching to the bending flank.[96] Together these troops went forward. As they passed the South Carolinians, who had been fighting for seven hours, Gregg—to quote one of his admiring Colonels—"collected the remnant of his regiments, and placing them in line . . . gave them instructions to lie down, and if our friends were overpowered and had to fall back over them to wait until the enemy was very near, then rise and drive them back at the point of the bayonet." [97]

That desperate duty Gregg's Brigade was spared. The mixed command of Early moved confidently against an enemy that had spent his strength. All the ground lost in Gregg's defensive was regained. The Federals were driven from the railroad cut and back almost to the positions from which they had launched their first attack. Early had been told, ere he advanced, that he should not proceed beyond the railroad. Consequently, as soon as he could, he recalled his troops to that position.[98] Proudly, and with a relief that words could not convey, Hill sent this message to Jackson: "General Hill presents his compliments and says the attack of the enemy was repulsed."

Jackson's face broke into one of his rare smiles as he answered: "Tell him I knew he would do it." [99]

In this attack, as in virtually all the fighting of the day, the infantry had been without artillery support; but the dauntless Pegram now had found a field of fire and had opened. As usual, his daring provoked a violent answer from massed Federal batteries.[100] Soon he was being mauled badly—so badly that officers asked, Are the Federals preparing for a final assault? Early and Gregg and Thomas and the others waited uncertainly. A long

---

[94] 13 S. H. S. P., 34. Cf. 10 ibid., 244.   [95] Early, 124.
[96] Early, 124. The Eighth Louisiana, which belonged to Hays's (Forno's) Brigade, had been to the rear to get ammunition. Lawton's Brigade included the Thirteenth Georgia.
[97] McGowan in O. R., 12, pt. 2, p. 681.
[98] O. R., 12, pt. 2, pp. 556, 646, 671, 712; Early, 124-25.
[99] Douglas, 138.   [100] O. R., 12, pt. 2, pp. 652, 674.

hour of suspense passed without a further move by the Federals. Tension imperceptibly diminished. The gallant Union troops had enough! "When the sun went down," wrote one Southern boy, "their dead were heaped in front of that incomplete railway, and we sighed with relief, for Longstreet could be seen coming into position on our right; the crisis was over, Longstreet never failed yet, but the sun went down *so* slowly." [101]

When darkness fell at last, Jackson's tired staff prepared to bivouac on the scene of the Army's hard battle. Dr. Hunter McGuire had a long list of casualties to report. Gregg had lost more than 600 men.[102] Ten of his officers had been killed; thirty-one had been wounded. In the whole Brigade, two field officers only were unscathed.[103] The valiant Thirteenth South Carolina had been robbed by Federal bullets of more than half its personnel.[104]

Among officers of rank, the casualties had been almost as severe as on the previous day. Lamentably at the head of the list, to the definite loss of the Division, was General Trimble, who had been wounded badly by a Belgian explosive bullet.[105] In the defense of the left, both General Field [106] and Colonel Forno [107] had been shot. General Pender had his usual combination of good luck and of bad: he had been knocked down by the explosion of a shell nearby, but he had escaped the fragments and had refused to leave the field.[108] Archer, too, had escaped narrowly. His horse had been killed under him.[109] Col. J. Foster Marshall of Orr's Rifles had been mortally wounded.[110] Maj. William Patrick of

---

[101] *Ham Chamberlayne*, 100–01. It is interesting to note that this quotation appeared in 3 *Moore's Rebellion Record*, 402, and was quoted in *Cooke's Jackson* (Richardson's pirated edition, 181), as early as 1863; but the identity of the writer was not known generally until the appearance of Chamberlayne's letters in 1932.

[102] The figures are given both as 613 and 619. *O. R.*, 12, pt. 2, pp. 672, 681.

[103] *Ibid.*, 646, 681.

[104] *Ibid.*, 693.

[105] *O. R.*, 12, pt. 2, pp. 557, 646, 712. In his autobiography, 125, though not in his official report, Early stated that Trimble had been wounded by "an explosive ball." This is asserted, also, in Hamlin's *Old Bald Head*, 129. The Federals believed, for their part, that the Confederates were using cartridges of this type. Denison's *Groveton*, 25. For the continuance of the sketch of Trimble, see *infra*, pp. 257 ff. and Chap. XXVI.

[106] *O. R.*, 12, pt. 2, p. 671.   [107] *Ibid.*, 646.

[108] *Ibid.*, 671.   [109] *Ibid.*, 671.

[110] *O. R.*, 12, pt. 2, p. 681. He had been a Captain of the Palmetto Regiment in the Mexican War, a lawyer of distinction at Abbeville, and State Senator. Said Caldwell, *op. cit.*, p. 38, in tribute to him: "He had succeeded Colonel Orr . . . and had displayed such ability in camp, and such courage on the field, as to secure him the highest regard of the brigade. He was a man of acute intelligence, great tact, of affable and cordial address, at home in all places, conspicuous in all assemblages."

the Seventeenth Virginia Cavalry battalion had received fatal injury in beating off the attack on the wagon train.[111] Stuart's loss through the death of Patrick was increased by the wounding of Redmond Burke, one of his most intrepid and observant scouts.[112]

As many of these casualties as were known at the time, Doctor McGuire reported to Jackson, who himself had made all observers hold their breath lest he be among the fallen. During the late forenoon, he had come to the front of Hill's Division and, on foot, had walked calmly down the railroad cut. At intervals he had stopped to peer at the Federal positions.[113] Doctor McGuire had shared the Army's concern for Jackson, and he shook his head as he spoke of the fallen. "General," he concluded, "this day has been won by nothing but stark and stern fighting."

"No," answered Jackson, "it has been won by nothing but the blessing and protection of Providence." [114]

---

[111] For the attack, which came to nothing, see *supra*, p. 113, and *O. R.*, 12, pt. 2, pp. 646, 735–36, 740, 755. Major Patrick was in his thirty-ninth year and a native of Augusta County, Virginia. See *Laurel Brigade*, 87–88 n. Stuart, *O. R.*, 12, pt. 2, p. 736, described the loss of Patrick as "irreparable."

[112] *O. R.*, 12, pt. 2, p. 746.   [113] 13 *S. H. S. P.*, 26.

[114] *Dabney*, 531.

CHAPTER VII

THE GALLANT RIVALRY OF MANASSAS

As JACKSON gave thanks at his bivouac for the success of the bloody 29th of August, James Longstreet was completing his first tactical maneuver on the right of the long line formed that afternoon. Although "Old Pete," prior to the move from the Rapidan, never had handled more than two Divisions in action, he had directed admirably his part in the movement up the Rappahannock. In marching to support Jackson, it has been recorded already that his infantry made as good time as had the renowned "foot cavalry" of the former Army of the Valley. At Thoroughfare Gap on the evening of the 28th, Longstreet had proceeded with confidence and decision.[1] His dispositions for the advance, via Hay Market and Gainesville, had been excellent. Now he was to face a new test, the leadership of four Divisions immediately and of five as soon as "Dick" Anderson arrived with Huger's old command. One of these Divisions was under D. R. Jones, who was experienced and of moderate abilities. Hood, with his own and Law's Brigade, could be trusted. Three Brigades of Longstreet's old Division, as already noted, had been detached and placed temporarily under Cadmus Wilcox. He was capable, though not brilliant. At the head of three other Brigades of that former Division, it will be recalled, was James L. Kemper, who as recently as at Seven Pines had been a Colonel.[2]

Perhaps Longstreet felt that he should be cautious; he certainly hoped that he could receive attack instead of having to deliver it.[3] Whatever the precise reasoning behind his calm mien and composed manner, he shook his head several times on the 29th when Lee asked if a forward movement was not in order. Deliberately,

---

[1] In this affair, described at length in 2 R. E. Lee, 313 ff, the First Georgia Regulars of Major John D. Walker had especially distinguished themselves. O. R., 12, pt. 2, p. 564.

[2] For the composition of these Divisions, as of August 30, see O. R., 12, pt. 2, pp. 546–48.

[3] 2 B. & L., 523.

almost stubbornly, Longstreet delayed any action until late afternoon. Then he ordered a reconnaissance in force by Hood, supported by Evans. Their troops speedily encountered an advancing
Federal column. Hood gained the better of the clash, but he concluded that a withdrawal under cover of darkness was desirable
and that an attack the next day would be dangerous. When he
extricated himself after midnight on the 29th–30th,[4] Hood found
that "Dick" Anderson had come up and, in ignorance of the
ground, had marched almost within the enemy's lines.[5]

With Anderson's arrival and Hood's return, Longstreet had all
his troops united and under the eye of Lee himself. Their position
was one of exciting military interest. They were thrown diago-
nally across the Gainesville-Centreville Road in such a way that
their line, following the best elevations, formed an angle of about
160 degrees with Jackson's front. The two commands were jaws
that opened widely to the Southeast. Would Pope be reckless
enough to thrust his infantry arm into those jaws? Longstreet's
men waited to see; Jackson's veterans remained where they had
dropped at the end of the fighting Friday evening. Their order of
battle from right to left was the same—Jackson's Division under
Starke, Ewell's under Lawton, and A. P. Hill's.[6]

The morning of August 30 was hot, silent and dry. Where the
scorched grass caught, it burned briskly and sent white smoke
across the blue sky.[7] Such activity as the Federals displayed during
the early forenoon seemed to be directed against the right of
Jackson, not far from the apex of the angle his flank formed with
Longstreet's left. To ascertain what was afoot, Jackson rode out
with his staff to his extreme right, where the few survivors of the
Stonewall Brigade were stretched out. Wrote one witness: ". . . all
for a time engaged in watching the Federals in their movements,
seemingly preparing for a great conflict. We saw them massing
in a woodland east of us, but keeping pretty well hidden and

---

[4] *Hood,* 35; *O. R.,* 12, pt. 2, p. 605.
[5] For all the details of Longstreet's objections to attacking on the afternoon of the
29th, see 2 *R. E. Lee,* 322 ff. To the end of his days, General Longstreet persisted
in his belief that his course on that day of Jackson's hard battle had been wise and
soldierly and that, had he attacked Fitz-John Porter, who was in his front, he would
have been repulsed bloodily. See 2 *B. & L.,* 523.
[6] Early had relieved some of A. P. Hill's troops on the night of the 29th, and when
he found on the 30th that the Light Division had not resumed the whole of its position, he insisted that it do so. *O. R.,* 12, pt. 2, pp. 712–13.
[7] Cf. *E. A. Moore,* 117.

moving many of their troops directly south, looking to our right."[8] Jackson studied the changing scene and speculated on the meaning of so much marching.

"Well," he said at last to Colonel Baylor, commanding the Brigade, "it looks as if there will be no fight today, but keep your men in line and ready for action."

Then Jackson rode back to the rear,[9] where he remained until the silence on his own front and curiosity concerning the situation opposite Longstreet's line led him to trot over to Army field headquarters. Lee was there with Longstreet and Stuart. Already the commanding General was pondering how he should stir Pope if the Federal leader permitted the day to pass without action.

Of this, perhaps, the four Confederate Generals talked. Nearby soldiers looked and studied the difference in the faces and wondered that the plainest of the four should be the first in fame. Wrote one New Orleans artillerist: "Jackson was then dressed in a sort of grey homespun suit, with a broken-brimmed cap, and looked like a good driving overseer or manager, with plenty of hard, horse sense, but no accomplishments or other talent—nothing but plain, direct sense. It was because his manners had so little of the air of a man of the world, or because he repressed all expression that he had the appearance of being a man of not above average ability. The remark was then made by one of us, after staring at him for a long time, that there must be some mistake about him—if he was an able man he showed it less than any man any of us had ever seen." [10]

After a while Jackson rode away. The curious silence persisted, a silence so complete that one would have thought the breathing of the 150,000 men lying in the fields would have been audible. Nothing happened till after midday. Then came the creak and rumble of artillery and the familiar rise of long clouds of dust. Longstreet had some doubt whether these things presaged an assault. Jackson, having concluded that Pope fought in the afternoon, went to the front of his old Division. There he found no change in the position of the Federal infantry, but he observed that the number of Union guns visible from the Confederate line had increased.

8 E. E. Stickley in 22 *C. V.*, 231.   9 *Ibid.*
10 "Soldier's Story" in *Mil. An. La.,* 98.

It would be well, he told himself, to drive them off before they did any mischief. One battery, in particular, must be sent back to longer range. About 2 o'clock, he ordered the Rockbridge Artillery, Poague's men, to harness, to move out and to persuade the Federals, by the argument of iron, to withdraw. It was accomplished promptly and exactly in the manner Jackson desired. "That was handsomely done, very handsomely done," he acknowledged.[11] This, for him, was almost a speech, but it showed that his battle blood was not aroused. Had it been, he would have said hoarsely, "Good, good!"

From the battery, which soon returned to its bivouac, Jackson guided his horse to the rear of his infantry line, dismounted and waited calmly. The gunners who were loitering nearby saw nothing in his manner to indicate that he anticipated a general attack by the enemy.[12] An hour, or thereabouts, passed. The drowsy time of day brought nods and yawns. Horses almost ceased to switch their tails. Conversation died away. Everything invited afternoon slumber. Jackson was beginning to doubt whether the attack would be delivered [13] when, with a suddenness that shook and startled, there crashed from the Confederate right the sound of many rifles. Through the woods, clipping off branches and flattening themselves against the stones, came the vicious minié balls. Here and there, among the artillerists around Jackson, a man was hit. A serious attack it manifestly was and not merely a skirmishers' dispute.

"Old Jack" knew the sound too well to be deceived. Without a word he mounted and rode off to see how his thinned regiments met the shock.[14] He found that the enemy was streaming forward in three lines against his right [15] and that a similar formation was developing an attack on his center and left. Things had an ugly

---

[11] E. A. Moore, 118.

[12] Cf. E. A. Moore, 119. Douglas, op. cit., 139–40, recalled that Jackson was not riding the little sorrel that day.

[13] Douglas, op. cit., 139, told a charming tale to the effect that at the moment the signal gun was fired for the opening of the Federal attack, Jackson was in the act of dictating a letter to General Lee. In this letter Jackson was reaffirming his belief that the attack would not be made. As Douglas is singularly inaccurate on the small details of Second Manassas, the less dramatic version of Moore has been followed.

[14] E. A. Moore, 119. The time is variously given. Heintzelman (O. R., 12, pt. 2, p. 413) reported that Porter attacked at 2, and that by 4, the action had spread to the center. Lee (ibid., 557) gave the time of the advance against Jackson as 3. Jackson (ibid., 647) said it was 4; A. P. Hill (ibid., 671) timed it at 2.

[15] Dabney, 532

look. The bluecoats were more numerous than they had been the previous day, and they pushed their advances farther. Their fire was telling. An officer rode up and reported that Colonel Baylor had been shot down and that his successor in command wanted help.

Jackson did not catch the names: "What Brigade, sir?" he asked.

"The Stonewall Brigade," Captain Stickley reiterated.

"Go back," Jackson answered instantly, "give my compliments to them, and tell the Stonewall Brigade to maintain her reputation." As the officer started to leave, Jackson reiterated the order to hold at all hazards and promised quick reinforcement.

When the survivors of the Brigade got the message of their old chief, they cheered and redoubled their fire.[16] Pender soon appeared in support from the left, but he faced such odds of infantry and so heavy a fire of artillery that he properly withdrew.[17] Left to fight alone, Jackson's Division contrived to hold its own, though narrowly. Ewell's men had little to do. Farther toward the left, Hill had to repair a break the Federals made.[18]

Sterner the assault became—violent, determined and in abundant force. It was watched sharply by "Old Jack." Usually he relied with pride on his own unsustained forces; this time—were the odds impossible? Would the right be overwhelmed? The danger existed; every minute it was more acute; assistance must be had. An officer must ride immediately to General Lee and ask for men from Longstreet to bolster the line.[19]

On Jackson's call for help, chief responsibility for the battle shifted to Longstreet. He was alert. At the angle between his line and Jackson's he had taken his station. Already he had dispatched to commanding ground nearby the artillery battalion of Stephen D. Lee, who last was seen in these pages while he was striving vainly to bring up his guns to support Magruder's attack at Malvern Hill.[20] Colonel Lee's position was far better now than it had been on the 1st of July. The moment his waiting batteries were ordered into action, they could fire eastward, directly across the left flank of the Federals who were moving stubbornly northward against Jackson's right. It was an incredible opportunity.

---

[16] 22 C. V., 231. The pronouns are those used by Captain Stickley.
[17] O. R., 12, pt. 2, p. 698.　　　[18] Ibid., 671.
[19] Ibid., 647.　　　[20] See supra, Vol. I, p. 599.

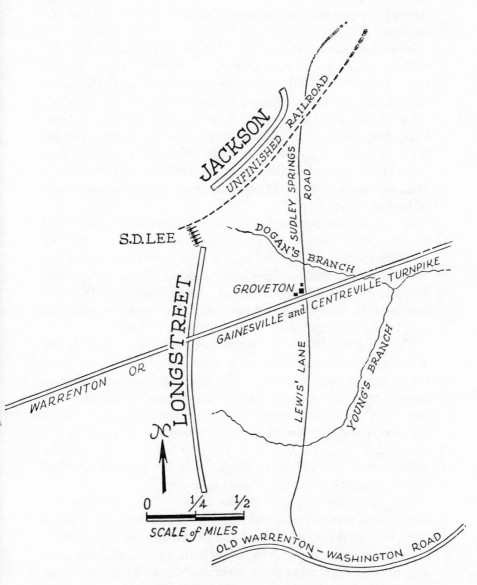

Sketch of the Position of Jackson's Right, of Longstreet's Left and of S. D. Lee's artillery, Aug. 30, 1862, near Manassas—after G. K. Warren

such as a gunner knows he will not have twice, an opportunity that Pope could not have allowed an adversary otherwise than through desperation or misunderstanding of the Confederate position.

When Longstreet received from Lee the request of Jackson for reinforcements, it was coupled with instructions to send a Division. "Old Pete" looked again at the exposed Federal flank, within easy range, and then, no doubt, he ran his eye across the wooded ridge whence rose the smoke of Jackson's defense. Far less time, Longstreet reasoned, would be required to break with gun-fire the lines assailing Jackson, than to dispatch a column to the ridge. "Certainly," he said in answer to the call for troops to relieve Jackson, "but before the Division can reach him, the attack will be broken by artillery." [21]

Wisely and unhesitatingly, Longstreet determined to disregard the letter of the order from Lee and to use the swifter method of relieving Jackson. "Old Pete" had to do no more than speak a few words. The observant artillery commanders had been anticipating instructions and had harnessed and hitched the teams. Within a few minutes after Longstreet had called for them, the guns had swept magnificently forward and were firing furiously.

The effect was all that Longstreet had expected. Although two of Colonel Lee's batteries were in action for the first time,[22] the fire of the battalion was overwhelming. Pope's second and third lines in front of Jackson were torn and blasted. Formation was lost. Bewildered men turned back under the swelling fire. When the heavily engaged front Union line found that its supports had vanished, it broke off the fight. Joyfully Jackson's men saw the enemy waver and fall back. Instinctively the grayjackets raised their foxhunters' yell and followed their foe.[23]

Longstreet, ere that, had seen his chance. Those waiting regiments could take advantage of the confusion in front of Jackson's line. They could sweep forward and overwhelm the enemy. With perfect composure but with the joy of battle in his soul, Longstreet sent word along the line for a general advance. Every man must

---

[21] Douglas's recollection, *op. cit.*, 140, was that he carried directly to Longstreet the request of Jackson for help; but if this was the case, some other officer went to Lee with a similar message. Jackson would not have called on another commander for aid without notifying G.H.Q. that he had done so.

[22] *O. R.*, 12, pt. 2, pp. 577–78.   [23] *Worsham*, 132

go forward! Before they could start, one of Lee's staff officers galloped up to inform Longstreet that the commanding General had
directed just such an advance. "Old Pete" must have been proud
to be able to answer that the line was in the act of throwing its
full weight against the enemy.[24]

For most of Longstreet's men, a furious, roaring attack soon
became a pursuit in which valor had full play. Daring raced
against the setting sun. Across the undulating fields swept the
Divisions of the right wing as if they were determined in that
single afternoon to win as much of fame as Jackson's "foot
cavalry" had gained from the hour Hill and Ewell and Taliaferro
had left the Rappahannock. To Colonels as to Generals, to Captains and to color bearers were credited feats that found an honorable place in reports. Col. Tom Munford of the Second Virginia
Cavalry made a charge that Murat would have envied. Tom
Rosser of the Fifth Virginia, Munford's rival, directed on the right
all the batteries that Stuart could requisition, and he used them to
scatter hundreds of bluecoats.[25] It was said of Lt. Col. F. G.
Skinner, of the First Virginia Infantry, that he rode ahead of his
regiment in a charge on a battery and with his saber struck a
gunner so frightful a blow on the collar-bone that the man's head
was well-night severed. Another artillerist the Colonel smote
through ribs and heart before he himself fell wounded.[26] Private
Jimmy Harris, heroic color bearer of the Fifth Texas, who insisted
on keeping many yards in advance of his regiment,[27] had a worthy
comrade in Private Sam Wallace of the Seventeenth South Carolina. Responsible for no flag, Wallace stepped out some fifteen
or twenty paces in front of his comrades and there, a target for
any and all, he calmly continued to load and to fire.[28] The sole
lament of Longstreet's men was that heavy clouds brought early

---

[24] Details and base-references are given in 2 R. E. Lee, 331 ff. Many descriptions of
the battle precipitated by the Confederate advance are in print. Perhaps the best, though
neither is dramatic, are those of Allan's Army, p. 262 ff. and of J. C. Ropes, The Army
Under Pope, 129 ff.

[25] O. R., 12, pt. 2, pp. 738, 750–51.

[26] 2 C. V., 184. Skinner was a picturesque giant, born at Annapolis, Md., Mch.
17, 1814. He was taken to France by Lafayette in 1826 and was educated with the
grandchildren of the Marquis. Skinner was credited with carrying the heaviest saber
in the Army, save only that of Stuart's aide, Maj. Heros von Borcke. At the beginning
of the charge, Skinner had insisted on using his horse, Fox. When the Colonel was
picked up, after his wound, his first remark was, "Didn't old Fox behave splendidly?"
(Ibid.)

[27] O. R., 12, pt. 2, p. 620.   [28] O. R., 12, pt. 2, p. 663.

darkness. Jackson's men said the advance of the Confederates from the right was across the front of the defenders of Groveton, who were denied their part in the pursuit. Longstreet's the afternoon was, though some of Jackson's Brigades were able, late in the evening, to strike a blow.[29]

As concerned Jackson himself, the final dramatic touch of the day was added while he was returning to his quarters. On the railroad embankment, weakly trying to climb it, was a Confederate soldier. To him "Old Jack" rode. Was he wounded?

"Yes, General," the boy answered, "but have we whipped 'em?"

In the same instant Jackson was reassuring the soldier and was dismounting to help him. To what regiment did he belong?

"I belong to the Fourth Virginia, your old Brigade, General. I have been wounded four times but never before as bad as this. I hope I will soon be able to follow you again."

Jackson had the boy examined. A deep flesh wound of the thigh was found, a wound exceedingly painful but not dangerous. All that the boy was suffering, Jackson seemed to sense. He put his hand on the soldier's head and said in his low, husky voice: "You are worthy of the old Brigade and I hope with God's blessing, you soon will be well enough to return to it." Staff officers were told to carry the wounded private to a safe place; Jackson's Medical Director was asked to relieve him; an ambulance was summoned to take him to a hospital. Kyd Douglas remembered: "The grateful soldier tried to speak but could not; sobs choked him and tears ran from his eyes over his ashen cheeks; words would not come and he submitted to everything in silence. But the General understood"—and understood, perhaps, that the plight, not less than the spirit of the old Army of the Valley, was described in the boy's remark: The Army was wounded, but it had "whipped 'em." [30]

Morning of August 31 found the roads heavy with mud and the streams high from the night-long rain.[31] The experience of the wet day after the struggle for Malvern Hill was in a fair way of being duplicated. Attempted pursuit could be little more than floundering. Boots seemed to lift more earth than the wearers covered. Besides, the Stone Bridge over Bull Run had been de-

---

[29] The pursuit is sketched briefly here because it is described fully in 2 *R. E. Lee*, 333 ff.

[30] *Douglas*, 142.   [31] *Wingfield*, 16.

stroyed. Only by roundabout roads could Pope be followed. Discouraging as was that prospect, orders were to strike the Federals once more before they found shelter in the defenses of Washington. Longstreet was directed to remain on the field of battle, to occupy the attention of the enemy, and to look after the victims of the action; Jackson was instructed to put his three Divisions in motion and to seek the flank of Pope. The line of advance was to be across Bull Run at Sudley's Ford and thence to the Little River Turnpike.[32] Down that road, in the direction of Fairfax Court House, Jackson might be able to reach the flank of the defeated Federal Army which, the cavalry warned headquarters, was now being reinforced heavily with more of the veterans of McClellan.[33]

Weary the Confederates were after marching or fighting for six days, but on Jackson's call, they started northward through the rain. Every man who held to his duty had reason to be proud. Equal honor had come to almost all the Brigades and to their commanders. It was a time for congratulation and it might well have been a time for wiping out old scores, such, for example, as those of Jackson against Powell Hill. If the chief of the Light Division had been negligent on the early marches, or had been careless in drawing his line at Groveton on the 29th, had he not redeemed all his blunders, actual or imagined, by the stubborn vigor of his fighting? Was he not, moreover, by Ewell's wounding, the senior divisional commander and, at least temporarily, Jackson's successor in the event that "Stonewall" fell?

If Jackson pondered any of this, it meant less at the time than did the fact that Hill was marching too fast. Because of the pace, men of the Light Division were said to be straggling. When Jackson heard of this, he sent to admonish Hill. Again in the evening, as the command approached Pleasant Valley on the Little River 'Pike, Jackson decided that the head of the column was moving too rapidly. Jed Hotchkiss, coming up from the battlefield, remarked that many stragglers were to be seen along the road in rear of Hill.[34] To this Jackson gave no reply, but in his mind he made another entry against A. P. Hill as a bad marcher. Previ-

---

32 This was the name given one section of the important highway that connected Alexandria and Winchester.

33 For the situation and for the references to the sources, see 2 *R. E. Lee,* 338.

34 MS charges against A. P. Hill, rough draft, *Jackson MSS.* Hotchkiss, in his *MS Diary,* did not mention the incident. to which, manifestly, he attached no special importance.

ously, the complaint of the exacting "Stonewall" was that the commander of the Light Division had been slow in moving; the reverse charge was in Jackson's eyes equally serious. Both, he told himself, involved a definite and reprehensible neglect of duty.

By Jackson's orders, Hill halted for the night at Pleasant Valley.[35] The other Divisions bivouacked nearby. They continued proud, of course, that they had Pope "on the run" after his ill-timed boast that he had come "from the West, where we have always seen the backs of our enemies";[36] but pride was dampened by the rain and then washed almost away by the news that no rations could be issued, because the wagons were far to the rear. The best that could be done by the most skillful forager was to get a "roasting ear" of corn, or two, from the fields of farmers.

By morning, appetite had triumphed over discipline. Even so devoted a champion of the Model Army as Jed Hotchkiss had to admit in his journal: "The soldiers were very bad, stealing everything eatable they could lay their hands on, after trying to buy it. They were nearly famished, our wagons being still behind. They were also very thirsty, water being very scarce."[37]

Progress with a parched tongue and on an empty stomach was slow that 1st of September. Stuart's troopers might dash about and somehow contrive to get a bite to eat,[38] but the infantry had to drag hungrily down the Little River Turnpike toward Fairfax Court House. Apparently, none of the Army's many diarists took occasion to note, if any recalled, that three months previously Lee had assumed command. Then the Confederates had been huddled around their own threatened and half-beleaguered capital; now they were within one day's march of the hills that looked down on Washington. Ninety days had carried the war from the Chickahominy to the Potomac! It was an amazing feat, but at the moment it was no substitute for bacon and cornpone.

Afternoon found Jackson's van near the fine old mansion Chantilly. Three miles only the men—men of the renowned "foot cavalry"—had covered in half a day's march. That of itself evidenced the virtual exhaustion. In wretchedness and emptiness they were continuing toward Fairfax Court House under black,

---

[35] O. R., 12, pt. 2, p. 682.
[36] O. R., 12, pt. 3, p. 474; address to the Army of Virginia, July 14, 1862.
[37] Hotchkiss' MS Diary, 81.
[38] For the operations of the cavalry September 1, see O. R., 12, pt. 2, p. 744.

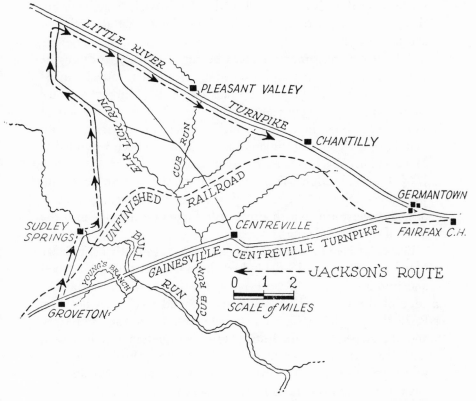

Jackson's March to Chantilly, after Pope's Map of August, 1862, *O. R. Atlas*, Plate VII. From this map it would appear that Jackson's approach to the Little River Turnpike was by the road West of Elk Lick Run. As the modern road crosses the Run, it is possible that the map is in error; but if the road did not exist at that time, the rain of the 31st may have rendered the declivity so heavy that a "short cut" across country would have been impossible

lowering clouds when the advance guard ran directly into the Federals. A defiant fusillade was taken to indicate that the enemy was waiting in force and was expecting attack. The Confederate column was halted; the Divisions were deployed on the south side of the road and were faced more nearly to the South than perpendicular to the highway. A. P. Hill was on the right; Ewell's veterans, under Lawton, held the center with two Brigades in line and two in reserve;[39] the men of Jackson's Division, directed now by Starke, guarded the left. To the North of the road, Jackson placed his artillery. The ground was such that the batteries could

[39] *O. R.*, 12, pt. 2, p. 714.

not support the advance, which had to be through woodland, but the guns, as located, could cover Confederate withdrawal and check pursuit.[40]

All these arrangements had to be made quickly, because the enemy was aggressive and seemed determined to attack unless driven at once from the field. By Jackson's order, Hill sent forward Branch on the extreme right, and Field's Brigade on the left of Branch to feel out the Union front.[41] Branch was in personal command of his North Carolinians, but as Field had been wounded at Manassas, his Virginia troops were in charge of the senior Colonel, J. M. Brockenbrough. To the uncertainty of this new leadership was added, in the midst of the advance, the disconcerting violence of a thunderstorm, which drove a lashing rain directly into the faces of the Confederates.

Branch pushed forward, despite the rain, as valiantly as at Cedar Mountain. He crossed a field, drove his adversary through a wood and into a second field, and halted his own men on the farther edge of the wood. There he delivered and received a hot fire. Particularly on his right, the Federals concentrated their musketry and threatened to flank him.[42] His ammunition ran low at a time when the Federals were believed to be sprinkling the line with explosive bullets.[43] Branch notified Hill of this and, in answer, received orders to remain where he was and, if need be, to meet attack with the bayonet.[44] He was isolated by this time, because Brockenbrough on his left was repulsed and was subjected to a counterattack.

Gregg then was thrown forward in support; Thomas followed Gregg; Pender's regiments moved up to relieve the pressure on Thomas, but in their advance they divided. One part joined Thomas; the other went to assist Branch.[45] Even the employment, in this manner, of all save one of A. P. Hill's Brigades[46] did not bring a decision. The fighting twisted the line until it formed to the southward an arc of a circle with the Little River

[40] See Crutchfield, O. R., 12, pt. 2, p. 654. For the disposition of the infantry, see Jackson, ibid., 647.
[41] For the order of battle, which is not clear from Jackson's or Hill's report, see Pender, O. R., 12, pt. 2, p. 698.
[42] O. R., 12, pt. 2, p. 677.   [43] 2 N. C. Regts., 552.
[44] Ibid., 31–32, 473; O. R., 12, pt. 2, p. 677.
[45] For the sequence of the advances, see O. R., 12, pt. 2, pp. 703, 698.
[46] Archer was in reserve. O. R., 12, pt. 2, p. 702.

Turnpike as the chord. Jackson's Division found itself involved in the extension of the battle to a weak point on the left, directly South of the road.

To that point, at Starke's instance, Early led his left regiment; but at that moment Hays's Brigade in the center was assailed by the Federals and was broken because the Colonel in command, new to such duty, lost his head and confused the Louisianians to such an extent that they could present no front to the enemy. In its break, Hays's Brigade ran through Early's rear regiments, which now prudently halted their movement to the support of Starke and beat off the attack on Hays.[47]

With advances here and repulses there, the fire raged furiously until one of the Federal commanders, Brig. Gen. I. I. Stevens, was shot down, and the other, Maj. Gen. Philip Kearny, was killed when he rode by mistake into Confederate skirmishers.[48] Then, sullenly, the Federals broke off the action in the gathered darkness. Kearny's body was recovered and was brought within the Confederate lines. "Poor Kearny!" said A. P. Hill, as he gazed the next day at the stiffened form of the gallant Federal, "he deserved a better death than that!"[49] Many another Southerner saw Kearny's body, as it lay on the porch of a cabin not far from the road, ere Lee sent it to the Federals under flag of truce. "He is a very soldierly-looking man," one Confederate wrote.[50] Another, who had seen Kearny a few days before, remembered him as a "spare, erect, military figure, looking every inch the soldier he was."[51]

To the Federals, any action was costly that had such a toll of leadership; to the Confederates, the Battle of Chantilly [52] was disappointing both because of the storm and because of the absence of fine performance. Branch had done well enough. The others, from private to commanding General, seemed at the time to have

[47] *O. R.,* 12, pt. 2, p. 715. The best map of the battlefield is that of Gen. C. F. Walcott in the back of 2 *M. H. S. M.*

[48] Kearny, it scarcely need be noted, during the fighting around Manassas, had led superbly the 1st Division of Heintzelman's III Corps. Stevens had commanded the 1st Division of the IX Corps and had charge of the field at Chantilly till he was killed while leading his men.

[49] 2 *B. & L.,* 538.

[50] W. M. Owen, *In Camp and Battle with the Washington Artillery of New Orleans* (cited hereafter as *Owen*), 128.

[51] 2 *B. & L.,* 537.

[52] Sometimes given the less pleasant name Ox Hill.

regarded the action as a skirmish rather than as a serious meeting engagement, in which more than 500 Southern casualties were sustained,[53] and probably 1,000 Federal.[54] No compensation was there for these losses save in the experience gained and in the addition made to the lore of the Army.

Col. William Smith made the chief contribution that day to the treasured humor of the troops. "Extra Billy," former Governor of Virginia, had lost none of his contempt for West Pointers and none of disdain for martial dress. He had brought his blue cotton umbrella with him and, for reasons he did not see fit to confide, he elected to top his uniform coat with a tall beaver hat. When the thunderstorm came on the battlefield of Chantilly, Colonel Smith calmly raised his umbrella and, so protected, moved nonchalantly among the men of Early's Brigade. Perhaps his own Forty-ninth Virginia, from respect or long acquaintance, restrained its mirth; but the other troops saw in the Colonel's appearance a variant of the oldest, most persistent joke of the Army. "Come out of that umbrel," the man cried, "I see your legs; come out of that hat, want it to boil the beans in!"[55] They had shouted the same thing a thousand times, of course, to dignified visitors to the camps, but the joke seemed new and sharp of point when the Colonel of one of "Old Jube" Early's fighting regiments appeared in battle with a blue cotton umbrella and a beaver hat!

A second addition there was to the Army's lore that day at Chantilly, an addition that was to take its place in the literature of war. During the advance of Branch and of Brockenbrough, the violence of the rain had made useless the rifles of hundreds of men. There seemed to be nothing to do except to withdraw the troops and to give them opportunity of pulling the charges and of drying the pieces. Some officer—his name mercifully has been forgotten—sent back an aide to Jackson with the message: "My compliments to General Jackson and my request to be permitted to take my command out of the line because all my ammunition is wet." Jackson listened critically and answered dryly: "My com-

[53] A. P. Hill (O. R., 12, pt. 2, p. 672) reported 306, and Ewell (ibid., 813) listed 200 casualties.

[54] General Walcott's estimate in 2 M. H. S. M., 161. His is the most detailed account of the battle. A supplementary paper, ibid., 173, is an interesting description of the fields of Manassas and of Chantilly as they were in 1883.

[55] Owen, 128, though the true born Confederate was far more likely to say "bile" than "boil."

pliments to Colonel Blank, and tell him the enemy's ammunition is just as wet as his!" [56]

The uncertain fire of those damp guns in the early [57] twilight of Chantilly ended what might be termed the Virginia phase of the campaign begun when Jackson, on July 13, was dispatched to Gordonsville. On the Federal side, the first part of the operations had been entirely creditable. Pope had ventured recklessly far beyond the Rappahannock, but he had discovered his danger and quickly had put the river between him and the Confederates. Thereafter, for five days, in guarding the fords, he probably had done as well as could any soldier of average ability who had so incompetent a corps commander as Franz Sigel.

It was on August 25–26 that the change came. From the hour Pope's lookouts reported Jackson on the march northward, the Federal commander lost his grip on the situation. He overworked his cavalry; [58] his infantry he was slow to concentrate. Some of his orders were cancelled so quickly, and his formal report was so much at variance with his current dispatches, that it is difficult, even after all the disclosures of seventy years, to say precisely what he thought of the developing situation. He undoubtedly believed that Jackson's march of August 25, which was observed by various officers, was a withdrawal toward the Shenandoah Valley. To that belief Pope held until he had established beyond all possible self-deception the identity of the troops that had reached Manassas Junction. Then, because his adversary disappeared promptly, he

[56] Cf. *Worsham*, 136. This exchange has been variously phrased, but the original form cannot be determined. A tradition, mentioned by Dr. Hunter McGuire (19 S. H. S. P., 311), that A. P. Hill was the officer who sent the message may have resulted from confusion of individuals. Hill it doubtless was who ordered Branch to hold his ground at the point of the bayonet when that North Carolina Brigadier was most hampered by wet, and then by depleted ammunition. A division commander in that mood was not apt to ask permission for his troops to leave the front. Precisely as Jackson had stated, some of the Federals were unable to advance because the charges in their guns were too wet to fire (cf. 2 M. H. S. M., 158). In general comment on Chantilly, it should be explained that Pope was tardy in issuing orders for the dispatch of troops up the Little River Turnpike to confront Jackson. General Walcott maintained that nothing but the initiative and rapid marching of General Stevens put a barrier at Ox Hill in the way of Jackson's advance. The Federals felt themselves outnumbered and in danger of being overwhelmed at a time when even Jackson indulged in unwonted adverbs to describe how "obstinately and desperately" the enemy "contested the ground" (O. R., 12, pt. 2, p. 647).

[57] 2 M. H. S. M., 157.

[58] Denison in his *Groveton*, p. 7, remarked of the 1st R. I. Cav.: "At one time we were in our saddles eighty-three consecutive hours . . . For more than twenty days we did not take our coats from our shoulders . . . That we were weary and wounded, covered with dust and vermin, and tanned in battle-smoke tells only our outward condition. Our mental trials, far greater than our physical, cannot be told."

concluded that Jackson was in full, hurried retreat, and that he could cut off and destroy the impudent raiders.

On the 29th, Pope did not know until late afternoon that Longstreet had arrived. The subsequent court martial and military disgrace of the able and courageous Fitz John Porter were based, in part, on Pope's conviction that Porter faced no hostile troops and could have turned the Confederate right flank. Porter failed to execute the orders for attack, Pope professed to believe, because Porter was one of McClellan's lieutenants and wished Pope to fail. Until the Army of Virginia was driven from the field and was in retreat on Washington, Pope insisted that the Confederates had been beaten.[59]

Lee, for these reasons, was fortunate in his opponent, but no less was he wise in judging how far he could gamble on Pope's confusion. To the Southern commanding General, more than to anyone else, credit for the victory was due. Press and public applauded him.[60] For the execution of the design of Lee, praise was given to Ewell,[61] to Longstreet,[62] and, in larger measure, to Stuart[63] and to Jackson[64] as equal partners in the enterprise. Lee's own dispatches and his final report presented the achievements of Jackson and of Longstreet with so balanced a hand that the reader suspects a deliberate purpose not to stir jealousies.[65]

So far did Lee go in his first dispatch, to avoid praise of one lieutenant to the disparagement of the other, that he noted how, "on the 28th and 29th, each wing under Genls. Longstreet and Jackson repulsed with valor attacks made on them separately." [66] Actually, Jackson both days had far more fighting than fell to the lot of his colleague. It was not till after Jackson was dead, and

[59] Probably the most complete and certainly the most detailed *exposé* of Pope's failures is that in G. H. Gordon, *The Army of Virginia.* The most judicious summary from the Northern point of view, though in some respects perhaps too generous to Pope, is that in 2 *M. H. S. M.* From the Confederate side, the account of William Allan remains the best.

[60] *Richmond Dispatch.* Sept. 3, p. 2, col. 1, Sept. 9, p. 2, col. 1; *Richmond Whig,* Sept. 8, p. 1, col. 2; *Richmond Enquirer,* Sept. 5, 1862, p. 1, col. 1. The most discerning comment of Richmond newspapers on the results of the battle was that of the *Examiner,* Sept. 4, p. 2, col. 2, Sept. 5, p. 2, col. 1, Sept. 8, 1862, p. 2, cols. 2–3.

[61] *Richmond Enquirer,* Sept. 5, 1862, p. 1, col. 1.

[62] *Richmond Enquirer,* Sept. 6, 1862, p. 4, col. 2.

[63] *Richmond Whig,* Sept. 1, 1862, p. 1, col. 1, with quotation from the *Lynchburg Republican.*

[64] *Richmond Dispatch,* Sept. 6, p. 1, col. 1, an excellent review; *ibid.,* Sept. 10, p. 1, col. 3, a reprint from the *Philadelphia Press.*

[65] *O. R.,* 12, pt. 2, p. 551.

[66] *Lee's Dispatches.* 60.

Second Manassas was compared with other battles, that he was credited with perfect fulfillment of orders and the flawless display of soldierly judgment. The special satisfaction of Lee was in the evidence that the Army at last had what every Army requires, capable corps commanders. Both Longstreet and Jackson, he felt, now were qualified to handle large numbers of men and to throw the entire force simultaneously into action. Could the contrast of two months have been more nearly incredible? June 30, Frayser's Farm; August 30, Second Manassas—the dates recorded a swift revolution. If, moreover, there was in Lee's mind any suspicion that Jackson was selfishly ambitious and was more interested in the furtherance of his own fame than in the advancement of the Southern cause, Jackson's behavior at Second Manassas began to remove that suspicion.

As possible doubts concerning Jackson faded, misgivings about Longstreet did not arise. It had been because he hoped Pope would assail him that "Old Pete" had stood out against delivering an attack on the afternoon of August 29; Lee's questions and hints had not been pushed with the vigor of one who believed his lieutenant definitely in error. Nor is it easy, even now, to say how much Lee lost on the field of Manassas by delaying the attack until the 30th. Had a general assault been made successfully on the afternoon of the 29th, Lee would have had the whole of the next day to follow up his advantage before the rain of the 31st halted him.

How reasonable was the basic assumption? Could Longstreet have driven Fitz-John Porter on the 29th? Who can say? The commanding General himself evidently did not believe that Longstreet's unwillingness to attack that day had any serious consequences. Lee is never known to have mentioned it, or to have considered it otherwise than as an entirely permissible disagreement on an open question. The effect on Longstreet may have been definite and deplorable, though here again there can be no certainty. In later years, after Longstreet had engaged in controversy with some of his Virginia comrades, they magnified his doubts on August 29 into costly, almost fatal insubordination.[67] Were they fair in this? Did Longstreet tell himself that he could say "No"

[67] This was part of the "Gettysburg controversy," for which see D. S. Freeman, *The South to Posterity*, 76–77.

and impose his will on Lee? Was there developing in his mind a belief that, no matter what the public might say of Jackson, he and not "Stonewall" had the large influence on Lee? A day was coming when these questions were to be asked again and perhaps with more reason.

To the divisional commanders under Longstreet and Jackson, the word most accurately to be applied at Second Manassas was *adequate*. The new organization has succeeded under the new men. There was nothing brilliant in the performance of any of them, unless it was in the withdrawal of Ewell from Broad Run, but there was no conspicuous shortcoming by a Major General anywhere during the campaign. A. P. Hill's failure to close the gap between Gregg and Thomas on the 29th and to secure his flank early on the morning of the final day in the railroad cut were forgotten, perhaps too readily, in admiration of his superb defense. "Dick" Anderson might have been negligent in not having his advanced guard where it could warn him on the night of the 29th that he was stumbling almost into the enemy's lines. If he was careless then, he hit furiously the next day. John B. Hood was magnificent. He had selected the position for Stephen Lee's guns.[68] Hood's Texans had set the pace in pursuit with all the contempt of danger they had shown in the swamp at Gaines' Mill.[69]

After Taliaferro was wounded, the handling of Jackson's Division by the new Brigadier, William E. Starke, was that of a veteran. Said Col. Bradley Johnson of him: "The buoyant dash with which he led his Brigade into a most withering fire, though then in command of the Division; the force he showed in the handling of this command; the coolness and judgment which distinguished him in action made him to me a marked man . . ."[70] It began to look as if the smashing Brigadier from civil life was worthy to be Charles Winder's successor. "This," a regimental adjutant wrote years afterward, "was [Starke's] first experience in handling a Division, but he did it with great skill." Adjutant Worsham continued: "He was conspicuous for gallantry, and seemed to be at the right spot at the right moment!"[71] Not quite

---

[68] *O. R.,* 12, pt. 2, p. 577.

[69] Cf. *ibid.,* 566. For the next references to Hood, see *infra,* pp. 182, 206 ff.; for R. H. Anderson, see p. 211.

[70] *O. R.,* 12, pt. 2, p. 668.   [71] *Worsham,* 134.

so large an opportunity as Starke's had come to James L. Kemper, but as the senior Brigadier of the half of Longstreet's old Division that previously had been entrusted to the wounded and absent Pickett, the stout-hearted Kemper had led gallantly.

In keeping with the curious custom of regarding the cavalry as an ally, whose excellence it was proper to commend, and not merely as an arm of the service that would be expected to perform its duty as the dust-eating infantry did, Stuart received prominent mention in Lee's dispatches. For his advance to Manassas Junction, "Jeb" received as much applause as had been awarded him for his "ride around McClellan." His subsequent operations around Manassas were no less commended, and no less were deserving of praise. His task had been simplified to the extent that the Federal horse had been sent galloping West, on one purposeless mission after another, until men and mounts were worn to utter weariness.[72] Stuart's troopers had taken better care of their animals and had kept their striking-power to the hour of decision. "During all these operations," Lee reported, "the cavalry under General Stuart, consisting of the brigades of Generals Robertson and Fitzhugh Lee, rendered most important and valuable service." He particularized: "It guarded the flanks of the army, protected its trains, and gave information of the enemy's movements." [73] Here, again, tributes to the subordinates were reassurance to the leader. It was not Lee's nature to be hasty in his judgment of men, but after Second Manassas he reasonably could feel that in the dread test of unequal battle he could count on such men as "Dick" Anderson and John Hood and "Jeb" Stuart.

To dwell on all the fine performances at Second Manassas of officers below Stuart's rank of Major General would be tedious. Although the details were different, the valor was the same. Gregg brandishing his scimitar on the rocky little knoll; Col. Bradley Johnson of the disbanded Maryland Line shrewdly directing the Second Brigade of Jackson's Division by special assignment of "Stonewall" himself; [74] "Shanks" Evans pursuing as hotly as he had resisted at the First Manassas; old "Bob" Toombs released

---

[72] See *supra*, p. 135, n. 58.

[73] *O. R.*, 12, pt. 2, p. 558. For continuance of the sketch of Stuart, see *infra*, pp. 154 ff.

[74] Cf. *Worsham*, 134: "It was the unanimous sentiment of the Second Brigade that they were never as well handled as they were by Col. Bradley T. Johnson. during this battle and the rest of the time he was with us."

from arrest and rushing to his cheering Brigade; [75] Cadmus Wilcox unhesitatingly and swiftly moving his troops to threatened points; [76] Beverley Robertson redeeming a late start by a gallant finish [77]—these and many exploits no less splendid were reported.

Of all the Brigadiers, perhaps the man most distinguished was none other than the most conspicuous figure at Cedar Mountain, the sharp-tongued, keen-eyed Jubal Early. To him, in large part, belonged credit for Ewell's withdrawal from Broad Run. Early it was, also, who relieved Gregg at the critical moment on the afternoon of the 29th. Even Jackson applauded the first of these operations.[78] Ewell was full of praise for his Brigadier; [79] Hill gratefully acknowledged Early's aid on the 29th; [80] Early himself was entirely satisfied with his performance and was convinced that he had earned promotion. Already he was hinting that if he could not get his deserts in Virginia, he would join Bragg in the Western Army. Ewell was afraid Early would go. Before he was wounded, Ewell wrote his sweetheart in Tennessee: "Early is very able and very brave and would be an acquisition to your part of the world." [81]

Of many shining performances by Colonels, at least one was credited to an officer destined to win fame. Stephen D. Lee, after a brief interval of cavalry service,[82] had returned to the "long arm." [83] His handling of his battalion of artillery on the great day at Manassas had won the plaudits of the Army at the same time that it had broken the final assault on Jackson's right. When the Federals had undertaken to silence Stephen Lee's fire by a direct charge, he had held his ground and had repulsed them, though some of them got within 200 yards of him. His feat was the finer because, as noted already, two of his batteries were in action for the first time.[84] Praise was awarded him both by Longstreet and by the commanding General.

Failures amid fine achievements were few. Along with much applause, there was some carping. After twenty years, Longstreet

[75] O. R., 12, pt. 2, pp. 566, 580; 2 B & L., 526.
[76] Cf. O. R., 12, pt. 2, p. 567.
[77] O. R., 12, pt. 2, p. 737. His report is ibid., 746–47.
[78] O. R., 12, pt. 2, p. 644.
[79] Cf. Hamlin's Ewell, 115.   [80] O. R., 12, pt. 2, p. 671.
[81] Old Bald Head, 122. For the next material references to Early, see infra, pp. 207 ff.
[82] As commander of the Fourth Virginia. Cf. O. R., 11, pt. 2, p. 745.
[83] August 17; O. R., 12, pt. 3, p. 933.
[84] Cf. supra, p. 126.

was to say that Jackson on the 30th "did not respond with spirit to my move"; [85] but Jackson, in his report, took pains to recall the "timely and gallant advance of General Longstreet" on the 30th.[86] In Longstreet's own command there was criticism of Brig. Gens. Featherston and Pryor for drifting away from their designated line of advance and for failure, later in the day, to strike the rear of Federals who were attacking Jackson.[87] No explanation of this was satisfactory to Cadmus Wilcox, under whom the two Brigades fought.

Still less explicable was the failure of Gen. Thomas F. Drayton.[88] When he was ordered to advance on the 30th, along with the remainder of Longstreet's command, he was delayed temporarily by a report of Thomas Rosser that the enemy was attempting to flank the right wing of the Army. D. R. Jones, to whose Division he belonged, sent repeatedly for Drayton, as the other Brigades became heavily engaged, but Drayton did not arrive until twilight was putting an end to the action. For failure in these circumstances, Jones did not think Drayton censurable,[89] though at least one other discerning South Carolinian had expected Drayton to fail.[90] Lee felt that Drayton, with the best of will and of effort, was not able to get his men into battle.[91]

These were trivial failures when set against the many fine deeds of individual prowess or against the general excellence of the Army's performance. Seven thousand prisoners, not to mention 2000 wounded Federals left by Pope on the field of battle, thirty guns, 20,000 small arms, and vast stores were impressive proof that the officers had learned how to lead and the troops how to fight together. Army unity, long lacking, was achieved. As always, the price had been high in the death or wounding of men not easily replaced. Total casualties exceeded 9100.[92]

To recapitulate losses in the high command: Ewell, losing a leg, would be absent for months, if ever he would be able to resume

[85] 2 B. & L., 524.

[86] O. R., 12, pt. 2, p. 647. In The Grayjackets, 191–93, is a lengthy account of adventures that are said to have befallen General Pryor while cut off and lost inside the Federal lines.

[87] O. R., 12, pt. 2, pp. 566, 598, 599.

[88] See supra, p. 63.   [89] O. R., 12, pt. 2, pp. 579–8o

[90] James Conner to his mother, Dec. 2, 1861: "I always knew Drayton would prove a failure . . ." (Conner, 72).

[91] O. R., 21, 1030.

[92] Alexander, 219. The same authority put Federal losses at 14,462. (Ibid.)

command. Neither Trimble nor Taliaferro appeared so badly injured, but they could not follow the Army on its next move. Besides these three, Brig. Gen. William Mahone,[93] Brig. Gen. Micah Jenkins [94] and Brig. Gen. Charles W. Field were wounded severely.[95] "His invaluable assistance," wrote Hill regretfully of Field, "was . . . lost to me during the balance of the campaign." [96] Pender was knocked down by the explosion of a shell but was unwilling to be accounted a casualty.[97]

The wounding of five of the thirty-five general officers then with the Army was a serious matter. Scarcely less serious was the continued slaughter of some who were rated among the ablest of the Colonels. On the 28th, it will be remembered, Jackson lost Col. John F. Neff. By the time the last gun was fired at Chantilly, nine other Colonels had been killed or mortally wounded. One of them, John H. Means of the Seventeenth South Carolina, had been Governor of his State.[98] Another, W. S. H. Baylor, senior Colonel in command of the Stonewall Brigade, was a general officer in all but title and soon would have had that.[99] Said Taliaferro, "No more exalted recognition of his worth and service can be uttered and no higher tribute can be paid him than to declare that he was worthy of the command of the Stonewall Brigade" in the fight with King's Division.[100] As much lamented as any man was Lt. Col. John C. Upton of the Fifth Texas, who had led the van in Longstreet's advance of August 29 from Thoroughfare Gap.[101] "Many gallant officers and men fell upon this memorable field of Manassas," wrote Hood in justified comparative, "and our country has cause to regret the loss of none of her sons more than that" of Upton.[102] At Chantilly fell Capt. W. F. Brown of the Twelfth Georgia, whose coolness at Cedar Moun-

---

[93] O. R., 12, pt. 2, pp. 559, 567; ibid., 19, pt. 1, p. 842.

[94] O. R., 12, pt. 2, p. 567; ibid., 19, pt. 1, p. 842.

[95] O. R., 12, pt. 2, p. 555.

[96] Ibid., 671.   [97] Ibid., 671.

[98] In 1850–51. Mrs. Chesnut, 26; for references to his death, see O. R., 12, pt. 2, pp. 567, 629.

[99] McHenry Howard, 177.

[100] O. R., 12, pt. 2, 657. The other Colonels who lost their lives during the operations of Aug. 29–Sept. 1 were: J. M. Gadberry, Eighteenth S. C.; J. V. Moore, Second S. C.; T. J. Glover, First S. C.; W. T. Wilson, Seventh Ga.; J. F. Marshall, Orr's S. C. Rifles; W. A. Forbes, Fourteenth Tenn., and R. H. Riddick, Thirty-fourth N. C. At the time, A. P. Hill feared that the "gallant [Henry] Forno," Colonel of the Fifth Louisiana and temporarily commanding Hays's Brigade, had been wounded mortally, but Forno recovered. (O. R., 12, pt. 2, pp. 671, 717 ff.)

[101] O R. 12, pt. 2, p. 605.   [102] O. R., 12, pt. 2, p. 606.

tain had won "Jube" Early's admiration. Brown had not been promoted, but by the casualties of action and the sickness incident to hard campaigning, he had been in command of Trimble's Brigade for three days when his own end came.[103] This was perhaps the extreme case of the transfer of command, from higher rank to lower, but extremes as great in the casualties among officers were reported. A. P. Hill in the aggregate lost three Colonels and one Lieutenant Colonel killed, and five Colonels and four Lieutenant Colonels wounded.[104] Jackson's Division ended the operation with no general officer besides Starke.[105] The regiments of the Stonewall Brigade at the close of action, September 1, were commanded by Captains and Lieutenants.[106] Gregg's Brigade, on the 29th, had all save two of its field officers killed or wounded.[107] For such tasks as lay ahead, the subordinate army command was suffering more from attrition than ever it had, but the high command had learned much that it was, by turn of circumstance, quickly to be called upon to apply.

[103] *O. R.*, 12, pt. 2, pp. 712, 714. On May 30, it will be remembered, Captain Brown had saved the Twelfth Georgia at Front Royal. See *supra*, Vol. I, p. 416, and Vol. II, p. 30. His last day was his greatest. Said Oates: "Captain Brown, our Brigade commander, seeing the retrograde movement of his regiment, with his conspicuous black plume in his hat, his long sabre in hand, his face aglow with excitement and indignation, looked like Goliath with his weaver's beam. His tall form was conspicuous along the line among the retreating men, trying to halt them, and cursing like a trooper, when a Federal bullet struck him in the head and killed him instantly" (*Oates*, 150).

[104] *O. R.*, 12, pt. 2, p. 672. Hill listed four Colonels wounded, but he forgot Col. Samuel McGowan of the Fourteenth S. C., who was wounded on the 29th (*O. R.*, 12, pt. 2, pp. 681, 682).

[105] Cf. *ibid.*, 548.

[106] *O. R.*, 12, pt. 2, p. 658. It will be noted that no report of the Fifth Virginia seems to have been filed. For this reason, it cannot be stated with absolute certainty that the Fifth had no field officer, but all the indications are to that effect.

[107] *O. R.*, 12, pt. 2, p. 646.

CHAPTER VIII

THE IMPONDERABLES OF INVASION

FROM CHARLESTON came the summons. Said the *Mercury:* "Our victorious troops in Virginia, reduced though they be in numbers, and shattered in organization, must be led promptly into Maryland, before the enemy can rally the masses of recruits whom he is rapidly and steadily gathering together. When the Government of the North shall have fled into Pennsylvania, when the public buildings in Washington shall have been razed to the ground, so as to forbid the hope of their ever again becoming the nest of Yankee despotism, then, at last, may we expect to see the hope of success vanish from the Northern mind, and reap the fruit of our bloody and long continued trials."[1] It was not the first demand of the year for an offensive,[2] nor, so far as the Davis administration was concerned, did it come from a welcome quarter; but it was urged vigorously,[3] and it was in accord with General Lee's appraisal of the military and diplomatic situation.[4]

[1] *Charleston Mercury,* Sept. 6, 1862, p. 1, col. 2.

[2] Agitation for the invasion of the North had been renewed as a result of Jackson's Valley Campaign and, after the Seven Days, had been more excited. Cf. *Richmond Dispatch,* Aug. 2, p. 2, col. 1; Aug. 11, p. 2, col. 1; Aug. 28, p. 2, col. 1; Aug. 29, p. 2, col. 1; *Richmond Examiner,* July 31, p. 2, cols. 1–2; Aug. 22, p. 2, col. 1; *Richmond Whig,* Aug. 4, p. 2, col. 1; Aug. 6, p. 1, col. 1; Aug. 7, p. 1, col. 1; Aug. 25, p. 1, col. 1; *Augusta Chronicle and Sentinel,* quoted in *ibid.,* Aug. 22, p. 2, col. 1; *Savannah Republican,* quoted in *ibid.,* Aug. 25, 1862, p. 1, col. 1. Notable among these statements was the warning of the *Richmond Dispatch,* Aug. 11, 1862, p. 2, col. 1: "Another 'Manassas lethargy' is gradually settling upon us . . . It is fated, it seems, that we are never to reap the fruits of our victory, no matter how decisive." The same paper, Aug. 9, 1862, p. 1, cols. 2–3, reprinted from the *Albany Evening Journal,* described as "Seward's organ," an editorial which had acknowledged the prowess and endurance of the South and had given the North this admonition: "We have learned that the contest between us and the Confederates is reduced to a question of pure brute force . . . that there is no middle ground—no half-way house—between absolute triumph and absolute vassalage."

[3] See *supra,* p. 136, n. 60; also *Charleston Mercury,* Sept. 2, p. 1, col. 2; Sept. 6, p. 1, col. 2; *Richmond Whig,* Sept. 8, p. 1, col. 1; *Richmond Examiner,* Sept. 8, 1862, p. 2, col. 3. The last of these references concluded: "From the ignoble exhibitions which have been already given by the North even at the distant threat of invasion, we may justly anticipate the dismay that will seize her armies, and the agony that will wring the hearts of her selfish people when our troops have once obtained a footing north of the Potomac."

[4] For the detailed consideration, see 12 *S. H. S. P.,* 504, and 2 *R. E. Lee,* 350–53. To the references given in *R. E. Lee,* the reader may wish to add the survey of the Washington defenses in *O. R.,* 21, 903. Although that document is dated December 24, it deals with fortifications that were not materially less strong at the end of August.

Before the men had time fully to rest their limbs from the strain of Manassas, or even to dry the ragged garments that had been soaked at Chantilly, the Army of Northern Virginia headed for the Potomac.

Small the invading force was to be, and in much of its equipment deficient; but Hampton's Brigade of cavalry, Pendleton's reserve artillery, and three Divisions of infantry now were added to the Army.[5] One of these Divisions was that of D. H. Hill, to the direction of which he had been returned after Lee's misgiving of Hill's capacity as an administrator had prompted the decision that Gustavus Smith should command at Richmond while Lee was on the frontier.[6] A second Division to rejoin the Army was that of McLaws. The third, which was in reality a half Division of two Brigades only, brought back to old associations a Missouri Brigadier, John G. Walker.[7] Of his Brigades, one was Robert Ransom's. The other, Walker's own Brigade, was under the command of its senior Colonel, Van H. Manning of the Third Arkansas, a valiant, hard-hitting regiment. Included in this Brigade, also, was the Twenty-seventh North Carolina. Its Colonel was John Rogers Cooke, who was known to some former officers of the "old Army" as the son of Gen. Philip St. George Cooke, and as the brother-in-law of "Jeb" Stuart. A Lieutenant of the Eighth United States Cavalry at the time of secession, Cooke had a good reputation in his regiment. Of his larger capacities[8] there had

5 *Allan's Army,* 324.

6 O. R., 12, pt. 3, pp. 932, 938, 948, 965. In view of Smith's protests that Lee previously had kept him in the dark, it may be proper to note that while Smith was in charge of the Richmond defenses, Lee communicated with him often, entrusted to him many tasks and confided in him more freely than in anyone except the President himself. Cf. O. R., 19, pt. 2, pp. 627, 640 ff.

7 For his career, see 9 *C. M. H.,* Missouri, 323 ff. He was commissioned Brigadier General Jan. 9, 1862, and Major General Nov. 8, 1862. *Wright,* 68. References to his service will be found in *Richmond Examiner,* Aug. 30, p. 2, col. 3; *ibid.,* Sept. 4, 1861, p. 3, col. 1; O. R., 5, 958; 11, pt. 3, pp. 392, 553, 648, 948; 51, pt. 2, pp. 357, 567. As Walker was ordered to the Trans-Mississippi after his promotion to the grade of Major General, he is not sketched at length in these pages as one of Lee's lieutenants.

8 He was born at Jefferson Barracks, Missouri, June 10, 1833, and was graduated from Harvard in 1854. As a civil engineer, he soon became so conscious of the defects of his professional training that he served for six months as an apprentice in the locomotive works of Palmer and Robinson in St. Louis. It was from this plant that he entered the army as a Second Lieutenant (see John R. Steeger to President, etc. Richmond and Petersburg Railroad, Dec. 21, 1868; *Cooke MSS*). When he resigned to join the Confederacy, he was convinced that his father also would fight for Virginia (John R. Cooke to Mrs. J. E. B. Stuart, July 12, 1861; *Cooke MSS*). Both he and "Jeb" Stuart were humiliated by the elder officer's decision to remain with the Union. Stuart wrote John R. Cooke, Jan. 18, 1862: "[Gen. Cooke] will regret it but once and that will be continually. Let us so conduct ourselves as to have nothing in our course to be re-

been little test, and of the quality of his regiment still less. It had been under fire two or three times, it was well drilled, and it was devoted to Cooke.[9] This was all that could be said of Walker's Brigade. To look at the men, as they started for the Potomac, no officer, unless it was Cooke himself, could have predicted what a fortnight was to prove them capable of performing.[10]

The accession of strength represented by Walker, McLaws and D. H. Hill was cancelled in part by the 9000 casualties of Second Manassas [11] and, more particularly, by the loss of commanders who could not be replaced immediately. In this appeared the first of two imponderables which, despite the care with which Lee weighed his plans for the campaign, either were overlooked or else were considered less important than they proved to be.

Through seniority, Lawton and not Early was in charge of Ewell's Division. The return of John R. Jones gave him, instead of Starke, the care of Jackson's old Division. A. P. Hill only, of Jackson's division commanders, had the rank appropriate to his responsibilities. Of the fourteen Brigades entrusted to Jackson, eight were under Colonels. Worst of all, in this respect, were the Brigades that Taliaferro had directed till he fell at Groveton. To repeat, not one general officer, save Starke, was there in the Division. The Stonewall Brigade, a stubborn fragment, was led by Col. A. J. Grigsby. He either knew at the time or learned soon afterwards that Jackson would not recommend him for promotion to Brigade command, and he felt himself aggrieved, though he displayed consistent courage.[12] For assignment to a leaderless Brigade, the one trained man available at the moment was "Dick" Garnett, whose court martial had been interrupted by the preliminaries of Cedar Mountain. He was released from arrest and,

gretted. Certainly thus far we have had nothing that we may not be proud of. It is a sad thing, but the responsibility of the present state of the separation in the family rests entirely with the Col. [i.e., the General]. Let us bear our misfortune in silence." (*Cooke MSS.*) Young Cooke soon became T. H. Holmes's Chief of Artillery (John R. Cooke to Mrs. J. E. B. Stuart, Mch. 20, 1862; *Cooke MSS*), but scarcely had entered upon his duties when, Apr. 16, 1862, he was elected Colonel of the Twenty-seventh North Carolina Infantry (2 *N. C. Regts.*, 427). For a sketch, see 18 *S. H. S. P.*, 323 ff; 4 *C. M. H.*, 302.

9 *Cf.* 4 *N. C. Regts.*, 511.
10 For continuance of the sketch of Cooke, see *infra*, p. 214.
11 Alexander, *op. cit.*, 219. See *supra*, p. 141.
12 *McHenry Howard*, 180–81.

as he could not be employed with the unrelenting Jackson, he was assigned to Pickett's Brigade, Longstreet's command.[13]

This gave Pickett's men an experienced leader; but if one fine Division of Longstreet's "wing" thereby was strengthened, two others equally good were weakened by arrests. At Manassas, on the evening of August 30, John B. Hood had seen in front of his troops several new Federal ambulances, which he had much coveted. Some of his Texas scouts obligingly had gone forward and had captured the vehicles. A few days later, "Shanks" Evans, who had titular authority over Hood's troops,[14] directed that the ambulances be given his Carolina Brigade. Hood refused. "I would cheerfully," said he, "have obeyed directions to deliver them to General Lee's Quartermaster for the use of the army, [but] I did not consider it just that I should be required to yield them to another Brigade of the Division, which was in no manner entitled to them." [15] For this, Hood was placed in arrest and was ordered by Longstreet to proceed to Culpeper and to remain there until the case was tried. Lee heard of the clash and overruled Longstreet to the extent that Hood was authorized to stay with his troops, though not to exercise command.[16] Doubtless this leniency was displayed by Lee both because of the trivial nature of the alleged insubordination and because of the probable need of Hood's services, regardless of arrest. Hood's feelings were eased somewhat by Lee's action, but his men became half mutinous in their resentment.[17]

The other arrest that might weaken the Army came through a renewal of Jackson's disciplining of A. P. Hill. On the night of September 3, Jackson gave instructions for the start of each Division the next morning at a specified time and, as usual, he rode out at dawn to see if his orders were being followed. They were not. Hill's Division was not moving; Gregg's Brigade was not

---

[13] O. R., 19, pt. 1, p. 805; pt. 2, p. 595. This, it will be remembered, was the second time subsequent to Garnett's arrest that he had been ordered to duty. On June 25, under suspension of arrest, he had been directed to report to D. H. Hill for assignment (O. R., 51, pt. 2, p. 597), which had not been made because the campaign was concluded before he was able to report for duty. See supra, p. 8.

[14] Evans stated, O. R., 12, pt. 2, p. 628, that on August 30 he commanded his own and Pickett's Brigades and Hood's Division, but Hood seems to have ignored this connection. In his report (ibid., 606), he mentioned Evans only to the extent of saying that the South Carolinian's Brigade came up and entered the battle.

[15] Hood, 38.   [16] Ibid., 39.

[17] Ibid. See also Sorrel, 100.

even ready to start. Every Brigadier, Jackson concluded, had been left to move his own column without the supervision of the division commander. In Hill's absence, Jackson asked why Gregg was not on the march, whereupon, perhaps with some resentment, the South Carolinian replied that his men were filling their canteens. Jackson waited until this was completed, and then ordered Gregg to take the road. Something in Jackson's manner, or some words that passed between the two men, created a bitterness that did not pass with the day or with the campaign. For the moment, Gregg merely obeyed orders.

Jackson felt that the Division had made a bad start and he kept his eye on the column, ahead of which Hill rode steadily onward. Neither Hill nor any of his staff trotted back to see whether the troops were moving properly. The corps commander observed this dereliction. He learned that some units of the Division were straggling badly; Hill seemed to be making no effort to prevent it. After a while, the hour arrived for the halt Jackson had directed the column to make in order that the men might have a brief rest. Hill paid no attention to the time and did not call a halt. Jackson's wrath was aroused. He accosted the commander of the leading Brigade, Ed Thomas, and told him to stop the column in accordance with regulations. Thomas did. Jackson stood by. At the end of the noon rest, Thomas ordered the men to fall in and to resume the march. In a few minutes Hill came storming back to Thomas and wished to know by whose order the troops had been halted.

Thomas said: "By General Jackson's."

Hill turned on "Stonewall," who was sitting silent on his horse. With some statement that if Jackson was to give orders, the General had no need of him, Hill unbuckled his sword and offered it to Jackson.

"Consider yourself under arrest for neglect of duty," Jackson answered, and subsequently directed Branch to take command of the Division.[18]

18 Rough draft of charges against A. P. Hill; charges and specifications of Oct. 4, 1862; E. L. Thomas to E. F. Paxton, A. A. G., Sept. 24, 1862 (*Jackson MSS*). The *Charleston Mercury*, Sept. 25, 1862, stated that Hill, in passing over his sword, said flatly that Jackson was not "fit to be a General." David Macrae, *The Americans at Home*, gave a post-bellum version of the colloquy between Jackson and Hill. In *Douglas*, 146, is an account of the affair, but the contemporary documents show that Douglas confused some of the details.

So, as the Army passed over the grassy hills of Loudoun, en route to the Potomac, Jackson sacrificed his only experienced divisional commander to his ideal of discipline. He insisted later that "under Hill's successor, Genl. Branch, my orders were much better carried out,"[19] but he could not have overlooked the fact that the troops of the "Left Wing" were facing new battles on hostile soil with all three Divisions under Brigadier Generals not one of whom had received professional training. Longstreet was better circumstanced, though he would miss Hood. All this constituted the first imponderable.

The second was straggling. Some warnings had come before the Battle of Manassas that men were leaving the ranks without proper excuse.[20] A few executions for desertion had occurred, though not without some public protest.[21] Officers and provost marshal guards had been sent to Lynchburg, where martial law had been declared when that city was found to be something of a rendezvous for deserters.[22] None of this had prepared the Army for what came en route to Maryland—straggling of a magnitude so appalling that it made Johnston's evacuation of the Peninsula appear orderly. Thousands of men fell behind or disappeared. Jackson characteristically met with sternness this ominous breakdown of discipline: His order was that men who left the ranks were to be shot without argument or ado.[23] Lee designated Brig. Gen. Lewis A. Armistead as provost marshal, gave him authority to call for guards,[24] and sorrowfully Lee had to admit that discipline was "defective."[25] Exhortation, orders, threats, penalties alike failed. As the campaign progressed, the weak soldier fell away with the indifferent until, as one of the indomitable Haskells wrote, "none but heroes are left."[26]

[19] Endorsement of Sept. 24, 1862, on Hill's request for a court of inquiry, *Jackson MSS*.

[20] *Richmond Examiner*, July 26, p. 2, cols. 2–3; July 31, p. 2, cols. 1–2; Aug. 4, p. 2, col. 4; Aug. 18, p. 1, col. 2; *Richmond Whig*, Aug. 4, 1862, p. 2, col. 1.

[21] *Richmond Dispatch*, Aug. 27, p. 2, col. 1; Aug. 28, 1862, p. 1, col. 5.

[22] *Richmond Dispatch*, Aug. 20, p. 1, col. 6; Aug. 21, 1862, p. 1, col. 4.

[23] *Jackson's MS*. Letter Book. p. 60.   [24] *O. R.*, 19, pt. 2, p. 596.

[25] *O. R.*, 19, pt. 2, p. 597; letter of Sept. 7, 1862.

[26] Louise Haskell Daly, *Alexander Cheves Haskell* (cited hereafter as *Mrs. Daly*), 84; letter of Sept. 23, 1862. Straggling was an aggravated and not a new problem of the army. Richard Taylor (*op. cit.*, 36) encountered it early in his command and attributed it to the fact that most Southerners, before entering the army, had ridden habitually and seldom had walked any distance. He found that proper care of shoes and of feet, coupled with stiff discipline, almost eliminated straggling in his Brigade. In many other commands, during and after the Seven Days, straggling became so general

The first reason for this straggling was the obvious one of worn-out shoes. Most of the troops were being called upon to make long marches immediately after a succession of battles that had themselves been preceded by hard, steady pounding of the roads all the way from Gordonsville to Bull Run. Never before had so many men become shoeless.[27] Apparently the Quartermasters had not realized that the shoes of so large a part of the Army would go to pieces at the same time and, in effect, would render many unshod men incapable of marching. After another six months of hardening, most of the troops were to find themselves possessed of feet so tough that shoes in summer were a nuisance. It was far from being so in September, 1862.

Another reason for much of the straggling was the diet on which the men had to subsist. Before the Army began its advance, Lee realized that the commissary could not supply the Army from bases in Virginia, and he doubted whether rations could be had in Maryland otherwise than by plundering the civil population through methods similar to those for which General Pope had been denounced by Confederates.[28] The final decision of Lee,

(*Richmond Examiner,* July 3, p. 2, col. 2, July 11, 1862, p. 1, col. 1) that Richmond papers had to urge the generous not to feed stragglers, or to countenance them in any way. (*Ibid.,* July 22, p. 2, cols. 1–2; *Richmond Dispatch,* July 19, p. 2, col. 1; *Richmond Whig,* July 16, p. 2, col. 1, July 23, p. 1, col. 1, July 24, p. 1, col. 1 and p. 2, col. 2, July 26, 1862, p. 1, col. 4.) Said *The Examiner* (July 21, 1862, p. 2, col. 1): "We have seen twenty of these sturdy, dirty villains seated in the shade on our streets, while they were fed by some poor woman from the last supplies in her kitchen . . . There are officers as well as privates among these absentees; drones in uniform, who smoke or guzzle about the hotels, and are made parlor pets by some of the social noodles of Richmond . . ." Examination of passes on city streets reduced straggling (*ibid.,* July 16, p. 2, col. 4; *Richmond Dispatch,* July 17, p. 1, col. 7, July 25, p. 1, col. 6), but absence without leave was on so large a scale through the summer that the imprisonment of stragglers was ordered (*Richmond Examiner,* July 29, p. 2, col. 5, and July 30, p. 2, col. 4). Even the imposition of the death penalty was urged (*Richmond Examiner,* July 21, 1862, p. 1, col. 2). On July 17, Adjutant General Cooper asked the Governors to co-operate in bringing back to the ranks the deserters and stragglers whose absence so weakened the army that it could not invade the North or get the fullest results of victory (IV O. R., 2, 7). Railroad agents and employees were required by Lee, July 22, to give aid in the recovery of stragglers and deserters (G. O. 84, *Richmond Enquirer,* July 25, 1862, p. 1, col. 2).

[27] Col. Edward McCrady, in the course of the best review of straggling and desertion at this period, 14 *S. H. S. P.,* 205, remarked that on August 27 not less than 100 of the 300 enlisted men of the First South Carolina had no shoes. In the *Wilcox MSS* is a letter wherein Brig. Gen. C. M. Wilcox gave his brother, Congressman John A. Wilcox of Texas, a detailed description (Sept. 26, 1862) of the need of shoes and of clothing.

[28] Pope's notorious orders concerning subsistence in the enemy's country and the behavior of citizens of occupied territory produced a furious response in Southern newspapers and inspired the "reprisal order" (No. 54, A. & I. G.O.) which announced that Pope's officers, when captured by Confederate forces, would not be regarded as prisoners of war. This order was approved with vigor and virtual unanimity. (See *Richmond*

regretfully made, was that the Army must live for the time being on green corn and fruit.[29] The Army did. For an average of probably ten days, during the first three weeks of September, the men had little other food. They added potatoes where they could,[30] and they devoured almost anything the commissary issued, but they had green corn, meal after meal, as their basal diet. Some of the soldiers discovered that they could roast the corn for breakfast and for supper and could manage to keep in health; but if they cooked corn in the morning for use in the middle of the day, they found that without salt it became sour. As the columns did not halt long enough at noon to allow time for preparing fresh corn, the prudent fasted then.[31] Many of those who ate too freely of the corn developed a serious diarrhea [32] which weakened them and inevitably caused much absence without leave. "We call this even now," Adjutant Owen wrote after some twenty years, "the green corn campaign." [33]

Besides bruised feet and diarrhea, the inexperience of some of the acting brigade and regimental commanders was a factor in straggling: numerous officers never previously had been charged with the care of a column, and were unable either to keep it closed, or to distinguish between the skulker and the sick. This may be stated simply and without elaboration, but it represented a weakness that was shown hourly and disastrously.

A fourth reason there was for the straggling, a reason that does not seem to have been anticipated in any degree. It was exemplified by the Twenty-fifth North Carolina of Robert Ransom's Brigade. The greater number of the men in this regiment had come from the extreme western counties of North Carolina. Until President Lincoln had called for troops in April, 1861, they had been Unionist in sentiment. They enlisted for the defense of their homes against invasion, and when they learned that they were to

---

Dispatch, Aug. 4, p. 2, col. 1, Aug. 25, p. 1, col. 3; *Richmond Whig,* Aug. 4, p. 1, cols. 5–6, Aug. 7, p. 1, col. 1, with quotation from *Wilmington Journal,* Aug. 9, p. 1. col. 6, with a most vehement editorial from the *Petersburg Express.* See also *Richmond Examiner,* Aug. 4, p. 2, cols. 2–3; *Richmond Enquirer,* Aug. 5, 1862, p. 2, col. 1.)

[29] To the details, as given in 2 *R. E. Lee,* 352, should be added the reminder that part of the Army had done this before Second Manassas. See 14 *S. H. S. P.,* 102.

[30] *Neese,* 117.

[31] W. F. Dunaway, *Reminiscences of a Rebel* (cited hereafter as *Dunaway*), 49. Hotchkiss noted that Jackson, during a halt, took out an ear of corn and ate it. Perhaps it had been salted (*MS Diary,* Sept. 6, 1862, p. 83).

[32] *Sorrel,* 110.   [33] *Owen,* 130.

cross the Potomac, they responded in varying confusion of mind. Some approved; others rationalized their instinctive objection by saying that a threat to Northern territory would strengthen the Federal army. Still others, in the language of their historian, "said they had volunteered to resist invasion and not to invade; some did not believe it right to invade Northern territory." [34] This was a feeling not to be repressed by orders or by punishment. Those of extreme conscience may have found opportunity of leaving the ranks for the duration of the Maryland expedition. The fighting of those who entered Maryland did not indicate that they had any compunctions; but they soon found that the enemy North of the dividing river fought in a spirit akin to their own on their native soil. "I believe," wrote one disgusted horse artillerist, "that the confounded Yankees can shoot better in the United States than they can when they come to Dixieland." [35]

Together, these conditions were responsible for so much straggling even before the Potomac was reached that the commanding General thought it dangerous alike to the stragglers and to the Confederate cause in Maryland for the thousands of hungry, scattered men to follow the Army across the river. He stationed his bodyguard at the principal ford and told its commanding officer to direct all stragglers to Winchester,[36] where they might be organized and forwarded in numbers large enough to avoid all risk of capture.

[34] 2 *N. C. Regts.*, 293, 296.		[35] *Neese*, 114.
[36] L. W. Hopkins, *From Bull Run to Appomattox*, 51. For Lee's effort to prevent depredation, see *O. R.*, 19, pt. 2, p. 592, G.O., 102, II. It is possible that Lee's orders not to permit stragglers to enter Maryland may have been the basis of D. H. Hill's statement, not confirmed by other testimony, that barefooted men had been excused "from marching into Maryland" (2 *B. & L.*, 565).

CHAPTER IX

GENERALS ON DISPLAY

THE PASSAGE of the Potomac on September 4–7 [1] was to the spectators a drama of incredible contrasts, to the boys in the ranks a diverting lark, and to the commanding Generals the beginning of a venture diplomatic, political and social, no less than military. Said von Borcke of the cavalry's crossing: "It was . . . a magnificent sight as the long column of many thousand horsemen stretched across this beautiful Potomac. The evening sun slanted upon its clear placid waters, and burnished them with gold, while the arms of the soldiers glittered and blazed in its radiance. There were few moments, perhaps, from the beginning to the close of the war, of excitement more intense, of exhilaration more delightful, than when we ascended the opposite bank to the familiar but now strangely thrilling music of 'Maryland, My Maryland.' " [2] The soldiers were naïve in their half-nakedness, fully conscious of their prowess, and interested above all in the prospect of seeing pretty girls and of getting something to eat besides green corn. Over them, the Colonels kept a vigilant eye to prevent any offense that would alienate the people the Confederacy was wooing.

The higher officers realized, each in his own way, that the curiosity of the Marylanders might be capitalized to the benefit of the South. All the Generals were determined to be agreeable; but, as ill fortune shaped it, Lee, Jackson, and Longstreet were in varying degree incapacitated. On August 31 Lee had fallen and had injured his hands when his horse became frightened and attempted to pull away while the General, loosely holding the reins, was afoot. Lee had to ride in an ambulance for a few days and then required the attendance of someone to lead his charger. [3] For this reason, Marylanders were denied the pleasure of seeing him at his superb physical best.

Jackson had an odd experience. On the 5th of September, when

[1] O. R., 19, pt. 1, p. 145. [2] 1 von Borcke, 185.
[3] 2 R. E. Lee, 340.

he crossed the Potomac at White's Ford, he did not wholly dis dain the dramatic. In mid-stream, he took off his cap. A band struck up "Maryland, My Maryland." The men gave the rebel yell and sang with the band.[4] No sooner was "Stonewall" on Maryland soil than he was presented with a "noble melon" and then with a "strong-sinewed, powerful, gray mare." Jackson accepted her thankfully, because he had lost the little Sorrel temporarily and was riding a cream-colored claybank,[5] but the next morning he paid unexpectedly for his new gift. After he mounted her and gave her the rein, she did not move, whereupon he touched her with his spur. She reared instantly, lost her balance and went over backwards. Jackson was stunned and for half an hour was compelled to lie where he fell. His pain was acute; there was momentary fear of spinal injury. He turned over the command of his troops to D. H. Hill and ingloriously spent the remainder of the day in an ambulance.[6]

The crippled Lee and the bruised Jackson, together with Longstreet, pitched their tents quite close to one another, that 6th of September, in Best's Grove, near Frederick, and soon they had visitors from town and farm. Lee was busy and perhaps uncomfortable from his hurt. As far as he could, he excused himself from callers. Jackson kept to his tent most of the day. Longstreet had to do the honors, though a badly rubbed heel was giving him trouble.[7] "Stuart," said Henry Kyd Douglas, not without a touch of envy, "was ready to see and to talk with every good-looking woman."[8]

Amid much enthusiastic coming and going of Southern sympathizers, nothing untoward happened until late afternoon. Then, as Jackson was on his way to answer a summons to Lee's tent, he passed a carriage in which were two Baltimore girls. They evidently had been in wait, and when they saw him striding past, they made for him. Douglas observed: ". . . one took his hand, the other threw her arms around him, and talked with the wildest

[4] *Cooke's Jackson*, 308; D. Augustus Dickert, *History of Kershaw's Brigade* (cited hereafter as *Dickert*), 144.

[5] *Hotchkiss' MS Diary*, 83; *Douglas*, 147.

[6] *Douglas*, 148; *O. R.*, 19, pt. 1, p. 1019; *Hotchkiss' MS Diary*, 83. D. H. Hill had passed the Potomac while unattached either to Jackson's or to Longstreet's command, but as Jackson, upon crossing, assumed by Lee's order the direction of all troops North of the Potomac, Hill came under his command temporarily. For the details, see *infra*, Appendix I.

[7] *Sorrel*, 104.   [8] *Douglas*, 148–49.

enthusiasm, both at the same time, until he seemed simply miserable. In a minute or two their fireworks were expended, and
jumping into their carriage, they were driven away happy and
delighted; he stood . . . cap in hand, bowing, speechless, paralyzed, and then went to General Lee's." [9] Well might "Old Jack"
have admired the ease, if not the performance of Capt. "Lige"
White of the cavalry, who lived nearby. When he was welcomed
by kinswomen, "he threw himself from his horse"—again to quote
Douglas, "among a group of mothers and daughters, and kissed
such a lot of them in five minutes" that his record stood until the
days of Richmond Pearson Hobson. [10]

Less adept in such matters, Deacon Jackson was so embarrassed
by his encounter with the Baltimore girls that he kept to his quarters that evening. Nor did he venture carelessly forth the next
morning, though it was the Lord's Day. After as quiet a time as he
could make for himself, he decided he would go to evening service. He duly had Kyd Douglas procure for him and for his staff
officers exactly the same sort of pass required for any private
soldier who entered Frederick. Armed with this, he rode in his
ambulance to the Reformed Church, which Douglas, who knew
the town well, had commended when it was ascertained that the
Presbyterians were not meeting.

The occasion was not altogether a success. Courageously enough,
in the presence of one of the most "notorious rebels," the minister,
Dr. Zacharias, prayed for the President of the United States. Jackson doubtless would have joined in that petition, with the mental
note that it was needed, but, unfortunately, he did not hear it. He
fell most trustfully asleep as soon as the sermon was begun. His
head dropped to his chest and crumpled his beard. Down to the
floor from his relaxed fingers slipped his cap. Dr. Zacharias's most
earnest periods, the flight of the peroration, the prayer of minister
and the response of congregation—none of this awakened Jackson.
He enjoyed a soldier's rest until the organ and the voices, in the
closing hymn, brought him back to a world of clashing armies
and divided churches. [11]

On the return to camp he said nothing of the edification he
derived from church attendance. So far as the testimony of witnesses is available, not a word did he speak to indicate that he most

[9] Douglas, 149.   [10] Ibid., 147.   [11] Douglas, 150.

reluctantly had violated the Sabbath by having his **A.A.G. reply** to a letter in which Powell Hill had asked on the 6th for a copy of the charges to be preferred. Wrote Jackson: ". . . should the interests of the service require your case to be brought before a Court Martial a copy of the charges and specifications will be furnished in accordance with army regulations. In the meantime you will remain with your Division." [12] Just that it was: No release from arrest, no certainty of trial—"remain with your Division."

The next day, September 8, witnessed the issuance of the commanding General's tactful address to the people of Maryland. [13] Of this, much was hoped, but, in an immediate social way, the dance given by the cavalry officers at Urbana had a more practical appeal. Hampton's troopers had been stationed at the village, seven miles Southeast of Frederick, in order to cover the infantry from any advance by a Federal force based on Washington, which was forty miles beyond Urbana. The other cavalry Brigades were strategically placed within easy communication. [14] Stuart himself proposed the dance while he was inspecting a disused academy on a hill at Urbana. The General promised to find the music. Major von Borcke volunteered to supervise the lighting and decorating and the issuance of invitations. To play tactfully the role of friend, rather than of invader, von Borcke saw to it that all the families in and adjacent to Urbana were invited, rabid Northerners as well as friends of the Southern cause. "The large halls of the Academy," he wrote in his memoirs, "were aired and swept and festooned with roses, and decorated with battle-flags borrowed from the different regiments." [15]

Guests, at the stated hour, arrived in gratifying number; the band of the Eighteenth Mississippi, Barksdale's Brigade, supplied gay music. Except for the blunder of von Borcke in starting a polka, when his fair partner would not indulge in a round dance with a gentleman not of her family, all began well. The Pomeranian quickly changed from the polka to "a very lively quadrille" with the young lady, who was styled "the New York rebel"; the gray and yellow of cavalry uniforms whirled in the candlelight with the lovely girls; "the strange accompaniments of war added zest to the occasion"; from the dames on the bench, as well as

[12] *Jackson's MS Letter Book*, p. 42.
[13] For text and the circumstances of publication, see 2 *R. E. Lee*, 356 ff.
[14] *O. R.*, 19, ᴘᴛ. 1, p. 815.   [15] 1 *von Borcke*, 193.

from the girls in the figure, came exclamations that everything was "perfectly charming." [16]

Suddenly, above the bass of the Mississippians' horns, there echoed the challenging bark of a field gun and a distant rattle which, to experienced ears, bespoke the clash of outposts. A dusty courier appeared at the door, looked swiftly about him till he saw Stuart, and then stamped across the floor and announced loudly to the General that the enemy had surprised and driven in the pickets and was attacking the Confederate camp.[17] The band crashed into a discord; girls turned pale; parents rushed onto the floor; officers made hasty bows and ran for their sabers which, as prudent soldiers, they had hung nearby on the walls. In five minutes the Academy was stripped of fighting men, though reassuring promises were shouted over tall shoulders that after the Federals had been driven away, the dance must be resumed.

About 1 A.M., under a full, high-riding moon, the troopers jingled back to the Academy lawn and reported that the alarm had amounted to little. They found that the band, which perhaps had been tendered hospitably some spirituous refreshment, had received no orders to leave. Many of the girls had remained, also. Some of those who had been hurried home by parents had been unwilling to go to bed in the midst of so much excitement. Blinking lights in their homes were an invitation to young officers to call and to bring them back to the dance.

Within half an hour after Stuart and his staff had returned, lilting feet were answering every rhythmic beat of the drum. Two o'clock, three, four, a sinking moon and a graying East—still the dance went on. Captain Blackford's partner, weary or wanting fresh air, stopped at length by the door, just at the moment when the grinding thump-thump of men with a load was to be heard on the stair. She looked through the door, blanched and screamed. The other couples stopped, her friends ran to her. What was the matter? Was she ill or . . . Their glances, following hers, lighted on dirty men who were carrying stretchers to the upper story. On the stretchers, gory, smoke-marked, dazed or stubbornly fighting pain, were the boys who had been wounded in the skirmish.

The dance was over. Its belles became nurses. The "New York rebel" who had been von Borcke's partner insisted on attending a

---

[16] *W. W. Blackford's MS Memoirs*, 205.   [17] *Ibid.; von Borcke, loc. cit.*

soldier who still was bleeding, and she kept at her task until she fainted. After she regained consciousness she refused to leave until she was satisfied that the wounded man was comfortable. To the troopers whose injuries were slight, the presence of these lovely young nurses in evening dress was more than a solace. Wrote Captain Blackford: "One handsome young fellow, as he looked up into their faces with a grateful smile, declared that he would get hit any day to have such surgeons to dress his wounds." [18]

Unless he were as luckily wounded as was his young cavalier, the infantry private did not attend any dance in Maryland, even on a stretcher. "Johnny Reb," if the truth be told, was less emulous of his superior officers in making a good impression on the people and more anxious to get something to eat. He did not find Frederick and nearby towns wholly inhospitable. Perhaps he was among the fortunate 600 who shared the open-handed bounty of one householder with a Southern heart, an ample pocketbook and a large table. Denied that pleasure, a lonesome, ragged boy might find a kindly woman who would feed him and perhaps would mend his clothes.[19]

By observing accurately when the sentry made his rounds, a light-footed soldier might slip into Frederick and contrive, somehow, to get a good meal. Said Adjutant Worsham: "A friend and I succeeded in passing the guard, and took a stroll through the town. We were invited into several houses and entertained handsomely at supper, eating enough for half a dozen men." [20] Ned Moore, despite his connection with the elite Rockbridge Artillery, also evaded the guard and had a gala day. Liquor was to be procured in the town and was not disdained, one might say, by some, even, of Jackson's Model Army.[21] Those who had no appetite for it, or no desire to drink it, had at least an opportunity of washing their persons and their clothing [22] and perhaps of buying a few toilet articles or garments.

It was through some of this purchasing that the most unpleasant incident of the days around Frederick arose. Complaint was made

18 W. W. Blackford's MS Memoirs, 206; 1, von Borcke, 197. The Official Records leave some doubt concerning the participants in the skirmish. Probably the clash was the end of an outpost affair in which the 3rd Indiana and 8th Illinois Cavalry had followed until after dark one of Hampton's regiments, which von Borcke remembered as the First North Carolina. See O. R., 19, pt. 1, p. 208.

19 Cooke's Jackson, 310.   20 Worsham, 138.
21 E. A. Moore, 130 ff.   22 Caldwell, 41.

to General Jackson that certain "foreigners" in his command, visiting a store, had been discourteous to ladies. Jackson concluded that if "foreigners" were involved, they must belong to one of the Louisiana regiments. He accordingly ordered General Starke to have his Louisiana Brigade form and march through Frederick, so that the miscreants could be identified for punishment. Starke, though Virginian by birth, was devoted to his Louisiana troops and was convinced that none of them was guilty. He had held them sternly in hand and previously he had arrested several of his officers for not controlling their men. In the belief that wrong was being done his men because some of them were French in appearance, he boldly refused to obey Jackson's order unless it was made applicable to all the troops who had been in town at the time the ladies had been affronted. Jackson, of course, ordered Starke under arrest, but fortunately a quarrel that might have become as bitter as the one between Jackson and Hill was avoided by the discovery that the offenders were not of Starke's command. The Louisianians subsequently asserted, with much satisfaction, that the men who had misbehaved were of Jackson's own Stonewall Brigade.[23]

While a courteous soldier was treated decently by virtually all the Marylanders, and was lionized by Southern sympathizers, the Army could not regard itself as welcome. Where hostility was not disclosed, public indifference was displayed.[24] Supplies of flour in the country around Frederick soon ran low.[25] Recruits from Maryland did not offer in numbers worth counting. Nowhere was there any movement to accept the help of the Confederates "in regaining the rights" of which Maryland had been "despoiled." [26] Some thoughtful leaders may have reasoned with Lee [27] that the people of the State would not rise, in any event, until there was assurance that the Confederate occupation would be prolonged, but most of the officers felt a biting, resentful disappointment. Removal from Frederick seemed desirable on all these accounts.

A final consideration for such a move was presented at Harpers Ferry. The expectation had been that when the Confederates entered Maryland, the Federals along the south side of the Potomac would be withdrawn to the vicinity of Washington as a re-

23 Monier's Diary, *Mil. An. La.*
24 *Cooke's Jackson*, 310.
25 *O. R.*, 19, pt. 2, pp. 596, 602
26 *O. R.*, 19, pt. 2, p. 602.
27 *Ibid.*, 596.

inforcement of the main army, which newspapers reported as
again under the command of General McClellan. No such evacuation of Harpers Ferry and nearby posts had occurred. Although
masked, they were held by the Federals.

As soon as Lee learned this, he asked himself whether he should
divert part of his forces to capture the towns the enemy still held
in Virginia, but at Longstreet's urging,[28] and perhaps for other
reasons, he deferred action. Now that he had to move to the
vicinity of Hagerstown, which from the outset he had intended
to occupy, he decided that a single wide-sweeping advance might
compass everything. While one column marched westward, another might envelop Harpers Ferry, take it, and then rejoin at
Hagerstown, whence communications with the Shenandoah Valley could be opened,[29] or, if circumstance justified, Pennsylvania
could be invaded.[30] With this in view, on September 9,[31] Lee
summoned Jackson to headquarters and, when "Stonewall" reported, Lee closed the flap of the tent and outlined his plan for
taking Harpers Ferry quickly. Jackson was to march with his
three Divisions and was to invest the town from the rear. Another
Division was to co-operate from Maryland Heights, which overlook the Ferry from North of the Potomac. A fifth Division was
to climb Loudoun Heights, across the Shenandoah from Harpers
Ferry. Surrounded, and subject to a triple fire, the arsenal town
and its garrison could be captured readily.

In the midst of this conversation, Longstreet came to Lee's tent
on other business. When he found Lee engaged, he started away;
but as Lee heard and recognized his voice, "Old Pete" was asked
to enter and was told then and there of the plan which otherwise
would have been explained to him at a separate interview. The
difference between his comment and Jackson's was revealing.

---

28 *Longstreet*, 201–02.   29 *O. R.*, 19, pt. 2, p. 603.

30 *Ibid.*, p. 592. This reference to Pennsylvania was made September 4. After Lee
entered Maryland, he did not often mention Pennsylvania in extant correspondence with
President Davis. On September 9 he wrote that he would move "in the direction I
originally intended, toward Hagerstown and Chambersburg" (*ibid.*, 603). As late as
September 12 (*ibid.*, 605), when his advance pickets were "at Middleburg, on the
Pennsylvania line," he told the President: "I await here the result of the movements
upon Harpers Ferry and Martinsburg." That was to say, the invasion of Pennsylvania
remained contingent. If Lee's hopes were correctly set forth in J. G. Walker's account of
an interview, the commanding General planned to push on to the Susquehanna while
McClellan cautiously reorganized the Federal army (see 2 *B. & L.* 604–05; 2 *R. E. Lee*,
362–63).

31 Or, possibly, on the 8th.

said to his staff, 'We evidently have no friends in this town.' The girls, abashed, turned away and lowered their tiny battle-flags." [35]

From Middletown, the column climbed Turner's Gap of South Mountain—no exacting pull for veterans who had crossed Massanutton and had surmounted Brown's and Swift Run in the Blue Ridge. A mile to the East of Boonsborough, Jackson called a halt in the evening and directed that his tent be pitched. The more sedate members of his staff were glad to stop with him and to wait while mulatto "Jeems" fried some bacon and boiled some coffee,[36] but the cavalry went on. With them rode Col. Bassett French, aide to the Governor of Virginia and attached temporarily to "Old Jack's" headquarters. The Colonel had bethought him to go into the village in the hope of getting a consoling, well-cooked supper. Perhaps—who knows?—he also may have desired a glass or two of something the General did not serve. After Colonel French went presently that young Adonis, Kyd Douglas, ostensibly to get information about the roads and fords. Jackson advised the younger officer against a visit to Boonsborough with no companion save one courier; but truth was that Douglas wanted to call on some maidens of the town and in their company to enjoy an evening more gracious than could be spent by Jackson's fire.

Jackson himself stayed at camp and, after a time, leading his horse, started on foot along the highway, probably to give the animal a bit of roadside grazing. Suddenly he saw coming over the hill toward him Douglas and the courier. They were riding fast. Douglas was hatless; his pistols were smoking. In chase of the staff officer and his companion was a troop of blue-coated cavalry, whom Douglas evidently had flushed. Jackson did not wait for further explanation than he could get at a glance. In a moment he was in the saddle and was spurring away. Without a word, he passed T. W. Latimer, a gallant soldier of the First Virginia Cavalry, who was rushing to assist Douglas and the courier.

As they saw Latimer approaching, the two Confederates halted and yelled as if they were calling to other troopers, and then the three wheeled and charged. After a moment of hesitation, the Federals wheeled, too, and went as they had come—only to run

---

[35] *Douglas,* 152.
[36] In the history of culinary art it must be remembered that few Confederate soldiers accounted coffee "fit to drink" until it had boiled five minutes.

into Lieutenant Payne's men who, at the sound of firing, had started from the other side of town.

Jackson drew rein as soon as the Federals were driven off, and when Kyd Douglas finally came back to camp, after sharing Payne's chase of the enemy, the General had congratulations, tinged ever so lightly with sarcasm, for the speed of Douglas's horse. Thereupon the young man produced Jackson's gloves which, he blandly said, he had picked up in the road. "Old Jack" had to smile at this mute but dusty evidence that he, too, had not stood on the order of his going.[37] As for Colonel French, that dignitary turned up later, somewhat besmudged, and had to tell a humiliating tale of being interrupted over his glass and plate in the hotel dining-room by the approach of the Federals. A friendly Negro had hustled him off to the dark security of—ahem—the coal cellar of the establishment.[38]

Powell Hill, all the while, had ridden at the rear of his Division but had not received copies of orders. If he knew anything of what Lee had planned and Jackson was about to execute, it was through the kindness of some friend and not through any confidences of Jackson. The General, in fact, ignored the officer in arrest; but when Jackson's column crossed back into Virginia, by way of Light's Ford on the Potomac,[39] Hill drew his own soldierly conclusion: a battle was brewing, perhaps more than one. He must have a hand in the fighting; but how? Soon he thought of Kyd Douglas, who seemed at the moment to be closest to Jackson because of intimate acquaintance with the terrain.

Douglas must help. Hill sent for the young man and explained his request. He made no apologies, though he voiced no defiance. His application simply was that his arrest be suspended and that he be restored to command for the duration of the pending actions. When the battles were over, he would report himself in arrest again. Douglas agreed to present Hill's case. Jackson listened and, without argument or explanation, assented. He knew how admirably Hill led his troops in battle and, no doubt, he felt a measure of relief that the most experienced of his commanders was again to be available. Branch was notified promptly that Hill was released from arrest and was to resume command of his Divi-

[37] This is merely rewritten from *Douglas*, 152 ff.
[38] *Ibid.*, 153.   [39] *O. R.*, 19, pt. 1, p. 953.

sion. All instructions relative to the force were to be turned over to Hill.[40]

Jackson proceeded then to make a wide sweep in the hope of catching the Federal garrison in Martinsburg, but the bluecoats slipped through his closing net and reached the larger force that was holding Harpers Ferry. The Confederates on the 12th entered Martinsburg. In that friendly town the soldiers consumed an incredible quantity of food,[41] and enjoyed themselves vastly, but Jackson had another embarrassing personal reception. Every person in town, it seemed to his staff, was determined to shake hands with the General. Children tore open a window in the hotel parlor where he took refuge. With affectionate cries, they threw roses at him. He had, ere long, to make the best of his plight. Smilingly he surrendered and told his attendants to "admit the ladies." Almost on the instant, he was overwhelmed. Both his hands were wrung, buttons were cut from his uniform, autographs were solicited. His muffled "Thank you, thank you, you're very kind" was drowned in the chatter. He seemed in a fair way of being stripped.

At length, to quote Kyd Douglas, "one woman, more venturous, hinted for a lock of hair—of which he had no superabundant supply." That alarmed Jackson. He "drew the line and put an end to the interview." [42] Except for a dinner with friends, he ventured no further reception that day. About "10 o'clock on the following morning (13th)," as he later reported, "the head of our column came in view of the enemy drawn up in force upon Bolivar Heights." [43] Of the success of the impending attack, there could be no doubt. "Harpers Ferry," a Federal officer subsequently said in disgust, "is represented as an immense stronghold—'a Gibraltar.'" Instead, he maintained, it "was a complete slaughter-pen." [44] The sole question was the familiar one of time. That same question was about to assume for D. H. Hill, on other ground, a mien more threatening than it bore at the junction of the Potomac and the Shenandoah.

[40] O. R., 19, pt. 2, p. 604. Douglas, op. cit., 158, supplied new details but misdated the incident.
[41] Cf. Caldwell, op. cit., 42: "I doubt not I saw a ton of bread devoured that day."
[42] Outside, his horse's mane and tail were being thinned by souvenir-hunters who did not realize the animal was a chance mount and not the Little Sorrel.
[43] O. R., 19, pt. 1, p. 953.
[44] Capt. Henry M. Binney in 5 Moore's Rebellion Record, 444.

CHAPTER X

HARVEY HILL'S BATTLE

THE DAY OF Jackson's march through Middletown, September 10, witnessed the removal of virtually all the other Confederate infantry to the West of the Blue Ridge, which in that part of Maryland is styled South Mountain. Lee's plan had been to hold Longstreet and D. H. Hill temporarily at Boonsborough in order to block Federal retreat in that direction from Harpers Ferry; but these dispositions had to be changed before they could be executed.

Rumors came of an impending Federal advance from Pennsylvania to Hagerstown, which Lee had selected as his advance base for operations toward the Susquehanna. Vague though the rumors were, they represented a possibility so sound strategically that precautions had to be taken. Besides, a large supply of flour and some other military supplies were believed to be in Hagerstown. These the enemy must not be permitted to seize.[1] Longstreet was directed not to end his march at Boonsborough but to leave D. H. Hill there and to press on to Hagerstown with the remainder of his force.[2] This meant thirteen miles on a warm day through dust that choked[3]—a prospect that did not please Longstreet. "General," he complained to Lee, "I wish we could stand still and let the damned Yankees come to us."[4] It was to no purpose. The march had to be made, though at the march's end there was not even the satisfaction of punishing the enemy. All was quiet at Hagerstown. Reconnaissance northward did not so much as uncover a vidette.

If the feet of thousands were made weary by so futile a march, the pride of a few soldiers was gratified. A man in the ranks might do without a blanket or an oilcloth. Shoes he might forgo in summer when his native soles were hardened, but a hat of some sort he must have. Loss of headgear he considered a personal

---

[1] See *infra*, Appendix VII.　　　　[2] *O. R.*, 19, pt. 1, pp. 145, 839.
[3] *Hotchkiss' MS Diary*, 85; *Pendleton*, 212.
[4] Lee to William Allan, *infra*, Appendix I.

calamity. Often a man risked his life to save his hat, which was at once his protection against sun and rain and, somehow, in that Army, the badge of his manhood. Quickly at Hagerstown, those who could do so purchased hats from the reluctant merchants, whose stock in so small a town was as "five loaves" for the multitude.

It chanced that one Hagerstown dealer, years previously, had been tempted to a reckless gamble on public taste, or else had been allured by what seemed to be a great bargain: he had acquired a gross or more of beaver hats with long nap. Unhappily, these had sold so ill to burgher and to farmer that about a hundred of them, bell crowned and old fashioned, remained on the shelves. When the Confederates arrived, they purchased all other hats the merchant had and then, boy like, they began to "try on" the beavers. So comical were those lofty headpieces that the laughing soldiers bought every one of them, and, so bedizened, took their places in the ranks or on the caissons. Jeering and cheers and the hoary shout, "Come out from under that hat" greeted the proud wearers, who, it safely may be assumed, thereupon perched their beavers at angles more arrogant and stuck out their chests.[5]

Not many hours were to pass before some of the owners of those beavers were to wear them into battle. At Boonsborough, where D. H. Hill had been left with the rearguard, trouble began to brew. Hill had been told[6] that his mission was, in his own words, "to dispose of my troops so as to prevent the escape of the Yankees from Harpers Ferry, then besieged, and also to guard the pass in the Blue Ridge near Boonsborough."[7] The first part of these orders entailed, primarily, the guarding of the roads that led northward from Maryland Heights on the Potomac.

To the Heights, it will be remembered, McLaws's march was directed. R. H. Anderson's Division was in the same column. These two were to force the surrender of Harpers Ferry, which Jackson and Walker were to assail from the South and East.[8] If any part of the defenders of the Ferry escaped into Maryland, they

---

[5] *Owen*, 136. It scarcely need be added that, as a divertissement, Owen's brief account is here expanded.

[6] Hill's language, *O. R.*, 19, pt. 1, p. 1019, would indicate that orders to this effect were given him "on the 13th," but in the chronological form of the report, six paragraphs, close together, begin: "On the" specified date. The orders almost certainly had been given prior to the 13th, though they became more important that day.

[7] *O. R.*, 19, pt. 1, p. 1019.   [8] Cf. *O. R.*, 19, pt. 2, p. 603, § 5.

would enter a natural "V". The western face was formed by the Potomac, which flowed at that point from Northwest to Southeast. On the opposite side of the "V", South Mountain ran down to the river. Hill was based on Boonsborough, in the upper center of the angle between river and range, where he could reach out

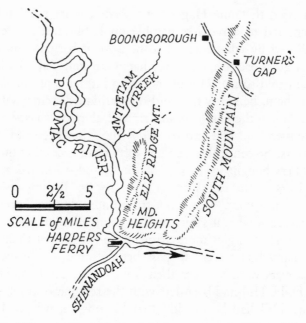

The "V" on the Maryland side of the Potomac opposite Harpers Ferry

with his regiments and gather in any Federals who might elude McLaws.

As for the second part of Hill's orders, the general plan of the Confederates did not contemplate any long defense of South Mountain.[9] McClellan was East of the range, watched by the cavalry, but he was advancing so slowly that the capture of Harpers Ferry by Jackson before the Federal Army reached the mountain seemed almost certain. If Harpers Ferry were taken ere McClellan could relieve the post, did not good strategy dictate an effort to draw McClellan West of the undefended mountain? The longer his communications, needless to say, the greater the Confederates' advantage in dealing with him.

[9] Lee in O. R., 19, pt. 1, p. 145.

On the basis of this reasoning at headquarters [10] Harvey Hill had been instructed. From headquarters three miles West of Turner's Gap,[11] the principal pass of South Mountain, Hill spread his outposts, but his vigilance was altogether toward the South, whither the roads from Harpers Ferry led. To the possibility of attack from the East, he gave little thought. In three days at Boonsborough he did not ride back to the mountains even once to study how, if an emergency crashed upon him, he might defend Turner's Gap.

This was not merely another familiar instance of a soldier's concentration of thought on the sector of assumed danger, to the neglect of precautions elsewhere. Harvey Hill relied on "Jeb" Stuart. East of South Mountain and of Catoctin, which is a still lower range between Frederick and Washington, the Confederate cavalry faced on all the roads the slowly advancing Federals. Stuart was in general command of an ample, vigilant force. Besides Fitz Lee's men and the Laurel Brigade, Stuart now could employ Hampton who, as noted already, had come up from Richmond with his troopers. The South Carolinian was in his grimmest fighting mood. At Burkittsville, during a brisk little action, he snatched off his overcoat and threw it to his son, who was riding with him. "Take care of my overcoat, Preston," he said and, drawing his saber, spurred into the fire. His high-spirited boy flung the garment into a fence corner and followed him where the squadrons clashed. "I've come to Maryland to fight Yankees," Preston explained later, "and not to carry Father's overcoat." [12] That was the spirit for which men loved the Hamptons and the spirit for which the South Carolinian was welcome.

Not quite so cordial, perhaps, had been a recent farewell. On September 5, Beverley Robertson had been ordered to report to the Department of North Carolina "where," the orders read, "his services are indispensably necessary for the organization and instruction of cavalry troops . . ." [13] His Brigade passed tempo-

[10] Ibid., 145.   [11] 2 B. & L., 560.

[12] 25 S. H. S. P., 148. For an example of South Carolina's confidence in him, see Carolina Times, n.d., quoted in Richmond Whig, Aug. 12, 1862, p. 2, col. 2. The sketch of Hampton is continued infra, p. 281 and Chap. XXV.

[13] O. R., 19, pt. 2, p. 595. McDonald, op. cit., 74, remarked: ". . . The Brigade won fame for the commander and not the commander for the Brigade." Longstreet subsequently noted that Robertson "was not deemed a very efficient officer in the field and was therefore relieved from duty with the Army of Northern Virginia" (O. R., 18, 900). Col. W. W Blackford noted in June, 1863, that Robertson was an excellent man

rarily to its senior Colonel, Tom Munford, who sought to do his full part in the skirmishing, though he could not overcome immediately the discord and bickering that had developed in the ranks of the old "Laurel Brigade." [14]

These three cavalry Brigades, by the early afternoon of September 13, were subjected to so much pressure from a heavy force of Federal infantry that they had to yield the Catoctin range and retreat to South Mountain. Stuart always withdrew reluctantly from the presence of the enemy, but in this instance he had no special concern. Through D. H. Hill, he notified G.H.Q. of his withdrawal, and he counselled Hill to watch Turner's Gap, which was the principal pass of South Mountain. Guard of the pass was regarded by Stuart as a precaution—and no more—because he thought that Harpers Ferry already had surrendered. He reasoned that Jackson, Walker, McLaws and Anderson soon would be on their way to rejoin Lee, and that no bullets need be wasted in defending South Mountain.

On receipt of the news from Stuart of the cavalry withdrawal toward the ridge, Hill ordered Col. A. H. Colquitt to carry his Brigade to Turner's Gap and to support Stuart. Colquitt's troops were seasoned and reliable. Part of them had belonged originally to Rains's Brigade and part to the old Manassas Garrison. As reinforcement of Colquitt, if needed, Garland's Brigade was ordered to make ready but was not told to reach the mountain top on the evening of the 13th. The remaining Brigades of D. H. Hill's Division were drawn closer to Boonsborough.[15] Hill himself remained three miles from the Gap,[16] and did not ride up that evening to

to train troops but that, in the presence of the enemy, "he lost all self-possession and was perfectly unreliable" (*MS Memoirs,* 336). General Lee himself believed that Robertson could be useful as a cavalry instructor. For Robertson's unhappy experiences in North Carolina during the next months, see *infra,* Chap. XXIX, and *O. R.,* 18, 121, 189, 891, 1007–08, 1059, 1071, 1074, 1088; 25, pt. 2, pp. 820–21.

[14] On October 7, unattached companies of cavalry, to the number of six, serving with Robertson's former Brigade, were organized as the Seventeenth Virginia Cavalry, under Lt. Col. O. R. Funsten. For the minor cavalry affairs of September 8–12, see *O. R.,* 19, pt. 1, p. 815 ff., 822–23, 825. Gen. J. D. Cox, in 2 *B. & L.,* 584, commended the account in 1 *von Borcke,* 203–04, to "those who have a fancy for learning how Munchausen could have told" the story.

[15] In *O. R.,* 19, pt. 1, p. 1019, and later in 2 *B. & L.,* 560, General Hill was under the impression that he sent Garland to Turner's Pass at the time Colquitt advanced, but Judge Geo. D. Gratton, who was Colquitt's aide, summarized the evidence and proved in 39 *S. H. S. P.,* 34–35, that Garland did not start for the mountain until later and did not arrive until about sunrise on the 14th. Hill indirectly set himself right in 13 *S. H. S. P.,* 422.

[16] 2 *B. & L.,* 560.

make reconnaissance. His eyes still were on the roads by which the Federals might retreat from Harpers Ferry.

After night had settled—a chilly night though the day had been warm—Hill received a curious message from Colquitt, who by that time was on the eastern side of Turner's Gap and well up toward the crest. Since darkness, said Colquitt, the campfires of the enemy had been lighted below him farther and farther toward the Federal rear. Many more fires were visible than would have been required for the two Brigades of cavalry that were, in Stuart's opinion, the only Union troops approaching the mountain.[17]

This news alarmed Hill. In an excited state of mind, he forwarded to Lee all the information he had received.[18] About midnight,[19] he received from Hagerstown a dispatch that probably was an answer to his report on the situation. Lee knew that Harpers Ferry had not yet been captured, and he could not disregard the possibility that a vigorous advance by the main Federal army might sweep past McLaws on Maryland Heights and relieve the town. Then, while the Confederates still were divided—Jackson and Walker South of the Potomac—McClellan might turn and attack the Divisions North of the river.

The one sure way of preventing this was to hold the passes of South Mountain against the advancing Federals. A defensive barrier that Lee had planned to disregard, in order to lure McClellan westward, suddenly had become indispensable to the plan of operations. Specifically, in new instructions, Lee ordered Hill to cooperate with Stuart in holding the passes. There followed a sentence that showed how seriously Lee regarded the situation. Longstreet's troops, said the commanding General, were returning from Hagerstown to join in the defense.[20]

[17] Judge Grattan in 39 *S. H. S. P.*, 36.

[18] E. C. Gordon, MS *Memorandum of conversation with General Lee, Feb. 15, 1868.* For the history of the interesting document, see Appendix I.

[19] 2 *B. & L.*, 560.

[20] The text of Lee's dispatch to D. H. Hill is not known to be in existence, but it was not so full, from the very nature of the risks of transmission, as the explanation in the text might indicate. Lee's reasoning is reconstructed from *O. R.*, 19, pt. 1, p. 140, 146. Hill remembered the letter as stating in effect that Lee "was not satisfied with the condition of things on the turnpike or National Road, and directing me to go in person to Turner's Gap the next morning and assist Stuart in its defence" (2 *B. & L.*, 560). Longstreet did not think it wise to return to South Mountain and urged that instead of ordering this, Lee should direct D. H. Hill to fall back and to join the remainder of the army at Sharpsburg. Subsequently, Longstreet wrote: "Lee listened patiently enough, but did not change his plans . . . After lying down, my mind was still on the battle of the next day, and I was so impressed with the thought that it would be impossible

When Hill read this letter, he had not seen Stuart, though the Chief of Cavalry continued to transmit through him all the dispatches forwarded to G.H.Q. Already, with a start, Hill had become conscious of his ignorance of the ground he was to defend and he hurriedly had dispatched General Ripley to Stuart[21] for information about the passes. Stuart felt some surprise, which he subsequently voiced in his report, that Hill was so poorly acquainted with the country.[22] Perhaps, also, Stuart was amused that the infantryman most notorious in the Army for his contemptuous sarcasms regarding the mounted arm should send to him for facts; but, he wrote later, "all the information I had was cheerfully given, and the situation of the gaps explained by map."[23] Among other things, Stuart doubtless told Ripley that he had left Col. Tom Rosser with a detachment of cavalry and the Stuart Horse Artillery to occupy Braddock's, also known as Fox's Gap, which was a mile and more to the South of Turner's Gap. Stuart no doubt explained, also, his intention of going southward to Crampton's Gap. That pass was on the shortest route

for us to do anything at South Mountain, with the fragments of a worn and exhausted command, that I rose and . . . wrote a note to General Lee, urging him to order Hill away and concentrate at Sharpsburg. To that note I got no answer, and the next morning I marched as directed" (2 B. & L., 665–66). No mention of this occurs in Lee's account of the events of the night. He merely said that he wakened Longstreet during the night. See Appendix I.

21 "About midnight," said Stuart. O. R., 19, pt. 1, p. 817.

22 As set forth in Appendix I, General Lee remarked in 1868 that Stuart was "very indignant" over the "lost order." Whether Stuart and Hill were at odds before the battle is not certain, but their failure to hold more than one consultation on the 13th may have been due to lack of cordiality.

23 O. R., 19, pt. 1, p. 817. D. H. Hill traditionally is supposed to have been the General who affirmed that he never had seen a cavalryman dead on the field of battle. Actually, Hill's complaint was less against the cavalry as an arm of the service than against incompetent leaders and inefficient use of mounted forces. While Hill was on semi-independent duty in North Carolina, in February, 1863, he wrote Secretary Seddon about the "wonderfully inefficient Brigade" of Robertson, but in proposing to trade it for Hampton's Brigade, he said, "If [Hampton] were in this State the Yankees would hug their gunboats everywhere" (O. R., 18, 891). In his address of February 25 to his troops, Hill exhibited in this remarkable paragraph his opinion of cavalry in general and, more vehemently, of the negligent mounted forces under his command: "The cavalry constitute the eyes and ears of the army. The safety of the entire command depends upon their vigilance and the faithfulness of their reports. The officers and men who permit themselves to be surprised deserve to die, and the commanding general will spare no effort to secure them their deserts. Almost equally criminal are the scouts who through fright bring in wild and sensational reports. They will be court martialed for cowardice. Many opportunities will be afforded to the cavalry to harass the enemy, cut off his supplies, drive in his pickets &c. Those who have never been in battle will thus be enabled to enjoy the novel sensation of listening to the sound of hostile shot and shell, and those who have listened a great way off will be allowed to come some miles nearer, and compare the sensation caused by the distant cannonade with that produced by the rattle of musketry" (O. R., 18, 895).

from McClellan's position to Harpers Ferry and, for that reason, was "as much threatened as any other" crossing of the mountains.[24]

During the night, Stuart received strange news from an unexpected visitor. A Southern sympathizer, residing in Frederick, reached him after a hard, hurried ride and informed him that McClellan had found in Frederick the previous afternoon a copy of Lee's order of September 9 for the movement of the various Divisions. In other words, according to Stuart's visitor, McClellan knew that the Confederate Army was divided and knew what forces had been detached for the capture of Harpers Ferry. Possession of that information would explain why McClellan, who usually proceeded most deliberately, seemed to be pushing westward fast.

Stuart probably was not alarmed by this disclosure. Still in the belief that Harpers Ferry already had been captured,[25] he reasoned that the Army would be reunited before the Federals could do great mischief; but he promptly forwarded to Lee the humiliating intelligence that McClellan was aware of the organization of the columns that had been dispatched to the mouth of the Shenandoah.

Whether Stuart received this information in time to explain it to Ripley, or whether he forwarded it later in the night to D. H. Hill, the records do not show. The facts, in any event, were substantially as they were reported to Stuart by the friendly Marylander. Soon after noon on September 13, Private B. W. Mitchell of the 27th Indiana Infantry had picked up in Frederick, on ground that D. H. Hill's troops had occupied, a crude package of three cigars. Around these was wrapped a paper. When Mitchell took it off, he observed handwriting on it and, upon closer examination, he saw that he had a copy of S. O. 191, Army of Northern Virginia. This was addressed to Maj.-Gen. D. H. Hill and was marked "Official, R. H. Chilton, A.A.G." Mitchell realized his find might be important and, in company with his Sergeant, he went immediately to his Colonel, who carried the paper to divisional headquarters. There, unluckily for the Confederates, the

[24] The quoted words are from Stuart's report, O. R., 19, pt. 1, p. 817. Before many hours, Stuart was satisfied that the Federal effort would be directed against McLaws and probably by way of Crampton's. Ibid.

[25] O. R., 19, pt. 1, p. 817.

staff officer on duty was a former friend of Chilton's and was able to identify the autograph. Probably from about 2 P.M. McClellan had the authenticated paper in his own hands and could act in documented assurance of what the Confederate plans had been on September 9, though he did not realize that only D. H. Hill, instead of the entire force of Longstreet, had been left at Boonsborough.[26]

After this unhappy night, Hill rode to Turner's Gap at dawn of the 14th of September. It was to be his day of opportunity, his first day of direct command of an entire field where large forces were engaged. On the mountain, at the moment, he had no other troops than Colquitt's Brigade, though Garland's North Carolinians were toiling up and were close to the crest. Three other Brigades Hill had, George B. Anderson's, Ripley's and the depleted but still magnificent Alabama regiments of Robert Rodes. These troops, about 3000 in number, were disposable, but Hill could not rid his mind of the possible escape from Harpers Ferry of the garrison Jackson was surrounding. His orders were so to dispose his troops as to prevent escape from Harpers Ferry *and* to guard the pass near Boonsborough. Somehow, he still could not attach the same weight to both parts of his orders. Stuart had said that two Brigades only had been following the Confederate troopers the previous day: Hill apparently did not regard seriously at dawn Colquitt's report of the previous evening concerning the vast number of campfires that could be seen from the pass. Even the fact that Lee was hastening back to South Mountain with Longstreet's troops did not convince Hill that a heavy thrust might be impending.

Soon enough, in a quick succession of surprises, the seriousness of his plight was disclosed. Hill had expected to find Stuart on South Mountain; instead, he received a message that the cavalryman had gone farther southward to Crampton's.[27] The resourceful trooper would not be with him to counsel or to share responsibility. That was not the worst of it. Colquitt was hopeful that the enemy had retired; but when Hill and he rode along the crest to reconnoiter, soon after sunrise, they scarcely had gone three-quarters of a mile before they could hear the rumbling of wheels

[26] See Appendix I. [27] Hill in 2 *B. & L.*, 561.

and the voices of Federal officers. The enemy was on the mountain, up the ridges and almost on the crest![28] If the Federals got much farther, they could flank Turner's Gap. South of it, a road

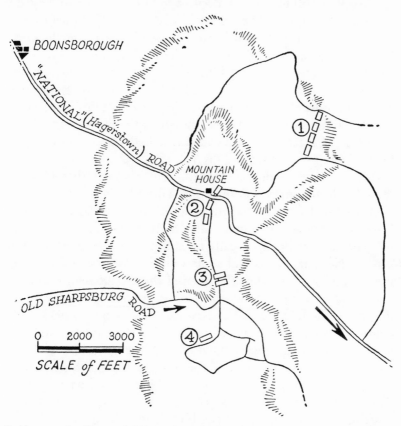

Positions on the Crest and Ridges of South Mountain, Sept. 14, 1862. (1) Rodes's advanced position; (2) Colquitt; (3) Hood in the late afternoon; (4) Garland's morning position—after 2 *B. & L.*, 568

crossed at Fox's Gap, whence several trails ran along the ridge toward the main highway through Turner's Gap. North of the pass were several higher knobs, cut by ravines and approached by several roads, one of which might be practicable for artillery.[29]

[28] *Ibid.*, 562; O. R., 19, pt. 1, pp. 1019–20.

[29] The map on p. 568 of 2 *B. & L.* is the one to consult for a ready understanding of the position. That in O. R. *Atlas,* Plate XXVII, 3, shows the contours but lacks graphic quality.

"Examination of the pass," Hill later reported, ". . . satisfied me
that it could only be held by a large force, and was wholly inde-
fensible by a small one." [30]

What was Hill to do? He decided to bring up a third Brigade,
G. B. Anderson's, and to dispatch a regiment of Ripley's to an
obscure gap to the northward. More than this, even when he knew
that the Federals were almost atop the mountain and beyond his
flank, Hill could not bring himself to do. "I felt reluctant," he
wrote in his official account of the battle, "to order up Ripley and
Rodes from the important positions they were holding until something definite were known of the strength and design of the
Yankees." [31] He did not state what he desired more "definite" than
the evidence brought him by his own ears.

Until George Anderson arrived, Hill planned that Colquitt
should hold the ground dominating Turner's Gap, and that Garland should defend the right. Colquitt already was in position.
Garland was ready to move. Since Malvern Hill, he had fought
no major action, but spiritually he had prepared himself for new
battles. New happiness had come to him, too. Social Richmond
was expecting at any time the news of the engagement to him of
one of the loveliest and most brilliant daughters of the city.[32] On
this day of danger, he had arrived early at Colquitt's field headquarters, had drunk a cup of coffee with the Colonel, and had
learned from that officer something of the ground. At Hill's
order, he led out along one of the obscure and narrow roads on
the western flank of the mountains his North Carolina regiments.
Some of these troops were green, but two of the regiments had
been Jubal Early's in the brave, blundering charge at Williamsburg, four months previously. The task assigned them now was
to hold at any cost the road that crossed at Fox's Gap and uncovered Turner's Gap. On keeping the enemy from getting control
of this road, Hill told Garland, the safety of General Lee's wagon
train depended.[33]

Garland swept through a belt of woods and soon met Col.
Thomas Rosser who, with some dismounted men and part of the
horse artillery, was awaiting further orders at Fox's Gap.[34] Pleased

---

[30] *O. R.*, 19, pt. 1, p. 1019.   [31] *Ibid.*, 1020.
[32] 39 *S. H. S. P.*, 35; *Ham Chamberlayne*, 111–12.   [33] 2 *B. & L.*, 562.
[34] Stuart gave it the older, more historic name, Braddock's Gap. *O. R.*, 19, pt. 1,
p. 817.

to find these stout soldiers at hand, Garland posted them and then deployed his own infantry. He sought, it would appear, to place his veteran regiments where they would meet the shock and to station on ground less contested those of his men who never had been in action.[35]

Reconnaissance established contact about 9 o'clock. In a few minutes a jumbled battle was joined. The Federals attacked vigorously and in strength, and seemed to have full knowledge of the ground. Everywhere that Garland attempted to advance, he met fierce fire. Where he stood on the defensive, the Federals massed. Almost from the initial clash, Garland was hard put to hold his own. Some of his Colonels were bewildered. The raw troops were brave and willing, but they scarcely knew what to do. Ere long, the drift of the fighting indicated that the enemy was trying to turn the flank of the Thirteenth North Carolina, with which Garland was standing.

"General," said Lt. Col. Thomas Ruffin, "why do you stay here? You are in great danger."

The fire was heavy at the moment,[36] but it seemed not to trouble Garland at all. "I may as well be here as yourself," he answered, casually.

"No," said Ruffin, "it is my duty to be here with my regiment, but you could better superintend your Brigade from a safer position."

Scarcely were the words spoken than Ruffin was struck. Coolly he turned to the General and remarked that if he had to leave the position, he would have to ask Garland to send someone to lead the regiment, because he was the sole field officer present with it. Garland calmly gave to one of his staff an order nobody else heard. In another moment, he himself dropped to the ground. One glance at him by the men who knelt to lift him showed that his wound was mortal. Already he was in his death spasm.[37]

Word of the fate of Garland was brought to Hill soon after he had examined from a lookout the Federals advancing toward him. The spectacle had stirred his fighting blood. After twenty years he wrote of it: "The marching columns extended back far as eye could see in the distance; but many of the troops had already

---

[35] Cf. McRae in O.R., 19, pt. 1, p. 1040.   [36] O. R., 19, pt. 1, p. 1046.
[37] 2 B. & L., 563–64.

arrived and were in double lines of battle, and those advancing were taking up positions as fast as they arrived. It was a grand and glorious spectacle, and it was impossible to look at it without admiration. I had never seen so tremendous an army before, and I did not see one like it afterward." [38]

Hill's emotions as he looked at the powerful blue columns about to be launched against him were strangely confused. He realized that his Division could be overpowered in time, but he had satisfaction in the thought that McClellan was attacking at the wrong place. Had McClellan turned southward and thrown his full strength against one of the thinly guarded lower gaps in the mountain, the Federal commander could have interposed between Lee and Jackson and perhaps with results too appalling to contemplate. The Confederate infantry might have cut their way out, but the wagon trains almost certainly would have been lost. As it was, Hill reasoned that if he could hold the gap till Longstreet arrived, their joint resistance might allow time for the wagons to get across the Potomac, or for Jackson to complete the capture of Harpers Ferry, or even for both these things to happen.

These consoling reflections were marred as soon as formed. Up the mountain from the southward rolled the sound of artillery fire. Listening between the throbs of field pieces not many miles away, Hill could catch the pulsing of more distant guns. Were two battles in progress? Where were they? Concerning the farther sound, Hill could hazard no guess. The nearer, he feared, might indicate that McClellan was forcing his way over the mountains, between Boonsborough and Harpers Ferry, and was attempting to cut Lee's Army in half.

A few minutes later, Hill had to turn all his thought to his own battle. He learned that Garland's Brigade had been broken. One small, green regiment had been driven from the field, though a few of its men rallied on the Thirteenth North Carolina. With the loss of some 200 prisoners, the other regiments were pushed steadily back and soon were too scattered to be of further use that day. Hill could not afford to move Colquitt to assist the remnant of Garland's command. No other troops yet had arrived at the top of the mountain. The best that Hill could do was to run out two guns and, with the flank regiment of Colquitt and a scratch

[38] 2 B. & L., 564.

contingent of "staff-officers, couriers, teamsters and cooks," to give some semblance of support to the artillery. Hill recorded later in a few revelatory words his sensations at the moment: "I do not remember ever to have experienced a feeling of greater *loneliness*. It seemed as though we were deserted by 'all the world and the rest of mankind.' " [39]

If Hill, however lonely, was to prevent the turning of his flank and the loss of his position, he had to forgo his purpose of continuing to guard with Ripley and with Rodes the route from Harpers Ferry to Boonsborough. The two Brigades across the line of the garrison's possible retreat must be ordered to join him as soon as they could climb South Mountain. He had waited too long already in sending for them. [40] Anderson was on his way. Not until 2 o'clock at the very earliest, and probably not until 3, could Rodes and Ripley reach the crest and complete the concentration of the Division in front of the enemy.

As for reinforcements, Longstreet had thirteen miles to cover from Hagerstown to Boonsborough on a hot day, over dusty roads. Even for veteran troops, that march would require approximately nine hours. Hill could be sure that Lee would press to his relief, but he did not know at what hour Longstreet started, and he could do no more than guess the time of arrival. His plight appeared well-nigh hopeless. Four Federal Corps, Hill estimated, were spread eastward from the crest of South Mountain. He had, at the moment, only Colquitt, the contingent under Rosser, a few guns [41] and the broken regiments of Garland. If the Union commanders realized how weak he was, they could destroy him.

Hill set himself for the worst; the Stuart Horse Artillery and

[39] 2 *B. & L.*, 566.

[40] Nowhere in his report or in the article he wrote for 2 *B. & L.* did Hill state the time of the issuance of these orders to Ripley and to Rodes. In general, it may be said that the arrival of Hill's troops, and most of the incidents of the action, were considerably later than usually has been assumed. Ripley stated that he was ordered about 9 A. M. to send up his artillery and that "soon after" he was directed to advance his infantry, but he reported that he was taking position when Drayton arrived (*O. R.*, 19, pt. 1, p. 1031). That could not have been prior to 3.30 at earliest (see *infra*, n. 50). Rodes said in his report that he got his orders "toward noon" (*O. R.*, 19, pt. 1, p. 1032). If "toward noon" be 11.00–11.30, a dispatch to him from field headquarters would have been given the courier not later than 10 or 10.30.

[41] Hill's report, *O. R.*, 19, pt. 1, p. 1020, would indicate that Bondurant was not employed until the arrival of Anderson, but the account by Hill in 2 *B. & L.*, 563, states that the battery went into action with Garland; which, needless to say, was the logical arrangement.

Bondurant's Battery put up much show of defiance; the flankers on Colquitt's right made inquisitive heads dodge quickly. The scattered little force waited for the overwhelming blow. It did not come. On Hill's right, the Federals could not believe they had cleared the crest. From the vigor of the artillery fire, and from what they could see through the underbrush, they thought the graycoats in heavy numbers had taken up a strong position.[42] To storm this successfully, the officers of the leading Division decided to wait for the arrival of more men. On Hill's left, the Federals had not yet woven their way through the ravines and ridges that covered the approaches to the main highway.[43] An incredible, a well-nigh miraculous delay there was. For the two hours from noon onward, when Hill most nearly was helpless, he had the mercy of a general lull.[44] Critics might have said that he was luckier than he deserved to be.

Before 2 o'clock, that stalwart Brigadier, George B. Anderson, had climbed to the pass and had filed to the right. Rodes and his fine Alabamians, including Col. John B. Gordon's distinguished Sixth, then were pressing toward the crest and, almost contemptuously, were striding past Ripley's well-blown Georgians and North Carolinians, who were halted to give them the road. By Hill's order, Rodes turned to the left and made for an eminence, well to the front, which it was manifest the enemy was preparing to seize. Ripley followed G. B. Anderson to the right but had difficulty in reaching his position.

Although his force still was feeble, Hill now had greater defensive strength than he had commanded at any time during the day. His prospect was less desperate. Word had come that Longstreet's troops were nearing Boonsborough. Hill's answer was a request that "Old Pete" hurry.[45] As the Federals seemed to be massing rapidly, Hill was anxious to assail them on his reinforced right, before they delivered their major blow, which he thought was apt to come on his left.[46]

As Ripley was fumbling through the mountain laurel, seeking the left flank of G. B. Anderson, the head of D. R. Jones's Divi-

---

[42] Cf. Brig. Gen. Jacob D. Cox's report, O. R., 19, pt. 1, p. 459.
[43] Cf. Hooker in O. R., 19, pt. 1, p. 215; Meade in ibid., 266-67.
[44] O. R., 19, pt. 1, p. 459.   [45] O. R., 19, pt. 1, p. 1020.
[46] Ibid.

sion of Longstreet's command climbed up the ridge from Boons-borough. Drayton was in advance. Behind him for miles spread the other Brigades.[47] Road weary they were after their all day struggle with heat and thirst and dust. The exhaustion of the weak and the straggling of the lazy had depleted regiments to battalions, to companies even. In the Eighth Virginia of Pickett's Brigade, the gallant Eppa Hunton's regiment, not more than thirty-four men were ready for action. In the Fifty-sixth, there were eighty muskets.[48]

Thin though they were, Drayton's Brigade and G. T. ("Tige") Anderson's, which followed it, immediately were placed under D. H. Hill's orders and were sent southward toward Fox's Gap. Hill rode down the ridge in the same direction, brought "Tige" Anderson, Ripley and Drayton together and explained that he wished them to attack in line with G. B. Anderson.[49] As the senior, Ripley assumed command of the four Brigades and attempted to deploy them. George B. Anderson was to be on the right, next was Ripley's own Brigade, next "Tige" Anderson, and, on the left, Drayton.[50]

Before Drayton could form, or G. T. Anderson close on Rip-ley's left, Ripley unwisely ordered an advance. It collided almost at once with an advancing Federal force, which quickly pene-trated the gap between G. T. Anderson and Drayton. Soon "Tige" Anderson found both his flanks in the air. Drayton's men were driven. Ripley's Brigade in some fashion was squeezed out of the line or was misdirected. For a time, it could do nothing. G. B. Anderson, as always, fought vigorously but accomplished little against such odds as he faced.

The whole effort, incompetently directed, soon was in baffling confusion. Then, toward evening, the tired troops saw what experienced, intelligent and determined leadership could accom-

---

[47] Jones was commanding that day his own Division and those Brigades of Long-street's Division which had been under Brig. Gen. J. L. Kemper at Second Manassas. Toombs's Brigade of D. R. Jones's Division had been left at Hagerstown. For a few days, Toombs had been in charge of his own, Drayton's and "Tige" Anderson's Bri-gades. See *O. R.*, 19, pt. 1, p. 888.

[48] *O. R.*, 19, pt. 1, pp. 898, 903. D. H. Hill, citing these figures, mistakenly called the Fifty-sixth the Fiftieth.

[49] *O. R.*, 19, pt. 1, pp. 1020–21.

[50] The only intelligible account of this operation is "Tige" Anderson's in *O. R.*, 19. pt. 1, pp. 908–09.

plish: John B. Hood with his magnificent fighting men came up on Drayton's flank and, with his soldierly promptness, drove back the enemy and restored the field.[51]

Hood had arrived after Hill had ridden back from the right to Turner's Gap and had become absorbed in the battle to the left of the highway. Robert Rodes had plunged boldly into action there. In advance and isolated, he occupied high ground but had to extend his line until its fire power was weak. Constantly, as he repulsed the enemy in front, he had vigilantly to watch lest his flank be turned. When, at length, he had to fall back, it was stubbornly, slowly, and with a bold front to the enemy. Although the other regiments of the Brigade were shattered, John B. Gordon's Sixth was held together by the flawless bearing and the singular moral leadership of its Colonel.[52] Another young officer, Col. Cullen A. Battle of the Third Alabama, caught many an eye by a magnificent display of valor. At nightfall, with the help of some of Longstreet's troops, these gallant men still were holding the key positions from which, reluctantly, the enemy withdrew.[53]

Hill saw all this and rejoiced in it. Precisely that type of battle was his forte—hard combat, where a man might fight with all his strength and cunning and not be responsible for strategy. In close, doubtful action he was superb. No man seemed able to get more fire power from a given number of troops. If Hill were charged with the direction of a campaign or with exclusive conduct of a large field . . . well, he justified all that had been said about him after the farcical bombardment of McClellan's camp and the unchallenged departure from the James of the Federal Army he was supposed to watch.[54]

During the morning on South Mountain, when he had responsibility, had not Hill felt a sense of loneliness? After Longstreet had come up and Lee was near at hand, Hill, the doubting independent commander, became once more the sharply critical subordinate. What he wrote in his report [55] he doubtless felt that evening. "I had now become familiar with the ground and knew

---

[51] O. R., 19, pt. 1, pp. 908–09, 922, 1021, 1031–32. The last of these references is to General Ripley's report which, though written just one week after the action, shows plainly that he did not know what had happened.

[52] O. R., 19, pt. 1, pp. 1021, 1034–35.   [53] Ibid., 19, 1, 1035–36.
[54] See supra, p. 54.   Unfortunately, it bears no date.

all the vital points," he said, "and had [Longstreet's] troops reported to me, the result might have been different."[56]

Technically, in a narrow sense, that strange statement may have been correct. Reinforcements that were thrown hastily to the right had to be recalled to the left before the Federal advance on that flank could be halted. The center was held firmly by Hill's own men of Colquitt's Brigade. Even so, the stiffened resistance that Longstreet offered on the left and the assured conduct of Hood on the right put an end to the action if they did not redeem the field. Hill was not satisfied. "Had Longstreet's Division been with mine at daylight," he asserted, ". . . the enemy would have been disastrously repulsed; but they had gained important positions before the arrival of reinforcements."[57] Not a word was there of self-criticism for failure to get the whole of his own Division on the mountain until after midday.[58]

[56] *O. R.*, 19, pt. 1, p. 1021.   [57] *Ibid.*, 1022.

[58] Those who might most reasonably have spoken in protest or complaint were dead—"undersized men mostly," said a Unionist who walked among them, "from the coast district of North Carolina, with sallow, hatchet faces, and clad in 'butternut' . . . " He added: "As I looked down on the poor, pinched faces, worn with marching and scant fare, all enmity died out. There was no 'secession' in those rigid forms, nor in those fixed eyes staring blankly at the sky." (2 *B. & L.*, 558). Confederate casualties at South Mountain were not separately reported, except for Rodes's Brigade, which lost 522. The total probably was about 2300. Livermore put it at 2863. Federal losses were 1831. (See *Alexander*, 239–40).

CHAPTER XI

THE TEST OF LAFAYETTE McLAWS

WHILE HARVEY HILL was fighting at Turner's Gap on the 14th of September, he surmised that the sound of one of the two engagements he heard to the South of him came from a gap McClellan was trying to force.[1] Precisely that was happening in circumstances of a sort to test the Georgian in command of the column sent to capture Maryland Heights and to force the surrender of Harpers Ferry.

Lafayette McLaws, 41 years of age and a Major General since May, had been denied any conspicuous part in the army's battles. At Williamsburg, on the afternoon of May 4, it will be recalled, he had acted with decision in manning Fort Magruder, but he had not fought at Seven Pines. Magruder, rather than he, had directed most of the operations of his small command at Savage Station and at Malvern Hill. His Division had not rejoined Lee in time for Second Manassas.

Now McLaws was given "Dick" Anderson's six Brigades in addition to his own four, but, according to the plan, he was to have opportunity without excessive responsibility. McLaws was not to be so far from Lee or from his immediate superior, Longstreet, that he would be called upon to make any important strategical decisions. Should some unexpected twist of circumstance, after arrival at Harpers Ferry, dictate a change in the general plan, without reference to G.H.Q., the responsibility would not rest on McLaws but on Jackson, his senior in commission.[2] On the other hand, the most difficult tactical operation in the effort to capture Harpers Ferry devolved on McLaws. From Middletown, he was, in the language of his orders, to "take the route to Harpers Ferry and by Friday morning [September 12], possess himself of the Maryland Heights and endeavor to capture the enemy at Harpers Ferry and vicinity."[3]

[1] 2 B. & L., 565.　　　　　[2] O. R., 19, pt. 2, pp. 603–04.
[3] O. R., 19, pt. 2, p. 603.

McLaws himself knew nothing of this terrain, but he had no difficulty in learning how completely the Maryland Heights commanded the town.[4] Some Confederate soldiers were natives of that district. Lee and Stuart, from their experience during the John Brown raid, and Jackson from his service at Harpers Ferry the previous summer, could acquaint McLaws with the dual obli-

Sketch of the Terrain between Turner's Gap and Maryland Heights

gation the ground imposed: He must command the Heights if he was to keep the garrison of Harpers Ferry from escaping westward into Maryland and, at the same time, he must guard well his rear. If he neglected this second duty, McClellan might fall upon him, overwhelm him, and divide the Confederate forces North of the Potomac from those South of the river. The importance of McLaws's mission and the necessity of discharging both phases of it explained the assignment to him of so large a force as ten Brigades.

[4] *Cf.* McLaws's topographical description in his report, *ibid.*, 852: "So long as Maryland Heights was occupied by the enemy, Harpers Ferry could never be occupied by us. If we gained possession of the heights, the town was no longer tenable to them."

McLaws began his movement early on the 10th of September. From the vicinity of Frederick, where he was encamped, the distance to the foot of Maryland Heights was not more than twenty miles,[5] though this included the passage of South Mountain at Brownsville Gap. His first day's march ended East of the pass. Most of the 11th was consumed in crossing the mountain to Brownsville in Pleasant Valley, the district between South Mountain and the upper end of Maryland Heights.[6] The plan had been to close on Harpers Ferry on Friday, the 12th, but nightfall of Thursday, the 11th, found McLaws's troops encamped around Brownsville. This village was distant six miles from the bank of the Potomac opposite McLaws's objective.[7]

Six difficult miles they promised to be. From the East, it scarcely seemed possible to assail Maryland Heights. A march down Pleasant Valley, parallel to the high ground, would subject the column to a plunging fire from Federal artillery. The one way of capturing the Heights seemed to be to climb them well to the North of the Potomac and then to proceed southward along the crest. For such an operation, access to the ridge could be had by way of Solomon's Gap, which was four miles North of the Federal batteries that overlooked Harpers Ferry from the Maryland side.[8] McLaws's information was that these gun positions were reached by a road along the backbone of the ridge.[9]

Carefully, on this basis, McLaws made his plan: He would send to Solomon's Gap the fine South Carolina Brigade of Joseph B. Kershaw, who had acquitted himself well in every engagement. Kershaw would be supported by Barksdale's Mississippians, another excellent command. His remaining eight Brigades, McLaws would dispose to meet any column that might seek to beat its way

[5] This is the outside figure. Accuracy is impossible because McLaws's exact line of march is in some doubt. He went by Burkittsville and Brownsville Gap (Dickert, op. cit., 147, so stated but made a mistake of one day in the chronology) and, to do this, logically would have moved from Frederick via Jefferson, but of that first stage of the advance, there is no mention. If McLaws's road was Frederick-Jefferson-Burkittsville-Brownsville, the distance was sixteen miles, more or less.

[6] This extension of the Heights is known as Elk Ridge, but the more familiar name is used here to reduce confusion.

[7] McLaws, in his report, O. R., 19, pt. 1, p. 852, stated merely that he "proceeded" on the 10th, and that he "reached the valley" on the 11th. Kershaw (ibid., 862) is authority for the statement that his command was at Brownsville on the morning of the 12th. It seems a safe inference from McLaws's sketch of dispositions (ibid., 853), that the remainder of the command was near Kershaw.

[8] On the Michler map of 1867, the gap is styled Salomo's.

[9] O. R., 19, pt. 1, p. 853.

into Pleasant Valley from South Mountain or to escape from Harpers Ferry.[10]

Under McLaws's own leading, the van of the larger Confederate force by nightfall on the 12th reached the Potomac at a point three miles downstream from the railroad bridge opposite Harpers Ferry. Kershaw, for his part, climbed to the northern end of Maryland Heights, met the Federal skirmishers and drove them back. He was compelled to advance on a narrow front, over boulders and along a mountainside so steep that the men sometimes had to pull themselves up by gripping the bushes.[11] On Kershaw pushed until, about one mile from the southern edge of the Heights, he encountered heavy abatis and perforce halted for the night.[12]

An early start by Kershaw on the morning of Saturday, September 13, carried the Seventh South Carolina past the abatis to another and heavier obstacle of logs and stones, 400 yards farther South. Barksdale already had been deployed on the precipitous eastern face of the Heights and there, by sheer tenacity, had been able to keep a line. He now received orders from Kershaw to turn the second abatis and to get in its rear. In co-operating, some of Kershaw's own men performed the difficult feat of loading and firing from positions where they had to use one arm to keep themselves from rolling into the abyss.[13]

The Mississippians speedily contrived to creep along the rim of the heights and to get on the flank of the Federals. Kershaw was encouraged by this and was hopeful of bagging all the defenders of the crude fort; but when a company of the Seventeenth Mississippi fired into some Union sharpshooters, a panic swept the bluecoats. They abandoned the whole position, plunged down the hillside and sought to make their way to Harpers Ferry.[14] By 10.30, Kershaw cleared the barrier completely; [15] by 4.30, the last Federal soldier was driven from Maryland Heights.[16] McLaws closed in from Pleasant Valley and occupied the little settlement, Sandy Hook, that nestles under the east edge of Maryland Heights

---

[10] For McLaws's dispositions, see *O. R.*, 19, pt. 1, p. 853.
[11] *Dickert*, 148.   [12] *O. R.*, 19, pt. 1, p. 863.
[13] *Dickert*, 148.
[14] *O. R.*, 19, pt. 1, p. 863. Col. William Allan, in 14 *S. H. S. P.*, 108, remarked that Kershaw deserved credit for this achievement, but that the smallness of the force opposing Kershaw should not be overlooked.
[15] *Ibid*.   [16] *Ibid.*, 854.

and on the main line of retreat northward from Harpers Ferry.

McLaws was satisfied. He reported subsequently: "The road, then, from Harpers Ferry which presented egress from the place, coming east, was now completely commanded. Up to this time I had received no notice of the advance of either General Jackson or General Walker, except that a courier from General Jackson brought a dispatch from him to the effect that he hoped his leading division would be near Harpers Ferry about 2 o'clock on this day [September 13], and some firing in that direction led to the belief that he was advancing. During the day heavy cannonading was heard to the east and northeast, and the cavalry scouts were constantly reporting the advance of the enemy from various directions, but the truth of these reports was questionable, as the lookouts from the mountains saw nothing to confirm them." [17] In short, it looked as if McLaws had outstripped not only Walker, but Jackson also, and that the honor of forcing the surrender of Harpers Ferry would be his.

Vigorously enough, on the morning of the 14th, McLaws pushed for the completion of his part of the enterprise. He set men to cutting a road to the crest of the Heights and by 2 o'clock he opened on Harpers Ferry with four guns. [18] All was going well and was promising high distinction to McLaws when calamity threatened suddenly. McLaws, it will be remembered, had crossed South Mountain at Brownsville Gap on the road from Burkittsville to Pleasant Valley. He never had seen the ground until that day, but he had learned that, under the lower end of the mountain, overlooking the Potomac, the railroad, the canal and a highway passed at Weverton and formed a line of communication with Harpers Ferry. McLaws had closed that route on the 12th

---

[17] *O. R.*, 19, pt. 1, p. 854. The evacuation of Maryland Heights by its commander, Col. T. H. Ford, 32nd Ohio, was one of the principal subjects examined in the autumn of 1862 by the so-called "Harpers Ferry Military Commission." Colonel Ford's report will be found in *O. R.*, 19, pt. 1, p. 541 ff. The testimony before the Commission is in *ibid.*, 549 ff. A full defense of Ford's actions appears in *ibid.*, 777 ff. The Commission's findings, *ibid.*, 749 ff., included this, as respects Ford: "In so grave a case as this, with such disgraceful consequences, the Commission cannot permit an officer to shield himself behind the fact that he did as well as he could, if in so doing he exhibits a lack of military capacity. It is clear to the Commission that Colonel Ford should not have been placed in command on Maryland Heights; that he conducted the defence without ability, and abandoned his position without sufficient cause, and has shown throughout such a lack of military capacity as to disqualify him, in the estimation of this Commission, for a command in the service" (*ibid.*, p. 799).

[18] *O. R.*, 19, pt. 1, p. 854.

and had posted troops to see that it was not reopened.[19] Every similar approach he protected with some of his abundant units. As far as his knowledge went, he picketed or garrisoned every exposed point.

In doing this, McLaws sent Paul Semmes, with his own and Mahone's Brigade, back to a point opposite Brownsville Gap. Semmes's instructions were to watch that crossing, to protect the road from which Kershaw had mounted to Maryland Heights, and "also to take precautions to guard the passes over the Blue Ridge." [20] Happily, Semmes took his duties in serious spirit and began reconnaissance. By the morning of the 14th, he ascertained that at a distance of a mile and three-quarters North of Brownsville Gap was another and important pass, Crampton's, which was undefended by Confederate infantry. To Crampton's Gap, accordingly, Semmes dispatched a battery and three regiments of Mahone's Brigade. These were under Col. William A. Parham, a competent officer.[21] "Jeb" Stuart, coming southward from Turner's Gap on the morning of the 14th, saw the danger of an attack on Crampton's Gap by a force too heavy for Parham to resist. Word of this was sent to McLaws. Until more infantry could arrive, Stuart explained, he had left Munford there with the Laurel Brigade.[22]

This may have been the first McLaws knew of such a place as Crampton's Gap.[23] He immediately directed that Howell Cobb move to the vicinity of Brownsville, and take command of Crampton's Gap. Semmes was told to recall from Solomon's Gap the troops sent there, except for a small guard, and to notify Cobb of all of McLaws's instructions.[24] Cobb's marching orders reached him at 1 P.M. He set out on his five-mile journey as soon as he could, and at 4 o'clock he was at Brownsville.[25] There he found no further orders.

To McLaws, these arrangements seemed adequate. He let

[19] O. R., 19, pt. 1, p. 853.
[20] The quotation is from McLaws's report, O. R., 19, pt. 1, p. 853.
[21] Ibid., 873.
[22] The message has to be reconstructed from Stuart's and McLaws's reports. O. R., 19, pt. 1, pp. 818 and 854.
[23] Cf. T. R. R. Cobb to his wife, Oct. 20, 1862: "The truth is McLaws didn't know there was such a gap until after the battle." (28 S. H. S. P., 297.)
[24] O. R., 19, pt. 1, p. 854. Through some error, Semmes understood that he was to withdraw his own troops from Crampton's Gap on the arrival of Cobb at that point. O. R., 19, pt. 1, p. 873.
[25] Ibid., 870.

them stand and climbed to Maryland Heights, whence he directed the employment of guns he had brought up for the bombardment of Harpers Ferry. After 2 P.M., McLaws was joined by Stuart, who had ridden down from Crampton's Gap. Not more than a Brigade of Federals, said Stuart, appeared to be moving against Crampton's Gap. That information reassured McLaws. He felt that, as he soon would have three Brigades close to the gap in addition to Stuart's cavalry, he need have no concern.

Later in the afternoon, McLaws heard firing from the direction of Crampton's Gap. At first it did not alarm him. He sent word to Cobb to hold the pass at any sacrifice [26] but he dispatched no reinforcements. As for Stuart, that officer seemed to be apprehensive of the nearer ground only. He dilated to McLaws on the importance of seeing to it that when the Federals had to yield Harpers Ferry, none of them should escape up the Potomac along the road directly under Maryland Heights.[27] McLaws listened and seemed to heed. If he was abstracted or appeared to have in hand more than he could direct, there is no record of it.

At length, when the firing from Crampton's became heavy and long sustained, McLaws decided he would ride in that direction. Stuart bore him company. Before they had proceeded far, Maj. T. S. McIntosh came galloping down the road and brought them appalling news: The Federals had broken through Crampton's Gap; Cobb was in mad retreat; the enemy was pressing hard.

It was true. At the gap, Munford's cavalry and Mahone's Brigade had been hammered by bluecoats who seemed to come up the mountain like a rain cloud. Both Munford and Col. William A. Parham, who commanded Mahone's men, had sent to Cobb for help. He had dispatched his two strongest regiments and then had led the remaining two. On reaching the gap, he had found Parham on the eastern side of the mountain, whither Mahone's troops momentarily had driven back the enemy. Even then it had been apparent that the farther Parham advanced, the more nearly the Federals were enveloping his flanks. Cobb threw out two of his regiments to the right and two to the left in order to cover Parham. Soon, Semmes' Tenth Georgia was at hand to help, though given conflicting orders.[28]

26 O. R., 19, pt. 1, p. 854.   27 O. R., 19, pt. 1, pp. 818, 854.
28 O. R., 19, pt. 1, p. 877.

Before the line could be rectified, the center gave way. The regiments thereupon broke wildly and ran down the western side of the mountain. Vainly Cobb and his staff, assisted shortly by Semmes, tried to stop them. As a color bearer passed to the rear with a regimental flag, Cobb took it from him and called to the troops to rally. Just then a bullet hit the flagstaff. Cobb dropped it and went back to see if he could get his men to form another line.[29] The best he and Semmes could do was to employ a battery to delay the pursuers until two of Semmes's regiments could be brought up and utilized as a rallying post.[30]

When Stuart and McLaws arrived, Cobb greeted them in vast distress. Said he: "Dismount, gentlemen, dismount, if your lives are dear to you! The enemy is within fifty yards of us; I am expecting their attack every minute. Oh, my dear Stuart, that I should live to experience such a disaster! What can be done? What can save us?" Soon it was manifest, upon reconnaissance by one of Stuart's officers, that the enemy had halted temporarily;[31] but the situation of the three Brigades remained about as dangerous as it could be, short of out-and-out slaughter. If the victorious Federals were in great strength, might they not overwhelm the remainder of McLaws's force, recover Maryland Heights and relieve Harpers Ferry? Would not Lee and Jackson be divided and then destroyed?

If McLaws's apprehension took this extreme form, when Cobb reported the disaster, there was no suggestion of such a state of mind in McLaws's subsequent report. He recorded this only: "I at once ordered up Wilcox's Brigade . . . and rode toward the gap. Fortunately, night came on and allowed a new arrangement of the troops to be made to meet the changed aspect of affairs. The Brigades of Generals Kershaw and Barksdale, excepting one regiment of the latter and two pieces of artillery were withdrawn from the heights . . . and formed line of battle across the valley and about 1½ miles below Crampton's Gap, with the remnants of the Brigades of Generals Cobb, Semmes, and Mahone, and those of Wilcox, Kershaw and Barksdale, which were placed specially under command of General Anderson."[32]

The enemy did not press hard in the twilight. For reasons that

[29] *Munford MSS.*
[31] 1 *von Borcke,* 217–18.
[30] *O. R.,* 19, pt. 1, pp. 870, 871, 873.
[32] *O. R.,* 18, pt. 1, p. 855.

are not altogether plain, even now, the Federal commanders, in the face of instructions to march for Harpers Ferry, seemed to think their day's work done when the pass was cleared.[33] Thanks to their willingness to let night overtake them ere they overtook the Confederates, McLaws's hastily drawn line was not assailed.

Even so, midnight on South Mountain was doubly black for the Confederate invaders. At Turner's Gap, Longstreet deferred, respecting the next move, to the judgment of D. H. Hill who, said Longstreet, knew the ground and the situation better than he did.[34] Hill himself and Hood believed the Army should withdraw before dawn, and they so advised Lee, who had learned during the evening that a prisoner reported Sumner's fresh Corps moving up to relieve the tired participants in the battle.[35] Added to what Lee knew of the outcome of the fight at the two gaps, this information made him doubt for a few hours whether he could attempt to remain longer in Maryland. He wrote McLaws to abandon the position in front of Harpers Ferry and to recross the Potomac. The forces with him, Lee explained in his dispatch to McLaws, would retire via Sharpsburg into Virginia.

Everything indicated a hurried and divided retreat. It might have been necessary, with excessive, perhaps ruinous losses, had there not spurred through the night a courier from Jackson with a message that changed the Army's plan.[36]

33 Cf. *O. R.,* 19, pt. 1, pp. 375–76, 380–81. Gen. W. B. Franklin was in command. His orders appear in *ibid.,* 45–46.

34 2 *B. & L.,* 571.

35 *O. R.,* 19, pt. 1, p. 140. This information was correct to the extent that the I! and XIII Corps reached the foot of the mountain "shortly after dark." See McClellan in *ibid.,* 52.

36 All the details are in 2 *R. E. Lee,* 371. The dispatch to McLaws is in *O. R.,* 51, pt. 2, pp. 618–19. For a critique of McLaws's handling of this operation, see *infra* pp. 270 ff. Caution is recommended in use of the account of the dispatch of orders in Jackson as given in 14 *C. V.,* 65.

CHAPTER XII

The "Wagon Hunter's" Great Day

When "Old Jack" reached the vicinity of Harpers Ferry at 11 A.M. on September 13, the day before the struggle for the gaps in South Mountain, his first move was routine. He placed his troops so that he could meet any maneuver on the part of the Federal garrison, which had been reinforced, he learned, by the regiments that had fled from Martinsburg on his approach. As soon as his own dispositions were made, Jackson sought a vantage point from which to study Loudoun Heights across the Shenandoah and Maryland Heights beyond the Potomac. John G. Walker and McLaws had been ordered by Lee to take those positions by the 12th. Jackson himself was a day late: Had the co-operating Generals completed sooner than he their shorter marches, or had they, too, found the logistics of Lee's plan too exacting?

Jackson scanned the picturesque eminences across the rivers, but he could see nothing of Confederate troops on Loudoun Heights or of any attack on the Federal positions in Maryland. His signal officer, Capt. Jos. L. Bartlett, was summoned and was instructed to establish contact with the other commands by flag, the sole means of ready communication among forces separated so widely.[1] Bartlett and his men worked to no purpose. Late in the afternoon, the sound of Kershaw's attack down the backbone of Maryland Heights could be heard, but there was no answer to the signal flags. Nor was there a visible reply to the calls sent Walker. Despairing at last of success that evening with a system of signals he much approved, Jackson decided to wait until morning for another effort at signalling and, meantime, to rely on couriers to find where the co-operating columns were.[2] Not until long after

[1] O. R., 19, pt. 1, p. 953.
[2] O. R., 19, pt. 1, p. 953. Failure to open communication with Maryland Heights was due to conditions described *infra*, but why Jackson's signals did not reach Walker on the afternoon of September 13 has never been explained. Walker stated (2 B. & L., 608–09), that signalmen joined him at the foot of Loudoun Heights about 10 A.M. He noted, also, that Col. John R. Cooke reached the crest by 2 P.M. Cooke reported that he saw nothing of Jackson, though "from the movements of the Federals he

darkness did one of these couriers return from the eastern bank of the Shenandoah and report that Walker was in position on Loudoun Heights.[3] Ere that, McLaws's approach had been verified, but Jackson could not be sure when McLaws could clear Maryland Heights and open fire on Harpers Ferry.

On the morning of the 14th, while D. H. Hill was fighting on South Mountain, Jackson proceeded deliberately, almost cautiously, with his preparations. Under his orders now were six of the nine infantry Divisions of the Army.[4] This was much the largest force he ever had directed. He was determined to co-ordinate it, but he was not inclined to wait on McLaws. Although Lee's orders indicated that the Georgian was to effect from Maryland Heights the capture of Harpers Ferry, Jackson acted as if the prime responsibility rested on his own troops.

The signal station nearest Jackson's headquarters was manned at daylight and ere long was in touch with Walker, but after several hours' effort, it still was unable to reach McLaws. About 10 o'clock, the signal officer under Jackson reported that Walker said he had six rifled guns in position on Loudoun Heights and wished to know whether to open fire or to wait on McLaws. "Wait," Jackson answered tersely, but in a short time he rode out to the signal station and had the flagmen spell out a joint order of about 130 words to Walker and to McLaws. The substance of it was that the battery commanders on the heights were to place guns, if possible, where they could drive the enemy from his strongest position. Suggestions for other action against the Federals were invited. The message concluded: "I do not desire any of the batteries to open until all are ready on both sides of the

thought [Jackson] was close at hand." Capt. James A. Graham stated (2 *N. C. Regts.*, 433) that Cooke's regiment, the Twenty-seventh North Carolina, quickly opened communication with McLaws by flag but was "unable to get any answer from Jackson." Was this an instance where signalling failed because of inexperienced men, or was it another case of breakdown through failure to agree in advance where the signal stations were to be located? Unfortunately, nothing is recorded of the signalmen who reported to Walker, beyond the fact that they were under Capt. R. H. T. Adams, a competent officer (*O. R.*, 19, pt. 1, p. 959). Little is known of the Confederate signal service, especially at this stage of hostilities. See *Alexander*, 13 ff, 16 *S. H. S. P.*, 98, 2 *C. V.*, 11–12; IV *O. R.*, 1, 1131; 2, 47, 199, 289, 371.

[3] *O. R.*, 19, pt. 1, p. 953. In the same manner, Walker had sent a courier and received an answer at 9 P.M. 2 *N. C. Regts.*, 433.

[4] Viz., Jackson's, Ewell's, A. P. Hill's, McLaws's, R. H. Anderson's and Walker's, though the last included two Brigades only. With Longstreet were left D. H. Hill's, Hood's and D. R. Jones's. The force of six Brigades, credited to D. R. Jones in *O. R.*, 19, pt. 1, pp. 804–05, was, as already noted, two Divisions, Longstreet's old command and Jones's demi-Division.

river, except you should find it necessary, of which you must judge for yourself. I will let you know when to open all the batteries." [5]

This message must have taken a long time to transmit. In answer to it, Walker signalled from Loudoun Heights that Mc-Laws reported the enemy in rear of him and said "that he can do but little more than he has done." Walker added, on his own account, that he was ready to open fire. Jackson had left the signal station ere this message was received. As Captain Bartlett had no courier, he was forced to take the copy and search along the lines until he found Jackson. Thereupon, Walker was told to withhold his fire while an effort was made to establish direct communication between Jackson and McLaws. In this effort, Jackson apparently failed once more. The file of his signal officer did not include even one message from McLaws, though Captain Bartlett later reported that messages may have been sent from other posts than his. Part of the trouble no doubt was due to the fact that McLaws's signal officer, Capt. J. H. Manning, had been seized with an attack of erysipelas, and had been incapacitated. One of McLaws's aides had to take charge of the detachment.[6]

The full text of the battle order, drawn by Jackson and approximately 150 words in length, next was sent from Jackson's signal station. Part of these instructions raised a question in Walker's mind [7] and led to more signalling. "Before the necessary orders were thus transmitted," Jackson recorded in some disgust, "the day was far advanced." [8] He did not on that account relax his

[5] *O. R.*, 19, pt. 1, p. 958. It should be noted that Captain Bartlett's report, here quoted, curiously omits reference to the time of the dispatch of all save one of the messages handled during the day.

[6] *O. R.*, 19, pt. 1, p. 857.

[7] *O. R.*, 19, pt. 1, p. 959. Mention in the order of firing "on the island in the Shenandoah" suggests that the order may have been sent in advance of the unsigned message to Jackson, "probably from Major Paxton," that precedes the order in Bartlett's log.

[8] In 2 *B. & L.*, 609, General Walker wrote that Jackson signalled him on the morning of the 14th: "Harpers Ferry is now completely invested. I shall summon its commander to surrender. Should he refuse I shall give him twenty-four hours to remove the non-combatants and then carry the place by assault. Do not fire unless forced to." General Walker then explained that from his position he realized that McClellan was pressing McLaws and that if the assault on Harpers Ferry were delayed twenty-four hours, "General Lee would be in fearful peril." In that knowledge, said General Walker, ne precipitated action. Walker's is the only direct testimony on this score, though Hotchkiss noted (*MS Diary*, 87) that Jackson had everything ready on the 14th, but for undisclosed reasons, delayed the attack. On the other hand, after the appearance of Walker's article, Bradley Johnson and Kyd Douglas promptly expressed the view (2 *B. & L.*, 615-16) that General Walker's memory was at fault and that Jackson had not delayed the attack by sending in a flag and allowing twenty-four hours for the

own efforts. A. P. Hill's Division, Ewell's under Lawton, and Jackson's own, led by Brig. Gen. John R. Jones, were disposed entirely across the neck in rear of Harpers Ferry, between the Potomac and the Shenandoah. By a mere demonstration on the part of the Stonewall Brigade and of one battery of artillery, commanding ground on the Federal right was carried.[9] Opposite the Union left, Dorsey Pender handled with much skill and small loss an advance to a good position on the left bank of the Shenandoah.[10]

By 8.15 P.M. Jackson felt that he could make a favorable report to Lee, though he characteristically refrained from incautious promises. He wrote R. H. Chilton, Lee's A.A.G.:

Colonel: Through God's blessing, the advance, which commenced this evening, has been successful thus far, and I look to Him for complete success tomorrow. The advance has been directed to be resumed at dawn tomorrow morning. I am thankful that our loss has been small. Your dispatch respecting the movements of the enemy and the importance of concentration has been received. Cannot you connect the headquarters of the army, by signal, with General McLaws?[11]

This was the letter that prompted General Lee to cancel orders for a withdrawal across the Potomac and to direct, instead, a new concentration West of the mountains. Jackson, meantime, gave orders that ten guns from Ewell's artillery be moved up the Shenandoah, be crossed at Kelly's Ford, and be brought into battery opposite the Federal left.[12] Hill's artillery also was advanced during the night to a position that had been reached about sunset by the men in charge of the rifled pieces of McIntosh's Battery, about 800 yards from the enemy's earthworks on Bolivar Heights.[13] With equal care, all Jackson's infantry were disposed skillfully for a general advance.[14]

Before dawn on the 15th, Jackson had all the troops aroused

evacuation of non-combatants. All the collateral evidence that has come to light since the publication of *B. & L.* bears out the contention of Douglas and of Johnson. When Jackson's own report is read in the light of Captain Bartlett's, the reason for deferring the attack becomes plain: the transmission of orders, under the conditions that prevailed, consumed the greater part of the day.

9 *Caldwell*, 43.   10 *O. R.*, 19, pt. 1, p. 954.
11 *O. R.*, 19, pt. 1, p. 951.   12 *O. R.*, 19, pt. 1, p. 962.
13 *Ibid.*, 984.   14 *Ibid.*, 954.

and put in line of battle. Ewell's gunners had not then reached their objective, but they were working furiously to open a road.[15] Walker's artillerists, looking down on a heavy mist that enveloped Harpers Ferry from the side of Loudoun Heights,[16] could do no more than wait and pray for a sight of their target. The moment the other batteries had sufficient light they opened a pattern of fire Jackson had designed. Soon afterward, Ewell's guns chimed in; then Walker's set rolling the echoes of Loudoun Heights. Jackson was fulfilling another dream of the officer of artillery: he had his guns precisely where he wanted them, he was firing as he desired, and he perceived ere long that he was silencing the enemy. It was an experience he did not forget. Months later, when his reports were prepared, he included in his account of Harpers Ferry a careful statement of the position of his batteries.[17]

An hour of steady hammering seemed to exhaust the Federals. Their fire became slack and discouraged and soon virtually stopped. Jackson directed that Hill's batteries cease fire. That was the prearranged signal for launching the infantry assault. Dorsey Pender began at once to move forward the Brigades that were to drive home the attack. The Federals then opened again, though their fire was slow and uncertain.[18] Pender halted. Two of Hill's batteries—one of them Willie Pegram's—dashed out. Four hundred yards they advanced and then, unlimbering, assailed the Federals furiously.[19] In about five minutes,[20] a horseman was observed on the Union works. He was riding from right to left [21] and he was waving something. What was it, and of what color? Eyes were strained to make sure.[22] It soon was unmistakable—white if not of the whitest [23]—the signal of surrender! As soon as the fact was realized, cheers swept the front.[24] Unfortunately, the more distant Confederate batteries were somewhat slow in discovering that the white flag had been raised. Some of them fired several more rounds before they found, to their humiliation, that they were punishing men who had ceased to resist.[25]

[15] Ibid., 962.
[16] Ibid., 914.
[17] O. R., 19, pt. 1, p. 955.
[18] Ibid., 955, 984.
[19] Ibid.
[20] Ibid., 984.
[21] Allan's Army, 340.
[22] E. A. Moore, 139.
[23] In fact, a piece of a tent. Allan's Army, loc. cit.
[24] Early, 137.
[25] O. R., 19, pt. 1, p. 528; 2 B. & L., 610.

Through the lines, shortly, came Brig. Gen. Julius White, who had been designated by the commanding officer, Col. Dixon S. Miles, to arrange terms of surrender.[26] With White rode A. P. Hill, who had met him en route.[27] As White drew rein in front of Jackson, the contrast in appearance of the two men made irreverent young staff officers grin. Kyd Douglas remembered: "There was nothing strikingly military about [General White's] looks, but he was mounted on a handsome black horse, was handsomely uniformed, with an untarnished saber, immaculate gloves and boots, and had a staff fittingly equipped. He must have been somewhat astonished to find in General Jackson the worst dressed, worst mounted, most faded and dingy looking general he had ever seen anyone surrender to, with a staff, not much for looks and equipment." [28]

White manfully asked for terms. Jackson answered in soldierly fashion that the capitulation must be unconditional.[29] When White perforce accepted, Jackson turned him over to A. P. Hill, with instructions that did not lack in generosity: All officers and men, other than Confederate deserters, were to be paroled; officers were to retain their side arms and private baggage; munitions and public property were to be turned over to the victors.[30] These were to be the signed, official terms. In addition, Jackson allowed the prisoners to retain their overcoats and blankets, loaned the Federals two of their former teams per regiment for the transportation of baggage, and gave the captives two days' rations, though that took all the subsistence stores at Harpers Ferry.[31]

After providing that the terms of surrender should be liberal,

[26] White outranked Miles, as their titles indicate, but when he reached Harpers Ferry from Martinsburg and faced a military situation with which he was entirely unfamiliar, he waived rank and offered to serve under Miles. O. R., 19, pt. 1, p. 525.

[27] In a few minutes, General White learned that he was negotiating surrender on his own account because, after he had left the Federal position, Colonel Miles had been hit in the leg and mortally wounded by one of the last shells fired. O. R., 19, pt. 1, p. 528.

[28] Douglas, 162.

[29] Cooke in his Jackson, 325, stated and the Count of Paris circulated more widely, a yarn that Jackson was asleep when White arrived. Kyd Douglas, who escorted General White wrote in 2 B. & L., 626, that Jackson was not asleep but was on his horse and "exceedingly wide-awake."

[30] O. R., 19, pt. 1, pp. 529–30. General White sought in vain to protect from punishment as deserters those Southern conscripts who had entered the Federal lines.

[31] O. R., 19, pt. 1, p. 528. A. P. Hill complained in his report, ibid., 980–81, that "the wagons . . . were not returned for nearly two months, and not until repeated calls had been made for them."

Jackson paid no further attention to them. While White and A. P. Hill still were negotiating, Jackson was writing to Lee about the next vital step in the campaign, the reconcentration of the forces:

> Near 8 A.M., September 15, 1862.
> General: Through God's blessing, Harpers Ferry and its garrison are to be surrendered. As Hill's troops have borne the heaviest part of the engagement, he will be left in command until the prisoners and public property shall be disposed of, unless you direct otherwise. The other forces can move off this evening so soon as they get their rations. To what point shall they move? I write at this time in order that you may be apprised of the condition of things. You may expect to hear from me again today after I get more information respecting the number of prisoners, &c.[32]

When the prisoners were counted, they numbered about 11,000.[33] The booty included some 13,000 small arms, seventy-three cannon and approximately 200 wagons, together with the provisions already mentioned and the quartermasters' stores usually kept at a busy post.[34] It was a noble haul, and one that much gratified Ewell's "wagon hunter." In writing his wife, Jackson listed what had been captured, and then commented: "Our Heavenly Father blesses us exceedingly. I am thankful to say that our loss was small and [your brother] Joseph and myself were mercifully protected from harm."[35]

To see that no time was lost in completing the surrender and in preparing the troops to rejoin Lee in Maryland, Jackson went with his staff down to Harpers Ferry about 11 A.M.[36] Along the road, many Federal soldiers were waiting. Those who saluted him received prompt acknowledgment, but he rushed along without a word to any of them. "Boys," remarked one prisoner, "he isn't much for looks, but if we'd had him we wouldn't have been caught in this trap."[37] A newspaper correspondent got an even more unfavorable picture of Jackson: "He was dressed in the coars-

---

[32] *O. R.*, 19, pt. 1, p. 951.
[33] According to the *New York Times*, quoted in 5 *Moore's Rebellion Record*, 448, the number was 11,583, but the table shows various approximations.
[34] *O. R.*, 19, pt. 1, pp. 951, 955, 960–61.
[35] *Mrs. Jackson*, 338.
[36] *O. R.*, 19, pt. 1, p. 599.   [37] *Douglas*, 163.

est kind of homespun, seedy and dirty at that; wore an old hat [38] which any Northern beggar would consider an insult to have offered him, and in general appearance was in no respect to be distinguished from the mongrel, bare-footed crew who follow his fortunes. I had heard much of the decayed appearance of the rebel soldiers, but such a looking crowd! Ireland in her worst straits could present no parallel, and yet they glory in their shame." [39]

Dirty or clean, the Confederates mingled with their captives, and, whenever the Federals cheered Jackson, the "Johnnys" added their yell. The only disagreement was over the remark of some of the bluecoats: "If we had *him,* we should whip you in short order." This, in language less like that of the copy-book, the Southerners would not allow.[40]

"Ah," said Jackson to von Borcke, as he viewed the prisoners and the booty, "this is all very well, Major, but we have yet much hard work before us!" [41] There was to be no holiday. All the energies of all the officers must be devoted to getting the men on the road as soon as they were fed. While the essential arrangements were being made, most of the troops were given liberty to explore the sutlers' establishments at Harpers Ferry.

Some of the Brigades of Hill's Light Division had been denied their proper part of the loot at Manassas, because Jackson had sent them to drive off Taylor's New Jerseymen. Now Pender's men and Branch's and the others, after establishing guard over the prisoners, could enjoy canned lobster or fill stomach and haversack with cake, or stuff pockets with candy. The historian of Gregg's Brigade added the touch that had been missing at Manassas for the infantry. Said he: "We fared sumptuously. In addition to meat, crackers, sugar, coffee, shoes, blankets, underclothing, &c., many of us captured horses roaming at large, on whom to transport our plunder." [42] When Walker's column came over the

---

[38] Here, it would appear, the New York reporter did "Old Jack" an injustice. Three days before, in Martinsburg, as Jed. Hotchkiss recorded in his *MS Diary* and mentioned often in later years, he bought and presented to Jackson a hat, which the General forthwith began to wear. His old cap was preserved and subsequently was given to Hotchkiss. That devoted staff officer preserved it for his lifetime and left it to his daughter, Mrs. George Holmes. In 1939, she deposited it at the Virginia Military Institute, where it now is. Jackson's hat, therefore, was almost new at the time of the surrender of Harpers Ferry, but doubtless it, as well as he, was dust-covered. The day was warm and, said the careful Hotchkiss, "quite dusty" (*MS Diary,* 87).

[39] 5 *Moore's Rebellion Record,* 447–48.   [40] *Caldwell,* 44.
[41] 1 *von Borcke,* 224–25.   [42] *Caldwell,* 43.

Shenandoah and McLaws's streamed across the Potomac bridge, on their way back to Lee, there was much grumbling, bitterness even, because the booty had all been devoured or appropriated. "Jackson's troops," wrote Comrade Dickert, resentful after more than thirty years, "fairly swam in the delicacies, provisions, and 'drinkables' constituting a part of the spoils taken, while Kershaw's and all of McLaws' and Walker's troops, who had done the hardest of the fighting, got none."[43]

Neither feasting nor complaining was for long. By 3 P.M., Jackson's Division was sent back to camp and was directed to cook two days' rations. In the late afternoon, Lawton led Ewell's Division up the Shepherdstown road and halted for the night four miles from Boteler's Ford. Jackson's Division did not finish cooking until midnight, but at 1 A.M. it started for Sharpsburg, Maryland, which Lee had named as the point of concentration.[44] The march by Jackson's own admission was "severe."[45] That is to say, it was all that even his toughened "foot cavalry" could endure. Twenty-four hours from the time he had received the flag of truce at Harpers Ferry, he was approaching the rendezvous, distant sixteen miles by road. As the regiments one after another, during the morning of September 16, reached the little town of Sharpsburg and halted, the men dropped silently down. Jackson, dust covered and gray, rode on to report to Lee, who was waiting, with more anxiety than he exhibited, the arrival of the detached Divisions to reinforce the thin line he had drawn behind Antietam Creek.

Already, on the opposite ridges, East of the stream, the Federals in vast numbers seemed to be deploying for an offensive battle. The assured character of McClellan's movements, the boldness of a cautious man, indicated that he might know the weakness of Lee. New credibility in this manner was given the report brought Stuart on the night of the 13th–14th, concerning the finding by Federals in Frederick of a copy of Lee's orders. Had McClellan attacked with his full strength before the arrival of Jackson, four-

43 *Dickert,* 150.

44 *O. R.,* 19, pt. 1, pp. 967, 1007. Von Borcke, *op. cit.,* 1, 224–25, either did a bit of romancing or else confused with some other the scene at the crossing of the Potomac. Jackson's troops were not, as von Borcke would have them, bivouacked "on either bank of the noble stream" with "thousands of camp-fires . . . reflected in the water." Nor was there in the two Divisions even one "Mississippi regiment" of "wild-looking, long-bearded men."

45 *O. R.,* 19, pt. 1, p. 955

teen Brigades of infantry, three of them still bleeding from the battle on South Mountain, would have been compelled to face six Corps in a hopeless battle. Now that Jackson was up, he raised the number of Confederate Brigades to twenty-two. These were not enough for successful prolonged resistance, but they might suffice to hold their ground until A. P. Hill, McLaws and Walker arrived with their eighteen Brigades. Jackson had relieved a desperate situation by a prompt march.

In the all-absorbing excitement of the field, Jackson probably did not recall the fact, but he was that day completing his third month in the school of the Army of Northern Virginia. On the 16th of June, he had been preparing to leave the Shenandoah and to aid Lee in the effort to drive McClellan from the Richmond front. Jackson had shown, ere that date in June, his ability to handle independently a small force and to co-operate admirably, at a distance, in the execution of a strategic plan. He had not shone, during the Seven Days, in co-operation with others or in the swift movement of four Divisions through the unfamiliar jungle of the Chickahominy. On his first test under his new teacher, he could not have been graded above "Fair." His next test, Cedar Mountain, might by lenient marking have been rated "Good," but no more than that. Then, sixty days after his march from Ashland to Polly Hundley's Corner, he made the superb advance of August 26 from Salem to Bristoe.

By that time, Jackson had mastered the essentials of the art of the executive officer. His operation against Harpers Ferry had not been perfect logistically or as an example of communication among co-operating columns, but the task had been performed, the garrison had been captured, and the next mission had been undertaken forthwith. All that the march from Jefferson to Manassas had marked in the improvement of Jackson, the advance from Harpers Ferry to Sharpsburg confirmed. The grade that had risen from "Fair" on July 1 to a doubtful "Good" on August 9, now had mounted from "Good" to "Excellent." An examiner might have asked himself whether that high adjective connoted quite the full measure of praise that Student Jackson, T. J., had earned.

CHAPTER XIII

DESPERATE HOURS ON THE ANTIETAM

LEE's WITHDRAWAL of Longstreet and of D. H. Hill from South Mountain, after the news of the impending capture of Harpers Ferry, had been directed to Sharpsburg for three reasons: At that point, Lee would be on the flank and potentially in rear of McClellan in the event the Federal commander sought to cut off McLaws; second, Sharpsburg was close to the Potomac across which the forces under Jackson were to move to reunite with Lee;[1] third, the terrain around Sharpsburg was moderately favorable for defensive action, though the position was not so deep as Lee would have desired.[2] Antietam Creek itself, running North and South, was scant protection. Across it were four bridges in addition to several fords which, though difficult, were by no means impassable.[3]

Over some of these, and onward to the pleasant rolling ridges between the Antietam and the Potomac, the march of Longstreet and of D. H. Hill on the 15th had been uneventful. Fitz Lee's cavalry Brigade covered the movement while Stuart was farther southward. Had "Jeb" himself been directing the squadrons, they scarcely could have been handled better.[4] Once arrived at Sharpsburg, the two infantry Divisions were disposed along the high ground to cover the Boonsborough road, by which they had marched, and the road from Hagerstown.[5] For the protection of these roads and for the defense of the ridges, the Confederate Army was alarmingly weak in comparison with an adversary who followed fast and boldly deployed. Even after Jackson

[1] McClellan, O. R., 19, pt. 1, p. 82, noted that at the time of the battle of Sharpsburg, the Potomac was "very low," but Alexander insisted, op. cit., 247, that one ford only, and that one "rocky and deep," was available to the Confederates.
[2] The first and the second of these reasons Lee avowed in his report, O. R., 19, pt. 1, p. 147. His third reason was set forth in Longstreet's report, ibid., 839. McClellan in ibid., 54, certainly exaggerated in saying that the position "was one of the strongest to be found in this region of country, which is well adapted to defensive warfare."
[3] Cf. McClellan in O. R., 19, pt. 1, p. 54.
[4] Cf. R. E. Lee in O. R., 19, pt. 1, pp. 147, 148.
[5] Fourteen miles to the North.

arrived on the 16th and took position on the left, the Army was weaker than ever it had been under Lee. The full effects of straggling and of dispersion of force were plain for every soldier to see. A strong attack by the whole of McClellan's command manifestly would threaten not merely defeat but ruin. The worst of all the succession of crises had come. An army of liberation was an army in desperation.

Could the new McClellan be beaten? Not unless all the missing Brigades could be brought up quickly and massed. Where were the troops that had been sent to envelop Harpers Ferry? Walker came up with his small force during the afternoon of the 16th and went to the right.[6] What of McLaws? In Anderson's Division and his own, McLaws had ten Brigades, or more than half the Army's reserve. His orders were to move over to Harpers Ferry and to hurry on to Sharpsburg. What delayed him? Why was he so slow? A. P. Hill, of course, was detained at Harpers Ferry to parole the prisoners and to secure all the captured property: how long would that require? If emergency demanded, could he be available on the 17th? None of these questions found an assured answer. Anxiety haunted every ranking officer who tried to sleep. Battle was in the air. Sharp clashes had occurred before darkness fell. All night long the restless pickets plied an intermittent fire. Each army seemed to think the other was massing for attack.[7]

With the dawn, the Federal artillery opened furiously. The battle was to rise with the sun. "Joe" Hooker's First Corps, as the Confederates soon ascertained, was moving against their left. Jackson instantly sensed danger. Stuart and his cavalry supported well-placed artillery near the Potomac. As that ground had to be held at any cost, Jackson moved "Jube" Early's men to serve as the flank infantry element—a wise assignment if deliberate and a fortunate one if made by chance. Next Early, to the right, was Jackson's Division. Beyond Jackson, whose men were under the direction of John R. Jones, was Ewell's Division, which A. R. Law-

[6] General Walker's narrative, 2 *B. & L.*, 611, might leave the impression that his two Brigades arrived with Jackson, but this was true only of Walker himself. Lee stated explicitly in his report, *O. R.*, 19, pt. 1, p. 148: "General Jackson arrived early on the 16th and General Walker came up in the afternoon." Although Walker stated that his van overtook the rear of Jackson's Division at 2 A.M., a considerable interval must have been allowed to develop thereafter. The delay was not serious.

[7] *Cf.* Hooker in *O. R.*, 19, pt. 1, p. 218.

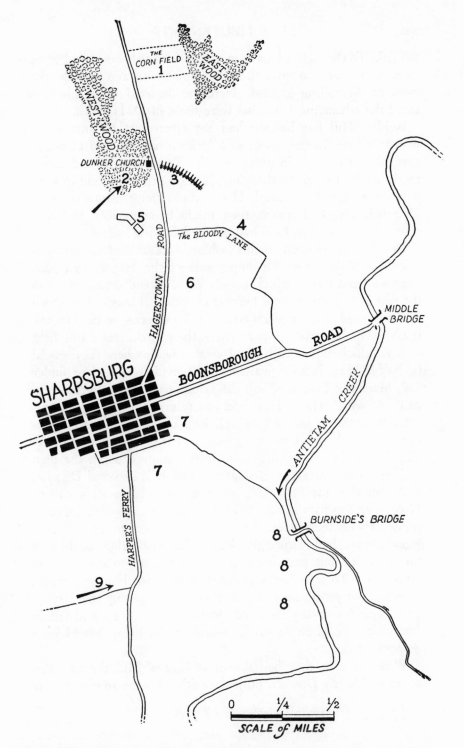

The Battlefield of Sharpsburg, Sept. 17, 1862. (1) The corn field into which first Lawton and Hays, and then Hood and the subsequent reinforcements advanced; (2) McLaws's line of advance; (3) first position of S. D. Lee's artillery battalion; (4) the scene of Rodes's disaster; (5) position from which John R. Cooke charged; (6) general zone of D. H. Hill's defense; (7) main body of Longstreet's troops on the right; (8) Toombs's advanced regiments; (9) the line of A. P. Hill's advance. Detailed sketches, based on the superb maps of the Antietam Battlefield Board, will be found in 2 *R. E. Lee*, 385 ff.

ton led. To the right of Lawton, the line turned southward from its easterly course to cover the Hagerstown road and to make the most of the rolling ground. Here the depleted regiments that faced the advancing Unionists were those of D. H. Hill.

Neither Hill nor Jackson had any reserves of his own command; but on the previous night, Jackson had relieved Hood, at that officer's request, in order that the Texas Brigade and Law's might cook rations. At that time, Jackson prudently had exacted a promise that if he called, Hood would move immediately to his relief. Hood's Division, then, might be counted as Jackson's reserve.[8] It was all Jackson had, all the left wing had.

For the line he drew in this fashion, Jackson had no fortifications and little cover. On either side of the Hagerstown road were scattered woods which, on the West, extended southward to the rear of a white-washed Dunker church that overlooked much of the ground of the Federal advance. To the East of the Hagerstown road, about 500 yards North of the church, was a fine field of corn, thick and head high. Into this field, where they would be half-hidden, Jackson was moving Lawton's Georgians under Col. Marcellus Douglass, and the Louisiana Brigade to the command of which Harry Hays had just returned.

On these troops and Jackson's Division to the left of the Hagerstown road, Hooker's sunrise attack was furious, overwhelming. The fire of the powerful blue regiments mowed down the men of Lawton and of Hays; it shattered Jackson's depleted Division and, almost at the first clash, it carried one of Lawton's staff to Hood with this panting message: "General Lawton sends his compliments with the request that you come at once to his support." Hood already had learned that D. H. Hill on his right could give him no help,[9] but, unassisted, he did not hesitate to answer Lawton's call. "To arms" was sounded at once for hungry privates who had not yet finished their cooking. They put up their frying pans, sighed over the food they had to throw away, and fell in for what they knew from the sound of the firing would be a desperate fight.

With the élan they had shown at Gaines' Mill the two Brigades of Hood's Division pushed swiftly into the southern edge

---

[8] *O. R.*, 19, pt. 1, pp. 923, 955, 967, 1007; *Hood*, 42.
[9] *O. R.*, 19, pt. 1, p. 923.

of the cornfield. Hardened though they were, they were appalled. Shambles, ghastly and streaming red, the Federals had created. By musketry in front and by the enfilading blasts of several Union batteries,[10] almost half of Lawton's and of Hays's troops had been slaughtered. Lawton himself had been wounded. Col. Marcellus Douglass had been killed at the front of the Georgians. A shell had exploded a little above the head of John R. Jones, and though no fragment of it struck him, he said it had stunned him so badly that he could not exercise command. W. E. Starke then had taken Jackson's withdrawing Division—only to fall in a few minutes with three fatal wounds. A. J. Grigsby, who was handling Winder's Brigade, assumed command—a Colonel in charge of a Division.[11] Never in all the Army's battles had so many high officers been put out of action so quickly. In the three Brigades of Ewell's Division, all save two of the regimental commanders either were down or soon were to fall.[12]

In the midst of this carnage, Hood deployed his men boldly. To aid the Texan, "Stonewall" directed Early to return from the support of Stuart on the extreme left. As ranking officer in Ewell's Division, Early must take command of it and give the utmost help to Hood. It was "hold or perish." In a time amazingly brief, the enemy had cut a gap on either side of the Hagerstown road. Every Confederate Brigade that had occupied the ground from Early's right to D. H. Hill's left had been swept aside. No organized force of more than a few score men remained to confront the enemy.

The Federals, still pressing on, now were close to the Dunker church. To stop them, Hood's hungry, mad Texans and their like-tempered comrades under General Law could not level 2000 muskets: Was it foolish for them to attempt to stop that fast, powerful and bewildering assault? If Hood thought so, or knew the odds he faced, he gave no sign. He must drive the enemy; he would. Gallantly his men entered the gap and pushed forward.

For the moment, they had the reward of daring. On Hood's right, D. H. Hill's line, which had bent but had not broken, contributed a steady, if not a heavy fire against the Federal left. On

---

[10] O. R., 19, pt. 1, pp. 978–79.   [11] O. R., 19, pt. 1, pp. 956, 1008.
[12] Ibid., 956.

the opposite flank of Hood and perpendicular to him. "Old Jube" was coming up. Already he had met some 300 men of Jackson's Division whom Colonel Grigsby and Colonel Stafford had rallied. With these and his own troops, Early was forming on the Federals' right. In short, if Hood seemed to have thrown himself into a gap, it now appeared that Hooker's Corps had advanced deep into a pocket, the three sides of which were held by D. H. Hill, by Hood and by Early.

It was not Jackson's nature silently to stand idle while his comrades fought. He had done that once—at White Oak Swamp—but he had come far since that last day of June. He must know how Hood fared and whether there was anything more he could undertake to help the Texans. Would "Sandie" Pendleton ride forward and ascertain? "Sandie" was off at the word. Said he afterward: "Such a storm of balls I never conceived it possible for men to live through. Shot and shell shrieking and crashing, canister and bullets whistling and hissing most fiend-like through the air until you could almost see them. In that mile's ride I never expected to come back alive." At last, unscathed, he found Hood and delivered his message.

A great moment that was for John Bell Hood. In an hour he might be dead. If he fashioned a fine, fiery sentence, it might become as famous as Barnard Bee's "There stands Jackson . . .", but Hood was too intent to be eloquent. In his reply was nothing sensational, nothing of exhibition or of declamation. Coolly observing everything the smoke did not obscure, Hood had sober judgment.

"Tell General Jackson," he said simply, "unless I get reinforcements I must be forced back, but I am going on while I can!"

On he went, not so fast as at Gaines' Mill or at Second Manassas, but as intrepidly and in the face of a heavier fire. As his veterans doggedly loaded and fired, they had to pass over dead men who lay in rows where the Federal fire had swept them in the first blast of battle. "Never before," said Hood, "was I so continuously troubled with fear that my horse would further injure some wounded fellow soldier, lying helpless on the ground." [13] Ere long, the fire faced by Hood's men grew fiercer, fresher, faster. Heavier resistance was being encountered. Although it

[13] *Hood*, 44.

was not plain at the moment, the I Corps had been repulsed, but Mansfield's XII—Banks's old Corps—was advancing in Hooker's stead. Hood had to halt. The best he could hope to do, with the help of D. H. Hill and a sharpening attack by Early, was to hold on till reinforcements reached him.

Jackson, ere this, had received Hood's brave message. "Stonewall," eyes ablaze, had not a soldier of his own to send into the cornfield. Every Brigade, every regiment save one that Early had left to support Stuart's guns, was engaged or shattered or wrecked altogether. The only recourse was the army reserve: Pendleton must ride to headquarters, find General Lee, repeat to him Hood's message and ask for help. Once more Pendleton dashed away. When he returned, it was to report that Lee had already dispatched Walker's Division from the right and had said, also, "I'll send McLaws." [14]

For these troops—for any who could come from any quarter— Hood waited and, as he waited, fought. Now with a sullen loss and now with a cheering gain of ground, his battle raged uncertainly but not long. By supreme exertion, Mansfield's attack was repulsed. The action fell away to an artillery exchange. What was left of Hood's Division slowly drew back to the Dunker church to rest and to replenish ammunition that in some regiments had been spent to the last cartridge.[15] "For God's sake, more troops," cried Hood.[16] When a brother-officer rode over and asked, "Where is your Division?" Hood answered grimly, "Dead on the field." [17]

Before Hood fell back, "Tige" Anderson had been called from the right and for a time had been able to beat off attack. During Hood's withdrawal, Walker's Division arrived and engaged. While these forces of Anderson and of Walker,[18] two Brigades

---

[14] *Pendleton*, 216. McLaws had left Harpers Ferry at 3 P.M. on the 16th but had halted after dark about two miles short of Shepherdstown. There, happily, a courier from Lee had found him and had delivered an order to speed his march to Sharpsburg. At midnight McLaws had taken the road again and, after sunrise on the 17th, he had the head of his column near the town; but even then, he lost time in finding General Lee. When McLaws did locate the commanding General, Lee prudently directed him to rest his men who, by exhaustion and a mismanaged march, were reduced to a mere fragment of their numerical strength. *O. R.*, 19, pt. 1, pp. 857–58, 883.

[15] *O. R.*, 19, pt. 1, p. 923; *Hood*, 44.   [16] *Pendleton*, 216.

[17] 8 *S. H. S. P.*, 528, where the question is attributed to "Shanks" Evans. In view of the difficulty between Hood and Evans at Second Manassas, it scarcely is possible that they were on intimate terms at Sharpsburg. The sketch of Hood is resumed *infra*, pp. 257, 273.

[18] *O. R.*, 19, pt. 1, pp. 909, 914–15.

and a half, were in confused action, McLaws reached the scene and started his troops forward.

The Georgian quickly met the impact of a fresh Corps, Sumner's II, but he repeated Hood's gallant feat in driving the enemy back to approximately the point where the battle had opened at sunrise. In doing this, McLaws's Division was scattered badly. Exposed and unsupported on its flanks, it was halted and, after a time, was forced to give ground.[19] Its front was broken in the movement, but it was not pursued. From a new position, McLaws continued to challenge the Federals with the help of "Tige" Anderson and of Ransom of Walker's Division. Jubal Early, who had done magnificently on the left, proudly re-formed his regiments and held his flank position.[20]

For the first time since sunrise, Jackson's front now was free of pressure. He now could mend his worn line, could carry off his wounded, and could prepare to meet another attack—if it came. Three Corps he had beaten off in successive assaults—the I, the II and the XII. At Groveton only had he ever been so long or so violently assaulted.

The reason for the lessened force of the hammer-strokes on Jackson was the shift of the fiercest action to the Confederate center. D. H. Hill's Brigades, Ripley's, Colquitt's and Garland's [21] had been battered in the previous onslaughts of the morning, but Rodes's and George B. Anderson's Brigades had been damaged little. They had been placed by Hill in a sunken road that branched almost at the perpendicular from the right of the Hagerstown highway about 500 yards South of the Dunker church. There they had been well protected from hostile fire. To the left of these troops, and somewhat at an angle on the west side of the Hagerstown road, were the Twenty-seventh North Carolina and the Third Arkansas of Walker's Brigade. These regiments had been stationed at that point when Walker went into action, in order that they might fill a gap between Jackson's right and D. H. Hill's left.[22]

Of these forces—indeed, of everything to the right of Jackson—

[19] O. R., 19, pt. 1, p. 858.
[20] Ibid., 858–59, 971. For the next phases of Early's career, see infra, pp. 259, 356.
[21] The last-named under Col. D. K. McRae of the Fifth North Carolina. O. R., 19, pt. 1, pp. 1022, 1043.
[22] O. R., 19, pt. 1, pp. 914–15.

the command was vested in Longstreet, but Hill handled Longstreet's left, which was the center of the entire Confederate position. The North Carolinian was as contemptuous as ever of danger. Perhaps he was more confident, more certainly full of fight, because the responsibility of the field did not rest on him. While his battle still was confined to his left, he received a visit from the commanding General, and with Lee he rode to the right of the Division where George Anderson and Rodes were waiting in the sunken road. Everywhere Hill heard Lee give the same exhortation to the men: they must hold their ground, because a break on their front would endanger the whole Army. When this was told the Sixth Alabama, and Lee and Hill were moving away, Col. John B. Gordon—the ramrod Georgian who had fought with glorious valor at Seven Pines, at Gaines' Mill and at Malvern Hill—cried after them: "These men are going to stay here, General, till the sun goes down or victory is won!" This, Gordon wrote afterward, he said "to comfort General Lee and General Hill, and especially to make, if possible, my men still more resolute of purpose." [23]

Hill bade farewell to Lee, who rode off toward Jackson's wing,[24] and then the North Carolinian turned back to face the coming storm. With soldierly calm, he watched the approach of the left of Sumner's Corps, which continued to press vigorously after the right had been repulsed by McLaws. Toward the sunken road, two blue Divisions, well led and well supported, advanced steadily if slowly. Hill beat off their attack without great difficulty.

A little later, when Harvey Hill learned that R. H. Anderson had arrived in support, he struck out, here and there, in counterattacks.[25] Anderson he frugally kept behind him as a second line, but soon he had word that Anderson had fallen, severely wounded, and that the command had devolved on Roger A. Pryor, senior Brigadier. From that moment, Anderson's Division ceased to act as a unit.[26] It sustained heavy casualties and it kept up scattered,

[23] *Gordon*, 84. For the next incidents of Gordon's career, see *infra*, p. 262.

[24] For a somewhat late account of the manner in which Lee rallied the stragglers on the left, see 8 *S. H. S. P.*, 528.

[25] Cf. *O. R.*, 19, pt. 1, p. 1037. Doubtless Lee had told Hill that Anderson would reinforce him, but of this there is no record.

[26] Longstreet, *op. cit.*, 248, stated that Pryor was "not advised of his new authority." D. H. Hill merely said in his report, *O. R.*, 19, pt. 1, p. 1023, that the "command devolved upon General Pryor." In Rodes's report, *ibid.*, 1037, reference is made to Pryor' presence on the field, but in the circumstances mentioned, Pryor might have been exercising divisional or brigade command. For Anderson. see p. 359 and Chap. XXXI.

sporadic fire from the vicinity of the Hagerstown road; but it lacked leadership, direction, drive or striking-power. Hill soon realized that his own Division, unsupported, would have to bear the brunt of the next attack.

That attack came speedily. The Federal left, driving gallantly forward, reached a position from which the bluecoats could enfilade part of the Sixth Alabama in the sunken road. By that time, Colonel Gordon was down and unconscious with his fifth wound of the day.[27] For orders, his Lieutenant Colonel, J. N. Lightfoot, hurried to Rodes, who was at his gallant best. In the knowledge that his losses had been light, except in the flank companies of the Sixth, Rodes was determined to hold fast to the sunken road by refusing his right. An order to this effect he gave Lightfoot, who turned at once to execute it.

Rodes started after Lightfoot to see that the Sixth took a proper position, but as the General moved, he heard a thud and, looking back, found that his aide was falling from a shell wound. Quickly Rodes led the young man to safety and, returning, got an ugly wound of his own in the thigh. He forgot it almost as soon as he felt the blow because, to his amazement, he saw almost the whole of his famous Brigade running back in confusion. Nothing had happened, so far as he could observe, to force a retreat. The enemy was not pressing the Alabamians. Artillery fire was no more destructive than it had been.

The reality continued before his eyes: From ground they had held valiantly, his veterans were breaking for shelter as if they had been raw conscripts. He must rally them. Off to them he galloped. Among them he wheeled and turned. He shouted, he commanded, he pleaded. It was to small purpose. Major Hobson of the Fifth Alabama succeeded in bringing to a stand the bravest spirits of his regiment, together with a few undaunted men from other commands. These soldiers, altogether some 150, Rodes assembled under the shelter of a ridge about 150 yards from his position. The other survivors scattered.

They had left the sunken road, Rodes learned, through a misunderstanding. Lightfoot had ordered the Sixth to an "about face and forward march." Major Hobson naturally had asked if the order was meant for the entire Brigade. When Lightfoot mis-

27 *Gordon.* 90–91: Rodes in *O. R.,* 19, pt. 1, p. 1036.

takenly had replied that it was, Hobson had started his regiment. The other troops had assumed that the position was being evacuated and they had broken for cover. George Anderson on the left of Rodes held his ground for a few minutes of furious fight; but soon the rushing enemy turned him. Anderson himself was wounded. His Brigade was driven and broken.[28]

The center now was wrecked. East of the Hagerstown road, for hundreds of yards, no organization of even 1000 men confronted the advancing Federals. "Lee's army," said Porter Alexander, "was ruined and the end of the Confederacy was in sight." [29] One more heavy thrust by McClellan on a widening front would divide beyond possible reunion the two wings of the Confederate Army and would bring the Federals to the rear of both fragments.

If Harvey Hill realized that the rout and ruin of the Army of Northern Virginia might come then and there, on his front, he did not exhibit new anxiety. Neither did "Old Pete." Fuming in the carpet slippers his injured heel compelled him to wear, Longstreet rode or hobbled in search of men and guns to mend the gap in the line. Hill found in a corn field Boyce's South Carolina Battery,[30] which was awaiting orders. Cheerfully, Boyce's men dashed into the open and began to unlimber. Instantly the closely watching Federal gunners opened on them. One of the first shots exploded a Confederate caisson, but that mishap served only to speed the Carolinians. In a few minutes they were sprinkling with canister the Union troops who now had crossed the sunken road and were creeping forward.

To Boyce's salvos, which made the Federals hesitate,[31] was added promptly the fire of Miller's Battery of the Washington Artillery.[32] Longstreet earlier in the day had employed this stout unit and, when the new situation demanded the instant use of every procurable gun, he thought of Miller and rode to the place where last he had seen the Louisianians. They were there, ready and unafraid, though they could use one section only of their battery. At Longstreet's word, that section was rushed forward and was put into action. On it, immediately, as on Boyce's pieces,

---

28 For the next section of the sketch of Rodes, see *infra*, Chap. XXXI.
29 *Alexander*, 262.   30 The Macbeth Battery, Evans's Brigade.
31 Hill in *O. R.*, 19, pt. 1, p. 1024. Curiously enough, Boyce in his report, *ibid.*, 943, mentioned no order from D. H. Hill.
32 Second Company, Capt. M. B. Miller.

the Federals opened with a devastating blast. Miller's men began to fall. Their fire was about to slacken. Longstreet's staff officers slipped off their mounts and took the stations of the stricken gunners. "Old Pete" himself held their horses and calmly assisted in correcting the range.[33]

At this instant, when oncoming disaster and improvised defense were balanced, Miller, Boyce and the scattered remnants of D. H. Hill's command found that they had on their left unbending support. The Twenty-seventh North Carolina and the Third Arkansas of Walker's Division originally had been deployed by their commander between Jackson's right and D. H. Hill's left. Now that the Federals had swept back the troops on either flank, these two regiments held an advanced position, which was both threatened and threatening. They were under Col. John R. Cooke of the Twenty-seventh, whose gallantry was matched by that of John W. Reedy, the senior Captain in command of the Third Arkansas regiment. From these officers' well handled regiments was pouring a volume of fire which the Federals might have credited to a strong and confident Brigade.

As the fire swelled, the fighting blood of John Rogers Cooke rose. In order that he might observe at closer range some suspicious movements of the enemy, Cooke ran out in front of his position some fifteen yards and stood behind a small hickory tree, whence he shouted back his orders to his men. The Federals soon saw him and did their utmost to hit him. They riddled the hickory but, incredibly, they could not touch the resolute Colonel.[34]

Cooke's bold fire and that of the two batteries began to tell. On Hill's center and right the blue line stopped. Then it wavered and slowly slipped back. Hill was quick to observe this. In the withdrawal he sensed opportunity, and he appealed to the men around him to organize a counter-charge. "I was . . . satisfied," he said afterward, "that the Yankees were so demoralized . . . a single regiment of fresh men could drive the whole of them in our front across the Antietam."[35] He did not have a regiment—not one, fresh or blown—but would not the still unwounded soldiers

[33] Walton in *O. R.*, 19, pt. 1, pp. 849–50; *Sorrel*, 112–13.
[34] 2 *N. C. Regts.*, 434; letter of Capt. Jos. C. Webb, Orange Guards, Oct. 9, 1862, printed in the *Hillsboro Record*, n.d.—*Cooke MSS.*
[35] *O. R.*, 19, pt. 1, p. 1024.

attack? One answered that he would go if Hill would lead. Instantly Hill agreed. Soon he had some 200 in a crude, uneven line. Hill seized a rifle, shouted a command and started forward. It was fine but it was fruitless. So small a force could not get far in the face of the fire the Unionists poured into it. Hill reluctantly had to recall his volunteers. The same fate met an attack organized by some of the North Carolina Colonels and delivered on the right center.

Cooke, for his part, saw from the uncertain shelter of his hickory tree that the Federals who had fallen back elsewhere were trying to bring up artillery against him.[36] Unmindful of odds, he ordered a charge.[37] Just as the willing Arkansans and North Carolinians were starting toward the enemy, an unidentified Confederate officer rode out in front—nobody observed whence—took off his hat, waved it and yelled: "Come on, boys; I'm leading this charge!" The men in the ranks were not too intent on their task to perceive on the instant that the gentleman already was well charged. They would have jeered him quickly into some consciousness of his condition, because they always had sarcasms for unidentified riders, but Lt. Col. R. W. Singletary of the Twenty-seventh did not give them time to express their opinion. Angrily he ran up to the mounted stranger and shouted: "You are a liar, sir! We lead our own charges!"[38] There scarcely could have been an encounter more perfectly typical of the Army of Northern Virginia. What became of the drunken officer, in the onsweep of Cooke's command, the record does not show. Rebuked, he was forgotten.

The two magnificent regiments now were moving forward. On the front of the Carolinians, the most conspicuous figure soon was the color bearer, William H. Campbell.[39] In the storm of bullets, waving the regiment's red flag, he pushed ahead of the line. Cooke had to call out to him to slacken his pace. "Colonel," protested Campbell, "I can't let that Arkansas fellow get ahead of me!"[40]

[36] 2 N. C. Regts., 434–35.   [37] Capt. Jos. C. Webb, loc. cit.
[38] 2 N. C. Regts., 436.
[39] Private, Company G, Orange County, North Carolina, killed the next autumn at Bristoe Station. Ibid.
[40] 2 N. C. Regts., 436.

Slow walking Federals were overtaken and sent to the rear. A rabble that took shelter behind some haystacks was told to stay there till it could be moved to ground less exposed. The two regiments, disdaining security for their flanks, pushed wildly on till they found the enemy behind a fence in a corn field.[41] Determined Federal officers were waiting there with unbeaten troops; the fight would be to the finish. Cooke halted his line, examined the ground and then, with a cold prudence that matched his hot valor, decided not to assault. His position was too advanced, his numbers too few and his ammunition too low.

After he ordered a withdrawal, the usual thing happened: the pace of his men became faster, formation was lost, retirement soon became almost a rout. The prisoners who had been left among the haystacks turned on the Confederates and shot down many a brave man. Both regiments were thinned and exhausted before they reached the position from which they had launched their attack, but they still were undaunted. Besides, even at the price of going forward, Cooke had divested himself of his thin hickory tree. When Longstreet sent once again to thank Cooke and to tell him he must keep his ground at any cost, the Colonel swore a breath-taking, hair-raising oath and assured the General, "We will stay here . . . if we must all go to hell together."[42] More formally, then or later, Cooke said: "Tell General Longstreet to send me some ammunition. I have not a cartridge in my command, but will hold my position at the point of the bayonet."[43]

Precisely that Cooke made ready to do. When the Federals came on again, though his men's rifles were silent, he had the color bearers wave their flags as notice alike to friend and to foe that he held his ground. Daring justified itself. This time the Unionists' advance was weak. It veered off to Cooke's right and soon collapsed under the fire of the artillery that now had been

---

[41] Captain Graham, *op. cit.*, remembered this as a stone fence. Actually, the corn field was fenced with rail on the northern and southern sides and with posts and rail on the eastern side. These directions are approximate only. It probably is not necessary to point out that this corn field was near the Mumma House and was about half a mile south of the corn field, below the Miller House, where Lawton and Hays were under heavy fire. The two fields have been confused.

[42] Sorrel, *op. cit.*, 114, gave what he, perhaps overmodestly, termed "a faint reproduction of the Colonel's gift of language."

[43] 2 *N. C. Regt* 436.

assembled to defend Hill's front.[44] After that, as much to the amazement as to the relief of the Confederate leaders, about 2 P.M. the attack on the center came to an end. Subsequently, the Confederates learned that at this stage of the battle Franklin's VI Corps had arrived on the field and had reinforced the II Corps, but that General Sumner decided against employing the fresh troops. McClellan later approved that decision. "The repulse of this, the only remaining Corps available for attack," the commanding General explained, "would peril the safety of the whole army." [45]

The battle was not over; it had undergone another shift. Other actors held the stage. At 7 in the morning, the scene of supreme danger had been on the Confederate left, where Jackson's line had been broken. Noon had brought the crisis of Rodes's withdrawal from the center. Now the Confederate right was being threatened with ruin.

From dawn, that wing of the Army had been numerically weak; hourly it had become weaker. Walker had been hurried to the left. No troops had remained to the right of D. H. Hill except the Division of D. R. Jones—six tragically small Brigades, whose "aggregate present" was 2460 men. From this force, "Tige" Anderson's five Georgia regiments had been sent to help Jackson. Scant reinforcement was at hand. Until A. P. Hill arrived from Harpers Ferry—if he could hope to complete his march that day —Jones could call up two regiments only.[46] Jones, in a word, with about 2000 infantry, had to defend more than a mile of front.[47]

If the assailed left was to be held, this risky thinning of the right was unavoidable. It had been ordered, also, in sound knowl-

---

[44] O. R., 19, pt. 1, pp. 150, 840, 915, 1024. Capt. James A. Graham, in his brief but admirable history of the Twenty-seventh, 2 N. C. Regts., 437, chivalrously expressed his regret that the Third Arkansas, which shared equally the dangers and duties of the field, did not receive proper recognition in the published reports. "It was a gallant regiment," said he, ". . . and was with the Twenty-seventh in every move." For the continuance of the sketch of Cooke, see infra, pp. 261, 360 ff.

[45] O. R., 19, pt. 1, pp. 61–62. On the Confederate side of the line, a suggestion that an entire Corps be held in reserve would have seemed fantastic. The Army of Northern Virginia thought itself opulent and fortunate when it had one Division in reserve. Hill reappears, infra, p. 274.

[46] These two regiments were of Toombs's Brigade and had been guarding wagons. O. R., 19, pt. 1, pp. 886, 890.

[47] From the Boonsborough road southward to the extreme right.

edge and shrewd appraisal of the terrain. The position assigned David Jones was, for the most part, on heights overlooking Antietam Creek. Artillery had been posted where it could cover the infantry though it was itself exposed [48] to the longer range Federal ordnance on the opposite side of the stream. An added defense, on the Confederate side, was the nature of the approaches. A narrow bridge, which after that day was styled Burnside's, crossed the creek at the foot of the heights midway Jones's position. This bridge offered so tempting an avenue of advance that the enemy was almost certain to attempt to force it; but the road leading to it from the East ran almost parallel to the creek for a quarter of a mile. A few hundred men on the heights to the westward could make that stretch of road a slaughter pen. It was worse than Jackson's road at White Oak Swamp.[49]

Command of the small force defending the crossing of Antietam Creek was in the hands of Robert Toombs, who had been restored to duty on the field of Manassas.[50] Toombs had written his wife that enemies were trying to drive him from the Army, but that he would not resign until he had distinguished himself in some great battle. "The day after such an event," he had said, "I will retire if I live through it." [51] His opportunity had come. The stage was his. On him were the eyes of all spectators. He had—or assumed he had—titular command of a nominal Division; [52] responsibility for the Brigade which would have to do

---

[48] So far as the writer knows, there never has been an adequate study of the artillery action on the front Burnside vs. Jones. Many of the artillery officers failed, apparently, to file reports. Other officers, including even Gen. Henry J. Hunt, reported sketchily.

[49] See supra, Vol. I, p. 572.

[50] Longstreet had released Toombs from arrest on August 30. Toombs then had ridden triumphantly to his Brigade, which was preparing to advance. He was received with much cheering. During the charge of his troops, according to one narrator, Toombs cried: "Go to it, boys! I am with you again. Jeff Davis can make a general, but it takes God Almighty to make a soldier." Inasmuch as the report for Toombs's Brigade at Second Manassas was filed by Col. H. L. Benning (O. R., 12, pt. 2, p. 593 ff), this story of Toombs's resumption of command that day is probably apocryphal. The more plausible account is that of Capt. H. L. French, Seventeenth Georgia, who quoted Toombs as saying: "Boys, I am proud of the report given of you by General Jones. I could not be with you today, but this was owing to no fault of mine. Tomorrow, I lead you" (Stovall, 261). Longstreet, who had the impression that Toombs returned to command on the 30th, wrote (2 B. & L., 526): "I had no more trouble with Toombs. We were ever afterwards warm personal friends."

[51] Stovall, 270.

[52] Toombs opened his report on the Maryland expedition by stating that on the day the Army left Leesburg, D. R. Jones notified him that he was assigned to command of a Division composed of his own, Drayton's and "Tige" Anderson's Brigades (O. R., 19, pt. 1, p. 888). In a later sentence, Toombs referred to the detachment of Anderson, and to the retention of Drayton in Jones's line of battle, but he wrote as if he still had

most of the fighting would rest on its senior Colonel, Henry L. Benning.[53] All was well. If Toombs the politician was to prove himself the successful soldier, the hour was striking.

During the morning the Federals had been demonstrating on Toombs's front as if at any moment they were going to plunge over the bridge and overwhelm the two regiments that Benning had stationed where he could command both the crossing and the approaches to it. Each time the Federals were advanced, they were repulsed bloodily. By noon, signs had multiplied that a major attack was coming. Above the bridge a column forced its way over the creek. About three-quarters of a mile downstream,[54] a Division was astride the Antietam. Troops manifestly were gathering to make another dash for the bridge.

How could these forces be resisted? The two Confederate regiments defending the stream-side opposite the bridge almost had exhausted their ammunition. They must be sacrificed or withdrawn. The decision was left to David Jones, who made his choice without hesitation: Nothing worth the price could be gained by leaving the Georgians to be slaughtered or captured. Jones designated a position, high on the hillside, where Toombs's Brigade could be deployed.[55] Benning—"Old Rock" to his men—

exercised divisional command. Actually, the only troops he commanded in addition to his own regiments were the Fiftieth Georgia of Drayton, five companies of the Eleventh Georgia of Anderson, and one company from Jenkins's Brigade. There seems to have been some question on the part of Jenkins's and probably of Drayton's men regarding his right to command them (see O. R., 19, pt. 1, pp. 889–91), but neither Longstreet nor D. R. Jones, in his report, mentioned Toombs's "Division." On the contrary, when Longstreet described the final Federal attack on the right, the reference was to "Jones with six Brigades,' which included all that Toombs had styled his own (O. R., 19, pt. 1, p. 840). Jones (ibid., 885–86) noted that his Division had been increased to six Brigades.

[53] Colonel Benning was 48 and, after a successful career as a lawyer in Georgia, had served for six years as a judge of the State Supreme Court. In July, 1862, he had disputed the constitutionality of the conscription act and had refused to obey orders based on it, but through the good offices of his fellow Georgian, Col. T. R. R. Cobb, he escaped arrest and court martial (Cobb in 28 S. H. S. P., 294). At Second Manassas, while in command of Toombs's Brigade, Benning lost control of his troops after a sudden stroke by the Federals. Astride an artillery horse, he rode to Longstreet and reported: "General, I am ruined; my Brigade was suddenly attacked and every man was killed; not one is to be found. Please give orders where I can do some fighting." Longstreet answered: "Nonsense, Colonel. You are not so badly hurt. Look about you. I know you will find at least one man, and with him on his feet, report your Brigade to me, and you two shall have a place in the fighting-line." This ridicule sobered Benning, who soon rallied his men and went back into the fight (Sorrel, 199). He was of impressive person, fully 6 feet tall. His voice was deep and guttural, his enunciation of each syllable distinct (6 C. M. H., 396–97).

[54] On an airline. As the creek bent, the distance was more than a mile.

[55] This position, shown on Antietam Board Map No. 12, is about 900 yards Southwest of Burnside's Bridge, in a corn field, with a rail fence in front and a stone fence to left and rear.

brought back to this ground the Second and the Twentieth regiments. The few co-operating companies from the other Brigades slipped into place.[56] By good chance, also, the two absent regiments of Toombs arrived on the field at this time [57] and went to the front line. The tired men who had defended the bridge all the forenoon were sent to the rear to refill their cartridge boxes.

About 1 o'clock, from across Antietam Creek, there came a sudden stir. Swiftly and in heavy mass, two Federal regiments [58] dashed for the bridge. Before the Confederate artillery could be trained on them, they were over! West of the stream, in a moment, the Stars and Stripes were floating. From every Federal position where the flag could be seen, wild, hoarse cheers were raised. Jones's infantry could do nothing but watch and steel their hearts for the coming charge. The Southern artillery, adjusting its range, tried to drop its projectiles in the ranks that were being formed near the creek. The fire was not effective. Although it forced the bluecoats to hug the ground, it did not prevent the crossing—at the bridge, above and below—of heavy reinforcements. Artillery bounced over the span and found shelter. Moment by moment the Union force was stronger, the threat to Toombs more desperate. Close to 3 o'clock, slowly and ponderously, the mighty line began to move up the hill.

The chief attack was to the left of Toombs and against those of Jones's Brigades on the crest directly East of Sharpsburg.[59] Small though these Brigades were, smaller than a corresponding number of regiments should have been, they had good artillery, which was being increased rapidly. The shells of these guns soon were exchanged for canister; the infantry opened as the irregular blue line appeared on the heights. For a time, it was a stand-off fight and therefore encouraging, because one of A. P. Hill's batteries already had arrived and had brought word that the Light Division was close behind it on the road. If the Union force could be held until Hill arrived, five veteran Brigades could be thrown

---

[56] O. R., 19, pt. 1, pp. 890–91.

[57] Together with five companies of the Eleventh Georgia of G. T. Anderson's Brigade.

[58] 51st N. Y. and 51st Penn. Sturgis's 2nd Div., IX Corps.

[59] Kemper and Drayton were South of the road to Burnside's Bridge, with their faces to the East. Between this road and that to Boonsborough were Jenkins and Garnett. Their line of fire also was eastward. Jenkins was on higher ground than Garnett and almost in echelon to the right and rear. The situation is shown admirably on Antietam Board Map No. 12.

against the left of the blue line that was creeping through the corn and across the open ground. Jones was diligent; Lee himself came to the Confederate right and brought to bear all the supporting artillery he could find.

It was not enough. Still slowly and cautiously, the Federals moved up, but behind their admirably led attack was a strength not to be resisted by Confederates so few. Kemper's Brigade was driven into the town and was pursued toward it.[60] Drayton's command was broken,[61] though his Fifteenth South Carolina [62] stubbornly kept its formation and fell back slowly. "Dick" Garnett held his ground for some time but when he at length gave ground, his men went far around to the north side of the town.[63] With a changed, front, and in danger of being cut off and surrounded, Jenkins's Brigade hung on.[64]

By 4 P.M. the battle on the right was almost lost to the Confederates. The Federals had gained nearly all the high ground East and South of Sharpsburg. If they could push 1200 yards farther westward, they would be across the line of retreat the left wing of Lee's Army would have to take to the Shepherdstown Ford. From the northern side of the town, Federal flags could be seen [65] as if the blue columns already were advancing toward the Shepherdstown road. Sharpsburg itself was aflame and under artillery fire; its side streets were filled with demoralized soldiers, who had become separated from their commands; above it, through the smoke and bursting shells, flocks of bewildered pigeons flew round and round; [66] on the left, at Lee's instance, Jackson had ridden out to see if he could create a diversion; sorrowfully "Stonewall" had concluded that the attempt would be too hazardous.[67]

Disaster should have been in the air, and with it the first signs of stampede. It was not so. The thrilling news had spread that A. P. Hill was coming. For fate or fame, his was to be the last

[60] O. R., 19, pt. 1, p. 886.
[62] Under Col. W. D. DeSaussure.
[64] Ibid., 891.
[66] E. A. Moore, 155.

[61] Ibid., and O.R., 21, 1030.
[63] O. R., 19, pt. 1, p. 897.
[65] Cf. Garnett in O.R., 19, pt. 1, p. 897.

[67] O. R., 19, pt. 1, pp. 956–57. This incident is not to be confused with the one regarding which Stephen D. Lee gave the account that appears in 2 Henderson, 264 ff. Although Gen. S. D. Lee was a gentleman incapable of deliberate distortion of fact, it is to be apprehended that in this instance, as in that concerning the details of the council of war held on the night of September 17, the memory of the General had become somewhat confused.

scene. Of his thoughts on that furious march from Harpers Ferry, there are no records, and of his acts not many. Half in complaint and half in admiration, soldiers were to say later that on the long, choking road from Shepherdstown,[68] he had urged the laggard forward with the point of his sword.[69] The impetuosity that had been his vice was now his spur. If regiments swooned by the road, to Sharpsburg he would go in time to reinforce Lee. Every sound of fire was a summons. Speed the march, close up, close up! The life of the Confederacy might depend on the pace of that one Division. Hill had on his red battle shirt [70] and though he was hurrying fast, he had an eye for everything. Once, as he neared the field, he drew rein by the side of a tree behind which a frightened second Lieutenant was crouching. Wrathfully, Hill demanded the man's sword, took it, broke it over the shirker's back [71] and dashed on.

When Hill met Lee, tradition has it, the reserved commanding General, eased of a cruel concern, embraced him in relief.[72] Where were Hill's troops; how soon would they arrive? The answer well might have been proud: Batteries already were arriving; not far behind Hill were the South Carolinians of Gregg. Although sixteen miles of weary road had worn them, Gregg's men marched as became the vanguard of Gaines' Mill. Closely following Gregg was Archer.

From the majestic presence of the commanding General, who was anxious but resolute, A. P. Hill rode to the right. In brief conference, he and David Jones agreed that Gregg was to occupy the corn field held by Toombs, and that Toombs then was to move by the left flank and attack the exposed right of the Federals who now were pressing into the very streets of Sharpsburg Archer's Brigade was to form to the left of Gregg and on the right of Toombs.

Not so readily was Toombs to be shoved from the stage to the

---

[68] O. R., 19, pt. 1, p. 988.   [69] Alexander, 266.

[70] Douglas, 173. Cf. 19 S. H. S. P., 178: "It was his habit when on the march to wear what was called then a 'hunting shirt.' "

[71] 19 S. H. S. P., 181.

[72] The writer heard this several times from Confederate staff officers present at Sharpsburg, but never has been able to verify it from a written record. Col. Alexander C. Haskell, writing years after the war, op. cit., 80, stated that Lee met Hill at Boteler's Ford and said: "General Hill, this is the last force we have. You must hold half in reserve and send in the other half." This is not reported by any other eye witness, and it may have occurred farther from the ford than Colonel Haskell thought at the time he wrote, but the remark he attributes to Lee has verisimilitude.

wing. In the outworking, he was ordered to the left before Gregg's Brigade could reach the corn field, but the Carolinians saved that position. When Toombs approached the ground chosen for him, he found it in the hands of the Unionists. His own account of his next move reads in this proud fashion: "[The Federals] held possession of all the ground from the corn field on [D. R. Jones's] right down to the Antietam Bridge road, including the eastern suburbs of the town of Sharpsburg, all the troops defending it having been driven back and retired to the rear or through the town. Under this state of affairs, I had instantly to determine either to retreat or fight. A retreat would have left the town of Sharpsburg and General Lee's rear open to the enemy, and was inadmissible. I, therefore, with less than one-fifth of the enemy's numbers, determined to give him battle. . . . As soon as possible I opened fire on the enemy's columns, who immediately advanced in good order upon me until he approached within 60 or 80 paces, when the effectiveness of the fire threw his column in considerable disorder, upon perceiving which I immediately ordered a charge, which, being brilliantly and energetically executed by my whole line, the enemy broke in confusion and fled." [73]

That was as Toombs saw it in retrospect. In the red reality of the field, the repulse involved far more troops than Toombs's Brigade and the fragment of Kemper's that Toombs credited his own aide with bringing into action.[74] A. P. Hill threw Archer's men forward in a direct charge. Gregg and Branch supported Archer and Toombs vigorously with a flank fire that alarmed the enemy as much as it hurt him.[75]

At the head of his Brigade, directing the fire, L. O'B. Branch fell.[76] Maxcy Gregg was just wheeling his injured horse when a

[73] Toombs added that he wished to pursue his charge and to drive the Federals across the Antietam, but that the artillery sent him for that purpose did not arrive before nightfall. *O. R.*, 19, pt. 1, p. 891.

[74] *Ibid.* For the next references to Toombs, see *infra*, p. 274.

[75] See 6 *C. V.*, 28. That the participation of these units of the Light Division in the counterstroke on the right was decisive, their losses attested. Hill's casualties of 346 occurred among Brigades that mustered on the field about 2000 rifles (*O. R.*, 19, pt. 1, p. 981). Toombs neglected to report the number of men he had present for duty, but he noted that his Second and Twentieth Georgia together numbered 400 (*O. R.*, 19, pt. 1, p. 889). On that basis, his total strength did not exceed 800. His killed and wounded were 139 (*O. R.*, 19, pt. 1, p. 811), of whom ninety-one belonged to the two regiments named. In terms of percentage, their casualties, 43 per cent., were heavier than those of any Brigade of Hill's command, but for Toombs's Brigade as a whole, the percentage of casualties, 17, was almost precisely the same as Hill's.

[76] *O. R.*, 19, pt. 1, p. 981. See *infra*, p. 251.

bullet crashed near his right hip and almost knocked him out of the saddle. His aide, Alexander Haskell, lifted him down and placed him gently on the ground in the belief that his hurt was mortal. Gregg would not permit the younger man to lose time in examining the hip. "Captain Haskell," said he in soldierly manner, "notify and put the next officer in command." When Haskell returned from this duty, the sergeant of the stretcher bearers was bent over Gregg. "General," the N.C.O. cried, "you aren't *wounded,* you are only *bruised.*" Up sprang Gregg and soon was directing his men from the back of a bony ambulance horse he stripped of its harness.[77]

By that time, the Confederates were driving the whole left wing of the Federals downhill to the banks of the Antietam. Above the din of battle could be heard the fox-hunters' call, the wild "rebel yell." Red banners were following stars and stripes. Ragged boys in butternut leaped over prone bodies in blue. The roar of the guns on the heights swelled to a pitch of triumph. Yard by yard the Union line, sagging and gaping but unbroken, fell back to the shelter of the low ridges near the creek. Slowly, after sunset, the fire died away By nightfall, the ghastly action ended. To the bark of the gun succeeded the wail of the wounded.

Never had the Army of Northern Virginia fought a battle so doubtful, save at Malvern Hill, and never one so long. "The sun," a soldier wrote, "seemed almost to go backwards, and it appeared as if night would never come."[78] During twelve hours and more of conflict, Lee had thrown into action every organized infantry unit North of the Potomac.[79] Within supporting distance South of the river, he had only Thomas's Brigade, which was guarding the guns and stores captured at Harpers Ferry. Though all were

[77] *Mrs. Daly,* 82. Colonel Haskell added that the next morning, when Gregg sat down to eat his breakfast of an ear of corn, "he reached back to the tail pocket of his frock uniform coat, pulled out his big silk handkerchief, and, as he opened it and spread it across his knees for a napkin, out dropped a rifle ball, flat as a half dollar— the ball that had given him the terrible blow the day before." Gregg observed, "Well, that is the second time this has happened to me," and he explained that prior to the war he had been hit over his vest pocket while acting as a second in a duel at Charleston. Surgeons vainly probed the surface wound but could not find the ball. After they left, his body-servant took off his boots and found the bullet in one of them. It had struck the contents of Gregg's pocket and had slipped downward (*Mrs. Daly,* 82–83). The sketch of Gregg is continued *infra,* pp. 355, 374 ff.

[78] 2 *N. C. Regts.,* 437.

[79] This will apply, at least technically, to Pender's Brigade and to Field's Brigade, under Col. John M. Brockenbrough, though A. P. Hill did not consider that these two Brigades shared in the action. Both Brigades were under fire (Cf. *O. R.,* 19, pt. 1, p. 981). The sketch of A. P. Hill is resumed *infra,* p. 233.

used, they were all too few. Straggling had reduced to 40,000 the men who had withstood the shock of the furious assaults that had rolled from left to right. Sharpsburg, indeed, was not one battle but three. Mercifully for the Confederates, the mismanagement of the battle by the Federals was such that after Jackson had been strained to the utmost and close to disaster, the Unionists had left his troops panting, and had attacked the Division of D. H. Hill and the reinforcements sent him. For an hour or two, Hill had been in danger of being overwhelmed. When it had seemed that one more thrust inevitably would drive him in rout to the Potomac, the enemy had desisted. Then the thin Confederate right had been assailed.[80]

Outside "Dick" Anderson's command, which had not been brought fully into the battle after the fall of its commander, every Division had suffered cruelly. To anyone with less faith than Lee had in his troops, it would not have seemed possible that the Army could face the enemy the next day. Retreat seemed as logical as, after so gallant a fight, it would be honorable; but Lee would not have it so. He held his ground all the next day, while his adversary hesitated, and not until the evening of the 18th did he begin an undisputed withdrawal to the south shore of the Potomac.[81] Dawn of the 19th found the remnant of Ewell's Division, the infantry rearguard, splashing through Boteler's Ford back to Virginia.[82] The price of the expedition had been 13,609 casualties or more. Of these, about 10,000 represented Sharpsburg. Federal losses were 27,767, of which Harpers Ferry accounted for 45 per cent. Twice as many men the Federals had lost as had the Confederates, but one for two was more than the South could afford to pay.[83]

[80] Perhaps the two fullest accounts of the battle are those in *Allan's Army*, 372 ff, and in F. W. Palfrey, *The Antietam and Fredericksburg*, 42 ff. The most lucid brief account is Alexander's, *op. cit.*, 241 ff.

[81] For the considerations that prompted Lee to remain at Sharpsburg, see 2 *R. E. Lee*, 403 ff. Allan's review, *Army*, 438 ff, is excellent. General McClellan's reasons for not renewing the attack on the 18th were set forth in his report, *O. R.*, 19, pt. 1, pp. 65–67. General Palfrey's conclusion was: "It is hardly worth while to state [McClellan's] reasons. It has been already strongly urged that he ought to have fought out the battle on the 17th, and there do not appear to have existed any better reasons for energetic action on the following day, except that two divisions then joined him after a hard march. The fault was in the man. There was force enough at his command either day, had he seen fit to use it" (*op. cit.*, 127).

[82] Early, in *O. R.*, 19, pt. 1, p. 972.

[83] *Alexander*, 239, 273–75.

CHAPTER XIV

Pendleton Fails to Count His Men

Like many another tragedy, that of Sharpsburg did not end at its high moment. It was prolonged to an anticlimax in which the embarrassed central figure was the Reverend William Nelson Pendleton, Brigadier General and Chief of Artillery, A. N. Va. Illness and circumstance had denied him any active share in the earlier part of the campaign. Via the North Anna [1] and ahead of his reserve batteries, he reported August 30 to Lee on the field of Manassas. Sick at the time, he was, as he told his wife, "urged by the general in the kindest manner to find some comfortable place, rest and get well." [2] Obediently, General Pendleton went with some of his staff to the Foote plantation, two miles North of Hay Market. Thence, on the 31st, he wrote further to Mrs. Pendleton: "Again I am writing you from a bed, and this time I am in it as an invalid. Not much, I hope, only the crisis of a diarrhoea of some two weeks' duration, rendered worse by my hard effort to catch up with General Lee." He explained that his guns would not arrive for two days and that he could "with an easy mind rest and recruit till then." To reassure his family he added: "I am as comfortable as I could be anywhere in the world away from home." [3]

A week later from Leesburg he wrote: "I am still unwell, but will try to take care of myself. Randolph blistered my right side to act on the liver; it has been very sore riding, but a quiet day has relieved it greatly." [4] He soon recovered sufficiently to follow the Army into Maryland: "About 12 [on the night of September 7] we reached Arcadia Farm. . . . There we have since been encamped on the banks of a nice stream." The community he found more than interesting. Before the war, he had been rector of All Saints' Church, Frederick; so, he duly recorded: "After reporting

[1] O. R., 12, pt. 3, p. 965.   [2] Pendleton, 209.
[3] Ibid.   [4] Ibid., 210.

to General Lee, Monday morning, I spent the day in calling on my old friends. . . . Greater kindness no one ever received." [5] The 13th of September found him near Hagerstown, and not in distress. He assured his wife: "I am myself much better; not quite sound and strong yet, but improving every day . . . we get along comfortably. Generally John and myself, with one or two others, find some place where we get wholesome food. At night we rest pleasantly in my tent." [6]

Thus introduced, the Maryland expedition did not prove a disagreeable or a dangerous adventure for Pendleton. He was in immediate reserve the day of the battle of South Mountain and he posted his batteries just before darkness. At midnight, Lee directed him to move back to Virginia the guns not needed with the Army, and to station them where they would command the fords. En route, Pendleton barely escaped an encounter with Federal cavalry who had slipped away from Harpers Ferry before the town was surrendered. Once across the Potomac, on the 16th, Pendleton so placed his guns—to quote the language of his report—that "the passage was thenceforward assiduously guarded." [7]

Although he was not under fire during the engagement at Sharpsburg, he found, as he said, that "other and arduous duties devolved upon the command and upon myself." He specified carefully: "By night and by day much labor was needed on the road; the passage of troops had to be facilitated, and important dispatches forwarded in different directions, all rendered the more essential toward [sic] General Jackson hastening to Sharpsburg after capturing Harpers Ferry. This continued through the 17th, while the battle (Sharpsburg) was raging, and during the night; especially in my having to meet a requisition for all the long-range guns that could be obtained and possibly spared from the fords. Instructions also reached me to have apprehended and sent forward all stragglers." [8] It was almost as hard for him, the General confided to his wife, on the 18th, the day the two armies held their ground and nursed their wounds on the ridges around Sharpsburg. "I should scarcely steal a nap," said he. [9] During the return of the Army to the Virginia side: "I had again to work like a beaver, as did all my officers and men, promoting the safe pas-

[5] *Ibid.*, 211.   [6] *Ibid.*, 212.
[7] *O. R.*, 19, pt. 1, p. 830.   [8] *O. R.*, 19, p 1, p. 830.
[9] *Pendleton*, 213.

sage of the army, with its immense trains of artillery and wagons, hence no rest again that night." [10]

Now, on the 19th, came what Pendleton termed "my great responsibility." [11] Under orders from Lee again to post guns to dispute the crossing of the Potomac at Boteler's Ford, Pendleton found positions for thirty-three and held eleven others out of range but within call.[12] Scarcely had this been done than the Federals appeared on the opposite side of the river. Long range rifles soon opened on Pendleton's batteries, which replied confidently but without wasting any ammunition. While an indifferent duel went on, Lee moved southward to get the men out of range. This withdrawal Pendleton described in his curious style: "Our troops that had been briefly resting in the valleys were now ordered farther inland, to be out of reach of the shells, &c., so numerously hurled by the enemy, yet near enough to turn readily upon and perhaps destroy the adverse army should it force the passage of the river and take position between it and our forces." [13]

To prevent this, Pendleton was given immediate command of the river bank and had assigned him the remnants of Lawton's and of Armistead's Brigades to support his guns and to act as sharpshooters. Pendleton's orders were to hold the crossing all day and for the night of the 19th–20th unless pressure became too heavy. In that event, he was to evacuate his position after nightfall and was to follow the track of the Army.[14]

The minister-artillerist never before had commanded infantry, nor had he now in the two Brigades assigned to him any officers experienced in the type of combat to which they were called. Lawton had been wounded at Sharpsburg; Armistead had been assigned as Provost Marshal of the Army.[15] The Colonels acting in their stead were courageous but knew little of handling a Brigade in the face of a long range artillery exchange. When they reported to Pendleton, he instructed them precisely. They were, he said, "to keep their force at the ford strong, vigilant, and as well sheltered as occasion allowed, and to have the residue well in hand, back of adjacent hills, for protection, till needed." Further, they were "not to fire merely in reply to shots from the other side,

[10] Ibid.
[11] Ibid.
[12] O. R., 19, pt. 1, p. 831.
[13] O. R., 19, pt. 1, p. 831.
[14] Ibid.
[15] O. R., 19, pt. 2, p. 596.

but only to repel any attempt at crossing, and to guard the ford." [16]
All this no doubt was enjoined firmly, perhaps eloquently. One
thing, if one only, General Pendleton omitted. That was to inquire of the Colonels how many men they had in the ranks of the
two Brigades. If the officers themselves knew, they did not volunteer the information.[17]

In due time, the commanding Colonels were sent to their posts.
Pendleton took pains, in his report, to explain where he went:
"My own position was chosen at a point central, moderately protected by conformation of ground, at the same time commanding
the general view and accessible from every direction, with as little
exposure of messengers as any one place in such a scene could be.
And here, except when some personal inspection or order had to
be given requiring temporary absence, I remained for best service
throughout the day." [18]

By midmorning, the superior Federal artillery on the northern
bank of the river was forcing the Confederates at most of the batteries to take cover. More than that, the Union fire covered the
advance of bluecoated sharpshooters to the parapet of the canal
that paralleled the northern bank of the river. "This," said General Pendleton, "proved to us an evil not slightly trying, since it
exposed our nearer cannoneers to be picked off, when serving their
guns, by the enemy's effective infantry rifles." [19]

The Southern artillerists did not exemplify the General's mod-
eration of speech. Those on the left, swearing sternly, called for
Confederate riflemen to give the enemy some of his own red medicine. "I was applied to," Pendleton went on, "for some infantry
to counteract in part this evil, by availing themselves of any cover
at hand to serve as sharpshooters on that part of our side." [20] Still
in ignorance of his disposable force of infantry, Pendleton ordered
200 men to move to the left. He did not know whether that depleted his reserves by 10 per cent. or by 30.

A second and somewhat similar request came ere long from the
cavalry posted two miles downstream: Officers reported that the
enemy's artillery was firing heavily there and that a crossing could
not be prevented unless infantry were sent. Pendleton did not dis-

[16] O. R., 19, pt. 1, pp. 831–32.   [17] Cf. Pendleton in O. R., 19, pt. 1, p. 832.
[18] Ibid.   [19] O. R., 19, pt. 1, p. 832.
[20] Ibid.

patch anyone to examine the ground, nor did he inquire whether the ford in front of the cavalry was practicable. He simply ordered thither, as he put it, "between 100 and 200 men" [21] and himself continued in calm ignorance of the number who remained at his command for the defense of the main ford.

The Federal fire from the opposite hills and from the canal bank quickened late in the afternoon. More sharpshooters seemed to be practising at the expense of the Confederates. Soon the Colonels in command of the Confederate infantry at the ford sent in their complaint. Pressure was getting too heavy, they said, to be resisted by the 300 men at their command.

Three hundred men? No more than that? "Of the extent of loss at Sharpsburg," Pendleton later wrote elaborately, "from the two brigades left with me, and of their consequent very small numbers all told, I had not been informed when their assignment to my direction had been made." [22] That was dignified enough and in contemporary print it may have sounded impressive. At the time, the news that he had not more than 300 riflemen opposite the ford must have made the gray parson look grayer still. With the equivalent of a good sized battalion, he had to protect forty-four guns, thirty-three of which were where withdrawal might be difficult!

That was not the full measure of Pendleton's perplexity. Battery commanders, one after another, sent to report that their ammunition was depleted or exhausted altogether. What was Pendleton to do? His solution theoretically was sound: He ordered to the ford the nearest cavalry, which Col. T. T. Munford told him he could expect at dusk, and then he assured the infantry that if they would hold their ground an hour longer, he would relieve them. The batteries not visible to the enemy were to pull out at once. Others were to follow as soon as darkness concealed them. The infantry next could leave. In their rear, nearest the enemy, would be the cavalry. Pendleton was quite satisfied—subsequently at least—that this was the soldierly move. Said he: "This plan, I judged it, under the circumstances, best on the whole to adopt, in the discretion left with me, as the reason of the case already indicated seemed not to justify the sacrifice incident to utmost resistance against any crossing." [23]

[21] O. R., 19, pt. 1, p. 832.   [22] Ibid.   [23] O. R., 19, pt. 1, p. 832.

The batteries began to slip off in the shadows. Those Captains who had any ammunition banged away. It was, said Pendleton, a "critical and anxious hour." In reviewing it later, Pendleton was careful to state precisely what he did personally: "My own position was taken near the point of chief importance, directly back from the ford, so that I might the better know of and control each requisite operation." [24]

Soon, past this post, infantrymen hurried to the rear. When Pendleton stopped them to inquire who they were, they said they were sharpshooters from the ford. Their thin line had given way, they asserted. Federal troops had reached the south side of the river. What Pendleton said in reply, none save the General himself has recorded, and he in this language: "Worn as were these men, their state of disorder, akin to panic, was not, justly, to be met with harshness. They were, however, encouraged to be steady and useful in checking disorder, and affording such tokens as they might, in the settling darkness, of force, to make the enemy cautious." [25] Whatever his phrasing of this exhortation at the time, in his orders to the men, Pendleton sent one of his staff officers to the ford to ascertain the exact situation. The other staff officer was to hurry to the rear the last batteries and the headquarters equipment. Of himself, left temporarily alone, Pendleton wrote: "My personal situation was all the while necessarily much exposed, and now to easy capture, accessible as it was to cavalry in a few minutes, should such have crossed and be coming forward." [26]

Naturally, Pendleton concluded that the enemy either would stick close to the ford or else would press on. He wrote: "In the former case, our guns &c., would as considerately instructed, get fairly out of reach, and this was, in the main, my expectation; still, the other course, a pushing hostile force, had to be provided for. I therefore proceeded to a point in the road probably not then reached by any part of the enemy, on foot and leading my horse, and accompanied by my adjutant and orderly sergeant, along a path still thundered over by the enemy's shells and crossing the road inland from the river." [27] This fire led Pendleton to decide that the Federals could not be pursuing rapidly or far. Otherwise they would come under the fire of their own guns.

[24] Ibid., 833.   [25] O. R., 19, pt. 1, p. 833.
[26] Ibid.   [27] Ibid.

Soon he ran into the rear of his own retreating artillery. "Mounting here, I rode with the column and employed the two young officers in moving our hospital camp and enforcing order along the entire column." [28] His statement to his wife, written two days earlier than his report, was somewhat different: "At the time I acted on the supposition that they [the Federals] would press on, and intending first, to save all I could, and, secondly, not to expose myself needlessly to capture, I passed, by a short path under a fierce fire from their heavy guns, toward the road which some of the artillery had, I knew, already taken. With this portion I passed on, leaving the rest to the result of my orders,—should the enemy not press on,—but rather anticipating its capture with William Nelson [29] and the other officers." [30]

The head of the artillery column, stumbling along in the darkness, passed the bivouac of Pryor's Brigade. There Pendleton turned out to ask the support of the infantry in protecting the guns; and from that moment, it would appear, he saw no more of his guns and did not know what befell them. He was referred by General Pryor to the nearest divisional commander, Hood, who was not to be found. "No one," wrote Pendleton, "could inform me where General Longstreet was." The last resort was to appeal to army headquarters. "This," said the General, "in the extreme darkness and amid the intricacies of unknown routes, proved a task of no little difficulty and delay." [31] It was, in fact, past midnight [32] when the alarmed Pendleton reached the apple tree under which Lee and his staff were sleeping. Pendleton dismounted, aroused Lee, recounted his afternoon's experience, and announced that the enemy had captured all the reserve artillery.

"All?" exclaimed Lee.

"Yes, General, I fear all."

Of what followed, a few scraps only of information survive. Pendleton's own account reads: "[Lee] was of course disturbed, but determined to do nothing until next morning, and I laid down. . . . My bed was a handful of straw, my covering an old

---

[28] *Ibid.*

[29] Pendleton's kinsman and Major commanding one of the battalions of the reserve artillery. Cf. *O. R.*, 19, pt. 1, p. 809.

[30] *Pendleton*, 214.   [31] *O. R.*, 19, pt. 1, pp. 833-34.

[32] *Pendleton*, 214. One of Lee's staff officers, quoted in Emily Mason's *Popular Life of Gen. R. E. Lee*, 151, said it was "about 1 o'clock."

overcoat, under the skies." [33] An anonymous staff officer, who heard Pendleton's announcement to Lee, wrote that the words "lifted me right off my blanket, and I moved away, fearful I might betray my feelings." The staff officer observed that Lee "exhibited no temper, made no reproach that I could hear, either then, or even afterwards . . ." [34]

With Jackson, it was different. Word of Pendleton's report to Lee brought from "Stonewall" more show of anxiety [35] and perhaps of disgust [36] than he exhibited on any other occasion during the entire war. "He took the matter in his own hands," wrote Kyd Douglas, "and his staff were little out of the saddle that night." [37] By 6.30 the next morning, September 20, Jackson had ordered A. P. Hill to return to the Potomac and to drive the enemy back across it. [38] Early was to move in support.

The movement was rapid, the action swift and decisive. Under artillery fire that A. P. Hill described as the "most tremendous" he ever heard, [39] the Light Division swept on, said its commander, "as if each man felt that the fate of the army was centered in himself." [40] Pender and Archer, co-operating perfectly, drove the Federal rearguard into the river and shot scores who were splashing vainly toward the northern shore. [41]

A frightful slaughter it seemed, but actually the Federal losses were not heavy, because the force was not large. The troops who had crossed the previous evening had captured two guns and had removed them to the north bank during the night. [42] Those Federals whom Hill encountered on the morning of the 20th had come to the south shore after daylight and, when they had found Confederates close at hand and in strength, they had started back. Only the 118th Pennsylvania had been caught by Hill's advance [43] and had been wrecked by his fire. [44]

---

[33] *Pendleton*, 214.
[34] Emily V. Mason, *op. cit.*, 151.
[35] *Mrs. Jackson*, 345.
[36] *Douglas*, 184; *McGuire MSS*.
[37] *McGuire MSS*. Dr. McGuire was of opinion that Jackson heard of Pendleton's difficulties before Lee had the news, and that "Stonewall" did not wait for orders to recover the lost ground.
[38] *O. R.*, 19, pt. 1, p. 982.
[39] *O. R.*, 19, pt. 1, p. 982.
[40] *Ibid.*
[41] *Ibid.* The river at that point was 300 yards in width and had, at the time, a depth of three feet (*ibid.*, 350).
[42] *Ibid.*, 350.
[43] *Ibid.*, 340.
[44] Its losses were 269. *O. R.*, 19, pt. 1, pp. 204, 340, 346–47, 348–49, 351–52. All the Federal troops in the engagement were of Morrell's and Sykes's Divisions, Fitz John Porter's V Corps. For the continuance of the sketch of Hill, see *infra*, p. 275.

To the relieved Pendleton, these events of the day were as agree-able as those of the night had been terrifying. Said he: ". . . I had the privilege of accompanying a force, under General Jackson, sent to punish the enemy; of attending that honored officer and friend in the exposure incident to his command, and of witnessing the destructive chastisement inflicted upon the several thousands that had crossed and remained on the south side of the river. . . . This severe work having been accomplished, I found that but four of our pieces had been lost. . . . About noon, returning from Shepherdstown along the Winchester road, about 4 miles on the way, I joined our batteries, commanded by Major Nelson. With others, similarly instructed, he had been diligently engaged the previous evening in causing batteries to be withdrawn in order, as directed, and the anticipated caution of the enemy had allowed them all to get back with no further damage than the leaving of one gun apiece by each of four batteries, as already mentioned." [45]

Nelson, in the estimation of the Army, had saved the reserve artillery; [46] Pendleton was told by Lee to file a report on the affair, "as well for my own sake," Pendleton explained to his wife, "as for [Lee's] satisfaction and the truth of history." The parson-general added confidently to his lady: "While I regret the loss and the occasion for Yankee glorification, I am so conscious of having done well my duty, and so thankful to God for ordering so re-markable a preservation, that for any temporary cloud over myself I am more than willing to compound." [47]

Others were not disposed to let the affair end there. One of the officers of Lawton's Brigade requested a court of inquiry, which in due time was ordered. [48] An indignant young artillerist assailed Pendleton in the *Richmond Whig* [49] and provoked an answer that seems, from its style, to have been written by Pendleton or, at the least, to have been revised by him. [50] Much mockery was made of a story, solemnly circulated, to the effect that "Old Jack" had caused men to abandon some of their guns as a ruse. This, said Lieut. Ham Chamberlayne, author of the article in the Rich-

---

[45] O. R., 19, pt. 1, p. 834.   [46] Miss Mason, *op. cit.*, 151.
[47] *Pendleton*, 215.
[48] O. R., 19, pt. 2, p. 671, as of October 18. No report of proceedings of the court has been found. Capt. (later Brig. Gen.) W. C. Oates, who was a member of this court, did not mention it in his memoirs.
[49] Oct. 13, 1862, p. 2, col. 1.
[50] *Richmond Whig.* Nov. 13, 1862, p. 2, col. 3.

mond paper, "was gotten up to shield Gen. P[endleton] and per-haps also to keep Gen. Hill from being credited with his due." [51] Harder things than these Chamberlayne had to say of Pendleton,[52] but he concluded in somewhat milder vein: ". . . Pendleton is Lee's weakness. He is like the elephant, we have him and we don't know what on earth to do with him, and it costs a devil of a sight to feed him." [53]

In the end, Lee's report of the Maryland expedition dismissed Pendleton's part in the affair with two cold sentences: "General Pendleton was left to guard the ford with the reserve artillery and about 600 infantry. That night the enemy crossed the river above General Pendleton's position, and his infantry support giving away, four of his guns were taken." That was all.[54] It seemed to satisfy Pendleton, but the time of its publication was not to find him happy. He was to write: "Few men have worked these two years as I have. And yet poor were the reward if the applause of men were my motive!" [55] Rarely, after that day in September, '62, did he command any infantry. Had he done so, it is safe to say that he would, at the least, have counted them.

[51] *Ham Chamberlayne*, 116.   [52] *Ibid.*, 111, 143.
[53] *Ibid.*, 134. See also *Sorrel*, 121.
[54] *O. R.*, 19, pt. 1, p. 151. On the morning of September 20, when Lee sent a preliminary report to Davis, he feared that "much" of the reserve artillery had been captured *ibid.*, 142.
[55] To Mrs. Pendleton, May 26, 1863; *Pendleton*, 272. The sketch of Pendleton is continued, *infra*, Chap. XXVIII.

CHAPTER XV

Longstreet and Jackson Step Up

DRIVING the Federals into the Potomac at Shepherdstown greatly relieved the feeling of the Army of Northern Virginia, which refused to admit that it had been worsted in Maryland. The Southern press was like-minded. Prior to the 22nd of September, the newspapers had no information about the battle. That day they published reports of a defensive battle and of the return of at least a part of Lee's troops to Virginia;[1] but the *Richmond Enquirer* assured readers that if there had been a withdrawal, it was to cope with a flanking operation against Harpers Ferry. Sharpsburg, said that authoritative journal, had witnessed "one of the most complete victories that has yet immortalized the Confederate arms."[2] This optimistic language did not stifle rumors that "created doubt and uneasiness."[3] On the morning of the 23rd, in Charleston, Rhett's *Mercury* gloomily remarked that the recrossing of the Potomac to Shepherdstown was a "movement which, to the unmilitary eye, with no more subtle guide than the map, would certainly resemble a retreat."[4]

Richmond papers still would not have it so. They clung to the theory that an attempted turning operation had prompted Lee to send troops back to Virginia, and they insisted that the greater part of the army still was in Maryland. The *Dispatch* even scolded its readers: "Our people," it said, "have been spoiled so thoroughly by the constant succession of victories that have marked the progress of our arms for the last four months, that they bear even the appearance of a reverse with less patience than we had a right to expect from the same men whose noble fortitude, at a time when our city was actually beleaguered by the enemy, made them the

[1] *Richmond Examiner*, Sept. 22, 1862, p. 2, col. 2.
[2] *Richmond Enquirer*, Sept. 22, 1862, p. 2, col. 2. Starke was acclaimed the hero of an inaccurately reported battle.
[3] *Richmond Examiner*, Sept. 23, 1862, p. 2, col. 1.
[4] *Charleston Mercury*, Sept. 23, 1862, p. 2, col. 2.

admiration of the world." [5] Some surprise was expressed, all the while, that the Federals had fought so well.[6]

In admitting a stubborn attack, the papers continued to assert a Confederate victory and the achievement of the objects of the campaign, which were described as the capture of Harpers Ferry and "the rousing of Maryland." [7] Not until after the 25th [8] were Richmond papers willing to concede that the entire Army was back in Virginia. Even then, they had vitriol for Northern boasts of victory,[9] and particularly for an assertion by the *New York Herald* that the "great victory of General McClellan and his noble army" meant that the "backbone of the rebellion is broken" and that 15,000 or 20,000 men, marching from Fredericksburg or from Fort Monroe, could capture Richmond.[10] In Richmond, the *Dispatch* republished on the 24th the article from the *Herald;* but the maximum the Virginia journal ever admitted was that "the victory, though not so decisive as that of Manassas, was certainly a Confederate victory." [11]

In none of the comment on Sharpsburg was reference made to the condition which was second only to the prowess of the individual fighter in keeping the tragic absence of the stragglers from ruining the Army. That condition was the success of the Confederate command in bringing into action every unit on the field. At Second Manassas, that same ideal of combat had been achieved offensively. Sharpsburg was cheering proof that the full cry of pursuit on Longstreet's front at Manassas had not been the result of lucky accident.

Among other reasons, Second Manassas was won and Sharpsburg was not lost because direction by two men, Longstreet and Jackson, under Lee's orders, had succeeded the system of semi-

[5] *Richmond Dispatch,* Sept. 23, 1862, p. 2, col. 1.

[6] *Richmond Examiner,* Sept. 23, 1862, p. 2, col. 1. This, said the *Examiner,* could be explained only "on the supposition that General McClellan retained the confidence of the Federal troops in a degree with which no other Federal commander could compare."

[7] *Richmond Enquirer,* Sept. 24, 1862, p. 2, col. 1; *Richmond Dispatch,* Sept. 24, 1862, p. 2, col. 1.

[8] Cf. *Richmond Examiner,* Sept. 25, 1862, p. 2, col. 1.

[9] Cf. *Richmond Whig,* Sept. 24, p. 1, col. 1; Oct. 2, 1862, p. 1, col. 1.

[10] This editorial, which assumed the speedy collapse of the Confederacy and discussed a program of reconstruction, was reprinted with derisive comment in the *Richmond Enquirer,* Sept. 25, 1862, p. 2, col. 1.

[11] *Richmond Dispatch,* Sept. 30, 1862, p. ? col. 1. The paper added, with some discernment: "If only as many as 5000 of the stragglers who left their colors and lingered behind had been present, McClellan's rout would have been irremediable."

autonomous, frequently jealous and often uncooperative Divisions. That awkward system, which had proved so nearly ruinous during the Seven Days, had been forced on Johnston and then on Lee by the fact that Confederate law had not provided for any unit larger than a Division. The device employed in the Army of Northern Virginia after June, of placing a number of Divisions under Longstreet and Jackson, scarcely would have been possible had not those two able men been senior Major Generals. If either of them held a commission of date later than that of, say, Magruder, "Prince John" could have insisted upon command of any group of Divisions that Lee wished to operate together. Had Lee in such a situation distrusted Magruder's leadership, the commanding General would have been compelled to maneuver the transfer of that officer. The sole alternative would have been to revert to the use of semi-autonomous Divisions.

This hampering restriction of law had been upheld by the War Department, it will be recalled, in the case of Beauregard, who had wished at Manassas to head a separate and self-contained Corps. He had been told, in words he did not like, that he was not first in command of half the Army but was second in command of the entire Army. No subsequent leader, however ambitious, had raised the question in Virginia. The restrictions of the statute had been accepted in theory and had been obviated in practice because the two senior divisional commanders fortunately were good soldiers.

Now the law was changed for the better. A brief amendatory act, approved by the President Sept. 18, 1862, provided for the organization of Divisions into Corps, which units were to be commanded by officers of the new grade of Lieutenant General.[12] Ten days after the modified act became operative, Davis asked Lee's opinion concerning the men who should be promoted. Outside his own Army, Lee recommended Kirby Smith. In it, he felt that two corps commanders would suffice.[13]

One of these should be Longstreet. To that conclusion Lee came so readily that when he wrote the President on the subject he did not think it necessary to elaborate on Longstreet's merit or record. Both had been distinguished during the Maryland expedition.

[12] IV O. R., 2, 198 No reference to debate on this measure is found in 46 S. H. S. P., which covers the proceedings of Congress for this period.
[13] O. R., 19, pt. 2, p. 642.

Longstreet's judgment in deferring attack at Second Manassas on August 29 perhaps was questionable; his mood may not have been the most co-operative when he learned on September 9 of Lee's purpose to detach Jackson for operations against Harpers Ferry; but after that, his counsel had been wise and his handling of his troops all that could be asked.

His A.A.G., Moxley Sorrel, did not overpraise the performance he thus described: "[Longstreet's] conduct on this great day of battle [at Sharpsburg] was magnificent. He seemed everywhere along his extended lines, and his tenacity and deep-set resolution, his inmost courage, which appeared to swell with the growing peril to the army, undoubtedly stimulated the troops to greater action, and held them in place despite all weakness." [14] At the critical hour on his front, after the Federals had seized the position Rodes's men had abandoned, "Old Pete's" calmness heartened the gunners who were struggling to halt the Union advance. Wrote one member of the Washington Artillery: "Longstreet was on horseback at our side, sitting side-saddle fashion,[15] and occasionally making some practical remark about the situation. He talked earnestly and gesticulated to encourage us, as the men of the detachments began to fall around our guns, and told us he would have given us a lift if he had not that day crippled his hand. But crippled or not, we noticed he had strength enough left to carry his flask to his mouth, as probably everybody else did on that terribly hot day, who had any supplies at command to bring to a carry." [16]

When the fight was over, and Longstreet was able to report to field headquarters, Lee rewarded him with words that made "Old Pete's" staff officers swell with pride: "Here comes my war horse from the field he has done so much to save!" [17] The next day, September 18, "Old Pete" concluded that the extension of the Federal right to the Potomac was in such strength that the Confederate Army should return to the Virginia shore. He so wrote Lee, but before his letter reached the commanding General, Lee came to the bivouac of Longstreet and expressed his intention of withdrawing from Maryland that evening. Longstreet was so much pleased his view coincided with Lee's that he recorded the fact in

[14] *Sorrel*, 115.
[16] *Mil. An. La.*, 138–39.
[15] This was because of his injured foot.
[17] *Sorrel*, 116.

his report.[18] This was a manly, forthright document, free of all bluster, modest and fair except that it was ungenerous in failing to credit A. P. Hill fully with the help the Light Division gave in the final charge on the right.

If, then, Longstreet was to be one of the two new Lieutenant Generals of the Army, was Jackson to be the other? On the basis of military performance, could there be any other choice? "Stonewall's" part in the operations around Manassas had been flawless. No allowance had to be made there for lack of experience in handling large bodies of men. Any soldier, though he had led a Corps for a decade with a veteran staff, would have been proud of what Jackson had accomplished from August 25 to the hour of departure from the field of the second victory on the grim ridges that overlook Bull Run.

Had Jackson done as well in Maryland? He undeniably had closed in slowly on Harpers Ferry and had shown there a certain awkwardness in the use of signals. An exacting critic might have disputed on the 17th the tactical wisdom of placing Lawton's and Hays's Brigades where they were at the time of Hooker's onslaught. These three matters apart, Jackson's capture of the Ferry and his tenacious battle on the left at Sharpsburg had been shrewd, vigorous and free of mistakes. His achievement was the more remarkable because A. P. Hill, Ewell and Trimble were absent, the trusted Winder was dead, and eight of the fourteen Brigades had Colonels, some of limited experience, at their head.[19]

That the Divisions on the left could be held together at Sharpsburg, even at the price of excessive casualties, evidenced not only Jackson's ability *in se,* but also his influence over his subordinates. This was pathetically illustrated by "Dick" Ewell. From the house where Ewell was lying after the amputation of his leg, Sharpsburg was distant thirty miles. All day on the 17th of September, the ceaseless roar of the artillery was audible on the plantation. Ewell became so excited that his brother spoke first to the attending surgeon and then to him about it. Somewhat reluctantly, with emotion he did not seek to hide, "Old Bald Head" confessed that he could not listen to the sound of battle without fearing that Jackson would be killed. On the preservation of Jackson's life, he

---

[18] O. R.. 19, pt. 1, p. 841. [19] Cf. O. R., 19, pt. 1, p. 952.

thought the future of the Confederacy in measure depended.[20] As with Ewell, so it was with many of Jackson's lieutenants: they were developing a faith in him as a leader comparable to that which great captains of the past had aroused. "Sandie" Pendleton wrote, when the expedition was ended: "I have been reading Carlyle's *Cromwell*. General Jackson is the exact counterpart of Oliver in every respect, as Carlyle draws him." [21]

Jackson proved himself at Sharpsburg as stubborn in conflict as "Old Nol" and as exacting. After Walker's Division had reinforced Jackson, one of Walker's regiments, Mat. Ransom's fine Thirty-third North Carolina, attempted to storm a battery and failed. From a distance, Jackson witnessed the charge and spurred over to order another effort. Colonel Ransom [22] said that he would try, of course, if so directed, but that he was afraid he would fail. Jackson demanded: "Why?" The reply was that in the previous charge, behind the rising ground he had reached, Ransom had observed in his front what appeared to be the greater part of McClellan's army. Jackson was skeptical. Looking about, he saw a tall hickory nearby. In a few words he called for a good climber. William Hood of the Thirty-third volunteered at once, and as he had no shoes to remove, he soon was high in the tree. From beneath, where he sat on his horse, Jackson asked how many troops Hood could see beyond the ridge.

"Oceans of them," the boy shouted.

"Count the flags, sir!"

Hood no sooner had begun to count audibly "One, two, three" than Federal sharpshooters noticed him in the tree and sought to pick him off. The "pop" of long-range rifles punctuated the count of Hood. The soldier himself was too brave to protest; Jackson seemed oblivious of the fire. "Nineteen, twenty," cried Hood. "Bang-bang," answered the sharpshooters. Hood's comrades waited breathlessly to see him tumble out of the tree; Jackson merely listened reflectively while the number mounted. "Thirty-two, thirty-three" sang out Hood to the accompaniment of whining

---

[20] 20 *S. H. S. P.*, 30. It is pleasing to note that Jackson had said in July, when urging an offensive, that he was willing to follow in such an operation Lee or "the gallant Ewell" (*ibid.*, 32, with quotation from *Dabney*, 487).

[21] *Pendleton*, 230.

[22] Who often is confused with his brother, Robert Ransom.

bullets. Thirty-three regimental flags visible, thirty-four—still Jackson refused to admit the odds too heavy to preclude a charge.

"Thirty-seven," Hood reported, "thirty-eight, thirty-nine"—close to ten Brigades in sight.

"That will do," said Jackson, "come down, sir!"

Hood needed no further order, but Jackson was not through with the argument. Why, he asked, had Ransom attacked so large a force as that? Ransom explained that when he first encountered the enemy, he had charged to delay an attack he knew he could not long resist. He had not understood the full strength of the enemy until he had reached the high ground in his front. That satisfied the Cromwell of the Valley, though it did not lead him to abandon his hope of an offensive. As he rode off, he bade the Colonel renew the attack when the rattle of small arms was heard on the left flank, where he proposed to strike.

Not a word of thanks, so far as the record shows, did Jackson have for William Hood, who was suffering from sore feet ere he started to climb the tree and, if truth must be told, was lousy besides. Three days later, Hood received unexplained orders to report at the headquarters of Gen. Robert Ransom, his Colonel's brother. That afternoon, as the Thirty-third North Carolina watched General Ransom pass at a gallop, there, behind the commander, Hood was riding. He was as dirty as ever and still he had no shoes, but he was astride one of the General's own mounts and somewhere he had procured a pair of spurs, which he had strapped to his bare feet. A courier he was now, a brigade courier, but he was not a man to forget friends because of fortune: when he recognized his old comrades he lifted his greasy old cap and saluted.[23]

Jackson doubtless was pleased if he heard of Hood's rise in the world, but on the day of battle, "Stonewall" scarcely was to be blamed for failure to commend the Zaccheus of the Army. After he rode away, Jackson sought out Walker and, while he made his lunch off apples plucked from a tree, "Old Jack" planned the counter-stroke on the left. "We'll drive McClellan into the Potomac," he said confidently;[24] but he found he could not challenge the powerful batteries the Union commanders skillfully had

[23] 2 *N. C. Regts.*, 604; 607.   [24] 2 *B. & L.*, 679.

placed near the river.[25] The next morning, September 18, Jackson
was at the front soon after daybreak. When he found John B.
Hood already there, his instant question was, "Hood, have they
gone?" A negative answer brought a regretful, "I hoped they
had," and he went on to see how fared his own exhausted troops.[26]
All day Jackson awaited, almost eagerly, the attack that did not
come. That night he worked as hard as Major Harman in getting the column back across the Potomac.[27] His action at Shepherdstown, after the fiasco of Pendleton, already has been
described.

One thing only marred Jackson's fine record during the entire
operation from Cedar Mountain to Shepherdstown. That was his
relations with A. P. Hill. The fiery commander of the Light
Division had no intention of accepting the stigma of arrest. At the
first moment the Army was free of pressure after Sharpsburg,
Powell Hill addressed to the commanding General an application
for a court of inquiry on Jackson's charges.[28] Hill had not been
rearrested after Harpers Ferry, nor had he been disturbed in his
command, but he had not been furnished with any statement of
the reasons for his arrest. He was determined that Jackson should
explain the public humiliation of a fellow-officer. If Jackson's
assumed charges against him were true, Hill reasoned, then he
was not fit to command a Division. Should he be absolved, as
he was sure he would be, he wanted to see Jackson reprimanded
for having arrested him. These were the reasons for his application, which bore date of September 22.

When Jackson received the paper from Hill for transmission
"through channels" to army headquarters, he was in duty bound,
of course, to forward it. In doing so, Jackson outlined in his
endorsement what he termed "the circumstances of Maj. Gen.
Hill's arrest." These were not set forth in definite charges and
specifications, but in a summary statement of the facts as Jackson saw them. The statement lost nothing of vigor because of its

---

[25] *O. R.*, 19, pt. 1, p. 957.
[26] *Hood*, 45.
[27] *Douglas*, 180; *Hotchkiss' MS Diary*, 89. In 25 *S. H. S. P.*, 102, Dr. Hunter
McGuire expressed his unbelief in Gen. S. D. Lee's story of Jackson's wish to retreat to
Virginia on the night of September 17. See on this incident also, 2 *R. E. Lee*, 404, n. 44.
[28] The text of this application has not been found, but the date and the nature of
the communication appear in Jackson's endorsement, *infra*.

form. Jackson outlined Hill's alleged shortcomings in the various
marches and, as noted already, said flatly: "I found that under
his successor, General Branch, my orders were much better carried out." [29]

In this manner and for the first time, the case came officially to
the attention of Lee. His was the difficult task of maintaining
Jackson's authority and of applying an emollient to the bruised
sensibilities of Hill, whom he regarded as an excellent officer.
Lee's immediate conclusion was that the circumstances did not
justify an inquiry. Even if a court could have been held, nothing
was at stake, in Lee's opinion, that would require formal examination of witnesses. Besides, at a time when any day might bring
an attack by McClellan, how could officers of appropriate rank
be detailed for a hearing that might be prolonged? Lee's own
unhappy experience before the war as a member of courts martial, and his knowledge of the character of his corps of officers—
proud, individualistic, contentious—disposed him to avoid courts
whenever he could. In this instance, he characteristically endorsed Hill's application:

"Respectfully returned to Gen. A. P. Hill who will see from the
remarks of General Jackson the cause of his arrest. His attention being
now called to what appeared to be neglect of duty by his commander,
but which from an officer of his character could not be intentional and
I feel assured will never be repeated, I see no advantage to the service
in further investigating this matter nor could it without detriment be
done at this time.

R. E. LEE
Comdg. Gen." [30]

For once, Lee's tact failed to relieve unpleasantness. The sensitive Hill was not willing to let the controversy end where Lee's
endorsement left it. Hill misinterpreted Lee's reference to "what
appeared to be neglect of duty" which "will never be repeated."
That, Hill thought, was acceptance of Jackson's charges. Vigorously, on September 30, Hill renewed his application for a court
of inquiry. He wrote Lee: "I respectfully say to the General that
I deny the truth of every allegation made by Major General Jack-

[29] Jackson's endorsement of Sept. 24, 1862—*Jackson MSS.*
[30] *Jackson MSS.*

son, and am prepared to prove my denial by any number of honorable men. . . . If General Jackson had accorded me the courtesy
of asking an explanation of each instance of neglect of duty as it
occurred, I think that even he would have been satisfied, and
the necessity avoided of keeping a black-list against me."

With this, Hill set forth his view of the alternatives: that he
was unworthy of command or that Jackson was subject to censure.
In phrasing this, Hill referred to Jackson as "the officer who
abuses his authority to punish, and then sustains his punishment
by making loose charges against an officer who has done and is
doing his utmost to make his troops efficient." In a postscript "to
show the spirit dictating the indorsement of General Jackson" on
his application, Hill cited one instance where Jackson definitely
was at fault in charges made against him.[31] Nor was this all: on
his own account, Hill drew up charges against Jackson and boldly
forwarded them to Jackson to be sent Lee.[32]

Jackson apparently felt no concern over the charges against himself, but the renewal of Hill's appeal for a court of inquiry presented him with something of a puzzle. He had no reason to find
fault with Hill's conduct during the Maryland expedition. Hill
had obeyed every order with promptness and with precision, and
he had won the plaudits of the entire Army. Jackson felt that
Hill had learned his lesson and would not be apt to err again.
What, then, did self-respect and the good of the service require?
Jackson concluded he should accept Hill's virtual challenge to
present charges and specifications, but "Old Jack" decided that in
sending these to Lee for such action as the commanding General
deemed proper, he would state that personally he did not think a
hearing was necessary.

With much scratching out of words and no little revision, Jackson presented the charge of "Neglect of Duty," and in eight specifications he reviewed every act of Hill's with which he had found
fault from the crossing of the Rapidan to the march toward the
Potomac. If these matters were to be reviewed at all, Jackson
thought they should go before a general court martial, not before
a court of inquiry, and, in effect, he so stated. Further, while he
explained with care that he was not presenting the charges and

31 O. R., 19, pt. 2, pp. 729–30.
32 Cf. ibid., 733. The text of these charges is not known to be in existence.

specifications because he wished Hill brought to trial, he could not forbear arguing the points Hill had made in the renewed application for an inquiry.

Jackson's language was not lacking in sharpness. Said he: "In regard to General Hill's statement respecting my not asking an explanation of each individual instance of neglect of duty, I would state that I spoke to him about the first neglect, and he did not give a satisfactory explanation. He had ample opportunity of knowing his neglect of duty. When an officer disobeys or disregards a known order, it is his duty to report it at once, with his explanation, without waiting to be called upon in each individual instance. No black-list has been kept against General Hill. The specifications only extend over a period of about four weeks, and are of such a character as would not readily escape the memory." Not content with this, Jackson insisted that Hill's second application for a court of inquiry contained evidence of "another instance of his neglecting his duty." [33]

A stubborn temper there was on both sides, a temper so stubborn the patient Lee did not attempt forthwith to bend it. Instead, he applied his usual philosophy and left to time what he could not himself settle: Hill's renewed application and charges against Jackson, along with those of Jackson against Hill, were put in the confidential files at headquarters and were left to slumber there. Lee's immediate justification for this was that he did not have time to give the papers close study. More fundamentally, he quietly exercised his discretion of deciding in any given case whether charges should be brought before a court.

Was this unhappy affair to be weighed against Jackson? Now that he might be made Lieutenant General and corps commander, was he to be denied that promotion because he always was having

[33] *O. R.*, 19, pt. 1, pp. 729–31, 732. The rough draft and the final text of the charges against Hill are in the *Jackson MSS*. Four of the seven charges related to Hill's alleged neglect of orders on the march of September 4. Hotchkiss, in his *MS Diary*, October 6, mentioned a report that Hill and Jackson had preferred charges against each other. The engineer commented: "So some trouble is anticipated. I hope all may blow over. General Hill is a brave officer but perhaps too quick to resent seeming overstepping of authority. No [doubt?] General Jackson intends to do his whole duty." In the *Charleston Mercury*, Oct. 11, 1862, was an accusation by "Hermes" that Hill had been "bragging" and twice had been arrested—once for "bragging over" Longstreet and once for insulting Jackson. The correspondent mused, "Giddy, giddy is the height." Douglas, *op. cit.*, 195, wrote of a conference at which Lee interposed sternly between Hill and Jackson, but the details are so vague that the account may be nothing more than an echo of the tradition that Lee called the two into his tent and insisted that the one who felt himself the more aggrieved should be the first to make a friendly advance.

difficulties with one or another of his subordinates? Apparently Lee did not take this into account at all, or, if he did, he counted it for righteousness on Jackson's part that discipline was inculcated, even though the method was stern.

If Lee had felt any concern about Jackson, it had been on different ground. In his letter of October 2 to the President, Lee wrote: "I can confidently recommend Generals Longstreet and Jackson in this army." Of Longstreet he said not another word. Concerning Jackson, the language of the commanding General was somewhat unusual. Ever since the text was published in 1887, students have been asking, Was Lee revealing his own previous doubts, or was he seeking to relieve the President's misgivings? Here is what Lee said: "My opinion of the merits of General Jackson has been greatly enhanced during this expedition. He is true, honest and brave; has a single eye to the good of the service and spares no exertion to accomplish his object." [34] What was behind the "enhancement" of Lee's opinion? Why should it be in order to speak of an eye to the good of the service? Had there been in Lee's mind or in the President's any suspicion of the sort "Dick" Taylor had felt that day in the Valley when, as Jackson had talked, a vast and consuming ambition had been disclosed? The evidence does not permit an answer, but the opinion Lee expressed to Davis, regardless of its antecedents, was one he never changed later. From the time of these operations in Northern Virginia, Lee's trust in Jackson and his confidence in the abilities of "Stonewall" were absolute. Every new experience was to increase the respect of General and of Lieutenant each for the other.

While recommendation of Jackson was as unqualified as it was justified, it was not phrased in a manner to humiliate the officer with whom Jackson was at odds. On the contrary, in presenting the names of Longstreet and of Jackson to the President, Lee wrote: "Next to these two officers, I consider A. P. Hill the best commander with me. He fights his troops well and takes good care of them." [35] If word of this reached Hill, he must have modified somewhat his belief that Lee credited Jackson's charges against him.

In the eyes of virtually all other officers, the promotion of Jack-

[34] O. R., 19, pt. 2, p. 643.   [35] O. R., 19, pt. 2, p. 643.

son and of Longstreet evidently was regarded as a matter of course. When the President appointed them and Congress confirmed, October 11, there was little comment.[36] The response of the two men themselves to their new honors was typical of the difference between them. Longstreet's reflections on his rise in military rank nowhere appear. Although he doubtless was much pleased at his promotion, he probably did not show it. He reorganized his staff and placed new responsibilities on its competent young chief, Moxley Sorrel. Everything was correctly but ostentatiously done at the new rank. If there was any change in Longstreet, it was an enlargement of his confidence in his own military judgment. In the close and costly fight at Sharpsburg, he had seen the vindication of his view that the Army should not have been divided for the capture of Harpers Ferry. Feeling that he was right and Lee wrong, he may have considered himself the better soldier of the two. The allegation has been made,[37] on the basis of Longstreet's writings in his old age, that after Sharpsburg he was immoderately critical of Lee's strategy, but of this there is little contemporary evidence.[38]

Jackson's feeling about his promotion was one of a deliberate subordination of the soldier to the Christian. When his wife joyfully congratulated him and asked if she might have an article prepared about him, he wrote back in Cromwellian spirit: "Don't trouble yourself about representations that are made of your husband. These things are earthly and transitory. There are real and glorious blessings, I trust, in reserve for us beyond this life. It is best for us to keep our eyes fixed upon the throne of God and the realities of a more glorious existence beyond the verge of time. It is gratifying to be beloved and to have our conduct approved by our fellow-men, but this is not worthy to be compared to the glory that is in reservation for us in the presence of our glorified Redeemer . . . I would not relinquish the slightest diminution of that glory for all this world can give. My prayer is that such may ever be the feeling of my heart. It appears to me that it would be

---

[36] The seven Lieutenant Generals appointed Oct. 11–13, 1862, and immediately confirmed by the Senate, were, in order of seniority: James Longstreet, E. Kirby Smith, Leonidas Polk, William J. Hardee, Thomas J. Jackson, T. H. Holmes and John C. Pemberton. Longstreet was to rank from October 9, Jackson from October 10. See *Wright*, 14–15.

[37] Eckenrode and Conrad, *James Longstreet*, 133–34.

[38] For the next part of the sketch of Longstreet, see *infra*, pp. 269 ff, 359 ff.

better for you not to have anything written about me. Let us follow the teaching of inspiration—'Let another man praise thee, and not thine own mouth: a stranger and not thine own lips.' " [39] Was it difficult for him to write that?

[39] *Mrs. Jackson*, 349–50. The sketch of Jackson is continued *infra*, pp. 273 ff, 310 ff

CHAPTER XVI

A CRISIS IN REORGANIZATION

PROMOTION of Longstreet and of Jackson legalized and facilitated the system of command Lee had created after the Seven
Days, but among general officers of lower rank, that organization
had now to be rebuilt. Choice of two Lieutenant Generals was,
in fact, the simplest part of the task now faced by the commanding General. The campaign in Northern Virginia had been
undertaken before all the officers wounded between Seven Pines
and Malvern Hill had returned to duty. Cedar Mountain, Second Manassas, South Mountain and Sharpsburg had taken exorbi-
tant toll. The loss of Winder at Cedar Mountain and the wounding of Ewell, of Taliaferro, of Trimble and of Field at Second
Manassas had been followed at South Mountain by the death of
Garland, who was among the ablest and most dependable of the
Brigadiers.[1] At Sharpsburg, the number of slain general officers
proved to be three, not two. George Burgwyn Anderson, who
appeared to have been wounded slightly, died on the 16th of
October. He was 31, had been graduated high at West Point,[2]
and had been trained in the 2nd U. S. Dragoons under Philip St.
George Cooke. In command of the Fourth North Carolina [3] and
then of a Brigade under D. H. Hill, he had displayed qualities of
stout leadership, though he never had been given opportunity in
independent command. All the physical excellencies coveted by
soldiers were abundantly his—a handsome figure, fine horsemanship, a clear musical voice, a commanding presence. His discipline had seemed as mild as his blue-gray eyes, but it had been

[1] Garland had, in the admiring eyes of D. H. Hill, "no superiors and few equals
in the service" (O. R., 19, pt. 1, p. 1020). Hill himself, for all his peculiarities, was a
man of great personal bravery, and he added by that very fact to the further tribute he
paid Garland: "The most fearless man I ever knew, a Christian hero, a ripe scholar,
and most accomplished gentleman" (ibid., 1026). Lee styled Garland "that brave and
accomplished young officer" (ibid., 146). Garland, it will be recalled, was in his 32nd
year. Said Ham Chamberlayne, in youth's estimate of leadership, Garland was "a man
of that mould and with those advantages of nature and accident that no position was
higher than his legitimate hopes" (Ham. Chamberlayne, 111–12).
[2] Cullum, No. 1545; graduated No. 12 in the class of 1852.
[3] Cf. Richmond Enquirer, May 22, 1861.

firm. In battle, as he rode calmly alert, with his golden beard flowing, he had inspired his fine regiments.[4]

A soldier's death, in combat, had come to Brig. Gen. W. E. Starke, who had succeeded to the field command of Jackson's old Division after John R. Jones had reported himself incapacitated.[5] The other General who fell in the Maryland expedition, L. O'Brien Branch, had won at Cedar Mountain honors that offset whatever loss of prestige he had sustained at Hanover Court House. In a Division where brigade command was above the average, he had learned rapidly and had won distinction, though he had received no professional training in arms before the war. "He was," A. P. Hill wrote sorrowfully, "my senior brigadier, and one to whom I could have intrusted the command of the Division with all confidence."[6] Besides these three whose names had to be stricken permanently from the rolls, five Generals had been wounded. They were "Dick" Anderson, Robert Toombs, "Rans" Wright, R. S. Ripley and Alexander Lawton.[7] Of these, the man whose absence would be most seriously felt was Anderson. His Brigadiers were of unequal ability. The senior of them was by no means the most skillful in combat. If Anderson were to be in-

[4] 1 N. C. Regts., 266. At Gaines' Mill, he had won Harvey Hill's praise (O. R., 11, pt. 2, p. 626) and affection (2 Land We Love, 464), and in every later action he had been steadfast. Anderson had been standing on a slight elevation, watching intently his troops, when a minié ball struck his ankle (14 S. H. S. P., 387). His death, which surprised the Army, occurred at Raleigh, N. C. For early references to him, see O. R., 5, 898; 11, pt. 1, p. 950 ff, pt. 3, p. 425; sketches appear in 3 Land We Love, 93–100, 14 S. H. S. P., 387–97. D. H. Hill described him as a "high-toned, honorable, conscientious Christian soldier, highly gifted and lovely in all the qualities that adorn a man" (O. R., 19, pt. 1, p. 1024). In 2 Land We Love, 464, Hill noted the pathetic fact that a few days prior to Sharpsburg, Anderson confided to him, "My wife and children are stereotyped upon my brain; they seem ever before me."

[5] See supra, p. 207. Starke's service with the veterans of the Valley had been brief, but his conduct at Second Manassas had marked him as a man of ability. While the left of Jackson's Division was reeling under Hooker's hammer-stroke, Starke had ridden into the mêlée, had seized a flag and had sought to rally the men. On the line of bitterest action, he had fallen with three—some contemporary accounts mentioned four —bullet wounds (Richmond Enquirer, Sept. 23, 1862). His body was brought off the field and was sent to Richmond, where it was buried in Hollywood Cemetery by the side of his son, Lieut. Edwin B. Starke, Adjutant of the Seventh Virginia, who had died July 17 from wounds received at Seven Pines (Richmond Enquirer, July 18, 1862, p. 2, col. 2). The weathered headstones stand now on the hillside within shouting distance of the burial place of thousands of Starke's comrades in arms (Cf. Mil. An. La., 32). For comment on Starke's promotion during the summer of 1862, see Richmond Enquirer, Aug. 13, p. 1, col. 3; Aug. 22, 1862, p. 2, col. 3. The fullest of numerous obituaries is in Richmond Enquirer, Oct. 2, 1862. In Lee's report on Sharpsburg, O. R., 19, pt. 1, p. 149, there is reference to the fall of "the brave General Starke."

[6] O. R., 19, pt. 1, p. 981. Lee, reporting the death, spoke of him as "brave and lamented" (O. R., 19, pt. 1, p. 150). The men of Branch's North Carolina regiments had regarded him with warm admiration (Cf. 7 C. V., 360–61).

[7] O. R., 19, pt. 1, pp. 150, 841, 956, 1027. For the reason given in the text, supra, p. 224, Gregg is not included here, though A. P. Hill, ibid., 981, listed him among the wounded.

capacitated for any length of time, transfer of at least one of the brigade commanders would be necessary to assure competent handling of the Division.

Below brigade command, the casualties had been grievous. Two Colonels had been killed at South Mountain [8] and eight at Sharpsburg.[9] One of these was the picturesque Dixon Barnes of the Twelfth South Carolina, a quiet, wealthy planter, who was familiar to soldiers for his flowing white beard. He had been distinguished in every action and was much beloved.[10] Another was C. C. Tew of the Second North Carolina, former head of a military academy in his State, who almost certainly would have been promoted in a short time.[11] Among the Lieutenant Colonels, the slaughter had been heavy.[12] For the corps of officers as a whole, 't never had reached such ghastly totals.

D. H. Hill, in five small Brigades at South Mountain and

[8] J. B. Strange of the Nineteenth Virginia and B. B. Gayle of the Twelfth Alabama (O. R., 19, pt. 1, pp. 839, 1026–27).

[9] These were: W. P. Barclay, Twenty-third Georgia (O. R., 19, pt. 1, pp. 1027, 1054); Dixon Barnes, Twelfth South Carolina (ibid., 981, 989); Marcellus Douglass, Thirteenth Georgia, temporarily commanding Lawton's Brigade (ibid., 956); P. F. Liddell, Eleventh Mississippi (ibid., 840, 923); W. T. Millican, Fifteenth Georgia (ibid., 887); L. B. Smith, Twenty-seventh Georgia (ibid., 1054); H. B. Strong, Sixth Louisiana (ibid., 965, 974); and C. C. Tew, Second North Carolina (ibid., 1026). In the absence of reports from R. H. Anderson's Division, it is possible that other deaths occurred among Colonels of his regiments. Numerous casualties, loosely listed as those of Colonels, were, in reality, those of Lieutenant Colonels.

[10] For A. P. Hill's tribute, see O. R., 19, pt. 1, p. 981. McGowan's moving reference is ibid., 989. On the march to Harpers Ferry, Colonel Barnes had been placed under arrest by Maj. E. F. Paxton, of Jackson's staff. The charge, which officers of Gregg's Brigade regarded as wholly false, was that of permitting his men to rob apple trees in violation of orders. When the Brigade had been preparing for action at Harpers Ferry, Colonel Barnes had approached General Gregg and had asked permission to go into the fight as a private. Gregg had been in the act of refusing most regretfully, when A. P. Hill had ridden up and, noting the strain, had asked what was amiss. Upon Gregg's explanation, Hill had said: "General Gregg, I order you to give Colonel Barnes his sword and put him in command of his regiment." Alexander Haskell commented: "Of course Hill was wrong to do this, but the case would stir the heart of a rock" (Mrs. Daly, 77–78).

[11] D. H. Hill, who was as generous to friends as he was unsparing of foes, described Tew as "one of the most finished scholars on the continent" and as a soldier with "no superior in the field" (O. R., 19, pt. 1, p. 1026). A sketch of Tew will be found in 10 C. V., 81–82. Cf. also 5 N. C. Regts., 641.

[12] Particularly lamented was Lt. Col. John T. Thornton, Third Virginia Cavalry, whom Stuart mentioned as a "brave and devoted member of the service . . . one of the brightest ornaments of the State" (O. R., 19, pt. 1, pp. 819–20). Another was Georges Coppens—in full Georges Auguste Gaston Coppens, of the First Battalion, Louisiana Zouaves, a French-speaking command (Cf. O. R., 19, pt. 1, p. 842; DeLeon, 329–30). He was succeeded by his brother, Major and former Adjutant of the Battalion, Marie Alfred Coppens, who signed as A. Coppens. The name more properly was de Coppens. The head of the family, Baron August de Coppens, had come to Louisiana from Martinique in 1853. He served for the greater part of the war as the quartermaster of his son's battalion. A fourth member of the family, Leon, the Baron's youngest boy, enlisted in 1862 and became a sergeant in 1864. See Ella Lonn, Foreigners in the Confederacy, 148 and n.

Sharpsburg, lost one Brigadier General killed, one mortally wounded,[13] three brigade commanders wounded, four Colonels slain, eight Colonels wounded, one Lieutenant Colonel killed and seven wounded.[14] Colquitt's Brigade of that Division had gone into action at Sharpsburg with ten field officers. Four of these were fatalities, five were badly wounded, "and the tenth was stunned by a shell."[15] In Lawton's Brigade, all save one of the regimental commanders were killed or wounded; Hays lost all his staff and all of the men who led his regiments across the Potomac; in Trimble's Brigade, the Colonel commanding and three of the four officers at the heads of regiments were casualties. The one surviving regimental leader was seriously wounded on the 20th at Boteler's Ford.[16] Every officer of the Fourth North Carolina present at Sharpsburg was killed or wounded as, with a single exception, were those of the Twenty-seventh Georgia.[17] In Jackson's Division, the higher officers had been massacred—no less. When the battle shifted from the left that red 17th of September, what was left of the Division was under command, as already noted, of Col. A. J. Grigsby. The famous Stonewall Brigade was commanded by a Major. Taliaferro's and Starke's Brigades were in the charge of Colonels. Jones's Brigade[18] was in the hands of a Captain who had succeeded two other Captains shot down.

Summarized for the Army, these frightful losses meant that for longer or shorter periods during the operations in Maryland, this situation existed: The commanders of nine Divisions, instead of being nine Major Generals, had been four Generals of that grade, four Brigadiers and, in the last hours of Sharpsburg, one Colonel. The end of action on the 17th found fourteen general officers only in command of Brigades. Colonels or officers of lower rank led the remaining twenty-six Brigades.[19] Some of these Brigades were smaller than regiments should have been. Regiments, which long had been too thin, were in numerous instances bare companies.[20]

---

[13] These were Samuel Garland and Geo. B Anderson.
[14] O. R., 19, pt. 1, pp. 1025–26.
[15] Ibid., 1022.   [16] O. R., 19, pt. 1, pp. 968 ff, 973.
[17] O. R., 19, pt. 1, p. 1029. The Fourth North Carolina belonged to G. B. Anderson's Brigade, the Twenty-Seventh Georgia to Colquitt's.
[18] Known in the Valley as Campbell's.
[19] See the organization of the army in O. R., 19, pt. 1, p. 803 ff.
[20] Secretary Randolph on Aug. 12, 1862, had reported that the number of regiments was too great and that the armies could not be maintained in "tolerable efficiency" unless authority was granted to consolidate weak regiments (IV O. R., 2, 44).

This was a crisis in command. The Army could not continue under temporary officers. Straggling, which so nearly had wrecked the Maryland expedition, was due in part to the inexperience or incompetence of many officers who had undertaken to lead Brigades or regiments in the absence of sick or wounded seniors.[21] Here, again, the law was at fault. Under existing Confederate statute, the Colonels, in order of seniority, exercised brigade command during the absence, however prolonged, of the Brigadier General. In the higher grades, the same rule applied. A Major General might be incapacitated for months; seniority might make the least competent of his Brigadiers the acting division commander; but nothing could be done under the law to replace the incapacitated Major General or to rid the Division of an acting commander who was not qualified to discharge his duties. In some of the units there was no prospect that the transfer of an incompetent would improve discipline because none of the juniors was qualified.

The statutes required, moreover, that vacancies below the rank of general officer be filled by promotion or election. For the amendment of this paralyzing law, Lee appealed to the War Department. Secretary Randolph on September 29 laid the issue before the President. Said he: "It is useless to increase the Army unless it can be properly officered." [22] Again on October 4, Randolph wrote: "The present condition of the Army of Northern Virginia imperatively requires" [the grant to the President by Congress of power to make appointments when neither election nor promotion secures competent officers]. The Secretary added: ". . . experience of the commanding General of that army has been unable to devise any expedient by which he may avoid the alternative of violating law or of exposing his army to ruin." [23]

Of all of this, President Davis was most unhappily conscious, but he also was aware of the political difficulties. He decided to make a gradual approach. On October 8, he asked Congress for authority to appoint from another unit of the same Brigade officers for any other regiment of that Brigade when neither election nor promotion within that regiment would assure competent leadership. In strong words Davis echoed the cry of the high

---

[21] Cf. IV O. R., 2, 98 and supra, p. 151.
[22] V O. R., 2, 97.   [23] Ibid., 109.

command in every major war: "It is vain to add men and munitions, unless we can at the same time give to the aggregated mass
the character and capacity of soldiers. . . . Tender consideration
for worthless and incompetent officers is but another name for
cruelty toward the brave men who fall sacrifices to these defects
of their leaders." [24]

Two days later, Davis faced the same issue in the higher ranks
and requested of the lawmakers "some provision by which Brigadier and Major Generals may be appointed when, by the casualties of service, commanders of Brigades and Divisions have become temporarily disabled." He explained the situation and went
on: "There is an obvious objection to multiplying the number of
general officers, but it may be readily removed by providing for
the subsequent reduction whenever there are supernumeraries
present for duty; and I would suggest that the determination as
to who should be discharged might be made to depend upon the
inquiry and report of an army board, to be organized according
to established law and usage." [25]

The Confederate Congress, which was about to adjourn, at once
proceeded to compromise between the counsel of the President
and the "democratic" organization of the Army. First, and without debate, so far as the record shows,[26] Congress set up a complicated arrangement whereby a general officer in charge of a Department could name an "examining board" to pass on the competency
of any officer of any grade to discharge his duty. Upon proof of
incompetency, the General could suspend and the President retire
the officer. A successor had then to be named from the same
command, by seniority and, if need be, by examination. Only in
the event that no qualified man could be found within the command, was the President authorized to make an appointment,
which had to be from the same State.[27]

In theory, by its title, this law covered disability as well as
incompetence; but the emphasis of its terms was on the officer
unworthy of promotion rather than on the wounded officer whose

[24] IV O. R., 2, 110. Public understanding of the importance of discipline was
growing. In the Richmond Enquirer of August 20, 1862, p. 2, col. 1, a letter to the
editor read, in part: ". . . The impression upon the public mind is that in the battles
before Richmond, we might have taken nearly, if not all, the army of McClellan if this
principle of cheerful obedience had rested in the bosom of all the Generals."
[25] IV O. R., 2, 114.
[26] Cf. Proceedings in 47 S. H. S. P., 95-96, 105.
[27] IV O. R., 2, 205-06.

long continued absence from his command raised a question of competent succession. The most that any General in charge of a Department could hope to accomplish under this act would be to remove, by a slow, complicated and often angry proceeding, an officer manifestly, perhaps notoriously, incompetent. Even then, the restrictions were so stiff that a department commander might have no assurance that the man who took the place of a removed officer would be any better.

A more acceptable if evasive compromise by Congress was a second law [28] which authorized the President, with the advice and consent of the Senate, "to appoint twenty general officers in the Provisional Army, and to assign them to such appropriate duties as he might deem expedient." This meant that in extreme cases where the promotion to brigade command of a senior Colonel of the same organization could not be justified, the President could go outside the Brigade and select a General for it. Twenty were too few appointments for all the forces of the Confederacy; but wise selection of some of them would strengthen the shattered brigade and divisional command of the Army of Northern Virginia.

Because Jackson and Longstreet had been promoted, two new Major Generals had to be named to take their old commands. In addition, as Ewell's return to the field was doubtful, there was a possibility that he might be invalided and that a General of appropriate rank would be appointed to lead Ewell's Division. A fourth promotion to the same grade also was being arranged. Whiting's Division of two Brigades, which Brig. Gen. John B. Hood had led, now was increased to the standard of four Brigades by the assignment to it of "Tige" Anderson's and Toombs's commands. The man who headed it then would be entitled to rank as a Major General.

Prospects of four promotions to coveted divisional rank excited the Army and aroused the ambitions of perhaps half a score. Trimble and Early made no concealment of their desire to change the buttons on their coat and to lead a Division. In Trimble's case, this ambition was so frankly avowed that it had been a theme of some quiet jest. Before the Army had started northward, Trimble had been heard to say to his chief. "General Jackson, before this war is over, I intend to be a Major General or a corpse!"[29] Jackson had made no reply, but he had been watching Trimble and he had a surprise in store for him. Lawton, for his part, could not see why he, the senior Brigadier of the entire Army and *ipso facto* the senior in Ewell's Division, should not have "Old Bald Head's" place. Toombs felt that he deserved, though he did not expect, promotion for his conduct at Sharpsburg.

These were the more conspicuous candidates, but they did not include two men in whose behalf Longstreet and Jackson were active. Longstreet sought promotion for George Pickett, who was his senior Brigadier and in spirit his younger brother. "Old Jack" felt that John B. Hood, though not under his command, deserved promotion and he so wrote the Adjutant General. In a careful letter he recalled the Texan's "distinguished service" at Gaines' Mill. Of Hood's conduct at Sharpsburg, Jackson wrote: ". . . it gives me pleasure to say that his duties were discharged with such ability and zeal, as to command my admiration. I regard him as one of the most promising officers of the army."[30]

Hood's record fully justified the praise. He had remained under arrest for almost a fortnight as a result of his controversy with "Shanks" Evans; but on the afternoon of September 14, as Hood had approached South Mountain, Lee had hinted that a word of regret over the affair of the ambulances would bring restoration of command. When Hood refused to apologize, because he thought the fault was not his, Lee had spoken: "Well, I will suspend your arrest until the impending battle is decided."[31] After Hood's stubborn and persistent fighting at Sharpsburg, no more was said about arrest. How could it be remembered in the light of the message Hood had sent back by "Sandie" Pendleton—"Tell General Jackson unless I get reinforcements I must be forced back, but I am going on while I can"? A fine motto that last clause is for any soldier.[32]

Hood himself described the fighting on the Confederate left

---

[29] In 19 *S. H. S. P.*, 314, Dr. Hunter McGuire said that Trimble was angry because he had not been promoted prior to the interview and that he prefaced his statement with a wrathful "By God." Douglas, *op. cit.*, 129, remembered that one of the staff had heard Trimble express the resolution, without the oath, but Douglas noted that Trimble spoke "laughingly."

[30] *Hood*, 45–46. Characteristically, Jackson never told Hood of this letter. Hood did not learn of its existence until after the war.

[31] *Hood*, 38–39; *O. R.*, 19 pt. 2, p. 600.   [32] Cf. *supra*, p. 208.

in the early morning as "the most terrible . . . by far, that has occurred during the war," but he believed that if McLaws had arrived earlier, the Confederate victory would have been complete.[33] The one regret of Hood's subordinates was that support did not arrive in time to prevent their withdrawal. Said Col. W. T. Wofford, who was commanding Hood's Texans: "They deserved a better fate than to have been, as they were, sacrificed for want of proper support." Never before, said Wofford, had that Brigade been compelled to give ground.[34] Col. P. A. Work of the First Texas, who entered the battle with 226 men and lost 186 of them,[35] wrote bitterly: "If required to carry strong positions in a few more engagements, and, after carrying them, hold them unaided and alone, this regiment must soon become annihilated and extinct without having accomplished any material or permanent good." [36] Perhaps the unique tribute to Hood's Division was the fact that not only Hood himself but his two Brigade commanders also were praised by Longstreet in his report for their conduct at Second Manassas, at South Mountain and at Sharpsburg.[37]

Of Hood's merit, Lee was equally aware and no less apprecia tive. Lee had approved if he had not suggested the enlargement of the Texan's Division. The one difficulty in the way of promot- ing Hood was to dispose of the difficult Whiting who, though still a Brigadier in rank, had exercised divisional command for months. Whiting now had returned from sick leave and had reported for duty.[38] If Whiting took the Division again, Hood's promotion would be blocked. Lee found a way of effecting his purpose. He knew better than did most officers the deep pes- simism of Whiting's nature, but he knew also that Whiting had exceptional ability as an engineer.[39] The simplest, fairest course to follow in all the delicate complexities was to suggest that Whiting be sent to some other post where engineering skill was

[33] O. R., 19, pt. 1, p. 923.   [34] O. R., 19, pt. 1, p. 929.
[35] Ibid., 933.
[36] Ibid., 934. Lee was conscious of this but was most anxious to get into the army more men of the same superb fighting quality. On Sept. 21, 1862, Lee wrote Sen. L. T. Wigfall, who at one time had commanded the Texas Brigade: "With a few more such regiments as those which Hood now has, as an example of daring and bravery, I could feel much more confident of the results of the campaign."—Mrs. D. Giraud Wright A Southern Girl in 1861 (cited hereafter as Mrs. Wright).
[37] O. R., 19, pt. 1, p. 841.   [38] O. R., 19, pt. 2, p. 680.
[39] Cf. O. R., 19, pt. 2, p. 697.

needed. This action he urged upon the War Department. Within three days, Whiting was ordered to repair to Richmond and to report to the Secretary of War for duty.[40]

When these orders were issued, October 27, the conclusion of the Army must have been that the way was being cleared for Hood; but who were the other new Major Generals to be? Here, again, while Longstreet urged Pickett, the pen of Jackson already had been employed. Four months before, at Swift Run Gap, Ewell would not have believed it conceivable—but Jackson was advocating the promotion of the insistent, the night-marching I. R. Trimble. On Sept. 22, 1862, Jackson wrote the Adjutant General: "I respectfully recommend that Brig. Gen. I. R. Trimble be appointed a Maj. Gen. It is proper, in this connection, to state that I do not regard him as a good disciplinarian, but his success in battle has induced me to recommend his promotion. I will mention but one instance, though several might be named, in which he rendered distinguished service. After a day's march of over 30 miles he ordered his command, consisting of 2 small Regiments, the 21st Georgia and the 21st N. C. to charge the enemy's position at Manassas Junction. This charge resulted in the capture of a number of prisoners and 8 pieces of Artillery. I regard that day's achievement as the most brilliant that has come under my observation during the present war." [41]

That was a tribute not lightly to be disregarded. "Brilliant" indeed was a feat which drew that adjective from "Old Jack." Such commendation gave Trimble an advantage that his comrade in Ewell's Division, the shrewd and cynical "Jube" Early, scarcely would have had a chance of overcoming; but Early's achievement at Sharpsburg had been entirely comparable to that of Trimble at Manassas Junction. "Old Jubilee," in fact, was one of the heroes of the battle of September 17. As surely as at Cedar Mountain, and with the issue more critical, he showed himself tenacious, cool

---

[40] O. R., 19, pt. 2, pp. 680, 681, 682.

[41] Jackson's MS Letter Book, p. 42. Trimble did not know of this recommendation, and on October 27 he wrote Jackson from Staunton a request for continuance in the command of "Stonewall." Doubtless it was a pleasure to Jackson to reply, October 30: "Your wishes respecting serving in my command have been anticipated. And if you were only ready to take the field, I am of the opinion that there would be no difficulty in your being made Maj. Gen. & put in command of my division . . . I have recommended your promotion and also a few days since recommended you for the commander of my division provided you were well." On November 5, Trimble replied appreciatively (Trimble MSS). His remarks when he subsequently learned that Jackson did not regard him as a good disciplinarian will be recorded in a later chapter.

and hard hitting. At one time, he was facing the Federals on three sides, but he made his dispositions shrewdly and he held his ground. In describing another incident of the day, he complained of the depth of a charge made by his Brigade, "which," he said, "I have always found difficult to restrain." [42] At the end of his report, which was not written until still another heavy battle had been fought, he was able to say that his Brigade—he must have been speaking of it as a unit [43]—"has never been broken or compelled to fall back or left one of its dead to be buried by the enemy." [44]

Lee was able to commend Early for attacking "with great resolution the large force opposed to him." [45] Stuart, who had been well placed to observe all that happened on the extreme left at Sharpsburg, reported that Early "behaved with great coolness and good judgment, particularly after he came in command of his Division." [46] Early received praise even in the report of Jackson, who noted that Early "attacked with great vigor and gallantry the column on his right and front." [47] Had that been said in a document made public soon after the battle, those who knew Jackson's reserve would have said that he was softening; but those only who disliked Early would have pretended that the compliment was undeserved. Early, in short, had shown himself capable of handling a Division. The sole question was whether the War Department would regard Ewell as incapacitated and would give his Division to Early or, failing that, could find a vacancy for "Old Jube." With his splendid magnanimity, Ewell would have done his utmost for Early,[48] but "Old Bald Head" still was too shaken to exert himself.

If three or four Brigadiers were to be Major Generals, a corresponding number of vacancies in brigade command would be created. In addition, successors to Garland, to George B. Anderson and to Branch had to be named. A leader for Starke's Brigade was named before the longer list was completed. He was Col. Francis T. Nicholls, of Taylor's old Louisiana Brigade, who had been wounded at Winchester and later had been captured and

---

[42] O. R., 19, pt. 1, p. 971.
[43] Else the retreat of his left at Cedar Mountain would have been proof to the contrary.
[44] Ibid., 973.   [45] Ibid., 149.
[46] Ibid., 821.   [47] Ibid., 956.
[48] Cf. Hamlin's Ewell, 115 ff.

exchanged.[49] Roswell Ripley, in addition, was to return to South Carolina at the request of Governor Pickens [50] but was not to take his troops. No successor ever had been named to Gabriel Rains or to Joseph R. Anderson. The Brigades that David Jones and J. G. Walker had directed before they assumed divisional command should have regular commanders. With eleven, twelve, perhaps fourteen or fifteen promotions thus in prospect, there must have been wire-pulling by the ambitious Colonels, but of the scale and direction of it, little evidence remains.

"Old Jack" wanted a Brigadier's commission for his acting A.A.G., Maj. Elisha Franklin Paxton,[51] 34 years of age, God-fearing, industrious, and prior to the war a lawyer and bank president. Paxton had entered the Army as a First Lieutenant of the Twenty-seventh Virginia, and had risen to be a Major in that valiant unit of the Stonewall Brigade, but he did not have the art of ingratiating himself with the men. It will be recalled that in the reorganization of the Spring of '62, he had failed of election. Jackson had a good opinion of him, used him for several months as acting successor to Major Dabney, and now wished not only to give Paxton three stars and a wreath on the collar but also to entrust to that officer the Stonewall Brigade itself. Said Jackson in a letter to the Adjutant General, September 20: ". . . there is no officer under the grade proposed whom I can recommend with such confidence for promotion to a Brigadier-Generalcy." [52]

In like spirit, Longstreet must have urged the advancement of John R. Cooke, whose performance with his Twenty-third North Carolina and the Third Arkansas was commended in every report from that of his own divisional chief [53] upward to Lee himself.

---

[49] *O. R.,* 19, pt. 2, p. 684. For the wounding of Nicholls, see *O. R.,* 12, pt. 1. p. 801, and *R. Taylor,* 61. He was at that time Lieutenant Colonel of the Eighth Louisiana, but immediately after his exchange, September, 1862, he was made Colonel of the Fifteenth Louisiana, a regiment formed of a former battalion and two detached companies. Before he was strong enough to assume command, he was, Oct. 14, 1862 (*Wright,* 92), made Brigadier General. His wound continued to trouble him so greatly that it was not until January, 1863, that he took over Starke's Brigade (see *O. R.,* 21, 1094). Nicholls was born at Donaldsville, Aug. 20, 1834, one of the six sons of Judge Thomas C. and Louisa Drake Nicholls. His mother was the sister of Rodman Drake. In 1851, Nicholls entered West Point, where he was graduated No. 12 in the class of 1855 (*Cullum* No. 1688). He served in the artillery till October, 1856, and resigned to study law. He was a practicing attorney when he volunteered. See *Mil. An. La.,* 35-36.
[50] 5 *Rowland's Davis,* 351.
[51] Almost universally styled Frank Paxton.
[52] *Paxton,* 65. For the defeat of Paxton in the election, see *supra,* Vol. I, p. 325.
[53] *O. R.,* 19. pt. 1, pp. 915-16.

Longstreet used the high phrase "very gallantly" in describing the charge of the young North Carolinian.[54] Lee described how Cooke stood "boldly in line without a cartridge." [55] An admiring Captain records the humanizing fact that Cooke, after the battle, was "certainly the proudest man I ever saw." When the Captain inquired how his company had done, Cooke answered: "Webb, you need not ask about any particular man or company, for all did more than I thought it possible for men to do." [56]

On a par with Cooke's performance, in the estimation of senior officers, was that of John B. Gordon. After the Colonel of the Sixth Alabama had received his fifth wound and had recovered consciousness,[57] he was carried to the rear and thence across the Potomac. His heroic young wife, who always was close to the front, arrived promptly to nurse him; but he was so blackened and disfigured that he feared she would be shocked to see him. To relieve her, he mustered all his strength and, as she entered the room, he cried, "Here's your handsome husband; been to an Irish wedding!" He soon developed erysipelas, from which she nursed him back to recovery. Years later he recalled: "The doctors told Mrs. Gordon to paint my arm above the wound three or four times a day with iodine. She obeyed the doctors by painting it, I think, three or four hundred times a day." [58] All the while, the ranks of D. H. Hill's Division were ringing with his praise. Rodes said that on South Mountain, September 14, Gordon handled the Sixth Alabama "in a manner I have never heard or seen equaled during this war." [59] D. H. Hill styled Gordon the "Christian hero" and the "Chevalier Bayard of the army" and asserted that Gordon had excelled his feats at Seven Pines and in the later battles around Richmond. "Our language," Hill concluded, "is not capable of expressing a higher compliment." [60]

In personal valor, many had shone on the hills above the Antietam. Former Governor Smith—"Extra Billy"—of the Forty-ninth Virginia had been conspicuous. When Early had succeeded temporarily to Ewell's Division, command of Early's Brigade had passed to "Extra Billy," who had just observed his 65th birthday.

---

[54] *Ibid.*, 840.   [55] *Ibid.*, 150.

[56] Capt. Jos. C. Webb, Oct. 9, 1862, in *Hillsboro Record*, n.d.—*Cooke MSS.*

[57] See *supra*, p. 211. An odd account of his sensations while wounded appears in *Companions in Arms*, 539. For Gordon, see further p. 265 and Chap. XXXV.

[58] *Gordon*, 88–91.   [59] *O. R.,* 19, pt. 1, p. 1035.

[60] *O. R.*, 19, pt. 1, pp. 1021, 1027.

He had not learned much of tactics and had not changed in the slightest his opinion of "West P'inters," but he had won the admiration of every beholder by his courage. Thrice wounded, he directed his troops till the battle was over. "Jeb" Stuart observed the old Colonel, dripping blood but fighting valiantly, and he went beyond the usual limits of report to say that Smith was "conspicuously brave and self-possessed." [61] Col. A. J. Grigsby, it will be remembered, late in the action had the somber distinction of leading Jackson's Division, because all his seniors were killed or wounded. He was rivalled in prowess by Col. Leroy A. Stafford, who handled Starke's Brigade [62] until an injury to his foot compelled him to leave the field.[63]

Other Colonels had distinguished themselves during the Maryland expedition not only for bravery, which had been shown by hundreds of men, but also, in a few cases, for intelligent leadership and for their administrative capacity, on which Lee put high valuation. All this had to be taken into account in recommendations for promotion. For some Brigades, seniority could be respected without risk to the service.

When certain other cases were considered, hope doubtless was cherished that seniors would resign or seek transfer or point to honorable wounds as a reason for not returning to field duty. "Monty" Corse of the Seventeenth Virginia had been commended by his Brigadier for "splendid gallantry" and had been mentioned by Longstreet as "one of the most gallant and worthy officers in this army . . . distinguished in at least ten of the severest battles of the war." Lee himself also had a word for the "gallant Colonel" of the Seventeenth Virginia.[64] If Pickett were promoted, Corse seemed the logical successor in brigade command. Similarly, if Trimble or the long-absent Arnold Elzey became a Major General, "Jim" Walker of the Thirteenth Virginia fitly could take his place. Carnot Posey of the Sixteenth Mississippi could measure up in the event that W. S. Featherston did not return from his sick leave. Should "Bob" Toombs conclude that he had won enough fame to avenge himself on Davis, then

[61] O. R., 19, pt. 1, p. 821.
[62] Cf. O. R., 19, pt. 1, pp. 149, 952, 956, 969–71, 1008.
[63] Ibid., 1017. In this reference, Stafford's temporary successor, the generous Edmund Pendleton of the Fifteenth Louisiana, said: "I beg leave to speak in the highest terms of the gallantry and fearlessness displayed by Col. L. A. Stafford."
[64] O. R. 19, pt. 2, pp. 677–78.

Toombs's Brigade could go to his fellow-Georgian, capable Tom Cobb, Howell's younger brother—a succession that Toombs could not protest.

A few other Colonels were believed to be ripe for promotion by seniority, but that list was not long. Recommendations, in some instances, may have been made with misgiving. Lee could not select from superabundant ability. Rather was it his to exclude those manifestly incompetent and, perhaps half doubtfully, half hopefully, to entrust the lives of the men in some Brigades to those Colonels who had made the fewest mistakes.

The decision at Army Headquarters was to fill the certain, the probable and the hoped-for vacancies. Here, in the end, were the names Lee submitted October 27 in answer to requests from the Secretary of War and the Adjutant General: [65]

To Be Major General:

George E. Pickett, for command of the larger part of Longstreet's old Division; [66]

John B. Hood, for command of the enlarged Division already in his care;

I. R. Trimble, for assignment to the command of Jackson's Division;

Jubal A. Early, for command of Ewell's Division in the event that a successor to Ewell were deemed necessary and Edward ("Allegheny") Johnson were unable to take the field because of his wounds.

To Be Brigadier General:

Carnot Posey, Colonel of the Sixteenth Mississippi, to succeed W. S. Featherston of Anderson's Division, who was absent sick;

M. D. Corse, Colonel of the Seventeenth Virginia, to have the Brigade of Geo. E. Pickett, promoted;

J. B. Robertson, Colonel of the Fifth Texas, to be in charge of the Texas Brigade;

G. T. ("Tige") Anderson, to permanent command of D. R. Jones's Brigade, which he had been directing as senior Colonel;

T. R. R. Cobb, Colonel of Cobb's Legion, in the event that the vacancy created by the absence of the wounded Robert Toombs should be filled;

[65] O. R., 19, pt. 2, pp. 681–82, 683.
[66] Pryor's, Armistead's, Kemper's, Jenkins's and Pickett's Brigades.

John R. Cooke, Colonel of the Twenty-seventh North Carolina, to command the Brigade of J. G. Walker, who was directing a small Division;

E. F. Paxton, Major and A.A.G., to have the Stonewall Brigade;

James A. Walker, Colonel of the Thirteenth Virginia, to command Trimble's or Elzey's Brigade;

William ("Extra Billy") Smith of the Forty-ninth Virginia to the Brigade of Ewell's Division not given Walker;

George Doles, Colonel of the Fourth Georgia, to succeed R. S. Ripley, detached;

S. Dodson Ramseur, Colonel of the Forty-ninth North Carolina, to have the Brigade of George B. Anderson, mortally wounded;

John B. Gordon, Colonel of the Sixth Alabama, to command Rains's old Brigade, which had been under Col. A. H. Colquitt at South Mountain and at Sharpsburg;

James H. Lane, Colonel of the Twenty-eighth North Carolina, to succeed L. O'B. Branch, killed in action;

Alfred Iverson, Colonel of the Twentieth North Carolina, to take Samuel Garland's Brigade;

E. L. Thomas, Colonel of the Thirty-fifth Georgia, to the permanent command of Jos. R. Anderson's Brigade, which he had been leading as senior Colonel.[67]

Unfortunately, this list was marred almost as soon as it was made. General Featherston returned, somewhat unexpectedly, from sick leave and resumed command of his Brigade, which Lee had planned to give to Col. Carnot Posey. It would not be possible to promote Posey at once unless service could be found elsewhere—perhaps in his adopted State of Mississippi—for Featherston.[68] Next, Lee found that Col. A. H. Colquitt had been promoted Brigadier without inquiry by the War Department at Army Headquarters. This closed the vacancy to which General Lee had been anxious to promote Col. John B. Gordon. Still again, Col. E. A. Perry of the Second Florida was named Brigadier [69] with a view to his assignment to the command of the Florida regiments. Whether or not this was engineered to re-

[67] O. R., 19, pt. 2, pp. 683–84. The name of Colonel Thomas does not appear in this list, but the final sentence of the reference to "Jim" Lane shows that the copyist omitted something. From the mention of "the senior colonel of the Georgia regiments composing Joseph R. Anderson's Brigade," it is manifest that Thomas was included. As will appear, he was commissioned.

[68] O. R., 19, pt. 2, p. 697.

[69] Sept. 30, 1862, to rank from Aug. 28, 1862.

move Roger Pryor from temporary command of Anderson's Division, it had that effect. What was more, in depriving the editor and ex-Congressman of his troops, it virtually stripped him of his commission. Lee made no effort to keep Pryor with the Army by providing another Brigade for him, but suggested that Pryor might be employed in the force Gustavus Smith was developing in Southside Virginia.[70]

When Lee's recommendations of October 27 had been hammered to fit these conditions and then had been rolled through the political mill by a President who sought to please both Lee and the Senate,[71] they emerged with these differences: Early and Trimble were not promoted; John B. Gordon was appointed, but immediate confirmation was not sought;[72] Carnot Posey, James A. Walker and "Extra Billy" Smith were passed over.

Those promoted to divisional command thus were Pickett and Hood. The new Brigadiers were Corse, T. R. R. Cobb,[73] J. B. Robertson, "Tige" Anderson, John R. Cooke, George Doles, S. Dodson Ramseur, Alfred Iverson, James H. Lane, E. L. Thomas and E. F. Paxton. These promotions, which were announced in orders of November 6,[74] included every man Lee had recommended in Longstreet's command. All the disappointments were among Jackson's troops[75] and were the result, probably, of a ruling by the War Department that general officers could be appointed only when they could be assigned to command.[76] This balked Trimble, in particular, to his disgust and to the regret of Jackson and of Lee.

One of the two recorded instances of outspoken resentment of

[70] *Ibid.*, 697–98, 708–09, 712, 715–16. The proposal was to use the First Virginia, Kemper's Brigade, and the Sixty-first Virginia, Mahone's Brigade, as the basis of a new command for Pryor. Both the Brigades to be reduced in this manner had five regiments. Cf. *ibid.*, pt. 1, pp. 804, 805.

[71] Cf. Davis to the editor of the *Louisville Courier-Journal*, May 5, 1887: "In Gen. Lee's army, I am quite sure, no promotions were made without his special recommendation, and no subordinate retained in his army whom he reported to be incompetent." 9 *Rowland's Davis*, 554.

[72] *Wright*, 95. Gordon did not mention this in his *Reminiscences*. Failure to confirm probably was due to the fear that he might be invalided by the wounds received at Sharpsburg.

[73] *O. R.*, 25, pt. 2, p. 699. He succeeded his brother Howell and not Robert Toombs, as originally planned. Howell Cobb did not resign though he did not resume field command in Virginia. On Sept. 19, 1863, he became a Major General. *Wright*, 36.

[74] *O. R.*, 19, pt. 2, p. 698.

[75] Which, by that date, included D. H. Hill's Division, and therefore John B. Gordon.

[76] Cf. Lee to Trimble, Jan. 2, 1863—*Trimble MSS.* "That," Lee added, in reminding ʰe wounded General of the law, "is the view taken of it by the Department."

the promotions was in Jackson's own cherished Stonewall Brigade, where the elevation of Maj. Frank Paxton made many faces red and loosed hot tongues. Jackson had asked the appointment because he did not think a single one of the regimental officers of the Brigade was as well qualified to direct a Brigade as was Paxton.[77] Within the Brigade, there was vehement disagreement. Jackson's judgment of men often had been disputed; some of his appointees had been failures; his partiality for Presbyterians often had been alleged. Never had all these criticisms been so combined as when the brigade officers learned that Charles Winder's successor was to be a fellow townsman of Jackson's, a staff Major who, in the spring election, had failed to receive the support of the Twenty-seventh Virginia.[78] The leader of the opposition to Paxton was the Colonel of that regiment, Andrew Jackson Grigsby. He felt that he had earned promotion, and when he failed to receive it, he resigned. "[He] told me," McHenry Howard remembered, "that for the good of the service he would do nothing while the war lasted, but that as soon as it ended he would certainly challenge Jackson." [79] The belief of some officers of the Brigade was that Jackson had declined to promote Grigsby because the Colonel swore as notoriously and as violently in the Valley as if he had been in Flanders. McHenry Howard did not believe that was the reason. Said he of Jackson: ". . . Stonewall appreciated a good soldier, although a swearer. His own quartermaster had the reputation of being the hardest swearer in the army, and soldiers used to say [Major Harman] could start a mule train a mile long by his strong language at the back end." [80]

The other protest was over the promotion of "Monty" Corse instead of Col. Eppa Hunton, who was his senior in commission and had been in more numerous battles. Other Colonels of Pickett's Brigade came to Hunton and proposed that all of them resign in order to show their disapproval. Gallant Eppa Hunton would not hear of it: all of them must remain and do their duty.[81]

This spirit eased the difficult task of General Lee, who had made the best of the material he had. Some good men he had

[77] Cf. Jackson's statement in O. R., 25, pt. 2, p. 645.
[78] Cf. Capt. Randolph Barton in 38 S. H. S. P., 281.
[79] McHenry Howard, 180–81.
[80] Ibid., 181. Howard, ibid., 152, remarked as evidence of the severity of the fighting at Malvern Hill that Major Harman stopped swearing while the battle raged.
[81] Hunton, 81.

found and promoted. In some he was to be disappointed. He could not hope quickly to replace such men as Winder and Garland, or to find division commanders to measure up forthwith to the stature of the wounded Ewell and "Dick" Anderson. When weak were balanced against strong, the unpromising against the able, the major gain of the reorganization was in the advance-ment of Longstreet and of Jackson.

CHAPTER XVII

The Balance of the Two Corps

THE REORGANIZATION of the Army of Northern Virginia into two Corps, the First under Longstreet and the Second under Jackson, was not announced formally until November 6,[1] but the assignments of troops were made prior to October 27. Longstreet was given McLaws's, Anderson's, Walker's, Hood's and his own Division, which last, it will be recalled, for some weeks had been consolidated with D. R. Jones's and had been commanded by that officer and, in part, by James L. Kemper. Now this unwieldy organism was divided. Two of Jones's Brigades, as recorded already, were given Hood. The others were assigned to George Pickett. To the Second Corps were apportioned Jackson's own sadly depleted Division, Ewell's Division, and those of A. P. Hill and D. H. Hill. This was substantially the organization of Jackson's command during the Seven Days, except that the Division of A. P. Hill had taken the place of Whiting's.

From this organization, at the outset, disappeared David R. Jones. This was because of the failure of his health, not because of the failure of his leadership. He had not been a brilliant division commander, nor had he displayed those qualities that win the interest or arouse the curiosity of youthful soldiers; but he had been capable, direct and honorable and he had won Longstreet's commendation for all his official acts on every field from Thoroughfare Gap to Sharpsburg.[2] Lee, in his final report, had praise for Jones, who "handsomely maintained his position"[3] and made a "determined and brave resistance."[4] Before his tribute appeared in the official accounts of the battle, Jones was to breathe his last, a victim of heart disease.[5]

John G. Walker disappeared, also, before he fairly could take his place in the new First Corps. Promoted Major General, he

---

[1] O. R., 19, pt. 2, pp. 698–99. [2] O. R., 19, pt. 1, p. 566.
[3] Ibid., 141. [4] Ibid., 150.
[5] Jan. 15, 1863, though the date of his funeral in Richmond, January 19, sometimes is given as that of his death. See D. A. B., 1 R. W. C. D., 241; 5 C. M. H., 406.

was ordered to the Trans-Mississippi Department.[6] His two Brigades, which had acquitted themselves most honorably, passed
temporarily to the direction of their senior Brigadier, Robert Ransom, Jr.[7] Almost at the same time, the Army lost the picturesque
"Shanks" Evans as the result of a call, early in November, by the
War Department for the dispatch of a Brigade to Weldon, N. C.
The choice of troops Lee left to Longstreet, who named Evans.[8]
This was done to the regret of McLaws[9] and doubtless of other
friends.

When these changes had been completed, and the new Corps
had taken on some permanence of character, it would have interested a critic to compare their divisional and brigade commands
and, in the light of the battles that had culminated at Sharpsburg,
to ask how well balanced they were. Was there anything in their
constitution to suggest that the First might be the corps of defense
and the Second of offense? Did the Second have in it men who
would see that it outmarched the First?

Of Longstreet's divisional commanders, after the transfer of
Walker to the West, Hood could be regarded as a leader of high
promise and "Dick" Anderson as a soldier of competence. Pickett
was untried at his new rank, but he had been an excellent brigade
leader and with Longstreet's full support was apt to direct with
wisdom his larger force. The one division chief of the First Corps
regarding whom the Maryland expedition had raised any doubts
was the senior of the four Major Generals, the stout and com-
radely Lafayette McLaws. During the greater part of the time
the Army was in Maryland, McLaws had exercised semi-autonomous command without conspicuous success. He erred in not
making better reconnaissance of Crampton's Gap, though he reasonably could assert that "Jeb" Stuart unintentionally had misled
him concerning the strength of the enemy in that quarter.[10] The
second time McLaws went astray was not because he followed but
because he neglected the advice of the observant cavalryman.
Stuart, on September 14, several times counselled McLaws to
picket a road that led from the northern end of the Harpers

[6] O. R., 19, pt. 2, pp. 697, 703, 710, 731; 9 C. M. H., Missouri, 225.
[7] O. R., 19, pt. 2, p. 703.
[8] O. R., 19, pt. 2, pp. 695, 697, 698, 715; ibid., 18, 770.
[9] Cf. McLaws to Evans, Nov. 8, 1862—Evans MSS.
[10] Cf. McLaws, O. R., 19, pt. 1, p. 854.

Ferry bridges [11] under the flank of Maryland Heights, and thence northward to Sharpsburg.[12] For some reason, McLaws did not guard this road. In consequence, on the night of the 14th, all the Federal cavalry at Harpers Ferry, some 1500 sabers,[13] escaped by that route, intercepted part of Longstreet's trains en route to Williamsport, burned forty-five wagons [14] and missed by an hour only the reserve artillery, which was being sent to Virginia.[15] So much for the mischief that can be wrought by neglecting even a road which may seem impracticable.[16]

More serious than this dereliction was the slowness of McLaws's march to join Lee at Sharpsburg. The terrain and the position of the enemy were such that McLaws made no effort to use the difficult road from Maryland Heights to Sharpsburg. He decided, instead, to cross the bridge to Harpers Ferry, to pass through that place to Halltown, thence to Boteler's Ford near Shepherdstown,[17] back across the Potomac and on to Sharpsburg. This entailed a march of approximately nineteen miles, for which, in all the circumstances, McLaws would not have been unreasonable in asking a day and a half. Jackson moved his own Division over the same ground, except for the distance between Maryland Heights and Harpers Ferry, in a single night.[18] A. P. Hill hurried his command, with its artillery, from Harpers Ferry to Sharpsburg in nine hours. The head of his column made the march in seven hours.[19]

McLaws, who received his marching orders during the early

[11] There was a pontoon crossing in addition to the regular bridge. O. R., 19, pt. 1, p. 584.

[12] See supra, p. 190.

[13] Stuart thought the number 500 (O. R., 19, pt. 1, p. 818), but Col. A. Voss of the 12th Illinois gave the strength of the contingent as 1500 (O. R., 19, pt. 1, pp. 758–59). Governor A. G. Curtin of Pennsylvania was informed that 1300 men reached Greencastle (ibid., pt. 2, p. 305). The troops were: 8th N. Y., 12th Ill., two companies 1st Md., Rhode Island Battalion and Cole's 1st Md. Potomac Home Brig. (O. R., 19, pt. 1, pp. 533, 538). For details of the conference preceding the departure of these troops at 8.30 P.M., see ibid., 583–84.

[14] These wagons, loaded chiefly with food and ammunition, had been started southward from Hagerstown, for safety, when Longstreet had started back on the 14th toward Boonsborough (O. R., 19, pt. 1, pp. 142–43, 818).

[15] Ibid., 830.

[16] Of this road, Lt. Col. Hasbrouck Davis said: "I should suppose that it was not a very good road at any time for artillery; I doubt whether it would have been practicable." O. R., 19, pt. 1, p. 629.

[17] For the relief of those puzzled by the occasional references to Blackford's Ford it may be stated that Blackford's and Boteler's were different names for the same crossing. Cf. O. R., 19, pt. 1, p. 344.

[18] Cf. supra, p. 201.   [19] O. R., 19, pt. 1, p. 981.

afternoon of September 15,[20] permitted his start to be delayed incredibly by paroled Federal prisoners who crowded across the bridge from Harpers Ferry whenever they had opportunity. Because of this and probably because of poor organization, Mc-Laws did not get his column under way until 2 A.M. of the 16th, and then he halted about 8 A.M. at Halltown, four miles distant. From that bivouac, Sharpsburg was distant not more than fifteen miles; but McLaws required about twenty-three hours to cover that distance. Even then, the last six miles he completed virtually as a forced march under orders from Lee to press onward.[21] That is to say, approximately forty-one hours elapsed from the time McLaws received his orders on Maryland Heights until he reached his objective. His men had not straggled,[22] but they were so weary that Lee had to allow them some rest before putting them into action.[23] McLaws attributed his slow march to the exhaustion of his men from the hardships of their fighting North of the Potomac, to their loss of sleep and to their inability to get or to cook rations.[24]

This excuse was not entirely acceptable to Lee. In his final report on the Maryland expedition, the commanding General came as close to censure of McLaws as ever he did in written comment on his officers' performances. After noting that McLaws considered the direct roads to Sharpsburg from Maryland Heights impracticable, Lee wrote: "Owing to the condition of his troops and other circumstances [McLaws's] progress was slow, and he did not reach the battlefield at Sharpsburg until sometime after the engagement of the 17th began." [25] What the "other circumstances" were, the commanding General, with his usual reserve, did not specify. His language did not carry with it any implication that McLaws had failed: it did raise a question whether McLaws would succeed, and, more particularly, whether he could make his Division march.

[20] 2 P.M. seems a fair guess from the statement of the facts, *ibid.*, 855.

[21] *O. R.*, 19, pt. 1, pp. 855–57. These logistics are calculated on the assumption that the middle of McLaws's column reached the vicinity of Sharpsburg about 7 A.M., September 17. This seems reasonable but may be an hour early. The head of his column, said McLaws, *ibid.*, 857, reached the vicinity of Lee's headquarters "about sunrise."

[22] This statement has to be limited to McLaws's Division but it is demonstrated by the tables of effective strength of that command (*O. R.*, 19, pt. 1, pp. 860–61). Nothing is known of the extent of straggling in Anderson's Division, which was in rear of McLaws.

[23] *Ibid.*, 858 and *supra*, p. 209, n. 14.   [24] *Ibid.*, 857.

[25] *O. R.*, 19, pt. 1, p. 148.

Longstreet's Brigadiers included five of the newly commissioned Generals. All of them had done admirably at their previous rank but all, of course, had to stand the test of promotion. Some at least of them might exhibit the familiar tragedy of being advanced beyond the grade for which they were qualified—and of remaining Colonels in ability though they were Generals in title. If Toombs refused to return to an Army in which he was not to be a Major General, his Brigade would be well handled by Henry Benning. In McLaws's Division, there was prospect of improvement in the odd circumstances that led Howell Cobb to stand aside in order that his brother Thomas might be a Brigadier. Howell Cobb was not held responsible for the bloody reverse that shattered his Brigade at Crampton's Gap,[26] but he was not considered as able an officer as his brother proved to be.

With the best of these men of brigade and of divisional rank, Longstreet could hope to make his Corps strong and reliable; but it scarcely could be said that any of his subordinates save one had by this date displayed qualities that would dispose anyone to expect a career of eminence. The exception was Hood. He was not a first class administrator, and when his troops were in camp he was inclined to be careless, but in battle there was about him some of the effulgence of the true captain of men. Anyone who had followed the operations of the Army after Gaines' Mill would have said that of all the officers under Longstreet, the most likely to be a great soldier was Hood.[27]

The Second Corps was to have as its Major Generals D. H. Hill and Powell Hill, but there was no provision for filling Ewell's place and none for supplying Jackson's Division with an officer of appropriate rank. In the case of Ewell, the law left his troops in the care of his senior Brigadier until he either was able to return to duty or was retired by formal action. This succession would put the Division under Lawton when that earnest but relatively inexperienced field commander recovered from the wound he had received at Sharpsburg. In the event that Lawton did not return, the Division would be well used by "Jube" Early. The Division of Jackson was intended for Trimble, but that vigorous fighter, it will be remembered, could not be assigned to command

---

[26] Cf. O. R., 19, pt. 1, pp. 818–19, 826–27, 870; 28 S. H. S. P., 297.
[27] For the next part of the sketch of Hood, see infra, Chaps. XXXI and XXXIV.

at new rank until he was well enough to serve with troops. Hope fluctuated on this score. At one time he was expected to return by November 20,[28] but he developed camp erysipelas and a malady that probably was an osteomyelitis.

Jackson's reliance, for the autumn, had to be on Harvey Hill and on Powell Hill. With the one his relations presumably were as cordial[29] as with the other they unhappily were strained. No less sharp was the contrast between the records of "the two Hills" during the Maryland expedition. Harvey Hill's handling of the action on South Mountain need not be reviewed further, but at the time it seems to have been unfavorably appraised, at least among certain irreverent junior officers. Said young Ham Chamberlayne: "D. H. Hill miserably failed to hold his position [at South Mountain], and we, not [the Federals] were flanked. . . . People up here are beginning very generally to call D. H. Hill a numskull. If Harpers Ferry had held out 24 hours longer, as it should have done, D. H. would have cost us our army, our life, our freedom."[30]

At Sharpsburg, Harvey Hill had been stubborn and personally courageous. He may not have used "Dick" Anderson's support to the fullest of its firepower, though there is doubt whether, after the fall of its leader, he could have done more with the Division. Hill had proved that day, by comparison with his performance at South Mountain, that he was at his best when he had good men on either side of him and was fighting without full responsibility for the field. In that type of combat, he had no superior.

After the campaign and its disappointments were behind him, different feelings controlled the North Carolinian. In his report, he stated tartly the reasons why, in his opinion, a "glorious victory" was not achieved at Sharpsburg: McLaws and Anderson arrived too late, the artillery was badly handled, the straggling was "enormous." On this last score he added: "The straggler is generally a thief and always a coward, lost to all sense of shame; he can only be kept in ranks by a strict and sanguinary disci-

---

[28] Trimble to Jackson, Nov. 5, 1862—*Trimble MSS.*

[29] "Presumably" has to be inserted because General Early, after the war, repeatedly said that Jackson and Harvey Hill did not get on well together. Early once wrote President Davis that he always had understood this was the reason for Hill's transfer to North Carolina after the Battle of Fredericksburg. Nowhere else is there anything to indicate that Hill did not have for Jackson during the war the admiration he subsequently voiced often.

[30] *Ham Chamberlayne,* 134.

pline." [31] All this was true, as far as it went, but as general comment on a battle another man directed, did it have a place in the report of a division commander? Was it calculated to promote harmony? Hill's sharp comments in this instance did not exhibit the qualities of a "croaker," [32] which Lee thought was one of his defects; but Hill's disposition to find fault with his comrades helps to explain the difficulty of using to best advantage his undeniable excellencies.[33]

Powell Hill's record during the Maryland expedition had been, all in all, the best attained by any division commander, except perhaps Hood. So much of the burden of maneuver and of preparation had fallen to the Light Division at Harpers Ferry that Jackson, who certainly had no partiality for him, gave Hill the privilege of remaining at the Ferry until the details of surrender had been completed.[34] Hill's march to Sharpsburg had equalled the best performance of Jackson's foot cavalry. Nothing had been lacking in the fierce and well directed attack of the Division at the moment the battle almost was lost.

For this, Lee saw to it that Hill received the credit his fine troops deserved. In the preliminary report on Sharpsburg, the commanding General described how Toombs "gallantly resisted the approach of the enemy" and then he told how Hill "drove the enemy immediately from the position they had taken and continued the contest until dark, restoring our right and maintaining our ground." [35] The final report gave [36] somewhat more credit to D. R. Jones and to Toombs, but it did not revise the conclusion that Hill's attack was the decisive move of the day. In this judgment concurred an officer of humbler rank but of complete familiarity with what actually occurred. This was Maj. B. W. Froebel, Chief of Artillery to Hood but at Sharpsburg under the direction of D. R. Jones. Said the honest Major, in his report of the fighting on the afternoon of the 17th: "At this time General A. P. Hill came up, and, charging, drove [the enemy] from the field." [37]

Longstreet would not have it so. He always was generous in

[31] *O. R.*, 19, pt. 1, p. 1026.   [32] See *infra*, Appendix I.
[33] For a general defense of D. H. Hill see Col. Archer Anderson in 33 *S. H. S. P.*, 26. The sketch of D. H. Hill is continued *infra*, Chap. XXI.
[34] *Cf.* Jackson to Lee, *O. R.*, 19, pt. 1, p. 951.
[35] *O. R.*, 19, pt. 1, p. 141.   [36] *Ibid.*, 150.
[37] *Ibid.*, 926.

praising his own subordinates, but he minimized what Hill did that ghastly afternoon. "Old Pete," in his report, praised Toombs's fight, described D. R. Jones's employment of Toombs on the enemy's flank, and added: "Two of the brigades of Maj. Gen. A. P. Hill's division advanced against the enemy's front as General Toombs made his flank attack. The display of this force"— there was not a word of its effective use—"was of great value, and it assisted us in holding our position." [38] D. R. Jones [39] scarcely was more generous to Hill.

Inasmuch as Jackson did not consider that A. P. Hill was under his command at Sharpsburg,[40] Hill, for justice, had to rely on his own report.[41] In doing so, he sent up no verbal rockets, but neither did he hide his light under a bushel. Here is the compact whole of his narrative of what happened after his artillery went into battery: "My troops were not a minute too soon. The enemy had already advanced in three lines, had broken through Jones' division, captured McIntosh's battery, and were in the full tide of success. With a yell of defiance, Archer charged them, retook McIntosh's guns, and drove them back pell-mell. Branch and Gregg, with their old veterans, sternly held their ground, and, pouring in destructive volleys, the tide of the enemy surged back, and, breaking in confusion, passed out of sight. During this attack, Pender's brigade was moved from my right to the center, but the enemy was driven back without actively engaging his brigade. The three brigades of my division actively engaged did not number over 2000 men, and these, with the help of my splendid batteries, drove back Burnside's corps of 15,000 men." [42] That was to say, if Longstreet would not recognize Hill's part in anything more than maintenance of the Confederate position, Hill had scant notice for other troops on the field and that notice scarcely commendation.[43]

Proud and sensitive the commander of the Light Division was, but diligent in camp and furious in battle. If he and Jackson could work together, Powell Hill's Brigades might prove to be the backbone of the new Second Corps. They were well organ-

[38] O. R., 19, pt. 1, p. 841. [39] Ibid., p. 887.
[40] O. R., 19, pt. 1, p. 957.
[41] It bore date of Feb. 25, 1863; O. R., 19, pt. 1, p. 979; Lee's was dated Aug. 19, 1863, ibid., 144.
[42] O. R., 19, pt. 1, p. 981. [43] The sketch of Hill is resumed infra, p. 341 ff.

ized; together, they were numerically stronger than any other Division; they had fewer officers of rank absent on account of wounds. In the Corps, six Brigades temporarily were under Colonels, not all of whom were competent. One only of Hill's Brigades, that of Charles Field, was without its regular commander.

The Brigadiers of Jackson's Corps were, at the moment, about on a par with those of Longstreet: Five new Generals looked to "Old Jack" for orders and instruction—the same number as in the First Corps. The gamble on individuals was in proportion. Nothing that was said at the time of the promotions indicated any particular doubt concerning Alfred Iverson, Colonel of the Twentieth North Carolina, who was advanced to the command of Garland's Brigade. Nor was there any open expression of relief that George Doles of the Fourth Georgia had succeeded Roswell Ripley.

The experience of Ripley in the Maryland expedition had not been happy. D. H. Hill complained in his report that "Ripley did not draw trigger" in the confused fighting on the right at South Mountain.[44] That night, in withdrawing, Ripley forgot altogether the Fourth Georgia, which would have remained in position, facing certain capture, had not Col. William L. de Rosset sent a courier to notify the regiment that the Brigade was retiring.[45] At Sharpsburg, Ripley's personal conduct, as always, was courageous and bold. In the thick of action, he was struck in the neck by a minié ball which probably would have been fatal had it not been deflected by his cravat. The choleric General was carried to the rear, where his wound was dressed, but within an hour and a half he was back with his men and was able to keep the field till action was concluded.[46] For this, he was commended by Harvey Hill,[47] but there seems to have been no distress over his departure for service in South Carolina. George Doles, who succeeded Ripley, was 32 years of age and had been a business man in Georgia before the war, but he had aptitude for the military life and as a Colonel had shown fiber and vigor.[48]

---

[44] O. R., 19, pt. 1, p. 1021.
[45] Thomas, 68–69. De Rosset commanded the Third North Carolina in Ripley's Brigade.
[46] O. R., 19, pt. 1, pp. 1027, 1033.   [47] Ibid., 1027.
[48] For a sketch see 6 C. M. H., 412 ff.

Although this shift from Ripley to Doles relieved one problem of brigade command in the Second Corps, nothing was done immediately in the case of President Davis's close friend, Thomas F. Drayton. The embarrassment that Lee had felt over the inability of the South Carolinian to maintain his organization had been constant. In Maryland, the poor performance of Drayton's troops at Manassas was twice duplicated. Even the considerate commanding General had to admit to the President that the Brigade "broke to pieces" at South Mountain and at Sharpsburg.[49]

These were minor weaknesses in the Second Corps. A majority of the brigade commanders were capable and some of them were rich in promise. Particularly was this true of Powell Hill's subordinates. Branch would be missed, but "Jim" Lane, who succeeded to the Brigade, was a two-fisted, vigorously human commander. So long as Charles Field had to nurse his wounds, his gallant Brigade would suffer. The others were in good hands. Especially had Archer and Pender distinguished themselves in Maryland. On the day of the hardest fight, Archer had arrived in an ambulance on the heights above Burnside's Bridge. He was so ill that he scarcely could keep his saddle during the battle,[50] but in his handling of his Brigade there had been nothing feeble, nothing doubtful. His colleague, Dorsey Pender, at Harpers Ferry and at Shepherdstown, had shown himself qualified to handle more than one Brigade. Of the fight on September 20 and of the general policy of invasion he wrote his wife characteristically: "Some of our miserable people allowed the Yankees to cross the Potomac before they ought and ours ran away making it necessary for us to go and drive them back. We did it under the most terrible artillery fire I ever saw troops exposed to. They continued to shell us all day. It was as hot a place as I wish to get in. It is considered even by Jackson as the most brilliant thing of the war. The fact is Hill's Division stands first in point of efficiency of any Division of this whole Army. . . . The whole of our time is taken up by two things, marching and fighting. Some of the Army have a fight nearly every day, and the more we fight, the less we like it. . . . I have heard but one feeling expressed about [Maryland] and that is a regret at our having gone there.

49 O. R., 21, 1030.   50 O. R., 19, pt. 1, pp. 981, 1000–01.

Our Army has shown itself incapable of invasion and we had best stick to the defensive. I think if it were hinted around in Yankee land that we would be satisfied with the Potomac as the line that the people would soon bring the government to it." [51] The forthright young General might not have won the fire-eaters' approval of this diplomacy, but in his own sphere, he had increasingly the confidence of his chief.

The artillery of the Army had won at Sharpsburg honors that equalled those of any of these infantry commands. Outranged, outgunned and exposed to better projectiles than they could return, the Confederates suffered frightfully, though few of their officers were killed. On Jackson's wing, control of a dominating hill to the left was necessary to the maintenance of the advanced line of battle: John Pelham held it with the spirit and fire the Army had come to expect of him.[52] In one move of the day, when the horses could not drag the guns across a plowed field, nearby infantrymen lent a hand and "almost carried" the pieces to the front.[53] On the center, where Boyce and Miller distinguished themselves,[54] the most shining figure was Col. Stephen D. Lee, who commanded a battalion of six batteries that were stationed near the Dunker Church during much of the heaviest fighting.[55]

On the opposite flank, A. P. Hill reported his satisfaction with the service of his "splendid batteries." As always, Capt. William Pegram was in the heaviest of the action and for the first time was wounded.[56] By September 20, his battery was so depleted through the accumulated casualties of many engagements in exposed positions that the survivors and their famous guns were distributed forthwith among other batteries. A. P. Hill would not have it so. He appealed to Lee, who directed that if batteries had to be dis-

[51] To Mrs. Pender, Sept. 22, 1862—*Pender MSS.* For the next part of the sketch of Pender, see *infra*, p. 358.

[52] *Cf.* Stuart in *O. R.*, 19, pt. 1, p. 821. Pelham had in his Stuart Horse Artillery, two rifles and two 12-pdr. Napoleons. *O. R.*, 19, pt. 1, p. 835.

[53] 13 *C. V.*, 21.

[54] See *supra*, p. 213. Longstreet never forgot Miller's gallant conduct at Sharpsburg Cf. *O. R.*, 19, pt. 1, pp. 840, 857; *Longstreet*, 395. D. H. Hill, who was critical of the handling of the artillery on September 16-17, had praise in his report for Boyce's Battery (*O. R.*, 19, pt. 1, pp. 1024, 1026). Lee's report commended both Miller and Boyce.

[55] Lee's Battalion had belonged to the reserve artillery, but on September 15 it joined Longstreet. For the conduct of Parker's Battery of this battalion, see *infra*, p. 282.

[56] *O. R.*, 19, pt. 1, p. 981.

banded, some unit less efficient than Pegram's be broken up. This was done [57] during the course of a reorganization through which Gen. W. N. Pendleton regained some of the prestige he lost at Shepherdstown. His best field of effort was in organization: in this crisis he outdid himself.[58] One important change only of personnel was involved. That fine artillerist, Stephen D. Lee, was promoted Brigadier General and was ordered to Vicksburg. In the campaigns of the Army of Northern Virginia he was to have no further part, though many achievements were to be his in the Gulf States.[59] To his battalion was assigned another young artil- lerist who was to win fame both as a participant in and as a his- torian of the campaigns of the Army of Northern Virginia—Lt. Col. E. Porter Alexander.[60]

In the cavalry, also, after Sharpsburg, praise was distributed and reorganization was undertaken. For "Jeb" Stuart's part in the campaign, there was no stint of the applause he loved. Jackson complimented the vigilant defense by Stuart of the Confederate left on September 17–18; [61] Lee paid tribute to the "great energy and courage" of his foremost trooper at Sharpsburg.

Performance justified praise, but for the first time Stuart almost had a rival. Fitz Lee's conduct was so fine that his Uncle, the commanding General, though careful never to display his deep pride of family, could not ignore what Fitz had done. In the absence of Stuart on other duty that had seemed more important, Fitz Lee covered admirably the withdrawal from South Mountain, delayed the advance of the Federals to Sharpsburg, and held the enemy in check the morning after the infantry recrossed the Poto- mac into Virginia. Three times, in the report of Gen. R. E. Lee, his gallant young nephew had to be mentioned approvingly.[62] For the same young officer, Stuart, too, had high words.[63] Either from affection for Fitz Lee himself, or out of regard for the com-

---

[57] *O. R.,* 19, pt. 1, pp. 623, 649. Similar action was requested for the Middlesex Artillery.

[58] Cf. *O. R.,* 19, pt. 2, p. 646 ff.

[59] Gen. R. B. Garnett paid tribute to Stephen D. Lee when, in reporting on Sharps- burg, he said: "[Lee's] bravery and intrepidity . . . should add fresh fame to the high reputation he has already won." *O. R.,* 19, pt. 1, p. 897. Longstreet, *ibid.,* 840, spoke of Stephen Lee's "distinguished part" in the battle. The commanding General felt him- self "weakened" by the departure of the newly promoted Brigadier. *O. R.,* 19, pt. 2, p. 697. For Lee's promotion, see *Wright,* 98.

[60] *O. R.,* 19, pt. 1, p. 156; pt. 2, p. 704.   [61] *O. R.,* 19, pt. 1, p. 957.

[62] *O. R.,* 19, pt. 1, pp. 147, 148, 151.   [63] *Ibid.,* 819, 820.

manding General, Stuart was not jealous of the chief of his second Brigade.

In commendation of Hampton, who had done splendid service, Stuart was not so warm; nor was he generous toward Col. Tom Munford, who had defended Crampton's Gap. There was praise for the "commendable coolness and gallantry" of the two regiments under Munford, but not a single clear word for their leader.[64] Of Col. Tom Rosser, who had held off the Federals atop South Mountain, Stuart said only that Rosser was left in position "with a detachment of cavalry and the Stuart Horse Artillery." [65] This silence may have been the result of oversight; it may have been the first expression of jealousy.

Reorganization of the cavalry was not dictated by casualties, as in the artillery, but by the increase in the number of units [66] and it involved, in effect, the creation of another Brigade. To the command of this, W. H. F. ("Rooney") Lee, Colonel of the Ninth Virginia Cavalry and second son of the General-in-chief, was named.[67] Stuart, and not the new Brigadier's father, doubtless was responsible for this.[68]

By the transfer of Beverley Robertson, a vacancy had been created at the head of the "Laurel" Brigade, which included Ashby's old command. In Maryland, this Brigade had been led by Col. T. T. Munford, of the Second Virginia, but, contrary to Stuart's wishes, the promotion went to William E. ("Grumble") Jones, Colonel of the Seventh Virginia [69]—an appointment that soon was to bring Jones into difficulties. For ill or for good, it was followed on November 12 by a transfer of a few regiments to give approximately equal strength to each of the four cavalry Brigades.[70]

Deserved as were most of the promotions of October and November, the real hero of the Army at Sharpsburg was, once more, the Army itself. Lee had said of it, soon after it had entered Mary-

---

[64] O. R., 19, pt. 1, p. 819.   [65] O. R., 19, pt. 1, p. 817.

[66] Between the Maryland expedition and the Battle of Fredericksburg, the cavalry Division increased from twelve regiments, and three "Legions" or battalions to seventeen regiments and three smaller units. Cf. O. R., 19, pt. 1, p. 810; ibid., 19, 544.

[67] October 3, to rank from September 15; Wright, 90.

[68] In July, it will be remembered, Stuart had said that "Rooney" Lee had shown capacity for higher command. O. R., 11, pt. 2, p. 522.

[69] Commissioned October 3, to rank from September 19; Wright, 90. Cf. O. R., 19, pt. 2, p. 705.

[70] O. R., 19, pt. 2, p. 712.

land: ". . . the material of which it is composed is the best in the world, and, if properly disciplined and instructed, would be able successfully to resist any force that could be brought against it." [71] When the 40,000 who remained to fight, footsore and hungry, had beaten off the attacks at Sharpsburg, Lee could have echoed the fine words with which J. R. Jones, describing the wane of Jackson's Division "to the numbers of a small Brigade," exclaimed at the end: "In this fight every officer and man was a hero . . ." [72]

How numerous and self-sacrificing were the examples that might have been cited to prove it! There, on the field, was little Charley Randolph, aged 13, who acted as Jackson's courier, won Stuart's praise in report,[73] had the rare tribute of open praise by "Stonewall" to General Lee, and received the grave acknowledgment by the commanding General of gratification that "my young kinsman" had merited Jackson's approval.[74] Who that read D. H. Hill's report could fail to see the pathos in his almost casual remark: "In charging through an apple orchard at the Yankees, with the immediate prospect of death before them, I noticed men eagerly devouring apples"?[75] Was there not defiance, if noble self-deception in Lieut. Ham Chamberlayne's letter home? "Don't begin to suppose we were driven out of Maryland; no such thing; our campaign is almost unexampled for quickness and completeness of success. We have done much more than a sane man could have expected." [76]

Could anything have been finer—or more typical of the Army —than the behavior of Capt. W. W. Parker's artillerists? These were boys of 14 to 17 who had joined the command of one of the noblest men of their native city.[77] They had been assigned to the battalion of Stephen D. Lee, who subsequently had the utmost delight in explaining how he had resented, at the outset, the addition of these boys to the responsibilities he bore. At Sharpsburg, the "boys' battery" fought until its guns no longer could be served;

---

[71] O. R., 19, pt. 1, p. 597.   [72] Ibid., 1008.
[73] O. R., 19, pt. 1, p. 821.   [74] Douglas, 131–32.
[75] O. R., 19, pt. 1, p. 1025.   [76] Ham Chamberlayne, 112.
[77] E. P. Alexander said of Dr. William Watts Parker: "If I want a Christian to pray for the dying soldier I call on Parker; if I wish a skillful surgeon to amputate the limb of a wounded soldier I call on Parker; if I want a soldier, who with unflinching courage will go wherever duty calls, I call on Parker."—MS Memoir of W. W. Parker. This beloved Virginian was born May 5, 1824, at Port Royal, was given his medical training in Paris, and thereafter, until his death, Aug. 4, 1899, was a practitioner in Richmond, where his humanitarian labors were as notable as his work in medicine.

then it withdrew. Later in the day, when the attack against D. R. Jones's position on the right threatened ruin, Stephen Lee called Parker's tired gunners together. Said he: "You are boys, but you have this day been where men only dare to go. Some of your company have been killed; many have been wounded. But recollect that it is a soldier's fate to die. Now, every man of you who is willing to return to the field, step two paces to the front!" Enough unwounded, courageous boys stepped forward to man a section, which was placed on the left of the road above Burnside's Bridge. The boys were so weak that when their guns recoiled, they did not have the strength to push the pieces back into position, but they held on with a slow and stubborn fire till the battle was over. Among their dead was at least one boy of 14.[78]

If the Maryland expedition had any incident finer than that of Parker's Battery it perhaps was the death of Lieut. Frederick Long of the Twenty-eighth North Carolina. He was hit on September 20, during A. P. Hill's move to redeem Pendleton's blunder of the previous evening. As the litter bearers were carrying Long to the rear, Col. "Jim" Lane called out to know who he was.

"Lieutenant Long of your regiment," the answer was.

Lane hurried to him and, with his regret, expressed the hope the Lieutenant was not badly hurt.

"I have been shot through the back," said Long in an even voice, "the ball has gone through me and I am mortally wounded."

With that, he took Colonel Lane's hand and put it inside his shirt on a slug that could be felt under the skin of his chest. "I am a young man," he went on; "I entered the army because I thought it right, and I have tried to discharge all my duties."

Then, still holding Lane's hand on the bullet, he asked: "Though I have been shot in the back, will you not bear record, when I am dead, that I was always a brave soldier under you?"[79] That spirit in Maryland—and not Early, or Cooke, or Hood, or Powell Hill or even Jackson or Lee—made the Army of Northern Virginia "terrible in battle."

[78] *Where Men Only Dare to Go*; the Story of a Boy Company, pp. 42. 44, 46; S. D. Lee in *O. R.*, 19, pt. 1, pp. 845–46.
[79] 2 *N. C. Regts.*, 474.

CHAPTER XVIII

How to Accomplish "The Impossible"

RESTFUL WEEKS those of the early autumn of 1862 were for an army that had been fighting since June. Monotonous weeks they were, too, for the men in the ranks. Worse they might have been if "Jeb" Stuart had not offered one question, at least, for camp fire debate. That question was whether he and his men ever should have attempted the October raid, or having undertaken it, should have escaped with whole hides.

The operation originated, so far as the records show, not with the Chief of Cavalry but with the Army Commander.[1] Lee wished to know what McClellan was doing and where the Union forces were spread. A reconnaissance in force seemed to be justified and might be extended to a raid. If conditions were favorable, the raid could be pushed as far as Chambersburg. North of that town, the Cumberland Valley Railroad crossed a branch of the Conococheague Creek. By burning the bridge there, the Southern cavalry could stop the southward movement of supplies to the Federal railhead at Hagerstown. Were this accomplished, McClellan would be forced to rely exclusively on the B. & O. for railway communication. That prospect was worth the risks of a brief "expedition," as Lee chose to style it.

Written orders were transmitted on October 8 to Stuart, who then had his headquarters at "The Bower," Stephen Dandridge's plantation near Charlestown and a place enshrined always in the mind of "Beaut's" staff as the ideal haven of a trooper.[2] Stuart

---

[1] In a letter of October 15 to his mother, R. Channing Price wrote a full account of this operation. He prefaced it with a statement: "I felt confident that some great movement was in contemplation, as General Stuart was sent for and had several lengthy consultations with Generals Lee and Jackson." This letter of Captain Price's appears to be the principal unpublished account of the expedition, apart from the *Memoirs of W. W. Blackford*.

[2] *Cf.* Blackford, *op. cit.*, 226 ff: "The family consisted of Mr. Stephen Dandridge, his wife and a house full of daughters and nieces, all grown and all attractive—some very handsome . . . The host and hostess were fine specimens of Virginia country gentry under the old regime, hospitable, cultivated, and kind hearted. Every afternoon, after the staff duties of the day were performed, we all assembled at the house for

was delighted with the assignment and was gratified by the discretion his orders gave him. If he could conceal his movement, he was authorized to take 1200 to 1500 well-mounted men and to strike for the bridge beyond Chambersburg. Any other legitimate damage he could inflict on the enemy while gathering information would be in order. Horses were to be collected. Hostages who could be exchanged for loyal Confederates imprisoned by Northern Generals might be taken and brought back. In language reminiscent of that used before the "Ride around McClellan" in June, Lee admonished Stuart: "Reliance is placed upon your skill and judgment in the successful execution of this plan, and it is not intended or desired that you should jeopardize the safety of your command, or go farther than your good judgment and prudence may dictate." The commanding General added: "Should you be led so far east as to make it better, in your opinion, to continue around to the Potomac, you will have to cross the river in the vicinity of Leesburg."[3] In other words, if the cautions that had preceded the raid of June 12–15 were repeated, the opportunities were duplicated. With daring and luck, a second, glorious "ride around McClellan" was ahead of those lucky enough to share in the expedition! "Old Blue Light," who was one of the few who knew of the plan, was openly envious. He was beholden at the moment to Stuart for a new and dazzling uniform he considered much too fine to wear,[4] and he was all regret that he could not

riding, walking or fishing parties, and after tea, to which we had a standing invitation which was generally accepted, came music, singing, dancing and games of every description mingled with moonlight strolls along the banks of the beautiful Opequan or boating upon its crystal surface. The very elements seemed to conspire to make our stay delightful, for never was there a more beautiful moon or more exquisite weather than during that month we spent there."

[3] O. R., 19, pt. 2, p. 55.

[4] See von Borcke's account of delivering the uniform, a present from Stuart Said von Borcke: ". . . I was heartily amused at the modest confusion with which the hero of many battles regarded the fine uniform from many points of view, scarcely daring to touch it, and at the quiet way in which, at last, he folded it up carefully, and deposited it in his portmanteau, saying to me, 'Give Stuart my best thanks, my dear Major—the coat is much too handsome for me, but I shall take the best care of it, and shall prize it highly as a souvenir. And now let us have some dinner.'" Von Borcke asked, as a special favor, that Jackson put on the coat. "Stonewall" did and then went outdoors to the waiting table. Von Borcke, doubtless with hyperbole, thus continued: "The whole of the staff were in a perfect ecstasy at their chief's brilliant appearance, and the old Negro servant, who was bearing the roast turkey from the fire to the board, stopped in midcareer with a most bewildered expression, and gazed in wonderment at his master as if he had been transfigured before him. Meanwhile the rumour of the change ran like electricity through the neighboring camps, and the soldiers came running by hundreds to the spot, desirous of seeing their beloved Stonewall in his new attire . . ." (1 von Borcke, 296).

accompany Stuart now as a private cavalryman.[5] Another evidence this was of the developing friendship between the two, a friendship that puzzled some of their associates. Said Kyd Douglas afterward: "How could Prince Rupert or Murat be on congenial terms with Cromwell? But Jackson was more free and familiar with Stuart than with any other officer in the army, and Stuart loved Jackson more than he did any living man." [6]

Stuart did not take literally Lee's instruction to conduct the raid with 1200 or 1500 troopers. He selected 1800 of his most reliable and best mounted cavalry and chose as the commanding officers Wade Hampton, "Rooney" Lee, "Grumble" Jones, Williams Wickham and Calbraith Butler. Four guns of the horse artillery were to go under Pelham's charge. Wednesday evening, October 8, Stuart and his staff danced with the young ladies at "The Bower" till about 11.00 o'clock. Then Stuart devoted two hours to work on official papers and, at 1.00 A.M., had "the music (violin, banjo and bones)" give "a farewell concert" to the ladies.[7] The General himself contributed no less than four solos to the program.

All officers selected for the expedition were told to prepare for the road and to assemble their forces around Darkesville at noon, October 9. That evening Stuart led them to Hedgesville, a village about five miles south of McCoy's, which was about ten miles up the Potomac from Williamsport.[8] At the bivouac was read this address to the men, written in a spirit distinctively Stuart's: "Soldiers: You are about to engage in an enterprise which, to insure success imperatively demands at your hands coolness, decision and bravery; implicit obedience to orders without question or cavil, and the strictest order and sobriety on the march and in bivouac. The destination and extent of this expedition had better be kept to myself than known to you. Suffice it to say, that with the hearty coöperation of officers and men, I have not a doubt of its success —a success which will reflect credit in the highest degree upon your arms. The orders which are herewith published for your government are absolutely necessary, and must be rigidly enforced." [9]

[5] Cooke's Jackson, 335.   [6] Douglas, 192–93.
[7] Price MSS, loc. cit. The "program" of this concert, in Stuart's autograph, is among the McClellan MSS.
[8] These distances are by road or by river. On an air-line, they are much shorter.
[9] O. R., 19, pt. 2, pp. 55–56. The accompanying orders related to the march, respect for public property, etc.

The next morning at daybreak, October 10, the column crossed the Potomac, overwhelmed a small picket at McCoy's Ford and started northward. When Stuart reached the old National Road, he learned that six regiments of Gen. Jacob Cox's Federal infantry and two batteries had passed only an hour previously, westward bound. They well might be left alone, Stuart reasoned, and so must be the Federal advanced base of Hagerstown. Stuart knew its warehouses were bulging with army supplies but, he wrote, "I . . . was satisfied, from reliable information, that the notice the enemy had of my approach and the proximity of his forces would enable him to prevent my capturing it." [10]

Accordingly, the Confederates pressed on toward Mercersburg, in which surprised town the advanced guard hurried to the first store and purchased every shoe that would fit. Not until they tendered quartermasters' receipts in payment did the merchant realize they were Confederates. [11]

So long as the column had been in Maryland, it kept in close order and turned not at all from the road for food or for plunder. Now that the Pennsylvania line had been crossed, before Mercersburg was reached, Stuart kept a "division" of 600 troopers in front under Hampton, and 600 to cover the rear. The central unit of 600 was sent out on either side of the road to collect horses from farmers who had no warning that graycoats were North of the Potomac. [12] Little trouble was encountered. As the ground was wet, nearly all the industrious Pennsylvania farmers were working in their barns and some were threshing wheat. The sound of this guided the detachments straight to the powerful draft horses, which were led off without the removal even of collars. Well was it so. No quartermaster on the Confederate side of the Potomac had any collars large enough for those animals. [13]

While the Confederates brought in horses by the dozen, the afternoon wore away. Before the column could reach Chambersburg, a steady drizzle [14] and then darkness descended. Was Chambersburg occupied by the enemy? Did the shining lights of the little town signify preparation or the lack of it? On nearer

10 *O. R.*, 19, pt. 2, p. 52.   11 *H. B. McClellan*, 140.
12 *W. W. Blackford's MS Memoirs*, 243. Channing Price, *loc. cit.*, wrote that "200 out of every 600 men were detailed to visit all the houses and seize horses."
13 *W. W. Blackford's MS Memoirs*, 244.
14 So Blackford remembered it. Channing Price, *loc. cit*, wrote that "the rain was falling torrents."

approach, the roll of drums was heard.[15] Wade Hampton, commander of the van, is his own best reporter of what followed: "Not being able to ascertain if there were any troops in the place, and having heard that some were there, I deemed it prudent to demand the surrender of the town. . . . In reply to this summons three citizens, on the part of the citizens at large, came forward to ask the terms proposed."[16]

These were arranged quickly. The troopers clattered in and established themselves. Stuart named Hampton "Military Governor," as if he were to spend the autumn there; and then he sent Butler to the bank for its funds and "Grumble" Jones to burn the bridge over the Conococheague Creek. Neither mission was a success. The money had been carried away from the bank at the first alarm;[17] the bridge was of iron and defied "Grumble's" words and axes.[18] Some compensation there was next morning, October 11, through the capture and parole of sick and wounded Federal soldiers. Moreover, in depot were many army overcoats, much clothing, underwear and socks, 5000 excellent new rifles and numerous pistols and sabers. From these the raiders made discriminating choice and then left the remainder, as well as the railroad shops, to be burned by the rearguard.[19]

As the morning was quite chilly, many of the troopers forthwith put on the blue army overcoats[20] and lined up at assembly call. Without discussion or orders, the men turned their horses' heads to the West, in the expectation that column would circle and return the way it had come. To their surprise, Stuart started eastward as if he were going to a college town of which, perhaps, few of the men ever had heard at the time—a place called Gettysburg. This choice of the longer road back to Virginia was not a display of bravado nor, as Stuart insisted later, was it the prompting of intuition. It was application of the sound old principle of strategy that the unexpected move often is the wisest.[21]

Stuart wished this to be understood. As soon as the troopers cleared the town on their way to the East, Stuart asked Captain William Blackford to ride with him a little ahead of the van, and

---

[15] Channing Price, *loc. cit.*

[16] *O. R.*, 19, pt. 2, p. 57.

[17] H. B. McClellan, 141.

[18] *O. R.*, 19, pt. 2, p. 52.

[19] Channing Price, *loc. cit.*

[20] *O. R.*, 19, pt. 2, pp. 52–53.

[21] H. B. McClellan, *op. cit.*, 163, reported General Williams C. Wickham as having asked Stuart later whether the move to the East was made by intuition. "No," replied Stuart, "rather say judgment."

out of earshot. After a long reflective pause, he began, "Blackford, I want to explain my motives to you for taking this lower route, and if I should fall before reaching Virginia, I want you to vindicate my memory." Then he took out his map and explained: Cox's command, the force Stuart barely had missed on the National Road, would halt as soon as it learned of the raid, and would await the expected return of the Confederates. This would be in hill country which the Unionists could defend easily. Farther down the Potomac, the Federals would not be on their guard. They would be at the fords, of course, but if attacked from the rear, those crossings were not easily held. The country was open; there consequently was scant danger of getting lost or of being ambushed. Every argument was for recrossing the river downstream; every advantage, Stuart insisted, would be on the side of the Confederates, except for the distance to be covered and the proximity of the large Union forces at Harpers Ferry. Quick marching and precautions against the dispatch of the news of the column's position, said the General, would overcome the two disadvantages.

Did Blackford understand? What did he think of the reasoning? The engineer assured his chief that he understood and that he believed it wise to make a wide sweep eastward and to cross far downstream. If, Blackford added, "the contingency you spoke of arises and I survive you, I shall certainly see that your motives are understood aright." The staff officer's eyes filled as he spoke; so did Stuart's. In a moment they shook off emotion and went about the work of making the march least arduous for men and mounts.[22]

Stuart's choice of a return route exhibited his developing strategical sense and one quality of military character that he had displayed on the ride around McClellan in front of Richmond. When Stuart had reached Old Church, it will be remembered, he had to make up his mind to return as he had come or to press on entirely around the Federal army.[23] He chose the bolder course in Maryland as on the Chickahominy. Nor was there any question of Stuart's authority to exercise discretion. In orders, Lee had said: "Should you be led so far east as to make it better, in your opinion,

22 *W. W. Blackford's MS Memoirs*, 249–50. In *H. B. McClellan*, 148, appears a second-hand account of this conversation.
23 See *supra*, Vol. 1, p. 287.

to continue around to the Potomac, you will have to cross the river in the vicinity of Leesburg." [24] That was the district toward which Stuart was heading.

"Of course I left nothing undone," Stuart related subsequently, "to prevent the inhabitants from detecting my real route and object." Specifically: "I started directly toward Gettysburg"—by the same road a part of Lee's army was to follow the next year—"but, having passed the Blue Ridge, started back towards Hagerstown for six or eight miles, and then crossed to Maryland by Emmits‑ burg . . ." [25]

As soon as Maryland soil again was reached, the seizure of horses ended. Captured animals to the number of 1200 or there‑ abouts remained with the central "division." Each trooper who was charged with the custody of horses had three of them hitched to the same halter by the side of his mount. These well broken Pennsylvania draft horses shared obediently in a march that de‑ liberately had been kept free of the encumberment of slow-mov‑ ing cattle.

The weather was itself good fortune. Although the skies were clear, the roads were damp after the rain of the previous evening. A column that extended five miles raised no dust.[26] Small pros‑ pect there was that from any of the remote Federal signal stations even a sharp-eyed officer could guess the direction of the Confed‑ erate march. At that, Stuart took no chances. He halted and held temporarily all travellers the column met or overtook.

Regretfully, when Stuart reached the friendly town of Emmits‑ burg, about nightfall of that long October 11, he had to deny his men the pleasure of chasing a party of 150 Federal lancers who, shortly before, had passed in the direction of Gettysburg. He rounded up a few Union stragglers and then moved directly south‑ ward, as if he were headed for Frederick, which he assumed to be garrisoned. At Rocky Ridge, about six miles South of Emmits‑ burg, vigilance was rewarded in the capture of a courier en route to the scouting lancers of whom Stuart had heard at Emmitsburg.

[24] O. R., 19, pt. 2, p. 55.
[25] O. R., 19, pt. 2, p. 53. Much the best map is that "showing Route of Stuart's Cavalry Division Oct. 9 to 12, 1862 and June 25 to July 2, 1863" in the back of H. B. McClellan. At some point prior to the turn-off from the Gettysburg road, Stuart halted briefly that the horses might be fed. Channing Price, loc. cit.
[26] Ibid., 251, 252. Rain had fallen most of the night of the 10th-11th, but the sun rose amid clearing skies on the 11th.

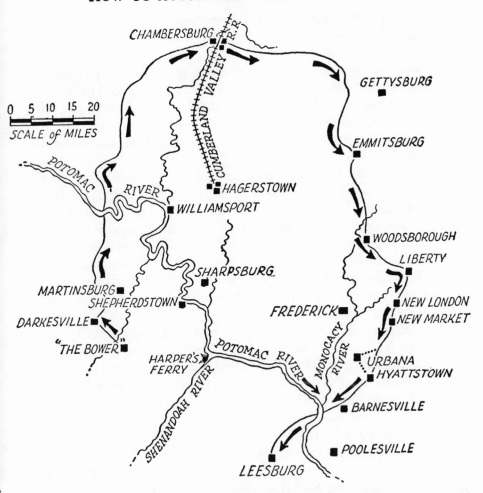

Route of Stuart's "October Raid," 1862

The courier's papers and his own admissions made it plain that, as Stuart had suspected, Union troops were in Frederick. Moreover, Stuart learned that Gen. Alfred Pleasonton and 800 Union cavalry were moving rapidly on Mechanicstown, four miles West of the point where Stuart then was. Prudence dictated veering eastward without delay across the Monocacy to a road that paralleled roughly the Frederick-Emmitsburg highway.

When Stuart changed route, silently and without a halt, he was approximately thirty-seven miles from Emmitsburg and a mile or

two farther than that from the Potomac—about halfway to safety.[27]
Long the march had been, long the road stretched southward
under a high-riding moon that was nearing its last quarter. The
men were hungry, yawning, nodding, numb or asleep. Weary
muscles ached or twitched. Tired nerves fairly screamed for relief.
Stuart, himself tireless, did not feel that he could afford to give his
men or his horses the rest even of an hour. They might nap in
their saddles if they could, but they must keep their column closed
and they must continue southward.

No enemy videttes were encountered. The sole disquieting
news gathered at the houses by the roadside was a report that
Gen. George Stoneman, who commanded the nearest stretch of
the Potomac, had between 4000 and 5000 men around Poolesville
and had been guarding the fords.[28] Although Stuart could not
have been free of anxiety, he outwardly was all confidence. As
"Jeb" approached New Market,[29] he recalled that from a point
about three miles westward, a side road led down to Urbana, scene
of the high festivities in September.

"Blackford," said he laughingly, "how would you like to see the
'New York rebel' tonight?"

"I should be delighted," answered Captain Blackford.

"Come on, then," Stuart challenged, and with several of the
staff and some of the couriers, he turned from the line of the
column's march.

It was not so desperate an adventure as it appeared to be. "The
night," Blackford later explained, "was light enough to see very
well, and the roads were perfectly familiar to us from our experience during the Maryland campaign, so there was really no
danger of capture even if we had fallen in with a force of the
enemy, for we could have scattered and rejoined the command."[30]
A brief, bold ride brought them to the Cockey home, where the
"New York rebel," a kinswoman of the family, had been visiting.
Stuart, it developed, had promised when he had left Urbana in
September that he would see the household again ere long. This
midnight visit was the fulfilment of the promise. In front of the

[27] H. B. McClellan, op. cit., 151–52, computed the distance from Chambersburg
to Emmitsburg at 31.5 miles. Rocky Ridge, where Stuart turned off, was six miles
South of Emmitsburg. From Emmitsburg to the Potomac, according to Major McClellan's map, was forty-five miles, and from Rocky Ridge, consequently, thirty-nine.
[28] O. R., 19, pt. 2, p. 53.
[29] On the direct road from Baltimore to Frederick.
[30] W. W. Blackford's MS Memoirs, p. 264.

hospitable home, the members of the cavalcade dismounted. They entered the yard. One of the officers gave the door a knock that resounded through the stillness. From an upstairs window, a frightened female voice asked, "Who is there?"

"General Stuart and staff."

Out of the window came a doubting head. After a swift glance the head was withdrawn with a half scream of surprise and excitement. The family began to stir. There was the stamp of unshod feet on the floor; questionings were heard within. Some of the more timid residents seemed to think a trick was being played. At the same window appeared now another head so pretty that even curlpapers could not mar its charm. "Who did you say it was?"

"General Stuart and his staff," Jeb himself replied with his unmistakable laugh. "Come down and open the door."

The doubts were resolved. Down went the window. Frenzied was the haste of dressing. Soon the listeners could tell from the sharpened sound that the girls had succeeded in getting on their shoes. Presently there was the creak-clonk, creak-clonk of feet on the stairs. Bolts rattled, bars were pulled back. The girls were on the stoop in the moonlight. The record holds no picture of a knightly cavalryman bowed low to kiss a throbbing hand. Nothing is said of rapturous glances or of grateful sighs; but frank, girlish smiles were no less pleasant because the moonlight made them pale. Feminine chatter was the sweeter for the bass laugh of the bearded troopers. Half an hour of this, and then "Goodbye, good-bye," waving handkerchiefs and graceful figures, and soon nothing but the beat of horses' hoofs, the jingle of spurs and scabbard, and the mumbled words of soldiers who never again were to see friendly Urbana or the lovely "New York rebel." [31]

It was at Hyattstown, soon after 7 o'clock, that Stuart and his staff rejoined his regiments.[32] Thirty-three miles and a little more the column had covered since it had left Emmitsburg. Twelve

31 Blackford's account, here followed, is the best, *op. cit.,* 264–65, where the name is spelled Cocky. In *H. B. McClellan,* 166, the spelling is that followed in the text. The same authority stated that Stuart in September had promised to return. As Major McClellan remembered the incident, Stuart did not dismount and stayed a few minutes only. Captain Blackford—to give him the rank he then held—said that the entire party dismounted and remained half an hour.

32 H. B. McClellan, *op. cit.,* 152, placed the arrival of the van at daylight. Channing Price, *loc. cit.,* wrote that the part of the column with which he was riding southward got to Hyattstown about 7. "The General joined us soon after." The map suggests no other route than that from Urbana to Hyattstown which Stuart could have used without doubling back on tired horses and passing the column for its entire length.

miles, the most difficult of all, still separated the raiders from Virginia soil. All the shrewdness, all the daring that Stuart and his officers possessed, they had now to muster. "Rooney" Lee commanded the van; Wade Hampton was in general charge of the rear "division." M. C. Butler commanded the rear regiment. Two guns under Pelham were in front, two behind. Guides who knew every foot of the ground, literally, went ahead with Stuart and with "Rooney" Lee. Orders were that the saber only was to be used if any outpost was met. Fire might spread the alarm. To silence, speed must be added. Though the column had been trot- ting nearly all night, it must keep that stern pace as it neared the zone of danger.

From the time Stuart had turned southward after crossing the Monocacy the previous evening, he had been paralleling that stream, which empties into the Potomac at a point where the river of division turns abruptly southward. For eleven miles below the mouth of the Monocacy, the Potomac keeps that general direction and even has a certain convexity toward the west. At Edwards' Ferry, opposite Leesburg, the river straightens out and runs east- ward. It was toward the long convex sweep of the river, between the mouth of the Monocacy and Edwards' Ferry, that Stuart was directing his column.

On this stretch of eleven miles, there were at least four crossings of the Potomac.[33] If the rains of the past days had rendered all of the fords impassable, then the jig was up; but if the Potomac was not out of bounds, by which of the fords would Stuart return to Virginia? He listened to a description of the approaches by his intelligent chief guide, Capt. B. S. White; he questioned that officer, and then, as a good soldier always should in the hour of decision, he put himself in the place of his adversary. Where would George Stoneman reason that the Confederates would try to re-enter Virginia? If the column struck for the nearest ford, it would turn off at a village called Barnesville and would proceed to the mouth of the Monocacy. If, again, a column moving to the Potomac from Hyattstown wished to give the widest berth to

---

[33] First is the ford at the mouth of the Monocacy, known as Noland's and later as Spinks Ferry. Nearby was Hauling Ferry. Then comes White's Ford, slightly less than three miles downstream. Next downstream, at approximately the same distance, is Conrad's Ferry. Five miles below that crossing is Edwards' Ferry. For the identification of some of these crossings the writer is indebted to the United States Coast and Geodetic Survey.

Federals descending the river, that column would keep on the straight road, which led via Barnesville, Beallsville and Poolesville to Edwards' Ferry.

Was the enemy, then, expecting Stuart at the mouth of the Monocacy or else at Edwards' Ferry? He would pretend to be going to one or the other, but would go to neither. Where, then, should the dash be made? For reasons that presently will appear, the guide recommended the little-used White's Ford, which was slightly more than three miles below the mouth of the Monocacy and nine miles above Edwards' Ferry.

The Captain was sure the approaches were favorable. Everything else depended on finding the ford undefended or occupied by a Federal force not too large or too strongly placed to be driven off before the nearby Union regiments could close in. No mistake could be allowed. Two miles to the West of the road the Confederates were following, Sugar Loaf Mountain arose. From its crest, Federals almost certainly would signal Stuart's movements. In answer, Union infantry and cavalry would concentrate rapidly. If there was delay or confusion at any point, the result might be the slaughter of the raiders. Crossing at White's Ford or anywhere else was a gamble. Stuart had made many and had won most of them.

From Hyattstown, southward for six miles, the column continued at a trot, and arrived at Barnesville just after a company of blue cavalrymen had left. Straight on toward Poolesville Stuart rode, rode ostentatiously, as if he hoped some Federal sympathizer would mount a swift steed and gallop across back fields to spread word that the rebels manifestly were bound for Edwards' Ferry. The ruse was to be executed below Barnesville, on the road to Beallsville. There, said Captain White, a forest extended for well nigh two miles on the right of the highway. Through this wood, White said, an old and disused road led southwestward. If the Confederates entered the wood and followed the obscure track, they would emerge into the main road that ran from Beallsville to the mouth of the Monocacy. Then, White explained, if the column moved on half a mile, as though it were going to the Monocacy, it would reach a farm road that led down to White's Ford in this wise:

Than such a situation, nothing better could be asked. The utmost must be made of the ground, as always should be, to the mystification and confusion of the enemy. Of course, if White had confused the route or had mistaken direction . . . Stuart

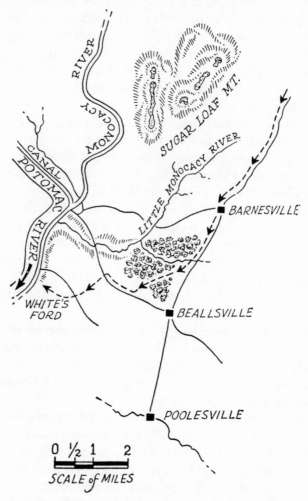

Vicinity of White's Ford, Potomac River—after *H. B. McClellan*

rode to the leading company and took his place beside Captains Tinsley and Southall of the advance guard. He would see!

Ahead on the right now was the wood Captain White described. Abundant cover it offered from any signal station on Sugar Loaf. So far, so safe. Presently, White turned his horse sharply out of the highway and into the wood. There, running southwestward, abandoned but scarcely overgrown, was the old road. At a few places it was crossed by fences that were pulled down easily enough. Otherwise it was entirely practicable. It led, after little more than a mile, to open fields, beyond which, at about 800 yards, was the road from Beallsville to the mouth of the Monocacy.

Boldly Stuart started up this road and soon saw ahead a column moving toward him. "Yankees!" the vanguard whispered and loosened their sabers. As it happened—or had it been so designed? —most of the men immediately with Stuart had not taken off the blue overcoats they had found at Chambersburg and had worn during the chill of the night. Because of this, the approaching Federals hesitated. Stuart rode straight toward them, quietly and without change of pace, until he was satisfied he was close enough to stampede the enemy. Then, with a shout, he set spur. Out flashed Southern sabers, up the road rushed the Confederates. Startled Federals gave them a wild volley and then wheeled and made off.[34]

Stuart did not pause. Behind the bluecoats he roared with as many troopers as the road would hold. On he went to a crest which seemed to his observant eye designed for the very purpose of holding off an inquisitive foe. There, as "Jeb" called a halt, he witnessed a sight he probably did not forget. Up galloped "Rooney" Lee's sharpshooters. Out they spread. Down from their horses they dropped, and almost before an inexperienced person could have discovered what was astir, they were firing briskly away at Federals who similarly were deploying.[35]

While the sharpshooters popped away, up came the blond young Pelham, aflush with excitement. Bewildered Pennsylvania horses were pulling two of his guns, but his veterans manned them. With the swift, sure observation he had employed in every action from Williamsburg onward, Pelham looked about him. He found that the crest was part of a long ridge which commanded the road of the Federal advance and, at the same time, covered the approaches to White's Ford, two miles distant. Pelham unlimbered; Stuart immediately directed down the lane

34 This paragraph is merely rewritten from H. B. McClellan, 155–56.
35 O. R., 19, pt. 2, p. 53.

toward the ford all the troopers not needed to support the artillery. The march of these exhausted boys and their dull-eyed,
dragging horses proceeded to Pelham's fast, staccato fire.

Thanks to the ridge, the farm track toward the ford proved as
safe as a covered way. To the West, the nearest enemy was on the
farther side of a creek known as the Little Monocacy, about a
mile East of the principal stream. If, now, the Confederate column was well closed and the rearguard safe, Pelham could be
relied upon to hold off the enemy until it was time for him to
withdraw. Then, with his familiar and dramatic tactics, he would
retire from position to position until he could make a dash for the
crossing.

Escape, therefore, seemed to depend solely on whether the
Federals held White's Ford in strength. Captain White had said
there was a troublesome old quarry near at hand. In addition, of
course, the Chesapeake and Ohio Canal ran along the Maryland
side of the Potomac. The canal probably was dry and might offer
as good protection for infantry as had the unfinished railroad cut
near Groveton. White's Ford itself admittedly was rough, but it
was passable . . . if the recent rains had not swollen the Potomac.[36]

These contingencies bulked larger as the proving time drew
nearer. Stuart himself remained near Pelham on the Beallsville-
Monocacy road, a post that must be held at any cost. Although
"Jeb" remained calm, he sent orders that the troopers proceed at
top speed, short of panicky haste, in seizing and crossing the ford.
Captain Blackford he directed to ride to the river bank and to give
an explicit, binding order that the horses must not be permitted
to stop and to choke the ford while they drank. Thirsty though
the mounts were, they must cross before they could be watered.
All the other details for occupying the ford were left to "Rooney"
Lee, that calm-eyed, amiable second son of "Marse Robert" whose
youthful beard concealed a jaw as firm as his father's. If there
were Federals at the ford, "Rooney" Lee must deal with them.

General Lee began at once to reconnoitre the ford, the approaches to which were banked with trees in the full splendor of
autumn. As soon as he was close enough to observe, he saw what
he had the best of reasons to dread—Federals on the rim of the
quarry. No artillery was visible, nor could the probable strength

[36] Cf. W. W. Blackford's MS Memoirs, 259.

of the enemy be discovered, but bluecoats undeniably were there in line on the quarry side and were awaiting attack. Once that was plain, "Rooney" sent a courier back to Stuart with a request that the General come down to the ford. Stuart answered that he was occupied imperatively on the heights overlooking the Little Monocacy and that Lee, using best judgment, must force the crossing. Truth was, Stuart felt growing concern for his rearguard, with which he had lost contact. Four couriers had been sent in succession to Colonel Butler with orders to hasten his march. None of the couriers had returned. Were they lost, or had Butler been cut off?

When "Rooney" Lee received Stuart's order to force a crossing, he took a little more time to study the ground,[37] and decided on his course: he would engage the Federals in front and on one flank and then, with the greater part of his force, he would make a dash for the ford. If he could get a gun across the river, he then could open on the rear of the Federals and could clear the way for the remainder of the column.

These seemed to be desperate tactics. If they failed, there might be slaughter or surrender. Was it not prudent, in the circumstances, to try to bluff the enemy? "Rooney" thought that the effort might be worth while, and he wrote a formal demand for the surrender of the position within a quarter of an hour. Impressively he said that General Stuart commanded in overwhelming force but wished to avoid unnecessary bloodshed. This note was entrusted to a cavalryman who advanced toward the ford with a pocket handkerchief tied to his sword blade. In a few minutes the paper was delivered.[38] "Rooney" Lee waited hopefully. Tired eyes were fixed on the field across which a Union courier would ride. No response came within the time limit of fifteen minutes.

A fight there must be. General Lee made his disposition. Men were designated for a frontal demonstration. A flanking force was told off. The other troopers and the gunners were ordered to push to the other side of the river at any cost. Just as General Lee

---

[37] Lt. Col. E. R. Biles, 99th Penn., reported that the Confederate column came within 800 yards or so, halted, "and remained in that position for some half an hour, sending small parties down toward the tow-path." O. R., 19, pt. 2, p. 50.

[38] H. B. McClellan, 157. Colonel Biles, loc. cit., made no reference to the demand for surrender.

was about to give the signal for the attack, a movement of men was observed along the tow path and on the nearer side of it. Confederate officers focused their glasses and, for the moment, almost held their breath. Then there were smiles and delighted gestures and a visible relaxation in the saddle: Undeniably, if incredibly, the Federals were filing out of their quarry fortress and were withdrawing downstream!

White's Ford was abandoned and open, but from the Monocacy the Federals were pressing. In rear, from the North, they might be closing. Danger, though reduced, was not past. Speed the crossing! Swiftly the horse artillerists drove forward the two field pieces that had been with the van. Down into the dry bed of the canal one gun was rushed, up the other side it was pulled and then, splashing and bouncing, it was on its way to Virginia through the startled waters of the Potomac, which, to the relief of everyone, were not high. The second gun was sent after the first, but when it was on the tow path, it was stopped and wheeled and unlimbered to command that approach.

Now followed the gray-clad cavalrymen as fast as weary mounts could be spurred. To the Captain of every company, Blackford repeated the order that the horses were not to be permitted to stop to drink. Some of the animals halted, despite their riders' blows, and buried their heads in the water, but these mounts were not numerous enough to block the wide ford. On the column pushed —a cheering and picturesque sight in the October morning.

By this time, Stuart had come down from the ridge to the ford. Pelham with his flawless sense of distance and of position was galloping near and halting and firing and then retiring again. Everything seemed to be shaping a triumphant climax. Men who scarcely could keep their saddles because of exhaustion smiled as they plunged into the water. Stuart did not.

"Blackford," he said, his voice choking and his eyes filling with tears, "we are going to lose our rearguard!"

Startled, Blackford shot back: "How is that, General?"

"I have sent four couriers to Butler to call him in, and he is not here, and you see the enemy is closing in on us from above and below."

"Let me try it, General," said the courageous young engineer. Stuart hesitated a moment, and then with a swift, impulsive gesture, he extended his hand: "All right. . . . If we don't meet again, good bye, old fellow."

Blackford pulled his horse up the bank, his wonderful horse Magic, and was starting to the rear when Stuart called after him: "Tell Butler if he can't get through, to strike back into Pennsylvania and try to get back through West Virginia." In more optimistic spirit he added, "Tell him to come in at a gallop!" [39]

Blackford spurred northward along the route the column had followed in reverse direction. There was no danger of losing the way, no mistaking the road that 3000 horses' hoofs had marked. Confidently Blackford pressed on. One after another, he met and questioned the returning couriers Stuart had sent out. Each man shook his head: he would be damned if he had been able to find Butler and those South Carolina cavalrymen of the rear guard. Blackford listened and then pushed northward. He would keep on if he ran squarely into the Federals. Three miles and more from his starting place he rode and then, without warning, around a turn of the highway, he found the missing regiment. It was calmly deployed and was facing the rear, whence it was expecting attack. Blackford was too experienced a soldier to shout orders. He searched out Butler, took him aside, and explained the situation. Butler understood, and with terse command, wheeled his troopers, got one gun [40] underway with some difficulty, and started at a trot for the ford. Blackford knew that speed was not enough to assure escape before the jaws of the Federal pincers closed.

He leaned over and told Butler they must move faster: Stuart's orders were that they should come in at the gallop. Butler was willing, but he was concerned about his gun, the team of which was fagged. Blackford urged that the piece be abandoned if it delayed the column. Butler was loath to agree. The gun had been entrusted to him. He would save it if he could. To his delight, if to his surprise, the strong-limbed team responded. The gun went bumping on.

All the way, as if it were sending a message of encouragement and reassurance from the direction of White's Ford, Pelham's rifle had been barking. Blackford heard it and felt sure that if the

[39] This is the language of *W. W. Blackford's Memoirs*, pp. 260–61. That of H. B. McClellan, *loc. cit.*, 158–59, is identical except for the instructions to Butler.

[40] Blackford wrote as if there were one only. Other accounts indicate that two may have been with the rearguard.

piece still were being fired from the tow path, the ford was clear.
Butler took no chances. As he approached the field that led down
to the ford, he prepared for a charge and had his men draw sabers
to cut their way through. With their blades flashing, the men of
the rearguard thundered into the open. Ahead, on the tow path,
they soon saw the smoking gun of Pelham. That dauntless boy
was standing by it and directed its fire. At a respectful distance,
to North and to South, Federal troops were to be seen. Butler did
not pause. Into the ford, his Carolinians splashed. As the last of
them entered the water, Pelham and his men limbered up and
followed. From the Virginia side, his other gun admonished the
Federals to keep their distance.[41]

The bluecoats crowded quickly to the ford but they did not
attempt to pursue. Near the Virginia side of the Potomac, the
thirsty horses meantime were drinking their fill. Stuart's men
were free to stretch themselves, to seek feed for their horses, and
then to move on to Leesburg and thence to camp. There the booty
was counted—full 1200 horses in exchange for about sixty animals
left behind as lame or broken down. Some thirty public men were
brought back as hostages for Southern sympathizers in Federal
hands. Public and railroad property estimated to be worth a
quarter of a million dollars had been destroyed.[42] Approximately
280 Federal soldiers, sick or wounded, had been paroled at Chambersburg. As a price of this, not one Confederate trooper had been
killed. Few had been wounded. Two had straggled and doubtless
had fallen into the hands of the Federals. Stuart himself was the
heaviest loser. His Negro servant, who was over-fond of a dram,
had fallen behind with Stuart's two spare mounts, both of
them splendid animals. While the groom slept off his liquor
and the horses stamped impatiently, Union troopers came upon
them.[43]

For this loss Stuart had the condolence of his friends, and for
his exploits he had both the praise and the criticism of the army.[44]
The proud troopers themselves reviewed the expedition endlessly,

[41] W. W. Blackford's MS Memoirs, 262–63. McClellan, op. cit., 159–60, gave part
of the conversation between Blackford and Butler, but as Blackford himself omitted it,
as unimportant or forgotten, it is not incorporated here.
[42] Channing Price, loc. cit., put the figure at $1,000,000.
[43] H. B. McClellan, 161–62; W. W. Blackford's MS Memoirs, 265; O. R., 19, pt. 2,
p. 54.
[44] W. W. Blackford, loc. cit.

stage by stage. In Channing Price's opinion, "The moral effects [were] great, teaching Pennsylvanians something of war and showing how J. E. B. Stuart can make McClellan's circuit at pleasure." [45] Each infantryman and artillerist, as far as he had any knowledge of the facts, joined critically in the exercise of the most cherished of his meagre prerogatives, that of sitting in judgment on the strategy of his superiors. This time, the chief argument was whether the results of the raid were worth the risks. "Jeb" and his men had marched thirty-two miles their first day out, and on the 11th–12th, by moving almost continuously, they had covered eighty miles in twenty-seven hours—all this close to a hostile army of 100,000. Had they been justified in an operation that involved this frightful strain of man and horse?

For that matter, how had Stuart contrived to do what seemed to be impossible? He himself had an explanation of the sort the commanding General and "Old Jack" usually gave for their victories. Said "Jeb" in his report, which was written without immodesty:

"Believing that the hand of God was clearly manifested in the signal deliverance of my command from danger, and the crowning success attending it, I ascribe to Him the praise, the honor, and the glory." [46]

To most men of a religious generation, this seemed proper acknowledgment of results that could not have been achieved without the interposition of the hand of God. Had not the raid been made in an open country of decent roads, a country far more favorable to swift pursuit than the tangled woodland, the sandy trails, the marsh-bordered streams of the Chickahominy? Were not the fords of the Potomac few; had not the Federals all the advantage of railways and telegraph and of signal stations on every eminence? [47]

If any Southerners were disposed to question whether the Almighty wore Confederate gray and employed his angels as videttes, the first of several mundane explanations of Stuart's success was the fact that he had a picked force. The 1800 men who went with him were among the bravest, best disciplined and most intelligent of the cavalry Division. All the raiders' horses were in

[45] *Loc. cit.*   [46] *O. R.,* 19, pt. 2, p. 54.
[47] Cf. *W. W. Blackford's MS Memoirs,* 241.

good condition. No man went along whose mount was worn or weak. Even von Borcke, whose soldierly presence dressed any occasion, had to be left behind for this reason.[48]

Picked men on strong horses kept their column better closed and made better time than a miscellaneous force would have thought possible. Even selected troopers, veterans all, could not have covered eighty miles, by continuous riding, had they not been able to use the captured horses. Whenever a trooper or one of Pelham's gunners found that his mount was failing, he would change to one of the strong animals seized in Pennsylvania. This was done even more frequently with the teams for the guns and for the caissons.[49] Stuart said nothing of this in his report, but it was an indispensable of success.

The certitude of Stuart's march contributed both to his roundup of invaluable horses and to his applauded escape. In the enemy's country he operated with assurance and in full knowledge of the terrain. He turned aside at the right time and at the right points where he had the best prospect of confusing the Federals. For his ability to do this he was obligated, first of all, to his guides, who were natives of the districts he entered. He could thank himself for having learned so well the State and county from which each troop of his cavalry came that he knew where to find quickly, at any time, men who had been reared in the community where he was operating. Besides this, a credit that Capt. W. W. Blackford never claimed for himself was due that excellent officer. He learned at Mercersburg that a map of Franklin County was in a private home and he rode there promptly and procured it. As this map had on it all the roads, Stuart could consider alternative routes and could check readily the information his guides gave him.[50] In these contributions to the success of the raid was illustrated the teamwork that Stuart had developed in the cavalry. Jealousies and vanities there were. Between Stuart and "Grumble" Jones, and between Munford of the Second and Rosser of the Fifth, deep animosities were to be aroused. Despite these and every attendant pettiness, the cavalry organization worked as a

48 W. W. Blackford's MS Memoirs, 241–42. Von Borcke, who did not lack admiration for the capital I, sought to create the impression that Stuart left him in charge of headquarters (op. cit., 1, 297).
49 H. B. McClellan, 153; W. W. Blackford's MS Memoirs, 250.
50 W. W. Blackford's MS Memoirs, 242.

unit. It had confidence, enthusiasm and faith in its leadership and in all its parts.

Luck, as usual, rode with vigilance. From the time Stuart crossed the Potomac northward bound until the morning of the 12th, no observer at any of the well placed Federal signal stations located him. On the 10th, fog along the river and misty weather on the road concealed the march from the lookouts nearest the Potomac. Those stations adjacent to the route Stuart followed on the 11th were not manned until noon. Even then no glimpse of the Confederates was had. The first direct observation of the column from any signal station was reported by Sugar Loaf, probably a short time after daylight on the 12th. "We can see heavy bodies of troops near Hyattstown," the station signalled, though it was not until 11.00 A.M. that the commanding officer, in answer to inquiry, said that the troops were in gray.[51]

Picked men, spare horses, good guides, an accurate map, excellent teamwork and fortunate escape from observation—all these scarcely would have sufficed if Stuart had not decided to keep moving. His night march of October 11–12, more than anything else, saved the raiders from the Federals who were set on their trails. Information that Confederates had entered Maryland reached the nearest Union brigade commander at 7.30 on the morning of the 10th. He subsequently reported that he forwarded warning immediately to Hagerstown and to divisional headquarters at Downsville.[52]

As for action by army headquarters, the first pursuit order that can be assigned a definite hour was written at 4.00 P.M.,[53] though others probably were dispatched earlier.[54] Whatever the fact, McClellan was slow in making preparations to cope with the raid, but was confident he could capture the whole force. When Halleck telegraphed at 9.10 P.M. on the 10th, "Not a man should be permitted to return to Virginia," McClellan replied coldly, "Every disposition has been made to cut off the retreat of the enemy's

[51] *O. R.,* 19, pt. 2, pp. 31–32.

[52] *O. R.,* 19, pt. 2, p. 36. Downsville is located about eight miles North of Shepherdstown and equidistant South and slightly West of Hagerstown.

[53] Marcy to Brooks, *O. R.,* 19, pt. 2, p. 61.

[54] Doubt is due to the slovenly system then prevailing at McClellan's headquarters with regard to the timing of dispatches. Many of those in *O. R.* give no indication of the hour. The dispatch Marcy to Brooks, dated "11.15" would seem from its reference to Greencastle to have been sent in the evening, not in the morning. *ibid.,* 62.

cavalry." [55] Months later McClellan admitted: "After the order, were given for covering all the fords upon the river, I did not think it possible for Stuart to recross, and I believed that the capture or destruction of his entire force was perfectly certain . . ." [56]

Gen. W. W. Averell, who was close to the point where the South Branch enters the Potomac, was ordered downstream to find Stuart's trail. From Knoxville, which was three miles below Harpers Ferry on the Maryland side of the Potomac, Gen. Alfred Pleasonton was directed to move northward to cut the raiders' line of march. The Union column which the Confederates barely had missed at the crossing of the National Road below Mercersburg was instructed to entrain and to prepare to move wherever there was a prospect of catching the "rebels." Two of Burnside's Brigades were sent to the mouth of the Monocacy and were told to stay on the cars, with steam up, so that the troops might be sent up or down the B. & O. on the click of the telegraph. Col. Richard H. Rush and his 6th Pennsylvania Cavalry—"Rush's Lancers"— were sent on scout northward from Frederick, near which they had their camp. These were the men who had left Emmitsburg shortly before Stuart's arrival there.

All the Union infantry along the Potomac, from Hancock to Harpers Ferry, were ordered to be on the alert for the raiders. Eastward from Harpers Ferry almost to the mouth of the Monocacy, McClellan's camps were spread so thick, and fords were so few that no special precautions were taken. At the mouth of the Monocacy and below it, George Stoneman had his small Division,[57] with which, he subsequently complained, he was expected to guard about thirty miles of river.[58] At the time, Stoneman reasoned, confidently enough, that if Stuart sought to recross the Potomac on that sector, the ford selected would be at the mouth of the Monocacy or nearby to the eastward. In obedience to orders, Stoneman spread his mounted men widely to watch the roads so that he could concentrate his infantry without delay when notified of Stuart's approach.[59]

---

[55] *O. R.*, 19, pt. 2, p. 59.   [56] *O. R.*, 19, pt. 1, p. 73.

[57] Nowhere is its exact strength given, but it consisted of eight regiments of infantry. The regiments mentioned by Stoneman in his report did not average more than 550 men each, but there is reason to believe these were his smallest units. A guess of 3000 to 3500 infantry probably is not greatly in error. Besides these troops, Stoneman had 500 cavalry and four batteries. *Cf.* Stoneman's report, *O. R.*, 19, pt. 2, p. 43.

[58] *Ibid.*   [59] *Cf.* McClellan in *O. R.*, 19, pt. 1, p. 73.

These were the Federal dispositions. If the Union cavalry had been diligent, early execution of prompt orders from army head-quarters should have sufficed to snare the raiders. These essential conditions were not met. Orders were not dispatched with promptness or delivered with speed. Averell did not leave Green Spring until 3.00 A.M. on the 11th; [60] Pleasonton received his instructions an hour later; [61] Rush got his at 6.30. [62] Stoneman, for some reason, had no notice until G.H.Q. decided, about noon of the 11th, that Stuart probably was heading for Leesburg, Virginia. It was 3.30 P.M. that day when Stoneman was told to be on the *qui vive*. [63] Some of his units did not learn till evening that Stuart had been operating in Maryland and was trying to return to Virginia. [64]

All this was miserably slow action for dealing with raiders who had been in Maryland almost twenty-four hours when the first and most remote Union cavalry were sent after them. Even in the face of the slow Federal orders, Stuart, it may be repeated, well might have met superior force at White's Ford, with Pleasonton pounding his rear, had the Confederates halted on the night of the 11th–12th. Stuart had learned early in the war the advantages of night marching, but he never applied his lessons better than in pushing steadily southward through the autumn night. Black-ford was of opinion that the Confederate commander reckoned deliberately on the slow transmission of Federal orders. Stuart believed he could get back before the Federals were at the ford to stop him. [65]

General McClellan at first was disposed to think that Stuart escaped because Stoneman did not keep his cavalry well in advance and did not give proper support to Pleasonton when that officer came up. [66] Subsequently, with all the evidence before him, McClellan decided that the principal error was made by Burnside's infantry in going to Frederick instead of remaining on the train at the mouth of the Monocacy. On the conflicting assertions of Stoneman and of Pleasonton, the retired McClellan did not attempt to pass judgment. [67]

Some of the Confederates had a different question which they

[60] O. R., 19, pt. 2, p. 40.
[61] Ibid., 38.
[62] Ibid., 41.
[63] Ibid., 43.
[64] Ibid., 50.
[65] Op. cit., 265–66.
[66] O. R., 19, pt. 2, p. 30.
[67] O. R., 19, pt. 1, pp. 73–74.

must have debated beside their campfires: Did the Federals avoid a fight? Those at White's Ford certainly did. Their commander, Lt. Col. Edwin R. Biles, in his report, described his dispositions and insisted that at the time of Stuart's attack, he had not more than 100 men to defend the crossing—a figure the Confederates considered about half his actual strength.[68] These Federals had no artillery support. but they were admirably posted around the quarry. Had they been determined to die hard, they might have held off the Confederates, or at least a part of them, until Stoneman came up. Instead, Colonel Biles reported: "Finding that I was not to be re-enforced, and that if I remained my small force must be cut off and captured without being able to do any good, I commenced slowly falling back over the hills and ravines . . ." [69]

This retreat the Confederates thought uncourageous, but Captain Blackford had sharper words for the Federal cavalry than for the infantry. Of the Confederate advance to Chambersburg on the 10th, he said: "During this long day's march everything indicated our coming to be unexpected, and not a shadow of opposition appeared. The truth was that their cavalry was afraid to meet us and gladly availed themselves of the pretext of not being able to find us. Up to this time the cavalry of the enemy had no more confidence in themselves than the country had in them, and whenever we got a chance at them, which was rarely, they came to grief." [70] If it was so, it was not so to remain.

Contempt for their mounted adversaries and recognition of good luck on the road did not lessen the pride of the Confederates in their own performance. Praise similar to that which Stuart

---

[68] H. B. McClellan, *op. cit.*, analyzed the strength of the 99th Penn. and found that on September 30, the aggregate present for duty was 477. "If only four companies were present," said Major McClellan, "they should have numbered nearly 200 men." W. H. F. Lee thought this an underestimate (*ibid.*). Stuart reported the number as "about 200 infantry" (*O. R.,* 19, pt. 2, p. 53). A proper comment might be that if there were not 200, there should have been. Apparently Stoneman had so convinced himself the attempted crossing would be at the mouth of the Monocacy that he recalled two regiments that marched downstream past White's Ford on the evening of the 11th (*ibid.,* 50).

[69] *O. R.,* 19, pt. 2, p. 50. Biles continued in the service and received his brevet as Brigadier General of Volunteers to date from Mch. 15, 1865, for gallantry in command of the picket line at Deep Bottom (1 *Heitman,* 218). General Pleasonton believed that if "White's Ford had been occupied by any force of ours, previous to the time of the occupation by the enemy, the capture of Stuart's whole force would have been certain and inevitable" (*O. R.,* 19, pt. 2, p. 40); but General Stoneman (*ibid.,* 44) denounced this as "simply ridiculous" because "the enemy could have crossed at almost any other point as well as there." Stoneman did not criticize Biles for withdrawing from the ford.

[70] *Op. cit.,* 246-47.

bestowed on his lieutenants was given him abundantly by the commanding General. Lee did not fail to report the failure of the prime object, the destruction of the bridge across the Conoco-cheague, but he pronounced Stuart's expedition "eminently suc-cessful." [71] Stuart's report was endorsed by Lee with applause of the "boldness, judgment and prudence [Stuart] displayed." To this Lee added commendation of Stuart's subordinates, and then the commanding General indulged in something of a verbal flourish: "To his skill and their fortitude, under the guidance of an overruling Providence, is their success due." [72]

That was a longer plume for "Jeb."

[71] O. R., 19, pt. 2, p. 51.   [72] O. R., 19, pt. 2, p. 54.

CHAPTER XIX

CHIEFLY PERSONAL TO JACKSON

Two weeks to the day after Stuart's return from his raid into Maryland, the Army of the Potomac crossed the river that gave it a name. Whither was "Little Mc" bound—up the Shenandoah Valley or southward on the coastal side of the mountains? Because the answer had to wait on the march, Lee divided his forces. On October 28, Jackson was directed to retire a few miles toward Winchester with his troops;[1] Longstreet was ordered to move over the Blue Ridge into Culpeper County. Care was to be taken to man all the passes, so that the two columns could not be assailed separately.

The cavalry, of course, had to screen this operation. A difficult task it proved. Hampton's men were at Martinsburg and could not unite with Stuart for several days. "Grumble" Jones's Brigade had to be left to guard the rear of Jackson's command in the Valley. Fitz Lee's troopers alone were available to protect the march of Longstreet's Corps, and they scarcely were able to count 1000 sabers. A malady among the horses[2] had left hundreds of men without mounts. Not until the grayjackets had been skirmishing for five days with the Federals did the arrival of Hampton give Stuart sufficient strength to risk a general action. Even then, at Barbee's Crossroads, "Jeb" had to break off the engagement because of a rumored threat to his rear.[3] Seldom had it happened previously that Stuart had declined to fight to the finish.

Some fine episodes there were to cheer the heart. On November 2, near Union,[4] Major Pelham boldly advanced one of his howitzers beyond a point where Stuart could support him. With sure eye, Pelham quickly found a masked position from which

---

[1] Headquarters were established that day at Pendleton's, near Blackburn's, Clarke County, on the Summit Point and Berryville Road, about four and a half miles from Berryville. *Hotchkiss' MS Diary*, 101.

[2] "Greased heel and sore tongue" Stuart styled it. *O. R.*, 19, pt. 2, p. 414.

[3] *O. R.*, 19, pt. 2, p. 144.

[4] About seven miles Northwest of Middleburg in Loudoun County.

he fired so furiously on a body of Federal cavalry in a valley below him that the bluecoats galloped wildly off. Pelham then sent down some of his mounted cannoneers and brought off the booty the Federals left behind. He was beginning to develop new tactics for horse artillery, that boy was.[5] In a different affair, Pelham personally aimed one of his pieces at a Federal color bearer, distant 800 yards, and brought down man and flag. Not to be outdone, Capt. R. H. Hardaway, who led a battery attached to Harvey Hill's Division, created much talk by a unique achievement with one of the British Whitworth guns under his charge. A shot of his drove off a Federal force at a range of more than three miles —an unheard of range with a light field piece.[6]

Besides these fine performances, Stuart found satisfaction that Col. Williams C. Wickham, who had been wounded at Williamsburg, was entirely qualified to exercise brigade command[7] in the absence of Fitz Lee. When Wickham again was wounded, Tom Rosser showed like skill in handling the Brigade.[8] More than that, Rosser won new reputation when, at Warrenton, he suddenly found Federals in his front and in his rear as well. With much cleverness, he sidestepped them all and got back to Stuart with not one saddle empty.[9] Still others acquitted themselves handsomely, but the operation as a whole was not one of which Stuart subsequently spoke often. His report was not written until February, 1864. By that time the most conspicuous actor in the drama of the Loudoun Valley, next to Stuart himself, was where praise no longer could make him blush.[10]

Undistinguished as was the record of the cavalry during those first days of November, Stuart's men assured an uneventful march for the First Corps. After its arrival in Culpeper, Lee made a brief visit to Richmond, during which time Longstreet, as senior officer, administered all three arms of the service. After Lee's return, "Old Pete" directed the whole of the infantry around Culpeper. He did

---

[5] *Ibid.*, 142.
[6] *O. R.*, 19, pt. 2, pp. 142–43.
[7] Wickham, said Stuart, deployed with "great zeal, ability and bravery" (*O. R.*, 19, pt. 2, p. 43).
[8] *Ibid.*
[9] *Ibid.*, 44. *Cf.* Lee's approving comment, *ibid.*, 703. The date of this affair was November 5.
[10] See *infra*, Chap. XXVIII. It is to be noted that Colonel Blackford, though wounded slightly during this operation, dismissed it in a paragraph. *Op. cit.*, 270. For continuance of the sketch of Rosser, see *infra*, Chap. XXV.

it unostentatiously and well.[11] Jackson, in the Shenandoah Valley, resumed virtually the semi-independent command he had exercised in the spring.[12]

Neither Jackson nor Longstreet had done more than make the first adjustments to the new divisional and brigade commands within their corps when Northern newspapers revealed the fact that the bluecoats, too, were undergoing a reorganization. McClellan had been displaced and had been sent home to "await orders," which never were to be sent him. Ambrose Burnside—he who had commanded opposite Toombs at Sharpsburg—had been given command of the Army of the Potomac.[13] Jackson made no recorded comment on this change. In the diary of his topographical engineer, it is not mentioned. Kyd Douglas may have been writing in after-knowledge when he observed in his memoirs: "The attitude of our officers and men toward McClellan at that time was peculiar. We seemed to understand his limitations and defects of military character, and yet we were invariably relieved when he was relieved, for we unquestionably always believed him to be a stronger and more dangerous man than anyone who might be his successor. His great professional ability was never questioned. . . . The appointment of General Burnside created no apprehension with us." [14]

The response of many Southern people to the news was, at the outset, one of disbelief. Said the *Richmond Examiner*: ". . . we are slow to give it full credence. It appears quite probable that the withdrawal of McClellan from the Army of Virginia will presently be announced as a return to the duties and position of commander-in-chief at Washington." [15] To the *Charleston Mercury,* which accepted the report as authentic, "the disgrace of McClellan [was] a happy omen," because the congressional elections had "shown the radicals that the days of their rule are numbered, and they must make the best possible use of the time that is left them." [16] Eagerly the South waited for the explanation given in Northern newspapers of the reasons McClellan had been

[11] *O. R.,* 19, pt. 2, pp. 698–99. For the details of McClellan's advance, see *ibid.,* pt. 1, p. 83 ff. The Confederate moves are described in 2 *R. E. Lee,* 425 ff.
[12] Cf. *O. R.,* 19, pt. 2, pp. 685–86.
[13] McClellan was superseded November 7; Burnside assumed command on the 9th.
[14] *Douglas,* 202. For the comment of Lee and of Longstreet on the removal of McClellan, see 2 *R. E. Lee,* 428.
[15] *Richmond Examiner,* Nov. 14, 1862, p. 2, col. 1.
[16] *Charleston Mercury,* Nov. 14, 1862, p. 1, col. 2.

stripped of power;[17] devoutly the Confederates hoped that Mc-Clellan would rise in revolt and overthrow Lincoln.[18]

As the possibility of this diminished hourly, some sympathetic words were voiced for the fallen "Little Napoleon"; [19] but these were cancelled, so far as the *Richmond Dispatch* was concerned, by the observation: "We are by no means sure that the removal of McClellan from command is calculated to do the Yankee cause any great harm. It is said that he is the best General they have, and we think it probable he is. Yet they could have fallen upon no man who could have made a more signal failure than he did in his campaign against Richmond. If he be the best, they must all be exceedingly bad." [20]

The one remarkable feature of the comment was the prediction of Burnside's future action. Said the *Richmond Enquirer*: "If [Burnside] fights and is whipped he can but fall; while if he fights and triumphs, his fortune is made. The effect of the change will therefore be, as we think, to make the war more urgent. A battle on the Rappahannock would now seem among the probabilities of the few remaining weeks of autumn." [21] The *Charleston Mercury* gave assurance: "The best thing . . . that can happen for the South, is a campaign of invasion towards Richmond. Freezing nights and boggy roads are incompatible with the safe retreat of a beaten foe. It may be a Russian campaign." [22]

While Burnside prepared as best he could to avoid all possibility of such a fate, Jackson's men were destroying railways. Every mile of track within their reach, from the Potomac to the southern terminus of the Manassas Gap Railroad, they sought to wreck beyond repair that autumn. "Old Jack," one soldier grumbled, "intends us to tear up all the railroads in the State, and with no tools but our pocket-knives." [23] The General would have disavowed the second part of that charge, but he held his men strictly to their task, and, with equal sternness, he combated their practice of burning farmers' fence rails to get a fire. One offending soldier,

17 Quite the best of these explanations was that of the *New York Times,* as quoted in the *Richmond Examiner,* Nov. 15, 1862, p. 1, col. 4.
18 *Richmond Examiner,* Nov. 14, p. 2, col. 1; *Richmond Whig,* Nov. 17, p. 1, col. 1; *Richmond Dispatch,* Nov. 20, 1862, p. 2, col. 1.
19 *Richmond Enquirer,* Nov. 15, p. 2, col. 1; *Richmond Dispatch,* Nov. 21, p. 2. col. 1.
20 Nov. 17, 1862, p. 2, col. 1.   21 Nov. 15, 1862, p. 2, col. 1.
22 Nov. 21. 1862. p. 1, col. 2.   23 *Cooke's Jackson,* 351–52.

who was sent to Jackson for special treatment as an incurable rail burner, was asked by the General why he persisted in the face of all punishment.

"Well, General," the cheeky private answered, "you see I've been enlisted eight months now in General Hill's Division, and in all that time I never could get a good look at *you,* so I thought I would steal some fence rails; I knew they would take me up and then send me to you, so I would see you."

The General smiled grimly and turned to the guard: "Take this man and buck him, and set him on the top of that empty barrel in front of my tent. The front is open, and he can look at me as much as he likes." [24]

With severity in the treatment of his men, Jackson mingled admiration for them. One night while he was in his tent, the Stonewall Brigade raised the rebel yell and split the air until the Brigade in the nearest camp joined in. Then another and another Brigade sent echoing through the wood the fox hunter's cry. "Old Blue Light" came from his quarters, strode to a rail fence, leaned on it after his fashion of resting, and listened till the last echo died away. As he walked back, he said as if to himself, "That was the sweetest music I ever heard." [25]

In somewhat kindred spirit, when the gift of a sword was accompanied by notice that some cavalrymen formerly with him were being held at Fort McHenry as guerrillas, his acknowledgment had a promise attached: "The beautiful sword which you have so kindly presented me, and also the other much prized presents have been received. . . . Please accept my thanks for them. I have watched with great interest your brilliant exploits. Your men may well feel proud of having such a leader. Press on in your successful career. Let your men know that their comrades who are maltreated at Fort McHenry are not forgotten. I deem it a solemn duty to protect, as far as God enables me, every patriotic soldier of my command. I regret being driven to retaliation, but the enemy from time to time, have been warned against their inhumanity." Jackson went on to explain that he was detaining three Federal Captains while he investigated the outrage to his troops and procured the exchange of the victims and indemnification for any wrongs they might have suffered.[26]

His officers, like his men in the ranks, found in him this odd combination of discipline and goodwill. Publicly, Jackson said nothing of the controversy with Powell Hill. To others of his lieutenants, if the relationship were close, Jackson on occasion spoke frankly of their military shortcomings. Hotchkiss was admonished that his "great fault" was "talking too much." [27] In another instance, there was a suspicion that Jackson was not all tears over the death of a man who had sent him many excited reports. Said Hotchkiss: "I think the General put him down as a decided sensationalist and so replied, though I know not. The General dislikes rumors, exceedingly; unless he can get substantial facts, I don't believe he likes to hear anything," [28]—which is not a bad rule for a soldier to follow.

Once, at least, Jackson took down with a bit of dry humor an officer who heeded a rumor. On November 18, young James Power Smith, who recently had joined the staff, concluded from camp chatter that the army was about to proceed eastward, and he went to Jackson with this request: "General, as we are going across the mountains tomorrow, I wish to go to Winchester early in the morning."

Jackson looked at him with just a flicker of the eye and with a queer smile: "Are you going over the mountains tomorrow? Then, certainly, Mr. Smith, you can go to Winchester; but don't tell anyone that we are going over the mountains," and he broke into a thin laugh.

Gratefully Smith made an early start, got to Winchester and was hurrying back when, on the road, he met Jackson, who was moving headquarters to Winchester.[29] As Smith rode up, Jackson laughed: "Are you going over the mountains, Mr. Smith?" [30]

Jackson was in a pleasant, almost a facetious humor. Prob-

[26] *F. M. Myers,* 129.   [27] *Hotchkiss' MS Diary,* 93.
[28] Hotchkiss to his wife, MS Nov. 11, 1862—*Hotchkiss Papers.*
[29] From Pendleton's or Blackburn's—both names were used—Jackson transferred headquarters on November 6 to Saratoga, on the Front Royal-Winchester Road, 11½ miles from Winchester, a place mentioned also as "McCoy's, Ninevah" (*Hotchkiss' MS Diary,* 103). Thence on November 14 (*ibid.,* 105), headquarters were removed to a point on Hogg Run, 2½ miles from Winchester.
[30] Smith in *Mrs. Jackson,* 377. The incident can be dated from the entry in *Hotchkiss' Diary* that headquarters were moved from Hogg Run to Winchester on the 19th.

ably this was because he was approaching Winchester. Even a day there was a delight because of the Christian associations he had established there. The soul of Deacon Jackson had been stirred anew that autumn, ere he visited Winchester, by the ministry of the eloquent Rev. Dr. Joseph C. Stiles. That eminent minister, who was unofficial chaplain general of the Confederacy, had come to the Valley to preach to Lawton's Brigade and then had gone over to Trimble's camp to assist in a series of meetings under Rev. A. M. Marshall, a devout, fighting private of the renowned Twelfth Georgia, who had received commission as chaplain not long previously. Soon, by his fervent preaching, he had aroused among the men of his regiment and of the Forty-fourth Georgia much interest in religion. Dr. Stiles joined Mr. Marshall in fanning this religious feeling into the spiritual fire of the great revival that subsequently spread through the Army and had historic influence on its morals and on the life of the South during drear and bitter years that were ahead.[31]

Early in the revival, Jackson heard Dr. Stiles preach, and he felt himself much edified. He wrote Mrs. Jackson: "[Dr. Stiles's] text was 1st Timothy, chap. ii., 5th and 6th verses. It was a powerful exposition of the Word of God; and when he came to the word *'himself'* he placed an emphasis upon it, and gave it a force which I had never felt before, and I realized that, truly, the sinner who does not, under Gospel privileges, turn to God deserves the agonies of perdition. . . . Dr. Stiles is a great revivalist, and is laboring in a work of Grace in General Ewell's division." The soldier's ambitions were forgotten in the elder's admiration of the preacher: "It is a glorious thing to be a minister of the gospel of the Prince of Peace. There is no equal position in this world." [32]

Now that Jackson again was in Winchester, these emotions were quickened. Gratitude had been evoked, too, by the many gifts that had poured in on him. "Our gracious Heavenly Father," he confided to his wife, "strikingly manifests his kindness to me by disposing people to bestow presents upon me." In proof, he

---

[31] J. W. Jones, *Christ in Camp,* 283. "Personne" of the *Charleston Courier* reported deep religious interest among the troops as early as August. See *Richmond Whig,* Aug. 18, 1862, p. 1, col. 5.

[32] *Mrs. Jackson,* 348. The text quoted by Jackson is: "For there is one God, and one mediator between God and men, the man Jesus Christ; who gave himself a ransom for all, to be testified in due time."

sent her a detailed list.[33] Said Mrs. Graham[34] in a proud note to Mrs. Jackson: "I never saw such admiration as is felt for him by every one, and his Christian character elicits the greatest reverence and affection. It would have done your heart good to hear the prayers that were offered for *him* on the day of Thanksgiving."

Not until the eve of his departure from Winchester was he able to call at the manse where Mrs. Graham lived, but when he came he was at his best. "He is looking in such perfect health— far handsomer than I ever saw him—and is in such fine spirits," was the report of Mrs. Graham, "seemed so unreserved and unrestrained in his intercourse with us, that we did enjoy him to the full."[35]

A special and most personal circumstance made doubly dear to him the few hours he was able to spend that 21st of November at the manse where Mrs. Jackson had been with him the previous winter. There, not long before he had to evacuate the town, she had conceived, and now she was close to the delivery of her first born. To all the bewildering experiences that had been his in the nineteen months since the outbreak of war, this was to be added. He did not confide to any of his companions in arms the probability that he was about to be a father, and in excess of modesty or in disciplined adherence to the military mandate of secrecy, he requested Mrs. Jackson to mail him privately and not to telegraph openly the news of the arrival of a child he fondly hoped to be a son.[36] In his concern and uneasiness, there must have been comfort in viewing the familiar room where she had sat while he and Dr. Graham had discussed religion and the ways of God with man.

The Second Corps had left Winchester before "Old Jack" went to call at the manse. He followed his troops the next day past the battlefield of Kernstown and on to the Old Stone House on Tumbling Run beyond Strasburg. On the 23d he rode almost to Mt. Jackson and spent the night at the house just beyond Mill

[33] *Mrs. Jackson,* 351.

[34] Mrs. James R. Graham, wife of the Presbyterian minister of the town. See *supra,* Vol. I, pp. 128, 304.

[35] *Mrs. Jackson,* 358–59. Dr. Henry Tucker Graham, distinguished son of those friends of Jackson's, most charmingly has described them and their homes in *An Old Manse* (2nd ed., Richmond, 1916).

[36] *Mrs. Jackson,* 360.

Run.[37] The march of November 24, when the van reached New Market, repeated for Jackson the move he had made the preceding May from the opposite direction on the Valley Pike: He turned to the East, passed over the wind-swept Massanutton and then, crossing the Shenandoah at Columbia Bridge, began to climb the Blue Ridge. Night brought the halt on Hawksbill Creek, within a mile of the hamlet of Hawksbill, on the road to Madison Court House.

This was new ground to Jackson. Through Swift Run Gap, to the South, "Dick" Ewell had entered the country of the Shenandoah; beyond that was Brown's Gap, up which miserably in the mud of early May, some of Jackson's troops had toiled on the march to help Ed Johnson drive Milroy back. Farther still up the Valley was Rockfish Gap, where hundreds of campfires shone in the soft June night when the Army of the Valley was moving across the mountain to join Lee in front of Richmond. That was the night Jackson had epitomized his creed as soldier and as Christian in the quotation he recalled to Jed. Hotchkiss—"Never take counsel of your fears!" [38] With like courage now, he was looking over this road of new adventure to the Rappahannock, whither Lee and Longstreet had preceded him.

In dealing with the enemy, the commanding General had continued to allow discretion and free movement to "Stonewall," though gradually Lee himself had become convinced that the two Corps of his army should be united.[39] Jackson had not resisted this in any way, and with his usual interest in the new devices of war, he had done his utmost to set up a series of signal stations through which, when wanted, he might receive prompt notice from G.H.Q.[40] When this method of communication proved impracticable, Jackson lingered in the Valley as long as he dared. Doubtless this was because he hoped an opportunity might offer for another thrust at the rear of the Federals; but as scant prospect

---

[37] Presumably on the south side of the Run, though on this point *Hotchkiss' MS Diary*, 107, which is authority for Jackson's movements and headquarters at this period, is somewhat equivocal.

[38] See *supra*, Vol. I, p. 469.

[39] O. R., 19, pt. 2, pp. 710, 720; O. R., 21, pp. 1021, 1027, 1031, 1033. On March 4, 1863, "Jeb" Stuart told Jed. Hotchkiss that Lee had wanted Jackson to follow Long-street—presumably at the end of October—but that Jackson had asked to remain in the Valley. By doing this, Stuart insisted, Jackson had deceived McClellan (*Hotchkiss' MS Diary*, 145).

[40] *Cf. O. R., 19, pt. 2, p. 711*

of a third Manassas developed, he reluctantly now was bound eastward.

Since his destination no longer could be concealed, he dramatized it in a manner somewhat unusual for him. The morning his camp was nearest the crest of the mountains, he dressed with a larger expenditure of time and care than he usually allowed himself, and when he came from his tent, he wore the dazzling uniform coat that Stuart had given him. Sometime before, he had put aside his old weatherbeaten cap for the tall black hat which Jed. Hotchkiss had given him at Martinsburg. As he wore this with the brim turned down all around,[41] he far outshone all previous appearance. To complete his adornment, he buckled on his sword. Before the incredulous gaze of his staff officers, he blushed and then smiled. "Young gentlemen," he said, with an expansiveness as rare as his fine appearance, "this is no longer the headquarters of the Army of the Valley, but of the Second Corps of the Army of Northern Virginia." They knew that this meant he was on his way to rejoin Lee.[42]

By the evening of November 25, Jackson had passed Fisher's Gap and had marched through Criglersville to Madison Court House and half a mile beyond to a camp site on the Gordonsville Road. He still hoped that the Lord would open a way to the rear of the Federal army and would deliver into his hand some part of the Union host,[43] and accordingly he kept his headquarters on the Gordonsville Road November 26 and 27.[44] As no victim offered, he moved on the 28th to Haxall's, one mile South of Orange Court House.[45] Perhaps a personal consideration was added to his military reasons for lingering within easy distance of Gordonsville. In the knowledge that Mrs. Jackson's pregnancy was nearing its end, he had told her about the time he left Winchester that she should address her next letter to him at Gordonsville.[46]

His forethought had its reward in a letter postmarked Charlotte, N. C., and addressed in the autograph of Mrs. Jackson's sister, Mrs. James P. Irwin. The General opened it privately, no doubt, lest his concern over the contents be visible to his staff

[41] Cooke's Jackson, 354.   [42] 43 S. H. S. P., 24.
[43] Cf. O. R., 21, 1035.   [44] Hotchkiss' MS Diary, 109.
[45] ibid. The timing of these marches in 1 Henderson, 303, is slightly in error.
[46] Mrs. Jackson, 352.

officer. As he read the opening lines he steadied himself and began again:

"My Own Dear Father—As my mother's letter has been cut short by my arrival, I think it but justice that I should continue it. I know that you are rejoiced to hear of my coming, and I hope that God has sent me to radiate your pathway through life. I am a very tiny little thing. I weigh only eight and a half pounds, and . . ."

Did he read expectantly on, or did he turn the page to see how it was signed? Anyway, the signature was, "Your dear little wee Daughter." A girl, then! [47] He had wanted a boy, but if God had sent a girl, then he not only would accept the Divine mandate meekly but he also would prefer a daughter to a son.[48] On that point his mind was fixed. As for sharing the news of his happiness, well . . . keeping one's secrets was an essential rule in war and might be no less proper in respect to one's private affairs. If friends learned of his good fortune, let it be from others.[49] In his first letter to Mrs. Jackson he let his delight drip from his pen, and took care to have the mother feel that he was not disappointed because the baby was not a boy: ". . . give the baby-daughter a shower of kisses from her father, and tell her that he loves her better than all the baby-boys in the world, and more than all the other babies in the world."

In this reconciliation to the ways of Providence, Jackson on the 29th of November started for Fredericksburg. Ahead of his infantry, he travelled fast, fully forty miles. Much of his afternoon ride carried him for the first time through a gloomy, wooded and infertile district known as the "Wilderness of Spotsylvania." The trees were mixed. Fine hard wood soared close to tangles of stumps and of laps left where small trees had been cut to feed a nearby iron furnace. Well clad and comely pines were elbowed by scrub oaks and stubborn little hickories that stood impudently

---

[47] *Mrs. Jackson,* 360–61. The baby was born at the home of Mrs. Jackson's sister, Mrs. D. H. Hill, in Charlotte. Mrs. Irwin, whose residence was a few doors distant, was the eldest of the sisters. Her name had been Harriet Morrison—Letter of Mrs. Julia Christian Preston to the writer, n.d., 1941. Douglas, *op. cit.,* 203, is authority for saying that when Jackson received the news of the baby's arrival, the General either was near Madison Court House or was at Orange. It is not quite clear from Douglas's language which place was meant.

[48] He subsequently so informed Mrs. Jackson. See her remark, *op. cit.,* 363.

[49] *Mrs. Jackson,* 360. Douglas, *op. cit.,* 203, did not learn until December 26 that his General was a father.

naked in the wind. On Jackson's mind, so far as the record shows, the Wilderness made no special impression. When someone told him that a road farther to the North and parallel to the one being followed by the infantry would serve better for the wagons and the artillery, the General merely sent back word for the vehicles to proceed via Chancellorsville.[50]

By the southerly road the staff and their leader pressed on and came about nightfall to Army Headquarters in the vicinity of Muscoe Garnett's home on Mine Run.[51] Jackson was welcomed most heartily by the commanding General, but as "Stonewall's" wagons would not arrive that night, the suggestion was made that quarters be sought at the Garnett home. Jackson's aide, his sole companion, who went over to the house and knocked, was greeted sourly.

"What do you want here?" Mr. Garnett demanded.

Two officers, the aide answered mildly, asked lodging for the night.

"I have no room for anyone," Garnett replied, "my house is full."

The young Confederate shifted his ground, and explained that the senior for whom he sought shelter was—ahem, er—General Jackson.

Instantly the door flew open and released some of the friendly warmth of a roaring fire within. Said Garnett: "What General Jackson? 'Stonewall' Jackson? Is he here? Go and tell him to come at once; all my home is his, sir!"[52] Jackson had a good supper, a pleasant evening and then a warm bed in which to think of his own home and his new daughter.

The more he reflected on the blessing, the more grateful and enthusiastic was he: "Oh, how thankful I am to our kind Heavenly Father for having spared my precious wife and given us a little daughter! I cannot tell you how gratified I am, nor how much I wish I could be with you and see my two darlings." He exhorted his wife not to write until her strength was restored and, as became a Lieutenant General, he was the disciplinarian: "Do not spoil it, and don't let anybody tease it. Don't permit it to

[50] 1 *Land We Love,* 291.
[51] *Hotchkiss' MS Diary,* 109. This Mine Run must not be confused with the more renowned stream on the western fringe of the Wilderness.
[52] J. P. Smith in 43 *S. H. S. P.,* 25.

have a bad temper." Immediately his mood shifted back: "How I would love to see the darling little thing! Give her many kisses from her father." That suggested ways and means by which, after a season, he might have them with him. His whole spirit was exalted:

". . . Wherever I go, God gives me kind friends. The people here show me great kindness. I receive invitation after invitation to dine out, and spend the night, and a great many provisions are sent me, including nice cakes, tea, loaf-sugar, etc., and the socks and gloves and handkerchiefs still come!

"I am so thankful to our ever-kind Heavenly Father for having so improved my eyes as to enable me to write at night. He continually showers blessings upon me; and that *you* should have been spared, and our darling little daughter given us, fills my heart with overflowing gratitude. If I know my unworthy self, my desire is to live *entirely and unreservedly to God's glory*. Pray, my darling, that I may so live." [53]

When Mrs. Jackson wrote that he might name the child, he chose to call the baby Julia, after his own long dead mother. And he found his deepest religious impulses stirred by every reference to his little daughter. Earnestly he wrote his wife: "Do not set your affections upon her, except as a gift from God. If she absorbs too much of our hearts, God may remove her from us." [54]

Joyfully, gratefully, and as often as he might, he attended religious service. One Sunday night, he went by invitation with several members of his staff to have tea with Mrs. French, who lived about five miles South of Fredericksburg. [55] The meal over, he seemed to have pleasure in talking to his hostess and to an old lady of the neighborhood. As the hour approached for his departure, he took the family Bible, at Mrs. French's request, read a lesson and conducted prayers. [56]

It could not be altogether so. An army that cannot fight an adversary is apt to war within its own ranks. New quarrels began in the Second Corps; old controversy was revived. Resentment over Jackson's alleged mistreatment of Powell Hill spread to the officers of the Light Division. A rumor that Lee had recommended Hill for promotion to the grade of Lieutenant General

[53] *Mrs. Jackson*, 361–63.   [54] *Ibid.*, 363.
[55] *Hotchkiss' MS Diary*, 111.   [56] *Mrs. Jackson*, 378.

was received with joy, not less because it would mean release from Jackson's command than because it would give Dorsey Pender a Division. Pender confided to his wife: "General rumor and general feeling both have pointed me out to be Gen. Hill's successor. He told me the other night that he hoped I would soon be a Major General. I had no idea that I was a man of reputation in the army until I got back." [57] If Jackson heard of these rumors, he said nothing, but he did not yield an inch in the controversy with Powell Hill.

Nor, for that matter, did Jackson fail to protest against a request his own brother-in-law, Harvey Hill, indirectly had made. Harvey Hill's Division was without Napoleons, the most favored field gun of the army. As Jackson's command had five more Napoleons than were allotted the First Corps, General Pendleton had suggested that Hill be supplied by a shift of the guns in the batteries of other Second Corps units. For sentimental reasons, Hill asked that he be given four Napoleons that had been captured by him at Seven Pines and had been assigned a Louisiana battery then with Longstreet. "Old Pete" was willing to oblige Harvey Hill, provided four Napoleons from Jackson's Corps were sent to replace those he turned over to Harvey Hill, who, it will be remembered, had been reassigned to Jackson's Corps.

The transaction seemed simple and fair enough, but it aroused the wrath of "Stonewall." Stiffly he wrote, in answer to a letter from Lee, that if the transfer had to be made, he hoped it would be entrusted to General Pendleton or to some other staff officer; "but," he went on, "I hope that none of the guns which belonged to the Army of the Valley, before it became part of the Army of Northern Virginia after the battle of Cedar Run, will be taken from it." If artillery, since that time, had come improperly into his command, he trusted that it would be taken from him, and that the responsible officer should be punished.

Somewhat self-righteously, he asserted, "So careful was I to prevent any improper distribution of the artillery and other public property captured at Harpers Ferry, that I issued a written order directing my staff officers to turn over to the proper chiefs of staff of the Army of Northern Virginia all captured stores." "Old Jack" concluded with a smack at his division commander:

[57] *Pender MSS,* Dec. 3, 1862.

"General D. H. Hill's artillery wants existed at the time he was assigned to my command, and it is hoped that artillery which belonged to the Army of the Valley will not be taken to supply his wants." [58]

This was a surprising letter, for the receipt of which Lee was not prepared. He stopped the correspondence then and there, and with his usual tact, sought to satisfy Harvey Hill without prejudicing Jackson against the North Carolinian. From the Secretary of War and from the Chief of Ordnance, Lee immediately solicited four 12-pounder howitzers "for a particular purpose." He did not say that the purpose, *inter alia,* was to salve the sensibilities of a General exceedingly proud of what the Army of the Valley had achieved. [59]

Jackson himself had no more to say on the subject. The very day he sent his protest to headquarters, he wrote his sister-in-law: "I fear I am not grateful enough for unnumbered blessings . . . I trust God will answer the prayers offered for peace. . . . Not much comfort is to be expected until this cruel war terminates" [60] —despite the blessing of a daughter.

[58] *O. R.,* 21, 1043–44.   [59] *O. R.,* 21, 1047, 1048.
[60] *Mrs. Jackson,* 363.

CHAPTER XX

THE BATTLE OF THE PONTOONS

JACKSON'S CORPS had been brought to the vicinity of Fredericksburg because Burnside had decided to attempt from the mid-Rappahannock a new drive on Richmond. The Federal commanding General had arrived at Falmouth, opposite Fredericksburg, on November 19;[1] Longstreet the same day had taken position on the hills behind the city.[2] Lee had reached the scene on the 20th.[3] The First Corps had established its camps and had organized its outposts and its service of supply before Jackson's troops passed in rear to extend the Confederate right. In its first phase, Lee's movement to Fredericksburg had been rapid, but his defensive plan was firm. He was determined, if the enemy advanced overwhelmingly, to retire toward Richmond and to tear up both the R. F. & P. Railroad southward from Fredericksburg and the Orange and Alexandria to Gordonsville. "I am loath," said he, "to add to the devastation of the country . . . and yet think it prudent to throw every impediment to the progress of the enemy to Richmond in the way."[4]

Once Burnside found himself resolutely opposed in this manner, he appeared to lose all zeal for rapid movement. The Army of Northern Virginia, in consequence, had another period of rest, during which headquarters undertook, as always, to improve the organization. One change only seemed to be imperative—the removal of Gen. Thomas F. Drayton from command of his South Carolina-Georgia Brigade. These troops had been placed in the Division of a diligent administrator, Lafayette McLaws, who had sought to rebuild a shattered command. The Colonels were absent; Drayton could not so much as keep his staff together. McLaws despaired of results; Longstreet considered that the service of potentially good soldiers was lost to the Army. Lee had been concerned for weeks, but as he had respect for Drayton as

---

[1] O. R., 21, 86.
[3] 2 R. E. Lee, 433.
[2] Ibid., 568–69.
[4] O. R., 19, pt. 2, p. 717.

a gentleman and a friend, he sought to ease as best he could the retirement of that officer.

The most direct procedure was to assign Drayton's regiments to other Brigades and, as the General then would be without command, to give him leave of absence. Later, perhaps, some useful duty might be found for Drayton. This course was followed: The Fiftieth and Fifty-first Georgia were transferred to Paul Semmes's Brigade; the Fifteenth South Carolina was placed with Kershaw. The Phillips Legion went to Cobb. Drayton left the Army of Northern Virginia to return no more. The whole unpleasant affair was handled with the least possible disturbance and publicity.[5] Addition of two of Drayton's Georgia regiments to Paul Semmes's Brigade released two Virginia regiments which, with one from Kemper and one from Cooke, were formed into a new Brigade for "Monty" Corse.[6] That officer thereupon was relieved of command of Pickett's old Brigade which was placed under "Dick" Garnett.[7] Nothing further was done in the hearing of Jackson's charges against Garnett.

Longstreet was entirely willing, so far as the records show, to have Garnett in the First Corps, which the new Lieutenant General industriously was preparing for the next battles. Although the correspondence of the last two months of 1862 contains few references to Longstreet, he was as active as efficient. The administration of his Corps was smooth. "Dick" Anderson had recovered quickly from his wound at Sharpsburg and now found that to his four experienced Brigade commanders, a fifth of less experience had been added—E. A. Perry with a small Florida Brigade.[8] Pickett of the curly locks at length had reported himself cured of the wound received at Gaines' Mill and, for the first time, he was directing a Division in the field. Its five Brigadiers, with the exception of "Monty" Corse, all were seasoned and all, without excepting Corse, were capable. As much could be said for John B. Hood and his four Brigades.

[5] O. R., 21, 1029, 1030, 1033; cf. ibid., 538. In D. A. B., 5, 446–47, James H. Easterby stated that Drayton was detailed as a member of a military court and subsequently had temporary charge of a Brigade in Arkansas and then of a sub-district in Texas. Still later he was president of the court of inquiry on Price's Missouri Expedition.
[6] Fifteenth and Thirty-second Virginia from Semmes, Seventeenth Virginia from Kemper, and Thirtieth Virginia from Cooke. O. R., 21, 1033.
[7] Cf. O. R., 21, 539.
[8] Cf. supra, p. 265. Perry had been assigned to command Nov. 10, 1862. His regiments were the Second, Fifth and Eighth Florida. O. R., 21, 539.

The most interesting accession to Longstreet's divisional commanders was Robert Ransom, Jr., though his rank still was that of a Brigadier. His has appeared as one of many names in these pages—during the Seven Days and again at Sharpsburg; but now that John G. Walker had left the Army of Northern Virginia, Ransom, as senior Brigadier, was in command of his own and of John R. Cooke's North Carolina regiments. From Cooke's command, to the distress of all, the renowned Third Arkansas, companions in the homeric fight at Sharpsburg, had been transferred to Hood's old Texas Brigade, outside Ransom's command.

To many of the officers of the "old army," and to virtually all those who had served with the cavalry, Ransom was known as a capable Second Lieutenant of the 1st Dragoons and later as First Lieutenant and Captain of the 1st Cavalry,[9] who had endured his full part, and more, of sickness.[10] He had resigned immediately upon the secession of his native North Carolina and had organized the First Cavalry of that State, a regiment that had inflamed much enthusiasm upon its arrival in Richmond, Oct. 18, 1861. The regiment numbered about 850 sabers, or, with its wagons, 974 men and about 1000 horses.[11] It had an early introduction to combat, in a brush near Vienna, Nov. 26, 1861,[12] and it soon earned a good name for discipline and courage. Before many more months passed, its men had a maxim that a commission in the First meant "a hole in your hide." Every field officer of the regiment was killed or wounded, with the exception of Ransom.[13] He probably escaped that fate by his subsequent transfer to infantry command.

A gallant spirit was Ransom's, but he was not altogether popular with his men. He was too much the regular, the West Pointer,

---

[9] *Cullum*, No. 1467; *Army Register of 1860*; 2 *N. C. Regts.*, 599; *Richmond Examiner*, June 11, 1861.

[10] 8 *Rowland's Davis*, 370.

[11] The First North Carolina Cavalry later was known, officially, as the Ninth Regiment of North Carolina Volunteers. *O. R.*, 51, pt. 2, p. 377. For its arrival in Richmond and its movements en route to Manassas, see *O. R.*, 51, pt. 2, pp. 301, 336, 350; *O. R.*, 5, 909; *Richmond Dispatch*, Oct. 18, p. 3, col. 1, Oct. 19, 1862, p. 3, col. 1.

[12] *O. R.*, 5, 446–47; *Richmond Dispatch*, Dec. 6, 1861, p. 2, col. 5.

[13] 1 *N. C. Regts.*, 484. *Cf.* Wade Hampton in 1 *N. C. Regts.*, 463–64: "I always attributed much of the efficiency of his noble regiment [First N. C. Cavalry] to its first Colonel . . . Robert Ransom. To him was due, in large measure, those soldierly qualities which won for his old regiment its high reputation (a reputation it deserved) for, in my opinion, there was no finer body of men in the Army of Northern Virginia."

in handling troops.[14] "If he had understood volunteer soldiers," one of his veterans subsequently said of Ransom, "and [had] realized that four-fifths of the men in the ranks were as careful of their personal honor, and as anxious for the success of the cause as he, he would have been one of the greatest generals in Lee's army. . . ."[15] In action he was cool, and in judging ground sure. Never was there hesitation in his orders or his tactics. In the heat of battle, his bald pate shone above the abundant hair on his temples; his eyes flashed; every inch of him was soldier. Then, if then only, his men ceased to grumble about his discipline, and told themselves that when the shells were bursting and the minié balls whining, they had rather have Robert Ransom than any other man as their commander, because he knew how to move them swiftly and with minimum losses.[16] Unfortunately, his health was most uneven and necessitated sick leave[17] but on the hills behind Fredericksburg, he now was fit and ready for action.

If Ransom was dependable as an acting divisional commander, the new Brigadiers, almost without exception, showed promise. Thomas R. R. Cobb, in particular, gave fully to his new Brigade the high abilities with which he was credited. Cobb was 39 and had behind him in Georgia a reputation for legal acumen and vast industry. As a member of the Provisional Congress of the Confederacy, he had asked relief from his work as a member of the committee on permanent constitution, in order that he might organize a "Legion." Without previous military training, he learned fast.[18] By August, 1862, he had so won Lee's confidence that the commanding General urged him to increase his Legion

[14] 1 N. C. Regts., 27.

[15] 2 N. C. Regts., 295–96.

[16] Ibid. His picture appears in 4 C. M. H., 340. For reference to his movements before Fredericksburg, see O. R., 51, pt. 2, pp. 474, 541; ibid., 11, pt. 2, pp. 628, 791, 794; 3 N. C. Regts., 115; O. R., 19, pt. 1, pp. 821, 914 ff, 919 ff. These references are in chronological order. Ransom relieved J. G. Walker in command of Walker's Division, Nov. 7, 1862. See O. R., 19, pt. 2, p. 703.

[17] Cf. O. R., 18, 255; 3 C. M. H., 345 ff.

[18] The best sketch of Cobb probably is that by Rev. R. K. Porter in 3 Land We Love, 183–97. Other biographical references are given in the article in D. A. B., by R. P. Brooks. For reports on the progress of his "Legion" see Richmond Dispatch, June 17, July 2, p. 33, col. 4; Richmond Enquirer, July 2, p. 2, col. 6; Richmond Examiner, Aug. 14, 1861, p. 2, col. 6. The article in the Enquirer noted that his father-in-law Chief Justice [Joseph Henry] Lumpkin of the Supreme Court of Georgia had seven sons in the Confederate army. It was on Sept. 11, 1861, that Cobb's Legion was directed to report to Magruder at Yorktown, Virginia. O. R., 51. pt. 2, p. 288.

to a Brigade.[19] Stuart protested against the employment of Cobb's cavalrymen apart from the main mounted force because they were one of the best of his regiments.[20] At that time, or a little earlier, Cobb had been annoyed by professional soldiers generally and, in particular, by the Lees. He had complained privately to his wife when Fitz Lee was made a Brigadier General, "I suppose in a few days we shall see the balance of the Lees promoted also." [21] As late as October he wrote: "Let me but get away from these 'West Pointers.' They are very sociable gentlemen and agreeable companions, but never have I seen men who had so little appreciation of merit in others. Self-sufficiency and self-aggrandizement are their great controlling characteristics." [22]

From this state of mind, which was alien to his known Christian character, Tom Cobb had been won by the tact and consideration of the commanding General himself. When Lee had remarked the lack of vinegar and had expressed a wish for pickles, Cobb had sent some and, in return, had received a friendly note he passed on to his wife. A little later, Cobb wrote: "General Lee has taken pains to show and express his confidence in me as an officer, and personally he has been as kind as I could ask or desire. He has ordered me to take command of Howell [Cobb's] Brigade on a march this morning." [23]

After his promotion as Brigadier,[24] Cobb wrote no more in criticism of Lees or of other West Pointers, and now, as he approached the first battle in which he was to command a Brigade, he wrote reassuringly to Mrs. Cobb: "Do not be uneasy about my being 'rash.' The bubble reputation cannot drag me into folly. God helping me, I will do my duty when called upon, trusting the consequences to Him. I go on picket tomorrow, and hence cannot write regularly." [25]

19 28 S. H. S. P., 295. Cobb remarked that Lee professed more reliance on Howell Cobb and on him "than any two officers in the civil part of the army." This is a unique reference to the euphemistic name—"civil part"—that Lee gave those of his high-ranking officers who had no professional training in arms. The less polite name for the seniors was "political Generals."

20 Ibid., 296. A "Legion," it will be remembered, included men of all three arms of the service. The form of organization was so cumbersome that it had to be abandoned.

21 28 S. H. S. P., 294. 22 28 S. H. S. P., 297.

23 Ibid., 296, 297.

24 O. R., 19, pt. 2, pp. 683, 699, to rank as of Nov. 1, 1862.

25 28 S. H. S. P., 301.

This was the spirit of the Army. By diligent and well reasoned care of the men,[26] morale was raised high.[27] Details for non-military work were reduced;[28] a separate command of scouts and couriers was planned in order to lessen the calls on the cavalry.[29] Back in Richmond, Rebel War Clerk Jones paid tribute to the soldiers at the same time that he drew an age-old indictment: "Our patriotism is mainly in the army and among the ladies of the South. The avarice and cupidity of men at home, could only be excelled by ravenous wolves . . ."[30] At the front, Lee was so confident of the spirit of his men that he became impatient of Burnside's delays. Dorsey Pender, meeting the Commander, sensed Lee's feelings and wrote his wife: "Gen. Lee is very anxiously waiting for a fight. He told me today he would be willing to fall back and let them cross for the sake of a fight. All accounts are to the effect that they will not fight, and their numbers are not so terrible as might be supposed."[31]

This confidence was heightened by the strength of the ground the Confederates, and especially Longstreet's Corps, held in rear of Fredericksburg. "We have a magnificent position, perhaps the best on the line," said Cobb.[32] The Division of McLaws was upon heights immediately behind the city; Anderson was on McLaws's left; Pickett on McLaws's right; beyond Pickett was Hood, who was drawn nearer after Jackson moved in beyond Longstreet's right.

It scarcely seemed possible that the strong ground held by McLaws would be assaulted, but its organization and defense represented the type of work at which Lafayette McLaws shone. Under Longstreet's direction and with the assistance of the corps engineers, he prepared pits for his batteries and strengthened some parts of his front with abatis and fire trenches.[33] At the foot of the heights was a road that paralleled McLaws's front. The outer side of this sunken road was protected by a stone wall, but McLaws was not content with this. He had a ditch dug on the

---

[26] For a detailed review of the measures instituted after Sharpsburg to restore the morale of the army, see 2 *R. E. Lee*, 415 ff.

[27] Cf. *O. R.*, 19, pt. 2, pp. 664–65, 679, 688, 722; *ibid.*, 21, 1037–38, 1050; *Ham Chamberlayne*, 141, 144.

[28] Cf. *O. R.*, 21, pp. 1012–03, 1069. The controversy continued after Fredericksburg. Cf. *O. R.*, 25, pt. 2, 609 ff.

[29] *O. R.*, 21, 1039, 1041, 1045.   [30] 1 *R. W. C. D.*, 200.

[31] *Pender MSS.* Dec. 3, 1862.   [32] 28 *S. H. S. P.*, 299.

[33] *O. R.*, 21, 569, 578.

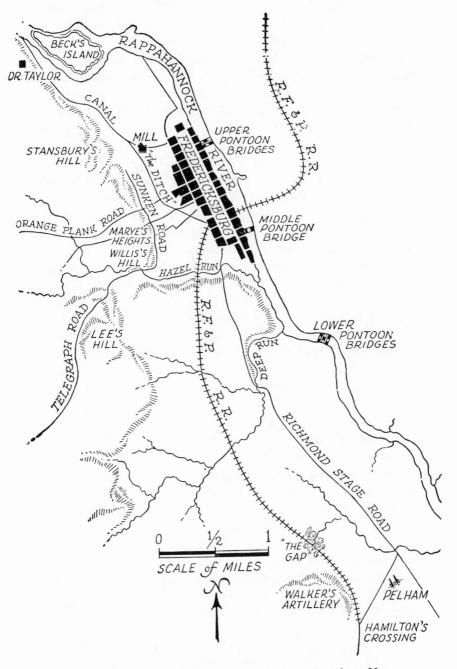

BECK'S
ISLAND

DR. TAYLOR

RAPPAHANNOCK

CANAL

MILL

STANSBURY'S
HILL

"the DITCH"

FREDERICKSBURG

RIVER

UPPER
PONTOON
BRIDGES

F. F. & P. R. R.

SUNKEN ROAD

ORANGE PLANK ROAD

MARYE'S
HEIGHTS

WILLIS'S
HILL

HAZEL RUN

MIDDLE
PONTOON
BRIDGE

R. F. & P. R. R.

TELEGRAPH ROAD

LEE'S
HILL

DEEP RUN

LOWER
PONTOON
BRIDGES

RICHMOND STAGE ROAD

0   1/2   1

SCALE of MILES

N

"THE
GAP"

WALKER'S
ARTILLERY

PELHAM

HAMILTON'S
CROSSING

Sketch of the Battlefield of Fredericksburg, December, 1862

lower or town side of the road, and had the dirt thrown out in front of the wall and banked against it—an ideal trench for point-blank fire.[34] This was to be Cobb's position.

Longstreet gave to McLaws, also, the more difficult task of guarding the river front. The stream itself was not beyond the range of the guns on Marye's Heights, but the terrain was such that the Confederate artillery could not reach the river without damaging the town, which sprawled downhill to the Rappahannock. Federals, therefore, could use the town as a screen when they decided to lay a pontoon bridge and to cross. From their side of the Rappahannock, moreover, the Unionists could employ their overpowering artillery to keep the Confederate batteries at a distance and to cover their own advance. The only defense was that of posting infantry in the houses and behind any cover the Southerners could find next the river.

This assignment was given the fine Mississippi veterans of William Barksdale, formerly under Richard Griffith.[35] They had been much diminished in number by the hard fighting of the summer, but in valor they were worthy of their stout-hearted commander. Barksdale himself had not enjoyed another such hour as the one in which, at Malvern Hill, he had displayed what no less a person than Lee had styled the "highest qualities of the soldier."[36] Lesser opportunities had not made him appear smaller. If all the animosities of the Gulf State politicians were his, so were most of their virtues.

He had not long to wait before he proved it. On the evening of December 10, numerous indications of activity on the Federal side of the Rappahannock were observable. From the stir and movement, Longstreet concluded that Burnside's men were about to cross the river. "Old Pete" shared the opinion of most of the experienced officers that nothing he could do could keep the Federals from crossing under the cover of their superior artillery, but, as a matter of course, he wished to meet the attempt boldly, and to harass and to delay it to the last moment of prudence. Word was sent to McLaws to have all his artillery harnessed by daylight. McLaws put his own interpretation on this order and gave

[34] *Allan's Army*, 468. A photograph of the trench, as it appeared in May, 1863, will be found in 2 *Phot. His. Civil War*, 123.
[35] Killed at Savage Station, June 29; see *Brent*, 18o.
[36] 1 *D. A. B.*, 607.

instruction that all infantry should be under arms by the same time.[37]

In Fredericksburg, along the river front and downstream as far as a quarter of a mile below the mouth of Deep Run [38] Barksdale was on the *qui vive*. He had part of the reliable Seventeenth Mississippi posted close to the river bank from the ferry to a point one-half mile above Deep Run. Thence, to a quarter of a mile below the mouth of the Run he had the Eighteenth Mississippi.[39]

At 11 P.M., Barksdale directed the commanding officers to double their pickets, and he himself rode ceaselessly along his front of a mile and a half. Often he drew rein and listened intently to that vague, subdued but unmistakable hum that rises in the night from troops on the march. Before 2 o'clock on the morning of the 11th, Barksdale felt sure the Federals were bringing down pontoons from the Stafford Heights. He gave the order to arouse all the men on advanced duty and he sent word to McLaws of what he had heard.[40] In the blackness,[41] nothing could be seen, but sound carried clearly. By 4 A.M., Barksdale was satisfied that the Union engineers were beginning to throw the pontoons at three points—one on the site of the rope ferry in the town, one near the railroad bridge, and one opposite the mouth of Deep Run.[42]

Barksdale, sensing all this, posted Col. John C. Fiser of the Seventeenth near the ferry in Fredericksburg whence came the greatest noise, and he trusted the judgment of Fiser in leaving to Capt. A. R. Govan the task of dealing with the bridge builders near the railroad crossing. The General decided, also, that in the

---

[37] *O. R.*, 21, 578.

[38] *Ibid.*, 604. Deep Run flows into the river from the right bank about a mile and a quarter below the railroad bridge.

[39] *O. R.*, 21, 601, 604.   [40] *Ibid.*, 578, 603.

[41] The moon had not reached its last quarter, but fog overhung the river bottom. Cf. *O. R.*, 21, 182.

[42] Statements in some of the narratives of the Battle of Fredericksburg differ widely concerning the number and location of the bridges. Actually, on the 11th one bridge was thrown opposite Hawk Street, site of the rope ferry; another was thrown near the railroad bridge; two were placed near the mouth of Deep Run. On the night of the 11th, a second bridge, which had been started early that morning in accordance with the preliminary plan, was finished near the bridge at the rope ferry. On the 12th still another bridge was put across the Rappahannock about one mile below the town and close to the two placed on the forenoon of the 11th. This made a total of six bridges—two at the rope ferry, one near the railroad crossing, and three near the mouth of Deep Run (cf. *O. R.*, 21, 167–68, 170, 171, 175). The three opposite the town were 400 feet each in length; the three lower bridges were, respectively, 400, 420, and 440 feet (*ibid.*, 171). For the exact location of the bridges, see the map in *O. R. Atlas*, Plate XXV–4.

darkness and the fog he wr uld be wasting ammunition if he opened fire before his rifles could take toll of the pontoniers. These developments were reported to McLaws, who looked at his watch and inwardly debated when he should give the signal of an enemy crossing. Days before, commanding officers had been informed that the firing of one gun, followed quickly by a second cannon shot, was to put the entire army on notice that the Federals were crossing the Rappahannock.[43] Barksdale had to leave to his senior to decide when the Army should be aroused, and, as he waited, he sought to assure himself that he had on his line every available man who could find shelter from which to draw bead.

A battalion of the Eighth Florida of Perry's new Brigade was at hand, and could be employed to prolong the front. In person, Barksdale led the small command to the ferry landing and told Colonel Fiser to assign it a position. Fiser put the force on his left, just above the ferry. Another and a smaller Florida contingent was placed on Govan's right, below the railroad bridge.[44] Barksdale rode on; Fiser decided that before he opened fire, he should give noncombatants an opportunity of vacating the houses from which he intended to pepper the enemy. By 5 A.M., the few women and children in the neighborhood had hurried away or had taken refuge in the cellars.

Then Fiser gave the word. His excellent riflemen opened. They could see nothing through the enveloping fog, but they could tell from the nearness of the sound that the head of the bridge was close to the shore they were defending. Their ears had to serve for their eyes. Almost at the moment they began to dispute the Federal crossing, the boom-boom of the signal guns from McLaws's position reverberated across the river valley.[45] Barksdale's men knew that every one of Longstreet's camps back of Fredericksburg soon would be astir, and that their comrades of the First Corps would be wishing them well, but that the fight would be theirs, altogether theirs. Southern artillerists scarcely

---

[43] Cf. O. R., 51, pt. 2, p. 653.

[44] O. R., 21, 603. Barksdale's line from left to right consequently was: Eighth Florida Battalion, Seventeenth Mississippi, companies of Eighth Florida, Eighteenth Mississippi. Inasmuch as the last named regiment had its right about a quarter of a mile below the mouth of Deep Run, the line defended by the Brigade with the help of the Florida troops was almost two miles in length.

[45] The battery of J. P. W. Read fired the signal guns. O. R., 21, 1070; 3 B. & L., 86. This battery, on the 13th, was to the right of Kershaw's first position. O. R., 21, 591.

could give more help than could the infantry on the bridge, because the understanding was that the batteries were not to be employed against the town.

The task of holding off the enemy at the ferry landing did not prove difficult. If the bullets from the rifles of the Mississippians reached few Federals, they made many cautious. The noise from the river was hushed or muffled. Every time a sound was answered with a minié ball, silence followed. At last, as wintry dawn slowly dissipated darkness and thinned the fog, the boys strained their eyes for a glimpse of the end of the closest pontoon. When finally they could distinguish it from the liquid gray, they calculated the distance as eighty feet from the west bank [46] where they were hiding. Their first shots drove off the working party. Every Mississippian within range fired as if he were a sharpshooter. The Florida troops above the ferry did their full part. Near the railroad bridge, Govan found it equally simple to keep the pontoniers at a distance.

Opposite Deep Run, the situation was not so favorable. The Unionists at work there were well led, competent engineer troops. They had to contend with ice, almost half an inch thick, but they worked steadily under a shielding and impenetrable fog,[47] which was heavier there than upstream. So well were the bridgemakers covered that the Confederates did not know that two bridges were being thrown. The Lieutenant Colonel in command of the Eighteenth Mississippi thought, apparently, that the lower bridge was one that had been started higher up and had been floated down.[48]

To the spiteful bark of the rifles along the river front after daylight,[49] the Federal artillery made wrathful answer. At first its fire was directed through the fog at the shelters from which the Mississippians were disputing with the bridge builders. Before long the nearness of the sound and the quick explosion may have made it plain to the Confederates that batteries had been brought from Stafford Heights down to the water's edge.[50] Barksdale's

---

[46] It should be remembered that the course of the Rappahannock, opposite Fredericksburg, is almost North and South.

[47] O. R., 21, 186.

[48] Cf. O. R., 21, 604. By 8.30 A.M. one of these crossings, and by 11 o'clock the other, was ready for use. Ibid., 186.

[49] There is some conflict of testimony regarding the time of the opening of the fire, both by small arms and by ordnance. Cf. O. R., 21, 182.

[50] Ibid.

men in the town were not to be shaken by random cannonade. They hugged the ground, or pulled close to stout brick walls, and waited till the fire slackened. Then, as the pontoniers ran out on the bridge again to resume their work, Barksdale's rifles mockingly picked the men off.

This resistance was prolonged beyond the possible endurance of a Federal commander who already was worn by unwelcome responsibility. Burnside ordered all artillery within range to open on the town in the hope of compelling Barksdale to withdraw.[51] A furious bombardment it was. It swept the streets, it shattered houses, it shook the very hills; but it did not drive out Barksdale's men. They took to the cellars or found deeper ditches and at intervals they would peer out to be certain the Federal bridge builders had not returned to work. Soon smoke and flame were rising; homes were burning. Barksdale sent to Longstreet to inquire whether he should try to put out the worst of the fires. Longstreet's answer was realistic: "You have enough to do to watch the Yankees."[52]

General Barksdale at the time was in one of the threatened houses, where he had established his headquarters in order that he could be reached quickly by couriers. In the heaviest of the bombardment, one of his staff entered the office, half startled and half amused, to say that a lady had come to the door, defiant of the fire, and insisted upon seeing the General. Barksdale answered that he could not possibly see her! The staff officer must tell her so and must urge that she run to some nearby cellar. All that, the aide replied helplessly, he already had explained; the lady had responded, blandly but firmly, that General Barksdale was a Southern gentleman and would not refuse to see a lady who called on him. Barksdale swore and fairly wrung his hands in annoyance. When he reached the door, there stood the lady as calm as if she were entering church on a Sabbath morning in spring.

"For God's sake, madam," Barksdale began, "go and seek some place of safety; I'll send a member of my staff to help you find one."

Indulgently, almost pityingly, the lady smiled at him. Said she: "General Barksdale, my cow has just been killed in my stable by a shell. She is very fat, and I don't want the Yankees to get her.

[51] *O. R.*, 21, 183. [52] *Hotchkiss' MS Diary*, 115.

if you will send someone down to butcher her, you are welcome to the meat." [53]

Barksdale's thanks were the more fervent because he wished to end the interview quickly. He promised, no doubt, that the cow would be salvaged and consumed to the glory of the Confederacy. Relieved of his guest, he got good reports from both the upper crossings. "Tell General Lee," the Mississippian said grimly to a messenger, "that if he wants a bridge of dead Yankees, I can furnish him with one!" [54]

He would have had trouble in making delivery. After the bombardment, the Union bridge builders tried again. Once more the Confederates drove them off and then waited for the next move. Soon from the eastern bank, loaded batteaux of Federals put boldly out and started to row across the river. Barksdale's men challenged the enemy as before, but this time the fire was weaker. Union batteries were beginning to search out the position of the Mississippi marksmen. On Fiser's left, the Captain in command of the Florida battalion had been wounded about 11.00 A.M. Thereafter his men had lacked leadership. One frightened and bewildered Lieutenant actually had drawn his pistol and had threatened to kill any of the Mississippians who, by firing at the enemy, disclosed the position.[55] Near the railroad bridge, the retirement of the small Florida contingent at 2 o'clock led Captain Govan to withdraw his men from the river bank.

Barksdale stuck stubbornly to his task, but at 4.30 he had to call his men back to Caroline Street.[56] Ere long, as Federal infantry continued to move fast across the bridges, McLaws sent orders to Barksdale to evacuate the town.[57] Barksdale had his blood up, and he decided that as he knew more about the situation than did his chief, he would defer compliance and meantime kill as many

[53] *Stiles*, 133. He had seen the lady as she had walked toward headquarters, whither he was riding. Stiles noted: "She apparently found the projectiles . . . very interesting—stepping a little aside to inspect a great, gaping hole one had just gouged out in the sidewalk, then turning her head to note a fearful explosion in the air." Years afterward, Major Stiles went to Fredericksburg to deliver an address, during which he related this story. He noticed, as he spoke, that his audience seemed especially interested and that many turned to look: ". . . Just as I finished my story and my eyes followed theirs—there before me sat the very lady, apparently not a day older." The audience rose and cheered her (*ibid.*). Unfortunately, with the passing of years, the identity of the patriot seems to have been lost. Effort to procure her name and story thus far (1943) have been in vain.

[54] *Owen*, 180.   [55] *O. R.*, 21, 603.
[56] *O. R.*, 21, 579.   [57] 3 *B. & L.*, 75.

bluecoats as he could. Doubtless Barksdale would have fought joyfully to the last soldier and the last cartridge, had not his orders been repeated. He had reluctantly to obey.[58] Courageous men went through shell wrecked streets to recall every guard and every sharpshooter. All fell back safely except one demoralized Florida company of twenty men. These were captured either through the inefficiency of their Captain or through fear of being killed when they ran from the river bank to the shelter of houses.[59]

Loss more serious suddenly was threatened in the last hour of withdrawal. The Twenty-first Mississippi, which had not been engaged along the river, was selected by Barksdale to cover the withdrawal. Nearest the enemy, at the rear of this rear regiment, was a detachment under Lieut. Lane Brandon, a graduate of the Harvard Law School. In some fashion, Brandon captured a few prisoners from whom he ascertained that the regiment pursuing him was the Twentieth Massachusetts. In command of the leading company, he learned, was his chum and former classmate, Henry L. Abbott. That was enough for Brandon. Cost what it might, he would whip Abbott then and there! Brandon halted his rearguard, turned about, attacked the Twentieth Massachusetts and momentarily pressed it back. He was preparing to carry the contest back through the town, if he could, when his delay in closing the rear was discovered. Orders the most peremptory were sent him to break off the fight. So mad was he, even then, to outdo his friend Abbott that he had to be put under arrest.[60]

Without further loss or incident, Barksdale marched through the darkness of the winter's early night to the foot of Marye's Height . . . across a wide, deep field, a field of execution.

[58] O. R., 21, 569.   [59] O. R., 21, 603, 604.

[60] Stiles, 130. Earlier use of this anecdote was made by Stiles in his address at the dedication of the Confederate monument at the University of Virginia, June 7, 1893. In the same address, Stiles recounted a sensational incident of the rescue of a small child who was cared for by the Twenty-first Mississippi and was carried as the "colors" of the regiment on its march through Fredericksburg after the retreat of Burnside (21 S. H. S. P., 30–31). As Stiles did not include this in his subsequently published memoirs, he probably had concluded that the story was apocryphal.

CHAPTER XXI

ON THE RIGHT AT FREDERICKSBURG

THE KNOWN completion of three or four pontoon bridges by nightfall of December 11 [1] led the Confederate commanders to conclude that Burnside was almost certain to attack somewhere near Fredericksburg. He scarcely could have afforded to put down that many pontoons, rich though he was in equipment, as a ruse to hold the Confederates at the town while he crossed at a remote point on the Rappahannock. The hour of battle must be near. Jackson at Guiney's Station was advised of the situation; Powell Hill, encamped around Yerby's, received orders directly from Army headquarters—Jackson of course repeated them—to move at dawn and to take the position previously held by Longstreet's right Division.[2] D. H. Hill and Early, who were watching the lower crossings of the Rappahannock, were left where they were until the probability of a Federal attack at Fredericksburg became a certainty.

On the morning of the 12th the fog was widespread, shifting and uneven. Where it lifted at intervals over the town, one house after another could be seen afire.[3] Troops in large numbers evidently had crossed from the Stafford Heights and had bivouacked both in Fredericksburg and near the bridges that had been laid opposite Deep Run.[4] Against these troops, whenever the fog thinned, the Confederate artillery directed its fire, but in every

---

[1] As explained *supra*, p. 335, the Confederates apparently were not aware during the forenoon of the 11th that two bridges instead of one had been constructed opposite the mouth of Deep Run, but the only reason for questioning their discovery of the second bridge during the afternoon is doubt concerning visibility. At the railroad bridge, the fog ceased to be troublesome by 1 P.M. (*O. R.*, 21, 606), but Maj. Gen. W. B. Franklin stated (1 *Com. Con. War*, 661) that he crossed all his troops under the cover of the fog. Strictly speaking, this would indicate that fog was pervasive both when Newton's Division passed over the bridges early on the evening of the 11th and when the same troops, less Devens's Brigade, marched back for security during the night (*O. R.*, 21, 536–37). On the other hand, none of the officers whose reports are on file mentioned fog or any limited visibility during the late afternoon of the 11th. Maj. Gen. J. F. Reynolds, who crossed the I Corps on the morning of the 12th, stated that he did so in a fog. Col. Adrian R. Root, 1st Brig., 2nd Div., I Corps, remarked that the fog overhung the river when he traversed at noon on the 12th (*O. R.*, 21, 453, 485).

[2] *O. R.*, 21, 645.   [3] *O. R.*, 21, 545, 547.   [4] *Ibid.*, 552.

instance it provoked instant, furious answer. This continued angrily long after the Confederate gunners broke off the duel.[5] As the morning wore on, with no news of Federal activity elsewhere on the Rappahannock, the question became that of where, on the Fredericksburg front, Burnside would concentrate his attack.

At first Longstreet thought the main assault would be against the Confederate right, but when he saw how heavily the Federals were massing in Fredericksburg, and how steadily they were pouring into the town, he concluded that the main assault would be against his right and the left of Jackson.[6] "Old Pete" accordingly summoned Ransom's Division from reserve and put it with the left units of McLaws's Division to guard Marye's Heights.[7] The special care of that part of the front was given to Ransom,[8] doubtless because McLaws had too long a line under his charge to devote to that sector the needed attention. The previous night, most of Tom Cobb's Brigade had been moved down to the sunken road under the heights in order to relieve Barksdale's tired men.[9] On Cobb's left, Ransom placed the Twenty-fourth North Carolina of his own Brigade.[10] John R. Cooke's great regiment, the Twenty-seventh, was placed near the crest.[11]

Jackson, for his part, had no enthusiasm for a battle on the banks of the Rappahannock, because he thought a victory could not be pressed. When he had sent D. H. Hill down the river, he was reported to have said: "I am opposed to fighting here. We will whip the enemy but gain no fruits of victory. I have advised the line of the North Anna, but have been overruled." [12] Now that the battle was about to be joined, "Old Jack" rose to it. Some time about noon, he dispatched orders for Early and D. H. Hill to join him.[13] No concern did he express that the distance they had to cover—

[5] Ibid., 552, 570.
[6] O. R., 21, 569; O. R., 51, pt. 2, p. 661.
[7] Ibid., 569, 609.   [8] Ibid., 553.
[9] Ibid., 579.   [10] Ibid., 625.
[11] See infra, p. 362.
[12] Dabney, 595, presumably on the authority of D. H. Hill. The words are not to be accepted as literally correct, because it scarcely was "in character" for Jackson to confide even to D. H. Hill that he had been overruled. As punctilious a soldier as Jackson might not have considered it subordinate to have said that superior authority had overruled him. Longstreet's reference, to the same effect as Dabney's, is in 3 B. & L., 71–72.
[13] The assumed time of transmission is based on D. H. Hill's statement that orders reached him "about sundown." O. R., 21, 643.

eighteen to twenty-two miles—was too long a march for a December night.[14]

The other preparations Jackson completed promptly and with his habitual care for detail and discipline. In particular, he instructed his Provost Marshal to prevent all straggling of the sort that had so dangerously weakened the Army in the Maryland operations. Jackson's orders were explicit: The Provost Marshal Guard was to shoot, first, all stragglers who refused to go to the front and, second, all soldiers who were said by two witnesses to be straggling for the second time.[15] There was a semblance of judicial process in this examination of two witnesses before a man suspected of quitting the front for the second time could be shot. The other course was simple: If the straggler would not go back into the fight—give him a bullet and end the matter. Instructions did not specify whether the straggler was to be shot in the head or in the heel.

All these arrangements were made while the Corps was moving into the combat zone. On the arrival at the front of Taliaferro, who had recovered from his wound and temporarily had charge of Jackson's old Division, that veteran command had an unusual privilege. All too often, as its thinned ranks showed, the Division had been in the "very front of battle." Now it was placed behind A. P. Hill,[16] out of the range of adventuresome minié balls—sure evidence that Lee, for once, had ample reserves. What a contrast to that dreadful September day at Sharpsburg, not three months previously![17] There was some suggestion, in this superabundance of strength, that Stuart's cavalry well might be employed against the Federal left, but the ground proved much too heavy for a charge by mounted men.[18]

One other subject only was there for debate while the Confederates filed into position on the ridge: Was that strong position weakened by the bit of woodland that projected toward the river from the line of A. P. Hill? The Light Division had a line that ran northwestward from Hamilton's Crossing approximately one and a half miles on a wood-covered ridge.[19] Immediately in front,

[14] O. R., 21, 630, 643.   [15] O. R., 21, 641.
[16] O. R., 21, 630.
[17] Cf. *Allan's Army*, 472–73. Colonel Allen estimated, *ibid.*, 481, that on the 13th, after D. H. Hill and Early had come up, Lee had on a front of 11,500 yards a total of 68,000 men, 11,000 to the mile or six to the yard.
[18] 2 *von Borcke*, 108–09.   [19] O. R., 21, 645.

for the entire distance, ran the R. F. & P. railroad.[20] About half a mile East of the railway was the old Richmond Stage Road, styled also the Bowling Green Road.[21] Another 800 yards or a little more, East of the highway, was the Rappahannock. From the railroad to the river, the ground was almost level and was clear of woods,[22] except at one point. About 1300 yards by air from Hamilton's Crossing, a boggy little ravine had its head close to the railroad track and extended eastward in the direction of the river. Along this ravine, and on its borders, for a quarter of a mile was a narrow triangle of woods, which had a base, at the railroad, of perhaps 200 yards.[23] To avoid this bad ground, doubly uncomfortable in winter, the nearest Confederate units had been placed on either side. Lane's Brigade, which was about 150 yards in advance of the general line of the Division, had its right flank about 250 yards from the left of the projecting triangle of woods.[24] Archer's Brigade was close to the right or Southeast of the tangled, sodden woods.[25]

That is to say, about 500 or 600 yards of front, between Archer's left and Lane's right, were not occupied by troops. Was it safe to leave so wide a gap? With the batteries placed as they were, Powell Hill apparently thought the gap would offer no danger, provided troops were placed on the higher ground in rear of the boggy wood. He accordingly stationed Gregg some 500 or 600 yards West of the railroad and roughly parallel to the gap between Archer and Lane.[26] As he was the Brigadier most directly concerned, "Jim" Lane took pains to make known the existence of the gap to Maxcy Gregg and Col. Peter Turney who, because of Archer's sickness, was directing the Tennessee Brigade.[27] Later, when Lane met General Hill, he explained to his chief where the

[20] It is on the same right of way now (1943).

[21] In some of the reports the name "Port Royal Road" also is used. This stretch of it is now part of U.S. Route 2.

[22] General Meade noted in his report: "Owing to the wood nothing could be seen of [the Confederates], while all our movements on the cleared ground were exposed to their view." O. R., 21, 510. Other descriptions of the ground, as seen from the Federal side, will be found in ibid., 449, 453, 511.

[23] The "boggy wood," as General Taliaferro termed it, O. R., 21, 676, appears clearly on the Michler map of 1867.

[24] O. R., 21, 645, 653.

[25] Von Borcke, op. cit., 2, 106, was mistaken in his memory of the dimensions of the wood. See the sketch infra, p. 353.

[26] Ibid., 654.

[27] It was so styled, though it included the Fifth Alabama battalion and the Nineteenth Georgia regiment along with three Tennessee regiments. Cf. O R., 21, 542

different units were located. In his subsequent report, Lane did not record any comment by Hill on his explanation.

Jackson probably heard nothing on the 12th about the gap in his corps front, though he rode the length of the line.[28] He devoted part of his day to a dangerous reconnaissance with the commanding General, who was anxious to know the strength of the Federals in order to be quite sure the movement across the river was not a feint to cover a thrust farther down the Rappahannock.[29] In the afternoon, Jackson rode to the river at a point beyond the extreme Federal left. So content was he that as he jogged back toward Hamilton's Crossing he whistled without arousing any protest from tone-sensitive members of his staff. He found his wagons near Powell Hill's headquarters and he pitched camp just in the rear of that officer. So far as is known, there was no visiting between corps and divisional headquarters that night.[30]

The remembered chill of that windy night of December 12 was relieved, for all save the pickets, by hundreds of camp-fires.[31] "Jube" Early and Harvey Hill were on the march up the Rappahannock.[32] Taliaferro had his men in the assigned reserve position behind Powell Hill.[33] To the left of Hill, the Division of Hood was moved nearer. Hood's instructions from Longstreet were to co-operate with Hill or with any other of Jackson's troops.[34] Where the men rested and warmed themselves and talked of the coming battle, confidence was complete. Why not? The position was stronger than any the Army of Northern Virginia ever had occupied. Reserves would be ample. Artillery that had been outranged in the duel across the Rappahannock would take its toll when those tens of thousands who crowded the fields and the town undertook to assault the ridge . . . if they were foolish enough to do so.

---

[28] On this point, Henderson unintentionally misled. In *op. cit.*, 2, 310, he quoted substantially the language of his *Fredericksburg* and said that Jackson "himself predicted" that the boggy woodland "would be the scene of the severest fighting." Henderson's uncited authority for this evidently was *Dabney*, 610; but that reference was to comment Jackson made on the morning of December 13, not to earlier prediction.

[29] 2 *R. E. Lee*, 450–51.

[30] *Hotchkiss' MS Diary*, 115, is detailed for December 12, but is without reference to any meeting of Hill and Jackson.

[31] Several nights were immoderately cold for the first fortnight of December. Jones remarked in his diary that on the morning of December 7 in Richmond there was ice on his wash-stand within five feet of the fire. "Is this," he asked, "the 'Sunny South' the North is fighting to possess?" (1 *R. W. C. D.*, 205).

[32] *O. R.*, 21, 643, 663.   [33] *Ibid.*, 630, 675.

[34] *Ibid.*, 622.

Much the worst of the day's happenings had been in Fredericksburg itself, where numerous noncombatants had remained
throughout the bombardment.[35] The plundering to which they
were subjected, Maj. Francis E. Pierce [36] thus described at the
time: ". . . Boys came into our place *loaded* with *silver* pitchers,
silver spoons, silver lamps and castors, etc. Great three-story
houses furnished magnificently were broken into and their contents scattered over the floors and trampled on by the muddy feet
of the soldiers. Splendid alabaster vases and pieces of statuary
were thrown at 6 and 700 dollar mirrors. Closets of the very finest
china were broken into and their contents smashed onto the floor
and stamped to pieces. Finest cut glass ware goblets were hurled
at nice plate glass windows, beautifully embroidered window cur-
tains torn down, rosewood pianos piled in the street and burned
or soldiers would get on top of them and kick the key-board and
internal machinery all to pieces. Little table ornaments kicking
in every direction—wine cellars broken into and the soldiers drinking all they could and then opening the faucets and let the rest run
out. Boys go to a barrel of flour and take a pailful and use enough
to make one batch of pancakes and then pour the rest in the street
—everything turned upside down. The soldiers seemed to delight
in destroying everything. Libraries worth thousands of dollars
were overhauled and thrown on the floor and in the streets . . .
I cannot begin to describe the scenes of destruction. It was so
throughout the whole city and from its appearance very many
wealthy families must have inhabited it." [37]

Well it was, perhaps, that the gray men on the gray hills behind
Fredericksburg knew nothing of this. Had they been aware of
the plundering and the purposeless destruction, the battle of December 13 might have been marked by hot vindictiveness and not
by cold, defiant repulse. A strange battle in any event it was to be
—unique for the Virginia campaigns in that officers and men of
one Corps could display their prowess and, when not engaged,

35 *W. W. Blackford's MS Memoirs*, 282: "In spite of all warnings many people had
remained in the town. When the cannonade began many of them came pouring out
in great fright, but even after the bombardment some remained, and some of them
were ladies."
36 Later Colonel of the 108th New York and Brevet Brigadier General.
37 F. E. Pierce to "Ed," Dec. 17, 1862, MS copy, *Pender MSS*. Major Pierce is not
mentioned in the Federal reports on Fredericksburg, but the verifiable statements in his
letter check completely with those of his brigade commander, Col. O. H. Palmer, 2nd
Brig., 3rd Div., II Corps, in *O. R.*, 21, 300.

could observe at a distance the soldierly conduct of the other Corps. Because the Army of Northern Virginia stood easily on the defensive, men were to look back on the events of December 13 with clear memory and were to recall the details of the wintry drama—

> "How such a one was strong, and such was bold
> And such was fortunate . . ."

The 13th of December dawned cold. Spotsylvania's hills were damp with the fog that covered the river valley. Though much was heard, little was seen of the enemy. At 7.17 the sun rose red and fiery behind the Federal left and promised from a cloudless sky to drive away the moisture.[38] Ere the fog began to thin, most of Lee's lieutenants were moving along their lines to see that all was in order. "Peter" Longstreet was in his battle mood—brusque but hearty, alert but perfectly composed, eager for a new adventure. When he rode to his right, he found Hood convinced, by the loudness of the sound carried in the fog, that the attack was to be on the front of Law and the Texans. Longstreet did not believe it. Burnside's chief assault on that flank, he told Hood and Pickett, would be South of them, and on Jackson's front. The two right Divisions of the First Corps, he explained to their commanders, must be prepared to deliver a counter attack on the Federal flank should Jackson's line be broken. As for his own front— again to paraphrase Longstreet's later narrative—he expected to be assailed farther North, near his left center, where he felt that he was strong enough to beat off the enemy without calling either on Pickett or on Hood.[39] In his judgment of the enemy's objective, Longstreet had changed somewhat during the morning.

Back to his left center, on Marye's Heights, Longstreet accordingly rode, and there he found Robert Ransom with Walker's demi-Division. Later in the morning, when the advance of the Federals from the town was visible, Longstreet again met Ransom and said of the high ground North of Hazel Run: "Remember, General, I place that salient in your keeping. Do what is needful and call on Anderson if you want help."[40] For the guardians of

[38] *Hotchkiss' MS Diary*, 117. *Cf.* the account of the battle as written by the correspondent of the London *Times*, reprinted in 6 *Moore's Rebellion Record*, 109: "The day . . . was one of those outbursts of that Indian summer which lingers long and fondly in beautiful Virginia . . ."

[39] 3 *B. & L.*, 75–76.   [40] 3 *B. & L.*, 94.

his field pieces, as for Ransom, the commander of the First Corps had confident words. When the men of the Washington Artillery told him atop Marye's Heights that the engineers had said the gunners had ruined their earthwork by heightening it, Longstreet approved the care displayed by the men of the red badge. Said he cheerily, "If we only save the finger of a man, that's good enough!" [41]

Soon, in conversation with Porter Alexander, who was about to fight his first battle as commander of a battalion of First Corps artillery, "Old Pete" suggested that the Lieutenant Colonel place an idle gun where it could command ground in front of Marye's Hill. Young Alexander answered, earnestly and with pride: "General, we cover that ground now so well that we comb it as with a fine-tooth comb. A chicken could not live in that field when we open on it!" That pleased Longstreet,[42] and sent him in high humor to the commanding eminence near the center of the line, where General Lee had established field headquarters.[43]

Thither Jackson was making his way. At his camp in rear of Powell Hill's headquarters, "Old Blue Light" had risen early, and had ordered the wagons packed and sent to the rear. His own toilet was made with uncommon care. For reasons known to himself only, he decided that he would wear that day the uniform coat "Jeb" Stuart had given him in October—the coat of resplendent gold braid—as well as the hat Hotchkiss had presented him at Martinsburg on the march to Harpers Ferry.[44] Thus glorified, "Old Jack" was dazzling to the eye if manifestly embarrassed.[45] The remarks of his men did not lessen his discomfort. Said one soldier, with a shake of his head, "Old Jack will be afraid of his clothes and will not get down to work." [46] Another private shouted: "Come here, boys! Stonewall has drawed his bounty and has bought himself some new clothes!" [47] Everywhere along the

[41] *Owen,* 176. [42] 3 *B. & L.,* 79.

[43] It should be noted that the sequence of Longstreet's movements on the morning of December 13 is not established positively, though the order followed here seems the most probable.

[44] Jackson must have worn this hat, with the brim turned down all around, from the time Jed Hotchkiss presented it to him. The "old gray cap" Jackson entrusted to Hotchkiss at Martinsburg and finally gave it to him Dec. 10, 1862. Cf. *supra,* p. 319 and *Hotchkiss' MS Diary,* 113.

[45] Cf. R. K. Charles in 14 *C. V.,* 66: "[Jackson] seemed to be a little ashamed of a splendid new uniform he wore . . ."

[46] Fitz Lee, *General Lee,* 227.

[47] *Douglas,* 205.

line, there was the same astonishment over Jackson's appearance.[48]

As he passed the front of Lane, the commander of the Second
Corps halted and, apparently for the first time, studied closely
the boggy wood that projected toward the Federals. "The enemy
will attack here," he said grimly.[49] On his arrival at the hill—
from that hour "Lee's Hill" [50]—where "Marse Robert" was waiting for the fog to lift, Jackson created no less of a sensation than
on the lines. Lee, of course, made no remark about the unwonted
smartness of Jackson's appearance; Longstreet trained his eye but
reserved his verbal fire; "Jeb" Stuart, who also had ridden up,
was delighted Jackson was using on so great a day a present from
affectionate hands.

When conversation turned to the battle that soon would begin,
Jackson forgot his clothes in zealous advocacy of immediate attack. He reminded the General that after the fog lifted the long-
range Federal batteries would have a clear target; but if the Confederates assailed the blue infantry while the fog hung low, the
Union artillery would be useless. By all means, said Jackson, the
order for a general advance from the hills into the plain should
be given. "Jeb" Stuart seconded his hero's proposal, but Lee shook
his head. The odds were too great, he said. It was the course of
wisdom to receive the attack, to reduce the odds, to wear down
the enemy and then to take the offensive.[51] This doubtless was
Longstreet's view also.[52]

Jackson acquiesced in the decision of the commanding General,
as he always did, heartily and without reservation, but he pondered the move he should make when the enemy's attack on his
front collapsed. Would there be opportunity of a counter stroke?
In the hope there might be, he would make ready.[53] While he
pondered, Lee rode off with Stuart to examine the position held
by the cavalry, and to ascertain whether the Federals were extending their left. Should that move be under way, the enemy might

---

[48] 2 *N. C. Regts.*, 556; 1 *Land We Love*, 75.

[49] *Dabney*, 610. See *supra*, p. 343, n. 28.

[50] For the range of vision from Lee's Hill, see *Stiles*, 134.

[51] See the references in 2 *R. E. Lee*, 454.

[52] That is to say, in none of his writings on the battle did Longstreet record disapproval of strategy and tactics which, at Fredericksburg, accorded with his oft-
expressed preference for the tactical defensive.

[53] See *infra*, p. 359 ff.

turn the extreme right, which appeared to be the weakest part of the Confederate position.[54] Stuart's horse artillery must be vigilant there.

By 10 o'clock, with a mystic majesty that made eyes brighten and cheeks flush, the scene visible from Lee's Hill began to change. The wide valley of the Rappahannock took on the appearance of a mighty vessel, filled with a shining, opaque fluid the level of which was being lowered every moment. Salvos from the Stafford Heights first gave warning that the loftiest Confederate positions already could be seen by the foe. Then, above the swirling silver of the fog, the church steeples of the little town could be distinguished. Down, down the fog sank toward the draining river until the mustered lines of blue, the ambulances, the ordnance wagons and the batteries could be discerned. The spectacle stirred Longstreet. He began to joke Jackson about the number of troops that manifestly were being concentrated to attack the Confederate right.

"Are you not scared by that file of Yankees you have before you down there?"

Jackson's retort was grimly honest: "Wait till they come a little nearer, and they shall either scare me or I'll scare them!"[55]

Presently, as Jackson started to mount, Longstreet inquired again, "What are you going to do with all those people over there?"

Jackson doubtless answered in the spirit of his deepest impulse as a soldier, "Sir, we will give them the bayonet."[56]

Back on the front of his Corps, Jackson was greeted with a swelling Federal fire and every evidence of a brewing infantry attack. He was prepared. With Colonel Crutchfield, he carefully had placed the guns of the Second Corps where they could enfilade at close range at least a part of any advancing line.[57] Jackson was re-examining the situation when Heros von Borcke, who happened to be near, availed himself of his privileged standing as a foreign soldier and voiced some anxiety over the near approach of the unchallenged Federals. Jackson was more than uncon-

[54] Cf. *Early*, 171.

[55] London *Times*, quoted in 6 *Moore's Rebellion Record*, 110. This may be an earlier and more nearly accurate version of the exchange than the one quoted in *Dabney*, 611.

[56] *Sorrel*, 138.

[57] Crutchfield's report, *O. R.*, 21, 636, contained his appreciation of the field of fire.

cerned: he was pleased. "Major, my men have sometimes failed to take a position, but to defend one, never![58] I am glad the Yankees are coming."[59] A few minutes later, Jackson directed that the horse artillery open against the Federal left flank, which he believed he could rake.

The duel that followed on the Confederate right was the most dramatic of all those in which John Pelham had been engaged. To a singular degree, he had been privileged at Williamsburg, at Gaines' Mill, at Evelington Heights, at Sharpsburg and at White's Ford to have the stage set for his performance, but never had he been so much observed as now he was.

When Stuart told him to prepare for action, Pelham asked if he might take two guns and advance on the road from Hamilton's Crossing to the intersection of the Richmond Stage Road. There he would be in advance of the Confederate line but in admirable position to send his missiles almost down the front of a column that was moving against Jackson. A bold, an almost foolhardy proposal this was—an invitation to a counter-bombardment that might kill the men and wreck the guns. Plain as that was to Stuart, his fighting blood triumphed over his judgment: Pelham might go!

Quickly the blond young Major chose his guns—a Blakely rifle and a twelve-pounder Napoleon—and amid the cheers of his comrades, he dashed off. At the crossroads, he found precisely the target he had expected: Union infantrymen were facing him as a flanking party. Others, by the thousand, were advancing toward the ridge where A. P. Hill was awaiting them. The moment his gunners could unlimber and load, Pelham opened with solid shot on the heavy column that was moving almost at right angles to his position. His first round startled the Federals, his second confused the line. For the moment, but for the moment only, he enjoyed the thrill of fighting a Division of infantry with a section of artillery. Furious Federal guns speedily were turned on him.

[58] Had he forgotten Kernstown?
[59] 2 *von Borcke*, 117. The Major was under the impression that Jackson was withholding his fire because Lee had given orders that the artillery were not to open until the Federals "had come within easy canister range." Official reports contain no reference to any such order. On the contrary, Crutchfield, *O. R.*, 21, 636, made plain that he it was who directed Walker to reserve fire for the Federal infantry until "it should come within effective range." The sequence of Jackson's various movements on the morning of December 13 is approximate only. Reports are at variance. Memoirs, in some instances, contradict official reports.

If he was accurate in his fire, the blue artillerists were far from blind. In exchange for a fine shot that broke the axle of a Union field piece,[60] he received a blast that put his obstreperous Blakely out of action. Four batteries soon were trying to hit[61] his solitary Napoleon. Undaunted, Pelham gave the only answer he could, the answer of redoubled fire. So fast did his men serve their gun that a Union General thought Pelham had a battery.[62]

Superb it was, but it could not persist otherwise than by the slaughter of the grimy boys who worked their bronze field piece as if the Confederacy hung on their fire. "Jeb" Stuart sensed this quickly and bade von Borcke ride out and say that the gun might be withdrawn whenever Pelham saw fit. Pelham would not hear of it. "Tell the General I can hold my ground," he answered, and kept his gun roaring. From time to time, he shifted his position, and of every undulation of the nearby ground he took full advantage.

Although Pelham's men were dropping fast, the loss seemed justified because the whole menacing Federal line now had halted. Evidently its commander intended to advance no more until Pelham was silenced. Again came word from Stuart that the gun might be moved to cover; again Pelham's reply was that he could continue the fight. When the fall of one other man left him without a full squad, Pelham himself assisted in serving the gun. Not until Stuart's third message had reached him and the caissons were almost empty did Pelham limber up and, amid a pursuing blaze of shells, drive back to Hamilton's Crossing.[63]

Ere that, from Lee's Hill, the glasses of the commanding General had been turned to the right. Lee's deep admiring voice had inquired to what battery that defiant gun belonged. When told that it was Pelham's, the comment was, "It is glorious to see such courage in one so young!"[64] Less dramatic but no less apprecia-

---

[60] The third gun of Battery A, 1st Pennsylvania Field Artillery. O. R., 21, 514.

[61] O. R., 21, 553.

[62] Cf. Meade in O. R., 21, 511. Union artillerists apparently were of the same opinion.

[63] The Blakely must have been sent to the rear as soon as it was disabled.

[64] 2 R. E. Lee, 457. Often, in the South, as old soldiers told the story of Pelham at Fredericksburg, they would say that when Lee was informed that the gun was Captain Pelham's, he announced, "Major Pelham he is from this day." In reality, Pelham had been promoted Major as of Aug. 16, 1862 (Mercer's Pelham, 70). Renowned as was the battle of one gun against four batteries, first-hand accounts are few. Neither Stuart nor Pelham filed any report on Fredericksburg. Colonel Crutchfield, though he paid tribute to Pelham's conduct (O. R., 21, 638), did not feel that a detailed accoun

tive was the tribute of one of the cavalrymen who supported Pelham. Said G. W. Beale: "Very serious fears were felt that our gun could not be extricated from its dangerous position, and that the Federal cannoneers . . . would cut deadly swaths through our ranks. Two circumstances saved us: one was the intrepid hardihood of Pelham, with his one gun and its rapid fire, and the other the fortunate fog, which wrapped us from view in its dense and friendly folds." [65]

Now that Pelham had withdrawn from the flank and the fog had lifted, the Federal batteries opened violently on the hill where fourteen of A. P. Hill's guns were hidden as well as the ground permitted. Jackson watched without anxiety. He believed that Hill's artillery would be able to beat off the infantry who evidently were about to resume their advance. To eliminate what he believed a remote risk, Jackson already had ordered up guns to lay a cross fire from the position to which Pelham had withdrawn. Until the proper minute arrived, all the Confederate batteries were to remain inactive. No matter how furiously the Federals belabored the hill, the divisional Chief of Artillery, Lt. Col. R. Lindsay Walker, was to forbid the dispatch of even one answering shell. Hard and humiliating it was for Southern gunners to hug the cold earth and passively to watch the shells break around them or over them; but for close to an hour, they had to do just that.

At the end of that time, the Federals apparently had concluded that the batteries on the hill had been destroyed and that the position could be stormed. Those long, awe-inspiring blue ranks began to move. Onward, straight for the ridge, came thousands of Federals across the open fields. No challenge met them; not even a skirmisher fired ere he fell back. To the mad music of the shotted guns, the Federals appeared to be staging a dress parade. Within 1000 yards they came; 900 it was; 800 yards. Then a hoarsely shouted order was repeated by each gray battery commander. Almost before the words were uttered, the lanyards

of the action by the guns of the Cavalry Division came within the scope of a report on the artillery of the Second Corps. Pendleton's report dealt primarily with the reserve artillery and contained bare mention of Pelham (*ibid.*, 566). It was much to Pelham's honor that the least meager official accounts of his fight were those of Jackson (*ibid.*, 631) and of Lee (*ibid.*, 553). The most intimate unofficial narrative is that of von Borcke, *op. cit.*, 2, 117 ff.
[65] *G. W. Beale,* 64.

were pulled. The shells of fourteen guns went screaming toward the blue line. Far on the Confederate right, like a distant pack that takes up the cry of the nearer hounds, Pelham's re-enforced horse artillery began instantly to bark. The startled Federal infantry hesitated a moment but responded gallantly to the words of their officers, and steadfastly pushed on again. Once more and still once more the artillery of Hill and of Stuart tore the ranks. There was a wavering, a halt and then a slow recoil.[66]

That is to say, the blue soldiers fell back, but neither they nor their officers quit the field. They merely withdrew beyond effective range. In a short time, as Jackson and Stuart watched, they saw the enemy mend his broken lines and perfect his formation. His artillery never paused in its fire. There was no hurry, no loitering in the Federal ranks. Cold, determined preparation was any man's to see through the smoke. About 1 P.M. across the fields the Federals advanced again in three long, massive lines. This time, evidently, a general assault was to be delivered and was to be supported by every gun the Federals could bring to bear.[67] The whole front of A. P. Hill was to be assailed. On the neck of woodland that extended beyond the railroad—the woods that represented part of the gap in the lines of the Light Division—the first blow would fall.

Hill's divisional artillery, which had beaten off the earlier attack, responded magnificently. As might be expected of men who had Willie Pegram and David McIntosh among their Captains, the Confederate gunners defiantly matched the Union fury. Again from the right, where he was reinforced by well manned batteries, John Pelham crossed his fire with Walker's.[68] For a few minutes, it looked as if this fire might drive back the Federals again. The lines slowed down, hesitated and retired ever so little. Jackson, Hill, every leader watched hopefully. Was it over? No! Instead of turning back, the Union troops pushed more furiously onward. Now they were within rifle range. Vol-

[66] O. R., 21, 553, 631, 638, 649. In this and the subsequent action on the Confederate right, the fire of the Union artillery was described by Southern observers as "remarkably accurate." John Esten Cooke recorded in his *Jackson*, 372, that when the graycoats opened with a Blakely gun, a Federal field piece answered "like an echo." The shot crashed among the Confederate cannoneers. "General," a soldier called to Stuart, who was nearby, "their very first shot has killed two men."

[67] O. R., 21, 632. [68] Cf. O. R., 21, 638.

leys echoed down the front. The Federals answered and came on.
Soon the volleys gave way to fire-at-will. Every man loaded and
rammed and pulled the trigger as fast as he might. Many a whining Southern minié ball found its mark, many Federals fell
under the artillery fire; but there was no halting now. Northern
blood was up. The front line was entering the apex of the triangle

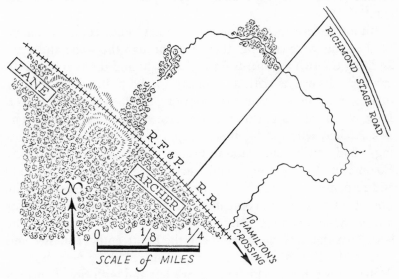

"The Gap" or "Boggy Wood" on Jackson's Front at Fredericksburg, Dec. 13, 1862. The
position of Lane and of Archer is approximate only—after N. Michler

of boggy woods. Lane's men on the railroad, in advance of the
main line, were at grips with the enemy.

From left to right, Lane had the Seventh North Carolina, the
Eighteenth, the Thirty-third, the Twenty-eighth and the Thirty-
seventh—veteran regiments all, but sadly diminished in strength.
Between the Thirty-third and the Twenty-eighth, a rise of about
twenty feet in the ground East of the railroad served to give the
three left regiments of the Brigade a measure of protection from
the hostile fire; [69] but this slight elevation served at the same time
to deflect the Federal attack toward Lane's right and directly into
the gap between him and Archer. The left element of Archer's
Brigade was the Nineteenth Georgia; next it, toward the right,

[69] O. R., 21, 654.

was the Fourteenth Tennessee.[70] Then came the Seventh Tennessee, the First Tennessee—a distinguished regiment—and on the extreme right, the excellent Fifth Alabama Battalion. As soon as Archer saw that the Federals were penetrating the gap, he started the Alabamians from his right toward his left and sent back word to General Gregg that it was time for the South Carolinians to advance from their reserve position and to close the gap.[71]

Almost before these precautions or any other could be taken, the Federals were crashing their way through the wood and were assailing the two regiments on Lane's right and the two on Archer's left. It was a critical moment for both Brigades and for their commanders. In his first hour of combat as a general officer, Lane was having a test that might have shaken steel nerves. The sick Archer, who got his first glimpse of the ground that morning,[72] had a well man's task and more. Fortunately for Lane, the Colonel of the right regiment, the Thirty-seventh, was a steady and responsible soldier, W. M. Barbour. Promptly he refused the line of his three right companies on the side of the gap and, for a time, maintained a bristling front. On the opposite side of the boggy wood, the Georgia regiment, the Fourteenth Tennessee and part of the Seventh broke under pressure of the attack, but the Alabamians came quickly to Archer's left and with fire of surprising power, held on tenaciously. The right companies of the Seventh Tennessee and the whole of the First, which occupied some shallow trenches, were able to stand their ground and to keep the enemy at bay.

For reinforcement, Archer sent directly to Hill,[73] and doubtless he called on Col. J. M. Brockenbrough, who was commanding on his right the excellent Brigade of Charlie Field.[74] Help was asked also by Lane. When he learned that his Twenty-eighth and Thirty-seventh were close to the bottom of their cartridge

[70] Hill's report, *O. R.*, 21, 646, mentioned these two regiments in the reversed order, but Col. J. W. Lockert's report, *ibid.*, 661, shows that the Georgia regiment was the flank element.

[71] *O. R.*, 21, 657.   [72] *O. R.*, 21, 656.

[73] *Early*, 172.

[74] Field, it will be recalled, had sustained a wound at Second Manassas and had not yet recovered fully. Neither Hill, *O. R.*, 21, 646, nor Brockenbrough, *ibid.*, 650, stated that Archer asked Field's Brigade for help, but as those troops were on the right of Archer and were not engaged, it is a safe guess that Archer sought the aid of Brockenbrough.

boxes, he hurried off an officer to notify General Thomas, who was to his left and rear, that the North Carolina Brigade was hard pressed.[75]

Before Thomas could do more than start his regiments toward the gap, the Federals slipped around the north side of the low hill on Lane's front and got between the right of the Thirty-third and the left of the Twenty-eighth. This meant that the Twenty-eighth and the Thirty-seventh, which was to the right and next the gap, were in danger of envelopment. They had to give ground. Stubbornly and in good order they withdrew a few hundred paces. The other regiments of Lane had to conform, though the left regiment did not yield more than fifty yards.[76]

Through the gap, the enemy now could pour thousands of men, but precisely what the Federals were doing, amid the smoke and confusion, Hill's subordinates could not ascertain. Of divisional staff work, there was none. Except as the brigade commanders informed one another, they were in the dark. Gregg must have known that he stood in rear of a gap,[77] but if he was cognizant of dispositions on the morning of December 13, he must have shared the general belief that the enemy could not penetrate the gap. He had been acting all morning as if he were in a secure second-line position. Arms had been stacked; under such cover as the woods offered, the men had been told to lie down in order that they might protect themselves from the Federal artillery.

Orr's Rifles, who were Gregg's right regiment, had obeyed in-structions; but, as the sound of musketry rolled toward them, they became restive. Of a sudden, without so much as a shout of warning, Orr's veterans found the Federals upon them. Up sprang the Carolinians to run for their stacked weapons. Some of the bluecoats, as surprised as the Confederates, opened fire. Men dropped. Others stood as if paralyzed by doubt. Many saw they could not reach the stacks before the Unionists did. Gregg heard the rattle and the yells, but in his deafness he became confused and mistook the attacking Federals for retiring Confederates who might be shot down by his men.

---

[75] *O. R.*, 21, 653.   [76] *Ibid.*, 655.

[77] Caldwell, *op. cit.*, 59, stated that "Gen. Gregg was not aware of the interval between Lane's and Archer's brigades," but, as stated already in the text, Lane reported, *O. R.*, 21, 654, that on the 12th he "informed General Gregg of this opening" and understood that Gregg was to be his support.

Swiftly toward the right of his line, Gregg galloped along a rough new military road. When he reached Orr's regiment, he yelled to the men to leave the stacked arms alone and to stop firing. There followed a moment of new hesitation, but it ended in a quick rush of the Federals. Before the Confederates could load their rifles, or even grab them, common sense demanded flight. Away ran as many of Orr's men as could escape. Gregg, directly between his retreating soldiers and the pursuing Federals, was shot from his horse.[78]

Gallantly the Unionists had thrust, but now they could not push farther the spearhead of their attack. The First South Carolina stopped the infiltration;[79] from either side of the gap, the Confederates began to close in. Field's Brigade sent aid to Archer;[80] Thomas hurried down the military road to relieve Lane;[81] farther to the rear, "Old Jube" was resolving a doubt. Archer's courier, searching for A. P. Hill, had found Early and had told him of the plight of the Tennesseans. While the courier was relating what he knew of the trouble at the front, a staff officer arrived from Jackson with orders for Early to hold himself in readiness to move to the right, where the enemy was making a demonstration. Which call should Early heed? He chewed and spat and inwardly debated. At the instant, Lt. Ham Chamberlayne, adjutant of Hill's artillery, dashed up and drew rein. There was, he said, an "awful gulf" between Archer and Lane. If it were not closed and the enemy driven, all the batteries to the right would be lost. That decided the question for Early, though he still felt some embarrassment because of lack of familiarity with the ground.[82] He ordered forward Lawton's Brigade and Trimble's,[83] and he had Col. James A. Walker advance Early's own Brigade to the flank of Gregg.

As Early's veterans overtook those of Hill's distinguished regiments that had been driven from the front, they had many jests: "Here comes old Jubal; let old Jubal straighten that fence; Jubal's boys are always getting Hill out o' trouble!"[84] To some of Archer's hard pressed men, the arrival of these troops was the first evidence they had that a powerful second line was behind them.[85]

[78] Caldwell, 59.
[80] O. R., 21, 650.
[82] Early, 172.
[84] 3 B. & L., 140.
[79] O. R., 21, 652.
[81] Ibid., 653, 655.
[83] O. R., 21, 664.
[85] Ibid.

The strength of that line they soon appreciated. Early launched his counter attack furiously. With help on both flanks, he pushed down the ridge and drove every Federal regiment out of the gap. Two of Early's Brigades were not content with that. Once started, they could not be stopped. They pressed far beyond the railroad and, in withdrawing, suffered heavily.[86] Some of the advancing officers remembered, after the affair ended, that as they ran over the ground where Orr's rifles had been stacked, they had seen a man pull himself painfully up by the side of a little tree, and wave them onward. It was Maxcy Gregg.[87]

The battle on the Confederate right did not end with Early's counter attack. Southern artillery had put a heavy price on the advance of the Federals and now it exacted a toll of the retreating bluecoats, but the batteries paid dearly on their own account. By repeated firing, the Federals had found the exact range of Walker's position, and they pounded it mercilessly. Several of the guns that had opened the engagements had to be withdrawn. In their place, Jackson advanced Poague with two 20-pounder Parrotts. Orders from "Old Jack" directly to Poague were that these long-range guns should be employed against the Union artillery till the counter fire was too hot. Then Poague was to turn his guns on the Federal infantry.[88] Poague did as he was told and did it so brilliantly that John Pelham, who came up to watch the firing, had nothing but compliments for the battery from Jackson's town. "Well," said Pelham, "you men stand killing better than any I ever saw!"[89]

It was "hot" everywhere on Jackson's right, though Poague and Walker were catching the worst of the fire. As an old gunner, Jackson observed this bombardment with keen eye. His spirits were high. During a lull, he rode out to the extreme right where all day he was more or less apprehensive of attack. Dismounting, he went forward with no companion except his aide, James Power Smith, whom both he and Lee delighted to tease. As Jackson and Smith were walking forward to reconnoitre, a bullet whizzed past between their heads. Said Jackson in calm delight: "Mr. Smith, had you not better go to the rear? They may shoot you!"[90]

86 *O. R.,* 21, 632–33, 664–65, 672. For Early, see *infra,* Chap. XXVI *et seq.*
87 *Oates,* 166. For Gregg, see p. 374.
88 *O. R.,* 21, 633; E. A. Moore, 163. For the possibility that a projectile from one of these guns may have killed Gen. Geo. D. Bayard, see *infra,* p. 393, n. 93.
89 *E. A. Moore.* 162.   90 *Mrs. Jackson,* 369.

Other leaders had escapes as narrow. "Jeb" Stuart, who usually was to be found where the rain of minié balls was heaviest, galloped up and down the right wing and reconnoitered several times beyond it. Once he rode within 200 or 300 yards of some Federal sharpshooters who were hidden behind a hedge. That square, stout figure of his on a tall horse was an ideal mark. The Federal marksmen strained over their sights and sent two bullets through his clothes, but they did not injure him.[91]

On Jackson's left, whither the fight seemed to be drifting, action was not close. The Federals advanced many skirmishers and sharpshooters and several times threatened an attack which they did not see fit to press. Spitefully their artillery explored the position before which the infantry hesitated. Two Confederate batteries answered, Carter Braxton's and Greenlee Davidson's; but Braxton was sick[92] and about 11 o'clock[93] was relieved by five guns sent from Early's Division. These pieces and their squads were selected by Capt. J. W. Latimer, acting chief of artillery, who posted them and then could not tear himself away from them. His men and Davidson's gallantly endured a steady fire; Pender's Brigade, which was supporting the guns, suffered even more. Dorsey Pender, as usual, was wounded—this time by a bullet that passed between the bones of his left arm. As he rode along the line, with the injured member hanging down and blood flowing from the fingers, Col. A. M. Scales came up and observed, "General, I see you are wounded."

Pender answered: "Oh, that is a trifle; no bones broken. I want you to send at least two companies down to the railroad and drive those scoundrels out!"[94] Pender had to go to the rear and have his wound attended, but he soon was back on the field.[95] He found little to do defensively on the lines of the Second Corps. Burnside had shifted his battle to Longstreet's front in one of the most ghastly and dramatic assaults of American war.

[91] *Cooke's Jackson*, 375.   [92] *O. R.*, 21, 648.
[93] *O. R.*, 21, 669.
[94] 1 *N. C. Regts.*, 665. The author of the anecdote had Pender continue, "They are killing Colonel Cutts' men and horses," but this manifestly was a confusion of names or of places. None of Cutts's guns was in front of Pender. Those of his troops in advanced position near the railroad were part of Col. John S. McElroy's Sixteenth North Carolina.
[95] *O. R.*, 21, 647. For the next episode in Pender's career, see *infra*, Chap. XXXII.

CHAPTER XXII

Longstreet Wins an Easy Victory

At 11 o'clock on the morning of December 13, three hours before the attack ended on Jackson's front, Longstreet had opened with his artillery in the hope of relieving the pressure on the Confederate right.[1] The Federals seemed to have been waiting for the artillery of the First Corps to disclose its position. Union batteries responded wrathfully and at once.

On the edge of the town nearest the heights, the Federals visibly were massing in great numbers for an assault. Nothing could have been more acceptable to Longstreet. He had abundant infantry on strong ground; ample reserves were nearby; the Confederate batteries had been located admirably. "Old Pete" had simply to wait for the oncoming wave to break itself in ghastly loss against the heights, but meantime, of course, he had to protect his advanced units. "Dick" Anderson's left Brigade[2] was somewhat exposed; if it were driven back, Anderson might be compelled to withdraw the whole of his Division to the high ground. Were this to happen, Cobb would be enfiladed and would be required to conform. Warning to this effect Longstreet put in writing and sent to Cobb through the Washington Artillery, which was on the hill above the Georgians. When Cobb read the note, he could not repress one proud assurance: "Well," said he, "if they wait for me to fall back, they will wait a long time!"[3]

[1] O. R., 21, 570.
[2] This was Cadmus Wilcox's Brigade, the position of which, close to the river bank and exposed to an enfilade, is explained in Wilcox's report, O. R., 21, 611-13.
[3] Owen, 184; 3 B. & L., 97-98. General McLaws related how he received notice from Cobb that Anderson planned to withdraw to the heights should the Union attack be directed against Anderson's Division. McLaws stated that he then went to Longstreet, who sent Pickett to reinforce Anderson and told Anderson to hold his ground until forced to yield it. This did not satisfy McLaws. After a ride to the left convinced him that "preparations for defense . . . were incomplete and inconsiderable," McLaws said, he brought over Kershaw to secure the flank of McLaws's Division and sent word to that effect to Cobb (3 B. & L., 91-92). In much of this, McLaws was confused. None of the official reports, including his own, bear out McLaws's memory of the incident. Some of the reports at least inferentially contradict him.

Almost as if to mock him, the Federals at that moment made the first move toward an attack. In front of Longstreet's left and center, close to the town, ran the spillway of a canal.[4] The bank of this, facing the Confederates, was high enough to serve as a trench. Across the spillway were several bridges, toward which the Federals now rushed. "Hi, hi, hi," they yelled and, crossing, deployed under the bank and in the field that led to the sunken road. In the line of advance from the spillway to the road, at a distance of about 400 yards from the wall, spread a swale that offered some shelter. Numerous obstacles there were--houses, boundary marks, gardens [5] and, heaviest of all, a long plank fence. None of these obstacles did the Federals intend to skirt. They manifestly purposed to drive straight to the road and to attempt to storm the heights. It seemed inconceivable that an effort would be made, but there before Southern eyes was the evidence of their preparation and, about noon,[6] the reality of their advance.

They were coming! As they moved forward, their artillery covered them from Stafford Heights and, to less degree, from the town. In the windows and on the tops of Fredericksburg houses were many sharpshooters who, with long range rifles, tried to pick off Confederates.[7] As the blue line pushed forward, it crumpled the board fence as if it had been paper. This élan availed nothing. Once the fire of the Southern batteries on the heights blasted the Federal line, it faltered, it halted, it fell back in bloody confusion.[8] Cobb's Brigade in the sunken road and Cooke's on the crest had opportunity of firing one volley and no more.

---

[4] This was the so-called "ditch" or "canal" mentioned in many of the Federal reports. The Michler map of 1867 shows that the canal proper ran down the west side of the river from the dam above Beck's Island. At a point on the canal a few hundred yards North of the monument to Mary Washington, was a mill fed from the canal. Past this mill ran the surplus water into the spillway. This ditch was impassable except at the bridges opposite the various Fredericksburg streets. Part of the planking of one of these bridges had been taken up. Advancing soldiers had to cross on the stringers. See Maj. Gen. D. N. Couch's report, O. R., 21, 223. Cf. also, ibid., 227, 287, 292.

[5] O. R., 21, 223.

[6] Most of the Confederate accounts apparently time the attack from the appearance of masses of Federal troops on the outskirts of the town, about 11 A.M. The Federals considered that the attack began with the advance from "the ditch." On this basis, Couch reported that French became engaged at 12.10 and that Hancock's attack was merged with French's at 1 P.M. Owen (3 B. & L., 98), was not far in error when he said that the first direct assault was at 12.30 P.M. After that, the Confederates regarded the appearance of each new unit on the nearer side of the "ditch" as a separate attack. General Couch seems to have considered the advance of his Corps as a continuing assault and not as a succession of attacks (O. R., 21, 222-23). The point to be remembered is that, on the whole, the repulse of the various attacks was somewhat later than the hour given by the Confederates.

[7] Dickert, 184-85.

[8] O. R., 21, 570.

When the smoke lifted, many Federal soldiers still were behind the rim of the depression through which the ditch flowed,[9] but from the Confederate side, only three stands of Union colors that had been planted at the point of deployment,[10] and the dead or writhing victims on the ground, showed where the attack had been delivered. The repulse was as well directed as it was easy. Longstreet's First Corps was justifying its name and was vindicating the record the separate Divisions had achieved. McLaws was at his best. Ransom was measuring up to every requirement. Cooke on the hill-top, with his famous Twenty-seventh and his other fine regiments, was as gallant a figure as at Sharpsburg.

Down in the sunken road, Tom Cobb was cool and self-possessed and was holding perfectly in hand his confident troops. Above the howl of conflict, his resonant voice had been audible. Every quality that should be possessed by a brigade commander in defense, he was exhibiting. Diligently, for ten minutes and more, after the repulse of the first phase of the assault, Tom Cobb prepared his men for the second test, which manifestly might come with the next bugle call. He was moving among the troops, in calm cheerfulness, when with a gasp, he dropped to the ground. A bullet from the rifle of a sharpshooter, in a house to the left [11] had shattered his thigh. Blood poured from severed arteries. Stretcher bearers carried him, still conscious, to the shelter of the nearby house of the Widow Stevens.[12] The first surgeon who reached Cobb did what he could to staunch the flow, but he looked grim. Cobb's chaplain and messmate, R. K. Porter, came dashing up from the left, dismounted, and began to bathe the General's head. "Porter," said Cobb, scarcely aware of his words, "it's very painful." They brought him whiskey and poured it down his throat, but he was past stimulation. Suddenly he became insensible. Soon his heart ceased to beat.[13]

9 Cf. O. R., 21, 580.   10 O. R., 21, 580, 608.
11 O. R., 21, 608.
12 For the courageous behavior of this lady, who tore up all her garments to bandage soldiers' wounds, see 3 B. & L., 100, and J. T. Goolrick, Historic Fredericksburg, 51-52.
13 This is nothing more than a rephrasing of the account by Rev. R. K. Porter in 7 C. V., 309, except that Mr. Porter mistakenly indicated that the wounding of Cobb occurred during one of the later assaults of the day. Col. Robert McMillan, who succeeded temporarily to the command of the Brigade, stated definitely in his report that Cobb fell "about twelve or fifteen minutes" after the first repulse of the Federals (O. R., 21, 608). The mistake of other authorities in stating that Cobb was struck later in the day was due, doubtless, to the fact that the news of his fall could not be transmitted immediately to divisional field headquarters.

Almost at the moment of Cobb's fall, John R. Cooke had been hit in the forehead while he was atop Willis's Hill,[14] as that part of the heights was styled.[15] An ugly wound Cooke had, and one that manifestly had fractured the skull. Whether it would be fatal, none could say. Odds were that his end had come, like that of Tom Cobb, in the first battle he had fought as a general officer. At best, then, the two Brigades that apparently were to be hammered hardest that day on the anvil of attack, were now to be commanded by their senior Colonels present.[16]

Before Longstreet could reflect whether this would make any difference in the defense, the Federal attack was renewed. From the high ground, McLaws as well as Longstreet watched the blue line deploy and then advance slowly. Did McLaws have enough men in the sunken road to beat back the bluecoats? He was not sure. Kershaw had better send two of his regiments to help Cobb. The reserve regiment of Cobb's should move down to the sunken road.[17] Thither, also, Ransom hurried two exposed regiments of Cooke's Brigade.[18] These North Carolinians, being nearer than Kershaw's men, got to the sunken road in time to share in beating off with small effort the second Federal attack.[19]

Not long did the Confederates have to wait for another. As the enemy fell back, he appeared to meet reinforcements, and before rifles began to cool in the December air, he was coming up

[14] In 2 *N. C. Regts.*, 439, Capt. James A. Graham noted the error of some early writers in stating that Cooke's Brigade was in reserve. "Yet," said Captain Graham, "I know the fact to be that Cooke was wounded while talking to General Cobb of Georgia, who was killed *at* the rock wall." Nothing in the reports can be cited in definite refutation of this, but the probabilities are strongly against it. If Cooke was hit, as Ransom reported, almost at the time Cobb was, and if Cobb fell, as Colonel McMillan stated, soon after the first Federal assault, then Captain Graham's statement can be supported on one assumption only. This is that in the first advance of the Brigade to the crest of Willis's Hill the Twenty-seventh, which was the right regiment, continued down the hill, and that Cooke went with it to the sunken road. Unfortunately, Col. E. D. Hall's report (*O. R.*, 21, 629) is not clear on this point.

[15] The term "Marye's Heights" was applied loosely to all the heights immediately West of Fredericksburg and North of Hazel Run; but, strictly speaking, Willis's Hill was the eminence between Hazel Run and the next ravine to the northward. That is to say, the present National Cemetery occupies Willis's Hill. Adjoining it to the North and extending as far as the crossing of the road styled "The Pike," directly South of the Plank Road, were Marye's Heights, site of the Marye home, Brompton.

[16] Robert McMillan of the Twenty-fourth Georgia took Cobb's Brigade; E. D. Hall of the Forty-sixth North Carolina succeeded to the direction of Cooke's Brigade. *O. R.*, 21, 608, 629. The time was about 12.30 P.M.

[17] *O. R.*, 21, 580, 588.

[18] They must have been the Twenty-seventh and the Forty-sixth North Carolina, though here, again, the language of Colonel Hall's report, *O. R.*, 21, 629–30, is not altogether clear.

[19] *O. R.*, 21, 608.

again. Along the sunken road the volleys flashed; down the hill-side roared the echo of the guns. Against the enemy the full weight of lead and iron was hurled. The repulse was swift, easy, ghastly. Dead men were piling up now between the ditch and the wall.

Word of Cobb's fall reached McLaws about this time. The surviving Colonels were good soldiers. They would fight hard. Of that McLaws was sure, but he reasoned that reinforcements and the firm voice of a leader who had nerves of steel would steady the Georgians if they had been shaken by the loss of Cobb. The man to replace him was Kershaw. Two of that excellent soldier's regiments already were on their way to the sunken road. Let Kershaw go there in person; let his remaining troops follow him.[20]

Upon receipt of that order, powerful Joe Kershaw, he of the blond mustache, the keen eyes and the resonant voice, became the central figure on the smoke-swept stage. Almost before he had finished reading the order, he was in his saddle. To get to the sunken road, he had to ride down the side of Lee's Hill, gallop over a stretch of the Telegraph Road and then climb the flank of Willis's Hill. Personally, he was quite capable of dashing straight down the Telegraph Road directly into the Federal fire, all the way to the stone wall; but he had to use the route that was least hazardous for his men. They must march fast behind him, he said. With that, he gripped his rein, touched the flank of his steed and rode out into the fire with no more hesitation than he would have shown on his way to a political barbecue in his native South Carolina. Down the Telegraph Road he dashed, swerved to the left, climbed the new military road and then emerged on the crest of Willis's Hill, a conspicuous and defiant target. Men said afterward that when he pulled up his horse, the Federals withheld their fire as if in admiration, and that he took off his cap in acknowledgment ere he disappeared on his way to the sunken road.[21] An army myth this may have been, but a tribute it was to bravery that thousands had seen and had admired.[22]

Kershaw reached the sunken road about the time his two ad-

[20] O. R., 21, 580, 589. By this order McLaws conformed to Longstreet's wishes, but whether he anticipated or obeyed the instructions of the Corps commander is not certain. See O. R., 21, 570, 580.

[21] 1 Land We Love, 70.

[22] Cf. O. R., 21, 625, where the route pursued by Kershaw admiringly is described by Ransom.

vanced regiments arrived.[23] Not long afterward, his other regiments reached Willis's Hill, where, unfortunately, through no fault of Kershaw's, they were assigned to an exposed position.[24] That did not keep them from sharing in the next repulse. When their volleys were added to those of the men in the sunken road, the enemy faced an impenetrable front of fire. Never had Lee presented so many muskets on so narrow a front. Said Kershaw afterward: "I found, on my arrival, that Cobb's Brigade . . . occupied our entire front, and my troops could only get in position by doubling on them. This was accordingly done, and the formation along most of the line during the engagement was consequently four deep. . . . Notwithstanding that their fire was the most rapid and continuous I have ever witnessed, not a man was injured by the fire of his comrades." [25] Firepower, then as always, bred confidence. The Federals could continue their assaults. They would get more than they could stand!

So thought the men, so their corps commander. "Old Pete" observed everything, kept his eye on everything. The sole difference that anyone could have noted in him, as he sat and smoked and watched the enemy through his field-glasses was an increased heartiness, an added forthrightness of manner. When Lee expressed some concern lest repeated Federal assaults break the front of the First Corps, Longstreet answered proudly, almost bluntly: "General, if you put every man on the other side of the Potomac on that field to approach me over the same line, and give me plenty of ammunition, I will kill them all before they reach my line. Look to your right; you are in some danger there, but not on my line." [26]

Longstreet believed this, but he was not a man to neglect pre-

[23] They had sustained a heavy fire on the crest of the hill and then had double-quicked to the sunken road, but on the way down the Eighth South Carolina had stopped to deliver a volley and had suffered severely from the counter-fire. Of the thirty-one men lost that day by the Eighth South Carolina, twenty-eight were struck while getting to the sunken road. O. R., 21, 598, 599.

[24] In the Third South Carolina, the veteran Colonel, J. D. Nance was wounded early. The Lieutenant Colonel, the Major and three Captains who took command in succession were hit. The regiment was to finish the action under its gallant fourth Captain, John K. G. Nance. Incidentally this regiment had a most confusing roster of officers—a Col. James Nance, a Capt. John Nance and a senior Capt. W. W. Hance, who died Jan. 6, 1863, of wounds received at Fredericksburg. See O. R., 21, 589, 594.

[25] O. R., 21, 589. Kershaw remarked, ibid., 591, that during the battle the men of his Brigade averaged fifty-five rounds per man. That was quite high for the era of muzzle loaders.

[26] 3 B. & L., 81.

cautions because he felt he was safe. After 2 o'clock, as the attack on Jackson was collapsing, he decided that he safely could reduce force on his right to strengthen his center. He sent, therefore, to Pickett for two Brigades. Kemper's he put in reserve for Ransom; the veterans of Jenkins were given the place in line that Kershaw had vacated.[27] To Longstreet it must have been an experience as gratifying as it was novel to control reserves in such numbers that he could do what all the books said a commander should do in battle. Usually, instead of debating how many reserves it was worth while establishing, Longstreet had been compelled anxiously to ask himself whether he could afford to maintain a reserve of even one Brigade.

By 2.45 p.m. it was evident that regardless of what reserves might or might not have to do, the front line units had to settle down to an afternoon of slaughter. Attacks seemed to come at intervals of scarcely more than a quarter of an hour.[28] Behind each assault was the might of all the guns the Federals could bring to bear. "Frequently," wrote Cadmus Wilcox, ". . . I counted as many as fifty shots per minute."[29] Stafford Heights blazed ceaselessly. Many guns were firing from the town. The Confederate batteries answered defiantly when the infantry advanced but at other times they husbanded their fast dwindling ammunition.

This was true even of the Washington Artillery which occupied the heights between the Telegraph and Plank Roads and bore the heaviest burden of defense.[30] The battalion's ordnance train was several miles to the rear. If the caissons were sent back to be filled in the usual way, they could not be returned before nightfall. For that reason, Colonel Walton held on as long as he could; but by 3.30 he realized that his gallant men had to leave the post of honor.[31] Longstreet, notified in advance, ordered up in place of the Washington Artillery a part of the battalion that had been

[27] O. R., 21, 570.   [28] O. R., 21, 580, 589.

[29] General Wilcox prefaced this by saying: "More artillery appeared to be used on this day than I had ever known before." O. R., 21, 612. C. M. Wilcox to his sister, MS, Dec. 17, 1862—Wilcox MSS.

[30] Walton's report, O. R., 21, 573. Battalion headquarters were at the Marye House, Brompton. Owen, 180–81. For the history of the interesting old mansion, see T. Sutton Jett and Ralph Happel, Brompton (MS Fredericksburg and Spotsylvania National Military Park Library, Fredericksburg, Va.).

[31] So Walton reported in O. R., 21, 574. Adjutant Owen, op. cit., 194, stated that Alexander received a request simply to send ammunition but replied that he had better dispatch the batteries complete, as the men driving the limbers might not find the guns they were to supply.

Stephen Lee's and now, slightly modified,[32] was Porter Alexander's.

It was a humiliation to the Washington Artillery to prepare to go to the rear while the shells were screaming over the crest of Marye's Heights; but the advance of the relief guns was to give the First Corps a thrilling spectacle and a proud memory. At the moment Colonel Alexander received his orders, about 3.40, some of his batteries were in slow action and the others were in reserve near the Stansbury House, a mile and a quarter North of Willis's Hill.[33] Alexander quickly told Pichigru Woolfolk to limber up his Virginia battery, Tyler Jordan to make ready two more Virginia guns, and George Moody to have his Louisianians man their 12-pounders.

It was about 4 o'clock when these pieces were pulled into the extension of the Telegraph Road and were headed southward toward the stone wall where the men of Cobb and of Kershaw were firing whenever they saw a Federal stir or lift his head above the ground. Alexander's task was to drive down the road and then, swerving to the right,[34] to mount to the crest and to occupy the emplacements from which, at that moment, Walton was removing his grimy guns and his tired men. Their withdrawal the Federals had seen and had mistaken for the beginning of a retreat. Loudly the bluecoats had cheered and swiftly they had pressed a little closer toward the unyielding barrier of the stone wall. Fast enough the Union fire had been before this time. Now it outdid its worst fury.

Into the zone of this bombardment, Alexander's drivers spurred their pieces. Guns careened as they hit the rocks. Caissons bounced as if the concussion of their fall would explode their charges. Wheels pounded or spun in air. How could men keep their seats on the ammunition chests of the limbers? By what Providence were the horses escaping shells that might have blocked the road with quivering masses of flesh? One gun did overturn crazily and forced every driver to the rear to pull madly on his reins to prevent collision; but hands by the score jerked and tugged and

[32] Rhett's in the place of Brooks's South Carolina Battery.
[33] O. R., 21, 576.
[34] Some of the teams doubtless turned up "the Pike," South of the Plank Road; others possibly, but not probably, went up the ravine between Willis's Hill and Brompton. Reports are vague.

righted the piece again. Out of the road and up the hill went the column, and then it raced at a gallop along the face of the ridge— a sight so stirring that watchers caught their breath and felt the tears of admiration rise in their eyes. Still at the gallop, the guns were brought to the earthworks where they were unlimbered and were put into action as smartly as if they had been at perfect practice for a dress review.[35]

The welcome opening of these guns was to the infantry under the hill music as sweet as the sound of the swelling rebel yell to the ears of "Old Jack." Every round raised confidence still higher in Southern hearts; but so far as the Confederates could ascertain through the smoke, the appearance of fresh artillery on the hill did not deter or even discourage the Federals. Instead, for the first time, Union batteries boldly crossed the ditch, took position within little more than 300 yards of the sunken road and attempted to cover the advance of the infantry.[36] Alexander answered these newcomers with fine discrimination and divided his fire scrupulously between the infantry and the batteries. The infantry he drove back with the firm help of Southern riflemen behind the stone wall and on the hill. From the Federal artillery he suffered little after he got in position.[37]

Repulsed, slaughtered, the Federals appeared indomitable. Again they came, again, again, till Confederates lost count of the advances. The sun set not so late, nor seemed to sink so slowly as at Sharpsburg, but the bravely mad assaults continued till twilight. When they ended, the field from the ditch to a point about 100 yards from the stone wall was a blood-soaked blanket of blue. Nearer the sunken road the bodies were less numerous, but some were within forty and a few were within twenty-five yards. Subsequently, the Confederates found that the intrepid men who had

[35] Dickert, 188–89; Allan's Army, 503; O. R., 21, 571, 574–76.
[36] Alexander thought that three batteries participated in this fine advance (O. R., 21, 576). Kershaw spoke only (ibid., 589), of a "mass of artillery." Statements of Federal battery commanders regarding their position are not altogether clear, but from the sketch in O. R., 21, 1127, it would appear that the guns were those of Capt. John G. Hazard, Baty. B, 1st Rhode Island Light Arty., and those of Capt. John D. Frank, Baty. G, 1st New York Light Arty. Some reports would indicate that Capt. William A. Arnold's Baty. A, 1st Rhode Island Light Arty. should be added to this list; but Arnold's statement that he "remained in position all night" (O. R., 21, 266), coupled with General Howard's reference to this battery as "near Hanover Street, in the suburbs" (ibid., 264), makes it certain that Arnold, though he fought admirably, did not cross the ditch. Lieut. George Dickenson, Baty. E, 4th United States Arty. had been beyond the ditch earlier in the day, but had been killed.
[37] O. R., 21, 576.

advanced farthest before Southern minié balls had laid them low
wore the badges of the 69th New York, the 5th New Hampshire
and the 53d Pennsylvania. All three of these regiments belonged
to Hancock's 1st Division of Couch's II Corps.[38] Gallant their
charge had been, but their repulse the most costly the war had
brought. Much truth and little exaggeration appeared in the dispatch of a Federal newspaper correspondent: "It can hardly be in
human nature for men to show more valor, or generals to manifest less judgment . . ." [39]

Nothing touching that indictment of the Federals could be said
of Longstreet. Every phase of the fighting he had watched. After
his brief exchange with Lee concerning the security of his position, "Old Pete" did not receive a suggestion from the commanding General, nor did he order a movement subsequent to the shift
of the two Brigades from Pickett. Confidently, Longstreet left the
defense of the heights to McLaws, to Ransom and to their men.
Easy his bearing had been, easy his handling of his Corps. A great
day for him that 13th of December was, a day that confirmed his
faith in the tactical defensive.

[38] *Allan's Army*, 507. It was to the honor of this Division, even more, that each of
these regiments was of a different brigade. *Cf.* Francis A. Walker, *History of the Second Army Corps*, 164 ff.

[39] Dispatch of the *Cincinnati Commercial*, 6 *Moore's Rebellion Record*, 100.

CHAPTER XXIII

THE NIGHT OF THE NORTHERN LIGHTS

AT TWILIGHT and from a position so much exposed to the Federal artillery, a counterstroke by Longstreet was not to be considered. On Jackson's front, the outlook was unpromising. After
the heavy attack had been repulsed at 2 o'clock, the Confederate
batteries had not been able to take advanced positions. The ground
was heavy. Many of the guns had been rendered immobile by the
slaughter of the teams. Continuous, forbidding Federal fire had
seemed to indicate that another attempt might be made to storm
the ridge.[1] Jackson had waited to repulse such an attack, but all
the while he had burned with a desire to throw his veterans
against the troops in the plain. His excitement was intense,
though suppressed; "his countenance," one officer wrote later,
"glowed as from the glare of a great conflagration." [2] For once he
spoke openly of his plans. "I want to move forward," he said, "to
attack them—drive them into the river yonder," and he threw out
his arm as he spoke.[3]

Jackson's military judgment quickly challenged his impulse.
To be sure, the foe was spread across the flats and was weakened
and discouraged by a vain assault. At the enemy's back was a
wide, deep river. As inviting a situation this was as any apostle of
the offensive could ask. On the other hand, the Federal artillery
was undiminished in strength and admirably was placed to mow
down infantry that descended from the ridge. If the Second Corps
could reach the Northerners, it could drive them; but how was it
to get at them? Were the Confederate infantry to attack and then
fail to come to grips with the enemy, Jackson's men would suffer
frightfully and, above all, in withdrawal across the open field.
Was there any solution? Jackson soon thought of one, but of one
only that had practicality: The counterstroke might be delayed
until nearly sundown and then might be launched after a heavy,

---

[1] O. R., 21, 638.   [2] Cooke's Jackson, 372.
[3] Caldwell, 61.

close range bombardment. If this demoralized the enemy for a few minutes, the Confederates might reach those masses of blue soldiery. Even if a swift, late thrust of this sort were repelled, Jackson's men would have darkness to cover their return to their own lines.[4]

Jackson decided that this plan was not unreasonably hazardous. He would put it into execution at once and, as a first step, would seek reliable artillery that could be advanced quietly for a surprise attack. Batteries that had been fighting all day could not be used for this duty. They did not have the horses; they probably did not have the ammunition. Fortunately, Maj. Tom Carter, always alert and diligent, had brought up D. H. Hill's ordnance on the extreme right while Colonel Crutchfield had been relieving the batteries on the right center. Among Carter's excellent gunners, who had not been engaged during the morning, volunteers assuredly could be found to dash out from the woods and open on the weary Federals. The call was made. Bondurant's Alabama gunners, Page's Virginia Battery and the King William boys who had won fame at Seven Pines, all offered to take the post of danger.[5] Quickly they prepared for the advance, which was to be followed in a few minutes by that of the infantry.

Four Divisions of infantry, no less, Jackson intended to use on the sound principle that if the attack was worth anything, it was worth maximum effort. D. H. Hill's men were somewhat rested after their march of the previous night; Hood's Brigades, which Jackson had been authorized to employ at any time that day, had scarcely been engaged. These two Divisions, if at hand, logically should deliver the counterstroke. Early and Powell Hill, who had

---

[4] This is one of the few instances where Jackson in a formal report (*O. R.*, 21, 634), so fully explained his reasoning that the student is able, as it were, to watch the working of the General's mind. Doubtless the assertion of some early writers that Jackson planned a night attack was due to misunderstanding of what he said about possible retirement "under cover of night" (*ibid*). No foundation whatsoever exists for the story, cited and denied in *Early*, 183, that after the battle Jackson fell asleep at a council of war called by Lee and, when aroused, and asked for his opinion, muttered, "Drive 'em in the river; drive 'em in the river." There was no council of war that evening. The experience about to be recounted in the text shows that Jackson most assuredly had no plan to "drive 'em in the river" on the night of the 13th.

[5] In *O. R.*, 21, 643, D. H. Hill mentioned "Captain Bondurant and Lieutenants [S. H.] Pendleton and [William P.] Carter," without identifying the units to which the second and the last named were attached. Pendleton and Carter reappear in *O. R.*, 42, pt. 2, p. 1221, as commanders respectively of the Morris Artillery, which was Page's Virginia Battery, and of the King William Artillery, which was Carter's Virginia Battery. Lieutenant Pendleton is identifiable, also, from a reference in Dr. R. C. M Page's *Sketch of Page's Battery*, 6–7.

fought that day, should in fairness be used in support only. That was reasonable, but it was not feasible. When an hour might mean success or defeat, there was not sufficient time to shift Divisions. As the formation then was, the advance had to be. All who could go forward must. Taliaferro's remaining Brigades must be called up from their reserve position.[6] "Captain," said Jackson to a staff cavalryman whom he pressed into service to deliver orders to the artillery, "if you and your horse come out alive, tell General Stuart that I am going to advance my whole line at sunset."[7]

To this point, everything went smoothly, but quickly and abruptly, like a wagon that lost a wheel, Jackson's staff work broke down. "Sandie" Pendleton, his A.A.G., was hit and stunned, though not forced to leave the field.[8] Without "Sandie," the transmission of Jackson's orders was slow, confused and wholly incompetent. D. H. Hill received word promptly,[9] but no instructions reached A. P. Hill until about dusk. Then he was directed, in few words, to advance his whole line and to drive the enemy.[10] Hood's orders, received as the sun was setting, bade him join in the movement on his right as soon as Powell Hill advanced.[11]

No intimation did Early receive during the afternoon of any plan to attack. The first he knew of the operation was the sight of D. H. Hill's men moving forward. Upon inquiry, "Old Jube" learned from A. H. Colquitt, one of Hill's Brigadiers, that the whole front line was advancing and that Colquitt and the other officers of the second line were instructed to follow. Harvey Hill, coming up, himself presently confirmed this. When orders for Early at last arrived through Jackson's young brother-in-law, they were that the Division was to hold itself in readiness to move. A moment later, one of Early's own staff brought word from Jackson that Early was to take command of all the troops on the right and was to proceed at once. The depth of the advance, the officer said, was to be regulated by the effect the artillery had on the Federals.[12]

Early was puzzled and confused by these instructions which, as

[6] Taliaferro, reporting on Fredericksburg, did not mention the receipt during the late afternoon of any order to make ready or to go forward; but "Sandie" Pendleton, when hit and stunned, was on his way to Taliaferro with orders to advance (*Pendleton*, 246).

[7] *Cooke's Jackson*, 386.   [8] See *infra*, p. 437.
[9] *O. R.*, 21, 643.   [10] *O. R.*, 21, 647.
[11] *Hood*, 49–50.   [12] *Early*, 177; *O. R.*, 21, 666.

he reported later with exemplary understatement, were "rather embarrassing." [13] He was directing a Division, to be sure, but in rank he still was a Brigadier General. How was he to take command of a line on which were parts of two of the Brigades of Powell Hill, a sensitive Major General? Besides, Early was unfamiliar with the ground in his front. As he previously had sent some of his men to Powell Hill's relief, the Division was scattered. Disconcerting as all this was, Early had to ride forward and to put his troops in motion.

When the fuming Early reached the position held by Trimble's Brigade—there was Jackson himself. Early explained where his Brigades were, and he waited for Jackson to clarify orders. "Stonewall" pondered a moment. Did Early have at hand Trimble's and Hays's Brigade and the Thirteenth Georgia of Lawton's Brigade —these and no more? What of it? Advance with them after the artillery opened; abundant support would be at hand. Not a word did Jackson say of Powell Hill or of any extension of command for Early.[14]

Jackson now recovered grip on the movement he had ordered. He knew where his units were and he could control the field. One Brigade and the Georgia regiment Early put in the first line. The other Brigade formed the second. Hood and Harvey Hill were ready. The valiant Light Division, though it had endured the hardest of the day's fighting, was prepared to push forward. Through fast gathering twilight, Jackson gave the word for the artillery to emerge and to deliver what he hoped would be a surprise bombardment. Speed the advance, speed it! Whatever was done at all must be done quickly. December twilight would not linger, even in Virginia, for the defenders of the soil.

Intently Jackson listened; anxiously he waited. The leading battery was out of the woods. It had advanced 100 yards. Soon it would be within easy range. . . . Then the Federals opened. At first there were a few shots, as if some vigilant battery commander had spied the advancing Southern artillery and had challenged it. A dozen, a score, a hundred guns joined in. On a wide arc they flashed and roared. Up the ridge and through the woods crashed the shell. Over the field that Jackson's line would have to cross there swept a scythe of fire. Impulsively, almost automati-

[13] *O. R.*, 21, 666.   [14] *Early,* 177.

cally, the Southern gunners took their station and answered. Jackson stopped them. They were wasting ammunition. The advance could not succeed. Halt all forward movement. Let all the troops except Early's advanced units return to their bivouacs. Tell A. P. Hill to relieve Early and to restore the front held by the Light Division.[15] Jackson was wise in this. Said Early afterward: "Nothing could have lived while passing over that plain. . . . I feel well assured that, while we were all ready to obey the orders of our heroic commander, there was not a man in the force ordered to advance, whether in the front or in support, who did not breathe easier when he heard the orders countermanding the movement." [16]

After cancelling abruptly his plan, Jackson rode back to his quarters. He did not seem especially disappointed because he had lost the twilight gamble on the plain. In fact, he was more talkative and less tired than usually he was at the end of a day of fighting. Although the glare of battle faded from his eyes, he did not abandon hope that God on the morrow would deliver the enemy into his hands. Had he thought of the many soldierly promises of his beloved Old Testament, perhaps the one he least would have wished to see fulfilled at that hour would have been that of the Prophet Joel, "I will remove far off from you the Northern army." [17]

Slowly the Federal bombardment, like the barking of a dog that has driven off an intruder, halted, rose again for an instant and then died growlingly away. Darkness fell, but not for the undisputed reign of the long December night. Soon from beyond the Confederate left, far up the Rappahannock, there rose a glow. What was it? Had some forage depot caught afire? Was Wade

15 O. R., 21, 634. Early noted, *ibid.*, 666, that Hill did not relieve him. O. R., 21, 634.

16 *Early*, 178.

17 Joel ii, 20. Doubtless on the authority of Col. A. R. Boteler, Jackson's friend, Mrs. Jackson (*op. cit.*, 369–70), described how, after Jackson returned to his tent, he shared his bed with Boteler, who had arrived during the General's absence. Jackson, the story has it, sat up late to write and, after two or three hours' sleep, got up again and resumed his writing. When he saw that the light by his side shone in Boteler's eyes, he carefully shaded it. There is nothing improbable about the story, except the time of occurrence and the statement that Jackson aroused himself after a few hours' sleep. That this happened on the night of December 13 seems most unlikely. After his battles, Jackson usually slept as if he were in a stupor. That particular evening, according to Capt. James Power Smith, the General was requested after supper to sit for some sketches by one of the Volck brothers—Adelbert or Frederick—who was visiting headquarters. Jackson consented; Volck went to work in the presence of the staff. Soon Jackson, bolt upright on his camp stool, was sound asleep (43 S. H. S. P., 32).

Hampton duplicating Jackson's feat at Manassas Junction? [18] The sky flushed and grew dark again. Now shining white, it reddened and dimmed and blazed once more till it lighted the faces of the marvelling soldiers. It could be nothing less than that of which Southern boys often had heard, though never had they seen it—"Northern lights," the fantastic sky-painting of the Aurora Borealis. The spectacle awed but it flattered. Wrote one Confederate: "Of course, we enthusiastic young fellows felt that the heavens were hanging out banners and streamers and setting off fireworks in honor of our victory." [19]

Mercy there was for the fallen along with splendor for the triumphant survivor. "The air," a Northern newspaperman reported, "was as mild in the night, as if the month were June, and the wind came balmily from the South." [20] Of all the wounded on the ridge or at its foot that night, the man most on the minds of Lee's lieutenants was Maxcy Gregg. He had been carried promptly to the Yerby House, not far from Hamilton's Crossing, and had been placed in a large bed, which was moved to the center of the room.[21] There, fully conscious, he dictated this proud dispatch to the Governor of his State: "I am severely wounded, but the troops under my command have acted as they always have done, and I hope we have gained a glorious victory. If I am to die now, I give my life cheerfully for the independence of South Carolina, and I trust you will live to see our cause triumph completely." [22]

This was in the spirit characteristic of Gregg. Politeness and courtesy were his second nature. Did not men say that not long before Gregg was shot down, "Sandie" Pendleton had shouted to him that the enemy was firing at him; and had not Gregg answered, "Yes, sir, thank you, they have been doing so all day"? [23] Now that the surgeons examined more carefully his injured

---

[18] Hampton on the 12th had raided Dumfries, had bivouacked that night at Morrisville, five miles North of Richards' Ford, and on the 13th was returning to camp. Cf. O. R., 21, 690–91.

[19] Stiles, 137. Some writers dated this aurora December 14, but Hotchkiss' contemporary note in his diary would seem to fix the time as the evening of the battle.

[20] Cincinnati Commercial, cited in 6 Moore's Rebellion Record, 100. Stiles, on the other hand, op. cit., 137, remembered the night as "very cold."

[21] 43 S. H. S. P., 42.

[22] Richmond Whig, Dec. 24, 1862, p. 2, col. 1.

[23] 8 C. V., 538.

spine,[24] they had to conclude that his hurt was mortal.[25] If they acquainted Gregg at the time with his condition, he received the death sentence without a tremor.

After nightfall, he saw by his bedside Capt. James Power Smith, who brought a message from Jackson. The General, said Smith, had sent him directly from the battlefield to present sympathy and regards. Gregg was much affected. He told the young officer to thank Jackson for this "thoughtful remembrance," [26] but after Smith left, Gregg continued to think of the corps commander. Not long previously, he had forwarded a paper on which he had written an endorsement that he now thought Jackson might have considered discourteous. That weighed on him through the dark hours of approaching death. At length, ere daylight, he directed one of his staff officers to go to Jackson's headquarters and to ask if the General would ride by Yerby's on the way to the front. Then Gregg renewed his wrestle with pain.

In little more time than would be required for a man to reach corps headquarters and to spur back to Yerby's on a fresh horse, one of Jackson's aides tipped up to the bedside to say that Jackson had received Gregg's message and would be at Yerby's as soon as he could get there. Ere long, in stalked Jackson—a Jackson very different from the stern-jawed, sharp-lipped General who once had put all of Gregg's Colonels under arrest by a single order.[27] The voice that greeted Gregg was low and husky and scarcely to be identified as that of the man who on the 4th of September harshly had told Gregg to take the road.

Down by the bed Jackson seated himself, and when Gregg began to explain about the endorsement, Jackson quietly slipped his hand into that of the dying officer. Exacting and unforgetting though Jackson was, he either did not recall the incident that was troubling Gregg, or else, for once, he stretched his conscience and professed to have no knowledge of it. Gently the Southern Cromwell insisted that Gregg had given him no offense. With deep emotion Jackson went on: "The doctors tell me that you have not long to live. Let me ask you to dismiss the matter from your

[24] His "wound was from a minié ball, which struck him in the side, traversing the neighborhood of the spine." *Richmond Examiner*, Dec. 16, 1862, p. 1, col. 3.
[25] Dr. Hunter McGuire, in 19 *S. H. S. P.*, 309.
[26] 43 *S. H. S. P.*, 32.   [27] See *supra*. p. 81.

mind and turn your thoughts to God and to the world to which you go." Tears were in Gregg's eyes. Deep patrician courtesy triumphed over pain. "I thank you," he murmured, "I thank you very much." Jackson said farewell and went out. "Silently we rode away," his companion reported, "and as the sun rose, General Jackson was again on the hill near Hamilton's Crossing." [28]

Long before that, the Northern lights had died away.

[28] James Power Smith in 43 *S. H. S. P.*, 34. A different version appears in *Companions in Arms*, 228.

CHAPTER XXIV

AFTER FREDERICKSBURG—LAMENT AND LAURELS

FROM Prospect Hill on the morning of December 14, Jackson could see nothing of the enemy until the fog lifted, and then, though the blue troops were spread line on line for a front of one mile, he could discern no activity. This itself was a surprise because a Federal courier who had been captured during the night had on his person a memorandum of plans for a renewal of the battle on the 14th.[1] Why, then, were the Union lines immobile? A little later, when Jackson reconnoitred with Lee and with Hood, not one Federal flag was visible. All the standards had been lowered—a circumstance that led Hood to assert that the Unionists would not give battle that day.[2] The Confederate front, moreover, had been strengthened during the night until earthworks frowned upon the plain. As the Federals could see something of this fortification, they might consider it a new and excellent reason for not attacking.

Occasionally the sharpshooters skirmished and threatened. At intervals, the Union batteries on both sides of the Rappahannock boasted of the abundance of their shells, but the Confederate guns, short of ammunition, replied briefly, like a man who wants no argument.[3] The infantry who were not engaged in throwing up dirt—with less complaint than in front of Richmond in June— were free to rest as they watched. Early and Taliaferro now held the front line of Jackson's Corps; Harvey Hill was in support, Powell Hill in reserve. To Jackson, as he rode up and down the lines, the enemy appeared to be awaiting attack instead of preparing for it.[4]

On Longstreet's sector that clear 14th of December, there was some spitting of the indignant batteries one at the other, and some outburst of the chronic contention between pickets.[5] In the swale on the Confederate side of the ditch, about 400 yards from the

---

[1] *Longstreet,* 316.   [2] *Hood,* 50.
[3] *O. R.,* 21, 555.   [4] *O. R.,* 21, 634.
[5] *O. R.,* 21, 577.

stone wall,[6] a considerable force of Northern boys held on. The braver or more aggressive of them would greet with a fusillade any Confederate who was reckless enough to lift his head above the wall. Most of the Unionists in the swale were content to keep their shoulders in subjection, to woo the wintry sun and to await the darkness that would protect their withdrawal.[7] To hasten their departure and to discourage any further tenancy of the sheltering ditch, "Old Pete" was bestirring himself to place artillery where it would enfilade the ditch side.[8]

The most gruesome and at the same time the most fascinating scene on the front of the First Corps was the field across which the assaults of the previous afternoon had been made. From the north window in the upstairs room of the house where he had his headquarters, General Kershaw could look across a sweep of ground covered with distorted corpses and with wounded men who writhed in misery or dragged themselves inch by inch toward the rear. "Water, water," they were calling as always the wounded do. Amid discordant screams and groans and oaths and the strange, mournful mutter of the battlefield, that pathetic cry ceaselessly was audible.

Presently Kershaw heard a different sound—the swift sound of sure feet on the stair and then a knock at his door. The General said, "Come in," and looked up. Before him, in a moment, stood Richard Kirkland, Sergeant of Company E,[9] Second South Carolina, a boy of 19 whose unpretending but substantial farm family Kershaw had known before the war.[10]

"General," broke out Kirkland, in tones of indignation and remonstrance, "I can't stand this!"

"What is the matter, Sergeant?" Kershaw inquired.

"All night and all day I have heard those poor people calling for water, and I can stand it no longer. I come to ask permission to go and give them water."

The fine eyes of Kershaw, as chivalrous as gallant, lighted with admiration as he said earnestly: "Kirkland, don't you know you would get a bullet through your head the moment you stepped over the wall?"

---

[6] See *supra*, p. 367.   [7] Cf. *O. R.*, 21, 571.
[8] *Ibid.*   [9] One account names Company G.
[10] Born near Flat Rock, Kershaw district, South Carolina, August, 1843, fifth son of John and Mary Vaughan Kirkland, 16 *C. V.*, 105.

"Yes, sir," Kirkland answered, "I know that; but if you will let me, I am willing to try it."

The blond General pondered. His handsome face was grave. Finally, he answered: "Kirkland, I ought not to allow you to run a risk, but the sentiment which actuates you is so noble that I will not refuse your request, trusting that God may protect you. You may go."

Kirkland's face lighted with pleasure. "Thank you, sir," he said, and with no further words, started down the stairs, but in a moment he stopped, turned, and came back up again. Kershaw heard him and concluded that the boy's heart had failed him. Instead, Kirkland had a question to ask: "General, can I show a white handkerchief?"

That did not accord with the rules of war. Kershaw had to shake his head in unqualified refusal: "No, Kirkland, you can't do that!"

"All right," said the Sergeant without hesitation, "I'll take the chances," and he smiled again as he closed the door and rushed off.

Kershaw waited and wondered and presently went to the window. Soon, from behind the wall of the sunken road, Kirkland quietly lifted himself. In an instant he had vaulted over and stood exposed to the fire of every Federal sharpshooter. Not one rifle challenged him. Did the men in the swale think him crazy, or did they suppose he had a white flag they did not see? As they watched, he walked, head up, straight toward them, and then he knelt by the nearest wounded man. Lifting the soldier's head carefully, Kirkland gave him a deep, long drink of water, placed a knapsack where the man could rest on it, put an overcoat about the prostrate form, and then moved on.

Kershaw saw this and must have held his breath, but later he could write: "By this time [Kirkland's] purpose was well understood on both sides, and all danger was over. From all parts of the field arose fresh cries of, 'Water, water; for God's sake, water!' More piteous still was the mute appeal of some who could only feebly lift a hand to say, here, too, is life and suffering."

Swiftly, if gently, Kirkland worked through the short December afternoon. An hour and a half he was in the open. He had to go back often for water and many times he crossed the field, because he was resolved not to leave a single wounded Federal unattended on that part of the front. At last, his task done, he climbed back over the stone wall. No cheers acclaimed his act either behind the wall or along the swale, but if John Bunyan had been there, he would have written that "all the trumpets sounded on the other side."[11]

While Kershaw's men talked that night of Kirkland's fine deed, word was passed that the enemy was preparing a great assault for the next day, December 15.[12] D. H. Hill's Division, which it will be recalled had not been in the action on the 13th, was brought up to the front line by Jackson to replace Early and Taliaferro. The second line was put in Powell Hill's care.[13] Longstreet kept a detail at work steadily on the gun pits from which he hoped to enfilade the Federals who clung to the ground on the Confederate side of the ditch. Ransom was instructed to strengthen his position with rifle trenches.[14] Expectancy was high everywhere and, most of all, in front of the ground Harvey Hill occupied. Said Col. Bryan Grimes, who temporarily was in command of Ramseur's Brigade [15]: ". . . there was commotion among the enemy, and [we] could see a light in the distance flash up and then again be darkened, and [we] inferred that the enemy were moving to the right, and that the light was obscured as the troops passed and flashed out at the interval between the passage of one regiment and the head of another."[16]

It was a thrilling experience but it did not result as Grimes had anticipated. No attack was there on the 15th, right, center or left. Artillery exchanges continued. If either side could be credited with the initiative, it was the Confederate. Some of Longstreet's artillery, from new positions, easily drove the Federals back into the town,[17] and silenced a detachment of annoying sharpshooters in a tannery.[18] During the afternoon, the Federals asked a truce on Jackson's front for the removal of the dead who lay unburied nearer the Confederate lines than the Federal burial squads had been willing to venture at night. Jackson granted the truce. For

---

[11] Kershaw's own account, in 8 *S. H. S. P.*, 187–88. Another account appears in 16 *C. V.*, 105.

[12] Cf. *O. R.*, 21, 571.   [13] *Ibid.*, 634.

[14] *Ibid.*, 571.   [15] Formerly G. B. Anderson's.

[16] Pulaski Cowper, compiler, *Extracts of Letters of Maj.-Gen. Bryan Grimes to His Wife* (cited hereafter as *Grimes*) 26.

[17] *O. R.*, 21, 577.   [18] *Ibid.*

a few hours, butternut and blue coat were mingled on the field.[19]

Still the Confederates could not believe the Federals would abandon the offensive; still Lee refused to throw away his defensive advantage and to launch an attack where his troops would come under the fire of those powerful batteries on the farther side of the Rappahannock.[20] So confident was Harvey Hill of a heavy Union attack that he solicited from Jackson and received cordial permission to continue another day in the front line.[21]

Men of the First Corps were equally hopeful they would meet the enemy on the 16th and give him another drubbing. When Col. Robert McMillan got orders on the night of the 15th to withdraw from the sunken road where he had asked the privilege of remaining, he was indignant that Cobb's survivors should be denied the post of honor.[22] They had to tramp to the rear through an ugly storm of wind and rain and had to give to their fellow Georgians of Semmes's Brigade the famous stonewalled trench the Federals vainly had assailed. Such rest as they could get in that storm, Cobb's tired veterans enjoyed. Their successors in the sunken road had some measure of protection under the hill. The wind blew directly from them toward the enemy, and howled, not at them, but at the invader.

Late, blusterous dawn on the 16th, disclosed the retreat of the Federals. Covered by the storm and muffled by the wind, the movement had been completed without the knowledge of the Confederates. Even the pontoon bridges had been removed or, when first seen that morning, were swinging inshore on the Federal side of the river. A more complete and humiliating failure the Army of the Potomac had not made since First Manassas.

Quickly the facts came to light at the demand of an indignant North. Burnside had planned a swift drive on Richmond precisely as the Confederates had expected, but he first had intended to cross at Skinker's Neck on the Rappahannock, about fourteen miles below Fredericksburg.[23] His preparations there had attracted early the notice of the Confederates, who had massed in superior strength, as he thought, to prevent his crossing. In addi-

[19] O. R., 21, 634. For some of the amusing and gruesome details, see 2 R. E. Lee, 471.
[20] Cf. Lee's statement, O. R., 21, 555.   [21] Ibid., 644.
[22] O. R., 21, 581, 590–91.   [23] O. R., 21, 87.

tion, the pontoon train he had ordered from Washington arrived too late for a surprise crossing at Fredericksburg or at any other point.[24]

A singular and unsubstantial plan of action finally was adopted by Burnside and reluctantly was accepted by the commanders of the three "Grand Divisions" into which he had divided his army. He had been brought by some process of reasoning to conclude that the Southerners would be more surprised by his crossing at Fredericksburg than elsewhere. Moreover, a Fredericksburg Negro had described for him the military road the Confederates had cut on the heights. Said Burnside in his official report: "I decided to seize, if possible, a point on this road near Hamilton's which would not divide the enemy's forces by breaking their lines, but would place our forces in position to enable us to move in rear of the crest, and either force its evacuation or the capitulation of the forces occupying it." [25] Tactical arrangements were not quite so vague as this strategic plan. Enough troops had been put on the Federal left, Burnside believed, to have pressed home the attack of George Gordon Meade, whose Division entered the gap between Lane and Archer. The fault, in Burnside's judgment, was with Maj. Gen. William B. Franklin, commanding the left Grand Division, who did not support vigorously the attack of Meade.[26]

The costly attack on Longstreet's front had been ordered by Burnside in the belief that Franklin already had attacked heavily on the Confederate right and had caused Lee to weaken his left to support his right.[27] Mistaken in this, General Burnside had continued the attack on Longstreet because, apparently, he could not think of anything else to do, and would not break off the fight.[28]

In these assaults on the Confederate left center, Burnside ex-

[24] For the much disputed facts concerning the delay in the arrival of these pontoons from Berlin and Harpers Ferry, see O. R., 21, 48, 84 ff.

[25] O. R., 21, 91.

[26] For Burnside's cautious—almost timid—review of Franklin's operations, see O. R., 21, 91 ff. Franklin maintained in his report (ibid., 449 ff), that he threw into the assault as many men as he could assemble without long delay. Franklin was relieved of command on the same day, Jan. 25, 1863, that Burnside was. The essential difference in the treatment of the two men was that in the published order relieving Burnside the words "at his own request" appeared. In Franklin's case, the phrase was omitted (O. R., 21, 1004-05). An extraordinary correspondence regarding Franklin, Burnside and Halleck appears in ibid., 106 ff.

[27] Ibid., 94; slightly amended in 1 Com. Con. War, 653.

[28] O. R., 21, 94.

hausted the II and part of the IX Corps of Sumner's Right Grand Division and the III Corps of Hooker's Center Grand Division [29] but he had intended to renew the action the next morning. On the 14th, while a column of attack from the IX Corps had been forming, Sumner had come to Burnside and had said: "General, I hope you will desist from this attack; I do not know of any general officer who approves of it, and I think it will prove disastrous to the army." As Sumner was a consistent advocate of the offensive, his advice had shaken Burnside. The commanding General ordered the troops held in position but suspended the attack, while he called to conference the divisional and corps chiefs who were near at hand.

Burnside's own words are the best report of what followed: "[The Generals] unanimously voted against the attack. I then went over to see the other officers of the command on the other side, and found that the same opinion prevailed among them. I then sent for General Franklin, who was on the left, and he was of exactly the same opinion. This caused me to decide that I ought not to make the attack I had contemplated. And besides, inasmuch as the President of the United States had told me not to be in haste in making this attack; that he would give me all the support that he could, but he did not want the Army of the Potomac destroyed, I felt that I could not take the responsibility of ordering the attack, notwithstanding my own belief at the time that the works of the enemy could be carried." [30]

Burnside later had decided to withdraw part of his troops from Fredericksburg but to hold the town and the bridgeheads for possible future use. The protests of General Hooker, concerning the danger of leaving a small force in Fredericksburg, had induced General Burnside to evacuate all ground on the right bank of the Rappahannock.[31]

Although the Confederate commanders were chagrined that the enemy had escaped with no more punishment than that of a costly repulse, the South was jubilant. Even the *Richmond Examiner,* which had expressed "regret and mortification" on December 13, at the success of Burnside on occupying Fredericksburg, proclaimed the battle a "stunning defeat to the invader, a splendid

[29] O. R., 21, 94-95. [30] 1 Com. Con. War, 653.
[31] Ibid., 653.

victory to the defender of the sacred soil." [32] The equally critical *Charleston Mercury,* though admitting concern lest the enemy deliver another blow, reflected confidently: "General Lee knows his business and that army has yet known no such word as fail." [33] In the eyes of the *Richmond Dispatch,* Fredericksburg was prob- ably the greatest battle ever waged on this continent and a com- plete Confederate victory: "Had the battle been fought twenty miles this side of the Rappahannock River there would have been such a rout as the world did not witness in the forty-six years that elapsed between the battle of Waterloo and the first battle of Manas- sas." [34] The *Examiner,* returning to the choir, confided that "much uneasiness has never been felt on Burnside's advance, and it is now evident that even less was needed." It added: "The news of Burn- side's defeat will act like a stroke of paralysis on all the Northern army which undertook to cooperate with him on the same day and the same hour." [35]

Burnside's return to the left bank of the Rappahannock spiced newspaper rejoicing with somewhat confused speculation but ended in the declaration that the Federal commander had admit- ted defeat and could do little further harm during the winter.[36] In the whole of this discussion there was no shadow of disappoint- ment that Lee had not been able to follow up his success. On the contrary, the *Richmond Dispatch* [37] waxed ironical in commenting on the assertion by the *Washington Republican* that Lee had "lost his opportunity" by not pushing his advantage after the re-

[32] *Richmond Examiner,* Dec. 13, p. 2, col. 1; Dec. 15, 1862, p. 2, col. 2. Defending on the 15th its earlier petulant criticism, the *Examiner* pointed out how Stafford Heights dominated the terrain of action, and it restricted its disappointment to the fact that "the passage of the river was not rendered rather more difficult and costly in life to the enemy than it was." On this the *Examiner* remained censorious. Its editor was even more dogmatic than usual because he knew the ground thoroughly.

[33] Dec. 15, 1862, p. 1, col. 2.

[34] Dec. 16, 1862, p. 2, col. 1. The *Dispatch* noted that Fredericksburg was the tenth pitched battle Lee had fought since he had assumed command of the Army of Northern Virginia. This was asserted to be a record equal to the campaign of 1796 in Italy and that of 1814 in France. Lee and Johnston, said the *Dispatch,* were "as superior to the Yankee generals in every quality that constitutes the military chief as the sol- diers they lead are to the thieves and cut-throats that Lincoln has sent to subjugate them."

[35] Dec. 16, 1862, p. 2, col. 2.

[36] *Richmond Enquirer,* Dec. 18, p. 2, col. 1; Dec. 22, p. 2, col. 1; *Richmond Whig,* Dec. 17, p. 1, col. 1; Dec. 20, p. 1, col. 1; *Richmond Dispatch,* Dec. 18, p. 2, col. 1; Dec. 20, p. 2, col. 1; Dec. 23, p. 1, col. 2. The *Whig,* Dec. 29, 1862, p. 1, col. 1, probably reflected prevalent opinion when it concluded: "No man calling himself a General ever undertook a more hopeless task than Burnside did at Fredericksburg. It is evident that he had no idea of what was before him, and that even yet he is in the dark about it."

[37] Dec. 20, 1862, p. 2, col.

pulse of Burnside. Said the *Dispatch*: "We are disposed to think
. . . that General Lee's opportunity presented itself [December
13], and that he took full advantage of it. What more would this
Yankee have!"

Along with laughter, was lament. Total casualties were 4201,
though the dead numbered 458 only. Many who were reported
"wounded" were seeking a Christmas holiday.[38] A remarkable
fact—unique in the major battles of the Army of Northern Virginia—was that not a single Colonel was killed. One, E. N. Atkinson, commanding Lawton's Brigade, was captured, wounded,
when Hoke fell back after the charge.[39] Sorrow was widespread
for Maxcy Gregg—Gregg remembered now as the soldier, not as
the proud student who had refused to share first honors at college,[40] nor as the extremist in State rights, the advocate of a reopened slave trade. There is no certainty that he received Governor Pickens's answer to his telegram; if Gregg did receive the
message, it comforted his last watch. Said Pickens: "I trust God
will spare you; but if you die, your glorious name will be loved
throughout all time. Every South Carolina heart beats for you
and your heroic men." [41] Ere the end, Gregg called in Capt. Alex.
Haskell, his young staff officer who exemplified so many of his
own best ideals, and to that gallant South Carolinian he gave his
dress sword. With "words of deep trust and affection" he did this,
and through Haskell he sent his last messages to his kin.[42] After
that . . . the silence of the last secret.[43]

Under the care of comrades, the body was brought to Richmond, was embalmed, and was sent sorrowfully to Columbia,
South Carolina.[44] That State and all the South mourned Gregg.[45]

[38] *O. R.*, 21, 562. Federal losses, in comparison, were 12,653. *Ibid.*, 142.
[39] *O. R.*, 21, 632–33.
[40] *Charleston Mercury*, Dec. 15, 1862, p. 1, col. 3; *Charleston Courier*, quoted in
Richmond Whig, Dec. 23, 1862, p. 2, col. 3.
[41] *Richmond Whig*, Dec. 24, 1862, p. 2, col. 1.
[42] *Mrs. Daly*, 88. She added: "To the end of his life, this sword remained Father's
dearest treasure."
[43] *D. A. B.* gives the date of his death as December 14; the *Richmond Examiner* of
December 16 (p. 1, col. 3), stated that he "expired yesterday morning."
[44] *Richmond Examiner*, Dec. 16, p. 1, col. 3; *Richmond Dispatch*, Dec. 17, p. 1, col.
5. There was complaint by the *Examiner*, Dec. 17, p. 1, col. 2, that the General's body
was not laid in state at the Capitol, instead of at the Provost Marshal's office, Ninth
and Broad. The *Enquirer* replied that Governor Letcher prepared a room in the
Capitol for the remains, but that General Winder, who had the funeral arrangements in
charge, did not avail himself of the Governor's tender.
[45] For obituaries, not of special merit, see *Charleston Courier*, quoted in *Richmond
Whig*, Dec. 23, p. 1, col. 3; *Charleston Mercury*, Dec. 15, 1862, p. 1, col. 3; *Richmond
Examiner*, Dec. 16, p. 1, col. 3.

Of him, Jackson wrote in formal report: "General Gregg was a brave and accomplished officer, full of heroic sentiment and chivalrous honor." [46] Said A. P. Hill: "A more chivalrous gentleman and gallant soldier never adorned the service which he so loved." [47] More deliberate was Lee's tribute to Gregg and to Tom Cobb: "[In them] the Confederacy has lost two of its noblest citizens, and the army two of its bravest and most distinguished officers. The country consents to the sacrifice of such men as these, and the gallant soldiers who fell with them, only to secure the inestimable blessing they died to obtain." [48] In a formal letter of condolence to Governor Pickens, the commanding General said: "From my first acquaintance . . . I have admired his disinterested patriotism and his unselfish devotion. He has always been at the post of duty and of danger, and his services in this army have been of inestimable value. . . . The death of such a man is a costly sacrifice, for it is to men of his high integrity and commanding intellect that the country must look to give character to her councils, that she may be respected and honored by all nations. Among those of his State who will proudly read the history of his deeds, may many be found to imitate his noble example." [49]

Although Tom Cobb's name was linked with that of Maxcy Gregg's in many like tributes, the Georgian did not lack distinctive honors of his own. Some of his comrades must have heard of that last word to his wife: "God helping me, I will do my duty when called upon, trusting the consequences to Him. I go on picket tomorrow, and hence cannot write regularly." [50] Said Lee, with a depth of feeling he often reached but seldom permitted himself to voice: "[Cobb's] death has left a gap in the army which his military aptitude and skill renders . . . hard to fill. In the battle . . . he won an immortal name for himself and his Brigade. Hour after hour he held his position in front of our batteries, while Division after Division of the enemy was hurled against him. He announced the determination of himself and his men never to leave their post until the enemy was beaten back, and, with unshaken courage and fortitude, he kept his promise." [51] Longstreet wrote, ". . . we have lost one of our most promising

[46] O. R., 21, p. 632.   [47] Ibid., 646.
[48] Ibid., 555–56.   [49] Ibid., 1067.
[50] See supra, p. 329.
[51] Letter to Howell Cobb. O. R., 21, 1067–68

officers and statesmen." [52] McLaws reported of Cobb: ". . . his devotion to his duties, his aptitude for the profession of arms, and his control over his men I have never seen surpassed. Our country has lost a pure and able defender of her rights both in council and the field." [53]

Lower in rank but not in esteem was Lieut. Col. Lewis M. Coleman of the First Virginia Artillery.[54] Coleman was of intelligent stock and was eminently related in Hanover County and elsewhere in Tidewater Virginia. He had won his Master's degree at the University of Virginia when 17 and, after teaching in private academies for twelve years, had gone back to his Alma Mater as Professor of Latin and Literature. As soon as his colleagues would permit, after the secession of Virginia, he left his chair and joined the Confederate army as a private soldier. In August, 1861, he organized a battery which he fought with a vigor that won him advancement to the grade of Lieutenant Colonel before the Seven Days.[55] His fidelity as a Christian had equalled his skill as an artillerist and had matched his distinction as a scholar. The wounds he received at Fredericksburg, while bringing two howitzers into action, were not regarded at the time as serious but they were to prove fatal.[56] Both Lee and Jackson mentioned him in reports; [57] his Colonel, J. Thompson Brown, praised him warmly and issued a special order at the time of his death.[58] Said Brown of Coleman in this order: "Patriotic and brave, his only motive was of duty, his only fear was of his God, his last earthly fight was a victory over the enemies of his country, his final struggle was a victory over death itself." [59]

Laurels followed laments. In addition to the slain, those officers most praised in official reports were those whose conduct already has been described—Barksdale for his defense of the water front

---

[52] *Ibid.,* 571. [53] *Ibid.,* 582.

[54] Otherwise Brown's Battalion, Reserve Artillery.

[55] The record is not complete, but as the First Virginia was fully organized as a regiment, probabilities are that Coleman was elected and not appointed Lieutenant Colonel.

[56] Born Feb. 3, 1827; died Mch. 21, 1863. His exemplary life became the subject of one of the few war-time biographical tracts—J. L. Burrows, *The Christian Scholar and Soldier,* Richmond, 1864, p. 44. A copy is in the Confederate Museum, Richmond. See D. S. Freeman, ed. *Calendar of Confederate Papers,* 527.

[57] *O. R.,* 21, 556, 633.

[58] *O. R.,* 21, 639; *Calendar cit.,* 210.

[59] *Brown MSS,* Confederate Museum. *Cf.* Ham Chamberlayne, *op. cit.,* 164: "There was no better nor more useful man."

on the 11th,[60] Pelham for his artillery duel on the right in the first stage of the battle,[61] Alexander for his dash under fire to the crest of Marye's Heights,[62] and Archer for his quick change of front after the break through on his left.[63]

Most of the men from whom the South had become accustomed to expect fine service sustained at Fredericksburg their reputation. Lee did no more than equal justice when he said in his final report: "To Generals Longstreet and Jackson great praise is due for the disposition and management of their respective corps. Their quick perception enabled them to discover the projected assaults upon their positions, and their ready skill to devise the best means to resist them. Besides their services in the field—which every battle of the campaign from Richmond to Fredericksburg has served to illustrate—I am also indebted to them for valuable counsel, both as regards the general operations of the army and the execution of the particular measures adopted."[64] This was tribute to the new organization as surely as to the men who directed it. Staff organization had not been perfect, to be sure, but the authority of the Lieutenant Generals had been adequate. The contrast with conditions during the Seven Days had been marked at Second Manassas and at Sharpsburg. Now that the system of corps command was legalized as well as tested, it was vindicated. One question only, in this connection, began to trouble Lee: were the Corps too large?

Had Lee's tribute to his corps commanders been reduced, for any reason, to comparisons, Longstreet would have been entitled to somewhat more distinction at Fredericksburg than Jackson would have been. During the whole of the day of battle, "Old Pete" kept his hand on every unit of his Corps. Though he had no task of especial difficulty, he did not make a faulty move. When the enemy was back across the river, Longstreet issued a

[60] McLaws's tributes appear in *O. R.*, 21, 579, 582. Longstreet in his report, *ibid.*, 571, said: "[Barksdale's Brigade] held the enemy's entire army at the river bank for sixteen hours, giving us abundance of time to complete our arrangements for battle. A more gallant and worthy service is rarely accomplished by so small a force."

[61] *O. R.*, 21, 547, 553, 631, 638. In Lee's reference to Pelham, *ibid.*, 547, the young artillerist was mentioned as "the gallant Pelham." The adjective was not unusual in reports, because gallant conduct was frequent; but in Pelham's instance the word "stuck." Cf. *infra*, p. 452 ff.

[62] For Alexander's promotion and fine conduct see the following: *O. R.*, 19, pt. 2, p. 704; *ibid.*, pt. 1, p. 156; *O. R.*, 21, 1046, 547, 571, 555–56, 576. These are in chronological order.

[63] *O. R.*, 21, 631, 656, 667.   [64] *O. R.*, 21, 556.

fine and restrained congratulatory order to the First Corps and concluded with an appeal for the Fredericksburg patriots who had been driven from their homes.[65]

Jackson had done nothing amiss and had done several things admirably; but there remains a question concerning the vigilance of his examination of his front before the battle opened. "Stonewall" himself was far from satisfied with the outcome. As he looked glumly across the fields on the morning of the 16th and saw no sign of the enemy save newly turned graves and the bodies of the unburied dead, he spoke gravely, almost bitterly: "I did not think that a little red earth would have frightened them. I am sorry that they are gone. I am sorry I fortified." [66] Compared with Jackson's part in the operations, that of Stuart was small, but it was marked in every phase by his limitless industry, his sleepless vigilance.[67]

If the most notable trio of Lee's lieutenants vindicated at Fredericksburg the reputation won by wise administration and hard fighting, at least one divisional commander regained standing that had been impaired. This man was Lafayette McLaws. In contrast to his course during the Maryland campaign, McLaws's handling of his troops had been sagacious. Reports both of his corps commander and of the General of the Army praised him.[68]

In his own business-like account of the action, McLaws distributed praise without inviting it for himself.[69] Privately he wrote his wounded friend "Dick" Ewell a letter that reveals the fineness of his own character in a manner of which he doubtless was not himself aware. Said McLaws: "Three Brigades of my Division were active participants and I can say with perfect conviction that never in the world has there been more determined devotion and dauntless courage than they exhibited. Their deeds make me prouder of the South than I ever was and the memory of those who have fallen makes me sad indeed to think that such men should be sacrificed to beat back such a causeless invasion. Let us give all praise to Him who gave the might to the right and blessed our arms with victory." [70]

[65] O. R., 51, pt. 2, p. 663. The next detailed reference to Longstreet is *infra*, p. 467.
[66] 1 *Land We Love*, 117. The sketch of Jackson is resumed *infra*, p. 495.
[67] O. R., 21, 556.   [68] O. R., 21, 547, 571. *Sorrel*, 133.
[69] O. R., 21, 579.   [70] *Old Bald Head*, 130–31.

From Lee's hastily prepared first report on Fredericksburg,[71] reference to Ransom's part in the defense of Willis's Hill unintentionally was omitted. This incensed the North Carolinian momentarily and seemed to exalt McLaws at Ransom's expense; but it was not due to any greediness for fame on the part of McLaws or to any depreciation of Ransom by the commanding General. Rather was it one result of the natural confusion which arose from the fact that McLaws had Cobb's Brigade and then Kershaw's of his Division directly in front of a position held by Ransom. The final report made plain the substantial service rendered by Ransom.[72]

Some of the new brigade commanders were distinguished at the same time that Ransom established himself and McLaws erased the question mark that Maryland Heights and Sharpsburg had put behind his name. John R. Cooke's serious wound in the head had not been received until he had shown that he could handle a Brigade with ability.[73] Jim Lane, who had succeeded to Branch's Brigade of A. P. Hill's Division, had the misfortune to lose more than 500 men in this, his first fight as a general officer,[74] but he was not held responsible for the gap on his right, and officially he was praised by A. P. Hill for his firm defense.[75] That Lane's men fared hard while fighting hard, a curious colloquy between Lane and Capt. Gold Holland of the Twenty-eighth demonstrated. Holland, a man of fascinating face, came up to Lane after the close of the action of December 13, and congratulated him on passing unscathed through the fight. When Lane made proper acknowledgment, Holland went on: "And I am indebted to a biscuit for my own life." With that, the Cap-

[71] December 14.

[72] See *O. R.*, 21, 547, 553, 571, 625, 1124; 3 *B. & L.*, 94; Ransom's address to the Ladies' Memorial Association of New Berne, n.d., MS, courteously lent to the writer by Eugene M. Ransom of Atlanta.

[73] *O. R.*, 21, 555–56, 571, 625. Cooke filed no report on Fredericksburg. That of his senior Colonel, E. D. Hall, appears in *ibid.*, 629, but is quite brief.

[74] *O. R.*, 21, 656.

[75] *O. R.*, 21, 646. Lane's report already has been drawn upon for its references to the discussion on December 12 of the gap in the "boggy wood." See *supra*, p. 342. The report itself is in *O. R.*, 21, 653–56. Lane had been the principal actor in an amusing episode at Gaines' Mill, where he had led his Twenty-eighth North Carolina with conspicuous valor. During the battle, he felt the stunning proximity of a minié ball and, stopping, he bent his head toward Sergeant Milton Lowe, his color bearer. "Sergeant," he asked calmly, "is my scalp cut?" Lowe, as cool as his Colonel, carefully examined the cranium of Lane. "No, Colonel," he said after a moment, "it is only scorched a little." 2 *N. C. Regts.*, 547–48. For Lane's promotion, see *O. R.*, 19, pt. 2, pp. 684, 689, 699; W. R. Cox, *Life and Services of James H. Lane*, 16.

tain ran his hand into his haversack and pulled out a large biscuit, which had been cooked without salt or fat and looked, the narrator stated, "Like horn when sliced—something that an ostrich could not digest." Imbedded firmly in the biscuit but relentlessly halted midway, was a Federal bullet meant for Captain Holland.[76]

Besides Lane and Cooke and other new Brigadiers who did not have equal opportunity, several Colonels attracted at Fredericksburg the notice that usually marked a man for promotion. In the absence of Gen. A. R. Lawton, who still was suffering from wounds, his Brigade had been under its senior Colonel, E. N. Atkinson of the Twenty-sixth Georgia. When Atkinson had fallen, Col. Clement A. Evans of the Thirty-first Georgia had taken command and had done admirably.[77]

Trimble's Brigade, in the same manner, had been under a tall, magnificent young North Carolinian, Col. Robert F. Hoke of the Twenty-first, who had fought gallantly in every battle his regiment had shared.[78] Hoke had perfect self-confidence and a certain ferocious quality of leadership, which was tempered later with discretion. Sent forward by Early to help in mending the gap between Lane and Archer, he aided in driving out the Federals and then rushed headlong past the railroad; but he soon saw his danger and carefully withdrew to the track. There he left a strong outpost and, with the remainder of his command, took advanced position on the ridge.[79] This was the work of a man who manifestly knew how to fight.

As much was to be said of James A. Walker of the Thirteenth Virginia, who was commanding Early's Brigade while "Old Jube" was acting for Ewell. The difference was that Walker had been tried frequently enough to make it clear that he was qualified already for brigade command. Hoke was having his first chance and, incidentally, barely escaped having his last. While he was riding along the line, a fragment of shell hit the head of his horse and threw the animal momentarily to the ground. Hoke fell and attempted to spring clear of the mount, but he could not get one foot out of the stirrup. The frenzied horse dragged him

[76] 2 *N. C. Regts.*, 745.   [77] *O. R.*, 21, 632, 667.

[78] For Hoke's earlier career, see *O. R.*, 51, pt. 2, p. 492; *O. R.*, 9, 259, 261; *O. R.*, 11, pt. 2, p. 839; 4 *N. C. Regts.*, 537; 21 *S. H. S. P.*, 118; 20 *C. V.*, 570–71. His fine conduct at Fredericksburg is set forth in *O. R.*, 21, pp. 554, 667, 672. For the next reference to Hoke, see *infra*, Chap. XXXV.

[79] *Loc. cit.*

off. Happily, some of the men caught the animal before Hoke had suffered any worse injury than a pounding that temporarily bewildered him.[80]

Still another Colonel who had his first opportunity, though a brief one, in brigade command at Fredericksburg was Alfred M. Scales of the Thirteenth North Carolina, whose whole career from the Peninsula campaign onward had been one of consistent stout service in Pender's hard fighting Brigade.[81] During the short time the exhaustless Pender required to go to the rear and have a wound dressed, Scales was in command of the Brigade. He met the test.[82]

The improved morale of the Army and the absence of straggling were commended in numerous reports.[83] Lee for the first time was able to say that "the calmness and steadiness with which orders were obeyed and manœuvres executed in the midst of battle, evinced the discipline of a veteran army." [84] Those final words represented the ideal toward which Johnston before him, and then he and Jackson and Longstreet and Stuart and the Hills and others less renowned had been working.

"A veteran army"—twenty months had been required to make it that, but now all the arms of the service had earned the title. The infantry spoke for itself through its volleys and its movements; the cavalry had caught the spirit of Stuart. At Fredericksburg the artillery, though still outgunned and outranged [85] by the Federals, gave a good account of itself. After Pelham and his men, the greatest honor went with the worst danger on Jackson's right, where Col. R. Lindsay Walker kept A. P. Hill's artillery calm and resolute under concentrated fire for a long time before it could reply.[86] As usual, where the fire was furious, there was Willie Pegram. By his side fought David McIntosh.[87]

The men with the long range guns had a hard, if not an encouraging day.[88] At the commanding General's field headquar-

[80] *Oates*, 166–67.
[81] For his career, see 4 *C. M. H.*, 349; 1 *N. C. Regts.*, 654; *O. R.*, 51, pt. 2, p. 377; *O. R.*, 11, pt. 1, p. 567; *O. R.*, 19, pt. 1, p. 1045.
[82] Cf. *O. R.*, 21, 647.   [83] *O. R.*, 622, 635, 641, 647, 656, 667.
[84] *Ibid.*, 556.
[85] Allan, in his *Army*, 469–70, credited the Federals with 143 guns on Stafford Heights, in addition to the pieces that had been brought across the river. Among the cannon on the left bank were six 20-pounders and seven 4½-inch siege guns.
[86] *O. R.*, 21, 638.   [87] *O. R.*, 21, 648.
[88] *Cf.* Pendleton in *O. R.*, 21, 567.

ters, two 30-pounder Parrotts exploded, though without injuring anyone.[89] Artillerists of both armies were dissatisfied with the performance of their 20-pounder Parrotts.[90] The only long range gun that won special praise was an English Whitworth, which was under the command of Captain R. A. Hardaway, a marksman of special skill.[91] This was the piece which in November had put to flight Federals at a distance of more than three miles.[92] In the action of December 13, Harvey Hill, who always found artillery very good or very bad, credited Hardaway and this Whitworth with killing Brig. Gen. George D. Bayard, because Hill did not believe any other Confederate gun could reach Franklin's field headquarters where Bayard was struck fatally by a fragment of shell.[93] Of Hardaway's conduct, Harvey Hill justly was proud. Similarly, General Lee was pleased to observe that Col. Armistead L. Long of his staff, who had been trained as an artillerist, had forgotten none of his art. Before and during the battle, Lee stated in his report, Colonel Long was "particularly useful . . . in posting and securing the artillery." [94]

Not all of the aftermath of that spectacular day on the heights of the Rappahannock was praise for the living and tribute to the dead. The long, ugly quarrel between Jackson and A. P. Hill probably explained the tone of part of the discussion of responsibility for the gap between the front of Archer and that of Lane. In Hill's report, which was dated Jan. 1, 1863, he mentioned an "interval" there and another between Lane and Pender, but he spoke of Gregg, in reserve on the military road, as "crossing" one "interval" and of Thomas as "crossing" the other. In later paragraphs reference was made to the "interval" once only.[95] There was no inaccuracy in anything Hill said about the gap, but there was no statement of the distances involved, nor was there any

---

[89] *O. R.*, 21, 565–66.

[90] *O. R.*, 18, 193; *O. R.*, 21, 189. Both commands insisted, also, that the ammunition was as bad as the guns were. *Ibid.*

[91] Cf. *O. R.*, 21, 37, 643.

[92] *Ibid.*, 643, Cf. *supra*, p. 311.

[93] *Ibid.*, 643, 451. Whether Harvey Hill was right in saying that Hardaway's gun killed Bayard would seem to depend, among other things, on the time Hardaway went into action. Hill in his report simply said this was "in the afternoon," *O. R.*, 21, 643; but he remarked that Hardaway went in with Brown, whose report, *ibid.*, 639, stated that Brown moved to the right "about 2 o'clock." Bayard was hit between 1.40 and 2.15 P.M., *ibid.*, 92. It is possible that one of Poague's 20-pounder Parrotts might have reached the post of this gallant Federal.

[94] *O. R.*, 21, 556.   [95] *O. R.*, 21, 645–46.

admission of negligence or error in permitting the gap to remain.[96]
Lee, in his turn, speaking of the "interval," noted that Gregg was
"in rear" of the gap. Hill's word, "crossing," was not used.[97]
There was no praise for Hill or for any other division commander
in the closing paragraphs of Lee's report; consequently there was
no implication of censure for Hill even by Lee's usual device of
omitting reference to those he could not commend.

Jackson's handling of the episode was different. He did not
attempt to describe the interval, but he made its existence a matter of record by stating that Gregg was in rear of it. Nothing
more was said of it until Jackson described the main assault of
the Federals: "They continued . . ." he wrote, "still to press forward and before General A. P. Hill closed the interval which he
had left between Archer and Lane, it was penetrated, and the
enemy, pressing forward in overwhelming numbers through that
interval, turned Lane's right and Archer's left." [98]

That was all, but it was unmistakable censure and deserved
censure. Hill had left a somewhat similar gap in his front at
Groveton. The Federals had penetrated it. A second offense of
the same character was not to be overlooked by Hill's corps commander. Jackson did not stop to ask whether the reason for not
occupying the gap was negligence, or a belief that the ground was
too marshy for infantry to pass, or an error of judgment in assuming, as Stuart had, that the artillery cross fire would keep out
the Federals. The gap was there; Hill was responsible for it; that
was the fact set down—that and no more. The report of Jackson,
as will appear in a later chapter, was written during an active
period in the controversy with Hill over the charges made the
previous summer. Who can say whether Jackson introduced
this censure of Hill merely because he felt it was his duty to do
so or because he intended to add new evidence of Hill's carelessness? [99]

Another controversy might have arisen readily enough over
the course of the action on Longstreet's right. John B. Hood held
that position. He had come to Fredericksburg after some question
had been raised concerning his administration of his Division.
Everyone knew him for one of the hardest fighters on any field to
which he was sent. Was he as careless in camp as he was diligent

[96] O. R., 21, 645–46.   [97] Ibid., 553.   [98] O. R., 631, 632.
[99] For continuance of the sketch of A. P. Hill, see infra, Chap. XXX et seq.

in action? An inspection of his Division in November had shown part of the famous Texas Brigade in poor condition. The arms of the renowned First Texas were in bad order. Camp was dirty. Sixty men were barefooted. A third only of the entire command were decently clad. The regiment, said the inspector, showed "inexcusable neglect on the part of its officers." [100] This had been to Hood's discredit but apparently it had not dampened his spirits. Two or three days after the receipt of the report, he had written cheerily to his friend Senator Wigfall: "Well, I think Mr. Burn- sides is coming in a few days, and what a fight! I think we will whip him badly. Our army is in good trim for an old-fashioned fight." [101]

At Fredericksburg, Hood was assured that he would witness the fulfillment of his prediction and that he would have full part in the fight. On the evening of the 12th, when he had resumed a position from which he had been shifted, he received orders, it will be remembered, to co-operate with Jackson should occasion require.[102] The next morning Hood had been told by Longstreet that the main attack of the enemy would be on Jackson, beyond Hood's right, and that when opportunity offered, the Texan must throw his Division on the flank of the enemy that was assailing Jackson. In addition, Hood was told that Pickett on his left would be ready to aid in any operation he undertook.[103]

Events had developed substantially as Longstreet had predicted. While the attack on Jackson was at its height on the early after- noon of the 13th, Pickett rode over to Hood and suggested that the moment had come for the flank operation.[104] Hood was not convinced that the main Federal attack was being delivered and he waited too long to be persuaded by the evidence of the field that a heavier assault was not impending. When Hood did send Law forward, that officer advanced with his usual dash and vigor. He could not offset what time had done or bring to battle a retiring foe.[105] Longstreet felt constrained in his report to state the circumstances but he generously took Hood's view of the strength of the attack.[106] Years later, Longstreet explained that he

---

100 O. R., 19, pt. 2, p. 719.   101 Mrs. Wright, 95.
102 O. R., 21, 622. See, also, supra, p. 343.
103 O. R., 21, 570.   104 Longstreet, 309; 3 B. & L., 84.
105 O. R.. 21, 622.
106 Said Longstreet: "[The advance of the enemy] did not appear to have all the force of a real attack, however, and General Hood did not feel authorized to make more than a partial advance." O. R., 21, 570.

reported Hood's failure to meet orders and deliberately stopped there: "As [Hood] was high in favor with the authorities it did not seem prudent to push the matter, as called for under the ordinary usages of war. 'Bis peccare in bello non licet.' " [107]

[107] *Longstreet,* 317. For Longstreet's order to Hood on the evening of December 13, covering the next day, see *O. R.,* 51, pt. 2, p. 662. The order was not put in execution because the Federals did not renew the attack.

CHAPTER XXV

Cavalry Raids and Quarrels

In the mind of the soldier, the winter of 1862-63 was dull and purposeless; in the history of the Army, the season was one of anxiety and alarms. It was marked by six developments. First came a series of cavalry raids that culminated, March 17, in the sharp and costly action at Kelly's Ford; second were two sets of promotions and a marked change in the status of Gustavus W. Smith; third, the Army acquired a better knowledge of its components, and more particularly of its staff, during the closer relationship of winter quarters; fourth, a basic and vital reorganization of the artillery was effected; fifth was a period of semi-independent command for James Longstreet; last of all was the climax of the quarrel between Jackson and Powell Hill at a time when Jackson was being prepared spiritually for his supreme achievement.

Through all of this, which in separate chapters will now be presented approximately in chronological order, the cohesives were three—the influence of the women, the sustained morale of the man in the ranks, and the leadership of Lee. Usually, if the soldier despaired, it was because he did not get letters from home, or else it was because those letters told of sickness and misery. When, as more often happened, he endured cold without complaint and short rations without grumbling, he had in his pocket a courageous message from wife or mother or sweetheart. While the women kept high the spirit of the men who carried the rifles, the commanding General resolved the problems and smoothed the ruffled sensibilities and settled the contention of those who bore the insignia of rank.

Of this care on the part of Lee, the cavalry needed little, except when jealousies were aroused among the officers. Stuart was abundantly able to direct operations. At the instance of Lee, even before the Battle of Fredericksburg had been fought, Stuart had bedevilled Burnside by raids North of the Rappahannock. At that time, virtually all the supplies and munitions for the Union Army were dispatched by water to the base on Aquia Creek; but cavalry reinforcements, sutlers' wagons and occasional trains used the Telegraph Road. That old highway ran South from Alexandria West of the Potomac and parallel to that stream. A difficult highway it was in 1862 and for more than half a century continued to be.[1] It followed the vagrant contours that looked down upon the Potomac and it crossed no less than six creeks between Occoquan and the Rappahannock.

Along the road were two small towns only that the Confederates could hope to reach—Dumfries and Occoquan. Guards of some proportions were known to be at both places, and, of course, were supplied with provisions and with quartermasters' stores. These troops and their possessions, together with the telegraph line from Burnside's headquarters to Washington, were avowed objects of the raids Stuart ordered. Another professed aim was to force General Burnside to make heavy detachments to guard the road and thereby to weaken him on the Rappahannock. Actually, so little could be accomplished in these respects by brief raids on a small scale that Stuart must be credited with a desire to keep his regiments alert by field exercises, even when these involved hardship and exposure. Stuart must be suspected, moreover, of cherishing the troopers' familiar hope of picking up sutlers' wagons. Any cavalryman not ruinously indolent and of incurable cowardice would affirm unhesitatingly that a well furnished sutlers' train was worth the risk of a wintry raid.

Not one raid was there, but four, and in rising strength or deeper objective. On November 27, Wade Hampton took 158 men from the Carolina and Georgia mounted units and with them crossed the Rappahannock. Under the very noses of nodding Federals he captured about 100 horses and ninety-two officers and men, who constituted, he thought, all save five members of the entire picket on two roads. This affair of Hartwood Church,[2] as it was styled in reports, was of interest because it was the first independent operation undertaken in Virginia exclusively

[1] The present U. S. Highway No. 1 pursues the general direction of the Telegraph Road. Until concrete foundations were laid, the bottom lands on Chopawamsic Creek were a terror to travellers. As late as 1918, it was not unusual there to see, hub-deep and helpless in the mud, half a dozen motor cars.

[2] Hartwood Church is about seven miles Northwest of Falmouth on what formerly was the Warrenton Road. The site is marked as "Brick Church" on *O. R. Atlas*, Plate VIII.

by cavalry from States farther South. The men and their leader won high praise for this raid, which started an angry hue-and-cry among the Federals.[3]

So successful was the foray of late November that Stuart permitted Hampton on December 10 to march on Dumfries. This time Hampton had 520 men, all of whom, as in his previous raid, were Georgians and Carolinians. Readily enough Hampton captured the guard of some fifty men at Dumfries, caught a wagon train and cut the telegraph line. Then, according to orders, he undertook to sweep the road all the way to the Occoquan. This proved a bit more than so small a force could accomplish, because Hampton discovered that Sigel's Corps was moving down the road. Prudently the Southerner turned back, but along with his prisoners, he brought seventeen wagons across the Rappahannock, and for his raid he did not have to pay with so much as a scratch to any of his men. Three nights in the snow did not daunt them.[4]

As soon as his adventurers were rested, Hampton tried again on December 17–18 to reach Occoquan. This time he ran into a green New Jersey cavalry regiment, which put up some show of a fight, but he managed to get off with about 150 prisoners and twenty wagons. The finest feat of this raid was the capture of all forty-one of the pickets on eight miles of guarded road. To take each picket post without alarming the men at the next was a tribute to the stalking skill of Hampton's troopers.[5] Excellent sutlers' supplies were captured on this raid though nothing was said of them in official reports. The booty, which disappeared from the wagons with remarkable speed, included 300 pairs of excellent boots, numerous baskets of champagne and claret, and some tooth-some cheeses.[6]

The fourth raid was conducted by Stuart himself and was the most ambitious of the series. With 1800 men and four guns, Stuart rode up the south bank of the Rappahannock the day after Christmas, crossed to Morrisville[7] and prepared, as he subsequently

[3] *O. R.*, 21, 13 ff.
[4] *O. R.*, 21, 69–91. For commendation of Hampton by Stuart and by Lee see *ibid.*
[5] *O. R.*, 21, 695.
[6] Channing Price to his Mother, MS, Dec. 23, 1862—*Price MSS.*
[7] The best map to use in following this raid is the one in *O. R. Atlas,* Plate VIII. It should be noted, in advance of any account of this raid, that Stuart did not write his report until Feb. 15, 1864 (*O. R.*, 21, 731 ff), by which time, apparently, many of the minor details had become confused in his mind. Channing Price's full account in his letter of Jan. 20, 1863, doubtless is much more nearly accurate both because it was

reported, "to take possession of the Telegraph Road, to capture all the trains that might be passing." [8]

His plan was to descend on the road in three columns: Fitz Lee was to strike the highway South of Dumfries and was to drive northward toward the town. Wade Hampton "was to move round to the left in the direction of Occoquan"; [9] "Rooney" Lee was to advance eastward, down the valley of Quantico Creek, [10] straight on Dumfries, where Fitz Lee was to meet him. Stuart himself was to see that the columns got under way and then he was to join "Rooney" Lee.

For once, "Jeb" picked for himself the wrong road of adventure. Fitz Lee and his troopers had the good fortune to overtake nine sutlers' wagons on the 27th; [11] "Rooney" caught a few pickets and wagons; but when the time came to close in on Dumfries, Stuart had to choke his combative impulse and to admit that he was not justified in sustaining casualties in order to storm a position of some strength and to occupy a town from which, as he had seen, the Federals had time to remove their supplies. [12] He sent back to the Rappahannock two Confederate guns that had used up all their ammunition at Dumfries in a fruitless exchange with a Federal battery, and, regretfully, he led the column of Fitz Lee and of "Rooney" westward toward an untroubled bivouac, nine miles Northwest of Dumfries. [13]

On arriving at this bivouac, Stuart met Hampton [14] who had a tale of confusion to tell. Apparently, there had been some misunderstanding of Hampton's mission. The South Carolinian probably thought that his instructions to move "in the direction of Occoquan" implied three tasks: to clear the roads, to take the

nearer the described events and also because it was written by a young man of memory tenacious and accurate (see *infra*, p. 443). Specifically, to cite the first point of difference, Stuart wrote that the bivouac was at Morrisville; Price gave the place as Bristersburg, nine miles farther northward.

[8] *O. R.*, 21, 731. [9] *O. R.*, 21, 731.
[10] Presumably by the Forest Road.
[11] Channing Price to his sister, MS, Jan. 20, 1863—*Price MSS*.
[12] *O. R.*, 21, 732. This reference is an amusing example of the manner in which Stuart always, in his reports, made out the best case for himself. He said he concluded "the capture of the place would not have compensated for the loss of life which must have attended the movement, there being evidently no stores in the place . . ." That was literally true: there were "no stores in the place," but Channing Price's letter to his sister, Jan. 20, 1863—*Price MSS*, stated plainly "the enemy had 2 or 3 hours to move the stores, which we could see them doing . . ."
[13] At Cole's Shop, close to Union Church, on the Wood Road from Dumfries to Brentville. *O. R.*, 21, 732-33.
[14] *O. R.*, 21, 736.

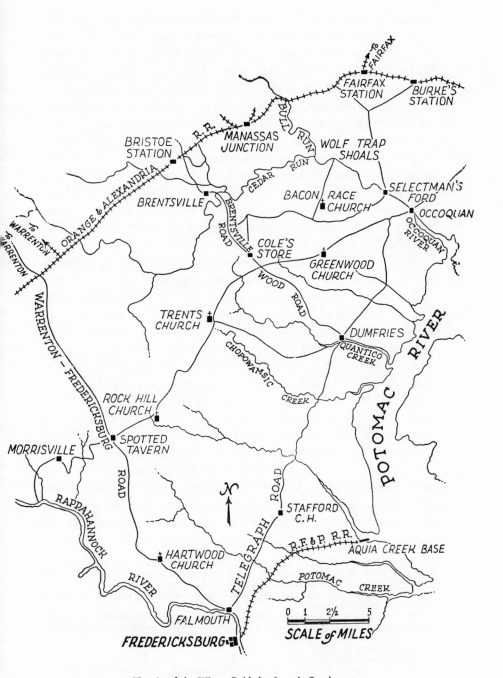

Terrain of the Winter Raids by Stuart's Cavalry.

town if he could and, in any event, to form juncture with the other columns near Occoquan.[15] Hampton had discharged without difficulty the first part of his assumed instructions and then had proceeded toward Occoquan. When he had reached the vicinity of the village, nightfall was near, but he sent Col. M. C. Butler directly forward to attack the place, while he turned aside to take position on the River Road and to cut off the Federal retreat toward Dumfries.[16] Unfortunately, Butler rushed into Occoquan before Hampton reached the point where fugitives were to be intercepted. The result was the capture of seven wagons only and of ten or fifteen prisoners.[17] With this small reward for his pains, Butler left the town and rejoined Hampton who, failing to find Stuart on the Telegraph Road, set out for the bivouac.[18]

Such were the scant results of much riding through the mud on December 27. So small was the recompense that Stuart was of a mind to end the raid and to start back to the Rappahannock, but on the basis of statements made by a man who had just arrived from Fairfax, he decided to continue on the enemy's side of the river.[19] He would seek to capture or chase any Federal force that might have been advanced to observe him, and then, if the outlook were favorable, he intended to move again to the Occoquan and to cross that stream and raid northward. In the event that the enemy tried to cut him off, he felt he could make a long detour in the direction of the Orange and Alexandria Railroad and could rejoin the Army on the Fredericksburg front.[20]

Fitz Lee had received the orders to start southward before Stuart changed his plan. Scarcely had Fitz got under way than scouts reported to Stuart that two Federal regiments were following the Confederate march, though still at some distance. As quickly as possible, Fitz Lee was recalled and was sent in the direction of the

[15] See Hampton in *O. R.,* 21, 736. Col. M. C. Butler, *ibid.,* 737, understood his orders, received through Hampton, to be that he should "move upon the town of Occoquan by the Telegraph Road and attack it."

[16] *O. R.,* 21, 736. This seems the most reasonable interpretation of Hampton's somewhat obscure language.

[17] *O. R.,* 21, 737. Although the Confederates seem to have expected that the detachment in Occoquan would try to reach Dumfries, the Federals actually withdrew northward across the river. *O. R.,* 21, 710–11.

[18] *O. R.,* 21, 736.

[19] Channing Price, *loc. cit.*

[20] This is not set forth explicitly in Stuart's report, but is unmistakable from his movements.

enemy's supposed advance. Hampton and "Rooney" Lee moved behind Fitz.[21]

When the column had ridden five miles through the chill December morning, Stuart directed Colonel Butler with 150 men to turn off to the left and to go four miles northward to the vicinity of Bacon Race Church. Thence Stuart believed Butler might flank the Federals who were said to be in front of the main column. Accordingly Butler swerved at Greenwood Church;[22] the other units kept on the road toward Occoquan.

Before Stuart and the main column had gone far, the Union cavalry were reported ahead in a wood through which the road passed. Hasty reconnaissance disclosed two regiments and, so far as Stuart could see, no more. He decided promptly that his men could ride over this force. Let Fitz Lee charge. Put the First Virginia in front. Clear the woods and pursue.

No time was lost in the execution of the order. Forward roared the First Virginia. It met scattered pistol fire[23] and brief resistance and then it had the target of fleeing men whom Union officers could rally for a few moments only. Some of the Federals were killed. Approximately 100 were captured. Pursuit became a race for the sheltering Occoquan. On stronger horses, the Federals outran the grayjackets, reached Selectman's Ford[24] and dashed through the chill waters.

Should the Confederates follow? The ford was "narrow, rocky and very difficult," but Tom Rosser had his Fifth Virginia in front and, being the man he was, did not hesitate any longer than the time required to put his regiment into files. Then, at bugle-blast, as many files as could get footing plunged straight ahead. A random, half-hearted fire greeted them, but it emptied no saddle. The Fifth was across; Fitz Lee's other detachments were close behind. Pelham, to the amazement of all, drove his guns through the ford, which always had been considered impassable for ve-

21 So wrote Channing Price, *loc. cit.* Stuart's account, from lapse of memory or unwillingness to make such an admission, contains no reference to any intention of abandoning the raid or of ordering Fitz Lee to start southward.

22 Five and a half miles North and slightly West of Dumfries.

23 Channing Price, *loc. cit.*

24 Upstream about 2½ miles from Occoquan. For the location of this ford, the writer is indebted to State Senator John W. Rust of Fairfax, who consulted James U. Kincheloe, Commissioner of Revenue of Fairfax County and a native of the Occoquan country. On the Federal map in *O. R. Atlas,* Plate VIII, the ford is marked "Snyder's." Mr. Kincheloe stated that never, to his knowledge, had that name been used in the locality.

hicles. Artillerists and troops together dashed for the Federal camps. These they found deserted and comfortably furnished, though reports mention no sutlers' establishments.[25] Everything of value that could not be carried off, the Confederates burned.[26]

Soon Calbraith Butler [27] arrived at Occoquan with a better tale of adventure to tell.[28] He had gone, as directed, to Bacon Race Church, in the expectation that the remainder of Hampton's troopers were to meet him there and were to form a column, as on the previous day, to co-operate with the forces on the roads to the southward. To facilitate this movement, Butler told the officer in command of the advance guard that if Federal pickets were encountered in any number not plainly superior, they were to be attacked at once and, if possible, captured.

Accordingly, when the advance guard was about one mile from Bacon Race Church, it ran into Federal pickets who were driven back to the eastward upon their support on the Brentsville Road. The resistance offered by this command led Butler to suspect that larger forces were at hand; but he held to the offensive in the belief that columns on parallel roads would strike the Federals. A moment later, his bold heart must have beaten faster at the sight of a formidable line, supported by two guns, in rear of the squadron he was pressing. The artillery fire made him recoil, but he determined not to retreat while there was a prospect that Hampton would swoop down on Federal flank or rear.

Minutes passed. Hampton did not appear. Neither sound nor movement of the enemy indicated the approach of another Confederate column of attack. Butler held on as long as he thought safe and then he started to withdraw westward along the Brentsville Road, but he found the Federals in his rear as well as in his front. He was in a trap. How was he to extricate himself? In his report he did not give any other explanation than that he had "to make a circuit of three or four miles," but the fact was, Stuart sent him a guide who knew thoroughly the forest trails and byways that led back to the road from Greenwood Church to

[25] O. R., 21, 733.
[26] Channing Price, loc. cit.
[27] Among his own people, M. C. Butler usually was called "Calbraith." In Virginia he was known as "Mat."
[28] Stuart reported that Butler rejoined the column as the rear was crossing the Occoquan (O. R., 21, 733-34); but Butler's account (ibid., 738), and Channing Price's (loc. cit.), indicate that Butler arrived later.

Occoquan.[29] By good luck and calm leading, Butler reached that road in time to fall in behind "Rooney" Lee's Brigade.[30]

On the arrival of Butler, Stuart had a reunited force of 1800 veteran horsemen; but he did not propose to take the desperate gamble of returning as he had come, by a route on which hostile troops might be collecting fast. As on the Chickahominy and the Maryland raids, the bolder course seemed more prudent, the longer road the safer. So, while Hampton made a demonstration toward Accotink,[31] the column turned westward. Hampton soon closed the rear; Stuart pressed rapidly on and, after dark, approached Burke's Station on the Orange and Alexandria Railroad.[32] There, "Jeb" was deeper than ever in the Federal lines, but was unshaken in his confidence that surprise and swift movement would get him safely out of any net the Union commanders might spread.

So sure was Stuart of himself that he sent two or three of his men ahead to pounce upon the telegraph operator before an alarm could be sent over the wire. Thereupon Stuart's own operator, Sheppard, who rode on all his expeditions, sat down at the sounder and read off the messages that excited Federal commanders were transmitting about ways and means of catching "the rebel raiders." Said Channing Price: ". . . it was very ludicrous, as [the Federals] were in great alarm, and orders were telegraphed to destroy everything in case of our attacking them." [33] To add the superlative of his own defiance to the enemy's dismay, Stuart drafted a telegram to the Quartermaster General of the United States Army and had the operator send it to Washington. A protest and remonstrance it was concerning the poor quality of the mules being supplied the Federal army. They were so inferior, said Stuart, that when put to captured wagons, they scarcely would pull the vehicles within the Confederate lines.[34]

---

[29] O. R., 21, 737, Channing Price, loc. cit.

[30] Ibid., 737–38. The heavy force that Butler encountered after he started back on the Brentsville Road must have been the advance of a Division of the XII Corps, which Gen. H. W. Slocum was moving via Wolf Run Shoals to reinforce Dumfries. Wolf Run Shoals is about six miles upstream on a straight line from Occoquan. The road southward from Wolf Run Shoals passed Bacon Race and Greenwood churches. Cf. O. R., 21, 892, 894.

[31] Six miles Northeast of Occoquan. Hampton is mentioned in the paragraphs immediately following but the main sketch is resumed infra, p. 418, n. 22.

[32] From this point, Stuart's route is best followed on Plate VII of O. R. Atlas.

[33] Loc. cit.

[34] O. R., 21, 734. The text, unfortunately, is lost. In 2 von Borcke, 168–69, the incident is stated in reverse: Stuart is represented as thanking General Meigs for the mules.

To this message Stuart attached his signature and, having revealed thereby his position at a given moment, he burned a railroad bridge and moved on. Even then he could not forgo an
effort once more to confront the Federals with the unexpected.
Did they assume that he would spur his jaded horses all the way
to the Rappahannock? Very well, he would surprise them: he
would go cross country northward to Fairfax Court House. That
famous outpost of contention was no nearer the Washington defenses than Burke's Station, nine miles, but it was garrisoned and was, so to say, the point where militarily the North
began.

To demand success in raiding Fairfax was to ask too much of
the goddess who favors the bold. As Stuart's column was moving forward, within a mile of the village, Federal troops, securely
ambushed, began to spit fire on the head of the column. Quickly
the veteran troopers withdrew and found, to their relief, that their
casualties were no worse than two horses killed and one man
nicked.

Because the Confederates sent not a shot in answer to this poor
fire, the Unionists were puzzled. A flag of truce was sent out to
the point, just beyond musket range, where the Confederate outpost had halted: Was the column friend or foe? the bearer of
the flag naïvely inquired. Some Southerner whose wit had not
been numbed by the cold replied that the flag would be answered
in the morning.

The Confederates then lighted enormous camp fires to deceive
the enemy, and by the time he began to shell the road they were
on their way by Vienna to Frying Pan—a singular combination,
surely, of continental and frontier names! From Frying Pan,
which was neither warm nor full, the column moved to Middleburg. Thence Col. Tom Rosser with fifteen men went on a
reconnaissance of the lower Valley. Stuart and the main force
made their leisurely way back to the Rappahannock, stopping
where hospitality was offered, and reached Fredericksburg New
Year's Day.[35]

Losses had not been large—one killed,[36] thirteen wounded and

[35] Diary of Lt.-Col. W. R. Carter, Third Virginia Cavalry, cited in *H. B. McClellan*,
202 n.; *O. R.*, 21, 734. Channing Price, *loc. cit.*, gave many details, nowhere else narrated, of the return.

[36] A most promising and gallant officer, Capt. J. W. Bullock of the Fifth Virginia

thirteen missing.[37] To these casualties, Maj. H. B. McClellan suggested an unhappy addition in this intriguing sentence: "The captured sutlers' wagons proved capable of inflicting nearly as much damage as the rifles of the enemy." [38] Stuart ignored that and, with high delight, counted about 200 prisoners, an equal number of horses, twenty wagons, 100 arms or more, and much miscellaneous loot.[39]

Of these gains, Stuart made the utmost. He reported that he had destroyed General Burnside's direct line of communication with Washington, had scattered the Union cavalry on the Occoquan, had made necessary the detachment of a large Federal force to patrol the country between Aquia Creek and Vienna, and had created the impression of an entry into Maryland, to prevent which the Federals had sent off large forces of cavalry and had broken down many of their horses.[40]

Compliments, too, Stuart handed out freely. Butler was commended for "coolness and presence of mind" in escaping from the Federals near Bacon Race Church; [41] Pelham was applauded for keeping up with the cavalry and for getting his guns across the Occoquan at Selectman's Ford.[42] Fitz Lee's praise of Tom Rosser for crossing at the same point in files—"one of the most admirable performances of cavalry I have ever witnessed" [43]—was echoed by Stuart in a dramatic recountal of the episode.[44] This was accompanied, also, by a generous sentence on Rosser's reconnaissance,[45] a tribute the more welcome by reason of a certain coolness that had developed. Stuart, in particular, had been pro-

[37] O. R., 21, 732, 734.   [38] H. B. McClellan, 202.
[39] Channing Price, loc. cit.   [40] O. R., 21, 735.
[41] O. R., 21, 734.   [42] Ibid., 735.
[43] O. R., 21, 739.
[44] O. R., 21, 733. Reports of this crossing by Rosser present an amusingly typical example of the familiar manner in which opposing sides view an episode that seems to one heroic and to the other merely a retreat in the face of overpowering odds. Stuart reported that the pursuing Confederates found the northern bank of the Occoquan "occupied by the enemy's dismounted sharpshooters in force." He went on: "Without waiting to exchange shots," and "in spite of the heavy volleys" the Confederates "pressed on, crossed the stream, suffered no loss, and captured or dispersed the whole party" (O. R., 21, 733). Capt. Charles Chauncey, 2nd Pennsylvania Cavalry, who led the detachment that was pursued across the Occoquan, described the effort made "to hold the ford" and the "heavy fire . . . poured into the advance of the rebels." They were driven back, he explained, and for a time were kept at bay. He continued: "Their superior numbers soon overpowered us. They brought down dismounted men armed with muskets, and, lining the whole bank, poured in a perfect shower of bullets. and at last crossed the river." (Ibid., 711–12.)
[45] Ibid., 734.

voked with Rosser on the 13th of December for withdrawing at Fredericksburg two 20-pounder Parrotts from an exposed position on the right.[46] Stuart himself, after the return from the raid on the Telegraph Road, did not receive formal congratulations on it in Army orders until Feb. 28, 1863. Lee then announced to the Army all the cavalry raids from November through February and commended the endurance, the gallantry and the promptness of the cavalry "in striking a successful blow wherever the opportunity offered." [47]

By that time, Stuart had spent what were for him two months of relaxing leisure in winter quarters, and there he had cemented old friends and had made new enemies. It always was that way with him. Women uniformly liked him. Men thought him an ideal soldier or an exhibitionist. There was no middle ground of opinion concerning him, no indifference to him. Of all his admirers, none was more fascinated than was Jackson. The affection of the Southern Cromwell was returned by the young Rupert in overflowing measure.

An incident of the autumn had become by this time a part of the anecdotal store of every staff officer. Stuart had ridden late in the night to Jackson's quarters and, removing nothing but his saber, had crawled under the blankets that sheltered "Old Jack." The coming of Stuart did not arouse Jackson—few things would —nor did the sleeper stir as Stuart, growing cold during the night, unconsciously pulled more and more of Jackson's blankets over himself. The next morning, "Jeb" was standing by a log fire when Jackson emerged from the tent. Greetings were exchanged. Said Jackson, in answer to a cordial good-morning: "General Stuart, I'm always glad to see you here. You might select better hours sometimes, but I'm always glad to have you. But General, you must not get into my bed with your boots and spurs on and ride me around like a cavalry horse all night." Kyd Douglas afterward insisted that Jackson stooped and rubbed his legs as he spoke, but that credits "Old Blue Light" with too much humor.[48]

Stuart made some facetious and now forgotten answer, but usually, in jest as in combat, he took the offensive. Few dared joke with Jackson; Stuart did often and never received a rebuke. He

[46] See R. Channing Price in *H. B. McClellan*, 194. For the next detailed reference to Rosser, see Vol. III.
[47] *O. R.*, 21, 1114-15.　　　　　[48] *Douglas*, 106.

had won the right to laugh sometimes because he supported always. "Jeb" had learned enough about the commanding General by this time to shun unfavorable comparisons; but during the winter, as will in its proper place appear, when Jackson's reports were being prepared, Stuart insisted that Jackson had earned credits that had not been claimed.[49]

Jackson's staff and his admirers were quite ready to admit what Stuart maintained in praise of their chief. Others there doubtless were in winter quarters who rallied the more heartily to Lee because Stuart was a "Jackson man." Lafayette McLaws, for example, himself honest, sincere and not overcritical, had undisguised contempt for Stuart's showmanship. The Georgian wrote "Dick" Ewell in February, '63: "Stuart carries around with him a banjo player and a special correspondent. This claptrap is noticed and lauded as a peculiarity of genius when, in fact, it is nothing else but the act of a buffoon to attract attention." [50]

Still other officers disliked Stuart without reference to any division into Jackson or Lee factions, factions which Lee and Jackson would have been the first to deplore and disown. One of Stuart's foes was Maj. 'Lige White, whom Stuart had provoked to wrathful tears during the Sharpsburg campaign.[51] Long and deep was his animosity toward "Jeb," though subsequently the division commander made honorable amends by frequent official praise of White's exploits.[52]

The Major's resentment against Stuart in the winter of 1862–63 was a feeble candle by the side of the flaming hatred of "Grumble" Jones. That strange man has appeared already in the story of Jackson's first weeks of command at Gordonsville after the Seven Days; but now he became a more conspicuous figure because of his promotion in the autumn at Jackson's instance [53] to the rank of Brigadier.[54] Besides, close to the year's end, Jones had been assigned, again on Jackson's recommendation,[55] to command the Valley District. For sentimental reasons, Jackson still was regarded at army headquarters as commander of that district.

49 See *infra*, Chap. XXX.
50 *Old Bald Head*, 133. For Stuart, see *infra*, Chap. XXXIV.
51 F. M. Myers, 107 ff.　　　　　52 Cf. *O. R.*, 21, 692.
53 *Hotchkiss' MS Diary*, 155.
54 As of Oct. 3, 1862; *Wright*, 90; *Cf.* his assignment to duty, Nov. 8, *O. R.*, 19, pt. 2, p. 705. See *supra*, p. 281.
55 *O. R.*, 21, 1092; *O. R.*, 25, pt. 2, p. 604.

Jones's orders, Dec. 29, 1862, to serve "during the absence of Lieutenant General Jackson" [56] added to the honor, though Jackson, at the time of Jones's appointment, had reversed his endorsement of Jones and had come to prefer Early.[57] It is possible that one reason for the assignment of Jones to the Valley was the wish of General Lee to utilize Jones's capacity for command to a more effective degree than was possible when Jones was under Stuart.

The differences between "Grumble" and "Jeb" ran back to the beginning of the war. Jones, who was 37 at the time of the secession of Virginia, had been born in Southwest Virginia, and had been graduated No. 10 in the class of 1848 at West Point.[58] He then spent three years in Oregon as a Second Lieutenant in the Mounted Rifles. Upon his return on furlough in 1852, he married Eliza Dunn and started with her by ship for his post. En route, March 26, 1852, the vessel was wrecked. The young bride was swept from her husband's arms by the force of the waves and was drowned.[59] Jones never recovered in spirit. Whatever there had been of gentleness in his heart seemed to have been destroyed. Embittered, complaining, suspicious, he resigned from the army in 1857 and, returning to the country of his birth, seemed to be determined to forget in farming everything military. Called to service as a Major in the Virginia service,[60] he had been made a Captain in the Provisional Army of the Confederacy and had been assigned to "Jeb" Stuart's regiment.

Although he was promoted Colonel when Stuart became a Brigadier General,[61] Jones, in the judgment of "Jeb's" friends, was jealous from the first of Stuart. This feeling, W. W. Blackford wrote, "ripened into as genuine hatred as I remember ever to have seen." [62] Jones had widened his animosity, though with less venom, to include his Lieutenant Colonel of 1861, who was Fitz Lee, one of Stuart's closest friends. As Jones was unpopular with the regiment and Fitz was much admired, an ugly situation developed. In the spring elections of 1862, Jones was displaced but, as already has been recorded,[63] was assigned to the Seventh Virginia. The so-called Laurel Brigade, placed under him later, had as

[56] O. R., 21, 1080–81.   [57] Douglas, 31–32.

[58] Cullum No. 1378, where it is stated that in 1847 Jones received the degree of M.A. from Emory and Henry College.

[59] 11 C. V., 266.   [60] O. R., 2, 823.

[61] O. R., 51, pt. 2, p. 320.   [62] W. W. Blackford's MS Memoirs, 18.

[63] See supra, p. 5.

its nucleus Ashby's famous command and it lacked nothing in valor [64] though its discipline out of action was defiantly low. "Grumble" had gone to work to correct this. He kept his men as busy as he could on raids, and if he had to hold the men in camp, he drilled them daily and made them obey the leter of regulations.[65] Saturday he designated every week as saber-grinding day —a routine that especially provoked the men of White's battalion.[66] They had, their historian protested, "a small opinion of the saber as a weapon to fight Yankees with, no matter how sharp it might be." [67] Jones insisted on the grinding and carried his point, with definite gain in obedience to orders.

Limited in equipment and in numbers, Jones had an unhappy experience at the beginning of the New Year, in executing orders General Lee issued for a raid on Petersburg and Moorefield in Western Virginia. Nothing went well during the operation. Jones himself lacked knowledge of the terrain and felt that the men on whom he relied to make good his deficiency failed him completely. His ammunition was bad, his guns no match for the Federal ordnance. The commissary virtually collapsed. Horses could not stand the strain. All these things "Grumble" Jones set down in his report of a futile march, which he described in a manner to justify his *nomme de guerre*.[68]

Lee commended and encouraged him, but the people of the Valley emulated him in grumbling. Certain members of the General Assembly of Virginia petitioned for better protection of the region of the Shenandoah. Ere long the Secretary of War went so far as to ask Lee to replace Jones with Fitz Lee.[69] In answer, the commanding General of the army defended Jones to the fullest and, while agreeing to make a change as soon as practicable, asserted that troops as well as commanders should be shifted.[70] Meantime, Lee continued to support Jones, who promptly grumbled that in general orders on the achievements of the cavalry during the winter months [71] Lee had failed to mention his Moorefield-Petersburg raid. The patient commander apologized and explained: "It was not from any want of appreciation of the serv-

---

[64] *Cf.* T. T. Munford, *O. R.*, 19, pt. 1, p. 828: "General Jones' brigade is second o none I have ever yet seen, in point of mettle."
[65] *Laurel Brigade*, 109.
[66] F. M. Myers, 150.
[67] *Ibid.*, 154.
[68] *O. R.*, 21, 747–48.
[69] *O. R.*, 25, pt. 2, pp. 604, 641.
[70] *Ibid.*, 654.
[71] *O. R.*, 21, 1114.

ices of your command, but was entirely accidental." [72] In answer to that, of course, Jones could say nothing, but his state of mind respecting Stuart and Fitz Lee, and the state of mind of the Valley people concerning him, promised trouble for the spring of 1863.

With division in the ranks of the cavalry itself, with horses dying and fodder scarce,[73] pessimists might question whether the mounted arm could keep safe the wings of the army, guard the outposts and bring back promptly accurate news of the enemy's movements. The grayjackets themselves never doubted. Nor did Lee, nor Stuart nor Hampton. When the time for field operations approached in the spring of 1863, they sought more cavalry but they did not lack faith in what they had.[74]

[72] O. R., 25, pt. 2, p. 682.
[73] 2 R. E. Lee, 491–92. See also 2 von Borcke, 153, Ham Chamberlayne, 154, 159
[74] O. R., 18, 1018; O. R., 25, pt. 2, 740–41, 747 ff.

CHAPTER XXVI

Promotion and a Fiery Resignation

WHILE Stuart's troopers were resting from the December raid and Jones's men were grinding their blades, one question endlessly was asked in camps around Fredericksburg: Would Burnside renew the attack? Against the background of the wintry sky, his campfires seemed to cover Stafford Heights and to gleam northward, Division by Division, mile on mile. Would the commander of that great army make no higher bid for victory and fame than that of one afternoon's assault on the pine ridge the shivering graycoats held? It seemed so improbable he would be content with a single blow that the cavalry were spread on a wide front to watch for any secret march. The infantry fortified heavily the Fredericksburg heights. If the numerically superior Federals made a feint there while preparing to attack at another point, a small Confederate force could hold the key position near the town. The remainder of the army could start after the enemy.

Burnside's next move was not the sole strategical perplexity. At the time of his attack on the line of the Rappahannock, the Federals took the offensive in North Carolina and pushed from New Berne to Kinston and Goldsborough. For ten days, the situation there had an ugly look. The government and the people of the North State were much alarmed. Reinforcements had to be snatched up wherever they could be found in lower Virginia and in South Carolina, and hurried to the threatened quarter.[1]

Almost immediately the competence of the command in the North State was brought into question and forthwith was entangled with rank and promotion in the Army of Northern Virginia. Because of the odd personalities involved, controversies of the weeks following the Battle of Fredericksburg were full of vexations but they illustrated some of the difficulties of organizing effective army command in an individualistic democracy. Grimly

[1] For more detailed reference to this operation, see *infra*, p. 420.

amusing, too, at least in retrospect, some of the complications appear.

In October, when Lee had wrestled with the choice of men to fill the vacancies created by the losses from the Rapidan to the Antietam, it might have seemed that he had expended enough effort to provide the best of available direction for all the Brigades and Divisions. Much that he had planned at that time was set at naught by the President's strict construction of military law. Mr. Davis would not promote officers who were unable physically to exercise immediate command, and, at the same time, he refused to retire some of those who seemed to be invalided. The patient Lee did not rebel against this, though he felt that failure to retire genuine invalids stopped sometimes the advancement of qualified men. As for the promotion of men temporarily incapacitated, he said: "It may appear hard that the honorable wounds of worthy and gallant officers should stand in the way of their promotion. But what can be done? Troops in the field must have Commanders, you know, and . . . none are so good as their permanent commander. Our cause is too momentous to allow private considerations to obstruct public interest, in which the individual concerned, as well as all others, has everything at stake." [2]

In application, this meant deferment of the promotion of I. R. Trimble, because he still was crippled by the wound received at Groveton. The converse application of the law postponed the advancement of "Jube" Early because Ewell might resume command Neither Ewell nor Trimble, if truth were told, had been doing any too well. Trimble had gone to Staunton, Virginia, and thence to Charlottesville, but, as noted, he had been dogged by camp erysipelas and later by what probably was osteomyelitis of the leg-bone that had sustained a compound fracture.[3] His temper, as will appear presently, was not one of sweet reasonableness.

"Dick" Ewell was in a healthier state of mind but not of body. In November, 1862, the great marcher had been moved to Richmond and had been received into the home of Dr. F. W. Hancock, who lived on Main Street [4] not far from the church of Dr. Moses D. Hoge, whose sonorous voice, Richmonders whis-

2 Lee to I. R. Trimble, MS, Jan. 2, 1863—*Trimble MSS.*
3 Dr. I. Ridgeway Trimble to the author, Nov. 22, 1940; see *supra,* p. 118.
4 *Old Bald Head,* 131. The address was 306 E. Main.

pered, had put "Old Jack" to sleep one July Sunday in 1862. Despite the care that Dr. Hancock had given, "Old Bald Head" had lost his temper because he had not recovered faster, and then one day had lost his balance, too, and had fallen. His amputated leg had hemorrhaged badly and had put Ewell flat on his back for weeks. Impatient and exsanguined though he was, he displayed—as sick men often do—the essential quality of his nature. Chivalrous he was at heart; chivalrous he showed himself to be in answer to a letter Jubal Early wrote in complaint over delayed promotion. From his bed, Ewell wrote: "The injustice you and Colonel [James A.] Walker have suffered has been a source of constant anxiety to me. And I should already have made efforts to have it repaired, but the absence of the President and the injury I have suffered have prevented me. I intend to go to work to have it corrected as soon as I am able, with strong hopes of success— but what ought to be most gratifying to you is that the injustice in your case is almost universally recognized. An officer of high rank in your Division"—Ewell did not say *my*—"told me the other day they had just discovered they had a trump and the Country is fast arriving at the same conclusion." [5]

This was not flattery on the part of Ewell. Although Early had won no popularity, he had earned increasing respect as a soldier.[6] Trimble had affection as well as respect. The promotion of these two to permanent divisional command seems to have been regarded as a continuing probability. In addition, General Lee had been watching Harry Heth, the guardian of the Kanawha road. Nor had the commanding General forgotten Arnold Elzey, who had been wounded in the head at Gaines' Mill, and Edward Johnson, who still was limping badly from the bullet he had received at McDowell.[7] In that operation, Jackson had formed a high opinion of Johnson. Doubtless on "Old Jack's" endorsement, when "Allegheny" began to recover, Lee recommended a Major General's commission.[8]

Of these five men marked for promotion to the grade of Major General—Early, Trimble, Heth, Elzey and Edward Johnson—

[5] *Hamlin's Ewell,* 115–16. The sketch of Ewell is continued *infra,* Chap. XXXVI.

[6] For evidences of the rising reputation of Early, see *O. R.,* 21, 647, 1022, 1026; *Douglas,* 31–32, 33. Early's own brief notice of his advancement will be found in his autobiography, 185–86.

[7] See *supra,* Vol. I, p. 354.

[8] Lee to Trimble, MS, Jan. 2, 1863—*Trimble MSS.*

circumstance gave the first set-up to Arnold Elzey. Although the injury to his face and tongue was such that he scarcely could speak,[9] he was thought to be physically able to administer a district. On Dec. 4, 1862, he had been commissioned at the new rank,[10] and the day before the Battle of Fredericksburg, he had been placed in command of the Richmond defenses and adjacent areas to the southward.[11]

This assignment of the bulky Marylander did not interfere with plans for the promotion of Trimble, or in any way thwart the ambitions of the sick soldier, but it infuriated him. He believed Elzey had discredited him, and he suspected also that he missed promotion because Jackson, in endorsing him, had stated, "I do not regard him as a good disciplinarian." [12] In a raging letter to Adjutant General Cooper, whom he knew well, Trimble spoke bluntly of Elzey's love of liquor. In his own behalf, Trimble defended himself against Jackson's charge. Said he: ". . the General knew but little of any Brigade, but his *old one*. It is well known to all, that I was most particular in my enforcement of discipline. My Brigade had fewer stragglers; burnt no rails, committed no thefts in the country, was more often drilled both by regiments and in evolutions of the line by myself, than any other in the Army of Jackson." Trimble insisted further to Cooper, "If I am to have promotion I want it *at once* and I particularly request, that my date may be from 26th August, the date of the capture of Manassas—which General Jackson was pleased to say he considered 'the most brilliant exploit of the war.' " [13]

More formally Trimble addressed the Secretary of War: "If any disparaging representations have been made to the Department to counteract this testimonial [*i.e.,* Lee's recommendation for promotion], in justice to me I should be informed of their nature and be allowed to correct them. If I am not to be promoted on such a testimonial, I wish frankly to know it, and shall continue to give the country my best service in my present grade. If however it be considered proper by you, that the promotion shall take effect, I feel bound to observe that if my services are deemed important to the Government they will probably sooner be obtained

9 *DeLeon's B. B. B.,* 318.   10 *Wright,* 31.
11 *O. R.,* 18, 764.   12 See *supra,* p. 259.
13 Trimble to Cooper, MS. Dec. 22, 1862—*Trimble MSS.*

by making the promotion at once, as my recovery from a painful wound is probably retarded by the suspense in which I have been kept for some months." [14]

Although Jackson inquired whether Trimble was well enough to direct a Division in camp [15] and Lee did his utmost to smooth ruffled feelings,[16] the Marylander did not improve rapidly. His feelings were not to be relieved, either, by an inquiry he was to receive later from Jackson concerning the operations of August 26 at Bristoe and Manassas. Out of that inquiry and Trimble's reply to it was to develop a controversy with "Jeb" Stuart, who was to maintain that he and not Trimble commanded the night attack on the Federal base.[17] When Trimble got on his legs again he was to knock the props, so to say, from under Stuart.[18] Meantime, Trimble was to find one outlet for his energies and imagination in planning a paper campaign against the Federal advanced base at Aquia Creek, a plan the patient Lee examined and praised but could not apply.[19]

Trimble's promotion was not delayed as long as he feared it would be. On Jan. 19, 1863—his own fifty-sixth birthday—Lee announced the promotion of Trimble and Early to the coveted rank of Major General.[20] To avoid any complication over Ewell's position or over the assignment of Trimble at a time when he still was unable to exercise field command, the army orders simply read that the two officers were to command Divisions of the Second Corps. Neither to this device nor to the promotions was there any recorded opposition except on the part of Brig. Gen. W. B. Taliaferro. As senior Brigadier in Jackson's Division, he felt that he should have had the divisional command, and when he did not get it, he told friends he would seek transfer to some other theatre of operations.[21]

Because of favorable circumstances in nearly all the units in-

[14] Trimble to Seddon, MS, Dec. 22, 1862—*Trimble MSS.*
[15] Jackson to Trimble, MS, Jan. 1, 1863—*Trimble MSS.*
[16] Lee to Trimble, MS, Jan. 2, 1863, quoted *supra.*—*Trimble MSS.*
[17] Trimble to Jackson, MS, Jan. 6, 1863—*Trimble MSS; O. R.,* 12, pt. 2, p. 720.
[18] This controversy came to a head in April. See *infra,* Chap. XXX and *O. R.,* 12, pt. 2, p. 720 ff.
[19] *O. R.,* 25, pt. 2, p. 658.
[20] *O. R.,* 21, 1099. The formal appointments were not made until April 23, 1863, when Congress was in session, but the commissions were to date from Jan. 17, 1863. *Wright,* 32.
[21] *Hotchkiss' MS Diary,* 133; Jan. 23, 1863. The sketch of Trimble is resumed *tra.* Chap. XXX; that of Early, *infra,* Chap. XXX.

volved, the vacancies at the grade of Brigadier General were not difficult to fill. General Lee understood that Wade Hampton, who fast was growing in fame,[22] had not accepted commission in the cavalry with the intention of remaining in that service throughout the war. Consequently, the Brigade of Gregg was offered Hampton.[23] He declined it.[24] If Hampton was not to lead Gregg's famous command, then the man to do so was Col. Samuel McGowan of the Fourteenth North Carolina,[25] who already was distinguished for quick perception and prompt, energetic action.[26]

For Tom Cobb's Brigade, the choice manifestly should be Col. W. T. Wofford of the Eighteenth Georgia, able and experienced.[27] As Trimble was to be promoted, his regiments well might go to the hard-hitting Col. R. F. Hoke of the Twenty-first North Carolina, who had commanded the Brigade at Fredericksburg ably, though in reporting on the battle he had marred his narrative by sprinkling the pages too thickly with "I's." [28] A fourth vacancy among the Brigadiers seemed probable in Paul Semmes's case.[29] To succeed him temporarily at the head of Georgia troops, no Colonel was so well qualified or so well known to the Army as "Old Rock" Benning, who had won fame with Toombs's Brigade and most notably at Sharpsburg.[30] Finally, as Gen. W. S. Featherston decided that he would prefer duty in the Gulf States,

[22] Davis proposed that Hampton be given command of the cavalry in North Carolina, but Lee had not been willing to part with Hampton (O. R., 18, 891). About the same time, when Seddon pressed for the substitution of someone for W. E. Jones in the Valley, Lee said that Hampton, senior Brigadier of cavalry, "and an officer of standing and gallantry" might do better in that command than anyone else who had been proposed (O. R., 25, pt. 2, p. 641). For Lee's thanks to Hampton for the patriotic importation of Blakely guns, see ibid., 694. Hampton's one shortcoming at this time was his failure to keep up the horses of his Brigade (cf. O. R., 18, 891). The sketch of Hampton is continued infra, p. 470 and Vol. III.
[23] O. R., 21, 1067.
[24] For commendation of Hampton for the winter raids of 1862–63, see O. R., 21, 15, 690, 696, 735; O. R., 51, pt. 2, p. 653.
[25] O. R., 21, 1100.
[26] Caldwell, 68.
[27] For references to Wofford, in chronological order, through September 1863, see O. R., 51, pt. 2, p. 356; 4, 689; 51, pt. 2, p. 369; Richmond Examiner, Nov. 9, 1861, p. 3, col. 3; O. R., 11, pt. 1, p. 631; 12, pt. 2, pp. 567, 606; 19, pt. 1, pp. 841, 929; 19, pt. 1, p. 1100; 25, pt. 1, p. 824; 27, pt. 2, p. 369; 29, pt. 2, p. 711.
[28] O. R., 21, 672; for the promotion, see ibid., 1099.
[29] The reason does not appear. It probably was sickness or necessary absence on account of business. Semmes was in the Battle of Fredericksburg and was reassigned to his old Brigade Apr. 3, 1863. O. R., 25, pt. 2, p. 702. For an interesting reference to Semmes at Sharpsburg, see 33 S. H. S. P., 102.
[30] O. R., 21, 1099–1100.

he was relieved. The delayed appointment of Col. Carnot Posey became effective.[31]

Such, then, were the promotions and changes in January— Trimble to take Jackson's Division when strong enough to do so, Early to continue in temporary command of Ewell's Division at appropriate grade, McGowan to have Gregg's men, Wofford to lead Cobb's, Hoke to take Trimble's former Brigade, Benning temporarily to have Semmes's, and Posey to be assigned Featherston's.

As these changes came little more than two months after the reorganization necessitated by the losses of the late summer, an optimist might have hoped that the Army would have stable command in the Spring of 1863. It was not to be. Resignations as well as casualties were in prospect. For the future as in the past the two dominant jealousies were to complicate and mar the promotions: Some of the officers who had entered the Army from civil life carped always at the West Pointers; others maintained that Virginians always were preferred. Even so honest and so good a man as Lafayette McLaws complained that if Longstreet had come from the Old Dominion the article about him in the *Illustrated London News* would have been much more laudatory.[32]

Not over Virginians or directly over West Pointers, but over competence in command, a situation of gravity was developing in North Carolina. Maj. Gen. Gustavus W. Smith, it will be remembered, had been able in August to report for duty after the so-called paralysis that had overwhelmed him on the second day at Seven Pines. On this happy recovery, Lee tactfully had assigned to Smith the "right wing of the army," which included Richmond and departmental command as far South as the Cape Fear River. As noted already [33] communication between Smith and the army commander thereafter was confidential and unrestrained con-

---

[31] See *supra*, p. 265. As of Nov. 1, 1862, Posey had been made one of the twenty "special" Brigadier Generals named under the act of Oct. 13, 1862, but it will be recalled that Featherston had returned unexpectedly to duty and that Posey had not been assigned to duty at his new rank (see *Wright*, 135). Apparently, till almost the eve of Featherston's decision to go South, the transfer of Posey to some other army had been in consideration. He had been ordered to Richmond, Jan. 17, 1863, with his adjutant—a course not usually followed unless assignment to another post was in prospect (*O. R.*, 21, 1095). For Posey's record, in chronological order, see *O. R.*, 51, pt. 2, pp. 200, 206, 217; 5, 979; 12, pt. 1, p. 783; 51, pt. 2, p. 604; 12, pt. 2, pp. 563, 567; 19, pt. 1, p. 841; 19, pt. 2, pp. 683, 697, 703.

[32] *Old Bald Head*, 133.   [33] *Supra*, p. 145 n. 6.

cerning both Lee's own plans and Smith's duties, which chiefly were those of watching an inactive enemy along the Virginia and North Carolina coast.

Nothing of large moment had arisen to disturb Smith until the seven Lieutenant Generals had been appointed under the act of Sept. 18, 1862.[34] As all those officers, with the exception of Leonidas Polk, had been Smith's juniors at the grade of Major General, the offended officer promptly inquired of the Secretary of War why he had been passed over.[35] Secretary Randolph did not answer this formally but he told Smith privately that the departmental command Smith was then exercising in Virginia and North Carolina was not considered one that rated the high grade within the intent of the law.[36] This explanation did not satisfy Smith. He sought another interview and hinted at resignation. Later he wrote a long protest at being overslaughed and closed this with formal tender of his resignation, but at Randolph's instance he agreed to continue in a post which the Secretary said he did not then know how to fill.[37]

For a few days in November, Smith seems to have been assuaged by appointment as Secretary of War between the resignation of Randolph and the acceptance of James A. Seddon.[38] The next month, he had to go to Eastern North Carolina when Federal forces under Maj. Gen. John G. Foster made the raid, already mentioned, on Kinston and Goldsborough.[39] The Unionists numbered 10,000 infantry, 640 cavalry and had forty guns,[40] and at the outset they encountered scarcely more than 2000 Confederates under "Shanks" Evans. That veteran put up the best fight he could, but before he got substantial reinforcement, he lost by capture over 400 of his men and six of his guns.

During the closing days of the affair, which covered December 10–20, Smith was on the scene and in general command. Beverley Robertson with his cavalry, Samuel G. French from the Suffolk-Petersburg district, Johnston Pettigrew—all these had some part in the affair. From Wilmington, W. H. C. Whiting sent many messages and such help as he could. In the end, the Fed-

[34] *Wright*, 14.   [35] *G. W. Smith*, 255.
[36] *Ibid.*, 256.   [37] *Ibid.*, 262–63.
[38] Nov. 17–21, 1862. See IV *O. R.*, 2, 1074; 1 *R. W. C. D.*, 191–94. Seddon was not nominated formally to the Senate until Jan. 15, 1863. See IV *O. R.*, 2, 358.
[39] All the reports of this operation use this longer form of the town's name.
[40] *O. R.*, 18, p. 54.

erals burned a main bridge on the Weldon-Wilmington Railroad, paroled 496 Confederates and carried off the captured guns.[41] Union losses were 591.[42] The Confederates had 71 killed and 268 wounded, in addition to the prisoners—a total of 835.[43]

"Our troops," wrote S. G. French in his autobiography, "were not properly handled at Goldsborough." [44] That was a moderate statement of the fact. North Carolina was puzzled and depressed by the outcome. Moreover, a great Federal fleet, then being made ready in Hampton Roads, was thought to have Wilmington as its objective.[45] So serious was the prospect of Federal invasion that North Carolina manifestly must be reinforced substantially and at once. On the 3d of January, though there was no diminution of force in his own front and every reason to expect a renewed Federal offensive, General Lee started Ransom's demi-Division for Richmond.[46]

Consideration had also to be given to command in North Carolina. Harvey Hill, the most conspicuous soldier from the State in the Army of Northern Virginia, was sick and depressed: Would it help him and North Carolina also, to detach him for service there? Despite misgiving of Hill's administrative capacity, Lee put the question to the President [47] and to the Secretary of War.[48] Both of them concluded that the suggestion was worth canvassing, but Seddon must have felt some doubts whether Governor Zeb. Vance would take Hill at the instance of the Confederate administration.

The Secretary proceeded to address the Governor of North Carolina with as much caution and deference as would be displayed to a sultan by a vizier who feared he might be marked for death: An extract from Lee's letter was forwarded. The commanding General was presented as anxious to know "whether the presence of one of his most distinguished generals (General D. H. Hill of your State) might not prove advantageous in rousing and stimulating the people and in counseling and co-operating with the State authorities?" Seddon continued: "On this subject I wish to defer to your judgment and wishes, of which I should be pleased to be advised." [49]

[41] *Ibid.*, 59.   [42] *Ibid.*, 60.   [43] *Ibid.*, 110.
[44] S. G. French, *Two Wars* (cited hereafter as *French*), 154.
[45] *O. R.*, 18, 810 ff.   [46] *O. R.*, 18, 818.
[47] *Lee's Dispatches*, 69.   [48] *O. R.*. 18. 819.   [49] *O. R.*, 21, 831.

Whether or not the Governor approved, the records do not show. The Senators and Representatives from his State previously had asked the promotion and assignment to North Carolina of Johnston Pettigrew, who had recovered from the wounds received at Seven Pines and now, as an exchanged prisoner of war, awaited larger duties than those of brigade command, though he did not complain of grade or duty.[50] Vance may have favored Pettigrew but he scarcely can have said "No" to the Department's suggestion, because on Jan. 14, 1863, Harvey Hill was ordered to proceed to Richmond and to report to the Adjutant General.[51]

Hill by that time must have been in serious plight physically. He sought relief from all service and talked of resigning,[52] though he agreed, at length, to go home and to withhold formal resignation. That much assured, Seddon addressed another note of rounded diplomatic phrasing to the Governor of North Carolina. He said: "It has occurred to me that from the appreciation of the Department of his proven valor and skill it might be pardonable in me to suggest that in view of the dangers from the enemy now menacing your State the benefit of [General Hill's] counsel and co-operation might be obtained by you on conference with him. His deserved influence with the people of North Carolina might prove advantageous in animating and encouraging them to effort and endurance, and his experience and judgment give valuable suggestions as to the best mode of commanding and guiding the means of the States for defense. Trusting to be excused for the liberty of such suggestion, I have the honor to be, with very high consideration and esteem, most respectfully yours."[53] Again there is no record of a reply from His Excellency Zebulon B. Vance, Governor, Captain-General and Commander-in-Chief,[54] but circumstances forced a decision of another sort.

General Smith had been pleading with the War Department for a heavy detachment from the Army of Northern Virginia to reinforce him, and in one of his arguments he showed that what he considered demotion still was rankling in his mind: "Before I was reduced in relative rank in this army," said he, "it was a question whether General Lee or myself should command the active forces in Northern Virginia, the other to command in Richmond,

[50] *O. R.,* 51, pt. 2, p. 627.   [51] *O. R.,* 21, 847.
[52] Cf. *O. R.,* 18, 851.   [53] *O. R.,* 18, 851.
[54] For the use of these exalted titles in a proclamation, see *O. R.,* 18, 861.

&c.," wherefore he wished Lee to consider the matter from the point of view of the Richmond command.[55] A week later he wrote in a tone of moderate confidence and concluded: "My health is not as good as I would wish, but I won't break down if [the enemy] will only come on." [56]

By that time, Robert Ransom had reached North Carolina with his half-Division and had observed something of Smith's handling of the command. He was much disturbed by what he saw and, as a loyal North Carolinian, he was resolved not to permit the State to remain under Smith's military care if he could prevent. In accordance with the usage of the "old army" he determined to write unofficially what he could not transmit to Army Headquarters without insubordination. In a personal letter to Gen. R. H. Chilton of Lee's staff he set forth his own unhappiness and enumerated some of the faults he saw in the defense of the State. As his letter subsequently was destroyed, in circumstances presently to be related, the exact nature of Ransom's disclosures is not clear but, inferentially, it would appear that he felt Smith lacking in energy and inclined to dodge matters that involved excitement.[57]

This state of affairs Chilton informally described to Lee, as Ransom doubtless had intended. Lee considered the situation so serious that he at once forwarded Ransom's letter to President Davis. If, the commanding General explained, Smith's health was impaired, it was more than ever to be desired that Kirby Smith, who had been under consideration, should take the command in North Carolina. Should it not be possible for Kirby Smith to go there, then, said Lee, it might be better for·Elzey to take the field in North Carolina and for Gustavus Smith to assume command of the Richmond District. Lee made plain that Ransom did not know the letter was being forwarded and he concluded with a request that the President, after reading the paper, destroy it.[58]

Action came quickly. As Kirby Smith would not be available

[55] O. R., 18, 847. The text of this letter to the Secretary of War, as received by Seddon, is perceptibly different from that in G. W. Smith, 289.

[56] O. R., 18, 855.

[57] This inference is based on Lee's remark, apropos of Ransom's letter, "I think it probable that General G. W. Smith's health makes him apprehensive of exertion or excitement." That almost certainly was Lee's charitable interpretation of evidence Ransom must have presented of inactivity on the part of Smith.

[58] O. R., 18, 856.

immediately, the President recalled Gustavus Smith to Richmond, sent S. G. French temporarily from Southside Virginia to North Carolina, and had the Secretary of War telegraph to inquire whether D. H. Hill would accept the command of his own State.[59] Hill hesitated to accept responsibility of that magnitude and he answered the Secretary that he would prefer to serve under Smith,[60] which he would have done anyway because Smith's departmental command included North Carolina.[61]

Smith previously had indicated that he would prefer the post in Richmond; [62] but when he got back there, he became restless and unhappy. A hint that he might be sent to Louisiana and Texas was not fulfilled. In a personal interview with the President, January 28, Smith was asked no questions of any importance and was given no instructions.[63] This fired new discontent, to which in a letter from Wilmington, W. H. C. Whiting added fuel. Said Whiting: "I have thought that I had grown callous to Mr. Davis's treatment, but every now and then the papers inform me of his promoting men who have served under me, and who have been placed under me because they couldn't be trusted to go alone —and the Old Adam in me rises. But let that pass." [64]

For ten days Smith fumed and kicked his heels, and then, February 7, he forwarded as a formal resignation a copy of his letter of October 21 to the previous Secretary of War. With this he coupled a new explanation and protest in the course of which he said: "The nature and amount of my duties in this city during the last summer and fall, and the annoyance consequent upon the action of the Government in reference to myself, have prevented the thorough re-establishment of my health. In this respect I have labored under some disadvantages, but I am not conscious of having failed on this account to perform satisfactorily the duties of my position, which are certainly not those of a commander of a division properly pertaining to my rank, but are higher, more important and more difficult than those of a corps commander. About ten days ago I was ordered back to Richmond from North Carolina, and now understand that I am expected to command, as heretofore, from the immediate theatre of General Lee's active operations on the North, extending South to Wilmington, with orders to remain in this

[59] O. R., 18, 861.
[61] O. R., 18, 872.
[63] G. W. Smith, 296–98.
[60] G. W. Smith, 338.
[62] G. W. Smith, 292.
[64] G. W. Smith, 299.

city. I cannot consent to remain here and be responsible at this time for operations in North Carolina. Neither am I willing to serve under the orders of those who were recently my juniors. There is no alternative left me but to resign my commission in the army." He added a statement of his resolution to work "in another sphere" for Southern independence and politely thanked the Secretary and the previous head of the War Department for their consideration.[65]

For another week and more, Smith continued complainingly to exercise command.[66] On the afternoon of the 16th one of the Assistant Adjutants General returned the letter of resignation with a stinging endorsement by Davis of what the President termed "this remarkable paper." The Chief Executive spared no sarcasm. If, said he, Smith's sole desire was to aid in achieving Southern independence "it might have been expected that less importance would be attached to provisional rank." Point by point, with all the sharpness of his logic, Davis dismissed the grievances that Smith had expressed in the letter to Secretary Randolph in the autumn. When President Davis came to the complaint that Smith had been superseded by Lee and had not been given the command of Johnston's army, the language of the endorsement left little to the imagination. "It . . . appears . . . that immediately after the battle, in which General Johnston was wounded, General Smith reported sick, and left the army, a fact not consistent with the supposition that he was willing and able to command it in active operations."

After another paragraph of like vigor, the Chief Executive dipped once more in acid and endorsed Smith's second and final resignation thus: "Secretary of War—If the alternative of resignation or appointment as Lieutenant General is presented as a claim founded on former relative rank as a Major General it will only be proper to accept the resignation, as to admit the claim would be in derogation of the legal power of the Executive and in disregard of the consideration due to service rendered in battle and campaign." [67]

Smith wrote nothing subsequently to indicate that he expected the President to accept the alternative of promotion; but as a sol-

65 *G. W. Smith*, 300–01. *Cf.* Smith to French, Feb. 7, 1863, *O. R.*, 18, 872.
66 *Ibid.*, 301 ff.   67 *G. W. Smith*, 305–07.

dier who had been a politician and was as quick to draw pen as
sword, Smith would not permit the President's endorsements to
pass unchallenged. He took his time and, on the 23d of February,
completed a letter of some 2400 words in which he reviewed again
his grievances, answered the President and no doubt satisfied himself that he had demolished Mr. Davis's argument. It was the
kind of letter a man writes in order to read aloud to his friends
at a club-table, where he pauses at the impressive flourishes as if
to say, "I got him there, did I not?"

The gravamen of Smith's letter was that he had been "overslaughed by wholesale," [68] that he had in effect commanded a
Corps at Manassas during the winter of 1861–62, and that, when
his juniors were promoted over him, he became convinced that he
was not "respected, supported and confided in by the government
to an extent sufficient" to authorize his remaining in service. Of
Seven Pines, Smith wrote: "You say that I complained of being
superseded by General Lee during the battle . . . I stated the
fact, nothing more. Is it denied? As to your lengthy argument
endeavoring to prove that because I reported sick the next day I
was not able and willing to command the army in active operations—passing by the covert insinuation—I have only to say in
answer to the plain substance of the remark, that no symptoms of
the disease—the same by which I had been stricken down more
than a year before—had shown themselves until the battle was
over, and I had been actually superseded by General Lee for more
than eighteen hours; of course a longer time had elapsed after
your order was given to General Lee directing him to take
command." [69]

All this Smith wrote with care and forwarded to the President,
but he got no answer. Davis did not take the time or the trouble
to enter into the same sort of controversy with Smith that subsequently he pursued with Governor Joe Brown of Georgia, a
polemic as stubborn as he. Smith went to Charleston as a volunteer aid to Beauregard, who was of a temper to welcome any
Confederate hostile to the President. Besides, Beauregard personally was fond of Smith. So were many of the officers and politicians who knew him intimately. [70] Governor Vance confided: "I

---

[68] G. W. Smith, 308.   [69] Ibid., 313.
[70] Cf. John R. Cooke to J. E. B. Stuart, MS, Jan. 18, 1863: "I have met G. W.
several times and like him exceedingly."—Cooke MSS.

was satisfied that you not only understood our military situation, but, what is of quite as much significance, the political status of our people; and I was always gratified to find that our notions and prejudices were respected." The sheet itself seemed to sigh with Vance's next sentence: "I fear that so thorough an understanding can never be obtained with your successor, though I shall endeavor that it shall not be my fault." [71]

Whether, in that, Vance was referring to a successor in the abstract or specifically to Harvey Hill, it is impossible to say; [72] but Hill himself was among those who lamented the departure of Smith from the service. The North Carolinian explained that he had expressed his preference for serving under Smith, and then he added a few words that confirmed all General Lee had written President Davis of Hill's unwillingness to assume exclusive responsibility. Said Hill: "At present I feel at a loss what to do. I have not yet assumed command and do not wish to do so. I came here [to Goldsboro] with the understanding that I was to serve under you. Honestly and truly I prefer that position and shrink from the other." [73]

[71] *G. W. Smith* 334. The next references to Smith are in Vol. III.

[72] Hill's formal assignment was published February 7, four days after Vance wrote Smith; but as orders usually were not published for several days, it is entirely possible that Vance knew on February 3 that Hill was to exercise command in North Carolina.

[73] Feb. 20, 1863; *G. W. Smith*, 338. The sketch of D. H. Hill is resumed in Vol. III. Not long after the resignation of Smith, another disputed figure of the times, John B. Floyd, yielded to the Confederacy the 200 or 300 men who remained of the Virginia "State Line," which was to have numbered 10,000 who would fight for Virginia if not for the South. For this and for Floyd's other military activities, apart (1) from his share in the controversy with Wise, Aug.-Sept. 1861, for which see 1 *R. E. Lee*, 580–93, and (2) his participation in the contest at Fort Donelson, the following references are chronological: *O. R.*, 51, pt. 2, p. 55; *Richmond Examiner*, May 18, 23, June 1, 10, 1861; *Wright*, 50; IV *O. R.*, 1, 374; *Richmond Dispatch*, June 25, July 1, 5, 8, 1861; *O. R.*, 51, pt. 2, pp. 152–53, 167, 213; *Richmond Examiner*, Aug. 31; *Richmond Whig*, Sept. 7; *Richmond Examiner*, Sept. 4; *Ham Chamberlayne*, 40; *Richmond Examiner*, Oct. 12, 16; *Richmond Dispatch*, Oct. 11, 23; *Richmond Examiner*, Dec. 4; *O. R.*, 51, pt. 2, p. 429; *Richmond Examiner*, Dec. 12, 18, 19; *Richmond Dispatch*, Dec. 13, 1861, Jan. 1, 1862; *Richmond Examiner*, Jan. 2, 1862; *Richmond Whig*, July 9, Aug. 25, 1862; *O. R.*, 12, pt. 3, p. 947; *O. R.*, 19, pt. 2, pp. 616–17, 625, 627–28; *O. R.*, 19, pt. 2, p. 691; *O. R.*, 51, pt. 2, p. 655; *O. R.*, 21, pp. 1022, 1059, 1065, 1068; IV *O. R.*, 2, 309; *O. R.*, 21, 1104, 1112–13; *O. R.*, 51, pt. 2, p. 672; *O. R.*, 25, pt. 2, p. 603 ff; *O. R.*, 51, pt. 2, pp. 655, 672, 686. Floyd died Aug. 26, 1863.

CHAPTER XXVII

THE DEVELOPING STAFF

THE CONCERN of the departing Gustavus Smith and of the incoming Harvey Hill for the safety of North Carolina was shared by the commanders of the Army of Northern Virginia. Those of Lee's lieutenants who lived in Carolina naturally were most deeply solicitous because they knew to what extent their State had been depleted of its garrisons in order that the enemy might be met and halted close to the Potomac, the northern frontier of the Confederacy. On the Rappahannock, Carolinians and Virginians and men from all the Southern States had continued their vigilant watch for a renewal of the offensive. With more of eagerness than of anxiety, the question asked so often during December was repeated in the New Year—When will Burnside advance; where will he strike?

On the 9th of January, 1863, the next development seemed to be foreshadowed by a cavalry reconnaissance in force against Catlett's Station and Rappahannock Station. This move suggested that General Burnside might be considering an advance by his right flank down the Orange and Alexandria Railroad in the direction of Gordonsville, but Stuart drove back the enemy with little difficulty in a day's confused skirmishing.[1] By the 19th, new evidence was accumulated of preparations for a Federal drive from Burnside's right, above Fredericksburg but much closer than the line indicated by the reconnaissance in force ten days previously. The shivering Brigades at the fords were strengthened.[2] Among the camps the feeling was, It's coming now. Scouts' reports on the 20th, a blustery, threatening day, indicated that the concentration was around Hartwood Church, that the offensive was to be undertaken by Hooker's and Franklin's Grand Divisions, and that the crossing would be in the vicinity of Banks' and United States Mine Fords.[3] Preliminary dispositions were

---

[1] The brief reports are in O. R., 21, 749 ff.   [2] O. R., 21, 755.

[3] O. R., 21, 755. These reports were correct, except that the scouts apparently did not ascertain that the newly formed Reserve Grand Division of the XI and XII Corps was to co-operate behind the lines of advance. Cf. O. R., 21, 754, 935, 986.

made by the Confederates at and near those fords to cope with the advance.

It did not come. Gray skies put on mourning. On the evening of the 20th a violent storm began and continued all night and for two days thereafter. Patriotic Virginia roads on the north side of the Rappahannock swam in defiant mud. Federal infantry could do no more than creep forward, heavy footed. Artillery had to double teams. Pontoon trains could not be moved at all. This "Mud March" simply stalled.[4] Before a wind of doubtful Southern loyalty could dry the mud, a second storm began early on the 27th and did not halt its attack until the morning of the 29th. By that time, six inches of snow covered the ground.[5] Said Lee in reporting this downfall, ". . . the probabilities are that the roads will be impracticable for some time." [6] That was not the only promise of a respite. Burnside on January 25 was relieved of command.[7] A new commander was given the Army of the Potomac in the person of "Fighting Joe" Hooker, who had commanded the Central Grand Division [8] and had been one of the most vigorous of Burnside's critics.[9]

As mud and the preparation of a new plan would preclude another advance for weeks, Lee's lieutenants at last could expect days and days of inactivity in shelter of such comfort as ingenuity could fashion. The Army actually was in winter quarters from about December 20, but not until the end of the "Mud March" was there any assurance it could stay there. Then the Army settled down for the first prolonged period of quiet the whole command ever had spent together. Many of the units encamped back of Fredericksburg had not joined until after the winter of 1861–62. Jackson during that first wintry season had been on detached service in the Great Valley. Lee had been in South Carolina. Now the Manassas Army, Magruder's men, Huger's Norfolk garrison, Jackson's Army of the Valley, Loring's men—all these, as the

[4] O. R., 21, 753, 754.   [5] O. R., 21, 755.
[6] O. R., 21, 755.   [7] Ibid., 96.
[8] Ibid., 1004–05.

[9] Cf. ibid., 998, for an order in which Burnside proposed to dismiss Hooker from the service of the United States, a step President Lincoln would not approve. This was a period of deep misgiving and of low morale in Union ranks. See Burnside's final report, O. R., 21, 96, where he speaks of "gloom and despondency." As early as Dec. 30, 1862, Quartermaster General M. C. Meigs, a most capable officer, wrote Burnside: "Exhaustion steals over the country. Confidence and hope are dying . . . I begin to doubt the possibility of maintaining the contest beyond this winter, unless the popular heart is encouraged by victory on the Rappahannock." O. R., 21, 917.

Army of Northern Virginia, shared the same camp sites and enjoyed the same period of rest.

A satirist only could have styled it a period of content. Although it was not a severe winter in the estimation of natives, it seemed to men from farther South intolerably frigid.[10] Some of the soldiers built log huts, and some dug themselves holes, which they covered with tent flies. Chimneys of many patterns rose. Even in Sibley tents, chimneys were erected of mud and wood or of stone and plastered earth.[11] To supply flues and huts and to feed the avid fires, forests disappeared from the ridges.[12] "Houses," Jed. Hotchkiss wrote his wife, "that never looked at each other in the almost century they have been standing, stare at each other, impudently, in the face—having barely the trees that surround them." [13]

The soldiers who cut down these trees and made fires of them often were close to hunger, especially during the first days of February.[14] They would have fared miserably worse had not parents and kinsmen stripped the pantries of Southern homes to provide for the boys boxes of provisions that were the subject of much correspondence. Thousands of letters were written from the Spotsylvania heights during those long wintry weeks. By far the greater part of what painfully was scratched on bad paper with balking pens related to three subjects—food, furloughs and clothing. The foremost of these was food.[15]

With hunger was joined the threat of smallpox, which had broken out in October but had diminished by February.[16] From hunger, sickness and nostalgia came desertions which, in the most flagrant cases, received the supreme penalty of a firing squad and a shallow grave in the woods.[17] Despite all these dark experiences,

[10] Dickert, 295; Caldwell, 71.   [11] Owen, 201; cf. Worsham, 155.
[12] 2 von Borcke, 152.   [13] March 15, 1863—Hotchkiss Papers.
[14] O. R., 51, pt. 2, p. 676.

[15] It scarcely is too much to say that nine letters in ten were devoted almost exclusively to these subjects. Health, inquiry about conditions at home and the death or wounding of friends were the other principal themes. A few officers and men in the Army of Northern Virginia wrote with vigor and charm and sometimes, it would appear, with consciousness that they were contributing to history, but the average "war-letter" is apt to be a disappointment to the present-day reader.

[16] Cf. O. R., 19, pt. 2, p. 679; O. R., 21, 1084; 1 R. W. C. D., 208, 226, 238, 245.

[17] Cf. Jed Hotchkiss to his wife, MS, Mch. 1, 1863; Hotchkiss Papers; 8 S. H. S. P., 29–31; 2 N. C. Regts., 400-01; O. R., 18, 821; O. R., 25, pt. 2, pp. 746–47; O. R., 51, pt. 2, pp. 669, 677, 680. For an especially pathetic case of a soldier who deserted and returned, see 7 C. V., 547–48.

most of the men maintained their morale, and found amusement in dramas, minstrel shows and snowball battles.[18]

Consolation and perhaps even a measure of reconciliation to the miseries of war came through religious meetings. The revival that had begun in the Valley during the autumn [19] deepened during the winter. For meetings, the first need was chapels. As became the men who had been from the outset the chosen soldiers of "Old Blue Light," the members of the Stonewall Brigade set the example in hewing logs and erecting a structure where they could assemble for worship. Other Brigades followed. Filling the pulpits was more difficult. A diligent chaplain was the exception. Franklin Paxton, speaking admiringly of the shepherd of one of the units of the Stonewall Brigade, commended him for remaining with the regiment and for sharing its privations. Paxton added sadly: "I am sorry to say we have few such in the army. Most of them are frequently away, whilst others stay at houses in the neighborhood of the camp, coming occasionally to their regiments." [20] Occasionally, too, in an hour of danger, a chaplain would leave his charges. One such chaplain "Jube" Early encountered during the action at Fredericksburg.

"Chaplain," cried Early, as he saw the minister running, "where are you going?"

"General, I am going to a place of safety in the rear."

Early snorted: "Chaplain, I have known you for the past thirty years, and all that time you have been trying to get to Heaven, and now that the opportunity is offered, you are fleeing from it, sir. I am surprised." [21]

Jibes and jests apart, Early was a consistent friend of the chaplains. Jackson and Lee did much to aid them. With the usual regard for discipline and organization, Jackson decided to name an unofficial chaplain general for the Second Corps. Such a man of roving ecclesiastical commission, Jackson reasoned, might be able to stimulate the other chaplains and to do effective preaching.

His choice fell on Rev. B. Tucker Lacy, a celebrated raconteur who long had been with the Valley troops. Mr. Lacy accepted the

---

[18] Cf. *Dickert*, 296; *Worsham*, 156. As might have been assumed, the soldiers most excited over these battles were those who came from States that rarely had snow.

[19] See *supra*, p. 316.   [20] *Paxton*, 92.

[21] 13 *C. V.*, 459.

assignment and widened labors that already were extensive. His sermons, like his stories, were not lacking in eloquence or, to modern ears, in originality. For example, late in March, before an audience so entranced that it scarcely dared breathe, Mr. Lacy expounded confidently what may have appeared to some others the obscure text in St. Matthew, xxi, 44: ". . . whosoever shall fall on this stone shall be broken; but on whomsoever it shall fall, it shall grind him to powder." The reverend gentleman laid the great cause of the destruction of the American Union "at the feet of the Unitarians of Massachusetts, who had denied the Divinity of Christ and so had fallen upon Him, and then from that evil had sprung all the fearful 'isms' that had ruined the land—and were sharers in the destruction and must suffer for their sins as well as our own." [22] That was a thesis to be maintained and disputed as vigorously as any political subject—for example the new emancipation proclamation of President Lincoln, which most of the soldiers regarded as proof that the Republican party from the first had aimed at the liberation of the Negroes.

Many of the officers were as diligent as any of the men in the discussion of Mr. Lacy's sermon and in the debates around the fires in winter quarters that varied greatly. Jackson, as will be set forth shortly, spent the bleak months amid comforts that might have shocked some of the admirers of the ascetic leader of the New Model Army. Lee lived simply in a tent near Hamilton's Crossing till illness compelled him to go to Yerby's.[23] Stuart was not far distant. The other Generals of Division found such comfort or bore such hardship as the location of their posts of command offered.

It was in liaison among these commanders and in arranging for the entertainment of guests that some of the staff officers first became familiar to all of their seniors. Most of the Generals, of course, knew Jackson's A. A. G., "Sandie" Pendleton, and as many of them had cordial comradeship with Moxley Sorrel, the Assistant Adjutant General of Longstreet. All officers above the grade of Colonel at one time or another had met Gen. R. H. Chilton, senior staff officer to Lee. Other officers of the staff who scarcely were known outside Brigades in December became familiar to

[22] Jed Hotchkiss to his wife, MS, Mch. 27, 1863—*Hotchkiss Papers.*
[23] 2 *R. E. Lee,* 502–03.

many of the Generals by May. Similarly, the Army reached a better understanding of the function of the staff.

Staff organization at the beginning of the war barely deserved the name. A crude distinction was made between the so-called "staff departments" such as those of the quartermaster and the commissary, and the "personal staff" of a commanding officer; but the modern conception of a general staff was not applied. Some Generals appeared to think that they were privileged to have in addition to the staff provided by the army regulations as many volunteer aides as they might desire. Beauregard before Manassas had the usual heads of the staff departments, two Assistant Adjutants General and no less than six volunteer aides, several of whom were powerful South Carolina politicians—a total of fifteen.[24]

The law did nothing to keep office holders from acquiring martial titles. A Confederate act of the summer of 1861 authorized the President, at discretion, on the application of a general officer "to appoint from civil life persons to the staff of such officer" and to allow them the rank and pay that would have been theirs if appointed from the regular army.[25] This opened wide the door to personal and political appointments and, what often was worse, to the designation of sons, nephews, cousins or brothers-in-law to positions for which they had neither training nor aptitude. Personal staff appointments were regarded all too often as personal patronage, with which neither the army nor the public had anything to do. Where nepotism was unabashed, a staff almost without exception might bear one family name.[26]

The scandal of these appointments and the manifest defects of organization had led Roger Pryor in February, 1862, to introduce a bill for the organization of a general staff of the army,[27] but this had been put aside after General Lee had assumed duties which

---

[24] O. R., 51, pt. 2, pp. 175–76, cf. *supra*, Vol. I, p. 2.
[25] Act of Aug. 3, 1861, amended Aug. 31, IV O. R., 1, 531, 594.
[26] For instances of this sort, see O. R., 25, pt. 1, pp. 841, 870. Conditions as disgusting prevailed in the departmental offices in Richmond. The *Examiner*, Dec. 4, 1861, p. 3, col. 4, had exposed the case of a clerk who held one position that paid $1800 and another that yielded $1200. He professed to discharge the duties of both by hiring for one of them an assistant at $400 per annum. Efforts to get positions that were safe, easy and remunerative were in strange contrast to the expectation Governor F. W. Pickens had voiced in a letter to Secretary Walker soon after the establishment of the Confederacy. The South Carolina executive had heard that no officer would be appointed to the army otherwise than on personal application. Pickens wrote at once to say, "I suppose this surely cannot be so, for so many delicate and sensitive gentlemen of the highest merit will not apply personally . . ." (IV O. R., 1, 176, 182, 185).
[27] 44 S. H. S. P., 56.

Congressmen thought would be essentially those of Chief of Staff. Not until the winter of 1862–63 was the subject again before Congress. At that time, the influence of Lee was exerted in behalf of the adoption of the French staff organization. Lee urged also a reduction in the number of aides and more adequate provision for adjutants and inspectors. He considered wasteful the authorization of superfluous aides and he pointed out that in action the chiefs of the staff departments often could serve the commanding General as aides. Of the staff as a whole, he told President Davis, "If you can fill these positions with proper officers not the relatives and social friends of the commanders, who, however agreeable their company, are not always the most useful, you might hope to have the finest army in the world." [28]

Although that ideal never was approximated, many men who began the war with no experience had become by the winter of 1862–63 qualified staff officers, and they still were developing. At army headquarters, Lee saw to it that the staff set an example in diligence, and not in mere sociability. This must be qualified in one respect: Although most of Lee's staff officers were alert either on their own initiative or under the prodding of the General, some of the staff grumbled because one of their number was disposed, they thought, to pass on to them the tasks he should discharge.[29]

Most of these officers who served the commanding General were older than the youthful average of the corps and divisional staffs. Col. Charles S. Venable—approaching 36 years of age and a Professor of Mathematics besides—in fact was considered of an age and dignity that equipped him, when necessary, to present staff grievances to the General. In extreme instances, he was expected to beard the General and to point out the lapses of the "Great Tycoon" as the staff sometimes among themselves made bold to style Lee.

Of all the personal staff at Army headquarters, the man best known to visitors and on most intimate terms with the aides of other general officers was Walter Taylor. He was the youngest of Lee's official family and much against his wishes had to serve as "inside man" because of his skill and accuracy in handling the

28 IV *O. R.*, 446–48.
29 Cf. *O. R.*, 19, pt. 2, p. 688; *O. R.*, 25, pt. 2, pp. 745–46. The Walter H. Taylor MSS contain several references to this affair.

official correspondence that Lee detested. Of unassuming personality was Taylor but magnetic from youth, friendly and understanding. Possessed of a memory as notable as his industry,[30] his one weakness was an impulse to steal off during a battle and to participate in a charge. Fortunately, he was never caught by Lee while thus indulging his love of martial excitement.

Jackson's staff was regarded by the Army as most unequal in merit. During the brief period from April to September,[31] when Major, the Rev. Dr. R. L. Dabney had been Chief of Staff, he had commanded respect for his intelligence and, in camp, for his activity; but on the march and in battle, he had been wholly lacking in experience.[32] Some opinion was expressed, sotto voce, that Jackson overestimated the value of Presbyterian clergy in the army, no matter how properly he esteemed them in their peacetime role. James Power Smith, one of Jackson's aides after Sharpsburg, was an exception to the army's low estimate of the soldierly value of "Old Jack's" Presbyterian coterie. This sober-faced young soldier, Smith, often teased by Lee and even by Jackson, was of fighting fibre and was as tireless as brave.

In sharp contrast to the clerical element of the staff, Maj. John A. Harman was the incomparable quartermaster, whose profanity retained in the winter of 1862–63 all the mysterious influence it had exercised on the pulling power of mules during the Valley campaign. The Major never professed to understand Jackson and perhaps never withdrew mentally his threat to quit so crazy and secretive a chief. Jackson, for his part, probably could not excuse the Major's oaths, inability to keep a secret, and general skepticism regarding the commander of the Second Corps; but Jackson knew that the Major could get a wagon ahead when nobody else could; and for that virtue Jackson was willing to overlook talkativeness and reports of shocking language. Of course, the Major never swore in the presence of "Old Blue Light."

During his eight months of service on Jackson's staff, Kyd Douglas gave to it virtually all the style and swagger it ever had, because he was one of the handsomest young men in the army, rode superbly and had a dramatic appearance. When he resigned

---

[30] D. S. Freeman, *The South to Posterity*, 65–66.
[31] Exact dates do not seem determinable. See T. C. Johnson's *Robert Lewis Dabney*. 263, 272.
[32] *Douglas*, 101.

in November to accept a captaincy in the hard bitten Second Virginia, he did not sever his social relations with the staff, but, of course, he could not be its representative on parades, reviews or formal missions.[33]

Less colorful than Douglas, but popular, vigorous and exceptionally competent was Jackson's topographical engineer, Capt. J. K. Boswell.[34] Rated with Boswell in ability, and almost unique in charm, was the Medical Director of the Second Corps, Dr. Hunter McGuire, then in his twenty-seventh year. He was from Jackson's beloved Winchester, was an ardent Confederate, and was distinguished as the quiz-master who, after the John Brown raid, had led the hegira of Southern medical students from Philadelphia. Young McGuire was as good a story teller as he was a surgeon and by the fireside was as charming as he was encouraging at the bedside.

The bulwark of Jackson's staff, its core, its driving force, was the lantern-jawed "Sandie" Pendleton who, though not yet 23, was one of the most promising staff officers in the Army of Northern Virginia. Born Sept. 28, 1840,[35] he was the son of the Chief of Artillery, Brig. Gen. W. N. Pendleton, and he had the best of the qualities both of his father's line and of the Pages and Nelsons, the forebears of his mother.[36] All his life, it was said, "Sandie" Pendleton had waked up in a good humor. He had been the medallist of his class at Washington College when 17 and had been graduated Master of Arts at the University of Virginia in 1861. About him there was a charming courtesy of manner, a cordiality and a magnetism that made every acquaintance regard him as a friend.

His mental endowment was in keeping. Judgment was as discerning as memory was retentive. Even Jackson was wont to say, when asked about an unfamiliar officer or about a regiment con-

[33] For the change of post, which in reality did not become effective until mid-December, 1862, see *Douglas,* 202.

[34] The other topographical engineer, introduced in Vol. I, p. 27, and often quoted in these pages, was the indispensable Jed. Hotchkiss, who at this time had not been commissioned because of limitations on the lawful number of topographical engineers. Although in every sense a member of the staff, he was in the winter of 1862–63, a civilian employee.

[35] *Pendleton,* 372.

[36] She was Anzolette Page, eldest child of Francis Page, third son of Governor John Page of Rosewell. Anzolette Page's mother was Susan Nelson, fourth daughter of Gen. Thomas Nelson. Five marriages occurred among Pages and Nelsons of that generation. *Pendleton,* 31.

cerning which he was in doubt, "Ask Captain Pendleton; if he don't know, nobody does." The skill, the mature wisdom, the promptness and the system with which this boy ran Jackson's headquarters were, perhaps, the best refutation of the oft-repeated assertion that Jackson lacked judgment in the choice of officers. Either "Stonewall" had observed at Lexington the excellencies of his young fellow townsman, or else he was incredibly fortunate in his choice. Pendleton distinguished himself with Jackson from July, 1861, onward and never missed a battle except that of Second Manassas, which was fought while he was ill. "Sandie's" escape from death in the Battle of Fredericksburg had been narrow. He wrote his mother, December 14: "I am here at headquarters and have a chance to write, because I was badly bruised in the fight yesterday. In the afternoon, as I went with an order to General Taliaferro to advance, I was struck by a musket-ball, which went through both my over- and under-coats, and was stopped by striking the knife in my pants pockets. It saved my life, as the ball would have gone through the groin and fractured the hip-joint. I am very stiff and horribly bruised. I did not leave the field, and shall return this morning." He did not state, as already has been noted,[37] that it was the injury to him that threw the staff work of the Second Corps entirely out of gear that afternoon.[38] As for risk, exposure and danger, he met them without thought. Seldom does one find a sharper contrast between the spirit of son and of sire than is presented by "Sandie's" comments on the war and those of his father during the autumn and winter of 1862.[39]

"Sandie's" fine conduct in every test won him, of course, the quiet admiration of Jackson, who was as quick to seek the recognition of rank for his proven lieutenants as he was slow to praise them. In December, 1862, before the Battle of Fredericksburg, "Sandie" was promoted. He was pleased and was frank in owning it. He wrote his mother: "Here I am a Major within two months after my twenty-second year is completed. I am proud of it and glad that the promotion has come from recognized merit, and accept it as a good omen of future success." [40] To this, the rightful addendum was phrased by his enthusiastic friend, Kyd Douglas. Said he: "The army never knew how much Jackson loved and

---

37 See *supra*, p. 371.   38 For his letter, see *Pendleton*, 246–47.
39 *Pendleton*, 235–36, 247–48.   40 *Pendleton*, 252.

was indebted to Sandy Pendleton . . . for he left small record of that regard." [41]

"Peter" Longstreet's staff was as different from "Old Jack's" as were the two corps commanders themselves. No ministers were there on Longstreet's staff, though after the tragic loss of his three children, the General had been more serious in his manner of living. Perhaps the essential quality that distinguished Longstreet's headquarters from Jackson's was a lack of austerity. Longstreet was efficient and administered army business promptly and with no noisy grinding of gears; but when his staff officers had finished their work and gathered in Maj. John Fairfax's tent for a nip, "Old Pete" said nothing to them. Nor did he frown and lecture them the next morning. Foremost among Longstreet's staff officers was G. Moxley Sorrel, a tall, trim Georgian whose Gallic grace, dark eyes and dash displayed the blood of a grandfather who had been a Colonel of Engineers in the French army. Moxley Sorrel was a clerk in the banking division of the Central Georgia Railroad on the outbreak of hostilities, but he came to Virginia, where his father had a large farm, and soon he found a place, without pay, as a volunteer aide to Longstreet. So much aptitude did Sorrel display that "Old Pete" quickly procured his commission and thereafter relied increasingly on him. Socially, Sorrel was charming; as a rider he was the envy of many a cavalryman; at work in Longstreet's headquarters tent, he need not have feared comparisons with any staff officer of the army.[42]

Maj. Osman Latrobe, physically and mentally a powerful representative of the Maryland family of that name, was Longstreet's A. A. G. and Inspector. Similar rank and title were those of John W. Fairfax, a Virginian of ancient line and positive habits. He was, wrote one of his comrades, "fond of his bottle, his Bible and his bath; always in front when danger pressed, but a fine looking fellow very much given to show." More than once, to his high satisfaction, on entering a strange town he was mistaken for Gen-

---

[41] *Douglas*, 211. It is to be noted that Douglas always wrote of his friend as "Sandy." The family spelt it "Sandie." A more detailed sketch of "Sandie" Pendleton than is permissible in these pages, without distorting historical perspective, should be written by some friend of American youth. Materials are not abundant but they will suffice. Numbers of his simple, graphic letters appear in *Pendleton*. Nearly all the diarists and autobiographers of the Army of Northern Virginia mention him and always with affection. He must have been one of the most popular boys in the entire army.

[42] *Sorrel*, 16, 17, 19; *Journal of Maj. Raphael J. Moses.* MS, p. 5.

eral Longstreet, whom he regarded with affectionate loyalty as the foremost Southern soldier. Wherever the Corps went, Fairfax carried a bath tub that bore an odd resemblance to a tin hat, and unless battle broke with the dawn, he had his bath and his toddy before he ate. On Sunday, he gave himself the refreshment of Holy Writ without neglecting his dram. This much amused his fellow staff officers and most of all the chief commissary, Maj. Raphael Moses. While Fairfax was out of his tent one Sunday, Moses attached to the bottle, which was hanging in one pocket of a "housewife," a bit of paper inscribed, "This in a moment brings me to an end." In the next pocket of the receptacle was Fairfax's Bible, between the leaves of which Moses placed another sheet that read, "While this informs me I shall never die."

When Fairfax came back and laughed at the discovery, he had no difficulty in identifying the culprit: "Moses, by the Lord," he cried. Major Moses was the wit and the story-teller of the staff. A lawyer of high distinction in Georgia, he owned a plantation on which he grew peaches that were among the first ever to be sent from that State to the New York market. He sought combatant duty in 1861, but General Toombs prevailed upon him to undertake the thankless but essential work of commissary. So admirably did Moses victual Toombs's Brigade that he soon had charge of the commissary of D. R. Jones's Division and, in due time, of Longstreet's Corps. "A most intelligent, efficient officer" Moxley Sorrel styled him. Sorrel probably would not have erred had he said Moses was the best commissary of like rank in the Confederate service. Moses's stories were endless; his narrative flawless. The darkest, dullest night at headquarters he could enliven.[43]

Two other of Longstreet's staff officers must have mention—Dr. J. S. Dorsey Cullen, Medical Director of the Second Corps, and Lieut. F. W. Dawson, assistant to the Corps Chief of Ordnance.[44] Dorsey Cullen, who was 30 years of age, had been born in Richmond and had been schooled at the University of Virginia and in the medical department of the University of Pennsylvania. So promising was he in his profession that one of the most renowned of Southern surgeons, Dr. Charles Bell Gibson, took him into partnership. When war came, Cullen went to the front as Surgeon of the First Virginia and soon attracted Longstreet's at-

[43] *Sorrel*, 125; *Moses, op. cit.*   [44] *Sorrel*, 124.

tention. Soon he was as secure in the affection of Longstreet as Hunter McGuire was welcome at Jackson's tent.[45]

Dawson was English and of an odd career. Born Francis Warrington Reeks, he early changed Reeks to Dawson and boldly challenged the London stage and the critics with a succession of comedies. Most of them succeeded moderately and made him, at 21, a dramatist of promise. The more exciting drama of the Confederacy fired him in 1861. He determined to enlist in its cause and, when he found himself rejected by the Captain of the C. S. S. *Nashville,* which had put into a British port, he employed a device that would have served in one of his plays: With care, he disguised himself as a sailor, went aboard ship in the absence of the Captain, signed up, and went to sea. As he found naval service dull in the winter of 1861–62, he got his discharge and volunteered in the Purcell Battery, of which William J. Pegram was then Captain. At Mechanicsville, where Pegram won his spurs, Dawson displayed a heroism and persistence that gained him commission as second Lieutenant. In the autumn of 1862, he was transferred to Longstreet's staff, as assistant to Maj. P. T. Manning, Chief of Ordnance. Dawson was a fiery youngster, ready to fight anybody at any time, though as quick to cool as to fire. Persistent he was, also, and self-willed but, along with some rasping qualities, he had a devotion his every act displayed.[46]

Because the cavalry under the energetic Stuart ranged far, his staff officers were widely known. For that matter, Stuart saw to it that everything connected with the cavalry was known. One of his staff officers, the oft-cited Heros von Borcke, lent himself admirably and willingly as an exhibit. Von Borcke was of vast bulk and appropriate height and had to ride a tall and powerful horse. He dressed in a fashion that emphasized his size at the same time that it suggested the rainbow. His blade was one a Crusader would have envied. Unquestioned valor was von Borcke's, a contempt for danger and an unfeigned delight in combat. Along with this he possessed polish, much experience and a

[45] It is an interesting fact that after the war the Medical Directors of both the original Corps of the Army of Northern Virginia practiced their profession in Richmond. Dr. Cullen died Mch. 22, 1893. It is from his obituary in the *Richmond Dispatch* of Mch. 22, 1893, that these facts are drawn. Dr. McGuire lived until Sept. 19, 1900. He is sketched in *D. A. B.*

[46] Dawson, *Confederate Reminiscences. D. A. B.* has a full bibliography. Sarah Morgan, who wrote the charming *Confederate Girl's Diary,* for which see D. S. Freeman, *The South to Posterity,* 146, was the second Mrs. Dawson.

familiarity with many charades, pantomimes and the like that had not reached the South. All these accomplishments made him useful and, to repeat, helped to advertise the cavalry. He could be ugly, selfish and graspingly ambitious when he relaxed either social suavity or self-mastery; but his most provoking quality was not revealed till the struggle was over. Then, in his published *Memoirs,* where none of his service lost weight in the telling, he calmly credited himself with many feats that had been performed by other members of the staff.[47]

Although von Borcke, among other honors, attributed to himself that of having been Stuart's Chief of Staff, the honor and the burden of that position, in the winter of 1862–63, again were Maj. Norman FitzHugh's. He had been exchanged at length after he had fallen into Federal hands at Verdiersville, and he had been prompt to return to active duty.[48] John Esten Cooke, the novelist, was Ordnance Officer and was sharing observantly, though not happily, all that Stuart was doing.[49]

Over these men and over all others attached to headquarters, the personality of Stuart shone so gaudily that it dulled the colors of their personalities, but two other of his staff officers had qualities that have not been forgotten after three-quarters of a century. One of these officers was Chief Engineer of the Cavalry Division, W. W. Blackford, who had married a daughter of Wyndham Robertson, former Governor of Virginia. Blackford was the son of William M. Blackford, at that time cashier of a bank in Lynchburg, Virginia. Four other sons Mr. Blackford and his wife, née Mary Berkely Minor,[50] had in the Confederate army—all of them excellent soldiers. William had received sound, disciplinary training as a civil engineer and in 1861 was operating, with his father-in-law, a plaster-of-paris plant in Southwest Virginia. As Blackford had helped to raise a volunteer cavalry company after the

[47] An amusing example is given in *W. W. Blackford's MS Memoirs,* 286. Blackford described how he invited von Borcke to go with him on a reconnaissance at Fredericksburg, only to find when the *Memoirs* appeared that von Borcke had invited *him* to be a companion on a mission assigned by Stuart to von Borcke.

[48] The FitzHugh homestead in Stafford County was "Eagle's Nest," a name that John Esten Cooke appropriated for one of his most popular war novels. Norman FitzHugh shifted from staff post of A. A. G. to that of divisional quartermaster.

[49] For his biography, see John O. Beaty, *John Esten Cooke,* a brief but wholly acceptable book. His MS *Journals,* now at Duke University, contain little of interest See J. B. Hubbell, The War Diary of John Esten Cooke, *Journal of Southern History,* Vol. VII, No. 4, p. 526 ff.

[50] Daughter of Gen. John Minor of Fredericksburg, whose wife was Lucy Landon Carter of Cleve.

John Brown raid, he adhered to that arm and in 1861 rode off with this command. Its Captain was William E. Jones—"Grumble" Jones himself. Among the privates, "rather a slouchy rider, [who] did not seem to take any interest in military duties,"[51] was John S. Mosby, destined to become, after John Morgan, the most renowned of the Confederate partisan leaders.

At Manassas, Blackford's gallantry was such that Stuart, for whom he was acting as adjutant, made his formal appointment as of that date.[52] In October, 1861, Blackford was commissioned Captain of cavalry and, just before Seven Pines, was appointed as Captain of Engineers on Stuart's staff. An inherently brave man, he always was ready for any assignment at any time and, though 32, was as dashing as Pelham. One of the obligations Blackford imposed upon himself was that of going over every battlefield he could examine after the action had closed. He said later in explanation: ". . . nothing cultivates the judgment of topography, in relation to the strategic strength of position, so well as to ride over the ground while the dead and wounded still remain as they fell. You see exactly where the best effects were produced, and what arm of the service produced them, for there lies the harvest they have reaped, each sheaf distinctly labeled with the name of the reaper in the wound received. Artillery tears its sheaves out by the roots and scatters the fragments, while infantry mows them down in well heaped windrows."[53] This was the viewpoint of a scientific but not of a cold-blooded officer. Along with dedication to the study of his temporary calling, Blackford had sympathy and chivalry and tears and laughter.

Best loved of Stuart's staff—if Pelham be regarded as a line officer—was the remarkable young A. A. G. that "Jeb" had found in his distant cousin, R. Channing Price of Richmond.[54] Son of a merchant of the Virginia capital, Channing Price had entered the war as a private in the Richmond Howitzers, and first on the Peninsula and then on the south side of the James had spent long

---

[51] W. W. Blackford's MS Reminiscences, 15.
[52] Ibid., 42.   [53] Ibid., 61.
[54] Both were descended from Thomas Price and his wife Barbara Winston in this wise: Elizabeth, a daughter of these two, married Capt. George Dabney. Their daughter, Nancy Dabney, married Judge Alexander Stuart, "Jeb" Stuart's grandfather. On the other line, Joseph Price, son of Thomas and Barbara Price, married Elizabeth Winston. Their son, Thomas Randolph Price, married Elizabeth Hall. Channing Price was the son of T. R. and Elizabeth Hall Price.

and tedious months. In the summer of 1862, Stuart gave him a place on the staff, and as Channing quickly learned his duties, "Jeb" never had occasion to regret the appointment or to apologize for the selection of a kinsman.

An exacting chief was Stuart. His aides had to justify their title at any hour and had always to be close at hand. By good temper and good health, as well as by character that shone in every utterance, Channing met the strain. At the "inside" work, the "paper work" as it was called, he was facile and unfailing. When he was acting as A.A.G. in the field, he had no superior in the Army. Said Blackford of him: "Repeatedly have I seen while on the march General Stuart dictate two or three letters to him, giving orders to the commanders of the different columns. Each one of [the letters] would state by what places the columns were to move, at what hours they were to leave these places and where they were to concentrate. Price would listen, and without asking him to repeat a single thing, or taking a single note, he would ride out to one side of the road, dismount, take his little portfolio out of his haversack and write the letters for the General's signature; and it was rarely the case that any alteration was made when Stuart read them and affixed his signature." This was attributed to Price's development of a retentive memory by acting as secretary to his father who, in late life, lost his vision and carried on his correspondence by dictating to his son.[55] A brilliant brother Channing Price had—Thomas R. Price—who had been studying in Berlin when the war began and, in January, 1863, joined Stuart as an aide. A singular misfit he was to prove.

Taylor for Lee, Pendleton for Jackson, Sorrel for Longstreet, Price for Stuart—these were not the only staff officers of outstanding capacity. Nor by any means did they carry all the burden of detailed staff work in winter quarters. Others of industry as great and ability almost as high labored patriotically, but these four, different in background though not in uprearing, were typical of the best of the Army and of the South.

[55] *W. W. Blackford's MS Memoirs*, 299.

CHAPTER XXVIII

Artillerists Get Their Stars

Along with the developing young staff officers, some of the ablest of the artillerists received one star or two during the months the Army was in winter quarters. The reorganization of the "Long Arm," it will be recalled, had been undertaken immediately after Sharpsburg. Small and inefficient batteries then were demanding far more horses than the quartermasters were able to supply. On the roster were batteries that had won the plaudits of the entire Army, and certain others that were an encumbrance of road and camp and battlefield. Which was the finest battery under Lee—if any one of them was in every respect better than any other—men might dispute; but which was the worst, Robert Ransom would have said he could establish. It started from Richmond with a wagon train bound for Northern Virginia, but it did not arrive until a week after the wagons reached their destination and then it was unfit for service. Left at Leesburg when the Army entered Maryland, the battery contrived to get across the Potomac. Although it did not fire a shot and held no exposed position, it succeeded in losing one of its guns and two caissons.[1] Such a battery, of course, had to be disbanded. Seventeen others, none of them quite so bad as this, similarly were stricken from the list. Their personnel was divided among other units; their guns were given to better batteries or were turned back to the army Chief of Ordnance.[2]

In the process, where so many sensibilities were exposed, not a few were bruised; among ambitions so numerous some were trodden upon. The only serious disturbance came before Sharpsburg

[1] O. R., 19, pt. 1, p. 921.
[2] For the armament of the corps and of the cavalry batteries, see O. R., 19, pt. 1, p. 835 ff. Details of the reorganization appear in ibid., pt. 2, pp. 632, 646 ff., 662. The date of the formal dissolution of the eighteen batteries was October 7 (O. R., 19, pt. 1, p. 153). After this, an effort was made to increase in the Army of Northern Virginia the number of bronze "Napoleons," which were 12-pounders, caliber 4.62 (O. R., 21, 1046 ff). The end of the year, which had been a hard one for the Ordnance Bureau, found the army moderately well armed. For this, thanks were due equally to Gen. Josiah Gorgas in Richmond and to the valiant units that had captured many of the fine, 3-inch Federal rifles. (Cf. William Allan in 14 S. H. S. P., 137 ff.)

and ended in a manner to discourage violent protests later. A curious episode it was, and one saved for narration here, out of its chronological order, because it shows with what fiery individuals poor General Pendleton had to deal.

Fleet's Battery, the Middlesex Artillery, a Virginia unit, had done admirably on several fields but it wore itself out in the opera, tions of August, 1862 and, by Jackson's orders, went to Leesburg to refit. While it was there, Pendleton got an order to forward four batteries to Maryland. To provide teams for them, he had to take eleven horses of Fleet's Battery. Its commanding officer, Lieut. William B. Hardy, called upon General Pendleton to pro-test. When the General informed him that he—but here is Pendle-ton's own shocked language—"that he must submit, under the rules prescribed by the commanding General, Hardy bore himself with strangely improper violence, stalking out of the room where I was and slamming the door, and gate, even, furiously." [3]

Not to punish Hardy, but no doubt in a desire to draw impar-tially on his lean resources, Pendleton the next day sent an officer over to the camp of Fleet's Battery: The Middlesex Artillery must supply a detail of cannoneers and more horses to reinforce bat-teries that were about to enter Maryland. The officer returned and startled Pendleton by reporting that Lieutenant Hardy refused to obey. Pendleton, as he later took care to report, was "extremely unwell," but when he got this message he rode over to the battery in person, with some of his staff, and handed to Lieutenant Hardy the written order for the detail of men. Did the Lieutenant, asked Pendleton, refuse to obey? He did. The other junior officer? He would not execute the order.

By this time, the whole personnel of the battery must have as-sembled to witness the affair and to support the battery officers. Dr. Pendleton did not yield an inch. He put the Lieutenants un-der arrest and sent them off forthwith, under guard, to another part of the artillery camp. Then the General looked about to see if there were any other officers. A bystander was pointed out as Captain of the battery, but, when faced by Pendleton, insisted that as he was under arrest he could not act.

The General was perplexed: Where was the orderly sergeant? The boys answered they had none. Point out some other sergeant

[3] O. R., 19. pt. 2, p. 651.

then. Solemn assurance was given that the battery had not a single sergeant. Where was the roll of the company? Nobody knew.

If there was no sergeant, no roll, let the company be formed! Some fifty men "fell in"—whether grinning or scowling the record does not say—but almost half of them insisted that they were sick and unfit for duty. Pendleton was fortified against this excuse. He had his surgeon along and he ordered an examination of the men who groaned or limped or rubbed their abdomens. Four of the men, the surgeon reported, probably were sick. The others were able to perform duty.

At this point, the gunners either began to haze the General or else they felt they had arrived at terms of sufficient intimacy to tell him their grievances. Everything was wrong. They had been seven months in service. Not a dollar of pay had they drawn. Bounty was due them: it had been withheld. Pendleton listened and could not credit them. Might they be mistaken? Where were the payroll and descriptive lists? The men assured him that none of these documents existed.

Were they making a jest of authority? Could conditions be as devoid of organization as the gunners alleged? There is no way of telling whether Pendleton asked himself those questions, but his temper rose. He was determined that the men should go into Maryland and that they should take their horses with them if the animals could stand the journey. The beasts were examined carefully. They were, Pendleton admitted, "in wretched condition," but a few of them could be used. He ordered them taken, and then by direct, individual appeal he got a few of the men to volunteer. Those who held back, he detailed by positive order. In the end Pendleton sent forty-six of the gunners to battery commanders who were about to start for Sharpsburg. The men did their duty in Maryland. Not a cowardly act or a mutinous word was charged against them there.

Fleet's Lieutenants continued under arrest; the battery was marked for disbandment. It had one hope only of escaping that fate: its service had been with A. P. Hill, who was nothing if not loyal to his own soldiers. Hill interceded, dwelt upon the previous good conduct of the battery, and said that he wanted it recruited and preserved. Pendleton was not opposed to this. As for the individuals, he was willing that the Lieutenants, "if suitably atoning to violated discipline by a proper acknowledgment, should be released."[4] Otherwise, no matter what happened to the battery, the young officers would have to stand court martial. They replied in writing with a defense of their conduct. The General sent back their letter, which he pronounced unsatisfactory, and offered them another chance to apologize.

In due time, the officers disclaimed any personal lack of respect for Pendleton, but said that, at the time he called on the battery, "disobedience was a necessity"—to quote Pendleton's vague words. The General shook his head again over this and said the officers must atone more acceptably. To Lee he had to report: "Further answer they decline. The case, therefore, must await a court martial. Charges shall be immediately submitted."[5] The records do not set forth the result of the court martial, though late in May, Federal raiders down the Rappahannock captured a "Lieutenant Hardy of the rebel artillery."[6] Despite Powell Hill's wish, the battery could not be reorganized. It disappeared as one of the eighteen that were stricken off the roster.

The reduction in the number of batteries was followed in February, 1863, by an historic, long needed change in the organization of the artillery as a combat arm. From the time the Brigades and Divisions had been formed in 1861, it will be remembered that designated batteries had been assigned to each of these units. A Brigade had one battery; normally a Division had four.[7] Soon the batteries had become so habituated to service with particular Brigades that any attempt to send the guns elsewhere was regarded as the darkest injustice to the gunners and to the Brigade—an act far worse than the detachment of a regiment for temporary service with another Brigade.

By the autumn of 1862, the artillery of most of the Divisions had come under the command of a divisional chief of artillery, who exercised a measure of discretion, but the permanence of the relations between certain batteries and one specific Division continued to be taken for granted. If a massing of guns or the reinforcement of an artillery position was necessary, the added units were expected to come from the general reserve, which consisted

---

[4] O. R., 19, pt. 2, p. 651.   [5] O. R., 19, pt. 2, p. 651.
[6] O. R., 25, pt. 1, p. 1116. For Pendleton, next see Chap. XXXV.
[7] This was about the average, but A. P. Hill's Division at Fredericksburg had seven. See O. R., 21, 542.

of fifteen to twenty batteries, rather than from the adjoining Division, even though the artillery of that Division might be idle.

This system patently was bad beyond defense. The employment of large forces of artillery was almost impossible. Field officers of artillery had little practice training. Batteries in isolated camps behind the lines often were neglected by supply officers who were busy with large infantry units and could not, to quote Pendleton, "devote to one or more batteries the time and attention they imperatively needed." [8] Lee and Pendleton both had concluded that battalions of four batteries, a total of sixteen guns, each battalion with two field officers, would be an organization far preferable. The Chief of Artillery went over with Porter Alexander and Stapleton Crutchfield the details of a plan of this character and, on Feb. 11, 1863, presented it, complete even to the assignment of batteries, for the consideration of Lee. [9]

When Lee sent to the corps commanders the proposed organization and the contemplated assignments for their commands, Longstreet apparently had no objection to offer. [10] The shifting of batteries and the few necessary advancements in rank seem to have been satisfactory to him. His old friend Col. J. B. Walton of the Washington Artillery Battalion was to be retained. Porter Alexander was to be made a full Colonel. The other promoted officers were meritorious and acceptable.

Jackson was not so ready to accept the men Pendleton proposed for him. The commander of the Second Corps had objections of principle to the assignment to his artillery of field officers who had not served with it, when he had good men of his own batteries whom he felt worthy of promotion. In addition, Colonel Crutchfield felt that one Major of artillery did not deserve promotion to the next grade. Besides, Capt. David G. McIntosh, whom Crutchfield considered one of the best of his artillerists, was not assigned a battalion.

These considerations "Old Jack" set forth earnestly in a letter to Lee and, in so doing, advanced the claims of one of his "boys" of the old Army of the Valley, Capt. R. P. Chew, who had commanded the famous battery that always had been barking where Ashby was slashing. Chew was in the Valley with "Grumble"

---

[8] O. R., 25, pt. 2, p. 614.   [9] Ibid., 614–19.

[10] That is to say, there is no hint of any in the records, though no correspondence with him on the subjects seems to be extant.

Jones at the time the reorganization of the artillery was under review, but Chew's detachment did not cause Jackson to forget what the young man had done in the spring campaign. Said Jackson somewhat clumsily on the general subject of promotion: "I am of the opinion, that when there are officers who have served with me, and whilst part of my command have rendered such service as to prove them worthy of promotion, that the interest of the service is promoted by promoting such officers to serve with me. Such a course is calculated to stimulate officers, as it will let them see that they will not be forgotten when an opportunity offers for advancing them."[11] Further complaint Jackson had to make, also, probably at the instance of Crutchfield, on the sore old subject of the comparative armament of the two Corps.

Lee satisfied Jackson quickly regarding guns, but he did not permit the broad argument about the good of the service and the value of the individual officer to pass unscrutinized. Said the commanding General: "I think the interest of the service as well as justice to individuals, requires the selection of the best men to fill vacant positions . . . I do not think it right, however, at any time to pass over worthy men who have done good service, unless you can get better." As for Chew, was it not a fact that he belonged to the artillery of the cavalry rather than of the Second Corps?[12]

Jackson did not take any of this in good part. He returned to the charge. With all the formality of quotation from Lee's letter, in order that he might refute its contentions, he sought to justify his own assertions and the arguments of Crutchfield. The conclusion of the letter lacked little of being rude. Said Jackson: "I have had much trouble, resulting from incompetent officers having been assigned to duty with me regardless of my wishes. Those who have assigned them have never taken the responsibility of incurring the odium which results from such incompetency."[13] With his lieutenant in this temper, Lee argued no more, but he sought, as best as he could, to reconcile Pendleton's suggestions and Jackson's objections to them.

Weeks passed before the commissions, on April 14, were brought from Richmond by Col. Lindsay Walker and were distributed.[14] The assignments were announced that day in Army orders.[15] Four

11 *O. R.*, 25, pt. 2, p. 633.   12 *O. R.*, 25, pt. 2, pp. 644–45.
13 *Ibid.*, 646.   14 *Ibid.*, 727.
15 *Ibid.*, 728–29.

battalions were attached directly to each of the Corps. In a deliberate effort to provide greater mobility and increased fire power, the best two battalions of Longstreet's command—the Washington Artillery and Alexander's Battalion—were designated as corps reserve for the First Corps. Two battalions that included some batteries not quite of the same level of distinction constituted the reserve of the Second Corps. The general reserve, which had been General Pendleton's particular charge, was reduced to two battalions. Jackson got all he had asked, except in two cases: Chew was not assigned a battalion; the Major whose promotion had been disapproved by Crutchfield was advanced to the rank of Lieutenant Colonel.

Although it disappointed these and other ambitions, the battalion organization was to justify itself many times over. Whatever lingering objection there was to the new system in February was to disappear on the 3rd of May. Some superb young men were given higher rank because of heavier responsibility. Tom Carter became a Colonel—he who had equalled on many fields, though he never could excel, his performance at Seven Pines. Snowden Andrews, though still unfit for active duty, because of the wound received at Cedar Mountain, had the stimulus of another star on his collar. A Lieutenant Colonel's commission was sent him. Willie Pegram, promoted Major, was made second in command of Lindsay Walker's battalion. David McIntosh stepped up to Major and to the head of a battalion that was thereafter to bear his name. W. T. Poague became a Major and second in command to McIntosh, though the shuffle necessary to put McIntosh as a chief of battalion necessitated the separation of the Rockbridge Artillery from the battalion of which Poague was second in command.

At least two other notable appointments there were: In the Second Corps, Maj. J. W. Latimer, who had handled Ewell's artillery with much skill at Cedar Mountain, was named as the junior field officer of Snowden Andrews's battalion. This meant that so long as Andrews was absent, Latimer would have four batteries, two of which were famous.[16] Second in command to Porter Alexander, in a magnificent battalion of six batteries, was Maj. Frank

[16] Carpenter's and Dement's.

Huger, son of Gen. Benjamin Huger and an officer whose judgment matched his heroism.

Older men of higher rank and of outstanding service there already were in the artillery; but as it chanced, most of the young men who appeared as battalion field officers for the first time in the order of April 16, 1863, were those who added most to the luster of the "Long Arm." Alexander, Huger, Tom Carter, Latimer, Pegram, McIntosh, Poague—take these from the roll of Lee's artillery and half its glory is gone. They had won their new rank by merit and they had the endorsement of Longstreet and of Jackson. Perhaps some of the aggressive battalion commanders would have been loath to admit it, but they owed something, also, to General Pendleton. Individual performance he had observed faithfully and, with a few exceptions, had appraised soundly. If he nursed the hope that the reorganization of the artillery might bring him promotion, he did not say so in any letter that has survived, nor did he voice disappointment because he remained a Brigadier. All he got—oddity and irony—was a larger wagon and more tentage. In answer to a letter regarding the transportation of the artillery, Lee wrote him: "Your duties in position are more nearly allied to that [sic] of a Major General than a Brigadier. If you find it necessary, therefore, the transportation and camp equipage of the former can be allowed you." [17]

If Pendleton was not disappointed—and well he might have been—Jackson soon was to be, through the failure of a private plan of his for the advancement of an officer he much esteemed. Under the act of January 22, 1863, which had made the other promotions possible, officers of artillery above the grade of Captain could be appointed "without reference to the number of batteries under the actual command of the officers so appointed." A final "however" was to the effect that the number was not to exceed "one Brigadier General for every eighty guns." [18] This inferentially authorized the appointment of a Brigadier General where an officer had charge of a minimum of eighty guns. Two days before the artillery commissions were brought from Richmond, Jackson wrote the Adjutant General and recommended that Col. Stapleton Crutchfield be made Brigadier General of Artillery. Crutchfield,

[17] O. R., 25, pt. 2, p. 749.   [18] See the text in Wright, 131.

said the former Professor, took first honors at V. M. I. and "of all
its graduates . . . is one of the most gifted." For more than eleven
months, Jackson set forth, Crutchfield had been chief of artillery
and had discharged his duty with great ability and fidelity.
Crutchfield had, his chief said, an extensive knowledge of his
profession and commanded more guns than were required by law
as the command of a Brigadier General.[19] Nothing came of this
effort. For the time, the decision of the government was against
the grant of commission as general officer to corps chiefs of
artillery.

On a footing different from Crutchfield's case or Pendleton's or
that of any of the artillerists who fought with the infantry units
was the recognition of John Pelham. His performance on the
right at Fredericksburg had underscored all his achievements
from First Manassas onward. In an army that did not lack brave
men, he was "the gallant Pelham." Students of war in the winter
quarters around Fredericksburg began to ask if he were not something of a military genius, who was developing new artillery tactics. It might not be daring or sheer combativeness that inspired
Pelham to dash with his guns ahead of all infantry support, to
pursue as if he led cavalry, and to withdraw so swiftly but with
so many halts on good ground that he could delay pursuit. Together, these might be tactical devices that would give a new function to artillery.[20]

No praise seemed in any way to affect Pelham. His eyes—
"gentle and merry, 'laughing eyes' "—were lighted with friendship;[21] his manner remained simple and unspoiled; he never
spoke of himself or of his exploits. If he was commended, he
blushed. "This modesty of deportment," wrote one of Stuart's
staff officers, "was observed by every one, and strangers often referred to the singular phenomenon in a youth bred in the self-
sufficient atmosphere of West Point, and whose name was already
so famous."[22] Apparently he gave no thought to death save as he
saw it about him or read of it in the Bible he studied reverently.
He told John Esten Cooke once that he had never felt he was destined to be killed in the war.[23]

If Pelham had any traducers, they dared not speak openly against

[19] *Jackson's MS Letter Book*, p. 55; Apr. 14, 1863.
[20] 38 *S. H. S. P.*, 381.   [21] 6 *C. V.*, 436.
[22] *Wearing of the Gray*, 135.   [23] *Ibid.*, 139.

one whose friends ranged from the humblest to the most exalted and were as numerous in one sex as in the other. A man's man he was by every act and impulse; yet he drew many a sigh and gentle glance from the young ladies of every town where he halted. How could it be otherwise? He was blond enough to match his dazzling blue eyes, and was "tall, slender, beautifully proportioned and very graceful." [24] Among Stuart's staff officers, who saw him at closest range and in the greatest diversity of cross lights, there was one criticism only of him, and that one half amused, half envious: If the girls looked, John Pelham looked back at them. When they smiled, he smiled too. He was, one of his closest friends had to admit, "as grand a flirt as ever lived," [25] though scandal never touched his name.

Most of his time when Pelham was not fighting, he had to remain, whether or no, at headquarters of the cavalry Division. Stuart insisted on that. He never restrained Pelham in action, but he had for his chief of artillery the same sort of older brother affection that Longstreet had for Pickett. If Pelham were missing from headquarters, Stuart always wished to know why, and, more often than not, would send for him. Pelham consequently lived with the staff and, to all intents, was one of them.[26] He did not have opportunity of riding in Hampton's raids of December, 1862, to Dumfries and the Occoquan; but he shared, it will be remembered, the sweep Stuart made after Christmas over the same ground. From that time until March, Pelham made occasional visits of inspection to the Rapidan, on which Moorman's Battery was stationed, or to Culpeper, where Breathed's Battery was serving with Fitz Lee's detached Brigade.[27]

Doubtless Pelham counted it ill fortune that he was not at Culpeper February 24. On that date, Fitz Lee took 400 of his men, crossed the Rappahannock at Kelly's Ford, and fell upon the Federal outposts. In this skirmishing around Hartwood Church, Fitz captured 150 men with their horses and full equipment, and himself lost fourteen only.[28] This much applauded feat [29] had the effect, among others, of giving the commanding General new

[24] W. W. Blackford's MS Memoirs, 126.
[25] Ibid.
[26] Blackford in his MS Memoirs, viii, so listed him.
[27] In 2 von Borcke, 180 ff is a diverting, if overdrawn, account of Pelham's success in procuring shelter from a free Negro on one of these inspections.
[28] O. R., 25, pt. 1, p. 25.   [29] Ibid., 16 and pt. 2, p. 640.

confidence in the ability and willingness of his nephew to perform any service that a cavalryman could render. There must have been deep satisfaction in the heart of Robert Lee, always a man of devotion to his family, when he was able to say, in answer to a suggestion that his nephew be sent to succeed Jones in the Valley, "General Fitz Lee is an excellent cavalry officer, and is extremely useful in his present position." Then the uncle of a brigadier nephew and the father of a brigadier son added of Fitz Lee: "I do not know how I can spare him upon the resumption of active operations, as I feel at liberty to call upon him and General W. H. F. Lee on all occasions." [30]

With either of "the Lees," with almost anyone else, and above all with the chief of cavalry, Pelham wished to ride on every raid, but during the worst mud of the wintry months, the horse artillerist had to content himself officially with his inspections. Socially he had the mild if pleasurable excitement of occasional visits to one or another of the many homes that were open to him.

When duty kept him idle at headquarters, in attendance on his chief, Pelham read, conversed and devoted himself to the care of his three fine horses. His tent was next to that of William Blackford, Stuart's engineer, in whose intelligent company he spent many hours. Together they mastered some solid books that winter. With Stuart himself, Pelham was as intimate as a Major could be with a Major General to whom he was responsible. So close was Pelham to his chief that he must have known of his inclusion among the artillerists who were to be promoted. His advancement to the grade of Lieutenant Colonel had been recommended by Stuart and had been proposed to the War Department by General Lee.[31] Doubtless Pelham looked forward to the receipt of a formal paper, with its red lines and signatures, but during the long, tedious and gloomy days of late February, he never intimated that he expected or felt that he deserved promotion.

At length came March, the month of mystery in Virginia. Often then the air is cold, the wind is searching, and the whole aspect of nature is blusterous. On the highways, deep in mud when they are not snow covered, winter seems unrelenting. In the woods, the buds are swelling confidently and unafraid. Spring was coming for John Pelham; spring and, his friends predicted, advance.

---

[30] *O. R.*, 25, pt. 2, p. 654.   [31] *O. R.*, 25, pt. 2, p. 651.

ment not only to a lieutenant colonelcy but to the rank of Brigadier General before winter descended again.

For the coming campaign, Pelham had an inspiring call to
arms. Almost daily, he and Blackford read aloud to each other in
turn Napier's clangorous narrative of the Peninsular war. All that
was written there of Torres Vedras, one might see anew in the
winding earthworks along the ridge of the Rappahannock. Odds
as severe as any that Wellesley had encountered, the Army of
Northern Virginia would face and overcome. No stranger tale
had Napier to tell of Spanish guerrillas than Stuart jubilantly reported about the 10th of March of that curious John S. Mosby who
had been half aide, half scout on the Chickahominy raid, and
now was operating a company of guerrillas, "Partisan Rangers" in
official parlance. On the night of March 8–9, Mosby and a few
companions had ridden boldly into Fairfax Court House and had
captured Brig. Gen. E. H. Stoughton and virtually all his guard.[32]
Omen this was—omen from Mosby and inspiration from Napier.

Pelham interrupted the reading of Napier one afternoon about
the middle of March. If he could get permission from Stuart, he
confided to Blackford, he was going to Orange to accept the implied invitation of one of Stuart's Richmond cousins. Miss Nannie
Price, who was visiting Miss Brill at the Court House, had sent
"Jeb" some of the product of a "candy stew" and had asked him
to give some of it to "the gallant Pelham." The Major thought it
would be proper to thank her in person.[33] Blackford marked the
place where the day's reading ended, and then he closed the book
and wished Pelham luck in coaxing Stuart to give leave for the
journey. Pelham needed the luck and needed shrewd planning,
also, because Stuart had a strange, upsetting way in dealing with
him and the others whom he liked to have around him. The
General might grant leave without much protest, but the next
morning if he missed the officer and thought of a mission for the
absentee, or even wanted companionship, he might cancel the
leave and recall a man already on the way home. That was one
peculiarity that Channing Price had in mind when he said that
a member of the staff had always to be at Stuart's beck and call.

[32] O. R., 25, pt. 1, pp. 43–44; 7 C. V., 156; Wearing of the Gray, 346 ff. This was
the performance that first brought Mosby to the attention of the army.
[33] Information courteously supplied by C. G. Milham of Williamsburg, Va., whose
MS biography of Pelham should be published.

Pelham resolved it should not be so on this occasion. He would ask at night for the leave. If he received it, he would get an early start the next morning and would not wait to have breakfast with the General, lest Stuart find some excuse for keeping him at head-quarters. Even if he started at sunrise, Pelham had to reason that Stuart forgetfully might ask "Where's Pelham?" and, when re-minded, might say: "Send for him." It was prudent to be so far on the road that a friend at the mess could answer, "General, he left so early that a courier could not overtake him now."

The first part of the plan worked perfectly. At supper, Stuart in benevolent mood granted the leave and said he would authorize it for an inspection of the horse artillery on the Rapidan, so that Pelham, in theory, would be on official duty and would not be violating any of the rules "Marse Robert" had laid down to dis-courage absence from the front. Major FitzHugh might issue the proper order. Quickly enough, the obliging A.A.G. prepared the paper. Pelham took it, thanked the Major, tucked away the sheet and made ready for an early departure.

Once on the road the next morning, he reached in good time an artillery camp where he had planned to have breakfast. He greeted friends there and drank a social cup of coffee, but he did not wait to fry bacon and cook bread. Prudence or impatience or both spurred him on. Beyond the camp, Pelham found the road through the Wilderness of Spotsylvania long. The mire slowed down his horse. Not until evening did he approach Orange and then, just as he had apprehended, he saw a headquarters courier behind him. When the man at length overtook him, it was to pre-sent an order from Stuart to return.

Pelham knew, of course, that Stuart did not intend for him to push a weary horse back through the mud that night. Conse-quently, he went on to Orange and spent the night there. Doubt-less he saw a young lady whose image previously had been smil-ing—who knows—between his eyes and the pages of Napier; but of what he said and of what she answered, there is no record.

Nor is there certainty of how, from Orange, he went the next day or the next to Culpeper. There is a story, which has verisimili-tude, that a train came roaring down from Culpeper to Orange to procure a supply of ammunition. Officers aboard the cars explained that the enemy was believed to be advancing in some force and that Fitz Lee, commanding at Culpeper, was preparing to give battle.[34] Pelham is said to have ridden back aboard this ammunition train in the knowledge that when an attack was threatened, Stuart of course would approve disobedience of the order to return to cavalry headquarters. Whatever the exact circumstances, Pelham reached Culpeper before night on the 16th and found Stuart there as a witness at a court martial.

The next morning, March 17, on borrowed horses, Stuart and Pelham began a hurried ride toward the quarters of Fitz Lee, who by that time had received fairly accurate and somewhat alarming intelligence of the enemy's movements. His information on the forenoon of the 16th had been that Federals in large numbers were moving in the general direction of Culpeper. About sunset on the 16th, scouts had reported the arrival of the Federals at Morrisville, in the southeastern part of Fauquier County, about nine miles East of the familiar crossing of the Rappahannock at Kelly's

[34] In his MS *Memoirs*, 293 ff, W. W. Blackford, who has been followed in this previously unpublished account of the circumstances, stated that the train went to Orange on the morning of March 17, and that Pelham returned with it, but reached Culpeper after Fitz Lee's column had left to meet the Federals. Insofar as he fixed the time of Pelham's arrival at Culpeper, Blackford must have been in error for these two reasons: First, Harry Gilmor, in his *Four Years in the Saddle* (cited hereafter as *Gilmor*), 59, stated that he saw Pelham in Culpeper on the night of March 16; second, H. B. McClellan, *op. cit.*, 217, noted that Pelham and Stuart had been attending a court martial in Culpeper as witnesses and had purposed to return to Fredericksburg on the morning of the 17th. When, said McClellan, they learned of the enemy's approach they borrowed horses and went out with Fitz Lee. As McClellan was then Adjutant of the Third Cavalry and was present, he, like Gilmor, can be regarded as an eye-witness. Captain Blackford was not. Pelham, then, almost certainly was in Culpeper when the column started on the 17th. He did not arrive aboard the ammunition train on the morning of the 17th and follow Stuart and Fitz Lee to the scene of action. Furthermore, all the accounts agree that Stuart and Pelham borrowed horses and rode to the scene of action. Fitz Lee reported that Stuart arrived at field headquarters before the fighting commenced. If Stuart and Pelham did not have their own mounts, it must have been because they came to Culpeper by railway—Stuart presumably by the Virginia Central to Gordonsville and then by the O. & A. to Culpeper. Pelham might easily have come from Orange aboard the ammunition train on the afternoon of the 16th when he learned that an attack was threatened. Fitz Lee stated, *O. R.*, 25, pt. 1, p. 60, that he heard from Hdqrs. A. N. Va., at 11 A.M. on the 16th, that the enemy was moving. Soon after that hour, he may have sent for ammunition from Orange. If Pelham returned on that train, he would have arrived at Culpeper in time to have been seen, as he was, by Gilmor, on the evening of the 16th. Gilmor did not list Pelham as a witness at the court martial, which was that of L. Col. H. C. Pate of the Fifth Virginia Cavalry, though Gilmor stated that Stuart was a witness. All the testimony can be reconciled, except for Blackford's statement of the time of Pelham's arrival at Culpeper, by concluding that Pelham went to Orange at some indeterminable date shortly before the 16th, that he was there on the 16th when he heard of the threat of a Federal raid, and that he hastened then to Culpeper on the ammunition train. Although this seems a reasonable theory, the conflict of evidence makes necessary the reservation in the text.

Ford.[35] About 1.00 A.M. on the 17th, Fitz Lee was notified that
the Federals had converged on Morrisville from three directions
and that they were encamped there. This might be the preliminary of an advance up either side of the Rappahannock toward
the Orange and Alexandria Railroad, or it might mean that the
Federals were preparing to make a dash toward Gordonsville or

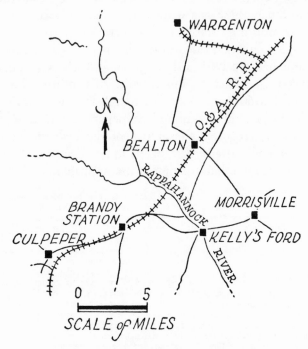

Vicinity of Kelly's Ford—after *H. B. McClellan*

some other point on the Virginia Central. The situation was somewhat confused later in the night by a report that hostile troops
were at Bealton, on the O. & A. From that point, manifestly, the
Federals might be planning a move toward Warrenton. On the
other hand, if Unionists intended to strike for any point South of
the Rappahannock, they probably would cross at Kelly's Ford.
Fitz Lee already had at the ford a picket of twenty men under a
gallant and careful officer, Capt. James Breckinridge of the Second

---

[35] The small settlement on the south side of the stream was known pretentiously as
Kellysville, wherefore the action of the 17th is styled Kellysville in some reports and
Kelly's Ford in others.

Cavalry; but during the night he had thought it prudent to send there an additional forty men. All the remaining sharpshooters of the Brigade had been ordered to move at daylight and to take position on the railroad at the point whence a road ran down to Kelly's Ford, distant three miles and a half. The Brigade itself was placed to the North of Culpeper.

By these dispositions, Fitz Lee seemed to be protected against surprise and in position to meet a Federal advance on either side of the Rappahannock. Now, at 7.30 on the morning of March 17, he was confronted with news that the Union cavalry had forced the crossing at Kelly's and had captured twenty-five of his pickets. If this were true, then the bluecoats might be riding straight for the Orange and Alexandria Railroad South of the Rappahannock. They must be met and defeated before they could reach the track. Confederate wagons and lame horses must take the road South and try to put the Rapidan between them and the enemy. The five regiments—First, Second, Third, Fourth and Fifth Virginia —must move to the road from Kellysville to Brandy Station.[36]

All this was done promptly. It was done grimly, too, because Fitz could not count more than 800 sabers and had no reinforcement near. If there was a clash, it might be a desperate one of the sort that most stirred the soul of John Pelham. Eagerly he rode on with Stuart till they reached the point on the Kelly's Ford road where brigade field headquarters had been established. There Pelham had to wait. At the moment, he could do nothing else. One of his batteries, attached temporarily to Fitz Lee's service, had not yet come up, but its commander, James Breathed, would get to the scene of action as quickly as straining horses and spinning wheels could bring him there.[37] If an onslaught came before the artillery arrived, Pelham could carry messages, perhaps, or might have a hand in the clash of horses and the crossing of sabers. That was a type of combat he never had shared in person, though often he had observed it from his guns. Fortunately, he had worn his sword when he went to Orange.

[36] H. B. McClellan, *op. cit.*, 209, stated that Fitz Lee advanced "to Miller's House about a mile and a half below Brandy Station," but he did not locate that property on his large map of the district. Vagueness of contemporary description makes it impossible to say precisely to what point Fitz Lee first advanced.

[37] Mr. Milham writes that he has seen a dispatch of March 17 in which Pelham told Moorman to be on the alert and added: "If everything is quiet here, I will be at Rapid Ann Station tomorrow."

The Federals did not come up the road from Kellysville to Brandy. Not a sound of conflict at the ford was borne on the brisk March air. What were the Federals doing? Had they headed southwestward for Orange, instead of westward for Culpeper? Fitz Lee determined to ascertain quickly. If Stoneman or Averell, or whoever was the commander, would not advance and attack, Fitz would. That was his nature. It was in his blood. Off he started his column.

With it rode Stuart [38] and Pelham through a country familiar from the experiences of the summer and autumn of 1862. Not far distant had been the road of Pelham's advance in August, within a few days after he had exchanged the three bars of a Captain's insignia of rank for the single gold star of the Major. Then he already had shared the actions at First Manassas and at Williamsburg, the ride around McClellan, the bloody battle of Gaines' Mill and the raid on White House which had culminated in that amusing chase of the gunboat. Ahead, when he had passed the Rappahannock, northward bound in August, 1862, were those pulse raising days around Groveton, the Maryland expedition, Sharpsburg, the October raid into Maryland, White's Ford, those exacting skirmishes while the First Corps was crossing to Culpeper, then Fredericksburg when the eyes of the army had been home, and after that the plunge through Selectman's Ford on the Occoquan, which the "old folks" said no wheeled vehicle could cross. Yes, the Kelly's Ford country, at the time of his first northward crossing of the Rappahannock, had been the half-way bivouac in the rise of John Pelham. Ahead of him now, as in August was . . . the promise of an exciting battle.

The column was approaching Kelly's Ford from the West. In front, the advance guard had located the enemy. He was about half a mile from the ford, in no great strength, and appeared to be deployed as if he expected to receive, rather than to deliver, an attack. Squarely across the road of Fitz's advance these Federals were. Their left seemed to be in heavy woodland; in a smaller wood on the opposite side of the road they probably were also, but at a distance little could be seen of them. No movement could be discerned where the woods on the Federal right opened on a field of C. T. Wheatley, whose family gave name to a little used cross-

[38] He and Fitz Lee always rode together when possible. See 35 S. H. S. P., 143.

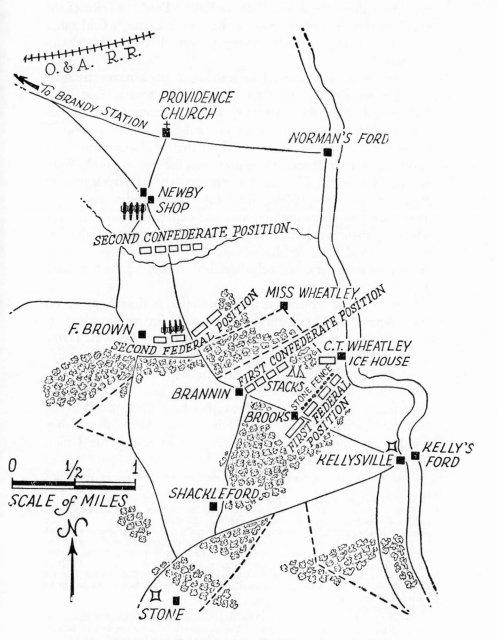

O. & A. R.R.

To BRANDY STATION

PROVIDENCE CHURCH

NORMAN'S FORD

NEWBY SHOP

SECOND CONFEDERATE POSITION

MISS WHEATLEY

F. BROWN

FIRST CONFEDERATE POSITION

SECOND FEDERAL POSITION

C.T. WHEATLEY
ICE HOUSE

BRANNIN

STACKS

STONE FENCE

BROOKS

FIRST FEDERAL POSITION

KELLYSVILLE

KELLY'S FORD

SHACKLEFORD

0   1/2   1

SCALE of MILES

N

STONE

Scene of the Action at Kelly's Ford. Mch. 17, 1863—after H. B. McClellan

ing three quarters of a mile [39] above Kelly's Ford. In front of the wood on the right of the road and across Wheatley's field ran a tall stone fence,[40] which evidently was defended by sharp-shooters.[41]

As much of this as could be seen on a quick reconnaissance, Fitz Lee scrutinized and then he turned to Stuart. Said Fitz: "General, I think there are only a few platoons in the woods yonder. Hadn't we better take the bulge on them at once?" Stuart always was agreeable to a fight that held any promise of advantage and this time he saw no reason for holding back. With his chief's approval, Fitz Lee sent word to the Third Virginia to push forward one squadron, dismounted, as sharpshooters. After these men had taken position and had peppered the enemy, the whole regiment would be ordered to charge.[42] Stuart remained at the front to observe the sharpshooters; Pelham galloped back to the rear to see if he could help Breathed in finding the best artillery position.[43]

When Pelham returned in a few minutes, he found the action developing fast. The skirmishers had gone forward but had recoiled in front of the stone fence; Stuart in person, with Harry Gilmor's help, had rallied the contingent that had wavered.[44] Now the Third Virginia, with drawn sabers, was yelling furiously [45] and, in column of fours,[46] was charging straight for the stone fence. There must be a gate somewhere, through which the men could swarm, or a low stretch of fence across which they could jump their horses. Then they could scatter the Union sharpshooters and press on.

[39] By air. The distance around the bend of the river was slightly more than a mile.
[40] O. R., 25, pt. 1, pp. 57, 61. The map in *ibid.*, 51, is inaccurate. The best is in H. B. McClellan, opposite p. 207, from which the sketch on page 461 was drawn.
[41] H. B. McClellan, 209–10. It should be noted that in most of the accounts of the battle the strength of the Federals and the formidable nature of their position are described as subsequently ascertained and not as observed during reconnaissance. Fitz Lee's report, O. R., 25, pt. 1, pp. 60–61, reviewed the preliminaries of the action and the first onset, but summarized the remainder of the fight in three sentences. Consequently, from this point onward in the narrative, chief reliance has to be on Gilmor and on H. B. McClellan. Warning must be added that Ware's *Kelly's Ford* (see the Bibliography, Vol. III), hopelessly confused memories of several battles and has to be discarded altogether.
[42] *Gilmor*, 61.
[43] *Jed Hotchkiss' MS Diary*, 151. This entry was made March 24 after Stuart had described the circumstances to Hotchkiss. The incident is of some importance because it explains why Stuart and Pelham separated and why Pelham happened later to be at the gap in the fence.
[44] *Gilmor*, 61–62.   [45] *Ibid.*, 62.
[46] H. B. McClellan, 210.

At the moment Pelham got his first view of the charging column, the van had reached the stone wall, and was galloping in
front of it toward the Confederate left. The men had drawn their
pistols and were firing at the blue line behind the fence, but they
had not been able to get over the barrier. Evidently they were
making for farm buildings on the left where, surely, there would
be a gate or a gap in the fence. This at a glance was plain to Pelham. Instantly he drew saber and put spurs to his horse. He
would share that charge, help as he could, and rejoin Stuart who,
of course, would be in the mêlée. Pelham's borrowed mount responded to the spurs and galloped toward the head of the column.
The joy of battle was in the boy's shining eyes. As he waved his
sword, he smiled and shouted "Forward!" [47]

"Forward!" he continued to shout and cut across the angle of
the column to reach its head. By the time he approached the farm
buildings, the men were streaming through a gap in the fence and
were filing off to the extreme left, whence their officers hoped to
attack the Federal flank. Pelham drew rein at the gate and yelled
encouragement to the men as they passed. In the high ecstasy of
conflict, he stood in his stirrups, sword uplifted, battle shout on
his lips. Overhead a roar, a flash, the loud explosion of a shell.
The horse leaped. Pelham fell. He lay on his back. The smile did
not fade. His eyes remained open; his face was not marred. He
looked as if at the next moment he would rise and shake off the
dirt and shout again, "Forward"; but in the back of his head, just
at the hair-line, there was a small bleeding wound where a fragment of shell had entered.[48]

The column had passed ere his fall was observed. A single rider
saw the body on the ground by the gate, recognized Pelham,
jumped down and tried to minister to him. A moment later, it
was evident the Union cavalry were preparing to countercharge.
Pelham must be carried off; otherwise he would be a prisoner.
While the officer, single handed, was trying to lift the wounded
boy over the bow of his saddle, Adjutant Henry McClellan fortunately rode up. Together the two got Pelham across the withers
of the horse. As the Federals came back with a rush, the over-

[47] 38 S. H. S. P., 382, a quotation that apparently is in excerpt from a private letter
of Maj. H. B. McClellan. The account in his life of Stuart is briefer and less dramatic
but essentially the same.
[48] Gilmor, 69.

loaded animal pluckily carried the rider and the limp form of Pelham to the rear.[49]

Almost from the time of Pelham's fall, the action lost its menacing character. Soon it degenerated into demonstrations. At nightfall it ended in the withdrawal of the Federals by the road of their advance.[50] Confederate casualties numbered 133.[51] Those of the Federals were little more than half as numerous—seventy-eight.[52] There was some complaint on Stuart's part over the bungling conduct of the reinforcements sent to Kelly's Ford during the night of March 16–17 by Fitz Lee,[53] but the brigade commander himself received nothing but praise.[54] Tom Rosser, too, was commended not only for his gallantry in the charge but also for his pluck in remaining on the field, though severely wounded, till the battle was won.[55] Sergeant W. J. Kimbrough of the Fourth Virginia had this remarkable citation in the report of Fitz Lee: ". . . wounded early in the day, he refused to leave the field. In the last charge he was the first to spring to the ground to open the fence; then dashing on at the head of the column, he was twice sabered over the head, his arm shattered by a bullet, captured and carried over the river, when he escaped, and walked back twelve miles to his camp." [56]

Most of all was there lament for the fallen and, above all, for the brave Maj. J. W. Puller of the Fifth Cavalry [57] and for the

---

[49] H. B. McClellan, 210–11; Gilmor, 66; 38 S. H. S. P., 383. It is quite impossible to reconcile the various accounts of the fall of Pelham and of the removal of his body. Gilmor and H. B. McClellan differed substantially concerning the status of the action at the moment Pelhalm was shot. Gilmor asserted that Capt. James Bailey of the Third Virginia Cavalry and Lieut. Charles Minnigerode assisted him in getting Pelham on his, Gilmor's, horse, op. cit., 66. H. B. McClellan, op. cit., 211, stated that he "saw a single cavalryman struggling to place the body" across a saddle, and that he assisted.
[50] The details, which are not of any strategical and of scant tactical interest, are given in H. B. McClellan, 211 ff.
[51] O. R., 25, pt. 1, p. 63. [52] Ibid., 53.
[53] Cf. Stuart in O. R., 25, pt. 1, p. 58. H. B. McClellan, op. cit., 207–08, explained that the horse holders of the picket reinforcement were too far in the rear and that the men who left their mounts and walked to the rifle pits, where Breckinridge's pickets were stationed, had so much distance to cover that most of them were captured before they reached the pits. Said McClellan: "This occasion, as well as many others, demonstrated the fact that the horse holders in a cavalry fight should be the coolest and the bravest men in the company. 'Number Four' has no right to be exempt from the perils of the battle. He holds the horses of his comrades only in order that they may more efficiently fight on foot; and he should always be near at hand to give whatever aid the occasion demands."
[54] See Stuart's commendation, O. R., 25, pt. 1, pp. 58, 59, and R. E. Lee's, ibid., 60, and ibid., pt. 2, p. 686.
[55] Ibid., pt. 1, p. 59. [56] O. R., 25, pt. 1, p. 62.
[57] O. R., 25, pt. 1, p. 63.

famous young artillerist. While Pelham's body was being carried to the rear, word passed that he was dead. Stuart heard this and bowed his head on his horse's neck and wept. "Our loss is irreparable," he said.[58] Half way to Culpeper, Harry Gilmor overtook the men who, in the belief that life was extinct, still were carrying Pelham's body across a saddle. Gilmor had them take the body off the horse and place it on the grass. To his amazement, he found the boy's heart still beating. Hopefully an ambulance was requisitioned. Carefully Pelham was placed in it and was carried to the home of Judge Shackelford in Culpeper,[59] where he was examined by three surgeons. They found that the fragment of shell, no larger than the tip of the little finger, had crashed through the back of the skull for two inches. Although the steel had not damaged perceptibly the structure of the brain, it had done fatal hurt to nerves. About 1.00 P.M. Pelham opened his eyes, drew a long breath and, without so much as a whisper, died.[60]

Stuart came back from the field of Kellysville to gaze in black sorrow at the magnificent boy and to make arrangements for the dignified return of the corpse to the soil of Alabama.[61] By the General's order, Heros von Borcke met at Hanover Junction the train that bore the corpse, and he attended it to Richmond where it was placed in the Capitol and, after transfer to a metal casket, was laid in state. "By special request," said von Borcke, "I had a small window let into the coffin-lid just over the face, that his friends and admirers might take a last look at the young hero, and they came in troops, the majority being ladies, who brought garlands and magnificent bouquets to lay upon the coffin." [62]

Then, with a guard of honor to the railroad station and with mourning dignitaries in procession, John Pelham's body made its long, last journey. Ere slow trains brought it to its native soil, the entire South had acclaimed him. "The gallant Pelham—so noble, so true—" said Stuart, "will be mourned by the nation." [63] A general order of the cavalry Division was devoted to his honor. The horse artillery and the division staff were directed to wear for thirty days the military badge of mourning.[64] Stuart named his

[58] *Gilmor*, 66–67; cf. *O. R.*, 25, pt. 1, p. 63.
[59] *Grimsley*, 7.
[60] *Gilmor*, 68-69. That writer believed that if surgical aid had been given soon after the wound was received, Pelham's life would have been saved. *Ibid.*, 68.
[61] *Gilmor*, 69.   [62] 2 *von Borcke*, 190.
[63] *O. R.*, 25, pt. 1, pp. 59-60.   [64] *Ibid.*, 60.

next baby Virginia Pelham. A comrade of the staff, John Esten Cooke, wrote memorial verses. Other poets were to pay later homage to Pelham.[65] Three girls put on mourning for him.[66] Blackford laid away the *History of the Peninsular War* and never again had the heart to resume the reading.[67]

The most notable tribute of all was paid by the army commander while Pelham's body still lay in state. Lee wrote the President: "I mourn the loss of Major Pelham. I had hoped that a long career of usefulness and honor was still before him. He has been stricken down in the midst of both, and before he could receive the promotion he had richly won. I hope there will be no impropriety in presenting his name to the Senate, that his comrades may see that his services have been appreciated, and may be incited to emulate them." [68] That was the place, unique if mournful, that Pelham had in the artillery promotions. It was as a Lieutenant Colonel that John Pelham went home.

Best may a kinsman, Maj. Peter Pelham, relate the end: "I was in the [Pelham home] the night his body was brought in its casket. He had been dead two weeks, and the news of his death had gone all over his native county, and they came, old men (the young ones were all at the front) and women, young ladies and children from all over that country to meet and honor the remains of one so loved and admired. It was a beautiful moonlight night the last of March and as the casket, covered with white flowers . . . [was] borne by white haired old men, followed by girls with uncovered heads, to us who stood in the porch at his home, waiting . . . it seemed a company, 'all in white.' . . . And I heard a voice near me say, 'made white in the blood of the Lamb' and I knew it to be the voice of his Mother. The Father and Sister were crushed and in sorrow kept their rooms, but that Spartan Mother met her beloved dead on the threshold as she would have done had he been living, and led the way into the parlor and directed that he . . . be laid where the light would fall on his face when Sunday came." [69]

[65] *Cf.* 2 *R. E. Lee,* 499 n.   [66] *W. W. Blackford's MS Memoirs,* 126.
[67] *Ibid.,* 293.   [68] *O. R.,* 25, pt. 2, p. 675; Mch. 19, 1863.
[69] Maj. Peter Pelham, n.d., 1898, MS to Edwin P. Cox; a letter which, with other material collected for an address on Pelham, graciously was presented the author by Judge Cox's able son, Col. Edwin Cox. Included is an unpublished account by Charles Pelham of John Pelham's first experience in drilling troops after secession.

CHAPTER XXIX

LONGSTREET TRIES INDEPENDENT COMMAND

THE DATE OF Pelham's fall, March 17, 1863, terminated the first month of "Peter" Longstreet in semi-independent command of a strange department and a stranger campaign. Early in January, General Lee had thought it probable that if Burnside went into winter quarters on the Rappahannock, part of the Army of the Potomac would be transferred South of the James for operations there.[1] A considerable Union force already occupied Suffolk, sixteen miles West of Norfolk. After reinforcing that command, the Federals might undertake an advance against the Petersburg and Weldon Railroad, which was for the Army of Northern Virginia the sole rail supply line East of the Blue Ridge. In Southside Virginia and in the corresponding part of North Carolina, the watersheds of the Nansemond and Chowan Rivers, were, moreover, a country of hogs and corn. Roger Pryor, who had exercised command slightly to the West of the Nansemond, reported that in a single month he had procured there the entire subsistence of his Brigade and something besides.[2] An easy country it was in which to live and not a difficult one to occupy.

For the remainder of January, nothing of any consequence occurred between the James and Cape Fear, though there was vast speculation over the probable objective of the Federal flotilla that now was believed to be moving down the coast. Was the destination Savannah, or was it nearer—Wilmington, perhaps, or Charleston? Could the naval force be bound for Port Hudson on the Mississippi? Confederate leaders had rival theories, all of which could be defended.[3] At length, February 14, Confederate Army Headquarters on the Rappahannock heard that Burnside's old Corps, the IX, had taken transports and was moving down the Potomac to Hampton Roads. Scouts reported Federal camp gossip that the Corps was going to Suffolk. General Lee had anticipated it might, but he remembered that the Corps had done well

[1] O. R., 18, 819.   [2] O. R., 18, 845.   [3] Cf. O. R., 18, 876.

in North Carolina and he counted among the possibilities a return there.

Regardless of ultimate objective, the presence in Hampton Roads of a Corps of veteran reinforcements placed heavy striking power in the hands of an adversary who commanded the deeper waterways. A swift voyage up the James and a surprise expedition against Richmond might be contemplated. Precautions had to be taken. Pickett's Division was started for the Confederate capital. Hood was directed to hold himself in readiness.[4]

If these first line troops were to be sent from the First Corps, Longstreet himself should command them. On February 18, orders were issued accordingly. They covered nothing more, at the outset, than that Longstreet should place the two Divisions in a sheltered position near Richmond and should report to the Secretary of War.[5] The one sentence that might arouse expectation was this: "Should the movement of the enemy from the Potomac render it expedient your other Divisions will be ordered to join you."[6] That suggested an independent command, perhaps of a separate army for "Old Pete."

Of Longstreet's reflection on that possibility, there is no record. Several times, during the absence of Lee, he had commanded the Army of Northern Virginia for a few days. On the occasion nearest the date of these new orders, he had been in charge when Burnside in mid-January showed some signs of activity. Curiously enough, and precisely as in March, 1862, Longstreet used his authority to remind Jackson that he was the senior of the two and had to be obeyed. The tone of one letter to Jackson was easily that of a commanding General, though the details were of no importance. Years later, in reviewing events of the winter of 1862–63, General Longstreet confused the preliminaries of the "Mud March" with the march itself, and told how Jackson disagreed with his view that the Federal advance would be above Fredericksburg, and that the Second Corps should move accordingly. Said Longstreet in 1896: "[Jackson] was not satisfied with the refusal to accept his construction of the enemy's purpose, and demurred against authority less than General Lee's, but found that the order must be obeyed."[7]

[4] O. R., 18, 876 ff.   [5] Ibid., 883–84.   [6] Ibid., 883.
[7] Longstreet, 323. The General forgot, apparently, that the "Mud March" proper did not begin until Jan. 19, 1863, by which date Lee had returned and had resumed command of the Army.

That sounded, at least in retrospect, as if a taste of power beyond the camps of the First Corps had not been unpleasant to Longstreet. Now, in a new field, he was to have more than a taste. On his arrival in Richmond, he was received with manifest relief and with flattering attention. The Secretary of War wrote Lee: "General Longstreet is here, and under his able guidance of such troops no one entertains any doubt as to the entire safety of the capital." [8] Longstreet was mentioned almost on the day of his arrival as commanding the Department of Virginia and North Carolina, which extended from Richmond to the Cape Fear River,[9] and on February 25, he formally was appointed.[10] The Department was in reality three—the Department of Richmond, over which Arnold Elzey presided, the Department of Southern Virginia, under Maj Gen. Samuel G. French, and the Department of North Carolina, which Harvey Hill reluctantly was taking in charge.

There was, at the outset, no clear definition of these Departments,[11] nor was the personnel all that could be desired. Officers who had been tried in Virginia and then had been shunted southward were so numerous that Longstreet might almost have thought he was back in the old Confederate Army of the Potomac as it existed before the coming of Lee. At Charleston was Beauregard, somewhat repressed perhaps in his Napoleonic ambitions, but otherwise the same as after Manassas. Wilmington on the Cape Fear, with elaborate defenses, had been since Nov. 17, 1862, under command of W. H. C. Whiting, comrade of Centreville days.[12] Harvey Hill, of course, was bound to Longstreet by all the ties of Seven Pines. "Shanks" Evans, another companion of Manassas, First and Second, was at Kinston, North Carolina.[13] Other officers in the Department were known to Longstreet from later association. Robert Ransom, it will be remembered, had gone to North Carolina with his own Brigade and John R. Cooke's. Johnston Pettigrew had been restored to health and had been assigned a Brigade of some 2500 men in the North State.

Along with varied excellencies, some of the best of these new lieutenants of Longstreet had more than their share of temperamental peculiarities. Doubtless because of his health Harvey Hill was in his most nervous, critical mood. He had more separate

8 O. R., 18, 890. Cf. 1 R. W. C. D., 263 (Feb. 24, 1863): "Richmond is safe."
9 O. R., 18, 889.　　　　　　　　　　10 O. R., 18, 895, 896.
11 This did not come until Apr. 1, 1863. See infra. p. 480.
12 O. R., 18, 848.　　　　　　　　　　13 Cf. O. R., 18, 865.

responsibility than he cared to assume, and he had permitted his prejudices to sour him. When at last he assumed command, which he had told Smith he was loath to do, he issued on February 25 an extraordinary address to his command. He praised the infantry and called upon it to "cut down to 6 feet by 2 the dimension of the farms which these [Northern] plunderers propose to appropriate." For North Carolinians who sought to escape military duty—"these abortions of humanity"—he has nothing but contempt. "Do your duty, soldiers," he said, "and leave these poltroons and villains to the execration of posterity." Artillerists were commended, but were told it "has been a mistake . . . to contend with the Yankee artillery." The men were advised: "Reserve your fire, as at Fredericksburg, for the masses of infantry, and do not withdraw your guns just when they are becoming effective. It is glorious to lose guns by fighting them to the last; it is disgraceful to save them by retiring early from the fight." After delivering this technical exhortation, Hill opened the sluices of his favorite prejudice—that against the cavalry—in language already quoted.[14] A subordinate who ended on that note, however friendly he was to "Old Pete" personally, might be expected to cause some puzzlement in the course of a campaign.

It developed speedily enough, and to Longstreet it was known at the time, that Harvey Hill's sarcasms were directed specifically against what he had described as "the wonderfully inefficient brigade of Robertson,"[15] the same Beverly Robertson who had provoked Jackson in the operations of the previous August. General Robertson had been sent to North Carolina, it will be remembered, after the Second Battle of Manassas, and had been there continuously but not, it would appear, to the satisfaction of all his superiors. Hill wanted Hampton in his stead.[16] One of Longstreet's first letters to the Adjutant General, after assuming command, asked that Robert Ransom supersede Robertson who, said Longstreet, "was not deemed a very efficient officer in the field and was therefore relieved from duty with the Army of Northern Virginia."[17]

Roger A. Pryor was on the Blackwater when Longstreet took command, and for a short time the ex-editor was retained,[18] but

14 O. R., 18, 895; see *supra*, p. 172.
15 O. R., 18, 891.
16 O. R., 18, 891
17 O. R., 18, 900.
18 O. R., 18, 906; O. R., 51, pt. 2, p. 667.

he soon was in a fair way of being deprived of a Brigade by the expedient employed in Northern Virginia in the autumn—that of transferring his troops to other stations or to different commands. It had been with some difficulty that Pryor had acquired on the Blackwater what Seddon subsequently termed a force, "dignified with the name of a Brigade." [19] To retain it, Pryor pulled many wires and even invoked the aid of Governor Vance, who wrote to Longstreet. As suavely as if he had been Lee himself, "Old Pete" replied that the Blackwater command was in good hands, and that Pryor was losing his Brigade because his regiments were being returned to Western Virginia, whence they had been sent to Eastern Virginia for the winter.[20] Sam French previously had spiked the assertion that while on the Blackwater, Pryor had subsisted his command from occupied territory. Orders to do that, said French, always had been in effect. Pryor had been able to execute them because he had been there after hog-killing. Before that time, the weather had been too warm. The hogs had not been in condition.[21] All the odds, in short, were against Pryor. He could do nothing to change them, and soon he once more was a Brigadier without a soldier.[22]

As for Chase Whiting, some of his peculiarities doubtless were familiar to Longstreet; but as departmental superior to the commander at Wilmington, Longstreet had yet to learn of the endless apprehension, the persistence and the prolixity of Whiting as a correspondent. Nor could Longstreet be expected to know at the outset the depth of Whiting's ambition to be an independent commander. As Whiting had affection for his friends and showed much loyalty to them, Longstreet probably would have been justi-

19 O. R., 27, pt. 3, p. 874. For Pryor's loss of this Brigade in November see *supra,* p. 265, and for his subsequent efforts to procure command, see O. R., 19, pt. 2, pp. 697–98, 708–09, 712, 715; O. R., 21, 1017, 1032, 1036.
20 O. R., 18, 1094–95.   21 *Ibid.,* 906.
22 Pryor's "scratch Brigade" had consisted in January of the Fiftieth, Fifty-fourth and Sixty-Third Virginia, to which temporarily were added the Twenty-seventh Battalion, some artillery and a few cavalry—altogether about 1800 men (O. R., 18, pp. 142, 145). The Fiftieth Virginia went into J. R. Jones's Brigade; the Fifty-fourth Virginia and the Twenty-seventh Battalion had belonged to the command of Humphrey Marshall, to which they were returned (O. R., 23, pt. 2, pp. 639, 792, 845); the Sixty-third Virginia had come from Sam Jones's little army in Southwest Virginia and went back there (O. R., 25, pt. 2, p. 678). In May, J. B. Jones (*op. cit.,* 1, 308) reported Pryor under arrest and serving as a volunteer to repulse an anticipated raid on Richmond. There is no other printed reference to arrest of Pryor at this time, nor is there so much as a hint of the reason Longstreet and Lee did not wish to have him under their command.

fied in concluding that if there was to be any jar in relations with Whiting, it would not be difficult to settle.

The last of the ranking commanders in the sprawling department was one of whom Longstreet knew little. Maj. Gen. Samuel G. French was a West Pointer, 44 years of age, and had been in the regular army from the time of his graduation in 1843[23] until 1856, when he had resigned to administer large properties left his wife.[24] In 1861, though a New Jersey man by birth, he unhesitatingly threw in his lot with the Confederacy. For the period from November, 1861, to March, 1862, French had been in charge of the heavy guns at Evansport on the Potomac,[25] and then he had been given command in North Carolina. For a time he had his headquarters at Wilmington, but subsequently he resided in Petersburg and directed operations all the way from Drewry's Bluff on James River to the Cape Fear. He has appeared in these pages at the end of July, 1862, when he was left by Harvey Hill in direct charge of the surprise bombardment of McClellan's base from Coggin's Point on the opposite side of the James.[26] His experiences subsequent to that time had been varied, though not spectacular.

Personally, French was sociable, blessed with more than a spark of humor, and quick to respond to every gallant gesture and every chivalrous act. As an "old army man" of thirteen years' commissioned service, including the whole of the Mexican War, he knew thoroughly his duties and his rights, and he was of a disposition to maintain his rights while discharging his duties. Not a soldier-lawyer in the offensive sense of the word, French was so well assured of his position that he was to meet Longstreet, if not with absolute composure, always with a firmness that was destined to puzzle "Old Pete" not a little.

These were a few of the men with whom and through whom Longstreet had to work. In ability they were about of the average of the Army. Temperamentally, they may have been somewhat more difficult than the average. That probability ought to be remembered in weighing the events that followed as a first test of Longstreet in separate command.

[23] *Cullum*, No. 1180. He stood 14th in the class with U. S. Grant.
[24] *French*, 32.
[25] Evansport, it will be remembered, was about one half mile South of the mouth of Quantico Creek on the Virginia, or right, bank of the river.
[26] *Supra*, p. 54. This period is sketched in *French*, 142–151.

Was "separate" to be synonymous with independent, in the sense that Longstreet no longer was under Lee's orders? Longstreet himself does not appear to have been quite sure during March. As soon as he assumed charge of the Department, he began to correspond directly with the Adjutant General, but that of itself was not incompatible with subordination to Lee. During these weeks, Whiting, without reprimand, did the same thing, though he may have sent his letters through Longstreet's office.[27] Longstreet's first extant letter to Lee,[28] in answer to one from the General, may be interpreted as assertion of independence or as the reverse. Said Longstreet: "I shall keep you advised of matters here that you may, by comparing notes, satisfy yourself of the enemy's position &c. I shall be guided by the information that I receive from you of the enemy's movements more than by what I hear here, for the present at all events." He added that he thought his force was "quite sufficient" for the defeat of the Federals if he could meet them.[29]

In so far as acts explained equivocal words, Longstreet in the first days of his command proceeded to order offensive operations without reference to Lee. Two days after he assumed command he suggested to D. H. Hill an enterprise which, among other results, was to open Longstreet's eyes concerning some of his subordinates. In North Carolina, the Federals had been occupying since March 14, 1862, the town of New Berne, on the Neuse River, which flows into Pamlico Sound. The place is of some importance strategically, first as a haven for patrolboats and, second, because the east-and-west coastal railroad, passing westward through New Berne reached at Goldsborough,[30] sixty miles inland, the major supply line of the East, the railroad from Petersburg to Wilmington and the farther South. New Berne consequently was an excellent base for a raid against Goldsborough not only to tear up the railroad but also to destroy its important bridge over the Neuse at that point. On Dec. 17, 1862, the Federals under Gen. J. G. Foster had made exactly such a raid and, in the face of slow and clumsy defense by some of Gustavus Smith's troops, had burned the bridge.[31]

[27] Cf. *O. R.*, 18, 913. [28] At least two, not found, had preceded it

[29] *O. R.*, 18 903.

[30] As noted *supra*, p. 420, the longer spelling of the name was used in nearly all the official reports.

[31] *O. R.*, 18, 57, 109–10.

A repetition of this Longstreet sought to prevent by the direct and soldierly expedient of nipping off New Berne. That done, he could hope to forage extensively in a district long closed to the Confederate commissaries.[32] He could see no reason why an attack on New Berne from both sides of the river, with the support of long-range Whitworth guns, would not force the Federals to surrender.[33] Although "Old Pete" was sick at the time with a troublesome sore throat that kept him to his quarters in Petersburg,[34] he proposed vigorously that Hill take the offensive. Later, in language that Lee might have employed, Longstreet wrote Hill: "If there is a chance of doing anything we should not be idle. We are much more likely to succeed by operating ourselves than by lying still to await the enemy's time for thorough preparation before he moves upon us." [35]

As it happened, Harvey Hill was of the same mind as Longstreet and believed that an offensive against New Berne was desirable in itself and would be a diversion that might lighten the attacks which most of the Confederates thought at the moment the Unionists were about to deliver against Charleston.[36] For the attack on New Berne, Longstreet reasoned that he could spare one long-range Whitworth field gun to operate on the north bank of the Neuse and that Whiting could send up another of these rifles from the Wilmington defenses. Of troops, Longstreet estimated that Hill would have 14,000 or 15,000 men, provided 4000 from Whiting's command co-operated.

It was over this proviso that Longstreet's calculations went astray. His first letter on the subject to Whiting was a matter-of-fact call to send "half of your force and as many more as can be spared from Wilmington garrison to re-enforce Major General Hill for foraging service." Longstreet added that he would like to have Whiting himself participate in the operation, "as some important service may grow out of it." [37] This letter had on Whiting as exciting effect as if it had been warning that the entire Federal Navy was concentrating for an attack on Wilmington. Promptly he wrote back that Longstreet evidently was unacquainted with

[32] O. R., 18, 905.   [33] Cf. O. R., 18, 920–21.
[34] O. R., 18, 903. This was one of the few instances when Longstreet ever referred to his physical condition. His health usually was perfect; his slight impairment of hearing seldom appeared to hamper him.
[35] O. R., 18, 903.
[36] Cf. ibid., 902–03.   [37] O. R., 18, 905.

the district. "So far from considering myself able to spare troops from here," said Whiting, "I have applied for and earnestly urged that another Brigade be sent here immediately." He continued: "The works here are by no means completed and I need the service of every man I can raise." [38]

Concerning the Whitworth gun, about which Hill and not Longstreet wrote him, Whiting was unyielding. He had no more than three of these rifles, he said, and he required the use of all of them to cover the movement of blockade runners. Whiting concluded in his reply to Hill: "Under these circumstances, unless for a matter of greater and pressing importance, I should not like to take the responsibility of detaching the gun from the coast defense. What is this expedition of which you speak? General Longstreet wrote me something about it, but wanted me to send off half my force and half my garrisons." [39] Nor did Whiting stop with this. Apparently in the belief that Hill was in large measure responsible for the raid on his resources, the next day he urged the Adjutant General to permit him to act directly under Longstreet and to report to that officer instead of to Hill.[40]

In the face of Whiting's manifest reluctance to co-operate, the expedition against New Berne was prepared. From Southern Virginia, Longstreet sent down Garnett's, formerly Pickett's Brigade; Hill moved eastward Pettigrew's and Junius Daniel's Brigades—all the infantry he had—and Robertson's cavalry. By arguments that do not appear in the records, Whiting for the time excused himself from sending either troops or gun.

Hill as usual was weighted down by his responsibility and from the outset was discouraged by his failure to get a Brigade from Whiting. In addition, Hill was suffering from sharp physical illness. "I started out," he wrote later, "with my throat in a terrible fix and thought it might cost me my life." [41] His attack on New Berne scarcely deserved to be called anything more than a reconnaissance in force. Feeble thrusts were made on both sides of the Neuse, March 13-15, but they were answered furiously by gunboats towed within range.[42] The Confederate fire was wholly wasted. Federal losses were two killed and four wounded.[43] No exaggeration appeared in the subsequent report of Maj. Gen. J. G.

38 Ibid., 907–08.   39 O. R., 18, 910–11.
40 O. R., 18, 913.   41 O. R., 18, 189.
42 O. R., 18, 184.   43 Ibid.

Foster: "The whole affair, meant to be effective and strong, was ineffective and weak." [44]

After Hill withdrew on the 15th, he insisted that the "expedition was partially successful," [45] but he was disappointed and bitter. He complained of the cavalry: "[Robertson] sent out a colonel who saw some Yankees and came back. Robertson did not go himself. We must have a better man." Garnett was accused of tardiness. Heaviest blame of all was put on Whiting for not sending Ransom's Brigade from Wilmington. Said Hill: "The spirit manifested by Whiting has spoiled everything. My order of assignment says, 'General D. H. Hill is assigned to the command of all the troops in North Carolina.' If I am to be cut down to two brigades I will not submit to the swindle. . . . I have received nothing but contemptuous treatment from Richmond from the very beginning of the war, but I hope they will not carry matters so far as to perpetuate a swindle." [46]

Longstreet was philosophical in dealing with this failure. When he got Hill's bitter report, he wrote back concerning new plans and in a postscript said: ". . . you intimate that there has been some desire on the part of the Department to 'perpetrate a swindle' upon you in putting you in command in North Carolina. I presume that this was not intended as an official communication and have not forwarded it. I hope that you will send up another account of your trip." [47] Hill made no reply, either to avow the report official or to confirm its private character, but he sent in no other account of his "trip." . . . Had there been sarcasm in Longstreet's employment of that word?

Complications now developed rapidly. From Hampton Roads to the Savannah every Confederate garrison was on the lookout for Federal ironclads and for the appearance of the troops that had left the Army of the Potomac. If vacillating Federal plans had been shaped deliberately to create the greatest confusion along the coast, they could not have accomplished that object more effectively. Up the James in Virginia, South of that river from the Suffolk area, into North Carolina via New Berne, at Wilmington, against Charleston, in Georgia—where was the blow to fall? Every commander had a theory; almost every guardian of an im-

[44] *Ibid.*, 184.   [45] *O. R.*, 18, 188.   [46] *O. R.*, 18, 189.
[47] *O. R.*, 18, 931. It will be noted that Longstreet quoted *perpetrate* though Hill had used *perpetuate*.

portant post believed that his was the most endangered. The major offensive, Lee thought, was apt to be on the Rappahannock, and for that reason he instructed Longstreet to keep Hood and Pickett close enough to the railroad for their quick return, in an emergency, to the battlefront of the Army of Northern Virginia. At the time of the raid on Kelly's Ford, Lee ordered the two Divisions to rejoin; but he cancelled these instructions as soon as he discovered that the movement on the upper Rappahannock was of no importance.[48] Longstreet, for his part, expressed willingness to return but explained that he could not keep two Divisions ready to move back to the Rappahannock and, at the same time, collect from Eastern North Carolina the large supplies of salt fish and meat known to be there.[49]

Increasingly the stores of that region were assuming importance in the minds of those operating nearby. To aid in getting the herring and much-needed bacon Longstreet and Hill simultaneously were considering plans for a demonstration against Suffolk,[50] for another against Wilmington, N. C., and for a possible third against New Berne once more. The hope of the Confederate commanders was that, if openings were found, these demonstrations could be turned into real attacks. At the least, it was reasoned, the Federals could be held at the threatened points while the Confederate commissaries scoured the country, which for a year they had not been able to enter.[51]

The importance of the North Carolina supplies to the Confederacy was developed in conferences and inspections voluntarily undertaken by Maj. Raphael J. Moses, Longstreet's corps commissary. Major Moses learned of the dangerous depletion of the reserve rations of the troops in Virginia and the Carolinas at the same time that he ascertained there were tons of bacon and unreckoned barrels of fish in the counties East of the Chowan River. First verbally and then in a written report, he laid these facts before his chief.

---

[48] *O. R.*, 18, 922–27; *cf.* 1 *R. W. C. D.*, 276.
[49] *Ibid.*, 926, 933. [50] *O. R.*, 18, 921.
[51] The assertion sometimes has been made—for example in *Sorrel*, 150—that Longstreet had been sent to the Tidewater district expressly to collect these provisions. Records show unmistakably that the two Divisions were dispatched southward to meet any offensive that might be undertaken by Federal troops when the IX Corps was reinforcing. Operations for the commissariat developed later, though, as indicated in the text, something had been known through Roger Pryor, as early as Jan. 6, 1863, and as French insisted, before that time, of the abundance of food supplies in the district.

When the commissary affirmed that he could get all salable supplies from Eastern Carolina, if the Federals were held at Suffolk, Longstreet smilingly replied that for an operation of such magnitude, the whole of the First Corps would be required. Moses answered that he knew nothing of army movements, but that he could not collect supplies in Eastern Carolina if his wagon trains were exposed to endless Federal raids.[52] Longstreet had a justly high opinion of Moses and he promptly forwarded to the commanding General the report prepared by the commissary. In doing this, Longstreet repeated what he had told Moses: "We can occupy that country and draw the supplies out with another Division of my old Corps, but I do not think it would be prudent to attempt such a move with a less force." [53]

While this and other possibilities were being considered, preparations were made for the investment of Washington, North Carolina, which was the western gate to a region from which the Confederacy was drawing no supplies.[54] To co-operate in the siege of Washington, General Whiting most reluctantly sent Ransom's Brigade from Wilmington[55] though he maintained that by so doing he lost two-thirds of his infantry and all that was "disciplined and efficient." He explained, "I place but little reliance on Evans' Brigade, which is certainly in worse condition than any I have ever seen. It had but about 1500 men for duty, a very large number of field officers absent or under arrest . . ." [56] Longstreet replied only, on this score, that "Evans reported his brigade 3000 strong when here a few days ago." [57]

Hill of course welcomed Ransom's excellent troops and, a little later, enjoined Ransom—to quote that officer—"not to go to Whiting under any circumstances unless the latter states that the enemy's fleet is directly off the forts below." [58] Ransom, for his part, was scarcely less unhappy with Hill than with Whiting, and he made his plea directly to Longstreet. Said Ransom: "If it be possible to prevent it do not let me be kept only to watch when others are doing better. I am not partial to service where there has been so little done and where there are poor opportunities to render real good." [59]

[52] Moses' MS Journal, 19–20.   [53] O. R., 18, 942.
[54] O. R., 18, 970.   [55] O. R., 18, 943; cf. ibid., 945, 947.
[56] O. R., 18, 943.   [57] Ibid., 945.   [58] Ibid., 961.
[59] O. R., 18, 961; April 4, 1863, Kinston, N. C.

There was no way of obliging Ransom. He must remain where he was and share what Hill did or did not accomplish. To add further strength to the expedition, Longstreet lent Hill the Brigade of Kemper and allowed Hill to retain Garnett.[60] At one time, Longstreet intended to entrust to his beloved Pickett the demonstration against Washington but, on redistribution of the troops, decided that Hill would be able to direct the movement.[61] Of the capture of Washington, Longstreet at the outset cherished small hope,[62] but he believed the investment of the place would help in pinning down the Federals to such an extent that his agents would be unhampered in purchasing provisions in the region North of the town.[63]

The "siege of Washington," as it formally was styled by the Federals, was begun on March 30 and was regarded by Hill one day as promising and the next as futile. "Dick" Garnett from the outset had no faith in the enterprise. Longstreet felt, despite his first misgiving, that the operation, once undertaken, should be pressed to success. Otherwise the confidence of the Federals would rise.[64] This seemed so plain that he was irritated by Garnett's continuing pessimism and by Hill's alternating hope and despair. At the end of the first week of maneuver and demonstration, Longstreet verbally set Hill before him for a reprimand, the substance of which was this: "Up to the 2nd instant you gave me no reason to hope that you could accomplish anything; on the contrary, you seemed to have but little hope. . . . Then came your letter of the 2nd which was full of encouragement and hope. I sent you, instead of four guns, as you desired, six, and sent you authority to retain General Garnett's Brigade. After your letter of the 2nd came one of the 4th which, I believe, was more desponding than your previous letters, and expressing the opinion that nothing but heavy artillery would answer any good purpose. I then sent my order for Garnett's Brigade to return and the six pieces of artillery. Your letter of the 5th revives much hope again . . ."[65]

Longstreet had more than the fluctuating moods of Hill to puzzle him. Should or should he not advance his outposts from Blackwater River and make an attempt to drive the Federals from

[60] O. R., 18, 931.
[62] O. R., 18, 942.
[64] O. R., 18, 960.
[61] O. R., 18, 931, 932, 938.
[63] Ibid., 942.
[65] O. R., 18, 969.

Suffolk? Had he force enough to invest the town? If not, would Lee send him additional troops? In the event that Longstreet could not get reinforcements and should not attempt formal siege, could he occupy the Federals by a protracted feint while he purchased and brought out the supplies from the district East and Southeast of Suffolk?

Longstreet's argument of these questions in his correspondence with Lee naturally is read with eagerness for the disclosure of his attitude toward the commanding General. Midway the discussion, April 1, 1863, orders from the War Department made clear the formal, military relationship. The "geographical limits of the command" of Longstreet were divided into three departments, respectively under Elzey, French and Hill; but the whole of the command was stated to be "under the supervision and general direction of General R. E. Lee." [66] As definitely as this placed Whiting under Hill, it asserted the subordination of Longstreet to Lee.

No change in the tone of the correspondence resulted. That Longstreet was coming to regard himself as a strategist who without abashment could dissent from the opinions of his chief, the exchange of opinions plainly shows. Beyond that, the letters are more easily read with one's prejudices than with one's judgment. If one is looking for a lieutenant who had come to consider himself the superior of his chief, and was anxious to advance his campaign at the expense of the main army, one can interpret Longstreet's language to confirm that view. With equal show of logic, one may read Longstreet's dispatches as the frank expression of a plain-spoken and somewhat cautious man who was anxious to have adequate force for the mission entrusted to him, but was not insubordinate or unreasonable.[67]

The first view of Lee was that Longstreet did not face heavy opposition and that there was no military justification for making further detachment from the Army of Northern Virginia, which Lee thought soon was to be attacked. For the rest, Lee was willing to trust Longstreet's judgment of what could be effected in front of Suffolk. If Longstreet were too heavily committed when Hooker attacked, Lee was willing to retreat from the Rappahan-

---

[66] O. R., 18, 953.
[67] The principal exchanges are O. R., 18, 922, 924, 933, 934, 943–44, 950, 954, 958–59, 970.

nock to the North Anna. Longstreet, for his part, remained doubt-ful of the results that could be obtained at Suffolk; but he felt that unless he had a stroke of luck, he would require for the swift cap-ture of the place a larger force than he had. Lee could defend the Rappahannock, Longstreet boldly maintained, with Jackson's troops and safely could dispatch to Southside Virginia the remain-ing two Divisions of the First Corps. Both Lee and Longstreet were agreed that, as far as time permitted, the area below Suffolk should be cleared of purchasable supplies.[68]

At length Longstreet decided that the removal of provisions from Eastern North Carolina was worth the risks to be encoun-tered in a heavy demonstration against Suffolk. He recalled Kemper's Brigade from North Carolina [69] though he left Garnett to help Hill. From Richmond, Longstreet sought with Lee's aid to procure part of Elzey's garrison of somewhat doubtful mobil-ity,[70] but he got nothing better than an assurance that part of Elzey's command would demonstrate on the Peninsula and in Gloucester County.[71] Hill, simultaneously, was to press the opera-tion against Washington which was unpromising but had not reached a stage of certain failure.

The advance was to be in the department of Maj. Gen. French and on a sector that French for months had been watching. Long-street would be compelled to use French's Division, which con-sisted of two Brigades only, but he was not disposed to employ French's services. In March, young Micah Jenkins had been trans-ferred from Pickett's Division to French's in order to relieve on the Blackwater Colston's Brigade, which was shifted from French's Division to Pickett's.[72] This arrangement made Jenkins the senior officer of the Division, after French himself. "Old Pete" had entire confidence in Jenkins and probably felt that the South Carolinian could handle French's troops better than their regular commander could.

Plans were developed. In a casual fashion, French was told that Longstreet intended to make the move on Suffolk. French's wag-

[68] It will be understood that these divergent points of view were not set forth fully in a single communication from either General but were developed gradually. They here are formulated from all the communications that passed. In the case of Longstreet, it should be repeated, judgment of what could be accomplished at Suffolk varied perceptibly from time to time. Cf. O. R., 18, 924, 942, 963.

[69] Cf. O. R., 18, 969.
[70] O. R., 18, 966.
[71] Ibid., 968.
[72] O. R., 18, 900.

ons would be required and would be used in the collection of supplies. Nothing was said of the date the operation was to be undertaken or of the troops that were to share it. "The next thing I knew"—General French is speaking—"[Longstreet], April 9, . . . put his command in motion and took from me a Division and a number of batteries, and was on his way to Suffolk without informing me in any way of his designs, or of his wishes." [73]

Immediately French concluded that the reason for Longstreet's secrecy was a desire to transfer the Division to Micah Jenkins. That Jenkins was able, French admitted, and he wished the South Carolinian well; but was French to acquiesce silently and to remain behind in Petersburg, where he had little to do and a small force with which to do it? Not Sam French! He had too much zeal for the cause and knew too well his rights to let himself be supplanted in this fashion. No notice of suspension from command had reached him, though the orders to his subordinates had not been sent through him as army usage prescribed. Regardless, then, of anything that Longstreet planned or desired, French reasoned that he still was in command of his Division. He would exercise that command. "The next day," he wrote later, "I put a staff officer in charge of the departmental headquarters, and with my other staff officers rode to Suffolk and took command of my own troops . . ." [74] That was all there was to it. Samuel G. French, Major General, P. A. C. S., blandly presented his compliments and awaited the orders of the Lieutenant General.

Longstreet showed no impatience when French rode up and reported in front of Suffolk, but he determined to use French otherwise than with infantry. As it happened, the artillery of the mixed command was active and was without a head. Neither Colonel Walton nor Colonel Alexander, on whom Longstreet relied day by day, was with the expedition. [75] Longstreet knew French's reputation as an artillerist and he promptly asked him to take charge of all the batteries. French may have regarded this as com-

[73] *French*, 160.   [74] *Ibid.*

[75] That is to say, Walton was announced February 26, as Chief of Artillery on the staff of the Department commander, *O. R.*, 18, 896, but he was absent on recruiting duty in the far South (*Owen*, 202–03). "Colonel Alexander" was mentioned by Longstreet on March 29 as inspecting ordnance. This doubtless was Porter Alexander, but he must have been on a brief tour of inspection which he did not mention in his memoirs. For the greater part of the winter, Alexander was with his artillery battalion in the vicinity of Carmel Church, about five miles North of Hanover Junction. See *Alexander*, 317.

pliment or as guile or as both; but he stood his ground. "I told him," French wrote of Longstreet, "I did not intend to give up the command of my division to any one, but that I was willing to give all the assistance I could, personally and through the chief of my artillery, to place in position guns to prevent gunboats going up and down the [Nansemond] river." [76]

Orders were issued formally by Longstreet on April 14 for all the artillery with the forces on the Blackwater to report to French.[77] He, in turn, promptly reassigned most of the batteries to the chiefs of artillery of Pickett's and Hood's Divisions. "Thus," French explained subsequently, the artillery was "scattered along the line for several miles, leaving me some spare batteries and a few siege guns in charge of my chief of artillery." [78]

To French, in other words, the whole incident, up to this point, appeared as an effort on Longstreet's part to get rid of him as divisional commander by assigning him artillery duties he was entirely justified in evading. He was suave in this; Longstreet was not awkward. Both proceeded so skillfully that many competent officers of less experience did not know what was afoot. For example, Maj. James Dearing, chief of one of the First Corps artillery battalions,[79] wrote to General Pendleton: "Major General French came down, and having no command (though being the ranking major general here), General Longstreet finally gave him the command of all the artillery." [80]

Out of French's anomalous position developed a sensation that might have been termed a scandal. It was on April 11 that Longstreet's command appeared in front of Suffolk. Pickett's and Hood's Divisions quickly were extended on a long concave front, which was fortified promptly. On the right, Pickett covered a flat and partly wooded country. His well drawn lines were of no particular interest except for the fact that they rested their right squarely on Dismal Swamp. From time to time Pickett's front was advanced by parallels precisely as if Longstreet intended to conduct a formal siege of the town.

Hood's line had to conform to the course of the streams, which

---

[76] *French*, 160–61.   [77] *O. R.*, 18, 988.   [78] *French*, 161.

[79] Strictly speaking, his battalion was the one usually operating with Pickett's Division, but Dearing seems, from the letter quoted in the text, to have been supervising temporarily, also, some of the other batteries with Longstreet.

[80] *O. R.*, 18, 334.

Longstreet had decided not to cross immediately because of the casualties he feared the operation would entail. Part of Hood's lines consequently faced South, part of them East. Longstreet sought to get help from the Confederate navy, to secure his ex-

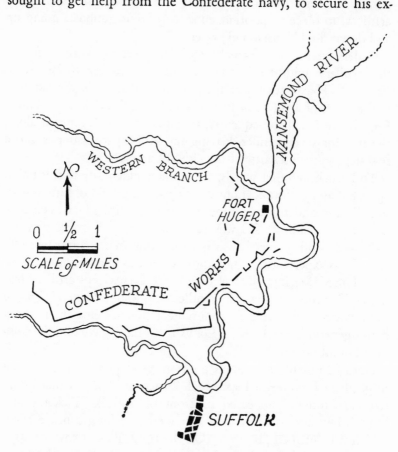

Vicinity of Fort Huger, Nansemond River—after *O. R. Atlas,* Plate XXVI.

treme left on James River,[81] and, failing in that, had to admit to himself that the flank was exposed. The best he could do for its protection was to construct earthworks between the upper stretches of the Nansemond and the western branch [82] of that stream which together formed three sides of a quadrilateral.

The eastern face of this was a navigable north-and-south stretch

[81] *O. R.,* 18, 910, 967–68, 999.
[82] A detailed map will be found in *O. R. Atlas,* Plate XXVI.

of Nansemond River, on which the Federals were operating gunboats. Near the point where the western branch of the Nansemond, flowing East, unites with the main stream, the course of which is North, stood Fort Huger, an open work that had been constructed by the Confederates in 1861 to protect Suffolk. This defense—"Old Fort" the Confederates usually called it—was without guns and in a bad state of repair, but it seemed to Longstreet to have value. Opposite it, within fifty yards of the shore,[83] was the channel used by the Federal gunboats that frequently patrolled the Nansemond. A battery in Fort Huger might close the river to the gunboats or make the passage of the stream unpleasantly warm. Longstreet accordingly directed French to put a heavy battery there. French sent in five of Stribling's guns—two 24-pounder brass howitzers and three twelve-pounder Napoleons[84]— and decided to dig pits and to put in rear of the fort two 32-pounders.

This was on April 16.[85] The next day, French dispatched three companies of Col. J. K. Connally's Fifty-fifth North Carolina to the vicinity of the river and directed that on the 18th the remainder of the regiment should take a somewhat advanced position in general support of the other batteries near the stream.[86] French placed the North Carolinians at some distance from the river, rather than on the bank and in Fort Huger, because he wished to protect a road and to guard the pair of 32-pounders in the pits. Connally's men were told that if they needed help, they should call upon Gen. E. M. Law, who was commanding one of Hood's Brigades downstream, i.e., North of the "Old Fort."[87] Law, on the evening of the 18th, marched into the fort, as a support, two companies of the Forty-fourth Alabama, approximately fifty men.[88] These troops, Longstreet and Law understood, were to be relieved by some of Connally's regiment.[89]

French was sick on the 19th[90] and did not visit the front. He gave no order to Connally to occupy the "Old Fort" and apparently concluded that Hood, through Law, was to garrison the work. Connally's sole duty, as French probably interpreted it, was

83 O. R., 18, 304.
84 O. R., 18, 331, 334.
85 O. R., 18, 336.
86 O. R., 18, 327.
87 Ibid., 325.
88 Lieut. George Reese, cited in French, 162 n.
89 Cf. O. R., 18, 326; Longstreet's endorsement of French's report.
90 O. R., 18, 326, 328

to guard the two heavy guns in the pits and to serve as general reserve. Certain it is that French knew Connally on the 19th was some distance [91] in rear of the fort but was under instructions to support the batteries if they were attacked.[92]

As always may happen when responsibility is not fixed, there came a surprise. About 6 o'clock on the evening of the 19th, some 270 Federals [93] landed 400 yards above the fort [94] and quickly and cleverly brought ashore four boat howitzers. These Federals encountered no opposition in getting a foothold. Neither Connally nor Law had picketed the river bank at that point, because each thought the other would or had.[95] With a rush, the Federals broke into the fort and after a brief mêlée forced its surrender. Five guns, seven officers and 130 soldiers were captured and were carried across the river.[96]

French, still sick, arrived on the ground after dark in the hope that he could recover the fort, but on reconnaissance, he agreed with Hood and Law that a successful attack would not be worth what it could cost. Although Longstreet dissented from this view when he looked over the ground the next day, he did not insist that the place be attacked by storm.[97] The Federals made a great show of strengthening the fort but on the night of the 20th they evacuated it as valueless.[98]

The "capture of Stribling's battery," as the affair was styled [99] in the Confederate army, created a tremendous stir. French in his report blamed the garrison of the "Old Fort." Said he: "It appears to me that if the garrison was surprised, they were negligent; if not surprised, they did not offer a sufficient resistance." [100] In his diary he expressed himself "tired of volunteering against gunboats" and resolved to confine himself to the immediate command of his own Division and to "take no more interest in Hood's line." [101]

[91] Longstreet said 600 yards, ibid., 326.
[92] Cf. O. R., 18, 327, 328.
[93] Ibid., 304.
[94] Ibid., 336.
[95] Ibid., 337.
[96] French insisted that the number captured was four officers and fifty-five noncommissioned officers and soldiers (O. R., 18, 329), but he curiously ignored the two companies of Law's Brigade. For the details of the capture, which was an admirable small operation, see the report of Gen. Geo. W. Getty, O. R., 18, 304, who, with Lieut. R. H. Lamson, U. S. N., planned the whole.
[97] French, 162.
[98] O. R., 18, 305.
[99] Cf. French, 163.
[100] O. R., 18, 325.
[101] French, 163.

Longstreet was altogether moderate in his judgment. He called for a prompt report from French [102] and, after he studied it, he endorsed it temperately. There seemed to have been "a general lack of vigilance and prompt attention to duties," he said, "on the part of most of the parties connected with this affair"; he expressed surprise that French should have thought Hood responsible for guarding the batteries. The fort, Longstreet reiterated, could have been recovered by a prompt counterattack, but he concluded: "Many of the officers were of limited experience, however, and I have no doubt acted as they thought best. I do not know that any of them deserve particular censure. This lesson, it is hoped, will be of service to us all." [103]

The sharpest resentments were among the field officers of the Fifty-fifth North Carolina, the regiment that had supported the 32-pounders. Colonel Connally heard that General Law had said the North Carolinians had behaved badly, and on the 20th, he rode over to the General's tent to demand an explanation. "General," said he, "I understand that you have reported that my regiment acted cowardly last night and fled before the enemy without fighting and in violation of orders; I wish to know if you so stated."

Law feared neither devil nor man, but he had to be precise in what promised to be an affair of honor: "I stated that Captains Terrell and Cussons of my staff so reported to me."

"Well, it's a damned lie," said Connally, "and I will see them about it." With that he dismounted and strode to the tent of the two young officers. It was wholly typical of the man and of the times that instead of restraining Connally or ordering him to go back to his quarters, Law followed to see what would happen.

Connally promptly questioned Terrell: Had the Captain made the report? Terrell said he had, that it was true, and that he would not retract. Connally turned to Capt. John Cussons, one of Law's scouts, a long haired, keen eyed Englishman, as fearless as his chief. "Captain," said Connally, "did you also make that report?"

Cussons was all politeness. "No, Colonel," he answered half regretfully, "I did not; but I will tell you what I now say: That if

[102] *O. R.*, 18, 1004.   [103] *O. R.*, 18, 326–27.

you gave your men orders to retire when the enemy appeared in their front, they obeyed damned promptly last night."

"I hold you responsible, sir, for that remark," the Colonel stormed.

Captain Cussons bowed gratefully: "All right, Colonel, I will be most happy to accommodate you." [104]

Back to camp rode the angry Colonel. A meeting of his field officers and Captains he called forthwith. After he recounted the circumstances, he asserted vigorously that the honor of the regiment was assailed. Satisfaction must be exacted of those who had slandered the Fifty-fifth. The field officers, he proposed, should first challenge the two officers of Law's Brigade. If they could not compose the affair and lost their lives in the duels that would follow, he wanted the company officers to pledge themselves to take up the fight and to continue it until the last Captain had been killed or proper amends had been made.

The first man to reply to this amazing proposal was young Lt. Col. Maurice T. Smith, a man of character and courage so manifest that the wildest champion of the duello could not accuse him of cowardice. Smith said, in few words, that he was conscientiously opposed to duelling and that he would not fight a duel to settle any question. All the other officers agreed to support Connally. As next in rank to Lieutenant Colonel Smith, the Major of the regiment, A. H. Belo, said that he would share with Connally the first challenge.[105]

This much settled, Major Belo prepared the challenge, mounted, and rode to the headquarters of General Law, where he sought out Captain Terrell and Captain Cussons. The challenge from Colonel Connally was delivered and accepted, whereupon the Major with much politeness informed Cussons that he would like to represent Colonel Connally and to meet the gentleman on the field where and when Connally faced Terrell. This was wholly acceptable to Captain Cussons. Details were left to be settled by new seconds, now that Major Belo had become a principal. In due time it was agreed that Colonel Connally and Captain Terrell

---

[104] This part of the narrative follows Col. W. C. Oates, *loc. cit.*, 176–77, and is the report, though late, of an eye-witness.

[105] This is the account of Charles M. Cooke, regimental adjutant, who apparently attended the meeting in his official capacity, though he was a Lieutenant, not a Captain. 3 *N. C. Regts.*, 292.

should use double-barrel shot-guns, loaded with balls, and should face each other at forty yards. Captain Cussons cheerfully selected the more deadly Mississippi rifle at the same distance.

Of these arrangements, General Law almost certainly was appraised. So probably was Hood, who was not of a temperament to interfere, otherwise than as a participant, in any fight. Whether Longstreet knew of the affair until it was over, there is no way of ascertaining. Neither he nor his A. A. G. mentioned it in memoirs.

If the duel was kept from the commanding General, it was the subject of fascinated interest among other officers. Few seem to have reflected that Southerners were in the field not to shoot one another but to kill Federals. For the day, at least, the code duello took precedence over the struggle for Confederate independence. As many officers as could procure an invitation or proffer a service assembled at the appointed time in two groups some distance apart on a large field. One group divided quickly for business. Major Belo and Captain Cussons took their stations, which duly had been paced at forty yards. The Mississippi rifles were examined and loaded. Each man took his weapon. At the word, they fired. The bullet from Major Belo's rifle clipped a hole in Captain Cussons's hat. Cussons's return fire did not touch the Major, though the Englishman was a bull's-eye marksman.

Again the guns were loaded and handed by the seconds to the principals; again the order to "Fire!" Major Belo winced slightly; Captain Cussons was unscathed. Said the Englishman with complete nonchalance, "Major, this is damned poor shooting we are doing today. If we don't do any better than this we will never kill any Yankees." The Major stood firm for a third shot, but when his second approached him, the Major's coat collar was found to have been cut by Cussons's bullet. Examination showed that the lead had grazed Belo's neck. Bleeding, he was unsatisfied.

A third time the rifles were loaded. The seconds were just placing them in the hands of the duellists when from the other company, there came a shout. A messenger ran toward the Major and the Captain: The difference between the Colonel and Captain Terrell had been composed. There was no reason for Belo and Cussons to continue the quarrel. Agreeably the two gentlemen advanced, solemnly shook hands and felicitated each other that the injury had been slight—one punctured hat, one skinned neck.

How had Connally and Terrell settled their mortal grievance? For once, a contradiction of historical evidence is gratifying. Said the historian of the Fifty-fifth: ". . . in the other part of the field, the friends of Colonel Connally and Captain Terrell were engaged in an effort to make an honorable settlement of the affair, and Captain Terrell, who was a gallant officer and true gentlemen, became satisfied that he had been mistaken in the report which he had made and which had been the cause of offense, and he withdrew the same, which action prevented further hostilities."[106]

That is to say, in the North Carolina version, the withdrawal came from the Alabamian. In toto this is denied by a supporter of the honor of Law's Brigade. Colonel Oates wrote: "As the weapons were handed to the Colonel and Terrell and the word was about to be given, Connally's second requested a parley. Terrell's second met him half way, and after the interchange of views Connally's second unconditionally withdrew the challenge . . ."[107] In short, the Carolinian who challenged the Alabamian underwent a change of heart.[108]

To this odd affair, if and when it was reported to him, "Old Pete" Longstreet paid no attention. Nor did he intervene or have reason to do so in a matter of unpleasant friction between Micah Jenkins and Jos. R. Davis, a nephew of the Confederate President. After French had re-established his command of the Division, he frequently—and of necessity—left Jenkins in charge while he himself was "volunteering against gunboats." Joe Davis did not like this and apparently did not know that whether or not he liked it, he had no alternative to it. Formally he wrote the A. A. G. of French: "I respectfully request to know if my Brigade belongs to the Division commanded by Major General French; and, if so,

---

[106] 3 *N. C. Regts.*, 292–93.   [107] *Oates*, 177.

[108] As several of the principals will not appear again, it may be noted that Captain Terrell was later Lieutenant Colonel of the Forty-seventh Alabama and was mortally wounded in October, 1863. Colonel Connally lost an arm at Gettysburg, and received also a wound in the hip. Left on the field he fell into the hands of the enemy but survived wounds and imprisonment. After the war he practiced law for a time in Richmond. In the collapse of a floor of the Capitol, in 1870, he narrowly escaped death and, as a result of that experience renounced the law and entered the ministry. Major Belo succeeded Connally as Colonel of the Fifty-fifth North Carolina, and, in restored peace, became proprietor of the Galveston *News*. Captain Cussons married a woman of large property and settled at Glen Allen, near Richmond, where he maintained a summer hotel, Forest Lodge, and a prosperous printing establishment. Cf. *Oates*, 178, and, for Connally, *infra*, Vol. III, Chap. V, and Cathcart's *Baptist Encyclopædia*.

am I to continue to receive orders and instructions from an inter-
mediate commander, or from the Major General commanding?"
French endorsed blithely: "I apprehend there is no difficulty in
this question. While I regard this Brigade, of course, a part of
my command as well as General Jenkins' Brigade, yet, as I must
be absent much of the time, the Division must be under the command of the senior officer present." Longstreet did not take his
time or that of Moxley Sorrel to answer a question so elemen-
tary.[109] Davis had to do as Micah Jenkins bade when French was
not at headquarters.

George Pickett was giving Longstreet trouble of a different sort.
The gentleman with the perfumed ringlets had married Sallie
Minge of Richmond in January, 1851, but had lost her through
death the following November. Now, at the age of 38, he was
desperately in love with LaSalle Corbell, not half as old. That
interesting romance would have been exclusively his affair had
not "the charming Sally," as he styled her, lived in the very county
where Pickett's lines now were drawn. The miles from his headquarters to her home at Chuckatuck were not too long to deter a
lover on a good horse; but double that distance between the end
of one day's duty and the labors of another was a heavy strain on
man and mount. Longstreet would deny Pickett nothing that a
chief honorably could grant a lieutenant and, again and again, he
gave assent for Pickett to rush to Chuckatuck, to make his avowals
and then to come back and get such sleep as he could in the morning. At length Longstreet must have sworn that for so many days
he would not authorize Pickett to leave camp. The gallant lover
did not despair. He went in the full panoply of his rank to Moxley Sorrel and tried to wheedle the Corps A. A. G. into giving
him authority to go.

"No," said Sorrel firmly, "you must go to the Lieutenant General."

"But he is tired of it and will refuse. I swear, Sorrel, I'll be
back before anything can happen in the morning."

The Georgian stood his ground. If the Division were ordered
to move or the enemy appeared during the night, how could he
explain the absence of a Major General?

Pickett's answer to this is not recorded. Sorrel wrote years after-

[109] O. R., 18, 993.

ward: "Pickett went all the same, nothing could hold him back from that pursuit. . . . I don't think his division benefited by such carpet-knight doings in the field." [110]

One other incident involved Pickett in a manner that disturbed a stout hearted Virginia Colonel, Eppa Hunton of the Eighth. Let him narrate how it occurred after he had returned with Garnett's Brigade from North Carolina: "In riding with Pickett along his lines, with his staff, we came to an exposed position, and to my surprise General Pickett and his staff laid flat down on their horses' necks. I felt surprised at this, and thought his example to his soldiers was exceedingly bad, and I, probably imprudently, rode along with him bolt upright in my saddle." [111]

To the other Major General on the Suffolk front, John B. Hood, little of interest happened. Hood was a bachelor and was becoming a social lion in Richmond, but he had no love affair on the banks of the Nansemond. He was bored, in fact, by the conduct of what had become a make-believe siege to cover the operations of the commissaries in North Carolina. Toward the end of the demonstration against Suffolk, Hood wrote Lee a boyish letter: "Here we are in front of the enemy again. The Yankees have a very strong position, and of course they increase the strength of their position daily. I presume we will leave here so soon as we gather all the bacon in the country. When we leave here it is my desire to return to you. If any troops come to the Rappahannock please don't forget me." [112] That was his temper; if there was to be a fight, he wished to share it. The Confederate capital might have attractions and offer opportunities, but wearing away spring days in idleness on the Nansemond was a vexation and worse.

Vexation there was, finally, for Longstreet in the situation in the Carolinas. In Charleston, over which Longstreet had no control, Beauregard was expecting attack; Whiting at Wilmington apprehended every day that on the next tide the Federal fleet would arrive off his sand forts. Harvey Hill in front of Washington insisted that he must have more troops if he was to recover the town. A long, involved and somewhat bickering correspondence developed.[113] Midway the exchange, Longstreet had to write

---

110 *Sorrel*, 152–53.
111 Eppa Hunton, *Autobiography* (cited hereafter as *Hunton*), 85.
112 *O. R.*, 51, pt. 2, p. 697.
113 *O. R.*, 18, 970, 983, 987, 990, 996, 1005, 100

rather sharply that if Hill required as many troops as then were being employed to besiege Washington, N. C., the operation had better be abandoned.[114] Soon afterward, the Federals ran in two vessels and replenished the supplies of the little garrison. That resolved all lingering uncertainty. Confinement of a small Federal force was not worth the effort and cost.

The siege was abandoned.[115] As an offensive, it would have been rated close to the bottom of military effort, but as a demonstration it served a purpose. The Federal commander, Maj. Gen. John G. Foster, was convinced, as he wrote the Chief of Staff, "that heavy operations will be necessary in this State, and that the most desperate efforts are and will continue to be made, to drive us from the towns now occupied." [116] Hill did not feel that he had labored wholly in vain. On April 24, eight days after his troops left the vicinity of Washington, he issued a long address in which he abused the enemy, thanked his men and loosed all his wrath against the exempts and the militia. He had suggested to Vance that the Governor issue another "stirring appeal" in the spirit of an earlier one which, said Hill, made "even cowards blush." [117] Without immodesty, Hill now might affirm that these concluding paragraphs of his General Orders No. 8 outdid anything of the kind that could be placed to the credit of his Excellency the Governor of North Carolina: "Others [of the skulkers] are warlike militia officers, and their regiments cannot dispense with such models of military skill and valor. And such noble regiments they have. Three field officers, four staff officers, ten captains, thirty lieutenants, and one private with a misery in his bowels. . . . Some [of the exempts] are kindly making shoes for the army, and generously giving them to the poor soldiers, only asking two months' pay. Some are too sweet and delicate for anything but fancy duty; the sight of blood is unpleasant, and the roar of cannon shocks their sensibilities. When our independence is won, the most trifling soldier in the ranks will be more respected, as he is now more respectable than an army of these skulking exempts." [118]

Here, again, if Longstreet read, he did not comment; and if he were disappointed with the direction of affairs in North Caro-

114 O. R., 18, 990-91.   115 O. R., 18, 1007.
116 O. R., 18, 211. This was written April 5, 1863, early in the siege.
117 O. R., 18, 1011.   118 O. R., 51, pt. 2, p. 694.

lina, he did not rebuke Hill further. Longstreet's own fruitless first experience in semi-independent command was drawing to a close. Had there been any real justification for an attack on the Federals at Suffolk—had it promised anything more than casualties on both sides—the time to have delivered it would have been immediately after Longstreet crossed the Blackwater. Then he had something over 19,000 men in French's, Pickett's and Hood's commands, and, in addition, he might have drawn on the garrison of Richmond and possibly on the forces in North Carolina.[119] The Federals in Norfolk and at Suffolk at the outset were of approximately equal strength with Longstreet's command;[120] but from the 12th of April onward, Union reinforcements arrived in the Department almost daily. The end of the month was to find about 9000 more bluecoats around Suffolk than had been there when the month opened.[121] Longstreet knew that these additional troops were arriving but of their number he had no solid information. He had to forgo any tenuous hope he ever cherished of assuming the offensive. All he could say of his situation on April 29 was, "I am of the opinion . . . that I can hold my position against any attack from the front." [122]

The day he wrote that letter, Longstreet received notice that the Federals were crossing the Rappahannock in the drama that was to represent the supreme achievement of his comrade Jackson.

[119] Cf. *O. R.*, 18, 915, 978.

[120] At the end of March, the Norfolk garrison was 3888; at Suffolk were 14,997—together 18,885. *O. R.*, 18, 574.

[121] *Ibid.*, 674. The precise increase was 8975.

[122] *O. R.*, 18, 1031.

CHAPTER XXX

"Old Jack" Prepares for Spring

JACKSON spent the winter in preparation for the call that came to him and to Longstreet the 29th of April, 1863. After Burnside evacuated the right bank of the Rappahannock during the black and blusterous night of December 15–16, Jackson reconnoitred and examined the abandoned camps. On the 16th, past midday, word came that the Federals again were crossing to the Confederate side of the Rappahannock, this time at Port Royal. Stuart set out immediately; Jackson put the Second Corps in the road and at 1 P.M. started after the cavalry. Early's Division, the army's pacemaker, was in front. Jackson rode with the van. During the afternoon's march—it was a bracing day—a message from Stuart announced that the report of a Federal crossing was untrue: All was quiet at Port Royal and on the opposite side; there was no need of bringing the infantry farther. Jackson promptly called a halt.

As ill luck ruled it, the Second Corps for virtually its entire length was strung out at the moment on a road that was bordered with pine forest and a tangle of impenetrable evergreen. To bivouac, at least part of the troops would have to countermarch until they came to open woods. In order to supervise this, "Old Blue Light" would have to ride back for the entire length of the sprawling column. He knew what that would mean—embarrassing cheers and homage that men should save for their Creator. Consequently, Jackson tried to find some parallel route, some woods' trail, along which he could ride unobserved to the rear. Search was vain. No other passage was there through the tangle. He must return as he had come. Reluctantly he started through the leading regiment that opened a narrow way for him. Single file he and his staff had to ride, and so close to the troops that his horse's flanks brushed the shoulders of the men. They raised a cheer that was kept up mile after mile. Even the staff officers were cheered, though with the sarcasms usually addressed to mounted men: "Close up!" was the shout; "You'll get lost" and, in fine contempt for staff officers' ability to see even the back of the rider directly ahead, "You'll never find him!"

Jackson came at length to open woods and rode to a sheltered spot close to a large tulip poplar. As he had no rations, the staff tried to persuade him to go to a private home. Moss Neck, the large Corbin home, could not be far distant: Let them search it out and ask hospitality there for the night. "Old Jack" shook his beard forbiddingly. They would bivouac where they were and would make the best of it. Fires were lighted. One staff officer of experimenting mind set sticks and leaves afire in the poplar tree, which he found to be hollow. A fine chimney this proved. It lifted sparks so gaily and so high that the staff began to discuss why sparks formed and rose. Jackson said little and soon gave his juniors the example of "early to bed."

About 10 o'clock, a crash shook the ground and brought dazed officers to their feet. The hollow tree, burned out, had fallen, but fortunately it had not struck any of the sleeping men. As all of them were now thoroughly chilled, they renewed their appeal to Jackson that he seek shelter under a roof. He refused, almost stubbornly, but he was hungry. When Capt. Hugh McGuire happened to come to the fire, Jackson learned that the young man had taught in the community and he asked if McGuire could find any food. McGuire confidently rode off and soon returned with a basket of biscuit and a half-consumed ham which he said he had procured at Moss Neck. The fires were stirred, the couriers were invited to share the food. When all had eaten, they stretched out again. Ere long Jackson stirred and sat up with a pulsing earache. "Captain," he said to one of his officers, "let's go to the Moss Neck House." [1]

"Old Jack" went to spend the night and stayed for three months. That protraction, though not alien to Virginia practice, was not deliberate. It was due, primarily, to the insistence of the Corbins. When they breakfasted with the General and his staff on the morning of the 17th, the ladies of the family offered him a

---

[1] This account is an attempted reconciliation of *Hotchkiss' MS Diary*, 119, of Mrs. Roberta Cary Kinsolving's account in 20 *C.V.*, 24–26, and of J. P. Smith's "Stonewall Jackson in Winter Quarters at Moss Neck," an address delivered in Winchester, Va., Jan. 19, 1898. A copy of this (cited hereafter as *J. P. Smith Address*) is in the Hotchkiss Papers.

wing of the mansion as headquarters. He declined promptly with the argument that a house was "too luxurious for a soldier, who should sleep in a tent."[2] He might, with the owner's consent, pitch canvas on Moss Neck, but that would be all. To this compromise the hospitable family regretfully had to agree. Jackson had his tents made ready and devoted himself busily to the self-assigned task of raising funds for the suffering civilians of Fredericksburg. He did this as splendidly as could be demanded even of a Presbyterian deacon, but physically he did not thrive. After about a week in the open, Jackson again developed an earache. His Medical Director insisting that Jackson go indoors, the Corbin family prevailed on him to utilize the office on the lawn—a separate building of three rooms.[3]

After Jackson recovered from his earache, he remained at the office. Both Lee and Stuart professed to be scandalized by such self-indulgence on the part of the Southern Cromwell. Unabashed, Jackson gave his chief and his beloved "Jeb" Stuart a Christmas dinner from the abundant food sent him for the holiday. Turkeys he had, a ham, oysters from down the river, unlimited white bread, pickle and even a bottle of wine, which had come in a box from Staunton ladies. The General's body servant Jim prepared all the dishes; the dining-room boy, John, put on a white apron. Because of this flourish, Lee protested that Jackson and his staff were playing soldier. To see how plain soldiers live, they must come to Lee's own headquarters.[4] Stuart was even more shocked. He pointed to the racing and sporting pictures that adorned the office walls and he called on his fellow-guests to say what would

[2] 20 C.V., 24.

[3] J. P. Smith Address. The office on most of the large Virginia estates stood opposite one of the angles of the front of the main house and quite often was balanced by a similar structure opposite the other front angle. At Stratford, the Lee mansion in Westmoreland County, Virginia, there was an outhouse of this type opposite each of the four angles of the dwelling. The office was for the transaction of plantation business and not infrequently it was used to house the books of the family. Over the office, in many designs, were sleeping quarters where the overflow of visiting boys might sleep. If the master of the plantation scheduled any heavy drinking with neighboring gentlemen, the office generally was the scene of it. Casual juleps and toddies might be taken in "the house." At Moss Neck, the office was a frame structure to the front and left of the mansion. The entrance door opened into a small lobby. On the right was a stairway to the second floor; on the left was a wood closet. Directly in front of the entrance was the door into the office proper. In the office, opposite the door, was a large fireplace; on either side was a window; flanking the door were bookshelves on either side of the wall that separated the office from the lobby. Above stairs was a half-story bedroom. Jackson put his table on one side of the fireplace, his cot on the other.—J. P. Smith Address.

[4] J. P. Smith Address; references in 2 R. E. Lee, 476.

be the judgment of the admiring old ladies of the South if they had this exhibition of the real tastes of their idol. Look at the print of butter on the table. Observe its adornment. What was it? Any man with two eyes could see for himself—it was a rooster, doubtless a game-cock. Jackson might protest that the print had been so made by the person who gave him the butter, but who could believe that? Jackson carried his sporting taste so far that he had to have a game-cock on the very butter he used at his table! It must be Jackson's coat of arms.[5]

Jackson remained at Moss Neck despite this and much similar banter, and, in the main, he enjoyed himself. By one thing only was he irked, the large number of callers at the office; but he met them pleasantly and entertained them courteously and simply, though with no wealth of small talk or of large. Over one peculiarity of his, irreverent young staff officers would smile privately: Whenever a guest would come, Jackson would say, "Let me take your hat, sir," and after he took it, he would look around in some bewilderment for a place to put it. Finding none, he would deposit it on the floor. Apart from such trifles, there was no denying the expansion of Deacon Jackson. He was dressing much better, even though the same envious young staff officers averred, in tribute to Jackson's thrift, that most of his adornment represented gifts to him.[6]

Even this might have passed without comment in the Corps, had not Jackson displayed small oddities of manner that soldiers loved to exaggerate when they spoke of him. He was not merely another general officer; he was not a corps commander only, though the army had no more than two. A personality he was, whose mannerisms plus his victories made thousands of boys believe that he had a mysterious genius, a special relationship to the Almighty. When he was not Cromwell, he was Joshua. Sometimes he was both.

In either role, he watched ceaselessly the discipline of his Corps. The Stonewall Brigade had, as always, to be the Model Army. If it had deserters, they must be punished with a severity that would make the example a deterrent. During the winter, when six men of Jackson's old Brigade were tried by court martial for desertion, the penalties meted out were: for one man, six months' hard labor

---

[5] This oft-told tale probably was published for the first time in *Cooke's Jackson* 391. J. P. Smith, *loc. cit.,* added the touch concerning the coat of arms.
[6] *W. W. Blackford's MS Memoirs,* 291.

with ball and chain; for two others, flogging; for the three worst
offenders, death. Paxton protested. Not more than one of the
three, he said, need be shot, and that one should be chosen by lot.
When this paper reached "Old Jack," he rebuked sternly his subordinate and fellow-townsman. Said the corps commander: "With
the exception of this application, General Paxton's management
of his Brigade has given me great satisfaction. One great difficulty
in the army results from over lenient Courts, and it appears to me
that when a Court Martial faithfully discharges its duty that its
decisions should be sustained. If this is not done, a lax administration of justice and corresponding disregard for law must be the
consequence . . ." Lee upheld Jackson; the President overrode
both in the cases that involved the death-penalty; [7] but in these or
in similar instances floggings occurred [8]—a penalty as humiliating
to the soldiers as bucking and gagging had been. Punishment of
this nature created the impression in the army that Jackson was
more severe than Lee in the punishments he inflicted.[9] Actually
this is not established by the small number of court martial records that survive. On the contrary, Jackson more often advocated
leniency in forwarding papers to Lee than did Lee in endorsing
court martial proceedings for the consideration of the President.[10]

Stern or merciful, Jackson adhered always to his ideas of justice
and, though he displayed prejudices, he bestowed no advantage,
save that of promotion, on those whose service disposed him favorably to them. In February, Brig. Gen. Alfred Iverson insisted that
he must have a furlough and that if he could not get it, he would
have to resign. Jackson answered promptly that while he would
dislike to have General Iverson resign, he would rather Iverson do
that than approve a furlough when a battle might be fought at
any time.[11] Nor would "Old Jack" follow the easiest way in dealing with those who lacked soldierly qualities. A request from
Hoke for the transfer to another command of a certain Major was
answered by Jackson with the assurance that if Hoke certified the
man to be a worthless and inefficient officer, he would have the
Major dropped, but he did not think it would be right to relieve

---

[7] *Douglas*, 213–14.

[8] *Hotchkiss' MS Diary*, 141. Flogging soon was prohibited under an act of the
Confederate Congress approved April 13, 1863, and published by the Adjutant General
April 16. See IV *O. R.*, 2, 476.

[9] Cf. *Douglas*, 214.

[10] Cf. D. S. Freeman, ed., *Calendar Confederate Papers*, 294 ff.

[11] *Jackson's MS Letter Book*, p. 50.

one Brigade of a bad officer by imposing that individual on someone else.[12]

In a darker matter of discipline that winter, Jackson stood firm.
Charges were filed against a Brigadier of Jackson's old Division
for the offense of which no General of Lee's army ever before had
been accused formally—cowardice.[13] Jackson was troubled and
humiliated because he had himself selected the accused General
for promotion; and he may have known that some of his subordinates were doubtful of his ability to judge the character of men.[14]
To Chaplain Tucker Lacy, the corps commander said: "I have
almost lost confidence in man. When I thought I had found just
such a man as I needed, and was about to rest satisfied in him, I
found something lacking in him." Then Jackson added, "But I
suppose it is to teach me to put my trust only in God."[15] In this
spirit, he had to face the prospect of a court martial of the assailed
officer.[16] Bluntly Jackson refused to accept the request of one accus-
ing Captain for permission to resign and to have leave of absence
until the trial was held. The Captain was told that he must remain on duty and either prefer charges or withdraw his allegation
that the General was deficient in courage in the face of the
enemy.[17]

Amid these continuing daily demands for the enforcement of
discipline, which was his prime duty that winter, Jackson had to
prepare the reports of his battles. It had been said in the army that
he never filed a report;[18] but the fact was that after Kernstown,
regarding which he had filed an official report,[19] he had been engaged in fourteen battles in eight months and during the intervals
had been occupied with much administrative work.[20] Of the

[12] Feb. 11, 1863; *Jackson's MS Letter Book*, p. 50.
[13] It is most unpleasant to have to mention a name in this connection, but as the
statement in the text might bring several gallant men under suspicion, the reference has
to be made specific to Brig. Gen. J. R. Jones, former Lieutenant Colonel of the famous
Thirty-third Virginia. John R. Jones must not be confused with the gallant John M.
Jones of the same rank.
[14] *Hotchkiss' MS Diary*, Feb. 27, 1863, p. 143; April 1, 1863, p. 155.
[15] *Ibid.*, 143. The remark is here changed from the third to the first person for
clarity.
[16] *Jackson's MS Letter Book*, p. 54; Mch. 23, 1863.
[17] *Jackson's MS Letter Book*, p. 52; Mch. 2, 1863.
[18] *Cf.* Ewell to Early, Jan. 7, 1863; *Hamlin's Ewell*, 116.
[19] *Douglas*, 210.
[20] The figure fourteen regards Front Royal and Middletown as one battle, includes
Frayser's Farm, and omits Ewell's fight against Frémont at Strasburg and the various
minor operations that followed to the date of Cross Keys.

action at McDowell only had he attempted to prepare a report and that he had not completed.[21] Now he had some leisure, but as he wrote slowly and painfully, with endless cancellation and revision, he manifestly needed literary assistance. To procure it, he turned to another native of Northwestern Virginia, Charles J. Faulkner, for eight years a member of Congress from the Martinsburg District and in 1859–61 United States Minister to France. Faulkner, who was 55, held a Lieutenant Colonel's commission in the Adjutant General's Department, and had the necessary skill in letters, but he knew nothing of the battles he was to assist in reporting.[22] He had, moreover, to adjust himself, as his work progressed, to the five conditions Jackson indirectly but firmly imposed: First, the reports must be simple; second, they must include nothing that could not be verified; third, they were to omit all matters of controversy; fourth, they must not be "laudations of anyone"; fifth, they must be subject to Jackson's revision in all respects.[23]

Jackson attempted to dictate some parts of the report; Lt. James Smith wrote parts of others.[24] The adopted procedure was for Colonel Faulkner to collect the material from subordinate reports, to settle controverted points by interviews with various officers and then, occasionally, to read completed drafts to the General's staff. Several engagements presented special difficulty. First and most debated was whether Cross Keys was to be regarded as a battle, as a skirmish, or as a reconnaissance in force. The disposition of staff officers was to make the action subordinate to Port Republic, but by the time they finished a long and oft-renewed discussion, they decided unanimously that the fight had definite importance in the Valley campaign and deserved treatment as a battle, not as a skirmish.[25] Another difficulty was presented in the report on the attack of May 24 at Middletown on Banks's retreating column. Who delivered it? Were the men Wheat's incorrigible Tigers or

21 A much-amended draft is in the *Jackson MSS.*

22 For Faulkner's career, see *D. A. B.* It would seem reasonable to guess that Col. A. R. Boteler probably was responsible for recommending and enlisting the service of Mr. Faulkner, whom Jackson could not have known well before Faulkner came to headquarters. Naturally one asks why Jackson did not name for this task his admired former A. A. G., Rev. Maj. R. L. Dabney. The reason doubtless was Dr. Dabney's ill-health, for which see T. C. Johnson's *Robert Lewis Dabney*, 272.

23 These matters developed one after another in the discussions Faulkner held with members of Jackson's staff. See *Hotchkiss' MS Diary*, Jan. 9, 12; Mch. 25, 26, 29, 31; Apr. 3, 6, 17, 1863; pp. 129–63.

24 *J. P. Smith Address.*

25 *Hotchkiss' MS Diary*, Mch. 25, 1863, p. 153; Apr. 17, 1863, p. 163.

were they of the other Louisiana regiments? Wheat was dead; Taylor was in the far South; the evidence offered by others was contradictory. The conclusion of Jackson was to write that "some of Taylor's Brigade" had struck the enemy.[26]

A third puzzle—and one that persists to this day—had to do with the position of the various Brigades at Cedar Mountain. Jed. Hotchkiss had drawn as carefully as he could the order of battle, but Jackson was almost petulantly displeased with it. He directed Hotchkiss to make corrections and then accepted the map, though the changes were slight. Even after he approved it, he insisted that the topographical engineer get more evidence from participants.[27] There was some feeling among Jackson's staff officers that Branch's report had overstated the achievements of his Brigade and had credited to his Brigade feats that had been performed by Winder's men.[28]

Most provoking of all, because of the rank of the men involved in the controversy, was a conflict between the reports of Trimble and "Jeb" Stuart concerning the famous night march from Bristoe Station to Manassas Junction, Aug. 26, 1862.[29] Each maintained that he was in command of the expedition and was responsible for the result achieved. Jackson on April 9 wrote Trimble of this "discrepancy" and invited an explanation. He stirred a hornets' nest. Trimble sent members of his staff to interview and to take the written statements of officers who had shared in the operation. These papers General Trimble reviewed and notified Jackson: ". . . I have not a word to alter, that [original] report stating correctly the main facts, but not all the circumstances, which I shall now briefly state." Trimble proceeded then to give Stuart even less credit than before.[30] Jackson held back his own report until Stuart found time to answer Trimble, which "Jeb" did in politest form but in a fashion not to take one feather from his own plume.[31] On the basis of this, Jackson—or Faulkner—wrote a tactful compromise: "Brigadier General Trimble volunteered to proceed [to Manassas Junction] forthwith . . . and capture the place.

[26] *Hotchkiss' MS Diary*, 155. The language finally adopted was "Taylor's infantry." *O. R.*, 12, pt. 1, p. 703.
[27] *Hotchkiss' MS Diary*, Apr. 3, 4, 6, 1863, pp. 156–57.
[28] *Ibid.*, Apr. 17, 1863, p. 163.
[29] Trimble's report, *O. R.*, 12, pt. 2, 720, was dated Jan. 6, 1862; Stuart's *ibid.*, 733, bore date cf Feb. 28, 1863.
[30] *O. R.*, 12, pt. 2, pp. 721–23.   [31] *O. R.*, 12, pt. 2, p. 741.

I accepted the gallant offer and gave orders to move without delay. In order to increase the prospect of success Major General Stuart, with a portion of his cavalry, was subsequently directed to move forward, and, as the ranking officer to take command of the expedition." [32] This made it plain that when Trimble was near Manassas Junction, he had no information that Stuart had been directed to assume command. Here the affair rested.

Three months Faulkner spent on the reports,[33] and then, with relief if not with full satisfaction, submitted the last of them to Jackson for final changes and approval.[34] Faulkner himself felt that Jackson had prescribed a "severe Roman simplicity." [35] In particular, Faulkner was disappointed because Jackson eliminated much that had been written with great care to show the reason for some moves. On this Jackson was unyielding. He did not wish to publish to the enemy, he said, why he did certain things, and thus enable them to "learn [our] mode of doing." [36] For his own part, Jackson realized how difficult it was to prepare accurate reports after a long interval. Said he to Faulkner, half seriously, half jestingly, "Now, Colonel Faulkner, when a battle happens—and I hope we may not have another—I want you to go where you can see all that is going on, and, pencil and paper in hand, write it down, so that we may not have so much labor and so many conflicting statements, and then write up the report at once after the battle." [37]

Discipline was first in the winter, reports next and, third, the endless question of promotions. Those of Jan. 19, 1863, had fol-

[32] *Ibid.*, 643.

[33] Jan. 9—perhaps earlier—to Apr. 17, 1863. The text of the report on Second Manassas bears date of Apr. 27, which may have been the time the revision of the paragraph on the disputed incident was completed. *O. R.*, 12, pt. 2, p. 641.

[34] The narrative of the Maryland campaign, for some reason, had not been completed. *Ibid.*

[35] *Hotchkiss' MS Diary*, Mch. 29, 1863, p. 153.   [36] *Ibid.*, Apr. 4, 1863, p. 155.

[37] *Hotchkiss' MS Diary*, Mch. 26, 1863, p. 153. For insistence that Jackson "carefully revised and corrected the facts before his official signature was appended," see *Cooke's Jackson*, 389. Douglas, *op. cit.*, 210–11, was most critical of the reports. Said he: "Generals and other officers who had done brilliant services under him did not get the recognition their services were entitled to; they had good cause to complain and did complain. . . . No one suffered from this so much as his staff, at least those who did not survive him." Apparently Douglas did not know of Jackson's resolve that the reports should not be "laudations of anyone." Nor, it would appear, did Douglas know that "laudation" of the dead was moderated in the reports of Jackson lest it be unjust to the living. Faulkner, for example, inserted in the tribute to Winder, in the report on Cedar Mountain, a sentence to the effect that the service of Winder still was missed. Jackson told Faulkner to strike this out because it might be considered a reflection on Paxton (*Hotchkiss' MS Diary*, 155).

lowed within a little more than two months the extensive promotions and reorganization of Nov. 6, 1862; but still there were
vacancies to be filled and ambitions to be gratified or denied.
Now, as formerly, most of these were in Jackson's Corps. From
Jan. 19 to Apr. 30, 1863, these vacancies had to be filled: First,
and far most important, as there was every reason to assume that
D. H. Hill would remain in North Carolina, his Division must
have a permanent commander. Next, there was scant prospect
that A. R. Lawton would return to command his Brigade of
Ewell's, now Early's Division. Third, Charles Field was still bed-
ridden with the wound received at Manassas:[38] His Brigade
needed a leader who would pull it together again as an effective
unit of A. P. Hill's Division.

Besides these three, a definite vacancy now existed in Toombs's
Brigade. At last, after having affirmed that he best could serve the
South in the army, where he intended to stay,[39] Toombs concluded that he could not "remain in the service with any advantage to the public or with honor" to himself.[40] The question of
"honor," so far as one could observe, simply was the honor of promotion; but he stuck to that explanation and, on March 5, he
formally bade farewell to his Brigade.[41] While "Rebel War Clerk"
Jones doubtless voiced public expectation in saying that it was
probable Toombs would "cause some disturbance,"[42] there may
have been more relief at having him out of the army than concern
over the prospect of having him in Congress. A year before, the
reverse would have been the feeling.

The sixth vacancy of the spring was due to the fulfillment of
William B. Taliaferro's threat, already noted, that if he were not
named to command Jackson's old Division, he would ask transfer.
Before either threatening or seeking another field of service, Taliaferro made an odd display of his authority as acting division commander. About a fortnight after the Battle of Fredericksburg, the
Judge Advocate of a court martial in the Stonewall Brigade forwarded to Gen. Frank Paxton of that command the sealed findings of the court in an envelope addressed to the A. A. G. of the
army. General Paxton endorsed the papers, still under seal, "Respectfully forwarded" to Colonel Chilton, and then sent them for

---

[38] 9 *C. M. H.*, Ky., 296.
[40] *Ibid.*, 611.
[42] 1 *R. W. C. D.*, 273; cf. *ibid.*, 267, 269.

[39] *Toombs, etc. Letters*, 608.
[41] Text, *ibid.*, 612.

transmission through Brigadier General Taliaferro, who was in command of the Division.

Taliaferro opened the findings of the court and returned the envelope and its contents to Paxton with a notation that the endorsement did not conform to army regulations. Paxton was sure of the practice at Jackson's headquarters, where he had served. Consequently, Paxton replied briefly to Taliaferro that the Judge Advocate was on detached service, that he himself did not think a communication from that officer to the commanding General was under the control of a brigade or division commander, and that as Taliaferro had broken the seal and returned the letter it would be forwarded through some other channel. Thereupon Taliaferro sent over and put Paxton under arrest on the ground that this was "very disrespectful."

Paxton was not ruffled. Continuing a letter he was writing when the staff officer came to notify him of his arrest, Paxton said: "Very good; there is a small chunk of a row to be settled, which I shall do in that calm spirit which becomes the man who means to vindicate himself and his conduct. . . . The offense of Genl. Taliaferro, in abusing his power as my superior officer, I think he will find, in the opinion of all disinterested gentlemen, is a much graver offense than any I have committed." [43] In about a week, in a manner not now known, the controversy was settled. Paxton was restored to command.[44] This probably did not anger Taliaferro, but the continued denial of a Major General's commission was an affront to his station as a landed aristocrat and a gentleman politician. He asked transfer, received it, and never fought again in the Army of Northern Virginia.[45]

To succeed Taliaferro, the choice of Jackson fell on Brig. Gen. Raleigh E. Colston, who had been in command under French on the Blackwater and then had been transferred temporarily to Pickett's Division.[46] Colston had been born in Paris of Virginia

[43] *Paxton*, 83–84. In the Paxton text the name of the Judge Advocate is given as "St. Pritchard," a name that does not occur in any available list of officers. "St." may be a misreading for "Lt." but that does not facilitate identification.

[44] *Douglas*, 209.

[45] As of Feb. 20, 1863, he was ordered to report to General Beauregard at Charleston. On March 6, Beauregard directed Taliaferro to report to Gen. Hugh W. Mercer in the District of Georgia. *O. R.*, 14, 787, 814. Subsequently General Taliaferro was in immediate command of Charleston, S. C. His MS papers are in the Confederate Museum, Richmond. A sketch will be found in 3 *C. M. H.*, 670 ff.

[46] *O. R.*, 18, 909–10; see *supra*, p. 417.

parentage but as a youth he had been sent to America and entered in the Virginia Military Institute, where he was graduated in 1846. In that year he was added to the faculty of the Institute and ere long was promoted Professor of French. Later he taught Military History and Strategy also. At the V.M.I. he held the rank of Major in Virginia service and to the students was "Old Polly" in an obvious pun on the *parlez* he required of the cadets.[47]

Colston had been mildly commended for his part in the Battle of Williamsburg,[48] but had been a subject of some contention because of the disputed part his Brigade had in the operations of June 1 at Seven Pines.[49] After that battle he had been stricken with a long and obscure illness, from which he had not recovered until December. During the Suffolk operations, he saw little or no action. He was brought now to the Army of Northern Virginia because Jackson, who had been his colleague at V.M.I., had a high opinion of him.[50]

Apparently Jackson had no concern because of Colston's limited combat experience. Nor did the corps commander note in any extant paper that Colston's commission as a Brigadier General dated from Dec. 24, 1861, which fact would make him the Senior Brigadier of Jackson's old Division, now Trimble's. If Trimble's recovery were again delayed, the Division in the next action might be under a man who had two battles only to his credit as a brigade commander and those two not at their hottest where he fought. There is no record of any reflection by Jackson on the seriousness of such a risk.

Charlie Field's Brigade of A. P. Hill's Division went to Harry Heth. This was as definitely Lee's choice as Colston was Jackson's.[51] Heth was 37, a cousin of George Pickett's and a graduate of West Point in the class of 1847. In the "old army" he had followed the usual career of an infantry officer with something more than average credit and, when he resigned in 1861, had been six years a Captain. The good opinion of Lee he won while serving as Acting Quartermaster General of the Virginia forces.

[47] The fullest sketch is in 25 *S. H. S. P.,* 347 ff. The following references give the chronology of his service in the Confederacy prior to his appointment to the command of Taliaferro's Brigade: *Richmond Dispatch,* Apr. 24, 1861; *O. R.,* 51, pt. 2, 123; IV *O. R.,* 1, 630; *Richmond Dispatch,* Jan. 3, 7, 1862; *O. R.,* 11, pt. 3, p. 481 ff; *ibid.,* pt. 1, 567, 945, 983–84; *O. R.,* 18, 807; *O. R.,* 51, pt. 2, p. 667; *O. R.,* 25, pt. 2, pp. 683, 705.

[48] *O. R.,* 11, pt. 1, p. 567.   [49] *Ibid.,* 945, 983–84.

[50] 25 *S. H. S. P.,* 348.   [51] Cf. *O. R.,* 25, pt. 2, p. 645.

Heth confirmed that esteem by his conduct in the column under General Floyd in the Kanawha operations of the late summer of 1861. The following December he was assailed in the press because Davis considered him as a possible appointee, at the rank of Major General, to command in Missouri over Sterling Price, then a popular hero. Heth himself discouraged this,[52] and instead of going across the Mississippi as a Major General, went as a Brigadier to Lewisburg, Virginia. There, through no fault of his own, he had the humiliation of a defeat and a panic in the ranks.[53] This minor disaster, which he frankly admitted to his superiors, did not impair his reputation. President Davis commended him heartily to Kirby Smith, who gave him posts of some importance. The last of these was the Department of East Tennessee, whence Lee asked his transfer to the Army of Northern Virginia.[54]

Tradition is that Heth was the one general officer whom Lee called by his first name; certain it is that Lee interested himself in Heth's advancement as in no other instance of record. The commanding General rated Heth so highly and endorsed him so solidly that Jackson, despite a disposition to keep promotions within the Second Corps, was anxious to have Heth.[55] A manly hold Heth had on the affection of Lee and of others. He was truthful, he was socially charming and he had the finest elements of character, but in war, he was to prove himself of a type not uncommon—the type that is capable but unlucky. Fortune smiled often on him in camp and salon but seldom in battle. When he arrived to take Field's old Brigade, of A. P. Hill's Division,[56] he became its senior Brigadier, as Colston did in Jackson's Division. Was this just to such men as Archer and Pender?

Toombs's Brigade went to "Old Rock" Benning who had been

[52] MS Memoirs of Henry Heth, p. 133.

[53] O. R., 12, pt. 1, pp. 812–13.

[54] Cf. Lee to Heth, Feb. 18, 1863; 44 S. H. S. P., 232. For Heth's career, the best brief sketch is the one in D. A. B., though that in 3 C. M. H., 601, is slightly more detailed concerning his career in Southern service. Another sketch will be found in 7 C.V., 569. The appended references in chronological order describe his early service in Virginia: Richmond Dispatch, Apr. 20, 1861; O. R., 51, pt. 2, p. 36; Richmond Examiner, Apr. 27, 30, 1861; O. R., 51, pt. 2, p. 121; Richmond Dispatch, July 1, 1861; O. R., 5, 772; O. R., 51, pt. 2, pp. 221, 303, 324, 341, O. R., 53, 190–91; Richmond Examiner, Dec. 3, 4, 1862; Richmond Dispatch, Dec. 4, 6, 10, 11, 16, 1862; O. R., 5, 1038; O. R., 51, pt. 2, p. 480; O. R., 12, pt. 3, p. 829 ff; O. R., 12, pt. 1, pp. 812–13; O. R., 51, pt. 2, p. 584.

[55] Cf. O. R., 25, pt. 2, p. 645, Jackson to Lee: "From what you have said respecting General Heth, I have been desirous that he should report for duty."

[56] Orders of Mch. 5, 1863; O. R., 25, pt. 2, p. 654.

temporarily in command of Semmes's troops;[57] Early's famous Brigade passed temporarily into the devoted if unskilled hands of "Extra Billy" Smith.[58] An appointment destined to mean far more to the army than either of these brought John B. Gordon at last to the head of Lawton's Brigade. Lawton, like Gordon, now had recovered from the wound he received at Sharpsburg but he despaired of receiving promotion to the grade he thought he had earned. He had, in addition, many calls and many opportunities in Richmond and in Georgia. Whether Lawton would come back to the Army of Northern Virginia Lee doubted, though a little later, when the question arose, he was willing that Lawton should resume brigade command.[59] If Lawton was not to return during the spring, then a vacancy existed among Georgia troops, a vacancy that John B. Gordon best could fill. The commission that could not be used in the autumn, because there was no Brigade for him, might be delivered him now.[60]

The most coveted of the promotions, that of Major General to head D. H. Hill's Division, who was to receive? Jackson was clear in his mind: He wanted Edward Johnson and he asked for "Old Allegheny." In a letter of February 10, he recommended the promotion and assignment. Johnson, said the commander of the Second Corps, "was with me at McDowell and so distinguished himself as to make me very desirous of having him as one of my Division commanders."[61] Lee was entirely agreeable to the promotion, which, in fact, he had urged in the previous October.[62]

The sole question was whether Johnson was able as yet to discharge field command. He had shown prompt improvement from the wound he had received in the ankle at McDowell, May 8, 1862;[63] but subsequently his leg had not lost its stiffness nor had his ankle bones knit satisfactorily. Johnson went to Richmond, where he owned property and had many friends,[64] and there, chafing at his slow mending, he made the best of misfortune: If he could not pursue the field of Mars, he enjoyed the domain of

[57] O. R., 19, 1099–1100; O. R., 25, pt. 2, p. 682.
[58] Wingfield, 24, entry of April 6. Formal assignment of Smith was not made until May 19, 1863; O. R., 25, pt. 2, p. 80.
[59] O. R., 25, pt. 2, pp. 710–11.
[60] O. R., 25, pt. 2, p. 717; Early, 192. For the continuance of the sketch of Gordon, see infra, pp. 619 ff.
[61] Jackson's MS Letter Book, p. 50.   [62] O. R., 19, pt. 2, p. 677.
[63] Richmond Enquirer, July 30, 1862, p. 1, col. 2.
[64] Cf. Richmond Dispatch, Dec. 16, 1861, p. 3, col. 1.

Venus. It was said with much amused shaking of pretty heads that his thunderous voice had been heard in a loud proposal of matrimony to one belle of the city and that, not a week later, he admitted "paying attention" to one of his cousins, whom he pronounced a "lovely girl." [65] A curious, somewhat uncouth and strangely fascinating man he was. He winked ceaselessly because of an affection of one eye, and sometimes by this he shocked strange ladies who thought him overconfidential if not impertinent. "His head," reported Mrs Chesnut, "is strangely shaped, like a cone or an old-fashioned beehive; . . . there are three tiers of it; it is like a pope's tiara." [66]

If and when his ankle mended, whether or not his suit had ended, "Allegheny" would join the Army of Northern Virginia, as a division commander. He would come solely on the basis of Jackson's estimate of him, and he would be among soldiers who knew him by reputation only Never had he fought with any part of that army save with the few regiments of his old command and with the survivors of the troops Jackson had moved to McDowell almost a year previously. This, manifestly, was as long a chance as Lee took with Heth.

Curious it was that Jackson, who insisted so often on the right of subordinates to the promotion he so seldom gave them, should in two instances have entrusted so large a part of his Corps to men of combat experience so limited. As Lee sponsored one of these assignments, that of Heth, and approved those of Johnson and Colston, much of the responsibility is his. In all three instances the aim of Lee and of Jackson was to bring to the army the most capable men available, but that had an ominous implication: The supply of men ripe and qualified for promotion within the army was, in the judgment of the commanders, at the moment exhausted. Good Colonels there were, but none of those who had the required seniority or could get it readily by transfer, was suited to brigade command. The attrition of two years, particularly in Jackson's Corps, now had offset the development of new men in the hard school of battle.

If there was more than the usual grumbling in the army over the appointments, no record of it has survived, but there was much chatter over the report that an additional Major General was to be appointed. This rumor may have spread from another to the effect that A. P. Hill was to be promoted and sent West,[67] and it may have had some connection with a petition North Carolina Congressmen had signed and filed with the War Department for the promotion of Dorsey Pender.[68]

Mrs. Robert Ransom heard of this and felt that her husband, instead of Pender, should be the North Carolinian next to be made Major General. Many wives, with little reason or less, think their spouses should be the men to get advancement, but comparatively few ladies adopt the direct method of Mrs. Ransom. She wrote indignantly to Lee's A. A. G. and complained much of the treatment accorded Ransom. As a faux pas, like murder, "will out," the mistake of Mrs. Ransom came to the ears of high officers. "Jeb" Stuart wrote his brother-in-law, John Cooke, with something of gusto and more of warning: "Now if Mrs. Jeb ever takes it upon herself to write to any official a letter of that kind in my behalf, she will have an account to settle with the aforesaid Jeb. It is *far better* to be neglected than receive promotion by such means. . . . Be sure, dear John, to keep out of snarls of every kind. They are perfectly abominable. Submit to almost anything but degradation to avoid them . . ."[69]

The method of advancement that Cooke was thus warned to avoid, with Mrs. Ransom as an example, was not one that Dorsey Pender himself had employed. His Congressmen, so far as the records show, were not inspired by him to circulate a petition in his behalf. Nor did he believe that he would win promotion with Jackson's approval while he was under A. P. Hill. Reports that he had been commended to Jackson as the best Brigadier in the Corps did not make his pulse beat faster.[70] Said Pender: "I do not believe General Jackson will have me promoted because I have been recommended by Gen. Hill. He wants some man in the place who will feel under obligations to him."[71]

Pender's pessimism was deepened, in all probability, by the knowledge that the quarrel between Jackson and Powell Hill had been renewed with more violence than before. In January, Hill asked General Lee for a trial on the charges preferred against him

[67] Cf. *Hamlin's Ewell*, 119.
[68] Pender to his wife, Feb. 21, 1863—*Pender MSS*.
[69] Feb. 28, 1863—*Cooke MSS*.
[70] Pender to his wife, Apr. 8, 1863—*Pender MSS*.
[71] Same to Same, Apr. 11, 1863—*Pender MSS*. The sketch of Pender is continued *infra*, pp. 656, 691 ff.

by Jackson. With a waiver of the right to be heard by officers of equal rank, Hill said: "Two of my important witnesses have been killed,⁷⁵ and others are leaving, and will not be available." ⁷³ Lee already had sent back the charges with his disapproval of a court martial and now he answered Hill patiently with a brief discourse on the necessity of the power of arrest in the maintenance of authority. He concluded: "Upon examining the charges in question, I am of opinion that the interests of the service do not require that they should be tried, and have, therefore, returned them to General Jackson with an endorsement to that effect. I hope you will concur with me that their further prosecution is unnecessary, so far as you are concerned, and will be of no advantage to the service." ⁷⁴

Hill did not concur. On the contrary, in a letter that shows the impress of a legal hand, he argued that while the return of the charges to Jackson was a rebuke to that officer, it was "not as public as was General Jackson's exercise of power toward me." Hill insisted to Lee's A. A. G., the addressee of the letter: "The General must acknowledge that if the charges preferred against me by General Jackson were true, that I do not deserve to command a division in this army; if they were untrue, then General Jackson deserves a rebuke as notorious as the arrest."

The whole tone of the letter was sharp and vindictive,⁷⁵ but as Lee did not answer, nothing developed until, in March, Hill wrote his report on Cedar Run. In that document, which he filed on the 8th, Hill set forth in restrained language his version of the disputed day's events that had been the beginning of the quarrel between him and Jackson.⁷⁶

This was the sort of challenge Jackson never failed to take up. When he received Hill's report, he sent staff officers to collect information from others concerning Hill's assertions,⁷⁷ and this he embodied in a detailed endorsement of Hill's report. Over this endorsement, from the appearance of his first draft, he must have spent hours.⁷⁸ When Hill was informed of the endorsement, he was aroused to press anew for a hearing of the charges against him. Painstakingly, at his own desk, Jackson revised his charges

---

⁷² Generals Branch and Gregg.   ⁷³ O. R., 19, pt. 2, pp. 731–32.
⁷⁴ O. R., 19, pt. 2, p. 732.   ⁷⁵ Ibid., 732–33.
⁷⁶ For the report, see O. R., 12, pt. 2, p. 314. The details of the day's march and the subsequent quarrel will be found supra, pp. 12 ff.
⁷⁷ Jackson MSS; Douglas, 215.   ⁷⁸ Jackson MSS

and specifications and, on April 17, 1863, had them ready for pres entation to a court.[79]

Before any action was taken by Lee, who was anxious to bury the whole affair, an entirely new controversy arose. Hill was a stickler. He always demanded that orders for his subordinates pass through him, and he applied this to officers of the general staff as well as to those of the line. His rule was that even the chief commissary of the Army or of the Corps must send his headquarters any communication intended for a commissary of the Division. Lee disapproved his practice and maintained that the general staff officer could communicate directly with any subordinate who, in turn, if the matter were one of importance, would inform the commander of the Corps or Division. Unless this were done, said Lee, the ranking general officers would "have to attend to all the staff operations of their commands in addition to their military operations . . ." This seemed the course of common sense, but apparently Hill, on March 11, insisted formally that he be the channel for all communication with the commissaries, the quartermasters, the ordnance officers, the surgeons and the signal officers of his Division. As the matter was not altogether clear in army regulations, Lee on March 20 referred it to the Adjutant General for a ruling.

The question was under examination by General Cooper when, about the 20th of April, Lee received a report that a message which had been copied from the enemy's signal line had been known and mentioned at General Lane's headquarters.[80] This was contrary to Lee's instructions. Standing orders were, first, that intercepted messages of the enemy be transmitted under seal to the officer to whom the receiving signalman was responsible; and, second, that messages from the Confederates' own signal line should be communicated to no other person than the one to whom they were addressed by the dispatching signal officer.[81]

---

[79] For events between the time Jackson drafted his endorsement and the date of his final charges and specifications, the evidence is inferential. The essential documents almost certainly were destroyed by General Lee when he decided he would not consider the case.

[80] Jackson said "spoken of," but he leaves the inference plain that the contents of the message were known at Lane's headquarters.

[81] Jackson in his endorsement of Apr. 24, 1863, is somewhat obscure on this point, but the substance of the standing order evidently was as here stated. A somewhat similar rule forbade spies and scouts to discuss their missions with anyone except the general officer to whom they reported.

As soon as Lee learned of what had happened in the handling
of the intercepted message, he directed Jackson to ascertain, if possible, the name of the officer who had disclosed the contents and,
if the man were identified, to relieve him of duty. Jackson was
instructed, further, to see that the regular rule was enforced.
Jackson's Chief Signal Officer, Capt. R. E. Wilbourn, an able man,
undertook an investigation. It soon was apparent that the "leak"
had occurred through Capt. R. H. T. Adams, signal officer of
Hill's Division. When Adams was told that he must conform to
the order from headquarters and deliver messages to those persons
only for whom they were intended, the Captain replied that he
could not obey Jackson's direct order, as he had contrary instructions from General Hill, to whom he considered himself responsible. Those instructions were that he must heed no orders that
did not come through Hill. On this statement, Jackson relieved
Adams of duty and sent him to the commanding General. Hill
immediately and indignantly defended Captain Adams and
started a correspondence that probably was designed to be the
foundation for a new controversy with his chief.

The time had come, in Jackson's opinion, when regard for his
duty as head of a Corps made further compromise between him
and Hill impossible. In the files of the Second Corps was a brief
letter of Nov. 13, 1862, from Hill to "Sandie" Pendleton on the
same general subject of transmission of orders through channels.
Whether Jackson had passed over the letter at the time for reasons
known to himself alone, or whether Pendleton had thought wise
to put the document away, lest it deepen the gulf between Hill
and Jackson, there is no way of determining. The note now was
brought to light. In it Hill said: "I have received but one order
from Maj. Gen. Jackson, to Capt. Adams to detail three signal
operators to report to Capt. Boswell. This order was received yesterday and obeyed the same day. A copy of this *same order* was
received by Capt. Adams direct, not through me, and I directed
him to pay no attention to it."

There, in plain words, written five months previously, was a
statement by Hill that he had told Captain Adams not to obey
orders sent directly from the corps commander to him. That same
defiance Hill now had repeated. The case must be put before
General Lee. Carefully Jackson prepared an endorsement for

Hill's letter of inquiry concerning the relief of Captain Adams from duty, and under the same jacket he put Hill's letter of November 13 to Pendleton. All the circumstances Jackson related. Every syllable he weighed. He spoke of Hill's letter as "improper," struck out the word, wrote it again and again cancelled it.

The point of the endorsement was in this startling climax: "When an officer orders in his command such disregard for the orders of his superiors I am of the opinion that he should be relieved from duty with his command, and I respectfully request that Genl. Hill be relieved from duty in my Corps. It is very important to have harmony in my command; but to do so, orders must be obeyed. The within letter [82] of yesterday from Genl. H. has not been replied to, as I deem it best not to countenance such an improper correspondence. If Genl. H. had properly asked for the information it would have been given." [83] To that the long quarrel had come: Jackson asked that the commander of his strongest Division—many thought, the best Division in the army— be relieved of command when a great battle manifestly was in the making!

Strange, strange the spirit of all this was in contrast to what had been happening at Jackson's quarters. He had been homesick during the winter months, as well he might be, because he had not been under his own roof in nearly two years, had not seen his wife for nearly twelve months, and had never looked on his own child. He had to stiffen himself with the reminder that officers had to stay at their posts and set an example. [84] At one period, his distress was heightened for days by the news that his baby had the chickenpox. Formally he summoned to his office the Medical Director of the Corps and had the doctor explain precisely the approved treatment for this malady. By attentive listening and diligent questioning, he mastered the procedure and meticulously put it into a letter for the guidance of Mrs. Jackson. [85] Although he permitted himself to hope that, if God willed it, his child be spared, he tactfully cautioned Mrs. Jackson not to call the baby a cherub, ". . . no earthly being is such." [86] When he went to

---

[82] It was before this word "letter" that Jackson had inserted and then had erased "improper."
[83] Rough draft of endorsement, MS. Apr. 24, 1863—Jackson MSS.
[84] Cf. Mrs. Jackson, 401.   [85] Ibid., 397.   [86] Ibid., 400.

church and saw the happy wives of other Generals there, he wished his *esposita* was among them.[87]

General Early saw the ladies, also, but not with approving eyes. In a long letter to Jackson he protested formally against the interruptions visiting wives, mothers and sisters created in the work of the army: Would not the corps commander order all these ladies to stay away? Jackson read indignantly and remarked with spirit to his staff: "I will do no such thing. I wish my wife could come to see me!" Staff and married officers who heard of Jackson's observation applauded him and frowned on the bachelor Early. Perhaps some of them decided they would make "Jube" pay in his own coin. Soon afterward there lay before Jackson a vigorous complaint by the medical department of the Corps that General Early had been using ambulances to escort ladies through the country. Immediately the staff officers began to prod Jackson: He must call on Early for an explanation. At length, half amused, Jackson consented and had one of the staff direct General Early to list the occasions on which he had so used the ambulances. "Old Jube" sent in a truthful and hence a long and embarrassing, if gallant report—and for some weeks thereafter did not appear at Jackson's headquarters.[88]

Jackson long had been planning to emulate the officers who somehow got their wives through Richmond and found quarters for them in the spacious country homes around Fredericksburg. With Mrs. Jackson, of course, the baby must come. All winter he had been hoping he could arrange it. In the very letter in which he had admonished Mrs. Jackson not to call the baby a cherub he had said wistfully: "I am still thinking and thinking about that baby, and do want to see her. Can't you send her to me by express? There is an express line all the way to Guiney's." [89] Again: "Last night I dreamed that my little wife and I were on opposite sides of a room, in the centre of which was a table, and the little baby started from her mother, making her way along under the table, and finally reached her father. And what do you think she did when she arrived at her destination? She just climbed up on her father and kissed him!" [90]

Till his own baby visited him, Jackson found such comfort as

[87] *Ibid.*, 397–98.   [88] *J. P. Smith Address.*
[89] Letter of Jan. 17, 1863; *Mrs. Jackson*, 400.
[90] Letter of Apr. 18, 1863; *Mrs. Jackson*, 407.

he could in Janie Corbin. She was the 5-year-old daughter of his hostess at Moss Neck,[91] and was, said Jackson, "one of the most attractive [children], if not the most so, that I ever saw at that age." [92] By special request, Jane came every day to his office, after work was done, and chatted with him. One of their chief delights was in cutting out paper dolls, in which enchanting art he had advanced to the moderate proficiency that permitted him to present many, many figures with hands joined. This particular arrangement always had the same name in conversation between Janie and the General: It was the Stonewall Brigade.[93]

Janie's hair was long and golden and sometimes it tumbled into her blue eyes. Then she would toss her little head and throw back her hair in one of the loveliest of all the gestures of girlhood. "Old Jack" may have seen the grace of the gesture, but he thought the falling locks annoyed her. So, one afternoon when he was explaining to her the mysteries of writing, he paused as she threw back the hair from her intent face. What, he asked, had become of her comb? It was broken, Janie explained. Jackson smiled as if a pleasant thought had come to him and he reached to his own gray cap with a gilt band, a present from his wife. Quickly he cut loose the band, picked out the threads and then bound it around Janie's hair. Holding her shining face between his hands, he said, "Janie, it suits a little girl like you better than it does an old soldier like me." Janie had much admired that particular band and, now that she possessed it, she had to run off in a gale of joy to show it to her mother. Thereafter, when she dressed for the evening or for some special event, she always wore her shining fillet.[94]

Life at Moss Neck was as pleasant as could be the existence of a soldier separated from home and vexed with all the problems of corps command, but as March days drew on, Jackson's military

[91] She was born Roberta Cary and was the wife of Richard Corbin. After his death, she married Rev. Dr. O. A. Kinsolving. See Wythe Leigh Kinsolving, *Early History of Virginia and Maryland*, 8, 12.

[92] *Mrs. Jackson*, 396.

[93] Mrs. Kinsolving, Janie's mother, in 20 *C.V.*, 24–26. A picture of Janie is printed in *ibid.*, 26. For much care and kindness in explaining the Corbin and Kinsolving connection, the writer is indebted to Rev. Wythe Leigh Kinsolving and to his book, already quoted.

[94] This account is a composite of Douglas's, *op. cit.*, 214—very beautifully done, too —and that of Mrs. Kinsolving, 20 *C.V.*, 24–26. The original band, dimmed but intact, has been presented by Rev. Wythe Leigh Kinsolving, Janie's half-brother, to the Confederate Museum, Richmond. Jackson's gift to Janie may have been made rather late in his stay at Moss Neck. The first time Jed. Hotchkiss observed the absence of the gilt band from Jackson's cap was on March 15. See *Hotchkiss' MS. Diary*, 149.

conscience began to prod him. The office afforded him too much worldly comfort; visitors continued to take an undue part of his time. They would trouble him less in a remote tent.[95] So, planning always ahead, he set his departure for the week of March 15 and selected a camp site not far from General Lee's near Hamilton's Crossing.

Before Jackson left, Janie was stricken with scarlet fever, but on the evening of March 16, when he went to thank Mrs. Corbin for her kindness and to inquire about Janie, his little friend was better. The next day he settled himself on his chosen ground, which General Early not long previously had vacated.[96] To the grief and dismay of Jackson, word was brought him on the 18th that Janie was dead. He who had gazed dry-eyed on the battlefield of Sharpsburg sat down and wept unabashed.[97]

He prayed for the bereaved mother, and for his own wife's sister, who almost at the same time had lost her first born.[98] In fact, loneliness, the thought of coming conflict and the surge of religious enthusiasm through the army made the days of early spring a season of prayer for Jackson. His appeals to the Almighty were made still more earnest by the illness of General Lee at the end of March. Jackson was alarmed for a time over the condition of the army commander, "for," recorded one of his officers, "[Jackson] thinks there is no one like [Lee], having unlimited confidence in him." [99]

Not in solitude did Jackson always pray. He shared the daily morning devotions that Chaplain Tucker Lacy held at headquarters, and unless army business demanded, he never absented himself from the somewhat longer prayer service Mr. Lacy conducted on Wednesday and Sunday evenings. The members of Jackson's military household were encouraged on Sunday afternoon to assemble and to sing hymns. Although he had not even then learned to recognize "Dixie," he could identify the tune of "How happy are they, Who the Savior obey" and he almost always called for it. Another favorite that he asked of the staff songsters, headquarters clerks and attendants, was "Come humble sinner, in whose breast

---

95 *Mrs. Jackson*, 404.
96 *Early*, 192. Hotchkiss in his *MS Diary*, Mch. 17, 1863, p. 149, described the site as "near William Yerby's, 2½ miles up Massaponax [Creek] from Hamilton's Crossing."
97 *Mrs. Jackson*, 396; *Douglas*, 215.   98 *Mrs. Jackson*, 397.
99 Jed. Hotchkiss to his wife. MS Apr. 2, 1863--*Hotchkiss Papers*.

LEE'S LIEUTENANTS

a thousand thoughts revolve." Still another was " 'Tis my happiness below, Not to live without the cross." A fourth was "When gathering clouds around I view, And days are dark and friends are few." [100] Nothing he thought more fitting for such an hour of praise than "Glorious things of thee are spoken, Zion, city of our God." [101] If he could not "raise the tune" or even join in the refrain, Jackson could "pray in public," and when called upon, or when Chaplain Lacy was absent, he did so. At a prayer meeting in Lacy's tent, on Sunday, March 29, "Old Jack" prayed fervently for peace and invoked the blessing of the Lord on his country's enemy "in everything but the war." [102]

There Jackson drew the line, because he was seeking Divine guidance and favor for the South and for himself in defeating the enemy. In February, most secretly, he had told Jed. Hotchkiss to make a map of the Shenandoah Valley and to extend it into Pennsylvania—proof enough of the direction of his military thought. "War," he averred, "is the greatest of evils," [103] but in talking casually of "the horrid sights" of life he put first a railroad wreck.[104] The difficulties that lay ahead he did not minimize. Some of them were unavoidable; some were the work of evil men. "The country," he once said when protesting the stupidity of the conscription bureau, "is being nearly ruined by political demagogues." [105]

Hampered though Jackson knew the Army to be by the cowardice of politicians, he awaited avidly the next move of Hooker, and made ready to meet it. Never did he work harder to have the Corps at its keenest fighting edge; [106] never during the winter or spring did he moderate his demand for war to the death. After Fredericksburg, Doctor McGuire had spoken of the wickedness of the invading Federals and had concluded, "What can we do?". Jackson's reply had been instant: "Do? Why, shoot them." Again

---

[100] Probably sung to the tune Yoakley.

[101] To the tune Harwell, by Dr. Lowell Mason. Mrs. Jackson, *op. cit.*, 406, is authority for these as Jackson's "favorite hymns." Students of hymnology may note that none of these hymns was by Isaac Watts, but that was by chance. "Show pity, Lord," though not mentioned by Mrs. Jackson, was beloved by the General and was by Watts. See *infra*, p. 677. Apropos of tunes and hymns, Mrs. Kinsolving noted, *loc. cit.*, that Mear was the air most used by the band of the Stonewall Brigade as a dirge that winter.

[102] *Hotchkiss' MS Diary*, 153. [103] *Hotchkiss' MS. Diary*, 119.

[104] *Ibid.*

[105] *Hotchkiss' MS Diary*, Mch. 5, 1863; p. 145.

[106] *J. P. Smith Address.*

he had told his staff, "We must do more than defeat their armies; we must destroy them." [107] The Army of Northern Virginia must be ready to maneuver and to fight. On April 13, Jackson renewed his orders for the conduct of the march: The troops were to rest ten minutes of every hour and, unless specifically ordered, were not to cover more than one mile in twenty-five minutes. When they halted they must not break ranks till they had stacked arms. [108] On every detail of this, he was insistent. If ever he had use for that map being drawn by Jed. Hotchkiss, the marches he traced on it beyond the Potomac would be arduous: the men must be steeled and trained.

A week after renewing his orders for the conduct of the march, Jackson ordered a reduction of transportation and a limit on personal baggage. [109] Any day now, the long roll might be sounded, the wagons started for the rear, and the lean gray infantry headed for the advancing enemy. A great battle was coming soon. Of that Jackson was confident. He explained his reasons to a member of his staff one day and, at the end, he paused. Then he added solemnly: "My trust is in God!" Again he paused as if he were musing. Suddenly his face flushed, his eyes flashed, he got up with a swift move: "I wish they would come!" [110]

Instead of a new army, calm descended on the Rappahannock for the leafing of the trees. Federal balloons mounted high over the new green of the forest, as if the enemy were tiptoeing and trying to see whether, beyond the ridge, "the rebels" were astir. "Everything is very quiet in our front," Lee wrote Stuart. [111] Said Frank Paxton, who had been thinking and writing that spring of the eternities, "I have hardly ever known the army so quiet as now." [112] Through a soft, enriching rain that deepened the mys-- terious quiet among the camps of 50,000 gaunt men, Jackson rode on the 20th of April to Guiney's Station. It was his great hour, the hour for which he had been waiting since he had the first news of the baby's birth: Mrs. Jackson and the little girl were coming, coming on the very train that was whistling now. No sooner had it stopped than he, in dripping raincoat and with that long,

---

[107] *McGuire*, 208, 213.   [108] *O. R.*, 25, pt. 2, p. 719.
[109] *O. R.*, 25, pt. 2, p. 739. General preliminary orders had been issued by Lee on March 21. See *O. R.*, 25, pt 2, p. 681.
[110] *Cooke's Jackson*, 394.   [111] *O. R.*, 25, pt. 2, p. 730.
[112] *Paxton*, 99.

farmer's stride of his, was on the crowded car and was pushing toward her. There she was and there the baby. He spoke to his wife and then, turning ever so little, for the first time gazed at his child. "She was at the lovely, smiling age; and catching his eager look of supreme interest in her, she beamed her brightest and sweetest smiles upon him." [113]

In his wet coat, he dared not touch her, but he shepherded mother and babe and nurse into the waiting vehicle, and he kept his eyes on the child. When he got to Yerby's, he threw off his raincoat the moment they were in their room, [114] took the little girl in his arms and caressed her again and again. For hours then and daily thereafter, he studied with fascinated eyes the child's face. While she slept, he often would kneel by the cradle and tell Mrs. Jackson that the baby looked almost as if she were . . . well, not a cherub, but, yes, and honestly, an angel! [115]

A blissful season it was for the Southern Cromwell. On the fourth day of the visit, Jackson arranged for Mr. Lacy to baptize the child. The Chaplain assumed that the rite was to be performed privately and he shook his head when Jimmie Smith asked the privilege of attending. Smith went to Jackson, who was in an expansive mood. "Certainly, Mr. Smith, you can go," said the General, "ask the others to go with you."

So, in their gray coats and with their youthful, strangely grim faces, the staff officers arrived at Yerby's for the baptism. They did not fail to observe that when there was some delay in bringing the child into the room for the ordinance, the father suddenly became the impatient General. He stalked out of the room, made short settlement of what had held Mrs. Jackson, and came back with the infant in his arms. [116] "That was 'Stonewall' Jackson's way." Whether it was in having Powell Hill cross the Rapidan, or Crutchfield post the artillery or Lacy baptize a baby, there must be punctuality!

The staff officers stood reverently by, praised the baby and then went to their daily tasks. They could not say that their General afterward neglected any of his duties as a corps administrator, but

---

[113] *Mrs. Jackson* 409.

[114] It was the room to which General Lee had been removed March 30 after he became ill in his tent. He remained at Yerby's until his convalescence was completed. See 2 *R. E. Lee*, 502.

[115] *Mrs. Jackson*, 409–10.   [116] *Mrs. Jackson*, 410–11.

it was well, perhaps, that they were not at William Yerby's house. A side of Jackson they may not have known they would have seen, and some things that might have made them smile. He spent every hour he could with his child and his wife, and he found time to bring over and to show his wife the presents given him. Among them was a new horse. After she had praised the steed and all things connected with it, he smiled and wheeled and galloped magnificently, because there was enough of the cavalier in this Cromwell to make him wish to exhibit his horsemanship. What would have startled his staff, and above all "Dick" Ewell, was this: In the speed of Jackson's departure, his cap blew rebelliously off, but he did not deign to draw rein and pick it up. Could anyone have imagined the "wagon hunter," the man who would halt an army to hunt a wheelbarrow, capable of such an act as that? He might never have recovered the cap!

By no means all the glamor of Mrs. Jackson's reception was provided by her husband. General Lee, of course, came promptly and resplendent, to pay a call on the wife of his lieutenant, and with him he brought several of the most captivating of his staff officers. Mrs. Jackson was a bit awed and nervous at this first meeting with the commanding General, but she was soon put at ease by the fatherly charm of his manner.[117] Equalling the visit of Lee—in fact, perhaps the greatest event of all—was the service of Sunday, April 26. Jackson had written his wife in February, "I don't know that I ever enjoyed Sabbaths as I do this winter"[118] and now he was to have the most gracious Lord's Day of all—an outdoor religious assembly and a full-length discourse in the noblest style of Chaplain Lacy. Moreover, Mrs. Jackson was to attend exactly as had the wives of other Generals whom he had seen at church during the winter when he had looked at them and had wished that she sat among them.

Mrs. Jackson rode in an ambulance to the meeting place and went to the tent that had been spread to shade the pulpit and the general officers and their guests. Lee was there and greeted her with his flawless courtesy; General Early, looking not at all out of place at church, paid her homage. In front of the tent were some 1500 to 2000 of her husband's soldiers. They sang the songs of Zion lustily; with reverence they listened as Chaplain Lacy ex-

[117] *Mrs. Jackson*, 412.   [118] *Mrs. Jackson*, 403.

pounded the parable of the rich man and Lazarus. As many of them as knew that Mrs. Jackson was visiting the General looked at her often and curiously, and gave her critical appraisal. She was, said one observer, "slightly built and tolerably good looking, and was somewhat gaily though modestly dressed" [119]—a tribute none too warm.

That Sunday afternoon the General and his beloved spent together, without interruption or reception of guests. Wrote Mrs. Jackson later: ". . . his conversation was more spiritual than I had ever observed before. He seemed to be giving utterance to those religious meditations in which he so much delighted." [120] Several times that winter he had opened his heart in much the same way. One day he had said to a friend: "Nothing earthly can mar my happiness. I know that heaven is in store for me; and I should rejoice in the prospect of going there tomorrow . . . I have as much to love here as any man, and life is very bright to me. But still I am ready to leave it any day, without trepidation or regret, for that heaven which I know awaits me, through the mercy of my Heavenly Father. And I would not agree to the slightest diminution of one shade of my glory there—no, not for all the fame I have acquired or shall ever win in this world." [121] In that same spirit he talked to her till the Sabbath shadows fell.

The 27th and the 28th, Monday and Tuesday, he was with her every hour he did not feel he should be at headquarters. Reports had come that the enemy on the other side of the Rappahannock had brought up all the troops from the rear; Stuart had written that Stoneman and the Federal cavalry were at Warrenton Springs. Lee had called on Longstreet to expedite the commissary operations in North Carolina because the two detached Divisions of the First Corps might be recalled at any moment.[122] That was all the information Jackson had Tuesday night.

Dawn of the 29th of April. Soft, regular breathing in the great bedroom at William Yerby's. The baby had not stirred. Suddenly a stamping on the stairs, a knock at the door. More readily than usual, Jackson awakened. What was wanted? "General Early's Adjutant wishes to see General Jackson." Jackson got out of bed. "That looks as if Hooker were crossing," he said to Mrs. Jackson.

[119] Hotchkiss' MS Diary, 167.   [120] Mrs. Jackson, 411.
[121] Mrs. Jackson, 294.   [122] O. R., 25, pt. 2, p. 752.

and then he tumbled quickly into his clothes. Down the steps he went to hear what the waiting officer had to say.

After a few minutes below stairs, he came hurriedly back—the General now. It was as he had expected. Hooker had launched the spring offensive. The Federal advance would be met. A battle would be fought. Mrs. Jackson might not be safe at Yerby's. She must prepare at once to start for Richmond. If Jackson could, he would return to Yerby's to see her off; if not, he would send her brother Joseph Morrison to escort her to the train at Guiney's. One last kiss; a long, long look at the baby . . Good-bye, good-bye!

CHAPTER XXXI

JACKSON GETS HIS GREATEST ORDERS

A MILD AND CLOUDY morning it was, that 29th of April, but rich
in the promise of spring. Along the Massaponax, the leaves of the
oaks were beginning to open. Around every well furnished farm
past which Jackson rode, the peach and the cherry trees were in
full bloom. In the woods and on the hillsides, the anemone could
be seen; the houstonia added its color; the bloodroot flew its flag
of truce.[1] Nature was dressed to entertain the daughter, not the
preoccupied father. His eyes were toward the Rappahannock,
whence battery-smoke already was rising; his first order probably
was for Robert Rodes to bring up immediately D. H. Hill's Division from its camps around Christ Church.

At the front, Jackson found that Jubal Early had deployed the
veterans of Ewell's Division, now Early's own, along the railroad
and had thrown three regiments forward to the old Stage road.[2]
Under the bank of the river were the Federals, who had crossed
on a pontoon bridge but as yet showed no disposition to attack.
Jackson could ascertain little concerning either their numbers or
their disposition, but he concluded that a fight was certain and
that Mrs. Jackson and the baby must leave at once—on the morning train for Richmond, if that were possible. He sat down and
wrote his wife a little note to this effect. Once more he used his
tender phrases, prayed God's blessing on her, and sent affectionate
messages to the baby. Then he sealed the letter and summoned
his brother-in-law, Lt. Joseph Morrison. Would Morrison take an
ambulance, go immediately to Yerby's, get Mrs. Jackson and the
child and put them aboard the cars?

Morrison was disciplined and not disposed to argue with a Lieutenant General, but he could talk plainly to his sister's husband.
Jackson, said Morrison, would have need of all the staff officers.

---

[1] *Hotchkiss' MS Diary,* 171. Major Hotchkiss, who usually made in his diary an
entry about the weather, never was so detailed, happily, as in his description of conditions during the first fortnight of May, 1863.
[2] *O. R.,* 25, pt. 1, p. 1000.

He would prefer to remain on duty and, if Jackson permitted, to send Chaplain Lacy in his place. The General acquiesced; Lacy got the summons, went forthwith to Yerby's where he found Mrs. Jackson, her maid and the baby prepared. He hurried them to Guiney's and arrived in time for the southbound train.[3] Their safe departure he duly reported to his chief.

Jackson ere that had seen the commanding General and had learned of various reports which indicated that the Federals might be crossing the Rappahannock West of Fredericksburg either for a movement against Lee's rear or for a drive against Gordonsville and the Virginia Central Railroad.[4] Upon Lee, not upon Jackson, rested the burden of sifting these reports and of deciding whether to start a column immediately up the river or to await a further development of the situation. Jackson's task was to watch the enemy in his front and to bring up his other Divisions. Rodes already was moving his men into position on the extreme right, perpendicular to the railroad, and was fortifying rapidly.[5] A. P. Hill was ordered to place his Brigades on the military road above the railway, behind the boggy wood and on the ridge where Maxcy Gregg had fallen.[6] Trimble's Division, then at Moss Neck and at Skinker's Neck, was directed to move up the river to Hamilton's Crossing.[7]

Provided the enemy did not undertake a sudden advance from the river, all this was simple. The only circumstance that would have disturbed a man less resolute than Jackson was this: Neither Edward Johnson, who was to take Harvey Hill's Division, nor Trimble, who was to lead Jackson's old Division, was with the troops. In place of Johnson, who had not yet reported for duty, Robert Rodes, the senior Brigadier, well might act. He had experience and in every battle he had fought, from Seven Pines onward, he had distinguished himself. What could have been finer, for example, than his behavior that day on South Mountain when his Brigade, almost alone, had held the left against a powerful and determined turning movement? In Jackson's own Division, which Trimble still was too crippled to direct in the field, Paxton led the Stonewall Brigade and, in Jackson's opinion, was qualified to

[3] Mrs. Jackson, 416.
[4] For the details of these reports, see the references in 2 R. E. Lee, 509 ff.
[5] O. R., 25, pt. 1, 939.   [6] O. R., 25, pt. 1, p. 901.
[7] O. R., 25, pt. 2, p. 1004.

handle the Division if the occasion demanded. The senior of the Brigadiers, the man who now must assume responsibility for the command, was Raleigh Colston. He had been with the Division less than a month and never had fought in it.[8]

While Colston was marching up the Rappahannock, the Federals threw another pontoon bridge, opposite Smithfield, the Pratt homestead,[9] but they did not move from the river bank. Every hour deepened Lee's belief that the major effort of the enemy would be elsewhere.[10] By evening, he was so well persuaded the principal attack would be directed against his left, upstream, that he started in that direction "Dick" Anderson, who already had four of his Brigades widely extended on that flank.[11] Anderson was to bring up the fifth, Wright's, and was to take command. On the Fredericksburg front remained Jackson's entire Corps, McLaws's Division of Longstreet, and part of the reserve artillery.

Dawn of April 30 was cool and misty and, on the flats, was fog laden, though as the morning wore on, the clouds scattered.[12] Jackson was awake early at his camp and from the first hour was full of fight. Together with Lee he observed the Federal dispositions and discussed the proper tactics. The commanding General was quite clear in his own mind: It was better to await the enemy's attack, if one was to be delivered. Presence of the Federal artillery on Stafford Heights imposed the same conditions that had prevailed in December. The Confederates would find it difficult to get at the enemy and still harder to get back across the flats after driving the Federals into the river or across their bridges.[13]

Jackson had abundant reason for knowing this, in the light of what had happened to his advancing batteries on the evening of December 13, but he could not bring himself to forgo the chance of striking an enemy who was hugging a river bank. As Jackson

[8] His orders from Lee to report to Jackson were dated April 4 and were of the form usually employed when an officer who had been sent to headquarters by the Adjutant General was ready for duty. *O. R.,* 25, pt. 2, p. 705.
[9] *O. R.,* 25, pt. 1, p. 1000.
[10] *O. R.,* 25, pt. 1, p. 796. *Cf.* R. E. Lee to R. H. Anderson, MS, Apr. 23, 1863. Lee told Anderson that the enemy might be making a feint at Port Royal and that Anderson must "be prepared and on the alert for any movement which they may make above."—*R. H. Anderson MSS.*
[11] *Ibid.* and 849; Lee to Anderson, MS, Apr. 29, 1863—*R. H. Anderson MSS.*
[12] *Hotchkiss' MS Diary,* 173.
[13] Fitz Lee's *Chancellorsville,* 22; the same article reprinted in J. W. Jones, *Army of Northern Virginia Memorial Volume,* 293 ff. For this reference, see p. 310. Further citations will be of this A. N. Va. edition.

stood unconvinced, Lee spoke again: "If you think it can be done, I will give orders for it."

That put the onus on Jackson. Willing as always he was to make decisions, he was loath to go squarely against the judgment of the man·whom, as he had told Boteler, he was "willing to follow blindfolded." Jackson asked now for more time in which to examine the terrain. Lee at once assented. Most of a rainy afternoon [14] Jackson then spent in more detailed study of the ranges, the gun positions, the ground across which his troops must sweep to reach the Federals. At length and most regretfully, he had to own to himself that an advance would be costly and that withdrawal would have to be under a devastating fire. In December he had thought of making a similar attack just before nightfall, so that if he were repulsed, the withdrawing forces could not be seen by the Federals. Now, as evening came on, the capricious skies cleared again. The moon, lacking two days of the full, already was high in the heavens. Its light would flood the flats. There would be no darkness to cover a possible retreat.

Back Jackson rode to the headquarters of the commanding General. Lee was correct, he said: "It would be inexpedient to attack here." What should he do instead? Lee was waiting with the answer. He was entirely convinced that the Federals below Fredericksburg were no more than a holding force, and that Hooker was striking through the Wilderness of Spotsylvania to turn the Confederate left. "Move, then," said Lee to Jackson, "at dawn tomorrow up to Anderson." [15] He went on to explain that McLaws with three Brigades would precede Jackson and that Early, with his Division, Barksdale's Brigade and part of the reserve artillery would be left to face the Federals on the river.

For these instructions, Jackson was not unprepared. Although he had hoped he could strike a blow where he was, he had realized that the main action might be upstream from Fredericksburg. During the afternoon, before he had made his final reconnaissance, he had called Jed. Hotchkiss to him and had told the topographical engineer to strike off eight maps of the country between the Rappahannock and the Rapidan as far South as the Virginia Central Railroad. His own copy, said Jackson, should be extended

---

[14] *Hotchkiss' MS Diary,* 173.
[15] Fitz Lee's *Chancellorsville, ed. cit.,* 310.

westward to Stevensburg.[16] He gave no explanation of the reason
for this last request, nor did Hotchkiss suggest one in making the
entry in a certain small diary; but the fact was, Jackson had
crossed the Rapidan on the road to Stevensburg, the previous
August, en route to meet Pope, and he knew what a trap to a
retreating army was the famous "V" between the Rappahannock
and the Rapidan. Perhaps Hooker might be caught where Pope
had escaped.

Soon after midnight, Jackson put on his full uniform[17] and
ordered the troops awakened. Rodes must proceed up the military
road on the ridge until he reached the point where it joined the
Plank Road from Fredericksburg to Orange.[18] Then Rodes was
to head westward. Hill would follow;[19] Colston, with Trimble's
Division, which had marched all day on the 29th,[20] would close
the rear.

With Ramseur's Brigade as the van, Rodes's troops went off in
the highest spirits. The sentiment of those who understood the
threatened turning movement against Lee's left may have been
voiced by Dorsey Pender on the 30th. Said he in a letter to his
wife: "If you hear that we have fallen back, you need not be uneasy, for we are all right. We are concentrated and can fight them
when we please, and whip them, too."[21] As the men confidently
tramped on, the setting moon was lost in a dense mist at dawn;[22]
but the morning proved pleasant—a "genuine May Day," wrote
Jed. Hotchkiss.[23]

Jackson rode ahead of the infantry and, at 8 o'clock, about five
and a half miles from Fredericksburg, he came upon Anderson's
Division which was facing West and Northwest and was entrench-
ing steadily on a front something more than a mile in length.
Soon Jackson found Anderson, who had a report to make of vigilant and prompt action. Anderson told it modestly, because that
was his nature, but it was a report to belie the persistent yarn that
he was indolent and that only under the spur of Longstreet could

[16] *Hotchkiss' MS Diary*, 173.   [17] *Grimes*, 29.
[18] *O. R.*, 25, pt. 2, p. 939. It should be noted that as there is no report for the
Second Corps, unusual reliance has to be placed on the report of the division commanders. Fortunately, those of Rodes and of Colston are quite full, though Hill was
not understating the facts when he spoke of his meager report as a "very imperfect
sketch." *O. R.*, 25, pt. 1, p. 885.
[19] *Ibid.*, 885.   [20] *Ibid.*, 1004.
[21] *Pender MSS.*   [22] 3 *B. & L.*, 203.
[23] *MS Diary*, 175.

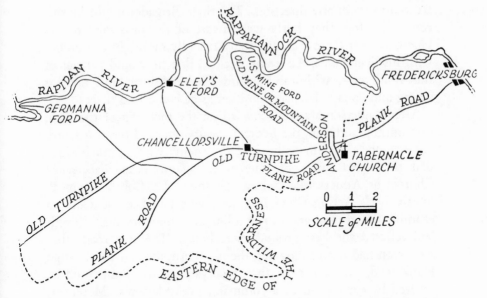

Anderson's Position and the Roads Leading to it in the Vicinity of Tabernacle Church, April 30, 1863—after Hotchkiss and Allan, *Chancellorsville*. The extension of this line, made during the night of April 30–May 1, 1863, appears on the sketch *infra*, page 535.

he be made to exert himself.[24] On the 29th, as directed by Army Headquarters, Anderson had advanced to the crossroads where, in the gloomy tangle of the Wilderness of Spotsylvania, stood the Chancellor House, a large brick structure used often as a tavern.[25] At the crossroads, which bore the pretentious name Chancellorsville, were "Billy" Mahone and Carnot Posey, with the greater part of their two Brigades. These officers had left a guard at United States Ford on the Rappahannock, about four miles North of Chancellorsville, and had themselves withdrawn on receipt of news that the Federals in large numbers were at Germanna and Ely's Fords, higher up the river.[26]

If the Federals had turned to the Southeast after crossing there, they were converging on Chancellorsville. To oppose the Union army, Anderson would not have three of his scattered Brigades until "Rans" Wright overtook him on the morning of the 30th. With that small force it would be foolish and worse to make a stand in that thickly wooded country where a man seldom could

24 Cf. *Sorrel*, 135.   25 *Cooke's Jackson*. 404.
26 *O. R.*. 25. pt. 2, pp. 850, 862, 870.

see 200 yards in any direction. The three Brigades might be surrounded before they fairly were aware of the proximity of the
bluecoats. For these reasons, after a friendly midnight conference
with his lieutenants, Anderson decided that he would get out of
the Wilderness, withdraw toward Fredericksburg and take as
strong and open a defensive position as he could find there.

After Anderson started eastward on the morning of the 30th,
through fog and rain, the Federal cavalry attacked the rearguard,
but Mahone's Virginians beat off the enemy with so much vigor
that the march was not interrupted again. Near Tabernacle
Church, as Anderson withdrew, he found Lt. Col. William P.
Smith, Lee's Acting Chief Engineer, who had been sent out to
examine the ground and to run a line of entrenchments.[27] Smith
had selected the best ground thereabouts. The two roads that
Anderson had been following, the old Turnpike and the Orange
Plank road, were not more than 1300 yards apart. Both could be
covered by even so small a command as Anderson's. Moreover,
with a refused right flank, the Division could guard reasonably
well against a turning movement from the North down the Old
Mine or Mountain Road which ran from United States Mine Ford
and entered the Turnpike at that point.[28] In front was forest, and
on both flanks, but the elevation was sufficient to afford a fair field
of fire.

As soon as Smith ran the line on April 30, Anderson put his
men to work on the field fortifications, a form of shelter the soldiers in front of Richmond had disdained eleven months previously. Now, in appreciation of the protecting works on the ridge
behind Fredericksburg, the troops worked willingly. During the
day of the 30th reports indicated that the Federals were advancing
on both the roads Anderson was covering. Occasionally the Union
horse would show itself and then would turn off. In the afternoon, the Third Virginia Cavalry arrived and, spreading widely,
threw out pickets. Their reconnaissance, which Anderson shared
in person, gave abundant evidence that a mighty force was moving
through the Wilderness toward Anderson's front. What was
Anderson to do? When someone asked him, his answer was as

27 O. R., 25, pt. 1, p. 850.
28 The position is shown in more detail on Map 12, opposite p. 245 of John Bigelow, Jr., The Campaign of Chancellorsville (cited hereafter as Bigelow), the most
detailed of the many accounts of the operations.

firm as brief—"Fight, General Lee says so." [29] To make resistance
the stouter, he kept detachments laboring on the field fortifications
all night. Shortly before sunrise on the 1st, he had the satisfaction
of welcoming Lafayette McLaws, who arrived from Fredericksburg with three of his Brigades.

Wright, Mahone and Posey of Anderson's Division, then, and
Kershaw, Wofford and Semmes of McLaws's—these six Brigades
were on the ground May 1, in a defensible position, which was being strengthened at 8 A.M., the hour of Jackson's arrival. [30] "Old
Jack" had—and could have had—no word of condemnation for
anything that had been done, but as soon as he studied the ground
and got word that the head of his own Corps was approaching
from Fredericksburg, he began in his convinced, staccato manner
to issue his orders.

Stop work on the entrenchments. Pack the tools. Get the
wagons ready. The column was going to advance on the enemy.
Send for Wilcox and Perry, still on the river, to rejoin Anderson
at once. Start Mahone back toward Chancellorsville over the old
turnpike. He knew the roads thoroughly. Give him a battery.
Behind him could move McLaws. When Wilcox and Perry
arrived, see that they co-operated with McLaws. On the Plank
Road, which Posey and Wright had traversed the previous day,
Wright could lead the way. [31] Let the remainder of Alexander's
battalion go with them. When the Second Corps arrived, it must
take the Plank Road behind Anderson. There was room for
maneuver on that flank. The other was too close to the Rappahannock. As soon as dispositions could be made, have the troops
go forward. The Third Virginia Cavalry could reconnoitre ahead
of the vanguard. Nothing was to be gained by standing on
the defensive. Instead of waiting for Hooker to strike, hit
him. [32]

At 11 o'clock, May 1, the Confederate advance began. Jackson
rode with the van and, as always, examined carefully the ground

29 C. Irvine Walker, *General Richard H. Anderson* (cited hereafter as *Irvine Walker*),
133.
30 *O. R.*, 25, pt. 1, pp. 824, 850.
31 This is almost but not entirely certain. Anderson, *ibid.*, 850, mentioned Wright
first, but neither Wright nor Posey referred to the other in reporting this stage of the
advance.
32 The sequence of these orders is, of course, no more than an approximation, but
Anderson's and McLaws's reports are specific enough to make the main facts clear.

ahead. In about fifteen minutes, from the direction of the old turnpike [33] came the challenging pop-pop of picket fire and then the bo-o-om of a few field guns. Evidently McLaws, who was commanding on that road, had encountered the Federals almost as soon as he had set his column in motion. Jackson continued to press forward on the Plank Road and, in a few moments, heard in his own front the dispute of the pickets. The column was halted. Reconnaissance was made. A heavy Federal force was discovered in the act of deploying. While Jackson's outposts were trying to ascertain where the Federals had their flanks and how many lines were forming, word came from McLaws. The Unionists in large numbers, said the Georgian, were advancing on him. Behind them, a mile or more in the Wilderness, many troops could be seen on higher ground. From what he could ascertain, McLaws went on, the better opportunity seemed to be offered for a flank attack from the direction of the Plank Road.[34]

Hooker, then, was ready for a fight on both roads and, if left alone, might attack. Jackson did not intend on this account to surrender the initiative. If McLaws could hold his ground, Jackson would try the effect of Alexander's guns on the Federals who were deploying. Should the artillery be unable to send them back into the Wilderness, Jackson would try to turn their flank and get in their rear.[35] McLaws was so advised. Alexander was told to put into action some of those guns he had carried at a gallop along the sunken road at Fredericksburg in December.[36] Rodes was halted where he was, back on the Plank Road, and was directed to send forward one Brigade to help Anderson.[37]

About the time these orders were given, a courier brought a note in which "Jeb" Stuart announced that he was coming up on the left and that Fitz Lee was still farther West and in position to observe any large troop movement in that quarter. Wrote Stuart: "I will close in on the flank and help all I can when the ball opens. . . . May God grant us victory." Jackson had no time for correspondence but he could not ignore the invocation of Divine blessing or forgo admonition to hem in the enemy. He turned over the sheet from Stuart, wrote out the hour, the date and the

[33] This road, almost abandoned at some points and at others a part of the Orange Plank Road, often was styled the "Old Stone Road" or the "Stone Road" or the "Old Orange Turnpike."
[34] O. R., 25, pt. 1, p. 825.   [35] O. R., 25, pt. 1, p. 825.
[36] O. R., 25, pt. 1, p. 820.   [37] Ibid., 940.

address and said much in fourteen words: "I trust that God wil! grant us a great victory. Keep closed on Chancellorsville." [38]

Having dispatched this note, Jackson saw Lee and his staff approaching. The commanding General had remained at Fredericksburg during the morning and had counselled "Jube" Early, Barksdale and Pendleton in the defense they might be called upon to make with their small force against the Federals on the plain. Now Lee was arriving to see how the battle was developing on the flank where he expected the heavier bolt of the Federals to be hurled. Cordial Jackson always was in greeting his chief; confident as well as cordial he now was. No serious opposition yet had been encountered: if it developed, said he, the ground to the South was favorable for a turning operation. In that direction, past the cheering line of Second Corps veterans, Jackson rode some distance with his senior. Lee had no suggestion to make, either of disposition or of direction, and soon turned around and started for the right to see whether any Federal attack was developing between the Rappahannock and the flank of McLaws. There was a decent road in that quarter. The enemy might be using it to march on Fredericksburg and to establish contact with the troops there. Lee disappeared; Jackson trotted back toward the Plank Road.[39]

Word may have come by this time from the old turnpike that Semmes's Brigade with some help from "Billy" Mahone's men had beaten off the attack, which had been delivered, prisoners said, by Sykes's regulars.[40] Those stout fighters still were in McLaws's front; but a rumor was spreading through the advancing ranks that Hooker was withdrawing from Chancellorsville. A. P. Hill had heard the rumor and had given it credence. Harry Heth, senior Brigadier, who was now fighting his first battle with the Army of Northern Virginia, already had been told by Hill to take three Brigades—his own, Lane's and McGowan's—and to hurry over to the turnpike. Thence Heth was to push straight for Chancellorsville.[41] Doubtless Hill reported this to Jackson,[42] who now

---

[38] 11 *S. H. S. P.*, 137–38.
[39] See 2 *R. E. Lee*, 517, where the sources are cited.
[40] *O. R.*, 25, pt. 1, p. 825, 833, 834.
[41] *Mrs. Daly*, 99–100, in direct quotation of Col. A. C. Haskell.
[42] The only references to the orders from Hill are those of Colonel Haskell and of Heth, *O. R.*, 25, pt. 1, p. 890. It is possible, of course, that Jackson gave Hill instructions to this effect. Without such orders, Hill was inviting another court martial; but the move was of the sort distinctly in keeping with Hill's ambition and impetuosity.

was again on the Plank Road and was urging Anderson's men forward. At 2.30, Jackson bade his brother-in-law, Joseph Morrison, give McLaws similar instructions to advance. Tell him, said Jackson, in effect, that the enemy is falling back and that I am pressing on the Plank Road; McLaws must do the same thing, but he must keep his skirmishers and flanking parties well out; the enemy may ambush him. Obediently Morrison wrote the dispatch and gave the paper to a courier.[43]

Soon, up the Plank Road from the East, came the fine North Carolina Brigade that had been George B. Anderson's and now was under its new Brigadier, S. Dodson Ramseur. This was the Brigade which Rodes was sending on Jackson's order, and it promptly was put in advance. "Rans" Wright was to South of Ramseur; northward was Carnot Posey, with the Mississippi Brigade, formerly the charge of W. S. Featherston. Between Posey and the left of McLaws, on the turnpike, there was no liaison.[44] Jackson rode with the center Brigade, which was accompanied by Alexander's guns. Ramseur was still farther in front, and personally was directing his skirmishers,[45] who soon were more heavily engaged than any Brigade had been that day.[46] Whenever the advance reached a point where the enemy might have set an ambush or formed an invisible line, Jackson would have the artillery "feel" the woods. Always his word to the regimental commander was the same, "Press them, Colonel."[47]

As the enemy appeared now to be at a stand, Anderson did not wait for Jackson to order the Federal flank turned. In midafternoon,[48] the division commander directed Wright's Brigade to sideslip to the left until it reached the unfinished railroad. Then the Georgians were to march westward along the right of way and were to get beyond the Federal right.[49] This was done swiftly and successfully. Without attempting to halt Wright, the Federals began to give ground again and more rapidly. The Confederate

---

[43] *O. R.*, 25, pt. 2, p. 764.

[44] Semmes probably was at this time still the left flank element of McLaws. Later, Kershaw came up in support of Semmes. In Kershaw's report there is no reference to any troops immediately on his left. *O. R.*, 25, pt. 1, pp. 830, 833, 871.

[45] *O. R.*, 25, pt. 1, p. 940.   [46] *Hotchkiss' MS Diary*, 175.

[47] *Grimes*, 28.   [48] *O. R.*, 25, pt. 1, p. 850.

[49] Anderson in his report, *O. R.*, 25, pt. 1, p. 850, stated that Wright "was directed" to make this move. By whom Wright was "directed," the report did not say, but as Anderson was most modest, this language almost certainly meant that he ordered Wright's advance without reference to Jackson. In Lee's report, *ibid.*, 797, the wording is: "General Wright, by direction of General Anderson, diverging to the left," etc.

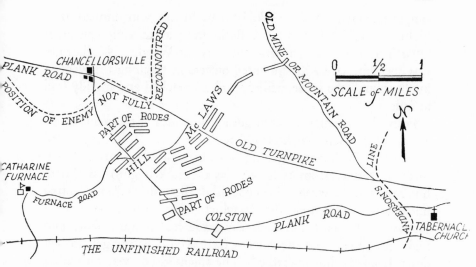

Jackson's Advance on the Afternoon of May 2, 1863—after John Bigelow's *Campaign of Chancellorsville*

advance was resumed on both roads.[50] It was now about 4 P.M.[51]

For a time, Jackson continued to watch the shrewd skirmishing of the North Carolinians on the Plank Road, and then he decided to see how "Rans" Wright was progressing and what the nature of the ground was to the left front. With a single aide,[52] he rode quickly to the vicinity of an iron furnace, properly called Wellford's but more often styled the Catharine Furnace, about a mile and three quarters South and slightly West of Chancellorsville.[53]

Near the furnace Jackson found "Jeb" Stuart with the First Virginia Cavalry and some of the horse artillery. Wright had arrived by that time and already was deploying to sweep a woodland to the northward. Jackson left to Wright what seemed to be a

---

[50] *O. R.*, 25, pt. 1, p. 850.   [51] *Cf.* McLaws in *ibid.*, 825.

[52] All the circumstances and the impersonal references in 1 *Land We Love*, 180, would indicate that this officer was Lieut. J. G. Morrison.

[53] Dr. Robert Welford, who came to America as a surgeon with the British during the Revolution and later settled in Fredericksburg, for personal reasons changed the spelling of the family name to Wellford. He married the widow Catharine Thornton, *née* Yates, and by 1820, perhaps before that time, was operating the iron furnace in the Wilderness, where he had bought large tracts of land. His son John Spotswood Wellford, and then a younger son, Col. Charles C. Wellford, later managed the furnace. In 1863, Colonel Wellford, whose home at Fredericksburg had been ruined the previous December, was refugeeing at the Catharine Furnace, which always was spelt with the "a" and not the "e." Colonel Wellford's son, Charles B. Wellford, not old enough at that time for military service, is the "young Wellford" mentioned as a guide. For this information, the writer is much indebted to his friend, Dr. B. Randolph Wellford. Jr.

simple maneuver, and he asked Stuart to ride with him to some higher ground whither, also, Beckham was moving several of Stuart's guns in order to clear the way for Wright. No difficulty was encountered by the mounted officers in reaching the wooded knoll, though the horse artillery had a wretched and muddy trail to follow.

From the elevation Jackson got a vague idea of the roads to the West. More than that he could not ascertain for the unpleasant reason that Beckham's opening salvo brought a furious and well directed answer from two batteries of masked guns. Beckham hung on, but, he wrote, "I do not think that men have been often under a hotter fire than that to which we were here exposed." [54] Jackson and Stuart and their cavalcade had to turn about and make for safety. All the riders except Maj. Channing Price got down from the hill unscathed. The splendid boy was hit with a bit of shell but proudly refused to think the hurt serious. No bone was broken, he asserted cheerfully. With fine pluck he kept his seat till the little company was out of range and then, with scarcely a sound, he fainted and dropped from his saddle. He was carried to the rear by some of the staff officers, while Jackson waited solicitously. Examination at the nearest farm house showed that the iron had severed an artery and that the Major had lost much blood. [55]

Stuart and Wright remained to watch the enemy, whose artillery fire was beginning to fall away; Jackson went back to the Plank Road where he met A. P. Hill and, no doubt, "Dick" Anderson. They told him regretfully that the advance had been halted again on that road in the face of what appeared to be a stubborn stand by the enemy. Everything indicated that Hooker was in great strength around Chancellorsville. Report of this Jackson dispatched immediately to Lee, who still was far on the right; [56] and then Jackson bade Hill ride with him to the turnpike, whence was rolling the sound of a brisk skirmish and a light artillery exchange.

On the turnpike, Jackson learned that McLaws was halted to the rear. About half a mile in front of McLaws was Harry Heth with the three Brigades that Powell Hill had sent to that road at

[54] O. R., 25, pt. 1, p. 1049.
[55] 1 Land We Love, 180; 2 von Borcke, 219-21.
[56] Cf. 34 S. H. S. P., 16.

the time the rumor of Hooker's withdrawal from Chancellorsville had spread. Heth had taken seriously his orders to press on
to Chancellorsville. As a newcomer, he had been determined not
to be found wanting in dash. When he had ascertained that he
was in front of McLaws, and was facing determined resistance,
Heth had sent to inquire whether the Georgian would support
him in attacking. McLaws had no words for such nonsense at
that time of day. All he did was to turn to one of his staff officers
and say, "Order my Division to halt here and bivouac for the
night."

Even in the face of that implied rebuke, Heth had not abandoned his mission. He must show Hill that he could and would
obey orders. McLaws or no McLaws, support or no support, he
would go on to Chancellorsville. Fortunately, Capt. Alex. Haskell,
quick witted as always, had said: "General Heth, let me go forward with two regiments. If the enemy have gone, we can sweep
through as your advance guard; and if they are there, the rest of
your command will be saved for the general fight." Heth had consented; Haskell had thrown forward two famous regiments, Orr's
Rifles and McGowan's old command, the Fourteenth South Carolina. A blasting fire had greeted them. The men had dashed
forward to the edge of the next wood, had re-formed their line,
and had begun to skirmish. Haskell had ridden a bit to the right
where there was a rise of ground.

This was the situation when Jackson and Hill and their staff
officers and couriers rode up. Haskell turned his horse and came
to meet them. Said Jackson quietly, "Captain Haskell, what is it?"

"Ride up here, General," said the South Carolinian, "and you
will see it all."

Jackson rode up, took out his field glasses and looked westward.
There, ahead of him, by happy chance was a vista to open ground
where, plainly visible, were three lines of battle and crude but
strong earthworks. McLaws had reported before noon that
Hooker occupied a strong position. Here was the proof of it.
Would Hooker stay there? Jackson did not believe so.[57]

Presently "Old Jack" lowered his glass and lifted his reins

[57] This statement of Jackson's opinion that Hooker would withdraw during the night
is based on the testimony of Col. Charles Marshall, who was present at the conference
of Lee and Jackson about 7 o'clock. See *infra* and Fitz Lee's *Chancellorsville, loc. cit.,*
315; *cf.* T. M. R. Talcott, General Lee's Strategy at the Battle of Chancellorsville, 34
S. H. S. P. (cited hereafter as *Talcott*), 13.

from the little sorrel's neck. "Hold this ground until 9 o'clock tonight," he said to Haskell, "when you will be relieved." [58] Then, he leaned over and—to the lasting pride of the young soldier— whispered the sign and countersign for the night: "Challenge, Liberty; reply, Independence." It was something for a young soldier not yet 24 to receive that confidence from the corps commander, the mysterious "Stonewall" himself!

Back to Heth's line and across to the Plank Road by the road that ran on to the Catharine Furnace, Jackson galloped. Near the junction of the Plank and Furnace Roads, Jackson halted and there, before darkness fell, he saluted General Lee, who rode up to investigate the report that Hooker had been brought to bay. With few words, the Confederate chieftains went back into the woods in order to get out of range of a Federal sharpshooter who could not be driven from his perch.[59]

Among the pines, Lee sat on a fallen log and asked Jackson to take a place beside him. What, Jackson was asked, had he found on the left? Briefly the corps commander told of Wright's attack near the Catharine Furnace and of the strength the Federals had displayed there. To this, Jackson attached no more than passing importance. He went on to describe how easily the Federals had been driven back into the Wilderness. They were making a feint, he insisted, or else in some unexplained manner, they had failed in their advance. "By tomorrow," he said, substantially, "there will not be any of them this side of the river." [60]

A polite shake of the head met this observation. It was plain that the commanding General did not agree. Lee expressed the hope that Jackson's prediction would prove correct; but, Lee went on, he believed Hooker's main effort was to be on that flank. What they were witnessing on the fringe of the Wilderness was no feint. Hooker had planned to give battle here and would not abandon the attempt so lightly.

Jackson hung to his own theory and maintained that the Federals would retreat during the night. The answer was that if the Unionists deceived him and remained in position the next day, they must be attacked. Where could that be done successfully?

[58] Colonel Haskell thought, when he wrote his narrative, that Jackson said he would be relieved by Fitzhugh Lee, but in this his memory played him a trick. Fitz Lee was far to the South and West. Heth remained where he was until morning, unrelieved. *O. R.*, 25, pt. 1, p. 890. This stirring episode, here paraphrased from Colonel Haskell's account, is given at length by Mrs. Daly, *op. cit.*, 99–101.
[59] *Talcott*, 17.   [60] Marshall as cited *supra*, n. 57.

Lee s reconnaissance on the right had convinced him that an effective blow could not be delivered between the old turnpike and the Rappahannock. The Wilderness was too thick. Was the situation immediately in front of the Confederate line equally discouraging? Apparently it was; but before the possibility was discarded, a careful reconnaissance ought to be made. Major Talcott was at hand and would act for Lee. Would Jackson name someone? Jackson chose the faithful and discerning Boswell. In a few minutes, the two engineers left the clump of trees and slipped forward. The moon so "filled the heavens with light," [61] that observation was easy. Talcott to the end of his life remembered the whole scene, even the appearance of a dead Confederate picket whose face was upturned.[62]

Lee made no motion to end the conference, or to defer discussion till the engineers returned. With Jackson, he canvassed the alternative that was shaping itself by elimination: If an attack on the Confederate right were ruled out, and his reconnaissance on the center revealed no opening, what could be done on the left? Beyond the Catharine Furnace where Wright and Beckham had fought, what were the prospects? Where was the Federal right? How securely was it anchored? Jackson knew only that from the hill where he had faced the hot artillery fire, roads stretched westward, and, presumably, northward. The maps, though not detailed, indicated that there were byways in that part of the Wilderness.[63] Were they adequate, and were they hidden from the eyes of the enemy?

"Jeb" Stuart rode up soon and jubilantly announced that Fitz Lee had been reconnoitring to the West and had satisfied himself that the Federal right was "in the air." That news gave more importance than ever to the location of a route that extended beyond Hooker's exposed flank. It must be a concealed route, but it should not be over-long, if the infantry were to cover it in time to give battle the next day. Nor need the roads be distant. They could, in fact, if covered, be near. Hooker most obligingly had given the Confederates that boon, because he had sent off virtually the whole of his cavalry on a raid to the southward. He had

61 *Caldwell*, 72.   62 *Talcott*, 17.
63 Colonel Talcott, usually accurate, undoubtedly was mistaken in saying, *loc. cit.*, 6, that Campbell's map of part of Spotsylvania, figured in *O. R. Atlas*, Plate XVI, was available to Lee and to Jackson at the time of this conference. The map included a full presentation of the works at Chancellorsville, Confederate and Union—proof positive that it appeared after the battle.

shown little cavalry in front of Stuart and he might have few squadrons elsewhere on the line to watch Confederate movements. A turning operation that would roll up his right seemed entirely practicable, if the Confederates could find any decent, adjacent roads out of sight of Federal mounted officers and infantry. Was there such a route? The tireless and resourceful Stuart said he would ascertain and, mounting quickly, he rode back toward the furnace through the moonlight.[64]

Jackson pondered the problem with the disciplined mind of a loyal lieutenant. He was as convinced as ever that Hooker would retreat during the night, but he did not on that account withhold for a moment his full co-operation. If Lee believed that the Federals would remain in the Wilderness and that the best way to attack them would be to turn their right, Jackson was ready.

Within an hour or two he found the probability of such a move developed to another stage. Talcott and Boswell came back from their reconnaissance and were of one mind: The Federal line in the Wilderness was too strong to be assailed. It was being fortified steadily; it was located where little artillery could be brought to bear on it. The whole country in front of the Confederates was a maze of mixed timber of all heights. Much of the "original growth" had been felled years before for charcoal and had been replaced with stubborn young hardwood. A Wilderness in truth that terrain was! [65]

From the chain of thought this report suggested, Jackson was recalled by Lee's voice. With his face still over the map, Lee was saying, "How can we get at those people?"

The corps commander did not argue again that "those people" would not be there in the morning. Nor did he assume that Lee was asking advice. Jackson knew that Lee often asked just such a question when he really was addressing it to himself. The answer then, was as loyal as it was understanding. "You know best," said Jackson, in effect; "show me what to do, and we will try to do it." [66]

[64] Marshall in *Talcott*, 13; Fitz Lee's *Chancellorsville, loc. cit.*, 315.

[65] *Talcott*, 16; cf. *supra*, p. 320.

[66] *Talcott*, 16. This important bit of conversation in the disputed account of what happened at the bivouac was overheard by Talcott and was narrated by him to A. L. Long, prior to 1886. Cf. *Long*, 254. Colonel Talcott never changed his version of this episode beyond saying (*Talcott*, 18) that he "may have been mistaken" in saying that Lee asked the question and Jackson made the reply *after* the two engineers returned

Lee's was the responsibility, Lee's the decision. On the map, in a few moments, he traced the approximate direction of an advance that should put the Confederates beyond the right flank and in rear of Hooker. Then Jackson had the pleasure of hearing Lee entrust the ascertainment of the exact line of march and the execution of the operation to him. "General Stuart will cover your movement with his cavalry," Lee added.

Designation of himself for this mission brought a smile to Jackson's face. Lee doubtless never had any other idea than that of committing the operation to Jackson but until that moment, he had not said so. Now the task and all the tactical arrangement were Jackson's. He rose quickly and saluted: "My troops will move at 4 o'clock." [67]

Lee bowed acknowledgment. He concluded, in effect: If you are in any doubt tomorrow morning whether the enemy still is in position, you can send a couple of guns to the point where Stuart's horse artillery was engaged last night; that will settle the question.

At so late an hour [68] Jackson did not dispatch orders to his troops to prepare for the march of the morrow. Perhaps he withheld orders for the reason that already he was planning to make a bold proposal to Lee in the morning.[69] Quietly, then, Jackson went back a little farther into the woods, and spread out his saddle blanket on the ground. Then he unbuckled his sword and placed it upright against a tree, and prepared to lie down. "Sandie"

from their reconnaissance. If the exchange occurred *before* the examination of the ground, said Talcott, what he heard on his return was "to some extent a repetition of what had been previously discussed in the presence of Colonel Marshall." The sequence of events in the conference on the night of May 1–2 is reviewed in Appendix II–5, of 2 *R. E. Lee*, 584 ff.

[67] *Talcott*, 16–17.

[68] The exact time is not determinable. Smith in 3 *B. & L.*, 204, stated inferentially that it was before midnight.

[69] On this point, the writer is compelled to dissent in part from the opinion that seems to have been expressed by his venerable friend of earlier days, Col. T. M. R. Talcott. That writer, *op. cit.*, 8, maintained that marching orders were given to "the Second Corps" before the conference between Lee and Jackson on the morning of May 2. If the implication of this is that orders were given on the night of May 1, after the designation of Jackson to make the march around Hooker's right, there is no evidence to confirm the statement. Rodes evidently was astir early on the morning of the 2d. He relieved Ramseur, who had been all night in an exposed position, and he prepared his other troops for the road. Significantly, all the Confederate officers whom Colonel Talcott quoted concerning a forward movement prior to 8 A.M. on the 2d were men of Rodes's Division. It is entirely probable that Jackson himself sent word early that morning that Rodes's Division was to continue in advance, but Rodes himself stated explicitly that "about 8 o'clock, the route was resumed" (*O. R.*, 25, pt. 1, p. 940) and he described the first stage of his march in a manner to make clear the fact that the start was from his bivouac of the night of the 1st.

Pendleton observed at once that in the preoccupation of the day, Jackson had not thought to bring with him any extra garment to protect him from the chill of the night. Immediately the boy proffered the General his overcoat. Jackson thanked Pendleton but would not deprive him of it. In full knowledge that his chief's politest "No" was final, "Sandie" did not persist. He unfastened the long cape of the overcoat and asked the General to take that. Jackson gratefully acquiesced in this division of the covering and stretched himself out.[70]

Staff officers and couriers came and went. Around nearby camp-fires was slow conversation and now and again a laugh, but the mournful whip-po'-wills in the thickets almost drowned the voices. Moonlight outshone the flickering fire and gave sleeping soldiers a strange look . . . as if they were dead already. What mattered ghastly faces? Tomorrow would bring Jackson as great an opportunity as ever Winchester had offered . . . or Port Republic . . . or Groveton or . . .

[70] This incident has been developed into a myth. Dabney, *op. cit.*, 675, stated that Jackson reluctantly accepted the cape, kept it over him until "Sandie" was asleep and then quietly arose and replaced it over the boy. Long, *op. cit.*, 258, saw Jackson take the cover, when he rose before daylight, and place it over the sleeping form of a "staff officer," who he thought was Gen. W. N. Pendleton. Actually it was the son and not the father Pendleton, and was the young man's cape, not Jackson's overcoat.

CHAPTER XXXII

"You Can Go Forward Then"

THE CHILL of the damp earth and the scantiness of his cover caused Jackson to awaken before daylight on the 2nd of May. He was shivering and felt the first symptoms of a bad cold; but he did not think he should keep "Sandie" Pendleton's cape any longer. He walked over to the sleeping place of the young officer and laid the garment carefully on the silent form.[1] Then Jackson went to a little fire a waiting courier had kept alive. With his rubber coat around him the General sat on a cracker box the Federals had left there. Over the fire he bent as if he were hungry for heat. Hand outstretched, he gazed into the feeble flames.

Presently another figure stirred among the silent men on the ground. Tucker Lacy, the chaplain, came to the fire. He had arrived during the night, after Jackson had gone to sleep, and he had told General Lee what he knew about the roads of the district, in which his family had large holdings of land. Jackson greeted him now and invited him to share his seat. Lacy thanked him but remained standing. Jackson looked up and saw that Lacy did not wish to crowd him. Quickly the General slipped toward one end of the box. "Come," he insisted, "sit down; I wish to talk to you."

Was there, Jackson asked when Lacy took a seat by him, any road by which either flank of the enemy could be turned?

On the Confederate right, Lacy answered, there was none; but on the left, a succession of roads, good and bad, led around to the old turnpike West of Chancellorsville.

From his pocket Jackson drew a rough map of the area. Into Lacy's hand he put a pencil. "Take this map," he said, "and mark it down for me."

Lacy sketched the road, but Jackson was not satisfied. "That is too near. It goes within the line of the enemy's pickets. I wish to get around *well* to his rear, without being observed; do you know of no other road?"

[1] *Dabney,* 675; *Cooke's Jackson.* 411.

543

No, Lacy replied, he did not, but West of the road with which he was familiar there must be some trail from the Catharine Furnace that would lead into the Plank Road.

"Then," asked Jackson eagerly, "where can you find this out certainly?"

The proprietor of the Catharine Furnace, Col. Charles C. Wellford, doubtless would know; he had a young son, Charles, who would make an excellent guide.

This fired Jackson. He woke up Jed. Hotchkiss and explained to the topographical engineer what he wanted—a concealed route, not too long, from the Catharine Furnace to the Plank Road West of the point where the Federal right was "in the air." Hotchkiss and Lacy were to find out from Mr. Wellford at the furnace whether such a route existed, and if so, what its length was and whether it was practicable for artillery. Hotchkiss would bring back this information as soon as it was established. Lacy must go on and find the guide and return with him.[2]

Hotchkiss and the chaplain got their horses and rode down the Furnace Road to consult Mr. Wellford. On the cracker box, over the fire, Jackson crouched alone until Colonel Armistead Long arose and joined him. Polite greetings were exchanged, but Jackson was too busy in mind and too uncomfortable in body to indulge in much conversation. At length the General did find words to complain of the cold; whereupon Colonel Long walked off and, after some minutes, came back with a steaming tin cup in his hands. The cooks, he explained, were beginning to prepare their breakfast, and from them he had procured a cup of coffee: Would Jackson have it? Gratefully the General accepted the comforting draft and began to sip it. Presently, in the silence, there was a momentary sharp clatter. Both looked in the direction of the sound. It was from Jackson's sword, which in some manner had slipped from its place against a tree and had fallen to the ground. Colonel Long was not superstitious but after he went over, picked up the weapon and brought it to Jackson, he reflected

[2] *Dabney*, 675–76; *Hotchkiss' MS Diary*, 175, 177. Colonel Talcott, *op. cit.*, 6, was mistaken in his criticism of Hotchkiss, because the Colonel wrongly assumed, as already noted, that Campbell's map of Spotsylvania was available to Jackson. It is probable that the map used by Jackson was the one incorporated into the map of April, 1864, which covered the area East of the Blue Ridge and South of the Rappahannock. If this were the case, the map did not show much detail of the country around Chancellorsville Jackson needed on May 2 all the supplementary details he could procure.

that this was ill omen. The sword of Jackson fallen to the ground in the night—what did that portend? Jackson himself asked no question and made no comment. He merely thanked Long and buckled on the blade.[3]

The flame was dimming; day was breaking; it gave promise of warmth and pleasantness.[4] Soon to Jackson's side came the commanding General. Refreshed and alert—always at his vigorous best in the early morning—Lee sat down by his lieutenant. Jackson did not have to repeat to his chief what Lacy had said about the roads, because Lacy had reported to Lee after "Stonewall" had gone to sleep;[5] but Jackson doubtless told of dispatching Hotchkiss and the chaplain to the furnace. The conclusion already reached by the two Generals was that the flank of Hooker must be turned. What now was to be decided was whether a march to the Federal right was practicable within the time that Hooker might be expected to remain on the defensive in the Wilderness.

Jackson had determined what he would propose in order to increase the prospect of success in a furious offensive that would hurl one Federal wing back on Chancellorsville and the fords of the Rappahannock. Of the nature of his bold proposal, Jackson said nothing. Everything was contingent on the report Hotchkiss would make on the roads. For that report, Jackson had not long to wait. Up the road from the furnace, Hotchkiss soon rode, and with good news. Mr. Wellford said there *was* a way! Hotchkiss had made a sketch and, if the Generals desired, he would show the route to them. He was asked to do so. Quickly he picked up another of the cracker boxes the Federals had left behind, and he placed it between Lee and Jackson. On it he spread the map, across which, with his usual clarity of description, he traced the route that Mr. Wellford recommended: From Catharine Furnace, you follow the Furnace Road South and Southwest till you come to the Brock Road, which runs North. You do not turn North into the Brock Road where you first strike it, because, if you do, you may be within sight of the enemy. Instead of taking that risk, you move South for about 600 yards, and then you make a sharp right turn and go back North again

[3] Long, 258.
[5] 2 R. E. Lee. 527.
[4] Hotchkiss' MS Diary, 181.

past the Trigg and the Stevens houses. You keep on parallel to the Brock Road until you get close to the place of a free Negro named Cook. There you get back into the Brock Road which you follow to the Orange Plank Road.[6] The route was not particularly bad, even for artillery, nor was the march long—estimated at 11 or 12 miles.[7] Most of the way, the road was concealed from the positions the enemy was supposed to occupy.

Always, in listening to Hotchkiss' explanations of routes, Jackson hung on every word and interrupted often if he did not understand. This time, all intent, he absorbed the information as Hotchkiss went over it. Lee, as an old engineer, grasped the whole of it instantly.

When Hotchkiss had finished, there was a moment of silence. Lee looked at Jackson, whose head probably was still bent over the map. "General Jackson," said Lee quietly, "what do you propose to do?"

The question was superfluous, of course, in view of the previous understanding, but it was polite. Jackson put his forefinger on the map and followed the line that Hotchkiss had traced with his pencil. "Go around here," Jackson answered.

"What do you propose to make this movement with?"

Undramatic the question was, and spoken in a conversational tone, but it presented on the instant a supreme test of both Generals. If Jackson asked for little he could do little, but if he asked for much, would he be fair to Lee? The answer had to be in terms of opportunities, not of sensibilities. Hooker's Army must be overwhelmed, hurled back to United States Ford, destroyed. Sufficient force to do this must be provided. So, without hesitation or preliminary, Jackson gave the answer he probably had been fashioning for hours. With what did he propose to make the movement?—"With my whole Corps."

With Rodes's, Jackson's old Division and A. P. Hill's; with every Division except Early's, which was at Fredericksburg? Must Jackson have all these men, fifteen Brigades, 28,000 bayonets? "What will you leave me?" the commanding General asked.

Without so much as an apologetic inflection to acknowledge

[6] The clearest large scale map is the one in the back of Hotchkiss and Allan's *Chancellorsville* that shows the operations of May 2, 1863.
[7] Actually, on Hotchkiss' map, from the bivouac of Lee and Jackson to the junction of the Brock and Plank Roads, the distance in 1863 was a fraction more than 9 miles.

that he was putting upon Lee the burden of facing perhaps 50,000 men with 14,000, Jackson replied, "The Divisions of Anderson and McLaws."

Why not? Lee had not forgotten that Jackson had started one flank march at Jeffersonton, the previous August, and had found his way, swiftly and surely, to the rear of Pope. In September, had not Jackson left Frederick with just such a column as he now wished to put on the road, and had not the reward been 11,000 prisoners at Harpers Ferry and more than seventy guns? Second Manassas, Harpers Ferry, Chancellorsville—retreat, sur·render, destruction—might not that be the ascending order of Jackson's achievements? [8] "Well," said Lee calmly, "go on," and he took pencil and paper to make notes for the orders he would issue.

Jackson then must have explained where his Divisions were, and how he proposed to place Rodes in the van and to follow with Trimble's Division and with Hill's. All his artillery would go with him. Stuart, he understood, was to cover the advance with Munford's Second Virginia Cavalry, and was to screen the column from the eyes of inquisitive Federal outposts. For all of this, Jackson had the instant approval of Lee.

Quickly, when Lee had assented, Jackson left the bivouac to prepare for the advance of the Corps. Already the blue of his eyes was beginning to burn, the line of his thin lips was sterner, his words were clipped. As he rode past the waiting Brigade of McGowan, the veterans who had fought that Homeric battle on his left at Groveton rose to cheer him, but they read "battle in his haste and stern looks" and merely gazed and wondered what he planned now.[9] Although he made his dispositions as rapidly as he could, much time was consumed in getting even the well disciplined men of Rodes's Division to cook and eat their breakfast and to move out to the road.

In advance was to be the Brigade of Colquitt,[10] which had watched from South Mountain in September the Federal campfires that had stretched mile on mile to the eastward. After Rodes's Division was to march Colston, with Trimble's Division, which had been Jackson's own. Powell Hill was to close

---

[8] For the conflict of testimony over this conference between Jackson and Lee, see 2 *R. E. Lee*, Appendix II–5, and text p. 522 ff.

[9] *Caldwell*, 74.   [10] *O. R.*, 25, pt. 1, p. 975.

the rear. A long, long column it would be, with its artillery, its ambulances and its wagons, on those narrow trails through the Wilderness.

It was about 8 o'clock when the head of the column crossed the Plank Road on the way down the Furnace Road toward Wellford's.[11] If this slow start irked Jackson, none of those who observed him that spring morning left any known record of the fact. He was alert but not impatient. Soon after the Second Virginia Cavalry had disappeared down the Furnace Road and Colquitt's Georgians had started after them, Jackson on his way to the front came back to the crossroads near the bivouac. There he saw again the commanding General. Few words Jackson had, because all was in order, and those few he uttered tersely. His sole gesture, wholly characteristic, was to point ahead. Lee nodded; Jackson rode on.[12] Under the brim of his cap, his eyes were shining fiercely now. When he spoke, it was swiftly "as though all were distinctly formed in his mind and beyond all question." [13]

Jackson did not force the march to the limit of the soldiers' strength, but he doubtless sought to keep the column at his standard—a mile in twenty-five minutes with ten minutes' rest every two miles.[14] Fortunately, the dirt roads were "just wet enough to be easy to the feet and free from dust." [15] As usual, Jackson placed the artillery, the ambulances and the ammunition wagons of each Division immediately behind the infantry; but even the heaviest of these vehicles did not make the road difficult for the troops that followed. The only discomfort that developed as the sun rose higher was lack of water. Few streams or farm wells were passed.[16]

The first danger point on the march was where the road crossed an elevation on the nearer side of Lewis's Creek close to

---

[11] The timing of Jackson's "flank march" has been neglected by some writers on the Chancellorsville campaign. Alexander, *op. cit.*, 330, remarked that the head of the column passed Lee "two hours after sunrise" but that manifestly was not intended to be exact nor, at the late date of Alexander's writing, could his statement be accepted as that of a prime authority. Nearly all the officers of Rodes's Division who specified any hour for their advance stated only that it began "early in the morning." Rodes, O. R., 25, pt. 1, p. 940, said that "about 8 o'clock, the route was resumed." As he was in charge of the leading Division, his timing may be accepted. Archer's Brigade, which was next to the last Brigade (Thomas's) on the march, did not start until 11 o'clock. Cf. O. R., 25, pt. 1, p. 924.
[12] *Alexander*, 333.
[13] J. P. Smith, an eyewitness, in 3 *B. & L.*, 205.
[14] Cf. O. R., 25, pt. 2, p. 719. For the uncertainties of his halts, see *infra*, p. 552.
[15] *Caldwell*, 76.   [16] *Ibid.*

the furnace. Both to the North and to the South of the road, as it crossed the hill that led down to the stream, the ground was open. Not long after the van had started the descent to the furnace, a shell from the direction of the Plank Road made an inquisitive flight over the heads of the Confederates. Another followed,

The Crossing of Lewis's Creek near the Catharine Furnace—after N. Michler

and another. A section of artillery, at the least, was being used against the column which, to his credit, some Federal officer had seen promptly.[17] As the fire continued, Jackson directed that when the troops reached the open space, they should double-quick. He had examination made, also, of the terrain to the South of him to ascertain whether there was a road by which the wagon train of the Corps could make a detour and escape a pounding on the exposed stretch. Reconnaissance showed just such a road,

[17] O. R., 25, pt. 1, pp. 386, 408, 443. The guns were those of Battery B, 1st N. J. Arty., at a range of about 1600 yards.

which came back into the route of the infantry about a mile and a half South of the furnace.[18] Orders were sent to the rear for the wagon train to follow the farther and safe route. The infantry and the combat train continued to make the best time they could over the eminence near Lewis's Creek. Happily, for the time, there was no increase in the volume of fire; but Jackson did not overlook the possibility that a Federal column might descend from the Plank Road through the woods to the furnace in order to ascertain the meaning of his movement. As soon as Colquitt's leading Brigade reached the furnace, Jackson directed Rodes to detach a regiment and order it to guard a trail from the North that entered the Furnace Road there.[19]

Past the furnace and thence southwestward through the farms of the numerous Lewises, Jackson rode with the van. All was going well. The men were thirstier than ever as the day grew warmer,[20] but they were in high spirits and had the zest of a great adventure. Their chaffing of young staff officers was as vigorous as on a leisured march—"Here's one of Old Jack's little boys, let him by,"—"Have a good breakfast this morning, sonny?"— "Better hurry up, or you'll catch it for getting behind!"[21] Neither the steadiness of the march nor the absence of any new threat of attack led Jackson to relax. His continuing exhortation was, "Press forward, press forward," or "See that the column is kept closed," or "Permit no straggling," or, terser still, "Press on, press on!"[22]

Only one circumstance showed, as the morning passed, that Jackson was satisfied with the advance: he talked somewhat freely and of other subjects than the closing of the column. For a time, he rode with Rodes and with Tom Munford, Colonel of

---

[18] This byway left the Furnace Road opposite the Brick House and ran southward slightly over one mile. Then it entered a road that ran Southwest from Aldrich's on the Plank Road to the Furnace Road, beyond the creek, at a point North of B. Lewis's house. On the Hotchkiss-Allan Chancellorsville map of May 2, this route is marked. Colonel Bigelow was misled by 5 *M. H. S. M.*, 371, into saying, *op. cit.*, 274, that the "regimental and main trains went by roads further to the South directed upon Todd's Tavern."

[19] *O. R.*, 25, pt. 1, p. 940.   [20] *O. R.*, 25, pt. 1, p. 992.

[21] 3 *B. & L.*, 205–06.

[22] Dr. Hunter McGuire, "Stonewall Jackson, an Address," etc. in McGuire and Christian, *The Confederate Cause and Conduct in the War between the States.* In this volume, also, is a reprint of Dr. McGuire's "Account of the Wounding and Death of Stonewall Jackson," which appeared originally in the *Richmond Medical Journal*, May, 1866. These two papers, which continue the pagination of the volume to which they are appended, will be cited hereafter as *McGuire.*

the Second Virginia Cavalry. As these officers wound their way through the woods, General Colston came up and reported that all was easy in Trimble's Division. Jackson remarked that all three of his companions had been associated with the Virginia Military Institute when he came there—Rodes and Colston as assistant professors and Munford as cadet adjutant.[23] As the conversation turned to V.M.I., one or another of the four began to name some of the numerous graduates of the school who then were with that very column—Stapleton Crutchfield, Chief of Artillery of the Second Corps, Henry Whiting, Rodes's A.A.G., who had been Munford's classmate, "Jim" Lane of the class of '54, Lindsay Walker, '45, who was Hill's Chief of Artillery, and field officers half a score.[24] These references lodged in Jackson's mind, though the conversation shifted again to the Federals and their reported great strength. Jackson remarked in his quiet, half-muffled voice: "I hear it said that General Hooker has more men than he can handle. I should like to have half as many more as I have today, and I should hurl him in the river! The trouble with us has always been to have a reserve to throw in at the critical moment to reap the benefit of advantages gained. We have always had to put in all our troops and never had enough at the time most needed."[25]

Noon came and passed but brought no word, so far as the record shows, that any part of the long column was in danger of attack.[26] By 1 P.M., after the men had eaten and had rested

[23] There was no apparent sensitiveness on Jackson's part or on Rodes's that Rodes had been an applicant for the professorship awarded Jackson and that, on account of non-promotion, Rodes had left V.M.I., which, a few months before the outbreak of the war, recalled him as Professor of Mechanics.

[24] General Munford's MS memorandum on this incident is in the *Munford MSS;* Col. Couper in his *One Hundred Years at V.M.I.,* 2, 171 ff cited a Munford letter to the same effect and listed, in an inspiring note, the V.M.I. men distinguished at Chancellorsville.

[25] Memo. of Gen. T. T. Munford in the *Munford MSS.* The MS is undated and, from the handwriting, was prepared many years after the war; but the observation was one that Munford would have been likely to remember, and as it is phrased in words that have the flavor of Jackson's speech, the quotation marks are believed to be warranted, with the reservation that these may not be *ipsissima verba.*

[26] It has been assumed by early writers, and was accepted by this writer in 2 *R. E. Lee,* 528, that Jackson countermarched Archer and Thomas, in the early afternoon, to repulse the attack on Hill's wagon train; but a review of all the evidence seems to vindicate the statement of Archer, *O. R.,* 25, pt. 1, p. 924, that he turned back to protect the trains on his own responsibility and without communicating even with Hill, much less with Jackson. If Bigelow, *op. cit.,* 282, was correct in fixing 2 P.M. as the hour that Archer started back toward the furnace, Jackson scarcely could have learned of the detachment from his rear until almost the time he began deployment on the old Turn-pike.

briefly,[27] the advance became more exciting. Not far ahead was the Orange Plank Road: Was it guarded? The Second Virginia Cavalry had turned eastward into that road. Did the enemy's flank rest there? Would battle be joined at that point?

Down the Brock Road toward the head of the column came presently a bearded officer on a galloping horse—Fitz Lee. Past the guards of his own Second Cavalry, Fitz hurried on till he met Jackson. "General," young Lee began as soon as he had privately the ear of the corps commander, "if you will ride with me, halting your columns here, out of sight, I will show you the enemy's right, and you will perceive the great advantage of attacking down the old turnpike, instead of the Plank Road, the enemy's lines being taken in reverse. Bring only one courier, as you will be in view from the top of the hill." [28]

It was entirely too much for a Brigadier of cavalry to be telling a corps commander, who was quite capable of deciding by which road he would advance, but Jackson overlooked Fitz's excess of counsel. The young trooper evidently was much excited. He had seen the enemy; he knew approximately where rested the flank which Jackson was marching to turn. With few words in reply, Jackson sent back word for the infantry to be halted under arms in the road. One of his couriers he told to follow him. Off with Fitz Lee the General rode across the Plank Road, down which, to the eastward, they knew the Second Virginia already was feeling its way. North of the Plank Road, Fitz turned to the right and took a path that led through the woods. Jackson followed and, for some minutes, saw trees only and the expansive back of the trooper. Beyond the Germanna Ford road Jackson went behind Lee, and then climbed a hill to a cleared crest.

There Fitz Lee drew rein and, with a broad gesture, bade Jackson see for himself. Spread out before the eyes, near enough for the movement of individuals to be observed, were long lines of Federals. Arms were stacked. The men were at ease. In the distance, beeves were being slaughtered. The smoke of campfires

[27] None of the participants who subsequently wrote of this march recorded any noon halt; but as such a halt "about 12 or 1 o'clock" was called regularly under Jackson's orders of May 13, 1862, MS Order Book, p. 37, failure to have rest at noon was more likely to be mentioned by one of Jackson's men than would have been the regular halt. Besides, road toughened troops scarcely would have required from 8 A.M. to 4 P.M. to cover 10½ miles unless there had been a halt of one hour at noon.

[28] Fitz Lee's Chancellorsville. 220.

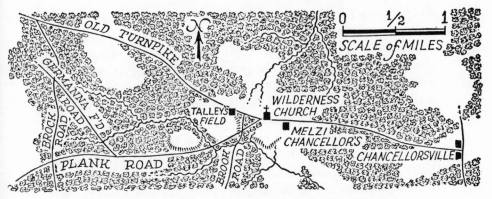

Talley's and Melzi Chancellor's Farms, Wilderness of Spotsylvania—
after Hotchkiss and Allan

already was rising. A few cannon were in position; some earth-works had been thrown up, abatis had been cut, but—challenging but—the enemy manifestly was not expecting attack. No warning whatever had reached the Federals that three Divisions of the Army of Northern Virginia were moving on them.

This Jackson saw quickly. It set his battle blood boiling. "His eyes," Fitz Lee said, "burned with a brilliant glow, lighting his sad face." All the while Fitz Lee was talking and was pointing out what he had observed on his earlier reconnaissance. Jackson made no answer and scarcely seemed to regard what the cavalry-man was saying. Eagerly, carefully, Jackson was measuring the Federal line and was trying to find exactly where, in the forest to his left, the right flank might be. "In the air" it was, precisely as the Confederates had hoped, and vulnerable it must be; but where stood the flank guards? How much farther must the Second Corps proceed before it would be beyond the Federal right?

As Jackson watched, his lips moved. Was he talking to himself to drown Fitz Lee's chatter, or was he praying? From his left, he turned his gaze to the front again to open ground around a farm house near the turnpike. Talley's Farm this was. Half a mile farther eastward beyond Talley's was another farm-clearing where binoculars showed some earthworks that seemed to be facing southward on good ground. This place was Melzi Chancellor's. Apparently the Federals intended to stand there.

Earnestly but swiftly Jackson made the reconnaissance. Not

five minutes after he had reached the hilltop, he had seen enough to justify decision. Abruptly he turned to the courier. His words snapped like a drover's whip: "Tell General Rodes to move across the Plank Road; halt when he gets to the old turnpike, and I will join him there." The man touched his horse and rode off. Jackson's eye swept once more the wide arc before him and then, without a word to Lee, he started down the hill. His arms flopped to the motion of the little sorrel. So intent was Jackson on his plans and so little was he mindful of his saddle that Fitz feared he might go over the animal's head.[29] Despite his seeming inattention, Jackson got to the bottom of the hill and wove his way along the path, back to the Brock Road and thence to the column. Said Fitz Lee afterward, in amusing candor: "I expected to be told I had made a valuable personal reconnaissance—saving the lives of many soldiers—and that Jackson was indebted to me to that amount at least." [30]

That debt Jackson left to the morrow. For today, his obligation was to destroy the Northern host. Were the Divisions in Rodes's rear well closed? They seemed to be. Was Rodes moving northward to the intersection of the turnpike? He was—rapidly. A Brigade must be sent to guard the road that came down from Germanna Ford and bisected the turnpike before the Plank Road was reached. If this road from the ford was secured and the Confederate cavalry were vigilant, the deployment of Jackson's infantry could be masked. Send Paxton, then, with the Stonewall Brigade eastward on the Plank Road and instruct him to report to Fitz Lee, who soon was in advance on that road and was skirmishing with a detachment of Federal horse.[31] As for the Confederate left: "Colonel," said Jackson to Munford of the Second Virginia, "look well to our left and, as we advance, endeavor, if possible, to seize the Ely's Ford Road and hold it and keep me posted on that flank." Then, remembering their conversation that noon, he added: "The Virginia Military Institute will be heard from today!" [32]

Now to notify the commanding General! Jackson did not interrupt any of his staff officers to take down a dispatch at his dicta-

[29] Fitz Lee's *Chancellorsville*, ed. cit., 319–20. The account in 5 *C. V.*, 289, seems to be a confused variant of the same incident.
[30] *Ibid.*, 320.
[31] *O. R.*, 25, pt. 1, p. 940.
[32] *Munford MSS.*

tion, nor did he dismount to write. Instead, he put a sheet of paper against the pommel of his saddle and scrawled this:

Near 3 P.M.
May 2d, 1863

General,

The enemy has made a stand at Chancellor's which is about 2 miles from Chancellorsville. I hope as soon as practicable to attack.

I trust that an ever kind Providence will bless us with great success.

Respectfully,

T. J. Jackson
Lt. Genl.

Genl. R. E. Lee

The leading division is up and the next two appear to be well-closed.[33]

As rapidly now as men could cover the mile and a half between the Plank Road and the old turnpike, Rodes's Brigades tramped northward through the brilliant May sunshine, and when they reached the turnpike, they headed eastward. Unopposed, unobserved even, Rodes led them almost a mile to a long, low ridge.[34] There Rodes's splendidly trained skirmishers under Major Eugene Blackford were advanced 400 yards.[35] The Division quietly was deployed.[36] Jackson's instructions to Rodes, who explained them carefully to each of his Brigadiers, were that when the bugles sounded the advance, the whole line was to sweep forward. The road was to be the guide. Talley's Farm was the first objective. It must be occupied at once and at all hazards, because that ground was thought to dominate the fortifications at Melzi Chancellor's.

---

[33] Facsimile in 3 *B. & L.,* 206. The statement that he wrote on the pommel of his saddle was an old tradition at the Virginia State Library, where the original of the dispatch for years was displayed.

[34] This ridge is a watershed between the Rapidan-Rappahannock and the Mattapony-York.

[35] *O. R.,* 25, pt. 1, p. 941.

[36] Iverson's and Rodes's old Brigades were on the left and to the North of the old turnpike; Doles's and Colquitt's on the right and to the South of the road. Beyond the right of Colquitt there would not have been space to place the fifth Brigade of the Division, Ramseur's, otherwise than by extending the right flank where, as it advanced, it might collide with the Stonewall Brigade at the junction of the Germanna and Plank Roads. The disposition is shown more clearly on the Hotchkiss-Allan map of May 2 than on any other. Consequently, Ramseur was placed in rear of Colquitt, who was told explicitly that he need have no fear of exposing his flank. Ramseur was directed to assume full responsibility for guarding the flank, so that Colquitt would be free to press straight on. *O. R.,* 25, pt. 1, p. 941.

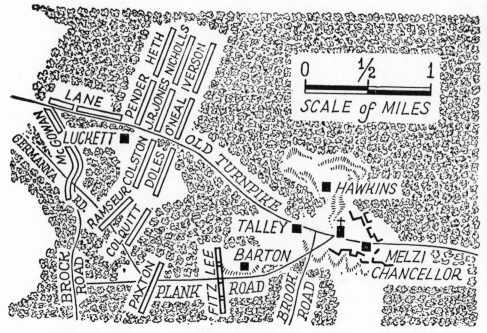

The Deployment for Jackson's Attack against the Flank of the XI Corps, May 2, 1863— after Hotchkiss and Allan

After the Division had stormed Talley's, it was to press on. If it found the Federals strong at Chancellor's, as Jackson expected they might be, Rodes's Division was to seek shelter until the Confederate artillery got into action. Otherwise the line was to pursue the enemy as far as he could be driven.[37]

While Rodes was instructing his Brigadiers, Colston was forming Trimble's Division.[38] Colston's orders were to follow Rodes and to support him. If any commander in the front line needed

---

[37] *O. R.*, 25, pt. 1, pp. 940–41.

[38] With the Stonewall Brigade detached at the mouth of the Germanna Road, Raleigh Colston, the senior Brigadier, had three Brigades only; but as Ramseur was in rear of Colquitt, the North Carolinians thus constituted the right flank element of a second line. On the left of Ramseur was Colston's own Brigade, now under Col. E. T. H. Warren of the Tenth Virginia. Three of the five regiments of this organization had been in Taliaferro's old Brigade. The added regiments were the First and Third North Carolina, formerly of Doles's, which previously had been Ripley's Brigade. Beyond Colston to the left were, in succession, J. R. Jones's Brigade and, on the extreme left, Nicholls's Louisianians. According to Colston (*O. R.*, 25, pt. 1, p. 1004), this line was deployed about 200 yards behind the first line. Rodes, who naturally would not have observed the deployment so closely, inasmuch as Colston was behind him, put the distance at 100 yards (*ibid.*, 940).

help, he would send back immediately for it to the officer of the second line, who would move up without waiting to refer the call to his Division chief.[39]

While the deployment of Colston's Division was being completed, Powell Hill's men were coming up. After Heth found that his Brigade could not form in accordance with orders, on Colston's left, both Heth and Pender were placed on the left of the road as a third line. Lane and McGowan, who were in column at the turn of the Brock Road into the turnpike, were instructed to move forward by the flank, eastward on the turnpike, as the lines advanced.[40]

About this time, probably, Jackson first learned that Archer and Thomas had turned back to repulse the attack on the wagon train and consequently were far to the rear. Their absence would not be fatal to the execution of the plan. In the three lines were ten Brigades. "Jim" Lane and Sam McGowan would be a reserve. Frank Paxton could advance the Stonewall Brigade when his front was cleared. The Federals seemed to have no more artillery at hand than could be engaged by Moorman's Battery of the Stuart Horse Artillery which was then waiting on the turnpike. Other batteries would come up quickly. The column of attack, with the favor of a kindly Providence, would suffice, Jackson thought, to destroy the Federals in his front who, to that moment, still had given no evidence that they even dimly apprehended danger. Every Federal command that could be glimpsed from any lookout seemed to have concluded that the day would end for them in a good supper by the campfire, a leisured smoke, gossip and banter and then the warmth of a blanket and the quiet companionship of the stars.[41]

Amid the underbrush and in woods where one could not see the length of a regiment, the Confederate deployment was slow. Five o'clock it was now. The sun would set in an hour and forty-eight minutes. By 7.30 darkness would fall. What was done that afternoon had to be done with the speed and force of a hurricane.

[39] O. R., 25, pt. 1, p. 1004.   [40] Ibid., 915–16.
[41] German troops most of those opposite Jackson were found to be—Howard's XI Corps, with some commanders of strange name, von Gilsa, von Steinwehr, Schurz, Schimmelfennig, Krzyzanowski (O. R., 25, pt. 1, pp. 166–67). Many of these soldiers had been Sigel's in 1862.

Otherwise night would salvage the wreckage surprise could create.[42] Jackson was in the high excitement of conflict. Under his cap brim, his eyes were blazing. His orders were thrust bayonets.

Robert Rodes, as full of fight as Jackson, rode up and drew rein nearby. With a bugler, Major Eugene Blackford followed presently to report that the skirmish line was extended fully and was waiting to go forward.[43] Jackson looked to right and could see part of Doles's Georgians, whose line extended through a bit of wood and then 600 yards across Luckett's field. Farthest on the right[44] was the grand old Twelfth Georgia that had fought gloriously with Jackson in nearly all his battles from McDowell onward. On the left of the road, where Rodes's own Brigade rested its flank,[45] the renowned Sixth Alabama was in line with regiments worthy of it. Nearby was Iverson's Brigade which, under Samuel Garland, had helped to delay the Federals at South Mountain. With those troops ready, their morale perfect and their ears straining for the first notes of the advance, what man worthy of the name of leader would fail that day to destroy the Amalekites?

Out from his pocket, under his rubber coat, Jackson took his watch and opened it. The hands were at 5.15.

"Are you ready, General Rodes?" the commander asked.

"Yes, sir," answered Rodes decisively.

"You can go forward then," Jackson said in even tones.[46]

Rodes with his long blond mustache and his penetrating blue eyes looked as if he were Wotan still young. A glance and a nod to Blackford were all the orders he need give. Through the forests rang the notes that set every soldier's heart to racing—

To right and to left, from each Brigade sounded the advance. Invisible, unheard, the skirmishers started. A moment later the

---

[42] The writer has not included in the text the conversation credited to Jackson by Maj. M. N. Moorman in 30 *S. H. S. P.*, 110 ff. This is not because Major Moorman was in any way lacking in credibility as a witness but solely because the existing version of his memoir is late and, unhappily, cannot be reconciled with some contemporary accounts. The Major's memory was not on a par with his often proved valor

[43] There is a measure of doubt concerning the exact duties that afternoon of Major Eugene Blackford of the Fifth Alabama. He certainly had been assigned to special duty

line was advancing behind them. Then a shouted order and an abrupt halt. Colonel O'Neal, who commanded Rodes's Brigade, or someone acting for O'Neal, had failed to instruct the skirmishers of that Brigade to advance. The line overtook them ere they started. Time had to be allowed for the skirmishers to get their distance.[47] Now—forward all and no stop, no pause! On the center and on the left, the gray line crashed through the woods. Ahead, terrorized, dashed deer and rabbits. Challenging shots came presently from the Federals, next some pretense of a volley, a few cannon shots. Instantly, as excited graycoats realized that they had flushed the enemy, they raised the rebel yell. It rolled and died away on the flank; it rose again and swelled and swept back along the line, and echoed through the forest. Soon a break was visible in the Federal front. It widened. Bluecoats ran back into the woods and disappeared. Now, on the right center they were visible again. The forest flamed—was it a rally? George Doles sent the Twenty-first Georgia to the left. His Twelfth he sent to the right; the Fourth and the Forty-fourth he ordered to make a frontal assault. The Georgians were instant in obedience and irresistible in attack. Nothing could stop them. Within ten minutes the Federals were being driven back toward Talley's.[48]

Vigorously Doles pursued. North of the road the other Brigades pressed on. Trimble's men were on their heels. Only on the extreme right did the line lag. There, in confusion, Colquitt thought his right was threatened.[49] In defiance of orders, he halted. That blocked Ramseur and immobilized the Stonewall Brigade on the Plank Road. Furious, Dodson Ramseur dashed to the front. He rode out and reconnoitred and found nothing. To Colquitt he crashed his way: Go on, continue the advance; leave to us any Federal forces on the flank! Colquitt caught his breath and, at length, ordered his Brigade to push on.

with the skirmishers (*O. R.*, 25, pt. 1, pp. 951, 958) and for that reason, he did not succeed to the command of the regiment when his seniors were put *hors de combat* (*ibid.*, 792). It may have been that Blackford was in general charge of all the skirmishers, and that through negligence, no other officer had been named to direct the skirmishers of Rodes's Brigade.

[44] *O. R.*, 25, pt. 1, p. 967.
[45] *O. R.*, 25, pt. 1, p. 951.
[46] 3 *B. & L.*, 208.
[47] *O. R.*, 25, pt. 1, p. 941.   [48] *O. R.*, 25, pt. 1, pp. 941, 967.
[49] *O. R.*, 25, pt. 1, p. 974.

It was too late now to straighten out the line.[50] By reason of the delay of the right wing, the attack on Talley's and on an open field to the North [51] had to be delivered by not more than six Brigades of the first and second line. That mattered scarcely at all. Few of the men who made the assault knew that the right was lagging. They did not stop to reckon numbers and to observe that the three Divisions had in the column of attack no more than half their strength. "Old Jack's" boys were fighting, not ciphering! Over the light works at Talley's the Georgians rushed; eastward through Hawkins's field charged Iverson and O'Neal.

Now for the pursuit to Melzi Chancellor's.[52] Not for a moment did Rodes forget his orders: If possible, he was to capture the ridge. Failing in that, he was to halt, seek shelter and wait for the artillery to dislodge the enemy. He would not fail. Boldly, immediately he would press on. The result would justify the risk and the losses. Part of the Federal works West of Melzi Chancellor's [53] looked South. They could be taken in flank. The flight of the men there might demoralize those in the heavier works that had been thrown across the line of the Confederate advance.[54]

The daring course proved the less costly. With a fiendish yell that froze blood in the gathering twilight, the Second Corps stormed up the elevation. A wild volley was all the resistance encountered. The few troops that attempted to make a stand were overwhelmed. Then, as Rodes's Brigadiers began to straighten their line for the next onslaught, Trimble's troops came rolling into the works behind them.[55] With two lines now united and the enemy on the run, Rodes hurriedly prepared to push on toward Chancellorsville.

As much of this as any man could see, Jackson, in the full joy of battle, had observed. Close to the front he had ridden; again and again he had shouted, "Press on, press on!" The ecstasy of conflict appeared to have seized him. Never had he been so transformed—never in such sure reliance upon the God of Battle. Every time the wild yell of victory swept across the fields or through the wood, he would lift his head and give thanks. He did, also, what he never had been seen to do before in action.

[50] *Ibid.*, 995.
[51] This was known as Hawkins' Farm.   [52] Often styled Dowdall's Tavern.
[53] Those directly South of Wilderness Church.
[54] Cf. *O. R.*, 35, pt. 1, p. 941.   [55] *O. R.*, 25, pt. 1, pp. 941, 1004.

If he passed a spot where some of his men lay dead, their blood still wet and red, he would draw in the little sorrel and raise his hand as if he were a priestly crusader who prayed for the souls of the fallen and blessed them for their valor. Said Jackson's principal companion on that advance, "I have never seen him so well pleased with the progress and results of a fight."[56]

Beyond Melzi Chancellor's, which was on open ground, the advance units entered a thick wood where, in an instant, they seemed to pass from twilight to night. That changed everything. The right of the line became entangled in an abatis. Officers lost touch with their men. Weary soldiers found themselves in the company of strangers. To Jackson came in a few minutes a report from Rodes that he had been compelled to call a halt but that he begged the General to throw Hill ahead of him so that, while Hill cleared the front, the original first line could re-form.[57] Rodes himself went forward to see whether there was any line of battle West of the high ground around Chancellorsville.[58]

By the time this message reached Jackson, the firing temporarily had ceased,[59] but Hill was anticipating Rodes's wishes. Pender was in support of Colston's left with his regiments in perfect control;[60] Heth's men were directly behind J. R. Jones's Brigade,[61] but were not past disentangling. McGowan and Lane had Brigades in the road, behind the third line.[62] They were no longer in the baffling blackness. The full moon was rising, as yet a dim red orb through the low hanging smoke.[63] A kindly Providence seemed to be lifting that lantern in the sky to light the Confederacy on its way to independence. Jackson resolved that as Gideon fell on the Midianites, so with the help of the Most High, Hill should deploy and drive the enemy back to Chancellorsville. Perhaps more could be done. It might be possible, ere that greatest of nights was over, to get between the Federals and United States Ford, to force the Federals to attack him there—and to slaughter them.

---

[56] Capt. R. E. Wilbourn in *Cooke's Jackson*, 416 n. Unfortunately, most of the highly dramatic accounts of this advance have to be rejected because they are more rhetorical than historical. Captain Wilbourn's is an exception. It was written soon after the battle and was not designed to present anything more than the remembered facts.

[57] *O. R.*, 25, pt. 1, pp. 941, 1004–05; 3 *B. & L.*, 233.

[58] *Ibid.*, 941.

[59] *Ibid.*, 1004.

[60] *O. R.*, 25, pt. 1, p. 935.

[61] *Ibid.*, 890.

[62] *O. R.*, 25, pt. 1, pp. 902, 916.

[63] Col. A. C. Haskell, in *Mrs. Daly*, 102.

Jackson touched his horse to ride still nearer to the front and to see for himself what the field promised. At the moment, Hill overtook him. Jackson turned abruptly. His order to his lieutenant sounded like picket fire: "Press them! Cut them off from the United States Ford, Hill! Press them!" [64]

[64] Hotchkiss in 3 *C. M. H.,* 385.

CHAPTER XXXII

A Night in the Wilderness

BEFORE JACKSON could get to the front, a furious cannonade swept the roads and the woods.[1] It forced him to seek shelter, and it compelled "Jim" Lane to halt the advance and to order the North Carolinians to lie down. Prone on the ground Lane kept them until, in answer to an inquiry from Hill, he explained that his advance was halted by fire which he believed had been precipitated by Moorman's horse artillery. If the Southern guns ceased fire, Lane said, he thought the Federals would stop. Hill gave the necessary order to Moorman. All firing quickly died away.[2] Jackson, tense and resolute, could resume his ride eastward along the turnpike. He went slowly forward until he was between Powell's field and an old schoolhouse on the right-hand side of the road. There he drew rein to receive at the hands of courier David J. Kyle a dispatch from "Jeb" Stuart. After Jackson had read this, he asked tersely if Kyle knew the ground around Chancellorsville. Kyle replied that he did. "Keep along with me," said Jackson.[3]

[1] This probably is the firing described, with some literary freedom, in *Caldwell*, 78.
[2] Lane's report in *O. R.*, 25, pt. 1, p. 916; the same officer in 8 *S. H. S. P.*, 494; Moorman in 30 *ibid.*, 112.
[3] David J. Kyle in 4 *C. V.*, 308, cited hereafter as *Kyle*. As presently will appear, Kyle insisted that Jackson turned over the turnpike to the Bullock Farm road, which is not stated by either of the two eyewitnesses to what followed. For this reason, Kyle's account, though published in 1896 and used by Hamlin, apparently was disregarded by Jackson's biographers and specifically was controverted by Rev. J. P. Smith in a letter of July 21, 1897, to Jed. Hotchkiss (*Hotchkiss Papers*). Any document relating to Jackson that Smith rejected and Hotchkiss did not accept as authentic has to be subjected to a stern critique. The results are not conclusive, because some of Kyle's statements cannot be verified, but the paper contains nothing that is improbable and little that is at variance with known facts. Much that Kyle stated from memory can be fitted into the established record. His statements, moreover, accord entirely with the tradition in the Wilderness, half confirmed by Jackson's own words, that the General started to reconnoitre in the direction of United States Ford. Aubrey Hawkins of Richmond, who acquainted the writer with that tradition, knew Mr. Kyle as a resident of Culpeper. During the 1890's Mr. Kyle came frequently to the Wilderness to buy cattle or to hunt. Mr. Kyle, says Mr. Hawkins, was entirely familiar with the terrain. Certainly Mr. Kyle's descriptions of the ground are more detailed and more confidently stated than those of other witnesses. It is to be noted, also, that neither Capt. R. E. Wilbourn nor Lieut. J. G. Morrison, the two eyewitnesses mentioned in note *infra* as primary authorities, had ever been over the ground until that evening. Morrison probably never went there again in daylight. Kyle was much more apt, in the darkness, to know where he was than was either of the others. Subsequently, he had ample opportunity of verifying the fact. See *infra*, p. 565, n. 10.

The General then went on to the schoolhouse, where he drew rein and ascertained from some officers there the little they knew of conditions ahead. With a touch of the heel he set the little sorrel toward the front again. About 200 yards he rode through shadows and in the uncertain light of a moon still low in the East. He passed Heth's Brigade and then Lane's. In the belief that he could organize quickly a night attack, he sent one staff officer after another to assist in the deployment and to urge Hill to hurry. The spirit of his speech, the sharpness of his commands, was that of a battle still raging. Not for a moment did he relax. Order followed order. Every detail of preparation he directed. Soon he had with him his couriers and guides only; but just then Lane came up. For whom was he looking? Jackson asked. The North Carolinian explained that he was drawing his line and was in search of Hill to ascertain whether he should begin his advance. Would Jackson give the order?

"Push right ahead, Lane," the General answered earnestly, and extended his own hand as if he were himself bodily pushing the Federals.[4] Without another word he rode on. It was then about 9 P.M.[5]

Almost immediately, Captain Wilbourn came up and began to describe Hill's deployment. Lieutenant Morrison returned from a mission. Captain Boswell was nearby, probably a little in advance on the turnpike.[6] Jackson himself, impatient, excited, anxious to strike the final blow, determined to ride out to the skirmish line to get some further understanding, if he could, of

[4] Lane in 8 *S. H. S. P.*, 494.

[5] 1 *Land We Love*, 181. This is one of the two primary accounts of events of the next fifteen minutes. No author's name is given, in accordance with the policy of D. H. Hill, who was editing the magazine, but there can be no doubt that the "aide" who is mentioned in the article was its author. He could have been no other person, in all the circumstances, than Jackson's and Hill's brother-in-law, Lieut. Joseph G. Morrison. The article consequently is cited hereafter as *Morrison.* The other primary eyewitness account is that of Jackson's signal officer, Capt. R. E. Wilbourn, which appeared first in a letter to Gen. Jubal A. Early, Feb. 19, 1873, 6 *S. H. S. P.*, 266, cited hereafter as *Wilbourn,* though essentially the same information had been given by Wilbourn to John Esten Cooke prior to the publication of that edition of *Cooke's Jackson* issued in 1866. Early quoted part of Wilbourn's letter as a footnote in his autobiography, pp. 213-17 n. The account by Capt. W. F. Randolph, of Jackson's bodyguard, issued as a pamphlet under the title *With Stonewall Jackson at Chancellorsville,* was written so late that details were confused by the gallant author.

[6] Dabney, *op. cit.,* 685-86, stated that Boswell had been sent to A. P. Hill, whom he was guiding, but Wilbourn included Boswell in Jackson's party. It is impossible to say, nor is it important to establish, precisely when the various staff officers joined Jackson for the reconnaissance. Almost every one of them, in describing what happened, unwittingly failed to mention the presence of some comrade.

the terrain in the direction of United States Ford.[7] By his side was Captain Wilbourn, who continued his report of Hill's deployment.

Jackson had to ride slowly in the darkness and over unfamiliar ground. With staff officers and couriers and signalmen, he now had a small cavalcade.[8] A few minutes' plodding by tired horses brought Jackson to an open space, to the left of Moorman's battery, where two roads diverged to the Northeast. The General halted again and sent back for the courier, David Kyle, who had brought the message from Stuart.

What, asked Jackson, when Kyle rode up, was the course of the roads on the left?

The farther of them, Kyle answered, led to the Bullock Farm, which was about three-quarters of a mile North of Chancellorsville,[9] and the nearer of the two was called the Mountain Road. It paralleled the turnpike and re-entered it about half a mile nearer Chancellorsville.[10]

Jackson's caution in dealing with scouts and couriers showed itself in his answer: If Kyle knew it, said the General, let him lead the way.

Some of Jackson's companions began now to be solicitous for his safety. They had passed the Confederate picket line, though they probably had seen none of the men who formed it. "General," said one of his staff, "don't you think this is the wrong place for you?"

"The danger is all over—the enemy is routed!—go back and tell A. P. Hill to press right on!" [11]

7 Wilbourn in 6 *S. H. S. P.*, 267.

8 Wilbourn, *ibid.*

9 Kyle reported himself as saying merely that the Bullock Farm was "behind Chancellorsville."

10 *Kyle*, 308. This is an important point in determining the credibility of Kyle as a witness. The Michler map of 1867 shows the Bullock road but not the one Kyle called the Mountain Road. Hotchkiss' map, *loc. cit.*, shows both, but places the terminus of Mountain Road in the marshy ground near the head of Lewis' Run. On this evidence one might be inclined to throw out Kyle's testimony; but Bigelow's maps, *op. cit.*, which were compiled from a variety of sources and most accurately represent the ground, show both the Bullock and the Mountain Roads. As sketched in the text, on the basis of Bigelow's map No. 28, page 356, these roads did not start from exactly the same point, but they were so close together that Kyle was entirely justified in speaking of one of them as the "road on the left" and the other as the "road on the right." Most of the authorities on the campaign seem to have been unaware that the Mountain Road ran parallel to the turnpike at a distance never much greater than 100 yards.

11 *Cooke's Jackson*, 419–20. The exact sequence of events at this point must not be regarded as positively established.

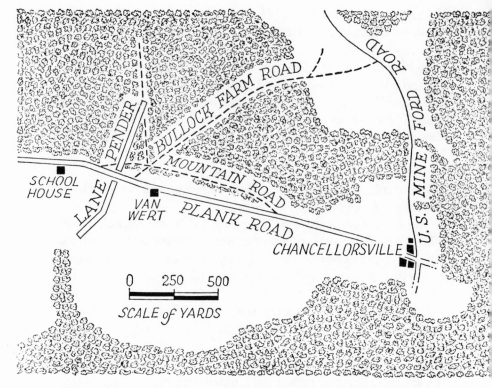

The Mountain and the Bullock Farm Roads, Wilderness of Spotsylvania. Lines of Pender and of Lane, as here shown, had not been formed completely when Jackson rode forward on the night of May 2, 1863—after N. Michler

Kyle started ahead. Jackson's impatience prompted him to over-take the young cavalryman. By the boy's horse, for a few hundred yards, Jackson kept the head of the little sorrel. Then, once again, he drew rein. Except where the moonlight reached the empty road, nothing could be seen ahead. There was darkness, but there was sound. Not far ahead, axes were being wielded nervously. Trees were being felled. Voices were audible, also. Union offi-cers apparently were trying to get troops into line.[12]

Jackson listened for a few minutes: was the enemy too strong to assail? Even for the prize of the road to Hooker's rear, was a night attack too hazardous? Was it possible to follow impulse and boldly, instantly, to drive the confused enemy? Jackson held to his plan. The attack must be pressed. Hill must cut off the

[12] *Kyle*, 308; *Bigelow*, 317.

Federals from United States Ford. Every man of the Light Division must be thrown against the enemy.

To assure speed in the attack, "Stonewall" turned his horse and started back the way he had come. Silently he rode along till he was nearly opposite a weather-boarded house in the woods by the roadside.[13] Suddenly from South of the dark road, there was a shot. Several others were fired. A volley roared through the woods.

"Cease firing, cease firing," Hill's voice rang out.

In the darkness, Jackson could not see who had fallen, nor did he have time. He felt the sorrel swerve suddenly away toward the North and dash into the woods. With his left hand, he checked the horse. His right hand he lifted to hold his cap and to protect his face from the low hanging boughs.

"Cease firing," Morrison yelled, as he ran toward the lines, "you are firing into your own men!"

"Who gave that order?" a voice shouted back. "It's a lie! Pour it into them, boys!" [14]

There was a long flash in front of Jackson—a volley by a kneeling line. Instantly he knew he had been hit.[15] His left arm fell limp; his grip on his bridle rein was lost; a bullet had struck his uplifted right hand. The sorrel, which he had headed toward the Confederate lines, swerved again and ran toward the enemy. Dazed, Jackson felt on his head a sudden blow from a bough that threw him back and almost off his horse. Somehow, he contrived to find the bridle rein with his right hand. Desperately he began to pull in the frightened horse. With a supreme effort he turned the animal once more toward his own lines, but he could not stop the sorrel. A moment later, he felt another and a strong hand jerk the rein. A voice was calling to the horse. Captain Wilbourn had come to his aid. On the other side, as Jackson felt himself growing dizzy, another officer dashed up. Together the two halted the sorrel and steadied the rider. Quickly Wilbourn sprang to the ground. "They certainly must be our troops," he exclaimed.

Jackson nodded but said nothing. He was looking up the road,

[13] Kyle said, *op. cit.*, Jackson was opposite the Van Wert House; Wilbourn, *op. cit.*, 267, called it "an old, dismantled house"; Cooke in his *Jackson*, 420, styled it "an unfinished weather-board house . . . whose shell torn roof may still be seen."
[14] *Morrison*, 181.
[15] The fire was from the Eighteenth North Carolina, Lane's Brigade. For the evidence on this point, see 2 *R. E. Lee*, 533 n.

toward his own line, as if he scarcely could realize that his soldiers had fired on him.[16]

"How do you feel, General?" asked Wilbourn. "Can you move your fingers?"[17] The General tried but replied weakly that he could not; the arm was broken. When Wilbourn reached up and tried to straighten the member, the pain was so torturing that Jackson had to say, "You had better take me down." As he fell toward Wilbourn, he almost fainted.

Jackson realized that Wilbourn and the other officer, Lieutenant Wynn of the signal corps, were trying to get him out of the saddle and on the ground, but he scarcely could help them at all. So nearly unconscious was he that he could not take his feet out of the stirrup. They were released by Wynn. At length, Jackson was on the ground. Half supported, half staggering, he moved ten or fifteen yards North of the road. Then, for safety, he was told to lie down under a small tree. There he perhaps heard Wilbourn tell an unidentified man by the roadside to ascertain what Confederate troops were ahead. Perhaps, too, Jackson heard Wilbourn direct Wynn to go into the lines and find Medical Director McGuire or some other skillful surgeon, but not to let anyone else know that Jackson was wounded. For the next few minutes, Jackson was alone with Wilbourn. As if in a dream, he saw Wilbourn loosen field glasses and haversack and put them over his own shoulder, and then he felt the pressure of rending cloth. Wilbourn was ripping off the sleeve of the gumcoat, that of the uniform jacket and those of the two shirts on the wounded left arm.

While the Captain was bent over the General, Jackson heard horse's hoofs and then the voice of Powell Hill. "I have been trying to make the men cease firing," cried Hill[18] and, with words of deep regret, he knelt by Jackson. One of Hill's staff officers, Capt. Benjamin Watkins Leigh, stood at the back of his kneeling chief. "Is the wound painful?" Hill inquired.

"Very painful," answered Jackson, "my arm is broken."

Gently Hill took off Jackson's blood filled gauntlets, to prevent further pain to the broken hands, and next he unhooked and

[16] *Wilbourn*, 268–69.
[17] The direct quotation is restored from Wilbourn's narrative.
[18] *ed. Hotchkiss' MS Diary*, 177

removed the General's sword and belt.[19] Then someone in the company asked if Jackson would have some whiskey. The fallen man hesitated but at Wilbourn's insistence, he swallowed all there was in the bottle—about a mouthful—and asked for water.[20] Under the stimulant, he revived slightly and began to wonder how long it would be till a surgeon arrived. When he was told what had been done to procure help, he said, "Very good." He knew that some of the surgeons were unskillful and he reasoned that the medical officer of the nearest Brigade might arrive before Dr. McGuire could get to the front. In a voice over which he fast was regaining control, he whispered to Hill to inquire whether the surgeon was competent. He had a reassuring answer.[21]

Hill continued to hold Jackson's head. Captain Wilbourn, who now had the aid of Lieut. James Power Smith, tied a handkerchief above the wound as a tourniquet and tried to make a sling for the General's broken arm. Fortunately, the blood had begun to clot by this time. Wilbourn, immensely relieved at this, asked where the other wound was.

"In my right hand," Jackson answered, "but never mind that; it is a mere trifle." [22]

The Assistant Surgeon of Pender's Brigade, who arrived in a few minutes with a litter, examined the major wound and decided not to apply an additional tourniquet.[23] Surgeon and attendants then had to decide what next should be done. To move the General might be to start the flow of blood again; to leave him where he was, between the lines, would be to risk capture or death from new projectiles.

Almost as soon as the question was asked, the voice of Capt. R. H. T. Adams—the same officer of the Signal Corps whom

[19] *Wilbourn*, 269. It will be observed that from the moment Jackson was fired upon Wilbourn and Kyle were the sole eyewitnesses who left printed accounts of the events of the next few minutes. Kyle may have been the "solitary rider" by the roadside whom Wilbourn ordered to ascertain what troops were in front. Morrison had run into the lines to stop the firing. After Hill's arrival there was another witness in the person of Capt. (later Maj.) Benjamin Watkins Leigh. Part of his narrative, written May 12, 1863, as a letter to his wife, appears in 6 *S. H. S. P.*, 230 ff. A more abbreviated version will be found in *Cooke's Jackson*, edition of 1866, p. 469 ff. The full text is among the *McGuire MSS.* This narrative of Leigh's is supplemented by that of Morrison, who returned quickly to the scene of the fusillade. On his heels came James Power Smith, whose memories of the night were published in 3 *B. & L.*, 209 ff. From the time of Leigh's arrival, there is no conflict of testimony except as respects minor details.
[20] *Wilbourn*, 273; *Cooke's Jackson*, 423.
[21] *Dabney*, 693–94.   [22] Wilbourn in *Early*, 216 n.
[23] *Dabney*, 694.

Jackson had relieved of duty the previous month—shouted from the road: "Halt! Surrender! Fire on them if they don't surrender!" Hill slipped Jackson's head and shoulders to someone else, got up quickly, drew his pistol and went off with the hasty explanation that he would form his troops and meet the attack. Thoughtfully he added that he would do his utmost to keep from the men the fact that Jackson was wounded. "Thank you," said Jackson faintly.[24]

Powell Hill reached the lines. With furious words he prepared Lane's men to repulse the expected assault. An order here, another there he gave and then, in a sudden burst of fire, he could not make himself heard. A moment later, he felt a sharp and stunning blow across his boot tops. Was it a wound, a serious one? In the uncertain light of the moon, he looked at his legs and felt for blood. The boot tops had been cut, apparently by a fragment of shell; both legs were numbed and bruised; but, apparently, there was no wound. With an effort he could stand. Soon he found that he could not walk otherwise than with an agonizing limp. So great did the pain become that he could not hope to ride a horse and to exercise command.[25] To attempt to do so would be to jeopardize the army.[26]

If Hill was disabled, who should command? In the whole of the Second Corps, not another Major General was present on the field. Colston, who commanded Jackson's Division, and Rodes, who headed D. H. Hill's, were both Brigadier Generals. Rodes was the senior of the two and, indeed, the senior Brigadier then with the Corps. For the time, he must assume command. Should he keep it? That day for the first time he had exercised author-

---

24 *Wilbourn*, 270.

25 *Cf.* W. D. Pender to his wife, MS, May 7, 1863, *Pender MSS.*

26 Hill had gone forward after Jackson, as he subsequently explained to Col. William H. Palmer, because he felt that if the commanding General had ridden out to a post of danger on his front, he should attend. When the first fire swept the road, Hill did not swerve into the woods, as the other riders did. Instead, with quick intelligence, he threw himself from his horse and lay down in the road. After the fire passed, he arose and shouted to the line to cease fire. Then he tried to assist his aide, Captain Murray Taylor, who was under a smitten horse. When word came that Jackson was wounded, Hill left Taylor to care for himself and ran to the General. The one adequate account of the circumstances is that written by Colonel Palmer in 13 *C. V.*, 233. Hill was said in Lee's report and in Rodes's to have been "disabled" (*O. R.*, 25, pt. 1, pp. 799, 942). Stuart spoke of Hill (*ibid.*, 889), as "wounded." Adjutant Wm. H. McLaurin, of the Eighteenth North Carolina, insisted: "Hill may have had a contusion from a bursting shell . . . but he certainly got a minié ball in his leg after Jackson was wounded" (2 *N. C. Regts.*, 38). Hotchkiss (*MS Diary*, 179), spoke of Hill as "struck on the leg by a shell and disabled for the time."

ity over a Division. Was it wisdom to entrust the Corps to him? Hill debated the question and probably discussed it with "Sandie" Pendleton. The conclusion was to notify Rodes that the command devolved on him and, at the same time, to send for "Jeb" Stuart and, with Rodes's acquiescence, to put the Corps in "Jeb's" hands. Stuart was not an infantryman, to be sure, but he was known to the Army as a leader. Rodes's abilities, though high, had not yet been recognized outside the Division he was leading. General Lee, of course, was to be notified as soon as he could be reached, so that, if he wished some other arrangement, he could make it.[27]

Capt. R. H. T. Adams was sent spurring after Stuart, who was supposed to be on the Ely's Ford Road, five miles away. Toward Lee's headquarters, through the night, was dispatched Captain Murray Taylor.[28] Meantime, with Hill still near at hand to counsel if need be, Rodes assumed temporary direction of the Corps. Neither he, Hill nor anyone else believed that the tired troops, without Jackson's leadership, could press farther that night. All that Rodes could do was to direct Colston, who kept his command of Trimble's men, and Heth, who now succeeded to Powell Hill's Division, to prepare for a resumption of the attack when daylight returned. Even in the darkness of approaching midnight, clashes continued. The right of the Corps repulsed sharply what appeared to have been designed as a Federal night attack.[29] Along the Confederate lines, also, there echoed the roar of a conflict that seemed to be waged between Federal Divisions that had lost direction and were firing into each other.[30]

During these hours of confusion, of abrupt bursts of fire and of sudden silence, Jackson was having an experience that never had been his before on a field of battle. It was the experience of evading an enemy he could not combat. After Captain Adams shouted "Halt! Surrender! Fire on them if they don't surrender!"

[27] All the circumstances of this transfer of command may never be known. Hill (*O. R.*, 25, pt. 1, pp. 885–86) stated only that "General Stuart was sent for, and the command of the corps turned over to him." Stuart reported (*ibid.*, 887) that the messenger from Hill "informed me of the sad calamities which for the time deprived the troops of the leadership of both Jackson and Hill, and the urgent demand for me to come and take command as quickly as possible." Rodes's testimony is printed *infra*, p. 582. Whatever the origin of the proposal, it speedily was approved by Jackson. See *infra*, p. 582.
[28] Palmer in 13 *C. V.*, 233.   [29] *O. R.*, 25, pt. 1, p. 942.
[30] This was Birney's clash with Knipe's and Ruger's brigades of Williams's Division near Fairview. See *Alexander*, 343; A. C. Hamlin, *The Battle of Chancellorsville*, 118 ff.

two Union soldiers—two only—held up their hands. They manifestly were much surprised to find themselves within the reach
of "Johnny Reb"—but what were they doing there? Were they
the scouts of an advancing column? Morrison hurried forward
to ascertain.[31] In a few minutes he was back, on the run and in
immense excitement. Jackson heard him shout, "The enemy is
within fifty yards and is advancing; let us take the General
away!" [32]

Wilbourn leaped to his feet at the cry. Said he: "Let us take
the General up in our arms and carry him off!"

"No," said Jackson faintly, "if you can help me up, I can walk."

Painfully, with help on either side, Jackson got on his legs.
Almost on the instant, a burst of Federal artillery swept the road
and thicket and then stopped as suddenly as it had started. Leigh's
horse received a wound from this fire and became so frantic that
the Captain had to dismount quickly, close to Jackson's side, to
keep the animal from running into the enemy's lines. It was fortunate that Leigh alighted there, because the General was barely
able to stand and was in need of the younger man's assistance.
Over Leigh's shoulder, Jackson put his right arm and bleeding
hand. With dragging feet he stumbled back to the road and along
it slowly walked toward the line. Wilbourn, who was trying to
hold three excited horses, sought also to keep them between Jackson and those of Hill's soldiers who were now coming forward in
a fumbling effort to form their line.

"Who is that?" the men began to ask, "Who have you there?" [33]

"Oh," the officers answered, "it's only a friend of ours who is
wounded."

That did not satisfy. Almost every soldier encountered in the
road had an inquiry and appeared suspicious. The number of
men assisting the wounded officer, the care being taken of him
and the presence of several horses multiplied the questions of
soldiers who, traditionally, are never more curious than they are
concerning the identity of killed or wounded men of rank. At
length Jackson himself suggested an answer: "When asked, just
say it is a Confederate officer."

[31] *Morrison*, 181.   [32] *Wilbourn*, 270.
[33] Wilbourn, it will be observed, was a realist: He did not pretend that a Confederate soldier would say, "*Whom* have you there?"

One soldier, dodging among the horses, got close enough to stare at the pale, bearded man who was walking with uncertain step along the road. "Great God," the soldier cried in an agonized voice, "that is General Jackson!" He was given a deceptive reply, which he did not dispute; but he looked again at Jackson and turned away in silence.[34]

Before Jackson had walked more than twenty paces, he was exhausted. Leigh stopped, called the litter bearers and prevailed upon the General to lie down on the litter. This done, Captain Leigh and Lieutenant Smith each took a handle, along with the two soldiers, to lessen the chance of a fall. The four had no more than adjusted the load than the forest and the road were swept with a new hurricane of fire—canister, grape, minié balls. One of the bearers was shot in both arms and was felled, but Leigh fortunately caught the other handle of the litter and saved the General from a fall.[35]

Almost at that moment, the other bearer quietly lowered his side of the litter and dashed off into the wood to escape the fire. Jackson now was on the ground. Over him the projectiles were shrieking; in the wood, by the roadside, severed branches and smitten saplings were tumbling to the ground. The horses became frantic; Wilbourn scarcely could hold them. While he struggled, Smith, Leigh and Morrison, without a word either to the General or to one another, but in obedience to the code by which they had been reared, stretched themselves out and made an embankment of flesh around the General. They could not protect him from a bullet that might fall straight on him, but as one officer was on the left, another on the right and the third in front of Jackson, whose feet were toward the enemy, they could shield him with their own bodies from missiles that might strike in the road and rebound.[36] Jackson, in a half daze, struggled for a moment to get up; but Smith threw his body over the General. "Sir," said Smith, "you must lie still; it will cost you your life if you rise!"[37] Jackson

---

34 *Wilbourn*, 270.

35 3 *B. & L.*, 212. The soldier shot through the arms lost one of them. He was John J. Johnson, Company H, Twenty-Second Virginia Battalion. 10 *S. H. S. P.*, 143; *Kyle*, 308–09.

36 3 *B. & L.*, 212; *Dabney*, 689, for the detail that Jackson's feet were toward the enemy; Leigh in 6 *S. H. S. P.*, 233.

37 *Dabney*, 689.

obediently restrained himself. He lay on his back and saw nothing but dim stars and the flight of shells overhead. The younger men, on their sides, could see again and again the spark of the grape-shot and minié balls that hit the stones of the road.[38]

Presently the Federal battery widened the range and opened with shell. As soon as this was manifest, the three young men lifted the General, who repeated, "I can walk." They turned off the road to lessen the danger and to avoid the troops who now began to pour from the woods. The General now asked for "spirits" and manifestly needed stimulation so badly that Wilbourn rode off [39] to see if he could find some whiskey. Jackson tottered along on the shoulder of Smith, while Morrison assisted [40] him and Leigh carried the litter.

This was for a few minutes only. Then Jackson, from weakness, had to stop. Leigh spread the litter; Jackson lay on it—but how was it safely to be conveyed? Should two of the officers carry the heavy load, and the third try to handle all the horses? Must help be procured from some of the soldiers who were deploying in the woods? Assistance was sought, but whenever a man was asked to lend a hand, he would give an excuse or back into the shadows and vanish. Leigh hestitated to tell any of the soldiers who was on the litter because he knew how quickly that depressing news would spread; [41] but when he vainly had asked one after another to help, he felt that he could not delay longer through a desire to conceal the identity of the man on the stretcher. Jackson's wounds might start bleeding again; the enemy might reduce the range and shell the woods. So, when next Leigh encountered men, he told them that he had Jackson on the litter and wanted aid in getting the General to a place of safety. They acquiesced instantly. From that moment, Leigh had all the assistance he required.[42]

As Jackson started slowly to the rear, Dorsey Pender came up, recognized him, and though himself wounded, spoke up manfully: "Ah, General, I am sorry to see you have been wounded.

---

[38] *Morrison*, 181.   [39] Cf. *Wilbourn*, 272.
[40] Probably with the horses.
[41] Cf. *Grimes*, 30. Colonel Grimes inquired who was on the litter and received in answer only, "Lieutenant Sumter." Rodes whispered to Grimes that the wounded man was Jackson, but that he, Rodes, "thought it advisable that it should be concealed from the troops, for fear of disheartening them, in view of the serious work ahead of us in the morning."
[42] Leigh in 6 *S. H. S. P.,* 263.

The lines here are so much broken that I fear we will have to fall back."

Jackson could not think in terms of his wounds when there was a suggestion of withdrawal. Instantly he was himself—the corps commander—and he raised his head to answer with flashing eye: "You must hold your ground, General Pender; you must hold your ground, sir!" [43]

The staff officers decided they would make better time if they turned from the road again For half a mile, on willing shoulders, the General was carried through the woods. He was weak, but conscious. Again he asked if a stimulant could be found for him. In answer, he was told that something would be provided speedily. With this assurance, the General relapsed into silence and seemed in perceptibly less pain when, without warning, one of the litter bearers on the left caught his foot in a trailing vine and went down head foremost. As the litter slipped from the man's shoulder, the General fell heavily and landed on the shattered arm. A groan of pain, the first he had uttered, escaped his lips, but he struggled hard with his nerves and soon recovered his composure.

Several times after he had been shot, it had flashed on the General that he might be dying. Each time, will had rallied him. Now he felt sure his end had come and he committed himself into the hands of his Maker. A sense of peace at once possessed him.[44] Calm and exaltation of spirit followed. There, helpless on the ground, he felt he had won the victory of faith in conflict with Death. A romanticist said afterward that as Jackson lay on the stretcher, the moon filtered through the clouds and lighted his face. His eyes were shut; his broad and lofty brow was lacerated and bloody; his breathing was spasmodic and difficult.[45] Was he dying? His companions half thought so, but none of them dared mention so dread a possibility.[46] Smith it was who spoke up finally.

[43] So Cooke's Jackson, 427. Dabney, op. cit., 690, gave the words as: "General Pender, you must keep your men together and hold your ground." McGuire, op. cit., 219, had still another version. Smith, op. cit., 212, placed this incident somewhat later. Leigh did not mention it.

[44] For Jackson's statement that he several times had thought he was about to die, see Dabney, 691. For his testimony concerning peace in the presence of death, see infra, p. 601.

[45] Cooke, op. cit., 428, is the sole authority for the moonlight on Jackson's face.

[46] Cooke's Jackson, loc. cit.

"General," he asked, "are you much hurt?"

"No, Mr. Smith," said Jackson steadily, "don't trouble ycurself about me."[47]

That reassured the young officers, who found themselves at the time no more than some twenty-five yards from what the natives called the Stony Ford Road.[48] Would it not be less dangerous, even under the Federal shelling, to go out into the road than to take the chance of a third accident to the litter in the woods? The bearers lifted the General again, felt their way across the turnpike and then, as confidently as men might under a shower of steel, walked southward with their burden in the hope of finding an ambulance.[49]

More quickly than they reckoned the time that anxious night, they were rewarded: in the road, under the charge of Sergeant Whitehead, was the covered vehicle. Although its springs were feeble and its floor was hard, any ambulance was a haven to the wounded soldier.[50] Unfortunately, this particular ambulance already contained Jackson's Chief of Artillery, Col. Stapleton Crutchfield, who had a shattered leg, and another officer, probably Capt. H. A. Rogers, who was less severely wounded.[51] For a moment only was this an embarrassment. As soon as Rogers learned that Jackson was on the litter, the junior insisted on being taken out of the ambulance, to provide space for the General.[52] Crutchfield was in pain so agonizing and had an injury so severe that

---

[47] So *Dabney,* 691, on information given by Smith. Cf. *Wilbourn,* 273. Later, in 3 *B. & L.,* 212, Smith quoted Jackson as saying, "Never mind me, Captain, never mind me."

[48] It was so named, Aubrey Hawkins remembers, because it led southward from the old turnpike to a stony crossing of one branch of Lewis's Creek which, lower down, is the Ny River.

[49] *Kyle,* 309; *Leigh,* 234.

[50] Leigh subsequently was told that Whitehead and the ambulance had been summoned for Jackson, *op. cit.,* 224; but if Whitehead had been coming for Jackson, the ambulance scarcely would have had two officers in it already. On the other hand, if it were an established fact that the ambulance was standing in the road when reached by the litter bearers, the natural conclusion would be that the vehicle was being held in waiting for someone.

[51] It is much to be regretted that this officer, despite much inquiry, cannot be identified positively. Cooke mentioned him as "Major Rogers," but the only Major Rogers listed in *O. R.* 25 was with Anderson. In Pender's report, *ibid.,* pt. 1, p. 936, reference is made to the gallant conduct of Capt. H. A. Rogers, Thirteenth North Carolina, who carried the flag of his regiment after being wounded in the arm. As this Captain Rogers subsequently became Major and Lieutenant Colonel of that regiment, he probably is the man mentioned by Cooke, but the identification is not certain, because the injury to Captain Rogers may have occurred May 3.

[52] *Cooke's Jackson,* 429.

he could not be moved. Neither he nor Jackson was told at the moment of the extent of the other's wounds.[53]

Carefully, Jackson was given Rogers's place in the ambulance. Morrison climbed in to hold the broken arm of the General and thereby to ease his pain.[54] From the Stony Ford Road, the ambulance soon turned to the Northwest, up the Hazel Grove Road, and came into the Plank Road at the corner of Dowdall's Field.[55] Thence the ambulance was headed westward in reverse of the line of Jackson's whirlwind advance that afternoon. Captain Leigh went ahead to clear the much encumbered way and to locate the "rough places." On the journey, the General spoke for the first time of the wound in his left forearm,[56] and in his pain and faintness he again asked several times for "spirits." Hotchkiss and probably several others besides Wilbourn had gone off in search of whiskey, but they had not yet returned.[57] All the wayfarers of whom liquor was solicited by surgeon or by attendants were men singularly abstemious or else they had drunk all the whiskey they had. Jackson got none until he reached Rev. Melzi Chancellor's, or until almost that time.[58]

At Mr. Chancellor's house, Jackson found his Medical Director and friend, Dr. Hunter McGuire, who was more welcome than spirits. Although the doctor was eleven years his junior, Jackson had for him not merely respect as a professional man but affection as an individual. On none of the officers of the general staff did Jackson lean so heavily. With relief he saw McGuire kneel by his litter and heard the warm inquiry, "I hope you are not badly hurt, General."

[53] Cf. *Leigh*, 234; *McGuire*, 221; *infra*, p. 578.

[54] *Morrison*, 182.

[55] That is to say, at the eastern end of Melzi Chancellor's farm.

[56] In the full text of his letter, *loc. cit.*, Leigh said that Jackson's worst pain at this time was from the wound in the right hand.

[57] *Wilbourn*, 272; *Hotchkiss' MS Diary*, 179.

[58] The vagueness of the text is due to an unimportant conflict of testimony. Leigh, *op. cit.*, 234, said that the party was "unable to find any spirits for a long time, but Dr. Whitehead at length procured a bottle of whiskey." Kyle wrote, *op. cit.*, 309, that this was at Melzi Chancellor's. Dr. McGuire stated that "some whiskey and morphia were procured from Dr. Straith," *op. cit.* 221. This officer almost certainly was Surgeon J. A. Strait, but where Strait was at the time, it is difficult to say. Dabney recorded, *op. cit.*, 691, that "Rev. Mr. Vass," Chaplain of the Stonewall Brigade, obtained the whiskey soon after Dr. McGuire reached Jackson. The reference to the Stonewall Brigade would fix the position of Mr. Vass, if he then was with his command, quite close to Melzi Chancellor's. Cf. *O. R.*, 25, pt. 1, p. 1013.

"I am badly injured, Doctor; I fear I am dying." The words were faint, but the tone was calm. A moment later he added, "I am glad you have come. I think the wound in my shoulder is still bleeding." [59]

McGuire at once applied a finger to the major artery above the wound and compressed it until he could get a light. Then he discovered that the handkerchief applied by Wilbourn had slipped.[60] This was quickly adjusted. Jackson's thanks were expressed with his usual politeness. In every respect he kept his grip on himself. Said McGuire: "His suffering at this time was intense; his hands were cold, his skin clammy, his face pale, and his lips compressed and bloodless; not a groan escaped him—not a sign of suffering, except the slight corrugation of his brow, the fixed, rigid face, and the thin lips so tightly compressed that the impression of his teeth could be seen through them." Even the restlessness and half convulsion so common in the wounded, Jackson put under the bar of his iron will.[61]

As soon as the bleeding was stanched, Jackson received from Dr. McGuire some whiskey and a dose of morphia. These had prompt effect. In a few minutes, the General was less sensitive to pain, and soon he was so much relieved that the ambulance could be started for the field hospital, which was nearly four miles to the rear. En route, beyond the range of fire and within the Southern lines, torches could be used to reveal the chuck holes in the road and to save the General from jolts. McGuire sat in the front of the ambulance and kept his finger on the severed artery so that, if the handkerchief-tourniquet slipped again, there would be no bleeding. Jackson spoke occasionally and once he took his right hand, lifted it to the doctor's head and pulled McGuire down to him. "Is Crutchfield dangerously wounded?" he asked in a low voice, lest the Colonel hear him.

"No," McGuire answered, "only painfully hurt."

"I am glad it is no worse."

[59] *McGuire*, 220. From this point onward, though Dr. McGuire confused his dates and forgot some details that others remembered, he is the basic authority. His account, it may be repeated, was published in May, 1866, and, with the exception of Leigh's letter, *Hotchkiss' Diary* and the composite narrative prepared by Cooke soon after the battle of Chancellorsville, *cf.* 6 *S. H. S. P.*, 267, is nearest to the events.

[60] This doubtless had happened when Jackson fell and it may have been one reason he had become sensitive to the wound in the forearm, which previously had been numbed by the tourniquet.

[61] *McGuire*, 220-21.

Presently, in much the same way, Crutchfield, though he was in the nerve-shattering pain of a broken leg, inquired about Jackson's wounds; but when he heard that the General was seriously wounded, the younger man could not restrain his emotion: "O, my God," he cried with a groan.

Jackson heard Crutchfield and, thinking the Colonel's anguish responsible for the outcry, ordered the ambulance stopped and something done to relieve his wounded comrade.

Often from the drivers of ambulances and ammunition wagons bound for the front [62] came the inquiry that had been so persistent in the thicket: Who was wounded? Every time Jackson heard the question, he would prompt McGuire, "Say, a 'Confederate officer.'" The General was determined that the confusion of the night should not be increased by the demoralization which often follows the report that a leader has fallen.

Back to Talley's he rode slowly in the rumbling vehicle, back to the ridge where the troops had deployed, back to the crossing of the Brock Road. Shortly after 11 o'clock the ambulance reached the Wilderness Old Tavern,[63] which then was the home of W. M. Sims.[64] At that point, the ambulance turned North into a field on the fringe of the Wilderness, where the Second Corps Hospital had been established.[65] The surgeon in charge, Dr. Harvey Black, had received the grievous news of the wounding of Jackson and had prepared and warmed a tent into which the General immediately was carried.[66] More whiskey Jackson received after he was placed on a cot, and then, slowly, under protective canvas and abundant blankets, he seemed to come back to life. His pulse became stronger; warmth returned to his body. Over him, Dr. McGuire and Lieutenant Smith watched quietly.

Midnight came and went. Except for the forlorn call of the whip-po'-will and the occasional agonized cry of a man under the surgeon's saw, there was quiet over the field. From the front there floated not an echo of conflict. One o'clock—still Dr. McGuire waited for a stronger pulse and a clearer mind. After a time the Medical Director slipped out, but about 2 o'clock he lifted the tent

[62] Leigh's letter, *loc. cit.*
[63] So Kyle styled it. On Hotchkiss' map it is marked "Old Wilderness Tavern."
[64] *Kyle,* 309.
[65] Kyle, *loc. cit.;* Hotchkiss' Map of May 2, *op. cit.*
[66] 3 *B. & L.,* 213; Leigh's letter, *loc. cit.*

flap again. With him were Dr. Harvey Black, Surgeon Walls [67] and Dr. R. T. Coleman, Chief Surgeon of Jackson's old Division.[68] As they stood around him, Jackson heard Dr. McGuire tell him that chloroform would be administered to permit the painless examination of the wounds. This examination might show the bone of the upper left arm so badly broken that the surgeons would consider amputation necessary. Should that be the conclusion, McGuire went on, did Jackson wish them to proceed with the operation immediately? The answer was weakly spoken but firm and instant: "Yes, certainly, Dr. McGuire, do for me whatever you think best." [69]

Preparations began. Dr. Coleman quietly rubbed over Jackson's face a protective unguent, and then the surgeon folded a cloth into the shape of a cup. Jackson never before had received an anæsthetic, and he had shared the feeling prevalent among many pious individuals of his day that a patient should not take chloroform when there was a prospect of dying while under its influence. A person about to face the Almighty, it was argued, should be in as full possession of the faculties as the disease or injury made possible. None of this misgiving about chloric ether troubled Jackson now. Dr. Coleman poured on the cloth about a drachm of chloroform from the container that had reached a Southern port aboard a blockade runner. The Surgeon bade Jackson exhale fully and, as the General drew breath again, Coleman placed the wet cloth about two inches above Jackson's nose and mouth. Another deep breath, then another: in a few minutes Jackson began to feel the effects. "What an infinite blessing!" he exclaimed. The same word, "blessing, blessing" came often but more slowly and jumbled. Then he was relaxed and was almost insensible, though he stated afterwards that he was dimly aware of what went on.[70]

The wound in his right hand was examined first by Dr. McGuire, while Lieutenant Smith held the light. A round ball had entered the palm, had broken two bones and had lodged under the skin at the back of the hand. Dr. McGuire took it out

[67] McGuire, 221.

[68] O. R., 25, pt. 1, p. 1009.

[69] Ibid. Leigh, loc. cit., stated that when he reached the hospital with Jackson, the surgeons spoke as if amputation of the arm was unavoidable.

[70] The statement of the manner in which chloroform doubtless was administered to Jackson is based on the technique recommended in the thirty-ninth edition (1864) of Samuel D. Gross's System of Surgery, the standard work of that period.

and, from his wide experience, could say at once that it had been fired from a smooth-bore Springfield musket. That weapon was much used by the Confederates but had been discarded by the Federals. The mute evidence of the projectile answered the question the army already was beginning to ask: Had Jackson been wounded by his own men, who mistook him and his companions for Federal cavalry?

McGuire put the bullet down and laid bare the General's left arm. An ugly wound was disclosed. A ball had entered about three inches below the joint of the shoulder, had divided the main artery, had shattered the bone and had passed out. In the forearm, a third bullet had struck about an inch below the uplifted elbow, and had come out on the inside of the arm just above the wrist.[71] McGuire shook his head as he looked: Conditions were as he had feared they would be. It was not possible to save a member so badly damaged. To prevent gangrene and useless anguish, the left arm should be amputated at once. The other surgeons were of the same mind.

It was an operation each of them had performed scores of times —a brief and usually not a dangerous operation. While Dr. Coleman continued to administer the chloroform and Dr. Black watched the heart action, Dr. McGuire swiftly made the approved circular incision and sawed off the bone. Dr. Walls ligated the arteries. With so many experienced hands at work, little blood was lost. After Dr. McGuire had applied the dressings, the anæsthetic was withdrawn. The salve was wiped off to permit treatment of the wounds of the face. All of these were found to be superficial, having been caused by limbs of trees when the sorrel ran under fire, and they were treated with nothing more than isinglass plaster.[72]

The operation now was ended. For half an hour Jackson remained on the border line of the unconscious and then he received a cup of coffee, which he was able to retain.[73] After this mild stimulant he was expected to have long, uninterrupted sleep, but within an hour, as he lay in the tent quietly under the eye of Lieutenant Smith, he was disturbed. Dr. McGuire entered with "Sandie" Pendleton. The staff officer had come with an impor-

71 This is almost verbatim the language of Dr. McGuire, *op. cit.*, 222.
72 *McGuire*, 222.   73 *Dabney*, 695-96.

tant message and, despite the surgeon's protests, had insisted on seeing the General. Jackson recognized him and spoke promptly: "Well, Major I am glad to see you; I thought you were killed." [74]

The faithful Pendleton did not stop to explain that when he heard of the tragedy in the woods he had ridden so far and so fast in quest of Dr. McGuire that when he found the Surgeon and told of the injury to their chief, he had fallen from his horse in a faint.[75] It was of the army, rather than of himself that Pendleton spoke. He reported that Hill had been disabled, and he told of the decision to send for Stuart. The cavalryman had arrived at the front,[76] said Pendleton, but knew little of the situation and sent to Jackson for instructions. Jackson was able to command his weary, drugged mind to ask a few questions in his brisk, military manner. With contracted brow and set lips he pondered the answers and struggled visibly to find a solution that would help Stuart. "For a moment," McGuire wrote, "it was believed [Jackson] had succeeded, for his nostrils dilated and his eye flashed its old fire, but it was only for a moment; his face relaxed again, and presently he answered very feebly and sadly, 'I don't know—I can't tell; say to General Stuart he must do what he thinks best.' "

With this message, Pendleton rode back to Stuart, who by this time had received the transfer of the command from Powell Hill. In the finest spirit, Robert Rodes acquiesced. His explanation, set forth in his report,[77] was as manful as logical: "I deem it proper to state that I yielded the command to General Stuart not because I thought him entitled to it, belonging as he does to a different arm of the service, nor because I was unwilling to assume the responsibility of carrying on the attack, as I had already made the necessary arrangements, and they remained unchanged, but because, from the manner in which I had been informed that he had been sent for, I inferred that General Jackson or General Hill had instructed Major Pendleton to place him in command, and for the still stronger reason that I feared that the information that the

[74] McGuire, 223. [75] Pendleton, 261 n.

[76] Stuart, O. R., 25, pt. 1, p. 887, stated that he arrived at 10 P.M. In this timing he undoubtedly erred. Rodes, ibid., 942, put the hour at midnight, which would correspond to the chronology of other known events. Marshall E. Decker of the Ninth Virginia Cavalry was serving as Stuart's guide that evening and was with the General when the courier arrived with the message. Decker had a stub of a candle and lighted it for Stuart to read the news of the wounding of Jackson—Letter of Dr. Henry W. Decker, Sept 24, 1942.

[77] O. R., 25, pt. 1, pp. 942–43.

command had devolved on me, unknown except to my immediate troops, would, in their shaken condition, be likely to increase
the demoralization of the corps. General Stuart's name was well
and very favorably known to the army, and would tend, I hoped,
to re-establish confidence. I yielded because I was satisfied the
good of the service demanded it."

Good augury this was for a situation that had no parallel in the
history of the army. Lee was distant by air not more than two
miles, but he could not be reached in time to advise Stuart what to
do at dawn. Tired though the troops were, and confused in organization, they represented three-fifths of the army, and they must
push the offensive on which the outcome of the battle, perhaps of
the campaign, would depend. For the direction of these 25,000
soldiers, there was a cavalryman who never in his thirty years of
life had conducted an infantry action. To execute his orders, he
had not a general officer who, till that 2d of May, ever had led a
Division in action.[78] Now that Pendleton was back from Jackson's
side, Stuart had his responsibility sharpened: he would not have
the benefit of his friend Jackson's sound judgment. "Jeb" was not
daunted by this, by lack of information or by the absence of all
Jackson's staff officers except Pendleton. Calmly and cheerfully,
Stuart made the best of his plight. The guns of the Second Corps
must be made ready, he reasoned first of all, to prepare the way
for the infantry. Where was Crutchfield? Wounded? Who was
next in artillery command? Porter Alexander? A capable man!
Send for him and have him locate and occupy the best positions
that could be found. Stuart himself would ride along the tangled
line, would impose silence on the troops and would prepare to
attack with the dawn.

[78] General Alexander, *op. cit.*, 341, made the singular mistake of saying that Rodes
ranked Stuart, when in fact, Stuart had ranked Rodes as a Brigadier (see *Wright,* 61, 63)
and Rodes, on May 3, 1863, had not been advanced to the grade of Major General,
which Stuart had held since July 25, 1862. See *Wright,* 28. Colonel Hamlin, *op. cit.,*
114, remarked: "Why Jackson felt impelled to [send for Stuart], and [to] overlook the
deserving claims of some of his able division commanders, is not yet clear." In this,
needless to say, the careful historian of the XI Corps erred in assuming that Jackson sent
for Stuart. Similarly, Colonel Hamlin had forgotten that after the injury to Hill, there
was no experienced divisional commander in the Corps.

CHAPTER XXXIV

The Young Commanders' Day

WHEN THE FIRST light of a warm and pleasant day [1] began to filter into the Wilderness of Spotsylvania on May 3, 1863, Powell Hill's Division was widely deployed in the front line. Harry Heth, though still a stranger to most of the officers and men, was undertaking manfully and intelligently to direct the force Hill was too badly bruised to command. The Division in two lines was across the Plank Road, almost exactly one mile West of Chancellorsville.[2] On the extreme right of the first line was Archer, with his front somewhat refused, not through design but because the advance of the right Brigades had been halted there. On Archer's left was McGowan. Next him, with left flank on the Plank Road, was Lane; on Lane's left, North of the road, was Pender and, as the left flank element, Thomas. Across the road, Heth's own Brigade,[3] now under Col. J. M. Brockenbrough, formed a short second line. The Division of Trimble, once Jackson's own and now led by Raleigh Colston, was from 300 to 500 yards in rear of Heth. The third line, Rodes's, was across the highway at Meizi Chancellor's. All these troops were hungry,[4] but most of them had slept a few hours on the field and were able to give battle, though manifestly they could not be expected to show the fighting edge they had displayed the previous afternoon.

The artillery was in somewhat better condition. Porter Alexander's well-made reconnaissance had shown that some guns could be employed advantageously in and near the Plank Road. Besides this, Alexander had found one place, though only one and that one curious, which seemed to afford good ground for batteries: On the right of the Corps, in the midst of a dense thicket of pines,

---

[1] *Hotchkiss' MS Diary*, 183.   [2] See Bigelow's Plan 3, *op. cit.*, 344.
[3] Formerly Field's.
[4] Rodes had brought up his commissary wagons and could issue rations. Cf. *O. R.*, 25, nt. 1, p. 887. Alexander, *op. cit.*, 345, stated that cooked rations were sent forward but could not be issued to all the troops before the advance was ordered. Neither Colston nor Heth mentioned in his report any issue of provisions. H. B. McClellan, *op. cit.*, 249, stated that "rations were on hand for a part of the command."

was an opening, about 25 yards wide, that led for 200 yards to what had seemed in the moonlight to be a cleared eminence where the Federals already had guns.[5] Alexander sensed the possibility of driving the Federals from this position and of occupying it with his own artillery. To this end, he had brought up several batteries before daylight and had concealed them as close as he could to

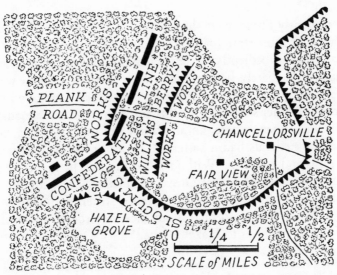

Terrain and Federal Works West and Southwest of Chancellorsville, about 5 A.M., May 3, 1863. The sketch shows, also, the Confederate Line and the "Vista" North of Hazel Grove—after *Bigelow*

the clearance. At dawn, from the Northwest, this high ground was hidden by mist, but as the sun drove away this screen, the hill appeared to be what Alexander had thought it was—an admirable position from which to assail the Federals.[6] Guides said the elevation was called Hazel Grove. Its strategical importance "Jeb" Stuart realized and, as Major Henry McClellan subsequently reported, the temporary commander of the Corps devoted a large share of his personal attention to the occupation and then to the strengthening of Hazel Grove.[7]

From the moment Stuart had gained his first knowledge of the situation, his determination had been to attack as soon as possible

5 This is almost word for word Alexander's own description in *op. cit.,* 342. which followed the language of his report, *O. R.,* 25, pt. 1, pp. 822–23.
6 *O. R.,* 25, pt. 1, p. 887.   7 H. B. *McClellan,* 249.

and with his full force.[8] He had been told by the half conscious
Jackson to do what he thought best. In Stuart's code of war,
where the offensive was not too hazardous, it always was the best
of any or many courses. He delayed now as long only as the
sun demanded time to rout the shadows. At last—it must have
seemed a long time—Stuart had full daylight. "As beautiful
and bright a day" it proved to be, "as one could desire, even for a
Sabbath." [9]

Confidently Stuart gave the first order: Archer and McGowan
on the right must straighten their front as a preliminary to a general advance. Obediently Archer began this movement at sunrise.[10]
Almost immediately he lost touch with McGowan, who was on
his left, but about the same time he established contact with the
enemy.[11] Archer's men drove this force through the woods and
out into the open, where, on an abrupt hill overlooking a spring
house, the Federals had a battery.[12] In his onsweep, Archer took
four guns and 100 men. Without knowing that he had seized the
strategic position of Hazel Grove, he pressed on, with his 1400
men, against bluecoats whose resistance stiffened quickly.[13] As
soon as Stuart got word of this advance, he ordered more of the
Confederate batteries to Hazel Grove.[14]

[8] H. B. McClellan, *op. cit.*, 249–50, stated that Stuart "had received orders, just before
day, from General Robert E. Lee, to begin the attack as soon as possible," but the statement of the time of the receipt of Lee's order was given second hand to McClellan and
may be early by an hour or two. Stuart himself, in his report, said nothing of the
receipt of orders from Lee and unmistakably left the impression that, from the time of
his arrival at the front, he intended to attack and "much against my inclination . . .
felt bound to wait for daylight." *O. R.*, 25, pt. 1, p. 887.
[9] *Caldwell*, 84.
[10] At least Heth, *O. R.*, 25, pt. 1, p. 891, so stated. This was in accordance with
the order Stuart said he issued, *ibid.*, 887, but there was some doubt whether Archer and
McGowan understood that their orders simply were to straighten the line.
[11] *Alexander*, 346. In their proper sequence and relation, the events that followed
on the Confederate right are past unravelling. Stuart attempted in his report, *O. R.*, 25,
pt. 1, pp. 887–88, to give a connected narrative but he succeeded in presenting a general
outline only. Heth's account, *ibid.*, 889 ff, though limited in scope, was reasonably clear
except for confusion of the order of events. Colston's official narrative, *ibid.*, 1003, was
vague; Rodes's, *ibid.*, 939, was no better. Many of the Brigadiers despaired of establishing what happened at a given time and contented themselves with general references
to fluctuations and to numerous attacks. Of the secondary authorities, Bigelow is
immensely detailed but at the last, *op. cit.*, 367, he could do no better than to say, in a
single sentence, that Stuart "push[ed] forward on the right and the left of the Plank
Road." Alexander, *op. cit.*, 347, frankly evaded any attempt at accurate narration of
all that came to pass. "It would be useless," said he, "to follow in detail the desperate
fighting which now ensued . . ."
[12] *O. R.*, 25, pt. 1, p. 925.   [13] *Ibid.*
[14] Presumably Stuart knew that Alexander during the night had placed artillery close
to Hazel Grove, but it is difficult to say whether Stuart's first orders were issued to those
batteries or to others.

On Archer's left, by this time,[15] Stuart had sent forward the other Brigades of Hill's Division.[16] These experienced troops, attacking on a front of about a mile and a quarter, had no difficulty in storming a crude Federal work of logs and brush, about 150 to 250 yards from their starting point. With a yell the men of the Light Division pressed immediately toward the second Federal line,[17] but they soon received on both flanks the challenge of angry fire. North of the Plank Road, Thomas's Georgians reached a struggling, smoke-covered mass of bluecoats. With the left units of Pender's Brigade, Thomas struck for the third Union line, but his own left soon became encumbered.[18] On the right of the road, McGowan pushed 100 yards past the first line,[19] only to find that Archer, on his right, had fallen back, about 6.30, to Hazel Grove and had exposed the right of the South Carolinians.

This formed between Archer's left and McGowan's right a gap

---

[15] About 5.45; sunrise was at 5.11. Rodes, commanding the third line, stated, *ibid.,* 943, that the "attack was renewed about 6 A.M."

[16] Those who study seriously the Battle of Chancellorsville will have occasion to use the detailed maps in *Bigelow.* The author saw fit, in locating troop positions, to give to each Brigade or part of a Brigade the name of the officer commanding it at the moment described. This is so confusing that the following list of changes in command May 2–3 may prove helpful:

Hill's Division became Heth's;

Heth's Brigade passed to Col. John M. Brockenbrough when Heth assumed divisional command;

McGowan's Brigade, after his wound, had as successive commanders Cols. O. E. Edward, A. Perrin and D. H. Hamilton;

Rodes's Brigade, while he served as commander of D. H. Hill's Division, was under Col. E. A. O'Neal and, after that officer was wounded, under Col. J. M. Hall;

Trimble's Division throughout *Bigelow* is described as Colston's, after its senior Brigadier, Raleigh E. Colston;

Paxton's Brigade, following the death of its chief, appears as Funk's Brigade, so styled from Col. J. H. S. Funk of the Fifth Virginia;

Jones's Brigade, when he left the field, passed to Col. T. S. Garnett, upon whose death Col. A. S. Vandeventer became commander;

Colston's Brigade entered the action under Col. E. T. H. Warren and then fought under Col. T. V. Williams, after Warren was wounded;

As Francis T. Nicholls was put hors de combat on the 2nd, his Louisiana Brigade on the 3d appears as J. M. Williams's.

In addition, for one reason or another during the course of the action of May 3, three of Rodes's Brigades were divided:

From Doles's Brigade, Col. J. T. Mercer with part of the Twenty-first and the whole of the Twelfth Georgia became separated. On some of Bigelow's maps these regiments are listed as Mercer.

Col. H. D. Christie, with part of his Twenty-third North Carolina, detached from Iverson's Brigade, appears under his own name in *Bigelow.*

The force figured by Bigelow as Hall's and as Pickens's was O'Neal's Brigade, which in reality was Rodes's own.

A detached unit on Bigelow's Map 31, marked 30 N. C., was the regiment of Col F. M. Parker.

[17] *O. R.,* 25, pt. 1, pp. 891, 913; 1 *N. C. Regts.,* 669.

[18] *O. R.,* 25, pt. 1, p. 913.   [19] *Ibid.,* 904.

which the Federals began to exploit. In heavy fighting, the old Brigade of Maxcy Gregg went back, almost step by step, to the first Federal line,[20] which it reoccupied and held. McGowan's withdrawal in turn uncovered the right of Lane, whose consequent retirement forced back all of Pender's regiments save the Thirteenth North Carolina on the left. That fine regiment, under the admirable leading of Col. Alfred Scales, continued its advance and ere long captured a Federal Brigadier, William Hays.[21]

By 7 A.M., then, Stuart had this situation before him: The right and the center of the Corps had been repulsed from the second Federal line and were being re-formed on the line captured in the first rush; the left of the Corps was precariously advanced. Inasmuch as the first line of the Federals had been at no point more than 250 yards from the jump-off, this phase of Stuart's advance represented a gain scarcely worth counting. The one substantial success was Archer's. Although his attack could not be pressed farther at the moment, it had won ground more valuable than most of the commanders yet realized. Hazel Grove was firmly in Confederate hands. Major Pegram had gone there, without further orders, as soon as he had observed the enemy evacuate the ground, and now he was opening with three batteries. Capt. R. C. M. Page followed immediately with his fine battery of Napoleons.[22]

When Stuart, through the smoke, saw the stars and bars at Hazel Grove, he may have sensed the possibility of defeating the Federal infantry by the fire of artillery massed there, but he did not rely exclusively on the "long arm." He would try the rifle, the minié ball and the bayonet, and with the fury of as many thousands as he could muster, he would wrest Chancellorsville from the enemy. Move guns to Hazel Grove; tell Colston and Rodes to bring up every man to support Hill's Division in a general assault. Press that assault straight to Chancellorsville.

---

[20] *Ibid.*, 891, 902, 904.

[21] *O. R.*, 25, pt. 1, pp. 891, 935, 936. Brig. Gen. William Hays commanded the 2d Brigade of French's 3d Division of Couch's II Corps. He is not to be confused with Alexander Hays, born the same year, who was killed May 5, 1864, in the Battle of the Wilderness.

[22] *O. R.*, 25, pt. 1, pp. 823, 925, 938. The Confederates did not know it at the time, but they could have had Hazel Grove without a struggle had they delayed their advance even a few minutes. For reasons never understood, General Hooker at daylight had ordered the abandonment of Hazel Grove and a concentration at Fairview. See *Bigelow*, 345–47.

Gloriously the first part of Stuart's orders was obeyed. Thanks primarily to the new battalion organization of the artillery, one battery after another climbed to Hazel Grove and wheeled into position. Never in the annals of the Army of Northern Virginia had so great a concentration of guns been effected so quickly or with comparable ease.

The infantry were not so fortunate. In the execution of the order to press behind Hill, the old Division of Jackson was poorly led. Colston did not have experience in handling so many men. In the whole Division, one only of the four Brigades had at its head a general officer.[23] The result of this lack of command was lack of confidence. When Colston's right wing reached the log works about 8 A.M.,[24] his troops crowded to cover behind Hill's men.[25] The utmost endeavors of perplexed officers failed for the time to get the line moving. While Pender and Thomas, on the left of the road, at heavy loss, were driving the enemy, the veterans of Jackson's old Division refused to face the fire. In Colston's own Brigade, three commanders quickly were shot down.[26] Soon, to quote A. P. Hill, men of the two Brigades of Colston on the right of the road were "somewhat broken and disorganized." [27] To their shame, officers had to admit themselves powerless. The assault must await the arrival of Rodes's Division.[28]

[23] Paxton was there, and was wholly capable; Francis Nicholls, a splendid soldier, though new in the direction of a Brigade, had lost a leg the previous evening. For that reason, Col. J. M. Williams of the Second Louisiana was in command of the Louisiana troops (O. R., 25, pt. 1, p. 1005). Colston's own Brigade, it will be remembered, was being led by Col. E. T. H. Warren of the Tenth Virginia. During the night, moreover, Gen. John R. Jones had complained of an ulcerated leg and had gone to the rear (O. R., 25, pt. 1, p. 1005). That put the second Brigade in the care of Col. T. S. Garnett of the Forty-eighth Virginia—in many ways a change for the better but a substitution of a sort to render united action by the Brigade difficult.

[24] Frequent references are made by Bigelow to "Slocum's" log works and to those of Berry and Williams. It may be convenient to remember that Slocum's works were the westward face of what appears on most maps of Chancellorsville as a "dipper," the handle of which is to the Northeast along Mineral Spring Road. The line in Slocum's care began in the neighborhood of Hazel Grove and ran convexly to a point about 350 yards North of the Plank Road, and almost directly North of the Van Wert House. On the road, the crossing of Slocum's works was about 1900 yards West of Chancellorsville. Williams's log works were South, and Berry's North of the Plank Road nearly three-quarters of a mile West of Chancellorsville and to the West of the swampy ground on the Confederate side of Fairview. The distance between the two Federal lines at the Plank Road was about 600 yards; South of the road, Williams's works apparently ran 400 yards only. At their southern termination they were approximately 420 yards from the nearest point of Slocum's works, which were to the West and Southwest. These works were not formidable. At the opening of the action they barely afforded shelter for kneeling or prone infantry, but they almost certainly were raised by the men who took refuge there.

[25] O. R., 25, pt. 1, pp. 902–03.   [26] Ibid., 1005.

[27] O. R., 25, pt. 1, p. 886.   [28] Cf. Bigelow, 353.

That was not the full measure of disgrace: it began to look as if the enemy, who now was advancing menacingly, might throw Jackson's men out of the shallow trenches. Said Colston: "This was a most critical moment. The troops in the breastworks . . . were almost without ammunition, and had become mixed with each other and with fragments of other commands. They were huddled up close to the breastworks six and eight deep." [29] So bewildered were these veteran soldiers, so completely without leadership, that they were not even keeping up a fire against the approaching enemy.[30] In this balance 'twixt death and doom, Colston decided he would bring the veteran Stonewall Brigade from the North of the Plank Road to the South and would throw it and Jones's [31] Brigade against the oncoming Federals. Unless Paxton stiffened the right, or Rodes arrived quickly, Stuart might lose his first infantry battle.

Paxton crossed the road, as ordered, and with Garnett on his right, prepared to advance.[32] At the works, McGowan, by that time, was wounded. His proud South Carolina officers were striving vainly to get the men to press forward and to repel the enemy. Some even of the tried, old soldiers who gained lasting fame at Gaines' Mill and at Groveton refused to budge. Now, through them, through *them*, the first volunteers of the Palmetto State, pushed Paxton's Virginians of the Valley. "[They] passed over us," wrote the historian of McGowan's Brigade, "some of them saying, with no very pleasant levity, that they would show us how to clear away a Federal line." [33]

The Stonewall Brigade made valiant effort. Garnett's men supported them with equal bravery.[34] Although both Paxton and Garnett were shot down, their men met the Federals in the spirit of the Valley campaign. The fierce fire of the two Brigades halted the enemy and made him waver. Soon he began to give ground. That put springs in the legs of Jackson's soldiers. They pushed on until they were within seventy yards of the Union line. There they faced precisely such a whirlwind of fire as they had thrown against their foe. Struggle though they might to continue their

[29] *O. R.*, 25, pt. 1, p. 1006.   [30] *Ibid.*
[31] Garnett's.
[32] Rodes noted, *O. R.*, 25, pt. 1, p. 943, that the Stonewall Brigade was crossing to the right as his Division came up.
[33] *Caldwell*, 80.
[34] Cf. *Bigelow*, 354; *O. R.*, 25, pt. 1, pp. 1006, 1025–26.

advance, they had to stop. "Hold your ground," they yelled one to another, but that was beyond their might. They were too few and were losing too heavily. Back to the log works, broken and decimated, they had to go. Not without a certain cold satisfaction did the same historian of McGowan's Brigade write of Garnett's men and of Paxton's: ". . . their reckoning was not accurate. They were forced back to the works with us." The South Carolinians had their own deeper humiliation: Col. D. H. Hamilton withdrew the First regiment from the works and went to the rear a short distance. He did so in order to renew his ammunition from a supply he knew the Federals had left there, and he acted wisely.[35] At the moment, his move may have seemed inexplicable to the bleeding men of the Army of the Valley who fell back to the log works.

It was now about 8.15. On the left as on the right, Stuart's attack had been beaten back. Thomas and Pender, North of the road, had withdrawn[36] from their advanced position. Fortunately, by this time, Rodes was close behind Heth and Colston, though he could not command his full strength. One of Rodes's Brigades, that of Colquitt, had been sent to the extreme left because of reports by the cavalry that the enemy was demonstrating heavily there.[37] Furthermore, in advancing through the thick undergrowth, some of his regiments were separated.[38] Rodes, in consequence, was not yet ready to push through Heth and Colston and to deliver his assault. The battle lagged.

In knowledge of this, even the buoyant "Jeb" might have been discouraged, had he not perceived that from Hazel Grove, gunners of the Second Corps, moment by moment, were increasing the weight of the metal they were throwing against the flank of the Federal line. The Union batteries were suffering, too. Near Chancellorsville on an elevation which the guide called Fairview, the Confederate shells were breaking among them. To the guns of Pegram, those of Alexander's own battalion under Frank Huger had been added. Tom Carter and David McIntosh had sent some

35 *Caldwell*, 80–81. It is not certain when this occurred. Neither Caldwell nor Colonel Hamilton, *O. R.*, 25, pt. 1, p. 905, is explicit in relation to the time of Colston's advance.

36 Cf. *Bigelow*, 353.

37 So Rodes reported, *O. R.*, 25, pt. 1, p. 943. He did not state whether the detachment was by his order or Stuart's.

38 These regiments were Doles's. Cf. *ibid.*, 943. The situation at 8.15 A.M. is represented about as accurately as reports permit on Bigelow's Map 28, opposite p. 356.

of their pieces. Before the morning was out, all of these and numbers from Poague, Hardaway, Hilary Jones and Lindsay Walker
were to be used.[39]

At Hazel Grove, in short, the finest artillerists of the Army of
Northern Virginia were having their greatest day. They had improved guns,[40] better ammunition [41] and superior organization.[42]
Officers and men were conscious of this and of the destruction they
were working. For once they were fighting on equal terms against
an adversary who on fields unnumbered had enjoyed indisputable
superiority in weapons and in ammunition. With the fire of battle
shining through his spectacles, William Pegram rejoiced. "A glorious day, Colonel," he said to Porter Alexander, "a glorious day!" [43]
Before either he or Alexander could see any definite evidence that
the Federal artillery was being outfought, there was an uncertainty, a nervous irregularity in the Federal fire.[44] Here and there
—the sight made the heart beat higher!—good eyes saw, through
the smoke, that Federal infantry were beginning to recoil under
the shells of the Southern batteries.[45] The right of Stuart might
suffer heavily in gaining the ground necessary to form a junction
with Lee, who was moving up from the South toward Chancellorsville; there might be much more of hard fighting and of costly
assaults; but if those gray batteries could continue to sweep the
field, the Federals must yield!

Stuart wisely devoted the greater part of his effort to seeing that
batteries which had to retire to replenish their ammunition were
replaced immediately. It was a joyous task. Had "Old Jack" been
fully conscious, back at the Second Corps Hospital, of what was
happening there on the hill at Hazel Grove, the soul of the
Chapultepec artillerist would have been renewed! The gunners
themselves realized that they were fighting a victorious action, and
they made a joke of their ghastly work. In one battery, a boy so
small that he seemed scarcely more than 12 years of age was at the
lanyard of a field piece. Every time he pulled the lanyard he
clownishly rolled over backward, to the delight of his laughing

---

[39] See *Alexander*, 347–48, and Alexander's report, *O. R.,* 25, pt. 1, p. 823. Part of
Walker's fighting was on and near the Plank Road.

[40] *Ham Chamberlayne,* 176.

[41] Except for that of the 20-pounder Parrott, *O. R.,* 25, pt. 2, p. 795.

[42] *O. R.,* 25, pt. 1, pp. 866–70.   [43] 5 *C. V.,* 288.

[44] Cf. *O. R.,* 25, pt. 1. p. 823.   [45] *Ibid.,* 938.

comrades. That was the spirit of the cannonade from Hazel Grove.[46]

Rodes's Division was now deployed for the advance.[47] In front of the left Brigade was a baffling tangle of woods and undergrowth, where a commander could not see his own men fifty yards away.[48] Everywhere else on the front, visibility was dangerously limited. In this maze, immediately North of the highway, where they could serve as Rodes's left center when he came up, were Pender and Thomas who, though repulsed and lying now behind Slocum's log works, were not disorganized. Rodes's right center was in rear of the weary and half demoralized units of McGowan. On the right, Rodes had in front of him the confused and irresolute command of Jones, which was under Col. A. S. Vandeventer of the Fiftieth Virginia. Of all the infantry ahead of Rodes's right, the one force that could be counted upon for strong and early co-operation was the Stonewall Brigade, which was a short distance South of the road. Even that renowned command, after its repulse, needed a little time in which to catch its breath and clot its wounds before it made another attack.[49]

At length Rodes was ready. As courageously as on the ridge by Jackson's side, he gave the order. Almost from the moment the first men clutched their guns and crashed through the bushes, the woods confused his line. Doles's Brigade split. Two regiments drifted to the right; the valiant Twelfth and four companies of the Twenty-first Georgia [50] pushed ahead.[51] Men began to drop. Colonel O'Neal, commanding Rodes's Brigade, went down. His troops divided. About half of them,[52] under Col. J. M. Hall of the Fifth Alabama, veered to the right. The remainder, led by Col. Samuel B. Pickens of the Twelfth Alabama, pushed on toward

[46] *Dunaway, 71.*

[47] From left to right the Brigades at the outset were: Iverson, then Rodes's under O'Neal, with its right on the Plank Road. Next to the South, its left on the highway, was Ramseur. On his right was Doles. The right flank element was Colquitt's Brigade, which, as noted, soon was moved to the extreme left of the Division. *O. R.,* 25, pt. I, p. 943.

[48] *Cf.* Iverson in *O. R.,* 25, pt. I, p. 986.

[49] The situation immediately before Rodes's attack is presented on Bigelow's Map 28, opposite p. 356.

[50] With some men of the other regiments, *O. R.,* 25, pt. I, pp. 968, 971–72.

[51] This is the force that appears on Bigelow's map as Mercer. It was commanded by Col. John T. Mercer of the Twenty-first, though the Twelfth was under a vigorous and able young officer, Col. Edward Willis. Cf. *supra,* p. 587, n. 16.

[52] With some isolated men of Brockenbrough's Brigade.

Berry's log works.[53] If there was disorder, there was valor to offset it. From Iverson's line in the baffling woodland North of the Plank Road, Col. H. D. Christie of the Twenty-third North Carolina soon became detached and started an attack all his own.

To Rodes, this sundering of his Division meant that he could handle those troops only that were close to the center of the line. Said he: "On account of the dense forest, the undulating character of the ground, and the want of an adequate staff, it was not in my power . . . to give a great deal of personal attention to the actions of any of my command, except Rodes's and Ramseur's Brigades, which were next to the road, but my orders were faithfully executed by each brigade commander." [54]

Rodes's embarrassment was Dodson Ramseur's opportunity. Until the afternoon of May 1, the North Carolinian [55] never had been privileged to lead in action the fine Brigade of George Anderson that had been committed to him. Now Ramseur went forward with a fury that had not been shown on the field that morning. Doles on the right was to have a gallant adventure, and Iverson and Christie on the left were to have high moments, but for the next hour, the battle was to be Ramseur's.

At the outset, during a pause on the Plank Road just before the attack began, Ramseur saw one of Stuart's staff ride up through the woods on the right and heard him order forward the troops that were crowding behind the log works. The officer who received the order answered that he could not advance without instructions from his division commander, Colston.

Instantly Ramseur spoke up: "Give me the order and I will charge."

Bryan Grimes, Colonel of the Fourth Carolina and a man lacking in no soldierly characteristic, felt that he should expostulate: The Brigade, said he, had fought hard for two days: Let Jones's Brigade charge; the North Carolinians would support it.[56]

---

[53] Which, it may be desirable to repeat, was the second or inner line, approached from the West, slightly under three-quarters of a mile West of Chancellorsville.

[54] O. R., 25, pt. 1, p. 943.

[55] He was not then 26 and had been promoted while he still was suffering from the severe wound he had received at Malvern Hill. See supra, pp. 265–66.

[56] Grimes, 31. At no point in the published text of Grimes's memoirs is the name of the Brigade in front of him mentioned, but in Ramseur's report, O. R., 25, pt. 1, p. 996, the reference is explicit to "a small portion of Paxton's brigade and Jones' brigade." Subsequently, Ramseur admitted that he was mistaken in his reference to the Stonewall Brigade. See O. R., 25, pt. 1, p. 1015. None of the reports of the Colonels of Jones's

Ramseur shook his head. No: he would advance if permission were given.

"Then you make the charge, General Ramseur," the staff officer said.[57]

"Let us hurry back," Ramseur said to Grimes. "Call your men to attention." [58]

In a few minutes, Ramseur's line was moving into the crowded works. Sternly he ordered the troops who were crouching there to advance. In his own indignant words, "Not a man moved." [59] Ramseur was as puzzled as he was wrathful. What should he do? He assumed that General Jones was on the field and he must have known that charges had been preferred against that officer, but as Jones's junior, could Ramseur order the men forward? If they refused to move, could he run over them? Quickly he decided to send back to Stuart, whom he knew to be close at hand, and to ask for instructions.

Word came back promptly for Ramseur to assume command and to force the shirkers to advance. Again Ramseur gave the order; again the men in the earthwork ignored it. He called for the commanding General and learned then, for the first time, that Jones had left the field and that Colonel Garnett had been killed. Apparently, Ramseur did not find Colonel Vandeventer, who was in command of Jones's Brigade. Undeterred, Ramseur exhorted and pleaded and denounced, to no purpose. Presently he stalked off to Stuart, who had reached that part of the line. In brief, angry explanation of what had happened, Ramseur asked if he might "run over the troops" in his front. Cheerful and approving permission instantly was granted.[60]

Ramseur hurried back to his waiting line, which was disgusted with the behavior of the men in front. Loudly he commanded, "Forward, march!" Without hesitation, his North Carolinians

Brigade admit any shirking. Ramseur is not mentioned. In the face of Ramseur's uncontradicted statement that Jones's Brigade was in the works, silence by the officers of that Brigade may mean nothing. A natural question concerns McGowan's men and the right of Lane. What had happened to these troops? Were not some of them still in the works; and were they not among those over whom Ramseur was prepared to advance?

[57] *Grimes*, 31. The absence of any reference of the matter to Rodes will be observed. Ramseur evidently felt that his orders from Rodes already were adequate, or else he could not communicate at the moment with Rodes. The report of the division commander would indicate that, at the time, he was devoting his attention to operations on his left.

[58] *Grimes*, 31. [59] *O. R.*, 25, pt. I, p. 996.

[60] *O. R.*, 25, pt. I, p. 996.

broke through the mob, climbed over the entrenchment and pushed forward. So wrathful was Bryan Grimes at seeing a cowardly officer prostrate, that he put his foot on the man's back and head and ground the face into the ground.[61] As Grimes went over the works, he heard a gloomy voice shout, "You may double-quick, but you'll come back faster than you go!" [62]

While Ramseur now pushed forward toward Williams's log works, two other parts of Rodes's Division were advancing with equal dash. On the left of the Plank Road, Iverson swept across the Bullock Farm Road. Colonel Christie, with his detached companies of the Twenty-third North Carolina, crashed around the rear of a Federal command and made a drive for Fairview. He failed to get there, but he held what he had gained and he forced the withdrawal of a Union battery that had been particularly troublesome.[63] This advance was to the left of Ramseur and it had the strong, gallant support of Pender and of Thomas. On Ramseur's right, Doles broke loose almost as furiously as the Fifth Texas had at Second Manassas. The Fourth and the Forty-fourth Georgia, under Doles's direction, pushed to the South of Fairview and for a time assailed the flank and rear of a strong adversary.[64]

Soon Doles had to withdraw, but Christie and Pender and Thomas, with some help from part of Rodes's own Brigade, fought to retain the advanced position near Fairview. Ramseur caught a furious fire. As he held to the offensive on his left, he had to defend his right.[65] That flank the Colonel of the Fourteenth North Carolina prudently guarded by halting a few hundred yards behind Ramseur's main advance.[66] Ramseur pushed his left across Williams's log works, but he had to draw his line at an angle beyond the works in order to get such shelter as he could against a fire that seemed to come from three directions.[67]

The young North Carolinian had a clear understanding of his position and realized that he must strengthen his right or fall back. If only the troops in the works behind him would sweep out and

[61] *Grimes*, 32; H. A. London, *Memorial Address on the Life and Services of Bryan Grimes*, 9.
[62] *Grimes*, 32.   [63] Dimick's. See *Bigelow*, 358.
[64] Ross. See *Bigelow*, 357. Bigelow's Map 29 gives this advance but, unfortunately, omitted Doles's name from the red mark that indicated his line. It appears immediately under the name of Bowman.
[65] *Bigelow*, 361.   [66] *O. R.*, 25, pt. 1, p. 996.
[67] *Ibid.*

fill a gap of some 500 or 600 yards between his right and Hazel Grove, all would be well! Several times Ramseur sent back to Colonel Vandeventer to move out Jones's Brigade. No more attention than previously was paid the order. Twice Ramseur went back in person, through a fiery hail. The result was the same. Jones's men insisted they would not move except on the orders of their own divisional commander, Colston, who, at that time, must have been on the other flank. At length, in manful distress and hot wrath, Ramseur had to notify Rodes that unless troops were sent to drive the enemy away from the exposed right, the Brigade would be compelled to withdraw. Rodes himself went up to the line but even he, always a commanding figure in battle, could move none of the troops behind the log works.[68]

Happily for the honor of Jackson's old Division, Stuart learned promptly of this sorry state of affairs and galloped up to the line of the Stonewall Brigade.[69] By a combination of authority and showmanship—by exhorting the men to avenge Jackson and by singing, "Old Joe Hooker, won't you come out of the Wilderness" —Stuart got the troops in motion.[70]

They advanced to the right of Ramseur, where they were most needed and, with the aid of a North Carolina regiment,[71] they made possible the orderly withdrawal of the other North Carolina units that had exhausted their ammunition.[72] Once started, the men who had fought with Jackson in all his battles continued to press on until they assailed Fairview, the dominant Federal artillery position nearest Chancellorsville. By that time, they were alone in their attack. Christie and Doles and all the others who had sought to break the Federal front had done their best but had withdrawn. With the Federal fire concentrated on him, Funk began to waver. A little before 10 o'clock, he found that he had lost

---

[68] O. R., 25, pt. 1, pp. 944, 996.

[69] Rodes throughout his report seemed to think that this Brigade had just arrived on the right when it was ordered to attack, but Col. J. H. S. Funk's report, O. R., 25, pt. 1, pp. 1013–14, shows plainly that the Brigade had made one advance and had suffered a repulse before Stuart came up and appealed to the men to relieve Ramseur.

[70] O. R., 25, pt. 1, p. 1014.

[71] Col. F. M. Parker's Thirtieth, which had been sent temporarily to support the artillery at Hazel Grove.

[72] O. R., 25, pt. 1, pp. 944, 996. It has to be noted that while Rodes gratefully acknowledged the advance of the Stonewall Brigade, Ramseur omitted all reference to the assistance given him by that command. The generous interpretation of this is that Ramseur was wounded later in the day and may have been unaware, when he wrote his report, that the Stonewall Brigade had come to his relief.

a third of his troops and that no support seemed forthcoming. The men of the Stonewall Brigade got the order to withdraw and slowly, unpursued by the enemy, as became veterans, they fell back to the log works.[73]

All the units of the Second Corps, save Colquitt on the extreme left, now seemed to be "fought out."[74] Stuart was forming a new line, was issuing rations and was replenishing ammunition. He would try again, but he had mustered all the might of seasoned troops and he appeared to have failed in his offensive. Then, abruptly—almost miraculously—the last of the Federal artillery, which had been leaving Fairview since 9 o'clock,[75] evacuated that position. From the high ground around Chancellorsville, where many guns had been massed, there was a perceptible decline in the volume of fire from Union guns. Was their ammunition near exhaustion? Always it had been enviably abundant by Confederate standards; had it failed now?

It had,[76] but something equally important had happened. By careful maneuver, hard fighting and the intelligent co-operation of Anderson and of McLaws, the commanding General, while pressing gradually northward, had extended to the West the left of the First Corps. Unknown to Stuart, part of "Dick" Anderson's Division had advanced from the direction of the Catharine Furnace and about 8 o'clock[77] had passed to the East of Hazel Grove. Two hours later, General Lee rode up to Archer's Brigade, which then was in support of the batteries at Hazel Grove, and ordered Archer to attack in the direction of Fairview. Junction of Anderson's left and Stuart's right then was effected. The united forces now could drive on a concave front against Chancellorsville.[78] Jubilant gunners raced from Hazel Grove to Fairview; yelling infantry poured northward through the woods and eastward on both sides of the Plank Road. By 10.30 or a little later, Lee was at Chancellorsville amid wild scenes of rejoicing. The price of the victory

[73] O. R., 25, pt. 1, p. 1014.
[74] Alexander, 347. Nicholls's Louisianians, who had fought admirably on the left, had been in danger of having their flank turned when Colquitt had arrived from the right. Colquitt at 10 o'clock was driving back Gen. Erastus B. Tyler. O. R., 25, pt. 1, pp. 943–44, 976, 1038.
[75] See Capt. C. L. Best's report, O. R., 25, pt. 1, p. 975.
[76] Cf. Bigelow, 375 ff. [77] Cf. Bigelow, 356.
[78] The operations of Anderson and of McLaws, under the immediate direction of Lee, are set forth in 2 R. E. Lee, 535 ff. Full details are given in Bigelow. For a curious story concerning Lee's handling of his dispatch to Davis on these events, see 21 C. V., 53

had not been unduly high. Mistakes could have been forgiven and losses endured if only, at the climax as at the beginning of the flank movement, Jackson had been there.

Jackson had awakened about 9 o'clock that pleasant Sabbath morning.[79] A heavy dew was on the ground. In the gardens the bloom of the apple and of the pear was added to that of the cherry

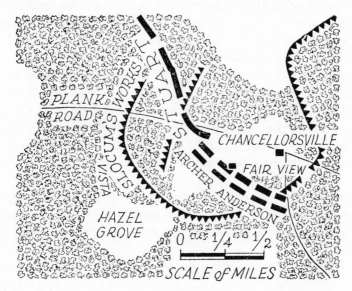

Confederate Infantry Dispositions in the Final Assault on Chancellorsville, May 3, 1863—
after *Bigelow*

and of the peach.[80] Calm the scene was, back from the hospital, among the farms that war had not befouled. To the wail of the whip-po'-will, the song of the robin succeeded; but over all, rolling and rising and ebbing and echoing, was the sound of the guns from Hazel Grove and from Fairview. Their bark was the best of tonics for the wounded Jackson. He took some nourishment and displayed a cheering resilience. The prognosis was favorable.

---

[79] After the departure of Pendleton with the message for Stuart to do as he thought best, Jackson had talked of the operation. He had some remembrance, he said, of what had seemed the most exquisite music. It must have been, he went on, the sound of Dr. McGuire's saw on the bone of the amputated arm. Chloroform, he repeated to James Power Smith, was a blessing but he would dislike to face eternity under its influence. Smith politely expressed interest and then suggested that the General refrain from all exertion. Jackson was as disciplined a patient as he was a soldier and he obediently stopped talking and soon fell into the deep aftersleep of his anæsthetic (*Dabney*, 696; *McGuire*, 223).

[80] *Hotchkiss' MS Diary*, 181

None of the surgeons seemed to have any fear for his recovery.[81] He was strong enough to dictate a note in which he informed General Lee of the success of the previous evening and announced his wounding and the transfer of command.[82] This done, Jackson sent all save two of his aides and other staff officers to assist Stuart on the battlefield. Lieutenant Smith was permitted to remain temporarily as nurse and companion. Morrison was to strike across the country overrun by raiding Federal cavalry and was to get to Richmond as best he could in order to bring Mrs. Jackson and the baby to the General's bedside.[83]

About 10 o'clock, after these arrangements had been made, Jackson felt so much pain in his right side that he asked Dr. McGuire to make an examination. It was probable, the General said, that in the fall of the litter he had struck a stone or the stump of a sapling. Carefully, inch by inch, Dr. McGuire went over the General's chest, abdomen and back. He could discover no bruise; there was nothing to indicate a broken rib; breathing seemed to be normal. The surgeon ordered some local applications and felt no special concern.[84] Jackson continued to suffer, but he seemed strong enough to be gratified in his wish to converse briefly with Tucker Lacy.

The Chaplain, on entering the tent, could not repress his emotion at the sight of the armless shoulder. "Oh, General," he exclaimed, "what a calamity!" Quickly Jackson reassured him. The loss of his arm, he said, was by the will of God. Later in life, or in the world to come, he would understand why that member was taken from him.[85] Jackson proceeded, almost eagerly, to recount

81 *Leigh*, 234; 3 *B. & L.*, 213; *McGuire*, 223.
82 The text of this dispatch has been lost. Contents have to be reconstructed from Lee's answer, for which see *infra*, p. 602.
83 *Hotchkiss' MS Diary*, 183; *Dabney*, 707.
84 *McGuire*, 223.
85 *Dabney*, 707. Jackson's religious experience during his illness became a favorite and, in time, almost a traditional pulpit theme. Chaplain Lacy "charged his memory" with Jackson's remarks, wrote them down promptly, and communicated them to Dr. Dabney within less than two years, perhaps much sooner than that. When this particular observation by Jackson, in answer to Lacy, came finally into print, the General's words, as reported "in substance" by Dabney, were these: "You see me severely wounded, but not depressed; not unhappy. I believe that it has been done according to God's holy will, and I acquiesce entirely in it. You may think it strange; but you never saw me more perfectly contented than I am today; for I am sure my Heavenly Father designs this affliction for my good. I am perfectly satisfied, that either in this life, or in that which is to come, I shall discover that what is now regarded as a calamity, is a blessing. And if it appears a great calamity (as it surely will be a great inconvenience to be deprived of my arm), it will result in a great blessing. I can wait until God, in his own time,

the circumstances of his wounding. He confided that when a bearer tripped and the litter fell, he thought that he would die on the field, and he gave himself into the hands of his Creator. Perfect peace, said Jackson, then had been his—a precious experience.[86]

While Jackson and Lacy talked of spiritual things, the sounds of the battle grew more distant and declined in volume. Jackson listened, so to say, with one ear to the sound of the cannon and with the other ear to the observations of Chaplain Lacy. That wise man had the good sense not to tire the General. Ere long, with fervent good wishes, Lacy left the tent.

Jackson's next caller had more to say about the battle than about religion. Smith told the General, after a time, that Kyd Douglas had ridden back from the front and had brought more news. Would Jackson care to hear it? In response to Jackson's immediate "Yes," Smith recounted as much of what Douglas had told him as he thought it prudent to disclose to a wounded man.[87] The death of Paxton and of other well-known officers of the Second Corps was announced to Jackson as gently as Smith could shape his words. The General was grieved and shaken, but he was even more stirred when Smith repeated Douglas's account of the charge by the Stonewall Brigade in answer to a special exhortation by Stuart. It scarcely was possible for Jackson to hold back his proud tears as he listened. "It was just like them to do so; just like them! They are a noble body of men!" [88]

shall make known to me the object he has in thus afflicting me. But why should I not rather rejoice in it as a blessing, and not look on it as a calamity at all? If it were in my power to replace my arm, I would not dare to do it, unless I could know it was the will of my Heavenly Father." Needless to say, so long and rhetorical a statement cannot be credited to a man eight or nine hours after an amputation. All that can be accepted as historical is that Jackson was reconciled to what he considered the will of God.

[86] *Dabney*, 708. Here again, Dabney's statement of Lacy's report credited to the wound-shocked Jackson "nearly the[se] exact words": "It has been a precious experience to me, that I was brought face to face with death, and found all was well. I then learned an important lesson, that one who has been the subject of converting grace, and is the child of God, can, in the midst of the severest sufferings, fix the thoughts upon God and heavenly things, and derive great comfort and peace: but, that one who has never made his peace with God would be unable to control his mind, under such sufferings, so as to understand properly the way of salvation, and repent and believe in Christ. I felt that if I had neglected the salvation of my soul before, it would have been too late then."

[87] So *Dabney*, 708–09, on the authority, no doubt, of Smith. Years later, Douglas wrote that he personally entered the General's tent and "was with him for an hour" (*op. cit.*, 227). Quotations of what occurred at the time make it seem probable that when Douglas wrote, he had Dabney's text before him.

[88] *Dabney*, 709. McGuire, *op. cit.*, 224, quoted substantially the same language but added the remark quoted, *infra*, p. 639, concerning the name "Stonewall."

The General relaxed after a time and probably was quiet and alone with Smith, in the early afternoon, when a courier brought a reply to the dispatch Jackson had sent Lee. By permission, Smith opened it and read:

Headquarters, May 3, 1863.

General Thomas J. Jackson,
 Commanding Corps.

General: I have just received your note, informing me that you were wounded. I cannot express my regret at the occurrence. Could I have directed events, I should have chosen for the good of the country to be disabled in your stead.

I congratulate you upon the victory, which is due to your skill and energy.

Very respectfully, your obedient servant,
R. E. Lee,
General.[89]

Smith stopped reading. Jackson paused for a moment and then —was it from modesty or from a desire that his aide should not see his pleasure over praise from such a source?—he turned his face away. "General Lee," he said in his quiet, half-muffled voice, "is very kind, but he should give the praise to God." [90]

[89] *O. R.*, 25, pt. 2, p. 769. For the dramatic circumstances in which this was written, see 2 *R. E. Lee*, 543.
[90] Smith in 3 *B. & L.*, 214.

CHAPTER XXXV

"Jube" Early Has a Right to Swear

While Jackson was affirming that the commanding General should give the thanks to God, "Jube" Early was wondering what perverse devil had placed him where he was. In the Army's strangest battle, he had the most incredible part to play. On the afternoon of April 30, Early received notice from headquarters of the Second Corps that he was to remain where he was on the ridge of the Rappahannock, and with his own Division and Barksdale's Brigade of McLaws's Division, was to observe the foe. An artillery battalion of the Corps, part of Pendleton's reserve guns and two units of a battalion attached to McLaws's Division were to continue, also, in front of the Federals who, it will be remembered, the previous day again had crossed to the Confederate side of the river.[1] Early's conclusion, of course, was that his infantry and this artillery were to be employed as a containing force while Lee moved with three Divisions of Jackson's Second Corps and three Brigades of McLaws, to support Anderson and to take the offensive against Hooker.

For coping with what manifestly was a superior Federal force, already on the right bank of the Rappahannock, Early estimated then or thereafter that he had about 9000 men and approximately forty-five guns.[2] He was not materially at fault in his figures on his infantry, but he overlooked some of the batteries at his command. He had fifty-six guns, not forty-five.[3] Strong or weak, he was resolute.

On the morning of May 1, "Old Jube" found Jackson and McLaws gone, and the commanding General about to depart.

---

[1] O. R., 25, pt. 1, pp. 1000–01. This is Early's report, which, for a General who had been both lawyer and politician, was unusually brief. It was elaborated in Early's military memoirs.

[2] Early, 198.

[3] What appear to be the correct figures are given in Bigelow, 268 n. Forty-six of Early's guns were "up"; ten were in reserve. Apparently Early's error was in underestimating the strength of Pendleton's reserve artillery and of the First Corps batteries available.

Early's own Division was South of Lee's Hill, on the front where Early believed the attack would be delivered. All four of the brigade commanders were present—John B. Gordon, R. F. Hoke, Harry Hays and "Extra Billy" Smith.[4] The bold Snowden Andrews was back after partial recovery from the frightful wound received at Cedar Mountain and, with the rank of Lieutenant Colonel, was in command of his artillery battalion. Early saw to it immediately that Andrews took full charge of the batteries on the right and that General Pendleton confined his energies to the guns on the left.[5]

Before these two officers began to shift batteries to cover as best they could a front that extended for no less than six miles,[6] General Lee gave Early final instructions for the employment of the containing force which was to be separated immediately by a few miles and perhaps later by many, from the main army. Orders were explicit: (1) Early was to observe and, if he could, to hold the enemy in the vicinity of Fredericksburg, and was to conceal the weakness of the Confederate force. (2) If compelled to retreat before an overpowering adversary, Early was to withdraw in the direction of Guiney's Station, the army's advance base, and was to protect the supplies and the railroad. (3) On the morning of May 2, Early was to feel the Unionists with his artillery. In the event that he found they had disappeared or had so reduced force that a move on his part was safe, Early was to post at Fredericksburg troops sufficient in his judgment to hold whatever the enemy left. With the remainder of his command, Early was to march to join Lee.[7]

The third of these clear and simple orders involved of necessity a discretion that Lee did not hesitate to entrust or Early to accept. Had not "Old Jubilee" fought for a time unaided and alone in the van at Cedar Mountain? Could the army forget his experience, ludicrous when it was past but serious enough in its occurrence, that night when the rising waters of the upper Rappahannock had separated him from Ewell? At Sharpsburg, had there not been a critical hour when Early had saved from a shattering blow the left flank of Jackson? Surely now, if someone had to remain

---

[4] Though neither Gordon nor Smith had been assigned finally to brigade command as general officers.
[5] O. R., 25, pt. 1, p. 810; Early, 199.   [6] Early, 198.
[7] Early, 197; O. R., 25, pt. 1, p. 811.

at Fredericksburg, and Jackson had to go and Longstreet was absent, Early, all in all, was the division commander best qualified to guard the heights and to protect the rear of the Confederate forces that were moving against Hooker. To this post of military trust, in less than two years, had risen the former Commonwealth's Attorney of Franklin County, Virginia!

He had little to do that 1st of May. Ere Lee rode after Jackson, there was a flurry over the dispatch of two batteries to Port Royal, where enemy gunboats were said to have appeared, but, with some fussiness, that mission was arranged by General Pendleton.[8] During the afternoon Early had to decide where he would dispose his few troops on his line of six miles. His judgment was that the main assault would be on his right, over the ground the Second Corps had defended in December. His entire Division he consequently determined to leave between Hamilton's Crossing and Deep Run. The stretch of nearly a mile and a half, between Deep Run on the right and Lee's Hill on the left, Early thought he could protect with no more infantry than a thin picket-line, because he could cover that part of the front with a crossfire of artillery.

Barksdale and the greater part of the artillery must watch Lee's Hill and Marye's Heights.[9] This task seemed not wholly beyond the capacity of Barksdale and his men, because, in the afternoon, the battalion of the Washington Artillery came up from the rest area. The guns of the New Orleans men, added to those already in position, should make the heights impregnable. Even Pendleton had no apprehension in answering later in the evening a call by Early for four additional guns on the right.[10]

The day ended quietly. At his camp, Early had no intimation that Lee and Jackson, bivouacking in the pines below Chancellorsville, were planning a movement that would sound for the Union force at Fredericksburg a peremptory call to brush Early aside and to march on Lee's rear.

The clear dawn and the friendly sun of May 2 revealed on his front no material change that Early could observe. If anything was different, it was that more Federal troops perhaps were visible

---

[8] *O. R.*, 25, pt. 1, p. 810.   [9] *Early*, 198–99.
[10] *O. R.*, 25, pt. 1, p. 811 For sending a battery of the Washington Artillery, instead of a battery from the general reserve, he subsequently was criticized.

on the opposite bank of the Rappahannock.[11] Early was prepared and hopeful: If the answer of the Federals to his test bombardment was feeble or perfunctory, he intended to start two of his Brigades to join Lee.[12]

The "feeling-out fire" began on a small scale. To the Southern guns in the vicinity of Deep Run, the Federals made no reply. In response to a challenge from the Confederate right, they were listless. Soon, Early observed that the Unionists in the most advanced positions opposite his right were withdrawing both their artillery and their infantry behind the protecting bank of the river.[13]

This encouraged Early to believe that he safely could attach troops to support his chief; but before he decided to give the order, he received from Pendleton and from Barksdale a somewhat perplexing note. From their position on the left, they said, they had observed a concentration of Federal troops at Falmouth. As that old town was opposite the upper end of Fredericksburg, and long had been a crossing of the Rappahannock, the two officers expressed the opinion that the enemy might be preparing to throw pontoons in that vicinity and to assail the Confederate left. Withdrawal of any part of the small Southern force, even to reinforce Lee, wrote Barksdale and Pendleton, might be dangerous.[14]

This note made Early delay his order. He rode to Lee's Hill and from that eminence examined the Stafford Heights. Beyond doubt, a Federal column was moving up the opposite side of the river. Whither was this force bound? Was it to reinforce Hooker, or to cross the Rappahannock and attempt a turning movement against Early's left, in the manner anticipated by Barksdale and Pendleton? Soon those officers joined Early on the hill, and with him they speculated on the Federal plan. Pendleton maintained that the marching bluecoats certainly would be thrown against the upstream flank of the Confederate force. He proposed to move some of his guns immediately so that he could open heavily on the Federals at Falmouth.[15]

Details were being discussed when, about 11 A.M., straight from

---

[11] Again the reminder may be in order that while the references usually are to the north and the south banks, the actual course of the river immediately at Fredericksburg made the Federal side the eastern and the Confederate the western.

[12] Cf. O. R., 25, pt. 1, p. 811.   [13] Early, 199–200.

[14] O. R., 25, pt. 1, p. 811.   [15] Early, 201–02.

the headquarters of the Army, arrived Col. R. H. Chilton, Chief of Staff. He at once took Early aside and communicated what he described as verbal orders from Lee: As soon as practicable, Early was to march toward Chancellorsville with the entire force at his command, except Pendleton's artillery and one Brigade of infantry. The artillery was to be divided. Eight or ten guns should be left on the heights to support the infantry. The remainder of the artillery, especially the heavy pieces, must be started at once for a place of safety down the R. F. & P. Railroad. Those batteries and regiments left behind were to do their utmost to keep the enemy from seizing the ridge; and if they failed in this, they were to retreat in the direction of Spotsylvania Court House. That part of the order concerning the artillery Chilton repeated to Pendleton.

The parson-gunner and, even more, "Old Jube" were stunned by these instructions. Early had Chilton and Pendleton sit down with him and, item by item, he went over the orders.[16] It was impossible, Early argued, to withdraw his force in daylight without being observed by the Federals: They overlooked his position and had up balloons besides. As soon as he abandoned the position to the care of a handful of troops, the Unionists would occupy Fredericksburg and Marye's Heights. Pendleton, in the language of his report, supported Early with "one or two suggestions." [17]

To these arguments, Chilton replied that General Lee presumably had decided that the advantage of having Early with him outweighed the loss of Fredericksburg, which could be recovered easily after Hooker had been defeated. To make clearer what Chilton assumed to be the reasoning of Lee, the Chief of Staff, who seemed quite cool, called attention to the Federals then in motion up Stafford Heights. He had no doubt, said Chilton, that those troops were marching to join Hooker and to oppose Lee.

Early still could not bring himself to believe that Lee had set aside the plain orders given the previous forenoon. The Union troops being held at Fredericksburg, Early expostulated, were more than he possibly could defeat in the Wilderness.

Was there any possibility that Chilton had misunderstood orders which were the more liable to misinterpretation because they were verbal? Chilton was sure there could be no mistake.

[16] *Early.* 200: *O. R.,* 25, pt. 1, p. 811.   [17] *O. R.,* 25, pt. 1, p. 812.

What, demanded Early, was the reason for dividing the artil-lery? It was, Chilton explained, because Lee did not need much artillery at Chancellorsville and wished to be sure that the guns at Fredericksburg would be sent to safety in the rear.

How long, asked Pendleton in his turn, was he expected to hold the heights against the overwhelming odds he would face? Long enough, answered Chilton, for the artillery and the trains to get to the rear and out of danger.[18]

"This," Early afterward wrote, "was very astounding to us . . . It is true that there was the force massed near Falmouth and the indications were that it was moving above, but still there was a much larger force of infantry stationed below, which evinced no disposition to move."[19]

This realistic argument the Fates set at naught. While Early was talking, a messenger brought word that the Federals who had retired under the right bank of the river to get protection from the "feeling-out" fire of the morning had evacuated the position, had crossed the river and had abandoned their bridgehead. Could anything have seemed more positively to confirm Chilton's asser-tion that the Federals were withdrawing from the district of Fredericksburg to confront Lee in the Wilderness? "Old Jube," a natural skeptic, was shaken but not wholly convinced. He pointed out that the troops near the mouth of Deep Run had not left the Confederate side of the river and that a number of guns remained.[20]

It was now between 11 and 12 o'clock[21] on the 2d of May Jackson at that hour was well advanced on his march to the left of Hooker. South and Southeast of Chancellorsville, Lee was play-ing a fine game of bluff with Anderson's and McLaws's Divisions and was trying to make the Unionists believe that he was prepar-ing to attack on that sector with his whole force. Of this general plan of operations, Chilton may have told Early something. All that either of the officers knew of the progress of the action was what they could determine from the sound of the distant artillery. It seemed heavy.[22] By it, and by the whole situation, Early was nonplussed. He could not see the logic of his orders, brought by Chilton, but when the Chief of Staff insisted that the instructions were explicit and positive, Early did not feel that his discretion

[18] Early, 200; O. R., 25, pt. 1, p. 812.   [19] Early, 201.
[20] Early, 201.   [21] O. R., 25, pt. 1, p. 812.
[22] Owen, 211.

extended to them. Foolish as abandonment of the Fredericks-burg front appeared to be, orders were orders. Lee must know more about the operation than Early could.

What Chilton required, Early set about doing as promptly as he could. Pendleton dropped plans for bombarding the force at Fal-mouth and began to designate the batteries that were to start for the rear. To cover their withdrawal he made a show of moving horses and vehicles as if he were increasing the number of guns on the heights. Early devoted himself to getting off his foot troops covertly. Barksdale had one regiment in Fredericksburg. As it could not be withdrawn without attracting attention, it must stay where it was. Harry Hays's Brigade, with one regiment of skir-mishers near the mouth of Deep Run, most conveniently could be left.[23]

Slow business it was to get the regiments on the ridge, in march-ing order, and to make them ready to start for the Plank Road. At length, about 2 P.M., Early said *au revoir* to Hays and Pendle-ton on Lee's Hill,[24] and rode off to expedite in person the move-ment of his men. To his dismay, as he was leaving, he observed that one of the Federal balloons had risen, most inquisitively, as if "Professor" Lowe had known that "the rebels" had afoot some new treason against the Union. Early concluded that the Federals had discovered his move [25] and he anticipated the worst, but,

[23] *O. R.,* 25, pt. 1, pp. 812, 1002; *Early,* 202. Early did not state why he left Hays instead of Barksdale, but he must have done so because the retirement of Hays's pickets, as of Barksdale's regiment in Fredericksburg, would have been observed. None of Early's Brigadiers filed report on the action; consequently, Hays is not available as a witness.

[24] *O. R.,* 25, pt. 1, p. 812.

[25] *Early,* 202. Lowe had reported on the 29th that the Confederate line "appears quite thin as compared with our force" (see F. S. Haydon, *Aeronautics in the Union and Confederate Armies,* 1, 318–19). During the morning of May 2, Lowe encountered high wind and, even when he ascended boldly in spite of it, he found his basket so unstable for a time that he could not use his field-glass. At 3.15 P.M. he observed the departure of a Brigade, which he assumed to be bound for Banks' Ford. It was 4.15 before he reported the withdrawal of the "advanced line with the exception of a small picket force." At 5.30 he notified Hooker's Chief of Staff: "Nearly all of the enemy's force have been withdrawn from the opposite side. I can only see a small force in the neighborhood of their earthworks." The aeronaut had to add that through inability to get elevation he could not say in which direction the Confederate column had moved. From the directions of the wagons, he judged that the troops were marching toward the Union right (III *O. R.,* 3, 315). As early as 9.30 A.M. on the 2d, Hooker had been correctly informed that the Confederate infantry left at Fredericksburg was Ewell's (Early's) Divi-sion (*O. R.,* 25, pt. 2, p. 362), but apparently the Federal ground forces did not discover until 5 P.M. that Early was evacuating his position (*ibid.,* 367). Sedgwick reported (*O. R.,* 25, pt. 1, p. 558): "I had been informed repeatedly by Major General Butterfield, Chief of Staff, that the force in front of me was very small, and the whole tenor of his many dispatches would have created the impression that the enemy had abandoned my front and retired from the city and its defences, had there not been more tangible evidence than the dispatches in question that the Chief of Staff was misinformed."

battling delay, he kept pushing men and wagons on. By late afternoon he had the last of his men in motion toward the Plank Road.

Now, abruptly, came another disconcerting messenger. He
brought a dispatch which Lee had written after Colonel Chilton
had returned and had reported the orders given Early. Those
orders, Lee wrote, had been based on a misunderstanding by
Colonel Chilton of Lee's wishes. It had not been intended that
Early should withdraw from Fredericksburg unless this could be
done with safety. The discretion given Early still was to be exercised.

How profusely "Old Jube" swore, and whether he went to the
extreme of shifting his quid of tobacco to the other jaw, the record does not show. He was relieved of a march but not of a quan-
dary. The enemy, he assumed, already had occupied—or was in
the act of seizing—his abandoned works. These he could not hope
with his small force to recapture. If he went back and made the
effort and failed, he would deprive Lee of any use of the Division.
It simply would have marched out, then have returned, and then
have wrecked or, at the least, have immobilized itself when Lee
most needed it. The start, under misapprehension of orders, had
been foolish; an attempt to go back might be equally so. Let the
column go on!

A mile the exasperated Early rode with his men along the Plank
Road and then—another messenger. This one had a note from
Barksdale, whose Brigade was following Early's Division. An offi
cer of Pendleton's—so the paper read—had overtaken the column
and had reported to Barksdale that the enemy was advancing
against the heights in great strength. Pendleton and Hays had informed the Mississippian that unless they had immediate relief, all
the artillery left behind by Early would be captured. The courier
who brought this information to Early added that Barksdale was
hurrying to help Hays.[26]

At the moment, this was all that Early knew about the situation. Later, it developed that the Federals farthest down the river
had moved up to the Richmond Stage Road.[27] On the whole
front, the Unionists had displayed an activity and a strength which
Pendleton had estimated at 15,000 to 20,000 men. He had assumed
that the bluecoats were about to storm the heights and he had re-

[26] Early. 202.   [27] O. R.. 25, pt. 1, pp. 558, 567.

solved that he must not again risk his guns as he had at Shepherds-town. In great excitement he had ordered one of his batteries to open before the enemy got in range.[28] Then Pendleton had sent for help from the column on the march toward Chancel-lorsville.

Barksdale, who had received this call and had turned back, soon saw guns moving toward him on the road from Fredericksburg. "What artillery is that?" Barksdale cried. The loud voice of Col. J. B. Walton shouted back: "The Washington Artillery."

Barksdale rode forward: "Colonel Walton," he said, "you are not going to desert me, are you?"

"General," said stout old Walton proudly, "I am the last man in the world to desert you or anybody else. I am acting under orders."

"Then will you obey an order from me?" asked the General.

"Yes," replied Walton with no hesitation.

"Then reverse your column and come back with me to Freder-icksburg. We must hold this point to the last." [29]

Of this development, though he lacked the details, Early got the substance. He had to make a decision on the changed basis: The enemy might not yet have occupied the heights, though cer-tain to occupy them in the morning. What was to be done? The march toward Chancellorsville had been resumed, in the first in-stance, on the assumption that the Confederates could not recover the ground the Federals were supposed to have seized. If the blue-coats had not actually taken the works, should Early reverse his march? As he pondered, John B. Gordon rode up and offered to take his Georgia Brigade to the relief of Hays and of Barksdale.[30] This was a gallant proposal, but manifestly Gordon could not go back alone. That would mean a further dispersal of force, an in-creasing risk that Early could neither reinforce Lee nor recover the Rappahannock Heights. The Division must be kept together! Either the entire column should push on to Chancellorsville or the whole of it had to return to Fredericksburg; which was it to be? "Old Jube" debated the question with himself and decided that he had a sufficient chance of success to justify him in secur-ing his old positions—and thereby of protecting Lee's rear. One

28 *Ibid.*, 813.   29 *Owen*, 211-12.
30 *O. R.*, 25, pt. 1, p. 814.

courier was sent Barksdale with approval of his counter-march; another messenger hurried off to Lee with a report of what was being done; on the Plank Road the troops and the trains were turned around and were started back to the ridge of the Rappahannock.

About the time that Jackson fell in the Wilderness, Early's weary and perplexed men were moving toward their former camps. On arrival, to his relief, Early found that the Federals had not advanced at Fredericksburg and, on the Confederate right, had not proceeded beyond the Richmond Stage Road. There even was an element of hospitable cheer in the return of the infantry. Barksdale, arriving first, had lighted many campfires on Lee's Hill, to create the impression that the positions were occupied and reinforced.[31] Warm, too, was the welcome given the returned column by Hays and by Pendleton. They had been waiting expectantly and without definite news. Previously they had decided that if they heard nothing from Early, they would evacuate the heights by 11 P.M. At that hour, instead, they again were under the direction of Early, who was posting his troops once more along the railroad.[32]

A singular episode appeared to have been closed with more of good luck than the Confederates could have hoped to enjoy. Exasperating and nerve-wearing had been the result of Colonel Chilton's curious and never-explained misunderstanding of orders, but it had involved no loss of life or of ground. The chief complaint was Pendleton's. Had he been apprised earlier, he told the division commander, that Chilton's instructions had been disavowed, the Confederate left would not have been weakened by the withdrawal of those guns that now had gone far southward. With what artillery he had, said Pendleton, he would make the best defense he could.[33] He made no effort, so far as the record shows, to recall during the night the batteries that first had been started to the rear.[34]

While Jackson was under the knife or was recovering from his anæsthetic on the night of May 2–3, little occurred on Early's front. The pickets disputed; the cannon cooled on the ridges; the officers and the men rested, but not for long. Before daylight,

[31] 3 *The Land We Love*, 448.   [32] *O. R.*, 25, pt. 1, p. 814; *Early*, 203.
[33] *O. R.*, 25, pt. 1, p. 814.
[34] Nelson's Battalion and Rhett's Battery. *O. R.*, 25, pt. 1, p. 842.

Early was aroused by Barksdale, who was not in placid mood. Apportionment of forces had not seemed to him either equitable or safe. The Mississippian at his camp had rolled and raged. When Col. B. G. Humphreys had come to his quarters and had asked if he was asleep, Barksdale had barked: "No, sir! Who could sleep with a million of armed Yankees around him?"[35] Now Barksdale was telling Early that the Federals had laid a pontoon bridge at Fredericksburg and were moving over. The attack would be delivered in rear of the town, the Brigadier predicted; reinforcements were needed there.

Early asked if the Mississippians had opposed the crossing of the enemy as they had in December.

No, Barksdale replied, the regiment had retired, skirmishing, because it had felt that resistance was futile.

"Old Jube" meditated and then told Barksdale that Hays's Louisiana Brigade would be ordered to the left. Barksdale could place it where his judgment of the ground told him it would be most useful.[36]

One Brigade seemed the maximum that Early could afford to shift to the left, if the main Federal attack was to be on the right; but the reinforcement was the minimum with which Barksdale could hope to offer successful resistance to heavy assaults on the Confederate center and left. At the moment, with somewhat formidable artillery but no more than 1500 infantry, Barksdale was occupying a front of about three miles.[37]

After Barksdale galloped off to arrange for the deployment of Hays's Louisianians, Early set out to ascertain what changes of position the Federals had effected during the night. Almost before he had sufficient daylight for reconnaissance, a rattle of picket fire and then infantry volleys and the roar of awakened cannon announced an attack on Willis's Hill. Ten taut minutes sufficed to show that this assault was premature. It was beaten off readily.

---

[35] Humphreys in 3 *Land We Love*, 448, 449.

[36] Early (*op. cit.*, 204) noted that General Barksdale was mistaken in saying that the bridge had been laid opposite the town so early in the morning. The troops with which Barksdale's men had established contact were those of Sedgwick's VI Corps, who had marched up the right bank of the river and had occupied Fredericksburg. Barksdale's pickets doubtless had been misled by the fact that preparations were under way before dawn for throwing pontoons for the crossing of Gibbon's 2nd Division of the II Corps. Three bridges were laid, but none was completed before 6.30 (*O. R.*, 25, pt. 1, pp. 215, 350).

[37] Cf. *Early*, 198; Barksdale in *O. R.*, 25, pt. 1, p. 839. Barksdale's front extended from the Taylor House to the hills in rear of the Howison House.

A second thrust met the same fate.[38] This success was a bracer for the Confederates. Still better was the stimulant of news Early now received—that the main army had won a victory the previous

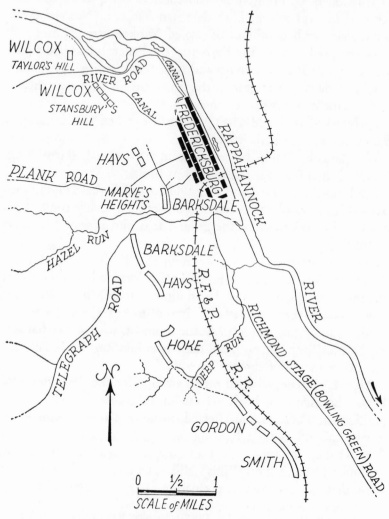

Early's Deployment, Morning of May 3, 1863—after *Bigelow*

evening and hoped on the 3d to complete a triumph. Early ordered announcement of this made to the Army.[39]

When it was light enough to see across the valley of the Rappa

[38] *O. R.*, 25, pt. 1, p. 839; *Early*, 205.   [39] Cf. *O. R.*, 25, pt. 1, p. 815.

hannock, Early looked eagerly for stirring camps and rising smoke, for moving guns and marching men. He was startled by what he did *not* see. Stafford Heights were "bare of troops." [40] Whither had the Federals gone—to reinforce Hooker or to mass on the right bank around Fredericksburg? What Early observed on a wide stretch of the right bank led him to conclude promptly that his thinly held lines and not the shattered Wilderness were the Union objective. The heaviest force visible to Early was near the mouth of Deep Run, a force that had some artillery and seemed to be prepared to advance up the left bank of that small stream. In front of Marye's Heights, as far as Early could ascertain, no heavy columns were deployed, though demonstrations were being made.

The attack assuredly was coming, Early told himself, and it probably was going to be on his right which, in December, all the Confederate commanders had known to be vulnerable. Burnside had found the heights near the town impregnable in December; Hooker had tried vainly to storm them; now that Hooker was in command, it was reasonable to assume that he would not repeat Burnside's costly blunder. Early felt that he must make ready for a stubborn defense on Jackson's old lines, and he rode off to see that his right Brigades were in position and in fighting trim.

Along nearly the whole of the divisional front, the Confederate skirmishers by this time were creeping out. They had no great trouble in reaching the Richmond Stage Road opposite the extreme right; but in the vicinity of Deep Run, they could not dislodge the enemy. Ere long the Federals in that quarter began to threaten the exposed left flank of Early's left Brigade, which was Hoke's and had been Trimble's. [41]

To combat this movement, Early was vigilant, because he thought the Federals might be trying to cut his force in half, [42] but in guarding his right, where his prediction of a Federal attack

40 *Early*, 205.

41 *Early*, 205. Although Early nowhere described his order of battle, May 2–3, scattered references make clear that from right to left at daybreak his Brigades were: Hays's, Gordon's, Smith's and Hoke's. Of these, Hays's Brigade had come up on the right during the night (*Early*, 204) but, as indicated in the text, already had been ordered to Barksdale on the left. Barksdale sent most of Hays's men to the extreme left of the line, in the vicinity of Taylor's Hill, but one of the Louisiana regiments was placed on the right of Barksdale (*O. R.*, 25, pt. 1, p. 839). If this regiment had any contact with Hoke's left, it was tenuous. Against any serious attack, Hoke's Brigade remained the left-flank element of Early's Division.

42 *Early*, 205–06.

appeared to be confirmed,[43] he could not and did not forget Barksdale's front. For a time, Barksdale and Pendleton reported frequently that all was well. Their batteries were keeping the enemy
at a distance. Ere long, Barksdale sent word to Early that a Union
column had moved upstream from Fredericksburg and, about
sunrise, had moved out to turn the Confederate left. The canal
had delayed this column. Before the Federals could repair the
bridge,[44] Hays's men had arrived, had filed into the trenches and
had repulsed the enemy. Another attempt at a crossing, a little
higher up, similarly had been frustrated.[45]

Of this new thrust, as of the events nearer Lee's Hill, Early got
prompt report and a further assurance that Barksdale and Pendleton, who had their post of command on Lee's Hill, believed they
could hold their ground. Early's concern for the left and center
was not relieved by these assurances. On the contrary, he was
alarmed to note that the Federals had abandoned their movement
against Deep Run and boldly had started upstream in heavy columns.[46] Were they preparing to attack on the left? Early thought
they might be, and he hurried off one of his staff officers, Lieut.
W. G. Callaway, to notify Barksdale and Pendleton and to
get information. From his own position, Early could see little
of what was happening on his center and left.[47]

Time slipped on. The activity on Deep Run was not renewed.
Another Federal demonstration, apparently more serious, on
Hazel Run, was halted easily by the artillery.[48] When the Federals who made that movement sought cover, the hands of Early's
watch were climbing toward 11 A.M.[49] Six hours of skirmishing
and demonstration had passed. Everything seemed favorable . . .
except that no further reports had come to Early from Barksdale.
Neither had Lieutenant Callaway returned from Lee's Hill,
whither he had been sent to get information. Northward, in

[43] Cf. 3 Land We Love, 450.
[44] Confederates had ripped the planking off both the canal bridges, but had not
destroyed the framework when the Federals came up and forced them to withdraw. 3
Land We Love, 449.
[45] Early, 206.   [46] Ibid.
[47] Early, 209.
[48] Although the mouth of Hazel Run is scarcely half a mile upstream from that of
Deep Run, the stretch of Hazel Run, directly North of the crest of Lee's Hill, is two
miles above the corresponding part of Deep Run on a straight line to the South. For
the details of the repulse, see Early, 207; O. R., 25, pt. 1, p. 815.
[49] Owen, op. cit., 216, 220, placed half an hour earlier the events about to be
described.

front of Marye's Heights, the Federals still were banging away, but they had been doing that all morning. Was anything amiss? What the devil could be keeping Callaway so long?

Early began to fume, perhaps to swear, and at length he determined to ride toward Lee's Hill and to see the situation for himself.[50] On the way, he soon heard behind the gallop of a horse and then a startling shout: A Union flag had been raised on Willis's Hill! The man on the galloping horse said, when questioned, that he had not seen the flag himself but got the news from someone who had seen the standard there. Early would not, could not believe this second-hand tale, but he spurred on the faster.

Now arrived a courier from General Pendleton: the enemy had been repulsed, the artillerist wrote; the position could be held. Almost before Early could draw a deep breath of relief, or adjust his mind to good news from bad, Lieutenant Callaway rode up with a rush. Pendleton and Barksdale, said Callaway, had been on Lee's Hill when he had left them, and they had told him they thought they could beat off the attacks; but as he had ridden down the ridge, he had seen the enemy mounting Marye's Heights and he knew the position was lost!

The Federals on Marye's Heights—that stirred instantly the combativeness of "Jube" Early's soul! By God, he would not retreat without a fight. Callaway must spur at once to Gordon on the right and must tell him to come up the ridge with three regiments. Early himself would gallop to the Telegraph Road and would rally any troops that might be making off.

Action followed orders. Soon Early was on the road. Down it, toward the rear, were rushing Pendleton's reserve batteries. "Old Jube's" clear and penetrating voice rose. "Halt! Halt!"—with added words, perhaps, not found in the manual of arms. He did not wait to see whether the excited gunners obeyed him. Furiously he galloped on until he came upon Barksdale.

The Mississippian was untouched by panic. Demonstrations on the Confederate left, he doubtless explained to Early, had been followed by the advance of one Federal column against Willis's Hill and of another against Lee's Hill. Twice the bluecoats had been beaten back from the stone wall at the foot of Willis's Hill;

[50] *Early,* 209.

then they had sent forward a flag of truce which a Colonel incautiously had received; no sooner had the men with the flag
seen the weakness of the Confederate line than they hurried back;
in a few minutes the Union line had advanced irresistibly;[51] the
Mississippi regiment and three companies that held the road under
the wall had been overwhelmed; the Federals had worked around
the flank of Willis's Hill and had stormed it; some field pieces of
the Washington Artillery and of Parker's Battery had been captured; on Lee's Hill, the gunners of Cabell's Battalion had held
on magnificently till the enemy was upon them.[52]

Early found the Washington Artillery angry and humiliated at
the loss of some of their famous weapons. When a reserve artillerist twitted one of the men who had fought on Willis's Hill and
asked where were the guns, the Louisianian broke out wrathfully:
"Guns be damned! I reckon now the people of the Southern Confederacy are satisfied that Barksdale's Brigade and the Washington Artillery can't whip the whole damned Yankee army!"[53]
Barksdale himself did not put it that strongly. "Our center has
been pierced, that's all," he said; "we will be all right in a little
while."[54]

At the moment, the Mississippi troops were scattered somewhat,
but the renowned Sixth Louisiana, one of "Dick" Taylor's old
regiments, which Hays had left on Barksdale's flank, had kept its
organization. With this regiment, Early and Barksdale quickly
formed a line along the plateau in rear of Lee's Hill. When the
Federals began to plaster this line with canister, Early ordered a
withdrawal for a few hundred yards. He continued to employ
these tactics until he was about two miles from the ridge. Then,
at Cox's house, on defensible ground, Early determined to make a
stand. Smith and Hoke had not withdrawn when the left gave
way; but their position was exposed to an enfilade from Lee's
Hill. For that reason, Early drew them back to the new second

---

[51] Gen. B. G. Humphreys, then Colonel of the Twenty-first Mississippi, noted that
the advance of the Federals was rapid because all the fences, orchards, etc., that had
delayed the enemy in the assaults of Dec. 13, 1862, had been destroyed during the winter.
3 *Land We Love*, 450.

[52] Barksdale's account is in *O. R.*, 25, pt. 1, p. 839. The reports of Colonel Cabell
and of various battery commanders follow. Pendleton's narrative is in *ibid.*, 815–16.
Probably the fullest treatment of the infantry action is that of Col. B. G. Humphreys in
3 *Land We Love*, 450. A somewhat dramatic account of the artillery fight is in *Owen*,
215 ff. The account in the history of Parker's Battery is sketchy.

[53] *Owen*, 22;.   [54] *Ibid.*, 218–19.

line. Gordon and Hays competently found their place in this new order of battle. By 2 or 3 P.M., though his strong position overlooking the Rappahannock had been snatched from him, Early could say that he had his force in hand, ready to fight, and that the infantry losses had not been excessive.[55] Artillery commands had not been so fortunate. The guns taken from the Washington Artillery proved to be six. Parker's "boy company" lost two; and Patterson's Battery, Cutts's Battalion, Pendleton's reserve, a like number, which subsequently were to be recovered.[56] Whether the withdrawal of Pendleton's other batteries had been marked by a precipitancy that some would have styled panic, critics might argue. Pendleton later was to report that personally he "proceeded slowly . . . along the Telegraph road, having remained some time on the hill near the signal station." [57]

If the balance of the morning's account was slightly, though no more than that, to the credit of Early, he had that afternoon remarkable good fortune, which he had not anticipated and, for that matter, did not deserve. Nearly five miles above Fredericksburg, as the river wound—three and a quarter miles as the crow flies—Cadmus Wilcox had been stationed with his Alabama Brigade. Banks' Ford, an interesting and picturesque crossing, had been his post. On Anderson's advance to the line taken up April 30, Wilcox had been left to cover the ford, which had much strategical importance; and after some movement on the 1st of May, he had been ordered back there. His instructions were to hold the position at all costs if it was assailed. In the event it was not, he was to notify the commanding General and was to detach a guard to watch the crossing. Then, with the remainder of his Brigade, he was to march via the Plank Road, toward Chancellorsville.[58]

The assignment suggested the possibility of detachment and lack of action for a Brigadier who had been sick for several days with dysentery.[59] Since his fine conduct at Second Manassas, Wilcox had been denied a conspicuous part in operations. At the time of the Maryland expedition he had been absent, sick; in December, he had been present at the Battle of Fredericksburg, but he had been on the left, where he had been able to do little. The

[55] Cf. *Early*, 208 ff. 219–20.   [56] *O. R.*, 25, pt. 1, p. 816.
[57] *O. R.*, 25, pt. 1, p. 815.   [58] *O. R.*, 25, pt. 1, p. 855.
[59] C. M. Wilcox to John A. Wilcox, MS, Apr. 30, 1863—*Wilcox MSS.*

winter had been one of disappointment for him. He had wished
in November to leave the Army of Northern Virginia in the belief
that he would have better prospects elsewhere. Lee had declined
to permit this, but efforts by friends of Wilcox to procure a major
general's commission for him had been futile.[60] Was he now
merely to watch a ford while his Division and his Army won
another victory that would bring praise and promotion to those
who led their men wisely?

The whole of the war brought few instances to demonstrate
more dramatically that vigilance often makes great the small
opportunity. Wilcox, in the first place, did not neglect the approaches to his position. From Banks' Ford to Falmouth, the
course of the Rappahannock is that of a bow bent to the North.
Once the Federals crossed at Falmouth, they might use the River
Road—the string of the bow—and assail Wilcox's right flank.[61]
Wilcox, who always was observant of ground, had familiarized
himself with the terrain during the winter. Now that he might
have to defend the ford against a heavy attack, he took care to
picket all the way along the string of the bow to Taylor's Hill,
which was opposite the head of the canal that had figured in the
action of December 13.

After Wilcox posted his pickets, on his return to Banks' Ford,
nothing of consequence happened along his immediate front.
Across the river, May 2, Wilcox observed large forces of Federal
infantry moving westward, and he saw much artillery that seemed
to be heading for United States Ford and the Wilderness. From
the direction of Chancellorsville, he heard the guns that Lee employed to divert the Federals during Jackson's march to the right
of Hooker. Although the Federal commanding General failed to
appreciate the importance of Banks' Ford, Wilcox did not. For
the night of May 2–3—the night that witnessed the tragedy of the

[60] Cf. R. E. Lee to Cadmus M. Wilcox, MS, Nov. 12, 1863: "I . . . am pained to
find that you desire to leave this army. I cannot consent to it for I require your services
here. You must come and see me and tell me what is the matter. I know you are too
good a soldier not to serve where it is necessary for the benefit of the Confederacy."—
Wilcox MSS. See also Featherstone, Posey et al. to James A. Seddon, Dec. 3, 1862, MS;
Landon C. Haynes and fourteen other Congressmen to President Davis, Feb. 6, 1863, MS.
A note on these papers indicates that officers of Wilcox's Brigade similarly had petitioned
for his promotion.

[61] The map for the operations of May 3, in the back of Hotchkiss and Allan, op. cit.,
is clear and explicit for Wilcox's movements.

wounding of Jackson—strong pickets were maintained vigilantly by Wilcox. If the enemy crossed, resistance would be instant and stiff.

On the morning of the 3d, Cadmus Marcellus Wilcox was—as soldiers always should be—early astir. He made carefully and in person the round of his picket posts from left to right, and at every lookout he observed with critical eye everything he saw of the enemy across the river. Fewer troops were visible—far less than on the previous day. Of that, Wilcox was sure, though at first he asked himself whether it might not be a ruse.[62]

Wilcox was not content to make general observation. He took pains to scrutinize through his glasses the individual Union sentinels who were visible to him. How were they accoutred? Were they acting as if they were prepared for a movement? Wilcox looked over the sentinels, one by one, and soon noticed that each of them had on his haversack. That was unusual. Why should sentinels, soon to be relieved, be carrying over their shoulders the bags in which they kept their rations? They must have been told to prepare for a march. As there was not the slightest sign of any attempted crossing at Banks' Ford, all the circumstances, Wilcox later explained, "induced me to believe that much of the force from Banks' Ford had been sent to Chancellorsville." He went on: "I relieved most of my pickets, being convinced . . . that the enemy . . . did not intend crossing there." [63] He directed that about fifty men, with two pieces of artillery, be detached to watch the ford and that the remainder of the command fall in at once and proceed toward Chancellorsville in the manner contemplated by orders.[64]

While Wilcox was far around on the right, making his preparations, one of his infantry pickets ran up to report that the Federals were advancing westward on the road between the river and the canal.[65] Wilcox spurred immediately to the canal bank, whence

---

62 Cf. O. R., 25, pt. 1, p. 855. This is Wilcox's own account. It ought to be read by every soldier who thinks he has an unimportant position in the face of the enemy.

63 Ibid.

64 Gen. H. J. Hunt stated vaguely in his report, O. R., 25, pt. 1, p. 248, that the position at Banks' Ford was abandoned by the Confederates on the afternoon of May 3. Even so close an observer as he probably did not see Wilcox's men slip away from the Ford.

65 This must have been Laflin's 1st Brigade of John Gibbon's 2d Division of the II Corps. See O. R., 25, pt. 1, p. 350 ff.

he could get a good view of the road. There, precisely as the picket stated, with their van not more than 1000 yards away, were three regiments. More might be following.

At hand to oppose this force were about twenty infantry pickets and no more; but Wilcox was rewarded immediately for having completed early his marching arrangements. Not far distant, with

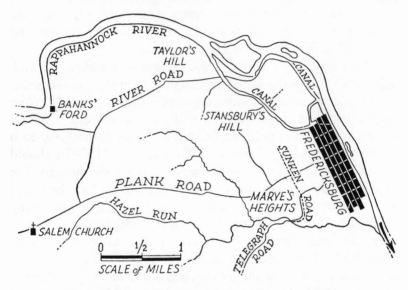

Terrain of Wilcox's Maneuvers, May 3–4, 1863—after *Bigelow*

horses harnessed, ready to start, were two field guns of Frank Huger's excellent battalion. Almost in the same breath that he told an officer to collect and to deploy the pickets on the crest of Taylor's Hill, Wilcox ordered the men with the two guns to hasten to a little work which he knew from his previous study of the ground was on an eminence across the River Road from Taylor's.[66]

Immensely to Wilcox's relief, the Federal column halted as soon as its officers saw his picket line on the hill. When Huger's guns opened defiantly with shell, the column took cover. By this time, too, Wilcox observed that Confederate troops, who proved to be Hays's men, were moving into the rifle pits at Stansbury's Hill,

[66] *O. R.,* 25, pt. 1, p. 855-56.

the eminence South of and to the right of the high ground where Wilcox had put his guns.

To Wilcox, the halt of the Federal column was too ready. It looked as if the enemy's troops might be demonstrating in order to hold the Confederates and to prevent the reinforcement of Lee. If that was the Federal game, Wilcox resolved not to play into his opponent's hand; but before making any move, at a time when his knowledge of the situation was incomplete, he rode over to Stansbury's Hill where he had seen two mounted officers. They were Barksdale and Hays, who gave him news of the heavy Federal threat against Marye's Heights. Barksdale said that he soon might require help on his right, but he had to hurry back to that part of the line before he explained what his needs were. Wilcox concluded, from what Barksdale had said, that his own Brigade should be brought up close to Taylor's Hill and held there until the designs of the enemy became somewhat plainer. He proceeded to do that. After he had shifted his troops and had placed them safely in a ravine near the Taylor House, Wilcox determined to consult Barksdale again and to ascertain what he should do next. This must have been about 10 A.M.

Wilcox rode as far southward as Brompton without finding Barksdale or any other general officer. While near the center of the line Wilcox saw many troops in the town and, as he was returning to his post, he observed a number of regiments on the march from the upper end of Fredericksburg. Whither they were bound, he could not be sure. Scarcely had Wilcox rejoined his command than a courier came from the General he had sought in vain: Barksdale, said the courier, was sustaining heavy attacks and asked for the help of a regiment. The entire Alabama Brigade at the moment was waiting in the ravine. A word sufficed to start the Tenth Alabama. Toward the endangered center Wilcox now himself rode ahead of his men, in order to ascertain where they should be placed. He had gone half a mile when, from the field in rear of the Stansbury House, he noticed that Hays's Brigade was on its way, apparently, to the Plank Road. This Wilcox took to be a movement to support Barksdale, but when he overtook Hays's men he learned for the first time that Marye's Heights had been taken by the Federals. Hays, under orders, was conforming to

Barksdale's withdrawal and was moving back, unhindered as yet, to the Telegraph Road.

Wilcox's keen eye for ground showed him that if he brought up his troops immediately to support Hays, where the two officers then stood, their two Brigades could hold off the enemy temporarily and, if need be, could retreat along the Plank Road. Hays was willing enough to share the fight, but his orders were to retire southward, not westward, whither the Plank Road led. These orders were supplemented, almost on the instant, by a courier who brought Wilcox from Barksdale the news of the lost fight on Marye's Heights and the suggestion of Barksdale that Wilcox, like Hays, proceed to the Telegraph Road.

The suggestion was both polite and permissible, but as Wilcox ranked Barksdale by almost ten months,[67] he had no obligation to follow the plan of the gentleman from Mississippi. Wilcox determined to follow his own judgment in the application of his orders from Army Headquarters. In doing so, he made the finest of his several wise decisions on that, his greatest day. He was alone; his nearest avenue for the execution of his contingent orders to join Lee was the Plank Road; down that same road it seemed reasonable to assume that the enemy, whose heavy lines were in plain sight, would be certain to advance. That Federal force, which must be several times his own strength, Wilcox would have to oppose; but, he said afterward, "I felt it a duty to delay the enemy as much as possible in his advance,[68] and to endeavor to check him all that I could should he move forward on the Plank Road." [69]

Wilcox got his Brigade safely out on the crest of hills in rear of Stansbury's, drew his line parallel to the Plank Road, on the best nearby ground he could find, and posted his four guns on his flanks. There, with the traditional tactics of delaying action, he held off the enemy for a time and then sideslipped to the left to see what the Federals would do. They seemed to be puzzled and hesitant. "From this slight affair with the enemy," Wilcox re-

[67] For that matter, Hays was Barksdale's senior but he either did not know it or else he accepted the guidance of the man who, of all the Brigadier Generals, probably had the most intimate knowledge of Fredericksburg.

[68] The statement in 2 *C. V.*, 51, that Sedgwick and Wilcox had been at West Point together has the implication that Wilcox was guided by his knowledge of his adversary. Fact is, Sedgwick was graduated in 1837, Wilcox in 1845.

[69] *O. R.*, 25, pt. 1, pp. 856–57. The account in the text follows closely the report of Wilcox which is the only detailed, first-hand Confederate narrative of the action.

ported, "I felt confident if forced to retire along the Plank Road, that I could do so without precipitancy, and that ample time could be given for reenforcements to reach us from Chancellorsville; and, moreover, I believed that, should the enemy pursue, he could be attacked in rear by General Early, reenforced by Generals Hays and Barksdale." [70]

That seemed irrefragable logic after the event. At the time, it represented risk as well as daring—a combination that must be balanced on the beam of judgment. Wilcox moved over to the Plank Road, threw his command squarely across the line of the enemy's advance and boldly offered shell for shell. With good troops, carefully employed where he expected he would not have to fight long without reinforcements, Wilcox did not suffer unduly from the attacks of a cautious adversary; [71] but he must have been pleased, in the early afternoon, [72] to hear from Maj. J. M. Goggin, of McLaws's staff, that three of the Brigades of that Division were on their way to reinforce the Alabamians. "These brigades," Wilcox reported in business-like fashion, "were directed to be halted in rear of the [Salem] Church, and out of the view of the enemy." [73] Wilcox did not know it at the time, but reinforcements for him and for Early had cost Lee dearly. In the hour of victory that morning, while Anderson's men were mingling with Stuart's at Chancellorsville, Lee had received word that Early had been driven from the heights of Fredericksburg. Further pursuit of Hooker had to be deferred that day. By no other course was Lee able to detach sufficient troops to deal with the Federals who were marching against Lee's rear. [74]

After the arrival of McLaws's men, the work of the afternoon was simple for Wilcox. Federal commanders skirmished with their infantry, blustered with their artillery and, about 5.15 o'clock, threw their regiments against the Confederate position at Salem

[70] O. R., 25, pt. 1, p. 857.

[71] He was pursued by Brooks's and Newton's Divisions of the VI Corps of John Sedgwick. Of this action Newton filed no report, nor did any of his brigade commanders except Frank Wheaton. In describing the preliminaries of the main action at Salem Church, few of the Union commanders credited Wilcox's infantry with special stubbornness but several of the officers mentioned his troublesome artillery.

[72] The time of the various moves on the first day at Salem Church is quite vague.

[73] O. R., 25, pt. 1, p. 857.

[74] See 2 R. E. Lee, 544–45. An amusing story of Lee's receipt of news of the fight at Fredericksburg from Rev. Wm. B. Owen of the Seventeenth Mississippi will be found in Stiles, 176.

Church. The repulse by the four waiting Brigades was bloody.[75] Wilcox then took the initiative and, with the support of Paul Semmes's Georgians, drove the column of attack back upon strong reserves. Darkness ended the action. While this success was easy, a long day's fighting had entailed for Wilcox 495 casualties, seventy-five of which were deaths.[76] As Wilcox lamented the loss, he could tell himself without vainglory that he had protected the rear of Lee and that he had made it possible for Early to reconcentrate scattered forces. Daring and devotion had their reward. Cadmus Wilcox that day gave military history an example far outliving his time, of the manner in which one Brigade, courageously led, can change the course of battle and retrieve a lost day.

Early owed more to Wilcox than he acknowledged then or thereafter, but as senior officer on the sector nearest Fredericksburg, he received on the evening of May 3 Lee's instructions and McLaws's request for counsel. Lee's first dispatch, which Early must have opened about 10 o'clock, was an expression of regret at the loss of Fredericksburg and an appeal for Early to unite with McLaws in an attack. "With McLaws' five Brigades[77] and you and your Division and the remnant of Barksdale's Brigade," Lee wrote Early, "I think you ought to be more than a match for the enemy."[78]

About the same time, and perhaps a little before he got Lee's note, Early received information of what had happened late in the day at Salem Church. McLaws told him that Lee wished McLaws's own men and Early to attack and to overwhelm Sedgwick.[79] What, McLaws naïvely inquired, did Early propose? The Georgian was in term of service the oldest Major General with the army, and the Virginian the most recently appointed; but that

[75] Robert Stiles, op. cit., 174, remembered that McLaws had been "boosted" to the top of a tobacco barn in a vain effort to give him a better view of the field.

[76] O. R., 25, pt. 1, p. 859.

[77] Lee counted Mahone and Wilcox of Anderson's Division with Kershaw, Semmes and Wofford of McLaws's own command.

[78] O. R., 25, pt. 2, pp. 769–70. Lee knew, by this time, from Stuart's report of a dispatch found on a captured staff officer, that John Sedgwick, who was in general command on that part of the front, then had—or that day had—two Corps at Fredericksburg. O. R., 25, pt. 1, pp. 886–87.

[79] Early, 220. Lee's language was: "It is necessary that you beat the enemy, and I hope you will do it." O. R., 25, pt. 2, p. 770. This, like Lee's note to Early, was dated 7 P.M.

circumstance neither deterred McLaws from asking for suggestions, nor led "Old Jube" to hesitate in giving them.

Early, in fact, felt entirely competent to direct McLaws's fight and his own. He determined to concentrate his Division during the night and in the morning to recover the high ground at Fredericksburg. When this was accomplished, Early would have secured himself against an attack from the direction of the town and would have separated the Federals there from the units on the Plank Road. Because the ground favored him, Early believed he could deliver successfully the first stroke with part of his forces. The remainder of his troops would extend their left to unite with McLaws's right. It would be easy, after that, for Early and McLaws to close in and to overwhelm the Brigades cut off on the Plank Road. In describing to McLaws this plan, Early did not use the word "envelop" but that manifestly was what he had in mind. It was a practicable operation, he thought, provided McLaws would co-operate heartily.[80]

After midnight on May 3–4, word came back to Early from McLaws that General Lee approved the plan and that the troops around Salem Church, under McLaws's command, would join in the attack the next day.[81] That was all Early remembered of the circumstances when subsequently he wrote of the occurrences of the night; but the fact was, McLaws had forwarded Early's letter and outlined plan of action to Lee, who thought the plan good, but had some doubt whether it was practicable.[82] Lee realized, in particular, that McLaws's active aid was necessary and he particularly enjoined that officer to "press [the Federals] so as to prevent their concentrating on General Early." [83]

In full expectation that the joint attack would be delivered soon after sunrise, Early sought a few hours' sleep. Nothing in his action seemed to indicate any misgiving, any unusual doubt regarding the effectiveness of the tactics to be employed, any unusual concern over the outcome. He was self-reliant, if not self-confident, and was not oppressed by his responsibility. Sure evidence this was that "Old Jube" was growing as a soldier.

[80] *Early*, 220. Cf. *O. R.*, 25, pt. 1, p. 827.   [81] *Early*, 220.
[82] *Cf.* Taylor to McLaws, midnight, May 3–4, *O. R.*, 25, pt. 2, p. 770: "General Lee . . thinks well of what General Early proposes, if it is practicable."
[83] *O. R.*, 25, pt. 2, p. 770.

McLaws's mental approach to the battle is more difficult to ascertain. He was not then, or at any other time, deficient in courage.
Personal risks he took without ostentation but calmly and as a
matter of course. If he was apprehensive at this time, it was on
three counts: First, he did not feel that he knew the ground of
probable action, though most of it was within half an hour's
canter of the heights where he had spent the winter. He undoubtedly was troubled, also, because he thought the enemy was
in superior force. Third, he had been much impressed by the
Federal bombardment on the afternoon of the 3d. "The batteries
of the enemy," he later reported, "were admirably served and
played over the whole ground." [84] It is possible, in addition, that
McLaws missed Longstreet and felt overwhelmed by his responsibility, but of this there is no positive evidence. Nor is there a
suggestion anywhere that McLaws missed the security of the
strong position he had commanded in the battle of the previous
December. Uneasy he was, and unconvinced that he should or
could carry the burden of the fighting the next day. That seems to
have been his state of mind.

Daylight of May 4 found Early's entire Division astir. The
General himself intended to march with John B. Gordon's Bri-
gade, which he had selected to lead the column that was to re-
cover the heights and to cut off the Federals from the town.
Snowden Andrews was to follow with his battalion of artillery.
Smith's and Barksdale's Brigades would be in support. When
Early had all these troops ready to advance, he rode off to show
Hoke and Hays where they were to cross Hazel Run and where
to take position on the right of McLaws.

This was a matter that called for precise lines of advance,
because the ravine of Hazel Run was so tangled that the crossing
had to be at a ford on Early's left. After that, deployment must
be undertaken, in woodland interspersed with steep hillside, where
troops easily might lose their way.[85] Early took care to see that
Hoke and Hays knew exactly what was expected of them. It did
not occur to Early or to either of the Brigadiers, apparently, to
acquaint the senior Colonels with the plan of action or with the
line of advance, though the division commander would not be

84 O. R. 25, pt. 1, p. 827.   85 Early, 222.

present to instruct the next in command, if either Hays or Hoke was incapacitated.

When satisfied that these two officers understood fully their part in the operation, Early hurried back across Hazel Run to the point on the Telegraph Road where he had left Gordon. The Georgians were not there. Neither were Andrews's guns. A moment's inquiry elicited the disconcerting fact that Gordon already had started on his mission and that Andrews had gone forward, also. Instead of waiting for Early, who would direct him and would deploy the supporting Brigades, Gordon already was moving toward Lee's Hill.

Early did not delay to ask why this had been done. Nor did he attempt to recall Gordon who, he reasoned, by that time might be assailing the Unionists. If Gordon had launched the attack prematurely, it must be supported. Let Smith proceed immediately along the road by flank; put Barksdale in advancing line of battle on the right; join Gordon with the least possible delay![86]

Fortune laughed—as Fortune rarely does—at a misunderstanding of orders. Gordon had an unopposed march to an invaluable objective. He found that Lee's Hill was not occupied by the enemy. Neither was Willis's Hill, though a surprised Federal force was on the road across the northern end of it. With the soldierly co-operation of the artillery, Gordon advanced from Lee's Hill to Willis's. General Early, arriving quickly, gave Gordon the support of Smith, and then ordered Barksdale to resume the familiar position under Marye's Heights and, if possible, to reoccupy Fredericksburg.

"Old Jube" was pleased with Gordon's fine performance but was a bit disposed to be overcritical and impatient in dealing with Barksdale. The Mississippi troops, in Early's opinion, had halted unnecessarily. After the heights were recovered, Barksdale seemed slow in advancing his pickets toward the town. Early sent to ascertain the reason. Barksdale replied that the movement was about to begin. A second messenger, dispatched to speed Barksdale, brought word that the Mississippi skirmishers found the rifle pits in their front manned and saw in Fredericksburg what appeared to be a heavy force.[87] Early had to content himself with

<hr>

[86] Early, 222; O. R., 25, pt. 1, pp. 840-41.   [87] Early, 224-25

ordering Barksdale to maintain position and to keep the Federals from advancing.[88]

What next? That part of the ridge recovered by Early was lower than the hills to the northward. If the enemy occupied in strength the upper end of the ridge, he now, of course, was aware of Gordon's presence. There could be no surprise attack on Stansbury's or Taylor's Hill. Capture of those eminences was not an essential preliminary of the attack along the Plank Road; but before Gordon and Smith started their attack in co-operation with McLaws, should not the strength of the enemy farther upstream be ascertained? No fire, other than that of muskets, had been directed at Gordon and Smith: could the Federals in that quarter be without artillery? All the small works that had constituted the second defensive line of the Confederates, on the plateau behind the ridge, were occupied by the enemy. Was he strong or weak up the ridge, which included many depressions where a large force could be sheltered? To answer his questions, Early "felt" the ridge with Smith's Brigade. Heavy fire from infantry and artillery, and consequent rough handling were the lot of these Virginians, whose deployment under a new Brigadier was awkward. Early did not have to hesitate in his interpretation of the result! The Federals evidently were manning in strength the upper part of the ridge. If they remained inactive there, they were better left alone.[89]

If Early's eyes, all the while, had been on the ridge, his ears had been straining for the sound of McLaws's guns. No echo had rolled down Hazel Run; no message had come. Why? Had the plan for a joint attack gone awry? Was McLaws waiting on Early? "Old Jube" still felt able to execute fully his part of the agreed plan without storming the upper end of the ridge, and he now hurried off a staff officer to explain his situation to McLaws. The Georgian was to be informed, with Early's compliments, that Hoke and Hays were in position on the right and were ready to co-operate with McLaws. As soon as those troops and McLaws's own engaged the enemy, Early would throw in Gordon and Smith.

[88] *O. R.*, 25, pt. 1, p. 841. As Early later admitted, somewhat casually, Barksdale had good reason for not attempting to reoccupy Fredericksburg: an entire Federal Division, Gibbon's of the II Corps, was there. Cf. *Early*, 225.

[89] *Early*, 225–26.

After Early's staff officer, Lieut. A. L. Pitzer, galloped off about 9 A.M., the center of interest shifted to Salem Church. McLaws received in some puzzlement the report that Pitzer brought. The terrain confused McLaws; the strength of the enemy in his front made him doubtful of success. He was willing to help Early, but should not Early open the attack? Moreover, General Lee had sent word that "Dick" Anderson was marching from Chancellorsville to reinforce the troops around Salem Church. Was it not prudent to wait until Anderson arrived and then to strike with a stronger force? So reasoning, McLaws bade Pitzer take back this message to Early: The advance would not be made until Anderson was in position; then three guns, fired in rapid succession, would be the signal for the general attack.[90]

About 11 A.M.,[91] Anderson arrived in the vicinity of Salem Church and reported to McLaws; but before McLaws could decide where he would put Anderson, the commanding General himself reached the ground and assumed the direction of affairs. This was a deliberate and not a chance appearance of Lee. He unwillingly left Hooker's main army among the thickets of the Wilderness. Preferably, if he could have mustered the men, Lee would have struck that day North of Chancellorsville. Instead, he came to deal personally with the Federals on the Plank Road, because he seems to have felt that McLaws was proceeding with too much caution and deliberation.[92] Soon after arriving, Lee

[90] *Early,* 226–27. Lee said, in his report (*O. R.,* 25, pt. 1, p. 801): "[Early] then proposed to General McLaws that a simultaneous attack should be made by their respective command, but the latter officer not deeming his force adequate to assail the enemy in front, the proposition was not carried into effect." McLaws (*ibid.,* 827) reported: "I agreed to advance, provided [Early] would first attack, and did advance my right [Kershaw and Wofford] to cooperate with him; but finding my force was insufficient for a front attack, I withdrew to my line of the previous evening, General Early not attacking, as I could hear." This language would seem to indicate that Kershaw and Wofford were advanced soon after the receipt of information from Early; but the next paragraph of McLaws's report begins "In the meanwhile" and proceeds to describe events that continue the narrative till nightfall. Wofford filed no report; Kershaw mentioned no advance until "late in the evening," by which he manifestly meant "afternoon." Then, he said, he and Wofford took position from which they were ordered at 6 P.M. to advance (*O. R.,* 25, pt. 1, p. 831). Kershaw made no mention of any withdrawal from this position prior to the attack. Federal reports contain no reference to anything more than casual skirmishing. Bigelow (*op. cit.,* 413) admitted himself unable to account for the long delay in the afternoon, but he found no evidence of any forward movement early in the day by Kershaw and Wofford.

[91] *O. R.,* 25, pt. 1, p. 852.

[92] This nowhere is set forth explicitly in Lee's dispatches or in his report. From what Lee did *not* say in commendation, rather than from what he might have said in criticism, his dissatisfaction with McLaws's performance is safely to be inferred. See *infra,* p. 661.

began, with manifest if unusual impatience,[93] to get into position Anderson's Division, the rear Brigades of which were slow in reaching Salem Church.

Even under the eyes of "Marse Robert" himself, progress was slow. Tired men did not show their old alacrity. Conditions were unbelievably different from those that had prevailed on the 1st of May. At length, in the afternoon, Lee rode out and met Early. By that time, the commanding General may have concluded that he could expect little of McLaws, and that the attack must be committed to the other Divisions. After Early had reviewed what had been done and what now could be undertaken, Lee sent this message: McLaws was to occupy the enemy in this front and, after Early and Anderson opened the attack, he was to throw in Kershaw and Wofford.[94]

Two difficulties still presented themselves. One was that of ascertaining precisely where the Federal lines had been drawn; the other was that of moving troops and guns to such tenable jump-off as could be found opposite those lines. From necessity, after Sedgwick had been cut off from Fredericksburg, he had made his dispositions on three fronts, East, South and West. If the Rappahannock be regarded as the fourth side, the able Union commander had a quadrilateral, the long side of which was South of the Plank Road for a distance of a mile and three-quarters.[95] That southern front covered the Plank Road. By possessing the thoroughfare, the Federals made slow and troublesome for the Confederates the detailed reconnaissance that had to precede a general assault in country where ridges and ravines might conceal a hostile column which readily could turn a flank. Had the Confederate staff officers been able to gallop along the Plank Road, liaison between McLaws and Early would have been simple. As it was, the commanding officer on neither Confederate flank knew what his comrade on the other flank was doing.[96]

It was close to 6 o'clock [97] when McLaws, who was on the right

[93] *Alexander*, 356.　　　　　　　　　[94] *O. R.*, 25, pt. 1, pp. 802, 828.
[95] The best map is No. 37 at the back of Bigelow's *Chancellorsville*.
[96] *Cf.* Lee's report, *O. R.*, 25, pt. 1, p. 802: "Some delay occurred in getting the troops into position, owing to the broken and irregular nature of the ground and the difficulty of ascertaining the disposition of the enemy's forces." See also McLaws, *ibid.*, 828.
[97] *O. R.*, 25, pt. 1, 802, 852.

of his divisional front, received word that Anderson and Early were about ready to attack, and that Alexander's battalion of artillery, which had been located with much care, should open fire.[98] In a few minutes, all along the line was heard the signal of three guns fired in swift succession.[99] On the right, Gordon started up the ridge toward the Taylor House; Hoke and Hays

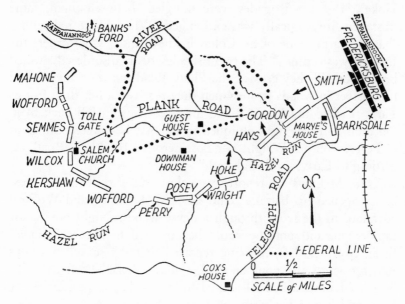

Final Confederate Disposition at Salem Church, about 7.00 P.M., May 4, 1863—
after *Bigelow*

immediately were set in motion by Early, who himself rode forward to join Hays; on the left of Hoke,[100] Anderson ordered forward Wright's Georgians. Beyond them, to the West, were Posey and his Mississippians; on their left, Perry and his Florida Brigade. Posey's orders were to advance. Perry was to remain where he was and was to guard a long gap between his left and McLaws's right, unless opportunity offered of striking effectively.[101] Mc-Laws's orders to advance Wofford and Kershaw stood.

Gordon encountered scant opposition at first; Hays, Hoke and Wright started magnificently out.[102] "Old Jube's" pulse beat up

98 *O. R.*, 25, pt. 2, p. 828.   99 *Early*, 228.
100 Hoke was on Early's left.   101 *O. R.*, 25, pt. 1, pp. 852, 872, 876.
102 Cf. *Early*, 228; *O. R.*, 25, pt. 1, p. 869.

and his sharp eyes shone more brightly than ever as he observed the North Carolinians and the men from Louisiana sweep on.[103] Wright defied a heavy fire of artillery and rushed through a wheatfield.[104] The onset was thrilling, the next stage was expectancy, the third was suspense. After that, gallantry did not suffice. Nothing went well. Hays's lines of advance converged with Hoke's; the two Brigades were mingled; between them, some mistaken fire tragically was exchanged. When Hoke fell with a shattered arm, none of his Colonels knew under what orders the Brigade was acting.[105] The two Brigades, badly disordered, pushed bravely on till they crossed the Plank Road but soon they found themselves in woods from which they received a hot fire. Just as Early reached the Plank Road, the two Brigades fell back to it. On their flank, Wright obliqued so far that he covered the front of Perry. Neither Wright nor Posey crossed the Plank Road, according to Early, until nightfall.[106]

As for McLaws, his report was a chronicle of confusion: "Alexander opened his batteries, and Generals Kershaw and Wofford advanced to the front through a dense woods. Night now came rapidly on, and nothing could be observed of our operations." Soon, from the left, Mahone reported that the sound of troops moving across the pontoon bridge above Banks' Ford could be heard. McLaws asked Alexander to fire as close as possible to the ford, which was not visible.

Next, when McLaws learned that Kershaw's advance had carried that officer to the Plank Road, the division commander requested Wilcox to take charge of Kershaw's regiments and, with such of the Alabama troops as Wilcox saw fit, to press on toward Banks' Ford. This, McLaws reported later, "was done in the most prompt manner, General Wilcox being acquainted with the localities, of which I knew nothing except by report." [107] McLaws knew nothing, either, of what had happened on the right of the Confederate line; but as he continued to hear the tremendous clatter made at Banks' Ford, as if giants were beating the long roll on the pontoons, he concluded that the enemy was retreating and that Kershaw and Wofford should pursue. They did so and picked up, by morning, a good deal of plunder.[108]

103 *Early*, 229.
105 *Early*, 229.
107 *O. R.*, 25, pt. 1, p. 828.

104 *O. R.*, 25, pt. 1, p. 852.
106 *Early*, 231.
108 *O. R.*, 25, pt. 1, p. 820.

Some of the other troops after nightfall on the 4th held to an unprofitable chase. Even Gordon, on whom the fates that day had smiled, was compelled to halt beyond Taylor's Hill in the face of darkness and stiffened resistance.[109] Commanders, in several instances, scarcely knew where they were or what they were expected to do.

Amid this confusion, protected by night, all the Federals in the vicinity of Banks' Ford got safely off. As a considerable force still was believed to be in Fredericksburg, Early was ordered back there during the night with two of his Brigades, to strengthen Barksdale. Ere dawn, varied alarms led Barksdale to call for reinforcements, but Early had none to send [110] and believed, moreover, that the enemy would quit the right bank of the Rappahannock before morning. Fact bore him out. By daylight of the 5th, the whole force of Sedgwick, from Fredericksburg to Banks' Ford, had the river between them and the Confederates.[111]

Of these events, "Stonewall" Jackson heard with a pleasure he physically was strong enough to express. During the afternoon of May 3, while Cadmus Wilcox was having his great day, Jackson was told by Dr. McGuire that General Lee had sent directions that the patient be moved to the rear as soon as this could be done without danger to Jackson. Meantime, Lee had said, troops would be sent to guard the Second Corps Hospital against a possible advance by Federals across one of the upper fords of the Rappahannock.

Jackson had accepted escape from death in the Wilderness as the dispensation of the Almighty, and he did not now propose to mock that mercy. He told Dr. McGuire that if in the surgeon's judgment a move to the rear would do him harm, he would stay where he was. To remain in a tent was no hardship. In fact, he would prefer to do so if, when Mrs. Jackson arrived, she could find quarters in a nearby house. "And if the enemy does come," he went on, "I am not afraid of them; I have always been kind to their wounded, and I am sure they will be kind to me." If it were better that he move southward, he specified that he should make the journey without special attention and that Dr. McGuire, in

[109] *Early*, 230.
[110] Hoke and Gordon, by Lee's orders, had been left North of the Plank Road. *Early*, 233.
[111] *O. R.*, 25, pt. 1, pp. 213–14, 561, 802; *Early*, 233.

particular, should not go with him. The Medical Director must remain with the wounded. There had been too many instances, said Jackson, where officers, to the neglect of the men in the ranks, had carried off their surgeons to care for them personally.[112]

To all of this, the Medical Director and the General's aide had to agree; but before they carried plans any further, they received late in the evening of the 3d another message from Army headquarters: Lee sent word that the military situation demanded the removal of Jackson to a place less exposed. Dr. McGuire was instructed to turn over all other duties to the senior surgeon, and was himself to attend the General, and to remain with him. Jackson heard this part of Lee's orders with a satisfaction he could not conceal. Unwilling himself to have McGuire detached for exclusive attendance on him, Jackson was satisfied that he could recover more quickly under the eye of his trusted and competent Medical Director. "General Lee has always been very kind to me," Jackson said, "and I thank him." [113]

As the commanding General considerately left to the patient the choice of a nearby haven, Jackson promptly said that if it was agreeable to the family, he would go to Fairfield, the home near Guiney's of Mr. and Mrs. Thomas Coleman Chandler, who had shown him many courtesies.[114] Whether the journey should be made the next day was left to be determined by Jackson's condition, which hourly seemed better. By nightfall he was rid of the pain in his side and, though not at a pitch of excitement, was anxious to get more details of the battle. "Good, good," he would say, at the recountal of some gallant deed, and with glistening eye he warmly would praise some officer to whom, had he been present on the field, he might have given at most a glance of approval.[115]

The 4th of May was the first anniversary of Jackson's arrival at Staunton en route to McDowell for the initial engagement of the

112 *McGuire*, 224. Unfortunately, Dr. McGuire misdated this incident and put it on the afternoon of Monday, May 4, not of Sunday, May 3. All the other authorities, including *Hotchkiss' MS Diary*, 183, fix the move on May 4. Many years later, some of Jackson's staff officers observed the difference in the reported date of these incidents. Jed. Hotchkiss made inquiry and, through Rev. James Power Smith, satisfied himself of the chronology. His dating is followed here.

113 *McGuire*, 224.

114 Statement of Mrs. Lucy Chandler Pendleton, Oct. 28, 1941. Mrs. Pendleton recalled distinctly, at the time she wrote, how she went as a little girl with her father to welcome Jackson to the vicinity of Fairfield after the move from Moss Neck, and how Mr. Chandler then invited Jackson to make Fairfield his headquarters.

115 Cf *Dabney*, 709.

"Valley Campaign." If he remembered the date, he said nothing to any of his attendants; but he had slept well and, in the judgment of his surgeons, he now could look forward to normal convalescence. Dr. McGuire told him the orders of General Lee could be executed without excessive risk. The weather was favorable, a fair and pleasant morning, though the atmosphere suggested a thunderstorm before the day was out.[116] Preparations to take the road already were being made. In Jackson's mind, that road to recovery did not end at Guiney's. The Chandlers' home was to be a temporary resting place only. From it, when his wounds began to heal, he would go to a pleasant village, such as Ashland, conveniently near Richmond but free of the bustle and excitement of the capital. Perhaps at Ashland, for a few days, it might be permissible to have the company of Rev. Tucker Lacy and to combine conversation on things of the spirit with delighted listening to some of the chaplain's stories.[117] Refreshed by this companionship, Jackson would travel from Ashland to Lexington, where, in the home he had not seen for more than two years, he would complete his recovery.[118] Then, in the mercy of God, with one hand he would smite the invader more heavily than ever he had with two!

At length the ambulance was ready. On the flooring, a mattress had been placed. Such Spartan comforts as the Corps Hospital counted in its scant equipment were made available to the General. His young Chief of Artillery, Stapleton Crutchfield, again was to accompany him as a fellow patient.[119] Jed. Hotchkiss was to choose the route and clear the road; Smith and Lacy were to remain at the General's side; Dr. McGuire was to direct everything and, in particular, was to see that Jackson did not become exhausted.

The safest road was one of the shortest—by way of Todd's Tavern to Spotsylvania Court House and thence southward and eastward to the R. F. & P. at Guiney's.[120] It would be an all-day journey, at the least, but it was begun auspiciously. Jackson was

116 *Hotchkiss' MS Diary*, 183.   117 Cf. *Pendleton*, 271.
118 *Dabney*, 711.   119 *Hotchkiss' MS Diary*, 183.
120 *Hotchkiss' MS Diary*, 183, but with no specific itinerary beyond Spotsylvania. The Spotsylvania map in his *Papers* and Campbell's map in *O. R. Atlas*, Plate XCI, indicate that from Spotsylvania, the ambulance in all likelihood proceeded down the New Court House Road to William Dickinson's and then headed eastward parallel to and on the south side of the Po.

placed in the ambulance without mishap. Almost as soon as the
vehicle got under way, the horses overtook lightly wounded men
who were walking toward the railroad. These veterans of the Second Corps sensed immediately from the equipage and the number
of attendants that Jackson was in the ambulance and they shouted
friendly messages to him. Over and over, the soldiers cried out
that they wished they could have been wounded instead of their
General.[121]

It was so even with the teamsters of the wagons coming up
from the South. In accordance with their own rule of the road—
that the heavier vehicle has the right of way—the drivers expected the ambulance to take the ditch. When they were commanded to wheel to one side, they told the man at the reins in
the ambulance and, no doubt, the pious Hotchkiss also, to go to
hell; but as soon as they heard that Jackson was in the conveyance,
they turned out and, in many cases, stood bareheaded and in tears
until he had passed.[122] Down the road, drivers and soldiers
shouted that "Old Jack" was coming. Before long, word had
passed so far that residents of that thinly peopled district had time
to come out to welcome the General and to offer him the few
delicacies they had—their bread, their milk, a little butter or a
handful of eggs. At Spotsylvania Court House, refugees and residents crowded sympathetically around the ambulance. Jackson,
needless to say, was pleased, as always he was by attentions.

The journey was rendered less tedious by conversation in which
Jackson shared freely. It almost was as if his staff officers were
gathered again in his tent at William Yerby's on one of those
evenings of the early spring when he had talked with them of
many things. As they chatted, someone spoke again of the part
Jackson's old Brigade had played in the battle of the 3d, west of
Chancellorsville. So gallant a command, said the speaker, deserved to have officially the title for which it had petitioned the
government—that of the "Stonewall" Brigade.

Jackson spoke up with enthusiasm: "They are a noble body of
patriots! When this war is over, the survivors will be proud to
say: 'I was a member of the old Stonewall Brigade.' The govern-

121 *Hotchkiss' MS Diary,* 183.
122 *Dabney,* 711. It should be noted that, almost beyond a doubt, Dabney got his
account of this journey from Chaplain Lacy.

ment ought certainly to accede to their request, and authorize them to assume this title; for it was fairly earned."

He paused, and then added: "The name 'Stonewall' ought to be attached wholly to the men of the Brigade, and not to me; for it was their steadfast heroism which had earned it at First Manassas." [123]

That remark was consistent with the little he previously had said about the *nom de guerre*. He never had associated it mentally with himself or had assumed that his men did. Once, during the winter at Moss Neck, when some of the young ladies had asked him, according to the fashion of the times, for a lock of his hair, he had replied that they must not cut any gray. To this they politely had answered that his hair showed no gray. His rejoinder had been that the soldiers called him "*Old* Jack." [124]

As the conversation in the slow moving ambulance revolved about the battle, the General was asked for his opinion of Hooker's plan of campaign. Jackson did not hesitate: "It was, in the main, a good conception, sir; an excellent plan. But he should not have sent away his cavalry; that was his great blunder. It was that which enabled me to turn him, without his being aware of it, and to take him by his rear. Had he kept his cavalry with him, his plan would have been a very good one." [125]

In this reply and in other exchanges of the morning, Jackson showed no confusion of mind and no fatigue. He had no symptom of distress until, later in the day, he became slightly nauseated. For this malady and for sundry other ills, Jackson previously had used the "water cure" of Farmer Vincenz Priessnitz, and he now asked that wet towels be applied to his abdomen. With Dr. McGuire's consent, this was done. The result, whether psychological or physiological, was entirely to Jackson's satisfaction.[126]

Once more, renewed talk turned to the battle. Usually, even

---

[123] *Dabney*, 712–13.   [124] *Hotchkiss' MS Diary*, 159.

[125] *Dabney*, 713. There is a distinct possibility that this remark was made later in the week. On the other hand, by the morning of May 2, when Jackson lost touch with army headquarters and with Lee's intelligence reports, it undoubtedly was known that most of the Federal cavalry were detached from Hooker and were engaged in a raid against Lee's lines of supply (cf. *O. R.*, 25, pt. 1, pp. 1046–47, 1098). Be this as it may, some Federals of rank shared Jackson's opinion. On Feb. 17, 1864, General Pleasanton, in disapproving plans for new operations against Richmond by the Federals, stated that the raid of May, 1863, had cost the Federals 7000 horses and had inflicted no damage that had not been repaired in a few days (*O. R.*, 33, 171).

[126] *Dabney*, 712; *McGuire*, 225.

when the last gun had been fired, Jackson said little of his
strategy for the reason he had advanced in eliminating from
Faulkner's draft of his reports most references to his planning: He
did not wish to disclose anything which ultimately might acquaint the Federals with his methods. Now it was different.
Responsibility no longer was upon him; from those to whom he
spoke in the ambulance, no word could reach the enemy. In
answer to tactful questions, Jackson confided that he had hoped to
press forward on the night of May 2 and to seize a position between Hooker and United States Ford, where the Federals would
have been compelled to attack him. With a grim smile, from the
mattress on the floor, he repeated, "My men sometimes fail to
drive the enemy from a position, but they always fail to drive us
away."

He spoke in unclouded memory of the attack on Hooker's left,
and in glowing words of those officers who most had distinguished
themselves. First in his praise was Robert Rodes. Previously,
Jackson doubtless had heard how Rodes had fought at Seven
Pines and at South Mountain, and how gallantly that officer had
stood at Sharpsburg until mistaken orders had caused the command to leave the "Bloody Lane." Now that Jackson himself had
seen Rodes's leadership in the woods West of Chancellorsville, he
had high admiration for the man who had directed against
Hooker's right the advance of Harvey Hill's old Division. Rodes,
said Jackson, should be promoted. He hoped it would be done
without delay, because promotion for valor, especially promotion
on the field, was the greatest possible incentive to gallantry on the
part of others.[127] Another whom Jackson singled out for special
praise was General Colston; [128] still another was Col. Edward
Willis of the Twelfth Georgia, Doles's Brigade, who swiftly had
cleared the right and then had re-formed his line and had continued the advance.[129] Of those who had fallen, Jackson spoke
again and with deep regret.

The long journey of twenty-seven miles [130] came to its end at

[127] McGuire, 225.					[128] See infra, p. 660.

[129] Dr. McGuire, op. cit., 225, mistakenly stated that Colonel Willis was in charge
of the skirmishers of Rodes's Division. See supra, p. 593. For references to the part
Willis and his famous regiment played in the battle, see O. R., 25, pt. 1, pp. 941, 946,
967, 968. He was mentioned by Rodes next after Brig. Genls. Doles and Ramseur
"for great gallantry and efficiency in this action." Ibid., 946.

[130] Dabney, op. cit., 711, estimated it at twenty-five.

8 p.m. Jackson was near the station where, in the rain, two weeks previously, to the very day, he had met Mrs. Jackson and the baby. They would return as soon as the Federal cavalry recrossed the Rappahannock and the railroad company could repair the damage done. Denied now the welcoming smiles of his *esposita*, he had accorded him a martial reception. The pleasant May skies had become overcast. Clouds were banking high. There was a distant rumble not unlike that which had echoed across the Valley from Cross Keys the morning he had waited at Port Republic. Louder the rumble grew, and nearer. Lightning swept the forest. All the new greenery of spring was in retreat before the wind. Salvo followed salvo. Every battery that had played at Second Manassas, on the ridge around the Dunker Church and on the rival heights of the Rappahannock was overwhelmed by the artillery of the firmament. Was it the challenge of battles to be fought, or was it salute to the victor of Chancellorsville? [131]

When Chaplain Lacy reached Fairfield, a little ahead of the ambulance, he found Mrs. Chandler busily putting the finishing touches to accommodations for the General in the parlors. At the same time, the parson heard over him much tramping and thumping and talking. Upon inquiry, he learned that the hospitable Chandlers already were entertaining a large company of refugees and sick and wounded soldiers. A less noisy place might be desirable. In that judgment, when he arrived, Dr. McGuire concurred with emphasis because he was told that a case or two of erysipelas had occurred in the "main house" at Fairfield. Instantly, Mr. and Mrs. Chandler placed at the General's exclusive disposal the office in the yard, a building quite similar to that which Jackson had occupied during the winter at Moss Neck.

This was ideal! Jackson was conveyed in the ambulance to the door of the office and then carefully was moved inside. On the left as he entered was a small room; to the rear were two chambers, in one of which, the one nearer the railroad, the General was placed on a bed. Above, reached by a small stair, were two half-story rooms. In front of the office were a pair of fine oak trees.

[131] Hotchkiss in his *MS Diary*, 183, stated that the thunderstorm was "late in the evening" but in his writings, as in the common Virginia usage of that period, "evening" often is synonymous with "late afternoon." As there is no record of the hour of the thunderstorm, the reference in the text has to be left vague.

To the side, almost on a line with the entrance, was the house well. In this setting, Jackson immediately was comfortable and relaxed. He ate some bread, drank a cup of tea and ere long he quietly fell into normal sleep.[132]

The cool [133] morning of May 5—the morning when Lee learned that Sedgwick had recrossed the Rappahannock—Jackson awoke in good condition,[134] though he felt he had rested less during the night than actually he had.[135] He was not told that the previous day, the wagons had been hurried off because of a rumor that Federal raiders were approaching. When the rumor had been proved false, the vehicles had been returned. Now, on account of a similar report, they were being reloaded in great haste. Nearly all the Confederate officers departed, but McGuire, Smith and Lacy remained in a determination to accept capture, if need be, in return for the privilege of attending their chief, to whom they gave no intimation of the reason for activity. Jackson consequently assumed that the officers who came to say good-bye were leaving in the regular line of duty. To Jed. Hotchkiss, the General expressed hope that he soon would be with his troops again. The engineer particularly was enjoined to give Jackson's regards to General Lee.[136]

Dr. McGuire, early that Tuesday morning, examined the wounds. The one in the right hand was giving little pain but McGuire thought the hand should be splinted to keep the fragments of bone at rest. No serious infection was discovered. The stump of the left arm was doing equally well. Some parts of it seemed to be healing by first intention. Granulation elsewhere was observable. Jackson ate with heartiness and began to speculate on the length of time he would be absent from duty. He was altogether cheerful. "Many," said he to Smith, "would regard [these

132 *McGuire*, 225; *Mrs. Pendleton's MS Statement*.
133 *Hotchkiss' MS Diary*, 185.
134 Here again the chronology has been confused. Dr. McGuire, it will be remembered, wrongly gave May 5 as the date of Jackson's journey to Guiney's. Concerning the date of arrival, May 4, Dabney was correct; but in his biography of Jackson he no sooner had the General arrive at Guiney's Monday evening, May 4, than, by a curious lapsus, *op. cit.*, 713, he described how Jackson waked up at Guiney's Monday morning, instead of Tuesday. The one safe guide for daily events seems to be Hotchkiss, who kept his diary with care but, unfortunately, left Guiney's on the morning of the 5th of May.
135 *Hotchkiss' MS Diary*, 185: ". . . went to see the General; found him cheerful, although he had not rested much. . . ." Cf. *McGuire*, 225.
136 *Hotchkiss' MS Diary*, 185.

injuries] as a great misfortune; I regard them as one of the bless-ings of my life."

" 'All things work together for good to them that love God.' " Smith quoted.

"Yes, that's it, that's it." [137]

[137] *McGuire*, 220.

CHAPTER XXXVI

Promotion for Rodes and for Jackson

At the hour of Jackson's fervent reaffirmation of his complete acceptance of God's way with him, three fierce Divisions of the Second Corps were waiting around Chancellorsville that 5th of May, 1863, for orders to renew the attack on Hooker. The remaining Division, Early's, was started toward Chancellorsville with the other troops that had fought at Salem Church, but it was ordered back during the morning to its old position on the heights of the Rappahannock.[1] After Anderson and McLaws rejoined the three Divisions under Stuart, preparations were made for a renewal of the general offensive on the morning of the 6th. Wasted effort it was. During the night of May 5–6, Hooker recalled the last of his troops from the right bank of the river.[2] Another "On to Richmond" had ended—as McDowell's and McClellan's and Pope's and Burnside's had—in retreat. The cost had been 16,804 Federal casualties. Lee's had been 13,156, of which number 5938 had been in A. P. Hill's and Rodes's Divisions.

Although Hooker proclaimed in general orders that "the events of the last week may swell with pride the heart of every officer and soldier of the army," [3] he personally had little of which to be proud. Strategically, his plan of containing a part of the Southern army at Fredericksburg, while turning Lee's left up the Rappahannock, was as sound as it was simple. Tactically, the whole operation was discreditable to commanders who previously on many occasions had done well.

For the failure of the offensive, five major reasons, administrative and tactical, may be cited. First, Hooker did not have a staff organization capable of conducting simultaneously an attack in

[1] O. R., 25, pt. 1, p. 802; Early, 233–34.
[2] For the familiar details, see Bigelow, 419 ff; 2 R. E. Lee, 554 ff. Hotchkiss noted, MS Diary, 187, that Stuart sent him to Lee's headquarters on the morning of the 6th with word that Stuart was satisfied the enemy was retreating. Lee, who was dressing at the moment, gave little credence to the report and sent back word to Stuart to press the movement on the left. Soon Lee rode to the front and conferred with Stuart and later with A. P. Hill.
[3] O. R., 25, pt. 1, p. 171.

the Wilderness and another at Fredericksburg. The General attempted to clear all communications with Washington and with Sedgwick through the office of his Chief of Staff, Maj. Gen. Daniel Butterfield, who was on the north side of the river, near Falmouth. Butterfield failed to maintain liaison. This was not because of any lack of effort or of understanding on the part of Butterfield, who did a prodigious volume of work. If anything, he tried to do too much. He certainly sent too many messages. Individual signal officers worked as hard as he did. It was not the men but the equipment that failed. On so long a front, the wires, the instruments and the signal stations were not equal to the demands made on them. In a few instances, also, general officers seem to have withheld from the Signal Corps information that would have helped to speed communication. Sedgwick, in particular, appears to have lacked confidence in the signal service.[4] As Hooker's own difficulties increased in the Wilderness, he made, in the second place, enlarged and perhaps excessive demands on Sedgwick, who during this campaign was much below the level of best performances. Next, the Federal command erred in its singular misapprehension of the strategic importance of Banks' Ford which, if attacked, occupied and used to the fullest by the Federals, would have permitted Hooker to separate Early and Lee and to keep them apart.[5]

A fourth important factor in defeat was the feeble employment of Hooker's artillery. Never had the strongest arm of the Federal service been so weak. This was due to the fact that when Hooker assumed command he limited Gen. Henry J. Hunt, the Chief of Artillery, to administrative duty. At the opening of operations, there was no unified control of the artillery. Hunt's exceptional abilities were wasted at minor tasks until, in Hooker's desperation, on the night of May 3, Hunt was restored to field command of all the guns—too late to use them effectively.[6] Misuse and nonuse of the artillery was one indication only of the fifth principal failure of the Federal army, namely, a singular lack of co-ordination of the forces in the Wilderness. At no time was their full strength

---

[4] The report of the Acting Chief Signal Officer, Capt. Samuel T. Cushing, *O. R.*, 25, pt. 1, p. 217 ff, sets forth the difficulties and explains many of the interruptions. It is a document that deserves more attention than has been given it by writers on Chancellorsville.

[5] *Cf.* Gen. D. N. Couch in 3 *B. & L.*, 157.

[6] Cf. *O. R.*, 25, pt. 1, pp. 250, 252.

utilized. In the main, they fought separately as Corps and more often as Divisions. Hooker lacked the power to elicit that confident, whole-hearted co-operation of his lieutenants which is the cohesive of command.

All five of these failings, administrative and tactical, were aggravated by two mistakes on Hooker's part that were capitalized fully by his opponents. His initial blunder, which of itself might have sufficed for his defeat, was in sending off virtually all his cavalry for operations against Lee's lines of communication.[7] It will be recalled that the wounded Jackson considered this the prime defect of Hooker's plan of operations, because the absence of Federal cavalry simplified the march of the Second Corps to the Federal right. Hooker could say in defense of this employment of his mounted forces that if the cavalry did their full duty, they could destroy Lee's lines of supply. The Army of Northern Virginia might then be compelled to retreat or to attack Hooker on ground selected by him. Such an argument, of course, prepared the way for blaming on the cavalry the failure of the campaign. Easily Hooker's apologists could insist that the cavalry itself should have dislodged Lee and should have made unnecessary a long struggle in the Wilderness.[8] If this was an honest contention, it assuredly demanded more of that arm of the service than previously the hardest riding, best led troopers on either side had accomplished.

Hooker's second blunder is full of instruction. On May 1, the day that Jackson arrived from Fredericksburg to reinforce Anderson near Tabernacle Church, Hooker had emerged from the Wilderness without substantial loss and had reached terrain that permitted some freedom of maneuver.[9] The first and most difficult part of his turning-movement was behind him. He was on Lee's flank; he was headed for the railroad that supplied the Confederate army; and he already had compelled the Southern commander to divide force. Both at Fredericksburg and on the edge of the Wilderness, Hooker was in superior strength.

With all this in his favor, Hooker about 1 P.M. suspended his

[7] For Stoneman's instructions, see *O. R.*, 25, pt. 1, p. 1065 ff, a document somewhat neglected.

[8] *Cf.* S. P. Bates, *The Battle of Chancellorsville*, 69: "General Hooker had anticipated that, if the cavalry, which he had sent out under Stoneman and Averell to sever the communications in rear of the rebel army, and break up its avenues of supply was successful, General Lee, when he found the Union army upon his rear, would retreat either in the direction of Gordonsville or Richmond."

[9] *Cf.* Couch in 3 *B. & L.*, 159.

advance and soon afterward ordered a retirement into the tangled Wilderness. Why he did this, he never explained fully. At the time, he informed his Chief of Staff he acted because of the "character of information" which he elaborated only as "news from the other side of the river." [10] This news may have been nothing more reliable than a tale told by a deserter to the effect that Jackson's whole Corps was at Fredericksburg, that rumor placed Longstreet in Culpeper, and that Lee had said this was the first time he would face the enemy with equal numbers.[11] Hooker may or may not have credited this yarn; he may have concluded that as Sedgwick had not attacked at Fredericksburg no help could be expected from that quarter. The result of this might be that Hooker "would be unable to deploy outside the Wilderness; that the heads of his columns would be crushed, and his forces beaten in detail." [12] Some vague concern there was, also, over the possibility that the right of the Army of the Potomac might be turned. These and other explanations may mean, in blunt terms, that when Hooker got out of the Wilderness he lost his nerve and drew back in the hope that the Confederates would attack him in a position of his choosing.[13] All the vast preparations of the Federal army and all the advantages that had been won by a surprise crossing of the Rappahannock were thrown away in that single decision. From that hour, the initiative on the Wilderness was with Lee. Had the Confederates been as lucky at Fredericksburg as they were on Hooker's front, the victory would have been overwhelming.

Notable the victory was, if not overwhelming, but it was no surprise to the people of the Confederacy. As always, some of those who knew least about the risks had been most confident of the outcome.[14] "A Glorious Confederate Victory" the *Richmond Dispatch* blazoned its editorial.[15] Wrote the *Enquirer:* "It is no disparagement to other great Generals and gallant forces in our service, to say that General Lee and his Army of Northern Vir-

---

[10] *O. R.,* 25, pt. 2, pp. 326, 328.   [11] *O. R.,* 25, pt. 2, p. 322.

[12] *Bigelow,* 248.

[13] *Cf.* Hooker to Butterfield, May 1: "The enemy may attack me—I will try it" (*O. R.,* 25, pt. 2, p. 326). Same to same: "Hope the enemy will be emboldened to attack me. I did (*sic*) feel certain of success. If his communications are cut, he must attack me" (*ibid.,* 328).

[14] *Cf. Richmond Whig,* May 1; *Richmond Examiner,* May 2, 1863.

[15] May 5, 1863. Cf. *ibid.,* May 16, 1863.

ginia may now be pronounced the most famous Chief and Army on earth at this day." [16] With this rejoicing was mingled much ridicule of Hooker. "So far as his reputation is concerned, Hooker might well envy the dead," said the *Dispatch*.[17] Some surprise was voiced that the North was not stampeded.[18] Inasmuch as the Union refused to admit defeat, the South must work to make the most of what the Army had gained.[19] A blow must be struck again before the enemy had time to recover.[20] Amid much uninformed comment, a correct understanding of the relationship between Lee and Jackson was shown by the *Richmond Whig*,[21] but otherwise no discerning appraisal of Chancellorsville appeared until the same paper on May 15, reviewing Northern comment, pointed out that Chancellorsville was "a battle of maneuver in which we beat the enemy utterly in strategy." In addition, the *Whig* summarized, "there was no straggling or disorganization" and "our artillery is at last perfected"—a most intelligent observation.

Satisfaction was dampened from the first by the news of the wounding of Jackson, but of other casualties, though they were many, little was said. "Our loss in officers was unparalleled," wrote Ham Chamberlayne, "in men not so great." [22] Of the subsequently reported total Southern casualties of 13,156, the killed were put at 1683. The wounded were 9277, the missing, 2196.[23] The most distinguished of those killed in action was Brig. Gen. Franklin Paxton, who fell, it will be remembered, on the morning of May 3.[24] Five Colonels had been slain and a larger number of

[16] May 8; cf. *ibid.*, May 12, 1863.

[17] May 7, 1863. Cf. *Richmond Examiner*, May 7; *Richmond Whig*, May 11 and 14, 1863.

[18] *Richmond Dispatch*, May 8 and 9; *Enquirer*, May 6. While the *Examiner*, May 13, 1863, shared this view, it expressed the fear that "despite the efforts of Lincoln the South is likely to lose the services of General Judas Hooker."

[19] *Richmond Sentinel*, May 9, 1863.   [20] *Richmond Whig*, May 8, 1863.

[21] May 9, 1863.   [22] *Ham Chamberlayne*, 176.

[23] Alexander, *op. cit.*, 360–61, made this careful computation.

[24] See *supra*, p. 590. For the reflections of this earnest man on the probability of death in battle, and for his meditations during the days preceding Chancellorsville, see *Paxton*, 74–75, 86, 89–00, 92, 93, 95, 98, 101, 104, 107. On March 15, writing his wife, he said: "I have received your miniature, reminding me of times when you and I were young; of happy hours spent, a long time ago, when I used to frequent your parlor in the hope that you might be what you now are, my darling wife. Then the present was overflowing with happiness, the future bright and beautiful. We have seen much of each other, much of life, its joys and sorrows, since then. By the grave of our first child we have known together the deep sorrow of parting with those we love forever. In this long absence of two years, we have felt the sadness of a separation with such chance of its being forever as we did not dream of when we began life

other field officers.[25] Besides Jackson, six general officers were wounded: The new Louisiana Brigadier, Francis T. Nicholls, lost a leg;[26] Samuel McGowan was injured severely;[27] Ramseur,[28] Heth,[29] Pender[30] and Hoke[31] were hit but not dangerously. Most of the men in Jackson's party at the time it came under fire were killed or wounded. Among the dead was the Chief Topographical Engineer of the Second Corps, Capt. J. K. Boswell.[32] Dead, also, was Channing Price who never rallied from the loss of blood he suffered in the reconnaissance of May 1.[33] Stanhope Crutchfield survived the wound that cost him a leg, but from his post as

together. May God in his mercy soon bring us together, in our dear home, never to separate again, to spend what of life is left to us in peace and happiness" (ibid., 93). In the final report of the battle, Lee mentioned Paxton for "conspicuous courage" (O. R., 25, pt. 1, p. 803). Paxton's case is one of many cited in alleged proof of the view that certain men have premonition of death. He showed much depression on the night of May 2 after he learned of the wounding of his chief, and he stated that he would be killed the next day. When first seen on the morning of May 3, he was reading his Bible. As soon as he was hit, he lifted his hand to his breast pocket where he kept that book and a picture of his wife.

25 The killed were Cols. Francis Mallory of the Fifty-fifth Virginia, O. R., 25, pt. 1, p. 890; T. S. Garnett, of the Forty-eighth Virginia, commanding Jones's Brigade, ibid., 1006; W. M. Slaughter, of the Fifty-first Georgia, ibid., 834; T. J. Purdie, Eighteenth North Carolina, ibid., 919, 920; and James M. Perrin, of Orr's South Carolina Rifles, ibid., 906; Caldwell, 84. In addition to these officers, Col. O. E. Edwards of the Thirteenth South Carolina was wounded, but was not thought to be in danger. En route home, he died. O. R., 25, pt. 1, p. 891; Caldwell, 84–85.

26 Cf. O. R., 25, pt. 1, p. 803. Cf. Mil. An. La., 33 ff. Nicholls's mother was Louisa H. Drake, sister of J. Rodman Drake. After the wound received at Chancellorsville, Nicholls had the tragic distinction of being an invalided officer "with one eye, one leg and one arm" (7 S. H. S. P., 525).

27 O. R., 25, pt. 1, pp. 803, 889.   28 Ibid.

29 Ibid.

30 Ibid., 803. Cf. Pender to his wife, May 5, 1863: "I have had better luck than usual having only been bruised a little by a spent ball." On the 23d, Pender apologized to his wife for failing to keep her informed about his wound. He had to admit "it turned out to be a little deeper than it appeared at first but still it is but trifling."—Pender MSS.

31 Early, 229. Hoke's wound, though not alarming, was most painful.

32 Hotchkiss entered in his diary a detailed account of the manner in which on the afternoon of May 3, he found the corpse of Boswell about twenty yards ahead of the spot where Jackson fell. Two bullets had passed through Boswell's heart. Another had struck his leg. The body had been rifled, but, said Hotchkiss, the look of Boswell "in death was peaceful and pleasant as in life." Hotchkiss had the remains carried to Elwood, the home of Maj. Horace Lacy, and had them interred in the graveyard there, close by the spot where the amputated arm of Jackson had been covered with earth. "We buried [Boswell]," wrote Hotchkiss, "just as the moon rose, wrapped in his martial coat." Hotchkiss confessed: "I wept for him as for a brother; he was kind and gentle and with as few faults as most men" (op. cit., 181).

33 See supra, p. 536. He expired on the 2nd. Among the Price MSS are letters of condolence from "Jeb" Stuart and from Fitz Lee. In General Orders No. 15, of May 10, 1863, Stuart announced a loss which "deprived the Division staff of its most efficient member; the country of a faithful and gallant defender, and an afflicted family of its brightest ornament" (Richmond Sentinel, May 15, 1863). An affecting presentation of the wounding and death of Price appears in Lieut. Frank Robertson's MS Memoirs In the Saddle with Stuart.

Chief of Artillery of the Second Corps he would be absent for months.

Crippled was the mildest word to describe the condition of the command of the Second Corps. In D. H. Hill's (Rodes's) Division, thirty officers were killed, 148 wounded and fifty-nine were missing—a total of 237.[34] Ere the battle ended A. P. Hill's Division had four successive commanders—Hill, Heth, Pender and Archer. The Brigade of McGowan, formerly Gregg's, finished the action of May 3 under its third Colonel.[35] Colston's Brigade entered the fight under its senior Colonel and emerged under its fifth ranking officer, a Lieutenant Colonel.[36] Lane's regimental leadership was almost destroyed. The Twenty-sixth Alabama of Rodes's old Brigade was led, during the final hours, by a Lieutenant.[37]

Like losses in command had been met and endured by the Army of Northern Virginia: was there a point beyond which competent successors to fallen officers could not be found? If that question occurred to any besides General Lee himself, an optimistic answer was taken for granted. Neither the civil authorities nor the press said anything to indicate that they considered attrition of command in terms of crippling cumulative loss of the bravest from Williamsburg to Chancellorsville, over a period of precisely one year.

The same grim process of attrition was wearing to feebleness some of the most reliable units of the Army. At Chancellorsville, several sustained heart-breaking losses. Jackson's old Stonewall Brigade never was itself in full might after that battle. The Twenty-second Virginia Battalion lost approximately forty-five of its 102 men [38] and, as the next engagement was to prove, had lost its fighting edge, also. In Lane's Brigade, nearly one-third of the entire command was put out of action during the first assault on the morning of May 3.[39] These casualties, men might say, could

---

[34] O. R., 25, pt. 1, p. 947.   [35] O. R., 25, pt. 1, p. 791.

[36] Ibid., 793. For the condition of Colston's Division, see supra, p. 589.

[37] Ibid., 792.

[38] O. R., 25, pt. 1, p. 901. The Battalion belonged to Heth's, formerly Field's Brigade, A. P. Hill's Division, which Brigade at Chancellorsville was commanded by Col. J. M. Brockenbrough of the Fortieth Virginia.

[39] His total losses were 909 in a total that could not have exceeded 2500 (cf. O. R., 25, pt. 1, pp. 917, 918). The kindred Second North Carolina of Ramseur's Brigade had its first and second color bearers killed and all four corporals of the color guard shot down (ibid., 998). One of the Wilson twins of Company F of that regiment was killed. His brother, bending over to save his watch, fell dead on the body (2 N. C. Regts., 118).

be made good by bringing into the Army the thousands who were evading military duty. The veterans would shame the conscripts into fighting. Perhaps it would be so. Was there not also a possibility that the best men were in the ranks already and, as they fell, would be irreplaceable from the small white population of the South?

Nor could the balance sheet of command and of enlisted personnel be drawn immediately after Chancellorsville entirely in terms of killed and wounded. The recovery of Jackson was taken for granted, after his fine rally from the amputation of his arm; but even if his return to his post would not long be delayed, the battle had created certain doubts at the same time that it had confirmed judgment. Competence as well as attrition had to be taken into account.

First might be written down the principal credit entries. At the head of the list of individuals, next to the commanding General himself, stood Jackson, of course. His performance had not been flawless. The start on May 2 had been late; the march had not been brilliant; Jackson had not maintained regular communication between van and rear; into the attack on the afternoon of the 2d he had been able to throw at the outset no more than six of his twelve Brigades.[40] All of this was defective technically; but the wisdom of the plan, the vigor of the whole conception and the fury of the attack were superlative. At the time, the secrecy of the march, the surprise of the enemy and the climax of the wounding of Jackson had an imaginative appeal that made men ignore minor shortcomings which today are plain and instructive. Lee himself spoke of the "matchless energy and skill" of Jackson in this operation.[41] After those words and earlier tributes even more eulogistic, anyone who criticized Jackson's leadership at Chancellorsville would have raised in Southern minds a question concerning his own sanity and patriotism.

For the manner in which "Jeb" Stuart assumed and exercised command of the Second Corps, he was most elaborately complimented by Lee and by Powell Hill. "Ably" had Stuart "discharged the difficult and responsible duties" unexpectedly assigned him. He had exhibited "great energy, promptness and intelligence" and had conducted operations with "distinguished capacity and

[40] Cf. *Alexander,* 335.   [41] *O. R.,* 25, pt. 1, p. 803.

vigor." [42] Within limits, this was true. Stuart had taken courage-ously at midnight the direction of a situation so confused that staff officers could not have explained it to a newcomer even had those officers been at hand. From daylight on the 3d Stuart pressed the attack. To be sure, his forces soon were piled up, immobile, on his right; but was that his fault? If, again, he offended some austere persons by his singing and his lack of dignity, had he not reanimated many tired troops? To an extent not fully realized even now, the advance of Confederate troops from South of Chancellorsville facilitated the last successful stage of Stuart's attack; but that advance was directed by Lee and was executed by "Dick" Anderson. Neither of those modest men was of a nature to dispute any assertion by Stuart, who never failed, in his reports, to make the most of his achievements. Probably the main consideration in just appraisal of Stuart's service is the difficult one of ascertaining his responsibility for the decisive concentration of artillery at Hazel Grove. Here, again, he had the same advantage he had enjoyed at the hands of Lee and of Anderson: what Stuart said in his own behalf was not disputed by the admiring Porter Alexander, who first had seen the importance of Hazel Grove during the night of May 2–3 and then had placed guns within easy distance of that eminence. [43] At least as much credit belonged to Alexander as to Stuart, but the entry at the time was made on the account of the cavalryman. [44] Even then, as will develop, Stuart was not satisfied with the praise given him.

---

[42] O. R., 25, pt. 1, pp. 803, 886.

[43] Stuart reported, O. R., 25, pt. 1, pp. 887–88, that he sent Alexander during the night "to select and occupy with artillery positions along the line bearing upon the enemy's position," but in the next paragraph Stuart said: "As the sun lifted the mist that shrouded the field, it was discovered that the ridge on the extreme right was a fine position for concentrating artillery. I immediately ordered thirty pieces to that point, and, under the happy effects of the battalion system, it was done quickly." Alexander never disputed this, though (op. cit., 342) he quoted H. B. McClellan as saying that "Colonel Alexander's reconnaissance convinced Stuart that Hazel Grove was the key to the Federal position, and to this part of the field Stuart directed a large share of his personal attention on the morning of the 3rd." As subsequently will appear, Alexander thought Stuart's performance on the 3d so fine that it qualified Stuart for command of an infantry corps; but in his own impersonal report on Chancellorsville (O. R., 25, pt. 1, pp. 822-23) Alexander explained dispositions which show clearly that he realized the value of Hazel Grove and had prepared to occupy it.

[44] In reporting somewhat hurriedly his infantry operations at Chancellorsville, Stuart omitted the usual summary of distinguished service, and he did not mention Alexander after stating the assignment of the Colonel on the night of May 2–3. A. P. Hill merely commended Alexander as one of four artillerists (ibid., 886). Lee listed Alexander second among the artillerists who deserved special commendation (ibid., 804). Nowhere at the time was the full value of the Georgian's service appreciated.

Next after Stuart, reports were to second Jackson in applauding the soldierly performance of Robert Rodes. Tactical details of all that Rodes did on May 2-3 are not determinable in their fullness, because accounts are vague, but the handling by him of D. H. Hill's fine Division was in keeping with the quality of the troops. On the field, astride his black, froth-covered horse, Rodes was a superb figure. His "eyes were everywhere, and every now and then he would stop to attend to some detail of the arrangement of his line or his troops, and then ride on again, humming to himself and catching the ends of his long, tawny moustache between his lips." [45] As far as the facts are known, Rodes made one mistake only—the minor one of not seeing that the skirmishers of his cwn Brigade were instructed properly before the offensive began on the afternoon of the 2d. To this lapsus, which did not influence the result, it does not seem proper to add on Rodes's account any blame for Colquitt's hesitation on the right after the attack got under way. In the midst of a rapid onslaught, Rodes scarcely could be expected to know that the commander of his right Brigade had disregarded specific instructions and had halted because of a false report that hostile cavalry was on his flank.[46] All in all, Rodes's leadership had about it something Jacksonian. As Lee wished both to reward Rodes and to please Jackson, the commanding General decided to ask immediately for the promotion of Rodes as Jackson had urged. Assignment was to be to the Division Rodes had led against the flank of Hooker. Although the President had to confess some legal compunctions, he appointed Rodes a Major General on May 7 to rank from May 2—the nearest approach the Army had known to promotion on the field for valor.[47]

Jackson, Stuart, Rodes—these three were honored, and next in the commanding General's report, Jubal Early. The language was this: "Major General Early performed the important and responsible duty intrusted to him in a manner which reflected credit upon himself and his command." [48] It would have been easy, even at the time, to have raised many questions concerning Early's hand-

---

[45] *Stiles*, 261.   [46] See *infra*, p. 664.

[47] Wright, 33; O. R., 25, pt. 1, p. 803, pt. 2, p. 774; *Lee's Dispatches*, 87–88; 5 *Rowland's Davis*, 481; O. R., 51, pt. 2, p. 703. Hill in his report, O. R., 25, pt. 1, p. 886, said: "Brigadier General Rodes distinguished himself much, and won a proud name for himself and his division." For the adjustments of brigade command necessitated by the promotion of Rodes, see *infra*, p. 702.

[48] O. R., 25, pt. 1, p. 803.

ling of the situation at Fredericksburg: Did he, for example, make proper dispositions, or did he concentrate too heavily on the right and leave too great a defensive task to Barksdale? [49] How much of the credit due Early for operations on the afternoon of May 3 belonged to Cadmus Wilcox? Was Early's plan of operations for May 4 too elaborate? Should he have foreseen that the lines of advance of Hays and of Hoke would converge dangerously? Could any part of the blame be placed on Early for the fact that no officer of Hoke's Brigade, other than its commander, was instructed in the plan? In describing events of May 4, did Early assert too much for Gordon and did he thereby depreciate Barksdale?

The last only of these matters came under review. Barksdale heard a report that Early had said the Virginian's troops "had recaptured Marye's Hill on the 4th that Barksdale lost on the 3rd." [50] This aroused the Mississippian. He adduced proof that one of his scouts, known as "Yankee Hunter" Roberts, had gone to Willis's Hill on the 4th before Gordon reached it. Roberts had found there, instead of Federal troops, a group of ladies from the town who were looking after the wounded. Further, Barksdale proved that a member of his staff and the commander of his advanced pickets were on the heights when Gordon "stormed" them. [51]

This brief controversy served to show that Early's achievements lost nothing in his recountal of them, but the achievements themselves were solid enough. Early had been subjected at a post of danger and difficulty to the impact of misstated orders and to the uncertainties of attack by an overpowering foe. In the face of all this, and of a doubtfully efficient handling of part of his artillery, "Old Jube" had kept his head. Without excessive loss of men or of ground, he, with Wilcox, had frustrated an essential part of the Federal plan, that of an attack by Sedgwick on the rear of Lee's Army.

[49] Bigelow's graph of density of force, *op. cit.*, 387, shows that from Hamilton's Crossing to the Brick Cabin, a distance of 5100 yards, Early's concentration was 1.2 men per yard and Sedgwick's 1.3. Between Hazel Run and the Plank Road—the critical sector of Barksdale's position—Confederate concentration per yard on a front of 1000 yards was .9; the Federal was 9. These figures, of course, do not take into account the relative strength of the artillery on these sectors.
[50] The language is that in which B. G. Humphreys summarized the allegation (3 *Land We Love*, 457–58).
[51] *Ibid.*

Following praise of Early in Lee's report, "Dick" Anderson received commendation he honestly had earned. He fought admirably at Chancellorsville and did much to hold the Confederate right while Jackson struck on the left. The South Carolinian, said Lee, was "distinguished for the promptness, courage and skill with which he and his division executed every order." [52] In this statement, especially in the reference to Anderson's "promptness," Lee made amends for some impatience he had shown on the 4th when Anderson failed to arrive at Salem Church as early as Lee had hoped [53]—a delay due to the fact that Anderson did not get his orders until after he had deployed his skirmishers and was preparing to engage the enemy in the direction opposite that of his directed march. [54] Even then he had to wait until Heth relieved him. [55] Always it was Anderson's nature to take the largest blame and the least praise. At Chancellorsville, as previously, he merited far more than ever he would have thought of claiming. He never seemed to realize that his side-slipping to the left and his subsequent attack to the northward exhibited tactics of the first order.

As well he should have been, Cadmus Wilcox was linked in Lee' report with these men. He was "entitled," said Lee, "to especial praise for the judgment and bravery" displayed in impeding Sedgwick on the 3d, "and for the gallant and successful stand at Salem Church." [56] A memorable example Wilcox afforded of the manner in which emergency and responsibility on occasion lift men of certain types far above their average performance. Wilcox always was observant of terrain. While stationed on the left of the line at Fredericksburg he must have examined closely and often the ground in his rear. When he had to fight there, he had the vast advantage of knowing the lines of advance, the short cuts, the shelter and the exposed positions. [57] His observation was not confined to ground. It will be recalled how quickly he had seen on the morning of May 3 at Banks' Ford that the Federal soldiers

---

[52] *O. R.*, 25, pt. 1, p. 803. In the *Anderson MSS*, an obituary from the Columbia *Daily Register*, June 29, 1879, contains the assertion that on May 3, Lee three times ordered Anderson to charge and came at length to ascertain why the order had not been obeyed. When Lee found that Anderson had beaten off two assaults by a far superior force, he shook Anderson's hand and said, "My noble soldier, I thank you from the bottom of my heart." Nothing in Anderson's report indicates that he received either the orders or the attacks. The anecdote probably is misplaced.

[53] Cf. *Alexander*, 356.   [54] *O. R.*, 25, pt. 1, p. 852.
[55] *Ibid*.   [56] *O. R.*, 25, pt. 1, p. 803.
[57] Cf. *O. R.*, 25, pt. 1, p. 828.

had on their haversacks. From that fact he reasoned intelligently and at once that the men were expecting to move. When Wilcox had reached this conclusion, he had prepared immediately to leave Banks' Ford. On receipt of Barksdale's call for assistance, he was ready, though circumstance prevented the actual reinforcement of the Mississippian.[58] After Hays had marched off toward the Telegraph Road, in accordance with his orders, Wilcox, left alone, might have felt that he had a right to cry, *Sauve qui peut.* Instead, he took his chance of being destroyed in order that he might delay the advance of the enemy. Never before had such an opportunity come to Cadmus Wilcox; never again was he to have another such; but it could be said that of the one supreme day he had made the most.

Others there were who had done well. Heth had not failed the expectations of Lee, his sponsor. Dodson Ramseur had given a fine example of what a fighting Brigadier should be. Jackson commended him in a message to Lee.[59] Both Hill [60] and Rodes [61] praised the North Carolinian. Said Dorsey Pender in full knowledge of what the words meant, "Ramseur covered himself and Brigade with glory." [62] Unflinchingly, after receiving a wound, Ramseur had remained with his men, despite pain and loss of blood, till the close of the action.[63] George Doles had proved himself the peer of Ramseur; [64] Fitz Lee's reconnaissance on the 2d and his skirmishing the next day on the Ely's Ford Road deserved the praise they received.[65] Gordon's quick movement on the morning of May 4 was commended, though Early had to say that if Gordon had not been successful, he would have been forced to court-martial the Georgian for starting before the other Brigades were prepared to move.[66] The sole stipulation of one of Lawton's men, whom the new commander was leading in action for the first time, was that Gordon should not again address them before they went into battle. When asked why, the soldier replied, "Because [Gordon] makes me feel like I could storm hell." [67]

---

[58] As Barksdale manfully stated in his report, "It was utterly impossible for either General Wilcox or General Hays to reach the scene of action in time to afford any assistance whatever" (*O. R.*, 25, pt. 1, p. 840).

[59] *O. R.*, 27, pt. 3, p. 871.   [60] *O. R.*, 25, pt. 1, p. 886.

[61] *Ibid.*, 946.

[62] To his wife, May 7, 1863—*Pender MSS.*

[63] Cf. *O. R.*, 25, pt. 1, pp. 889, 947.   [64] *O. R.*, 25, pt. 1, p. 946.

[65] *O. R.*, 25, pt. 1, p. 889.   [66] *Gordon*, 100–01.

[67] *Companions in Arms.* 540.

As always, the impersonal army itself deserved more praise than any person. Company officers and men in the ranks of the infantry had distinguished themselves so greatly that few officers were disposed to dwell on the unhappy morning hour of May 3 when hundreds of veteran soldiers had huddled under the breastworks South of the Plank Road. Nearly all the commanders had valiant deeds to report. Wilcox thought the finest feat of his gallant Brigade was that of his numerically weakest regiment, the Ninth Alabama, in advancing to fill a gap created by temporary panic in the strongest of his regiments, which was immediately in front of the Ninth.[68] Barksdale had boundless praise for the fight made by his Twenty-first and part of his Eighteenth Mississippi in the gallantly futile defense of Marye's Heights.[69] Lieut. John R. Ireland, of the Thirteenth North Carolina, Pender's Brigade, had rushed forward and had captured a Federal Brigadier General and his staff.[70] Private William Savage of the Twelfth North Carolina had as his haul of prisoners a Colonel, a Captain, two Lieutenants and eleven enlisted men.[71] J. S. Webber, a private in the same regiment, hunted standards, not men, and brought in three—the flag of the Forty-sixth and a cavalry and an artillery flag without markings.[72] Not least among the heroes of the infantry was a boy, so badly wounded that his arm hung by some shreds of flesh. When he met Henry McClellan, he began bravely: "Mister, can't you cut this thing off? It keeps knocking against the trees and it's mightily in my way." McClellan, somewhat aghast, proceeded to cut off the arm with his pocket knife, and, as he did so, asked: "Which is your regiment?"

"I belong to that North Carolina regiment in there. I'm just sixteen and I've just come from home. Don't you think it's a hard case that I should get hit in my first fight? We drove them out of one line of breastworks, and I was on top of the second when I got hit. But oh, how we did make them git!" [73]

Of like spirit were thousands of infantrymen. Their fighting quality, long tested, long had been applauded. Often, too, from the beginning of the war, particular batteries or brave cannoneers had been praised. Like commendation now for the first time could

[68] O. R., 25, pt. 1, pp. 858, 860.   [69] Ibid., 840.
[70] Brig. Gen. William Hays. O. R., 25, pt. 1, p. 935. See supra, p. 588.
[71] O. R., 25, pt. 1, p. 990. The regiment belonged to Iverson's Brigade
[72] Ibid.   [73] 8 S. H. S. P., 445.

be given the artillery as a whole. This was to be Lee's language: "To the skillful and efficient management of the artillery the successful issue of the contest is in great measure due. The ground was not favorable for its employment, but every suitable position was taken with alacrity, and the operations of the infantry supported and assisted with a spirit and courage not second to their own. It bore a prominent part in the final assault which ended in driving the enemy from the field at Chancellorsville, silencing his batteries, and by a destructive enfilade fire upon his works opened the way for the advance of our troops." [74]

Jackson, from his bed, credited the new power of the artillery arm, as did Stuart, to the recently established battalion system.[75] "The effect of this fire on the enemy," Stuart reported, "was superb." [76] Without referring directly to this new organization, Porter Alexander's account of the ease with which guns were concentrated at Hazel Grove [77] confirmed all that his superiors said. The ammunition was much better, also. Even the imported Whitworth gun, which had required British-made ammunition, was served with shells fabricated in Richmond. These were reported to have done "admirable execution." [78] Without difficulty, Maj. R. H. Hardaway used this gun with "home-made" ammunition to fire on a wagon park three miles distant,[79] and he massed rifled pieces for some excellent long range bombardment.[80] On the night of the 4th–5th, Porter Alexander conducted indirect fire against Banks' Ford.[81]

Of distinguished individual and battery service, there was enough for a chapter—Alexander, Pegram and the others at Hazel Grove, the superb defense of Marye's Heights by part of the Washington Artillery,[82] the brave, unhesitating act of Private Richard W. Saye of Carlton's battery in picking up and throwing from the parapet a live shell with a sputtering fuse that exploded a minute later.[83] These were a few of many. The struggle for Fredericksburg included nothing more heroic than the manner in which, after the enemy had stormed Willis's Hill and was advancing

[74] O. R., 25, pt. 1, pp. 803–04. [75] O. R., 25, pt. 1, p. 887–88.
[76] Ibid. [77] Ibid., 823.
[78] O. R., 25, pt. 2, p. 795. The exception of the ammunition for the 20-pounder Parrott already has been noted.
[79] O. R., 25, pt. 1, p. 879. [80] O. R., 25, pt. 1, pp. 851–52.
[81] Ibid., 216, 821. [82] Owen, 226, 228 n.
[83] O. R., 25, pt. 1, pp. 818, 843, 846.

obliquely across Howison's Farm toward Lee's Hill, Capt. H. D. Fraser of Cabell's Battalion [84] kept firing at the oncoming Federals until the service of another round would have meant capture. The limber chest of his howitzer was blown up, but he took the piece off with the limber of the caisson and bore away, also, the body of his slain lieutenant.[85] Perhaps the most effective though by no means the most spectacular firing of all on the Fredericksburg front was that of a rifled gun section under Lieut. James S. Cobbs, of Lewis's battery, Garnett's Battalion. Cobbs's detachment was so small that when he was badly wounded he had to withdraw his pieces, because he had no one to whom he could pass the command; [86] but he did not leave until an observer on the other side noted that the fire of these two guns, admirably placed, virtually halted the advance of Sedgwick's entire force.[87]

Fine as much of this conduct was at Chancellorsville, a few men had failed or, at best appraisal, had not fulfilled safely their opportunities and had made doubtful or dangerous their retention in command. Brig. Gen. Raleigh Colston, in particular, was not commended in Lee's report, which was detailed and exceptionally well stocked with praise of those who had distinguished themselves. Usually, in the reports of the reserved commanding General, when mention was honor, omission was not usually discredit. In the official narrative of Chancellorsville, where there had been so much to approve in the conduct of so many, failure to include a word of praise for the commander of one of the three Divisions that delivered the attack on Hooker's left, could not be regarded otherwise than as censure. Powell Hill, moreover, in his report, stated in plain terms that on the morning of the 3d "Colston's division [had] become somewhat broken and disordered." [88]

Why had this happened; what was the nature of Colston's failure? In answer, the records are vague. Some of them are complimentary, even. As far as Jackson had witnessed Colston's conduct, he had applauded it. When "Sandie" Pendleton was telling Jackson how the fight had gone, he said, "General Colston behaved with conspicuous gallantry and . . ." Jackson had interrupted with an admiring "Of course, of course," as if praise were

---

[84] For the armament of this battalion, see *O. R.*, 25, pt. 2, p. 802.
[85] *O. R.*, 25, pt. 1, pp. 841, 846–48.   [86] *Ibid.*, 857–58, 884.
[87] G. K. Warren, then Chief Engineer, Army of the Potomac, *ibid.*, 203.
[88] *O. R.*, 25, pt. 1, p. 886.

unnecessary. En route to Guiney's, Dr. McGuire had remarked in the ambulance that two of Jackson's Divisions were commanded by Brigadier Generals. Jackson answered, "Yes, Doctor, but those Brigadiers are soldiers, Colston and Rodes, both soldiers!" [89] In Rodes's own report describing the advance on the afternoon of May 2, he spoke of the "brave and accomplished Colston." [90] Lt. Col. Hamilton A. Brown, the fifth commander of Colston's Brigade in the battle of May 3, asserted that the "knowing ones" credited Colston's and the Stonewall Brigade with saving the day on their part of the line.[91]

Other reports are curiously, perhaps deliberately, reticent. When silences are probed and obscure references are traced down, it would appear, in the first instance, that Colston lost his grip on his troops during the early morning hours of May 3 and did not recover it that day. This was not surprising, if again it be recalled that Colston had led men in battle only twice before—once briefly at Williamsburg a year previously and again, May 31–June 1, 1862, at Seven Pines. In neither instance had his responsibility gone beyond his Brigade. At Chancellorsville, he had a Division with which he had little acquaintance, a Division that was alarmingly deficient in officers. One only of the four Brigades went into the action of May 3 under a Brigadier General. Nicholls of the Louisiana Brigade had been wounded seriously the previous evening; his troops were under a Colonel. Jones's Brigade had lost its regular commander because he complained that an ulcerated leg incapacitated him. A regimental officer consequently led Jones's Brigade. Another Colonel handled Colston's Brigade. During the Battle of Chancellorsville, the different Brigades of the Division fought under twelve and lost eight commanders. Three of these had been killed, five wounded. Of the six members of the division staff, one was killed and two were wounded.[92] In the entire Division two regiments were all that fought both May 2 and 3 under a Colonel. Four regiments finished the battle under a Captain.[93] In these circumstances, surely, it was not surprising that the Division became "somewhat broken and disorganized."

This could not have been the full measure of Colston's failure. Had it been, he would have escaped criticism, if for no other rea-

---

[89] Hunter McGuire to R. E. Colston, MS, Aug. 11, 1863—*Colston MSS.*
[90] *O. R.*, 25, pt. 1, p. 941.   [91] *Ibid.*, 1032.
[92] *O. R.*, 25, pt. 1, p. 1108.   [93] *Ibid.*, 793.

son than that other commands, with a less depleted corps of officers, had done scarcely better than Colston's Division. A black
entry must have followed an occurrence of the afternoon of May
3. After Chancellorsville had been reached, Lee temporarily
halted the advance in order to get entangled units separated and
to prepare for an advance that would drive Hooker back against
United States Ford. During this pause in the battle, Lee received
news of Early's evacuation, by Chilton's order, of the heights at
Fredericksburg. In the confusion of the field, it was 3 o'clock before the Confederates around Chancellorsville were in place to
resume the attack on Hooker. As a first step, Colston was ordered
to undertake in a specified manner an advance up the road to
United States Ford. Colston, in turn, directed his engineer to take
the skirmishers and make a reconnaissance. When the engineer
returned, he reported the position stronger than could be taken by
Colston's weakened Division.[94] Colston thereupon told Stuart—
to quote Colston's own words—"that my Division was not able to
attack with any prospect of success the position of the enemy."
Stuart evidently was disgusted that an officer of rank should say,
in effect, that he could not. The acting corps commander consequently ordered Colston to shelter his men in some abandoned
Federal entrenchments.[95] In addition, it would appear, Stuart
placed Colston and his Division under the general direction of
Rodes.[96] This episode may have been judged a failure of a hopeless sort on the part of Colston, a failure that meant he did not
have and could not hope to gain the confidence of his men. If
there was any other consideration than this in the appraisal of
Colston, the records give no hint. Lee's conclusion, soon to be
reached, was that Colston was not suited to active field leadership.
By May 20, Colston was to be relieved of command—a course of
action Lee seldom took. Even to the President, no written explanation was given by Lee. He wrote only: "I think it better to relieve
Colston from duty." [97] It was a curious case.

The next man of rank who came through the campaign with
diminished reputation was McLaws.[98] He, like Colston, received

94 *O. R.*, 25, pt. 1, pp. 1007, 1011-12.   95 *O. R.*, 25, pt. 1, p. 1007.
96 All that Rodes said on this subject in his report was: "Colston's Division, now
attached to my command, was located on the Turnpike road." Dispositions evidently
were made of Colston's men after that time by Rodes (*O. R.*, 25, pt. 1, p. 945).
97 *O. R.*, 25, pt. 2, p. 810.   98 See *supra*, Chap. XI.

no praise in Lee's report. Instead, a somewhat stiff reference was made to McLaws in Lee's account of operations at Salem Church on the morning of May 4: "General Early then proposed to General McLaws that a simultaneous attack should be made by their respective commands, but the latter officer not deeming his force adequate to assail the enemy in front, the proposition was not carried into effect." [99] In another paragraph of the report, McLaws's own statement why he did not join in the attack on the afternoon of the 4th was paraphrased and by that fact accepted as correct, though not on that account satisfactory. This cold treatment could mean only that Lee was disappointed in McLaws's performance, which the commanding General must have considered below the opportunities and the requirements of the situation. The reasons for McLaws's conduct were inherent in the facts as he presented them. Ignorant of the ground and doubtful of his strength, as compared with the enemy's, McLaws had not been aggressive. Nothing had he risked that more he might gain. Again the question: Was it overcaution, or hesitation in dealing with Early; or was it that McLaws missed the cool direction of "Pete" Longstreet, his absent corps commander? The record is silent.

That Brigadier General Pendleton was considered the third failure of the campaign is plain from the manner in which he, like Colston and McLaws, was denied commendation. There even was, perhaps, an unpleasant nuance in the principal reference Lee made to Pendleton in the final report. Lee praised the artillery in his report, as already quoted, and then wrote: "Colonels Crutchfield, Alexander and [R. L.] Walker, and Lieutenant-Cols. [J. T.] Brown, [Tom] Carter, and [Snowden] Andrews, with the officers and men of their commands, are mentioned as deserving especial commendation." Then Lee added—it scarcely could have been through carelessness in phrasing: "The batteries under General Pendleton also acted with great gallantry." Not the General, but the "batteries under" him were praised.[100] Early, who directed Pendleton's operations part of the time in the fighting at Fredericksburg, mentioned him casually and without a syllable of approbation.[101] Later, unofficial criticism of Pendleton included the charge that he made faulty dispositions in sending to Taylor's Hill

[99] *O. R.*, 25, pt. 1, p. 801.   [100] *O. R.*, 25, pt. 1, p. 804.
[101] *Ibid.*, 1001–02.

on the night of the 3d a section of the Washington Artillery when he might as well have called a battery from his reserve.[102] This was alleged to have weakened the artillery defense at the redoubt on the Plank Road—a vital position.

With equal justice, complaint might have been made that Pendleton did not recall on the night of the 3d or early on the 4th any considerable part, if indeed any, of the reserve batteries he had hurried to the rear at the time Chilton told Early to evacuate the heights. Pendleton, in his report, stated correctly that these batteries had been sent away with Early's consent, and the artillerist somewhat labored the fact that he had told Early he would make the best fight he could with the armament he had at hand.[103]

At the moment, amid rejoicing over the efficiency of the new battalion organization of the artillery, nothing derogatory of Pendleton seems to have been said publicly. He had not shone; he had not disgraced himself; it was doubtful whether the best of artillery employment would have prevented on May 3 the capture of the hills behind Fredericksburg. The worst that could have been said of him was that he had seemed more interested in saving than in serving his guns.

Pendleton's record at Chancellorsville, in short, might have been considered merely negative had not the General himself become somewhat unhappy and discouraged. It was during the weeks following these events that he wrote his wife the words already quoted: "Few men have worked these two years as I have! And yet poor were the reward if the applause of men were my motive!" [104] Subsequently, he heard through his kinsman, Maj. Thomas J. Page, that Lee had been dissatisfied with the handling of the artillery at Fredericksburg. Pendleton got Major Page to write out what he knew, and this the artillerist forwarded to the commanding General with a copy of the report on what happened under Pendleton's eye. The covering letter, now lost, may have been a request that Lee, in effect, pass judgment on the conduct of his chief of artillery.

Lee returned the papers with a note which seemed to indicate

---

[102] 3 *Land We Love,* 451. Pendleton asserted, in his report, that still another gun was withdrawn without his knowledge. *O. R.,* 25, pt. 1, pp. 814–15. See also *supra,* p. 605.
[103] *O. R.,* 25, pt. 1, p. 814. For his account of his personal movements, see *supra,* p. 619.
[104] *Pendleton,* 272; see *supra,* p. 235.

that even his superb patience had been shaken. The commanding General said briefly that he had no recollection of the circumstances in which he was supposed to have shown his displeasure at Pendleton's defense of Fredericksburg. Then Lee made this non-committal statement: "The guns were withdrawn from the heights at Fredericksburg under general instructions given by me. It is difficult now to say, with the after knowledge of events, whether these instructions could, at the time, have been better executed, or whether if all the guns had remained in position, as you state there was not sufficient infantry support for those retained, more might not have been captured." [105] That was all. It might be read as reserved judgment; it might be considered a tactful evasion; it certainly was not, even remotely, commendation of the General Chief of Artillery.

After Colston, McLaws and Pendleton, the man who probably had to be written down next as of doubtful achievement at Chancellorsville was Alfred H. Colquitt. Concerning him, the question fundamentally was one of judgment. Had he lessened the victory of the evening of the 2nd by his halt on the right, in the belief that cavalry was threatening his flank? Admittedly, Colquitt not only deprived Jackson of hundreds of good Georgia rifles but he also blocked Ramseur, whose fine Brigade showed the next day what it was capable of doing. In reporting the events of May 2, Rodes had to say that Colquitt had halted in disregard of orders,[106] and in his list of those who had distinguished themselves on the field, Rodes did not include Colquitt.[107] The Georgian made the best defense he could of his action, and he might well have said that if he erred on the 2d, he redeemed himself on the 3d,[108] but apparently he did not clear himself in the estimation of his superiors. At first opportunity, as will appear in another chapter, his Brigade was exchanged for one then in North Carolina.

Had reappraisal been made the day Hooker recrossed the Rappahannock, Chancellorsville would have produced substantially this estimate of change and of stabilization in an army from which the senior Lieutenant General and two of his Divisions were detached:

[105] O. R., 29, pt. 2, pp. 724–25.
[106] O. R., 25, pt. 1, p. 942. Cf. 2 N. C. Regts., 232–33.
[107] Ibid., 946.
[108] See his report, ibid., 975. He admitted the delay and the smallness of the cavalry that caused the halt, but he evidently felt that the delay was too brief to affect materially the general result of the advance on the 2d.

Second Corps command:

Jackson—at his superlative best in the dash and the dramatic success of his march to Hooker's right.

Divisional command of the Second Corps:

Early—resourceful, unafraid and manifestly capable of acting on his own;

Rodes—full of fire and drive; amply qualified for divisional command;

Colston—disappointing;

Hill—disabled but co-operative and courageous;

Heth—not brilliant as a second to Hill, but steady and reliable.

Among Second Corps Brigade commanders:

Paxton—dead and difficult to replace;

J. R. Jones—probably had written himself off the army roster by leaving the field because of an ulcerated leg;

Ramseur—full of promise in the spirit of Jackson and of Rodes;

Doles—of the same mould as Ramseur;

Pender—as always, valiant and hard-hitting;

John B. Gordon—daring, quick, courageous, and with a singular grip on his command by reason of his personality and eloquence;

Francis Nicholls—justifying his commission but probably invalided permanently by loss of a leg; no successor among his Colonels.

First Corps Division commanders:

"Dick" Anderson—admirably efficient, despite the tradition that Longstreet only could elicit his full powers;

McLaws—shown to be hesitant and unaggressive.

Among the First Corps Brigade commanders:

Cadmus Wilcox—one of the most conspicuous and useful officers in the campaign; promotion almost imperative;

"Rans" Wright—in the spirit of Malvern Hill, the first to reach Chancellorsville [109] in Anderson's fine advance from the South;

Carnot Posey—like Nicholls, justifying promotion, and of the same hard-hitting, indomitable spirit as Ramseur and Doles.

Artillery and Staff:

W. N. Pendleton—all the misgivings of Malvern Hill and of Shepherdstown deepened, but nothing of a positive nature to warrant displacement;

[109] *O. R.*, 25, pt. 1, p. 851.

Battalion commanders of the artillery—almost without exception qualified for their new rank and able to use their battalion organization most effectively; Alexander especially distinguished;

Stapleton Crutchfield—outstanding but now incapacitated for months; none of his battalion commanders pre-eminently marked as the man to act in his stead.

J. Keith Boswell, of Jackson's staff—dead and deplored but survived by his capable comrade Jed. Hotchkiss, who could succeed him;

R. Channing Price—by Stuart's admission the most useful staff officer of the cavalry Division; an able man required to fill the place made vacant by his death.

Longstreet, of course, had been missed greatly. It was difficult to think of any part of the First Corps in battle without the calm direction of "Old Pete." When John B. Hood also was absent with his shock troops, the Army of Northern Virginia scarcely seemed itself. If these Generals returned ere long with their troops, then, in corps and divisional command, Chancellorsville had wrought no harm that was beyond repair. Rodes could be trusted with D. H. Hill's Division; someone—most probably Edward Johnson or Arnold Elzey—would take Trimble's Division if its commander remained a cripple. New Brigadiers would be needed. They always were. To procure qualified men in any considerable number might be more difficult now than to get one or two new Major Generals. Reorganization, in short, might be vexatious and troublesome, but it would entail no impossible task, provided, of course, Jackson soon were back in the field.

Every soldier had been hoping "Old Jack's" return would not be far distant. Tuesday morning, May 5, after Jackson had agreed that "all things work together for good," he welcomed Chaplain Lacy, who arrived at 10 o'clock to conduct bedside worship and to give the General the satisfaction of discussing religion. Jackson asked that Lacy come every morning at the same hour, but he had made up his mind that he ought not to gratify his wish of having Lacy go with him to Ashland. He explained to the chaplain: "It would be setting an example of self-gratification to the troops, and you had better stay at your post of duty. I have always tried to set the troops a good example." [110] Meantime, he could enjoy to the

110 *Pendleton,* 271.

limit of his strength the privilege of Lieutenant Smith, who was of his same Presbyterian faith and was minded to the ministry.

That morning or the next, Jackson took occasion to expound one of his favorite views—that the Bible supplied rules for every action of life. He had contended many times that if an army rested on the Sabbath, it could cover more ground in a given week than if it marched all seven days. Now he argued that the Bible was rich in lessons for each exigency of a soldier's life. For instance—and he turned to Smith with a smile, "Can you tell me where the Bible gives Generals a model for their official reports of battles?"

Smith answered that he never had consulted Holy Writ to find examples of battle reports.

"Nevertheless," Jackson insisted, "there are such: and excellent models, too." He went on: "Look, for instance, at the narrative of Joshua's battle with the Amalekites; there you have one. It had clearness, brevity, fairness, modesty; and it traces the victory to its right source, the blessing of God." [111] Lee's battle, as well as Joshua's, came in for discussion, but not with any excited concern that day on the part of the wounded man. When someone told him that Hooker had entrenched North of Chancellorsville and seemed to be inviting attack there, comment was brief: "That is bad; very bad." [112] Beyond that, Jackson expressed no doubt of the result. As hopefully as the day began, it ended, but to the accompaniment of a hard, chilling rain. [113]

Like rain was falling on the morning of the 6th when, in the Wilderness North of Chancellorsville, the pickets sent back word that the enemy, whom Lee intended that day to attack, had crossed during the night to the north side of the Rappahannock. If anything of this was said to Jackson, there is no record of his observations. He passed that day, Wednesday, as he had spent Tuesday with no symptoms of other involvement, and with some delectable discourse on theology. Did Dr. McGuire suppose, Jackson asked, that the sufferers of the New Testament, who had received the healing touch of Jesus, ever were afflicted afterward with the same disease? McGuire had no opinion. Jackson was

---

[111] This and the references in these pages to other phases of Jackson's religious experience at this time, merely are paraphrased from *Dabney*, 715 ff. Joshua's battle with the Amalekites is described in *Exodus* xvii, 8 ff.

[112] *Dabney*, 715.   [113] *Hotchkiss' MS Diary*, 187

firm in his conviction that one healed by the Saviour of any malady never would suffer from it again. "Oh, for infinite power!" Jackson exclaimed.

For a time he was silent, and then he asked of Smith, "Where were the headquarters of Christianity after the crucifixion?"

Smith could answer that as readily as he could describe the road to Yerby's or tell a stranger how to get to Moss Neck. Jerusalem, said Smith, remained for a time the chief seat of the church; but after the dispersion of the disciples, by reason of persecution, the Christians had no home city until they established Antioch, Iconium, Rome and Alexandria as centers of influence.

That was fair enough an answer for most men, but the wounded Cromwell of the South, a military realist, would not have it so: "Why do you say, 'centers of influence'? Is not 'headquarters' a better term?" That reiterated, he urged Smith to proceed with the account of the manner in which those cities had become head-quarters of the faith.

Smith hesitated to deliver to a wounded soldier a discourse on church history, and before he answered, he looked inquiringly at McGuire. An encouraging nod was assurance that Jackson might be helped, rather than hurt by learning more about the divisional headquarters of Christendom. Smith must have thanked inwardly his instructors and his good memory, because he was able without hesitation or vagueness to explain, in the approving words of Dr. Dabney, "how the Apostles were directed by Divine Providence, seemingly, to plant their most flourishing churches, at an early period, in these great cities, which were rendered by their political, commercial and ethnical relations, 'headquarters' of influence for the whole civilized world." [114]

Jackson was loath to have the explanation end without supporting topographical data. He wanted, especially, to know where Iconium was, and he bade Smith "get the map" and point out the place to him, just as Jed. Hotchkiss, a year before, had made clear to him, after some effort, that Fisher's Gap and Swift Run Gap were *not* the same pass.

Smith deferentially suggested that perhaps no map at hand would show Iconium. "Yes, sir," Jackson corrected, "you will find it in the atlas which is in my old trunk." To satisfy his chief,

[114] *Dabney,* 720.

Smith is said to have examined the trunk [115] and, when he did not find the atlas, to have asked if it might be in Jackson's portable desk. "Yes," said Jackson, "you are right, I left it in my desk," and he mentioned the shelf, but by this time his attention was lagging. Exhaustion was creeping over him. "Mr. Smith," he said, once more the General, "I wish you would examine into that matter . . . and report to me." [116]

Despite weariness at the end, this theological meat helped to make a day of consistent and encouraging gain. Ere its close, Chaplain Lacy went to Army Headquarters to request the detail of Dr. S. B. Morrison of Early's Division, who had been the General's family physician and was, besides, a kinsman of Mrs. Jackson's. He would be an excellent medical counsellor and a relief chief nurse in the place of Dr. McGuire, who could not endure much longer his vigils at the bedside.

With word that Dr. Morrison would be sent as soon as practicable, Lacy in due time returned. The chaplain brought also a thoughtful message from General Lee: "Give [General Jackson] my affectionate regards, and tell him to make haste and get well, and come back to me as soon as he can. He has lost his left arm; but I have lost my right arm." [117] This, of course, was gratifying to Jackson and was perhaps the most pleasant incident of the day.[118]

That night, Wednesday, May 6, Dr. McGuire was so weary that instead of trying to stay awake by the General's side, he decided he would sleep on a couch in Jackson's room and would leave the patient in the care of Jim. The General's body servant, who was sponsor of many picturesque stories about his master, was devoted to Jackson and was quite competent to act as assistant nurse. With Dr. McGuire on the couch and Jim silent in the chair, Jackson went to sleep without difficulty.

About 1.00 A.M. Thursday, May 7, the General was awakened by nausea. As quietly as he could, he aroused Jim and told the Negro to get a wet towel and to apply it to his stomach. Jim was

[115] The text follows Dabney, but W. N. Pendleton, in an order of Apr. 15, 1863, for a reduction in the baggage of officers, remarked: "General Jackson takes no trunk himself, and allows none in his Corps" (*Owen*, 210).

[116] *Dabney*, 720–21. There is some doubt concerning the time of this curious incident, but the 6th, rather than the 8th, seems the more probable date.

[117] *Dabney*, 716.

[118] *Dabney*, 715; *Hotchkiss' MS Diary*, 187.

vaguely conscious that this was the wrong thing to do. Might he
not wake Dr. McGuire and ask him? Jackson refused: The doctor
had been very tired; let him sleep; get the towel. Obediently Jim
went out, wet a towel thoroughly in cold water, and helped in
applying it to the General's stomach.

The cold and the dampness did no good. Paroxysms in the right
side were added to the nausea. Moment by moment, pain increased until it almost passed endurance. The General's frame was
shaken but his resolution was firm: he would not wake the sleeping surgeon if he could endure till morning. Soon Jackson observed, though without panic, that the pain was sharpened every
time he drew breath. Agonizing as that was, he held out until the
gray of dawn and the first stir out of doors. Then he had to permit
Jim to awaken McGuire.

In a moment the tall young physician with his long face and his
understanding eye was by the bedside. He listened intently to the
General's breathing and he examined the painful area of the chest.
All too readily, McGuire became convinced of what the patient
himself may have suspected: Jackson was developing pneumonia.

Hope and planning and confident expectation now were halted.
Instead of an early removal to Ashland, a peaceful convalescence
at Lexington and a prompt return to the head of the Second Corps,
there must be a sterner battle there in the cottage at Chandlers'. If
it was won, Chancellorsville was a double victory. Were the battle
lost—were it possible, even, to think that Jackson might not recover
—then the North would be repaid for all the boys who had been
slain or maimed there in the Wilderness of Spotsylvania, where
the burnt forest still smoked and the dead lay unburied.

Jackson was not afraid. He did not believe pneumonia would
kill him. Judgment, confidence, faith, ambition—something had
convinced him that he had more work to do. Attack, then, the
disease that was assailing him! Preliminary to cupping, which
would bring more blood to the affected member, Jackson was
given morphia.

This of course made him less sensitive to his pain but it threw
him quickly into a stupor. From that hour, the personality of
Jackson, as his officers knew it, seemed in a haze, obscured, uncertain. He began to mutter and occasionally he used connected sentences, but it was difficult to tell whether he was rational or was

babbling. His attendants disagreed, at least in retrospect, regarding his consciousness at particular moments. What seemed to one auditor the expression of clear religious faith seemed to another hearer the uncontrolled expression of the formal words the General had loved and learned. In the first offthrust of reason, he seemed to be carried back again to the attack on Hooker's right. "Major Pendleton," he exclaimed, "send in and see if there is higher ground back of Chancellorsville." [119]

About noon, when the doctors had done what they could for him, he asked for a glass of lemonade. This, after some whispering and considerable delay, was brought him by Smith. The General sipped it and then said quickly: "You did not mix this, it is too sweet; take it back."

He was correct in saying that Smith had not prepared the beverage, but had he known by whose anxious hands it had been prepared, he would have been less critical. Soon he was aware of another presence in the room. There by his bed, white-faced but composed, was his wife. He stirred himself to greet her and he found words to express his thankfulness that she had come, but so deeply was he under his opiate that he dropped off again quickly. When she spoke or ministered to him he was able to show by smile or glance that he knew her. At length, looking steadfastly at her he observed the emotion she was trying to conceal. With an effort, but seemingly in full command of his faculties, he said, "My darling, you must cheer up and not wear a long face. I love cheerfulness and brightness in a sickroom." [120]

Had he known all she had endured, he would have been proud that she held back her tears. On Sunday morning, May 3, after

119 *Dabney*, 715. In *Pendleton*, 271, on the authority of Chaplain Lacy, Jackson is quoted as saying: "I must find out whether there is high ground between Chancellorsville and the river. . . . Push up the columns. . . . Hasten the columns. . . . Pendleton, you take charge of that. . . . Where's Pendleton? . . . Tell him to push up the columns." It is necessary to give warning that Jackson's delirious and semi-conscious remarks during his illness did not have anything that approximated the order and the dramatic quality assigned them in some of the contemporary accounts. Mrs. Jackson, *op. cit.*, 451, undoubtedly stated the fact correctly when she said: "From the time I reached him he was too ill to notice or talk much, and he lay most of the time in a semi-conscious state; but when aroused, he recognized those about him and consciousness would return."

120 *Mrs. Jackson*, 451. From noon, Thursday, May 7, Mrs. Jackson, though she wrote years afterward, is the fullest authority on the General's illness. She made some errors, confused certain events and omitted a few incidents, but she did not yield to the temptation, as more than one of the other first-hand authorities did, of "dressing up" every occurrence in the sickroom.

672					LEE'S LIEUTENANTS

family worship at Dr. Hoge's home in Richmond, she had been
told as gently as possible that the evening before her husband had
been wounded severely but, it was hoped, not dangerously. Her
instant wish, of course, was to hasten to him. That was impossible.
North of Richmond, railway service was suspended because of
Stoneman's raid; private travel over more than forty-five miles of
road was dangerous until the Federal cavalry were driven back.
Communication by telegraph and by mail was uncertain. It was
Tuesday before Mrs. Jackson's brother Joseph, who left the General Sunday, got to Richmond and told her the circumstances of
the wounding and of the operation.

This report increased her solicitude. She begged to be permitted
to start immediately and to take her chances of eluding the
enemy; but she received word that the railroad company expected
at any time to reopen the line to Guiney's. Thursday, this was
done. Then she started on the first passenger train that left
Richmond.

As soon as she arrived, she sensed danger. All that could be said
for her encouragement by the staff officer who met her was that
the General was doing "pretty well." When she reached the house,
Mrs. Chandler greeted her with womanly understanding and invited her to rest there until the surgeons, who were then "dressing
the General's wounds" were ready for her to see her husband.

Mrs. Jackson could not sit still. She went out on the long
porch [121] and walked up and down and waited, as it seemed to her,
for hours. At length she noticed men digging in the family graveyard at no great distance from the house. As she watched, she saw
them bring to the surface a coffin which was being exhumed for
shipment elsewhere. Horrified, Mrs. Jackson asked whose was the
body. It was, she was told, that of General Paxton, of whose death
she had not heard. A scene of 1861 flashed over her: "My husband's own neighbor and friend! and I knew the young wife, and
remembered how I had seen her weeping bitterly as she watched
his departure from her in those first days of the war, when all our
hearts were well-nigh bursting with foreboding and dread. Now
the cruel war had done its worst for *her*, and she was left widowed, and her children fatherless." [122] No wonder, when Mrs.

---

121 Which was on the level of the basement—*Mrs. Pendleton's MS Statement.*
122 *Mrs. Jackson,* 449–50.

Jackson was assigned the task of preparing her husband's lemonade, as a means of occupying her unhappy mind, she spoiled it with too much sugar! [123]

He was trying to tell her something else: "I know you would gladly give your life for me, but I am perfectly resigned. Do not be sad; I hope I may yet recover. Pray for me, but always remember in your prayers to use the petition, 'Thy will be done.' " [124] Although he dozed off again then, every time he opened his eyes and saw her, he would murmur, "My darling . . . you are very much loved" or "You are one of the most precious little wives in the world." [125] He seemed able to look at her and to speak to her without emotional strain, but more than once, when she asked, "Shall I bring in the baby for you to see?" he answered, "Not yet; wait till I feel better." The last time he had seen the child, spring was coming to the valley of the Massaponax and the peach trees had been blooming.

About 2.00 P.M., Dr. Samuel B. Morrison arrived and came at once to the General. As the surgeon leaned over him, Jackson opened his eyes, recognized Morrison, smiled and said simply: "That's an old, familiar face." [126] Morrison and McGuire now held a consultation and decided that if Mrs. Jackson was to be gratified in her wish to attend the General, she must have some capable, cheerful friend to help with the baby, who had not yet been weaned. Mrs. Jackson agreed to this and asked that Mrs. Moses D. Hoge of Richmond be asked to come. For their own part, the surgeons determined that they could call from the capital its most distinguished authority on pneumonia, Dr. David Tucker. To summon him and to escort Mrs. Hoge to Guiney's, Lieutenant Smith was sent to the city on the next train.[127] Mrs. Hoge was one of the wisest of women and would strengthen the young wife.

Jackson all the while seemed half asleep, half delirious. He continued able to rouse himself when called but he had to ask Mrs. Jackson to speak distinctly, so that he could hear every word.[128] When left alone, his mind would turn to the battlefield. More than once he seemed to be thinking of his troops as weary at the end of a long conflict. He wanted the commissary at hand, wanted the soldiers fed. "Tell Major Hawks to send forward provisions

[123] Dabney, 716–17.   [124] McGuire, 227.
[125] Mrs. Jackson, 451.   [126] Dabney, 717; Mrs. Jackson, 453.
[127] Dabney, 717–18.   [128] Mrs. Jackson, 451.

to the men." The name stuck in his mind . . . "Major Hawks
. . . Major Hawks" he muttered.[129]

Despite his delirium, the doctors did not feel discouraged. When
the cool evening closed in rain,[130] they could not dispute the nature
and progress of the malady, but they believed he was holding his
own against it. There were some reasons for thinking him better,[131] though these may have been nothing more than the effect
of the opiates the surgeons continued to administer. At bedtime,
Morrison took his seat by Jackson to watch and to give the medi-
cines. The doctor had little to do. Jackson lay in stupor but kept
a grip on himself. Once, during the night, when the doctor offered
him a draught and asked, "Will you take this, General?" Jackson
seemed almost to reprimand with a terse answer—"Do your duty!"
As Morrison paused, uncertain what Jackson meant, the General
said again, "Do your duty!" [132]

Friday, May 8, the anniversary of the Battle of McDowell,
dawned cool and misty.[133] Among the camps, there was profound
concern. For the first time, men seriously were asking, Was "Old
Jack" in danger? How could the Army do without him? For a
year, a rounded year that very day, his name had been the symbol
of victory. Others had failed or had fallen; he had defied rout and
death. Many who had seen him in battle, those blue eyes ablaze,
had shared Dick Taylor's belief that the bullet which could kill
"Stonewall" never had been moulded. The enemy had not struck
him down; his own troops had; and if they, even they, had not
been able to slay him, could pneumonia? Veterans of the old
Army of the Valley, in particular, argued and wondered or feared
and prayed. In the name of all of them General Lee was to speak
when he said, "Surely, General Jackson must recover; God will
not take him from us, now that we need him so much." [134]

In the cottage at Chandlers', that Friday, some of the surgeons
were not so sure. Dr. Tucker had not yet arrived from Richmond,
but Surgeons Breckinridge and Smith, men of high repute in the
Army Medical Corps, had come at Dr. McGuire's request for consultation. These three and Dr. Morrison made as thorough an ex-

---

[129] *Mrs. Jackson*, 452; *Dabney*, 719. Again it must be noted that these remarks cannot be given their proper sequence, but apparently they were spoken on Thursday and
not, as usually stated, on Sunday.
[130] *Hotchkiss' MS Diary*, 189.   [131] *McGuire*, 227.
[132] *Dabney*, 718–19.   [133] *Hotchkiss' MS Diary*, 189.
[134] *Cf.* 2 *R. E. Lee*, 562. This remark was made Sunday, May 10.

amination as Jackson's condition allowed. The wounds appeared to be doing well. Although the discharge had diminished, healing was continuing. Pain in the side no longer was troubling the patient.

The ominous condition was his difficult breathing and his great exhaustion. Of his sense of weakness, Jackson spoke; but when Dr. Breckinridge expressed hope that a blister would help, Jackson voiced his own confidence in that treatment and maintained that he would get well.[135] Later in the day, Dr. Morrison had to express a fear that the disease might not be overcome. To this, Jackson listened without emotion, and then, rallying his mind and tongue, he said deliberately: "I am not afraid to die; I am willing to abide by the will of my Heavenly Father. But I do not believe that I shall die at this time; I am persuaded the Almighty has yet a work for me to perform." [136] The General demanded that Dr. McGuire be summoned to pass on Dr. Morrison's opinion; and even after his own Medical Director admitted doubt concerning the outcome, Jackson still insisted that he would recover. He had a restless night, but he did not appear to be shaken in his confidence that he would beat his new adversary.

Out of doors, the brightest day of a changeable May week was Saturday, the 9th.[137] It found Jackson's breathing apparently less difficult and his pain diminished. His weakness manifestly was worse.[138] He still observed intermittently what was going on in his sick room, and he noticed dimly that to the intelligent faces of the doctors around his bed, another had been added—that of David Tucker, the Richmond authority on pneumonia, who at length had arrived. Jackson did not remark at the moment how many consultants had been summoned. Later in the day he said slowly to McGuire: "I see from the number of physicians that you think my condition dangerous, but I thank God, if it is His will, that I am ready to go." [139] Ready though he was, he still was determined to fight for recovery. He asked to see his baby and, when she came, he beamed at her in no spirit of farewell. With his

135 *McGuire*, 227.
136 These sentences are put in quotations because Dr. Dabney, *op. cit.*, 719, insisted that Jackson used "precisely these words." Further, Dr. Dabney insisted that Jackson distinguished with care and purpose between "my Heavenly Father," when speaking of his own relationship to God, and "the Almighty" when he referred to the divine plan.
137 *Hotchkiss' MS Diary*, 189.   138 *Dabney*, 721; *McGuire*, 227.
139 *McGuire*, 227.

splinted hand, which the child did not seem to fear, he caressed her. "Little comforter . . . little comforter," he murmured.[140]

In the afternoon, he bade his attendants summon Chaplain Lacy. At the time, the lungs of Jackson were so nearly filled that his breathing was difficult again. Such respiration as he had was shallow and cruelly fast. For these reasons, Mrs. Jackson and the physicians tried to dissuade him from conversing with Lacy. The General would not be balked. He must see the Chaplain. It was important. His attendants yielded. Tucker Lacy came in as if for another of the theological discussions in which Jackson delighted. This time the General had a more practical question of religion: Was Lacy working to promote Sunday observance by the Army in the manner previously enjoined on him? Lacy was able to report that he was. Jackson was pleased and relieved, but as the subject was one regarding which he had positive convictions, he tried to explain them once again, slowly and painfully, to the Chaplain.[141] When Lacy at length arose, he offered to remain with the General on the Sabbath Day; but Jackson insisted that Lacy go to second corps headquarters and preach, as usual, to the soldiers.[142]

Evening came, clear and warm. A week before, at that very hour, Jackson had been driving furiously through the Wilderness and, looking backward at the sunset skies, he had wished for an hour more of daylight.[143] Now, what was it he desired as he lay there and lifted his arm above his head again, in his familiar gesture, and shut his eyes and seemed to pray? [144] Was it for another day of life—for recovery—for opportunity, with blazing batteries and the cheering line of his veterans, to drive Hooker into the river? He talked more of battle than of anything else and he commanded and exhorted—"Order A. P. Hill to prepare for action . . . Pass the infantry to the front." [145] Most of his other words were confused or unintelligible.

Now, again, into the deepening silence, came the voice of Mrs. Jackson: Might she read to him some of the Psalms of consolation? He shook his head vaguely; he was suffering too much, he said, to be able to listen. No sooner had he spoken than his disciplined conscience stirred and smote him even in his stupor. Would

[140] Ibid.
[141] Mrs. Jackson, 453; Dabney, 721.
[142] Mrs. Jackson, 453.
[143] Cooke's Jackson, 419.
[144] McGuire, 227, with no certainty concerning the hour this occurred.
[145] See supra, p. 671, n. 119.

he not heed the Psalms, the Word of God? "Yes," he corrected himself, "we must never refuse that." He managed to add briefly: "Get the Bible and read them."

She brought the book and in her soft voice read. He tried to fix his attention on the promises of the Most High but he grew weary. "Sing to me," he said presently, and when she asked what she should sing, he bade her choose the most spiritual of the hymns. The brave woman thus far had endured the emotional strain but she was afraid to trust her voice alone on the hymns beloved by the man she loved. Her brother Joseph—the Lieutenant Morrison who had been with Jackson in the Wilderness—was there at the cottage. Would he help her? He came. She got the hymn book. Together in the dim light of the room, brother and sister sat by the bed and sang . . . to the ominous accompaniment of Jackson's wild breathing.

"Sing, 'Shew Pity, Lord,'" Jackson gasped.

They knew what he wanted—Dr. Watts's rendering of part of the Fifty-first Psalm, which was marked "A penitent pleading for pardon"—

> Shew pity, Lord; O Lord, forgive;
> Let a repenting rebel live;
> Are not thy mercies large and free?
> May not a sinner trust in thee? [146]

Doubtless, as it was written, they sang it through its sixth and last verse:

> Yet save a trembling sinner, Lord,
> Whose hope, still hov'ring round thy word,
> Would light on some sweet promise there,
> Some sure support against despair.

"The singing," Mrs. Jackson said afterward, "had a quieting effect, and he seemed to rest in perfect peace." [147] When Dr. Morrison hinted again, later in the evening, that the end might not be far distant, the spirit of the soldier asserted itself once more. "I don't think so," said Jackson; "I think I will be better by morning." [148]

---

[146] In Winchell's *Watts*, this is assigned the tunes German, Bath and Limehouse; but Dr. Dabney, *op. cit.*, 722, stated that it was sung to the tune Old Hundred.
[147] *Mrs. Jackson*, 473.   [148] *Dabney*, 719.

Determined as he was to fight on, he lost ground as the night passed and, half conscious, he seemed to get no relief except from cold sponging of his face and forehead.[149] As he appeared to be sinking steadily, one of the physicians tried to get him to take a drink of brandy. Jackson tasted it but refused to do more. "It tastes like fire," he said, "and cannot do me any good."[150]

The soft spring night ended at last in warmth and promise of sunshine.[151] It was the 10th of May. Two years ago that day at Harpers Ferry, when he was a Colonel of Virginia Volunteers, he had named as Surgeon the man who now was leaning over him. Orders had been issued also, May 10, 1861, for regimental commanders to superintend the drill of their regiments. Captains had been directed to inspect their companies before marching them to dress parade.[152] Jackson's mind then had been intent on training the superb raw manpower he had. Plans he had been maturing to increase the artillery of his command.[153] A year later, May 10, 1862, as a Major General in the Provisional Army of the Confederacy, he had been in pursuit of Milroy after the action at McDowell, and he had been writing Ewell: "My troops are in advance. Should circumstances justify it, I will try, through God's blessing, to get in Banks' rear . . ."[154] In Richmond, on the 10th of May, 1862, there had been rejoicing over the brief telegram he had sent on the 9th to the Adjutant General: "God blessed our arms with victory at McDowell yesterday."[155] Was all that ended now—McDowell, Front Royal, Winchester, Cross Keys, Port Republic, Cedar Mountain, Groveton, Harpers Ferry— those battles of his own and all those he had fought with Lee? It was Sunday; was the day to witness the last contest? In his mind there was contention—muttered references again to A. P. Hill, orders to Major Hawks, directions for the battle.

Mrs. Jackson slipped out of the room. If he observed her depar- ture, he said nothing. Breathing hard, he lay there and said nothing. Jim sat drowsily by. One of the surgeons helplessly watched. Minutes passed in silence. Presently, as the morning light grew brighter, Mrs. Jackson came back. The others left the chamber. Alone, she sat down by him. On her face were the

[149] Dabney, 722.
[150] Mrs. Jackson, 454.
[151] Hotchkiss' MS Diary.
[152] Calendar Confederate Papers, 286.
[153] O. R., 2, 823–24.
[154] O. R., 12, pt. 3, p. 386.
[155] O. R., 12, pt. I, p. 470.

marks of an emotional battle, but she was calm. Long before, he had told her that he did not fear to die but that he hoped he would "have a few hours' preparation before entering into the presence of his Maker and Redeemer." Now she felt she had to discharge the hard, hard duty that remark imposed.

Her voice came to him on the border of the far country. He stirred in evidence that he heard it but at first he could not arouse himself. She was talking to him: "Do you know the doctors say, you must very soon be in Heaven?"

He said nothing. She repeated it, and added: "Do you not feel willing to acquiesce in God's allotment, if He wills you to go today?"

Again she had to ask him the same question. Slowly the words and their import sank into his mind. He opened his eyes and looked at her. "I prefer it," he said slowly and with much difficulty. If he could focus his eyes to see her expression, he must have noticed that she seemed uncertain whether he was babbling or knew what he was saying. More carefully he framed the syllables: "I prefer it."

"Well," she said, incredibly keeping her self-control, "before this day closes, you will be with the blessed Saviour in His glory."

He steadied himself for the effort of speech and said deliberately, "I will be an infinite gainer to be translated."[156]

She talked with him further and asked his wishes about many things, but she could not hold his attention.[157] Nor did he appear to be convinced that his end actually was at hand. The man who had beaten off all the foe's attacks at Groveton was not of the spirit to believe that even the Last Enemy could rout him.

After Mrs. Jackson conversed with him, the surgeons must have made their examinations, but they did not attempt to dress his wounds. He was disturbed as little as possible. About 11 A.M.—the day continued warm and beautiful—he was aroused again by Mrs. Jackson. This time she was kneeling by his bed and was telling him again that before the sun went down he would be in Heaven.

---

156 *Dabney*, 722–23.

157 Mrs. Jackson wrote as if all the wishes expressed by Jackson were voiced in a single interview which occurred in the early morning. Dr. McGuire mentioned a second conversation at 11 A.M. The sole way to reconcile the difference between Mrs. Jackson's account and the earlier narrative of Dr. McGuire is to assume that Mrs. Jackson forgot, after thirty years, that she had the second and longer conversation with her husband later in the morning.

Often, in battle, he had met on their way to the rear unnerved men who had told of calamity and death at the front. He had rebuked them; he could not fail now to chide even her. Full consciousness seemed to return. Clearly he said: "Oh, no! you are frightened, my child; death is not so near; I may yet get well."

With this she threw herself on the bed and in a flood of tears told him that the doctors said there was no hope for him. He listened and seemed to reflect, and then he asked her to call Dr. McGuire.

Almost on the instant, the man who so often had come to his campfire to report the wounded and the dead, was at his command. "Doctor," said Jackson, still distinctly, "Anna informs me that you have told her that I am to die today; is it so?"

As gently and as sympathetically as was possible, McGuire replied that medicine had done its utmost.

Again Jackson seemed to ponder. He turned his eyes from McGuire's face to the ceiling and gazed upward for a few moments. In battle, when orders were well executed or some shining deed was performed, he often would say, "Good, good"; but now he thought the orders of Higher Command had been given, his response was stronger: "Very good; very good; it is all right." [158] With that he turned to the weeping woman and tried to comfort her. Much he had to tell her, he said, but he was too weak.[159] After a struggle, she undertook to inquire what he desired for himself and for her and the baby? Should she go back to her father when it was all over? she asked.

"You have a kind and good father," he said, scarcely conscious, "but there is no one so kind and good as your Heavenly Father." [160]

Where did he wish to be buried?

He did not seem to be interested. "Charlotte," she understood him to say, and she inquired again. "Charlottesville," he said half consciously.

There was no reason for that, no association other than that of names. She prompted him: Did he wish to be buried in Lexington?

[158] *McGuire*, 228.   [159] *Ibid.*
[160] It is possible that he made this remark in the first conversation of the morning with Mrs. Jackson, cf. *McGuire*, 227–28, but the probabilities would seem to favor the discussion of all the family arrangements at one time.

"Yes," he answered, "in Lexington, and in my own plot," but he spoke of it casually, as if it scarcely mattered.[161]

In accordance with the customs of the day, it seemed proper that he say farewell to his child. Mrs. Hoge accordingly brought in the baby, with the nurse. Jackson recognized the child at once and seemed far more pleased to see her than to talk of funerary details. His face, now emaciated and strangely ascetic in appearance, lighted up with a smile. "Little darling," he said, ". . . sweet one!" The baby smiled back and did not seem in any way frightened. She alone, of all the company, was the embodiment of life without knowledge or fear of death. Through the fog of morphia and weakness he played with her and called her endearing names until he sank back into the unconscious.[162]

When next he aroused, "Sandie" Pendleton in his martial gray was standing by his bed—"Sandie" who had so much of his unvoiced affection and soldierly admiration. The presence of the young soldier brought Jackson back for an instant to a world of camps and sinning soldiers. "Who is preaching at headquarters today?" he asked. Pendleton told him that Lacy was,[163] but he thoughtfully refrained from reminding Jackson that the Chaplain was there by the General's own forgotten order. Jackson was gratified that the men were to hear so eminent a preacher. Still more was Jackson pleased when "Sandie" told him that the whole army was praying for him. "Thank God," he murmured, "they are very kind . . ." Presently he spoke again. "It is the Lord's Day. . . . My wish is fulfilled. I have always desired to die on Sunday."[164]

"Sandie" went out to weep and not to weep alone. Everyone was in tears. The faithful Jim was overwhelmed. Not one of the doctors, looking at Jackson and listening to the struggle for breath, dared hope that the General could live even till night, but Dr. McGuire thought he should stimulate Jackson with some brandy. The next time the man on the bed seemed conscious, McGuire asked him to drink from the glass. Jackson shook his head: "It will only delay my departure, and do no good; I want

161 Mrs. Jackson, 456. Dabney said, op. cit., 723, "his tone expressed rather acquiescence than lively interest."
162 Mrs. Jackson, 456.
163 Lacy's text that day was, "And we know that all things work together for good. . . ." Romans viii, 28. Hotchkiss' MS Diary, 189.
164 McGuire, 228.

to preserve my mind, if possible, to the last." [165] Once more he slipped back into the land of far and near, where faces change instantly and scenes melt one into another. He murmured again, gave orders, sat at mess with his staff, was back in Lexington with his little family, was fighting, was praying.

From another world came presently the voice of McGuire, with kindly but solemn warning that the sands were running low. It was 1.30: Jackson might not have more than two hours to live.

Feebly but firmly the assurance was given: "Very good; it is all right!" [166]

More there was in the same mutter—Hill, Hawks, orders to the infantry—and then a long, long silence, such a silence as might have come that May night the previous year when he had pushed the Stonewall Brigade forward toward Winchester and had halted and heard only the breath of his companions, and then had seen the fire of the Federal sharpshooters run along the hillside. Great events had been impending then. Long marches and hard battles and wide streams had been ahead. Now . . . the clock striking three, the spring sunshine in the room, the rustle of new leaves in the breeze, peace and the end of a Sabbath Day's journey. Fifteen minutes more; breathing now was in the very throat; and then from the bed, clearly, quietly, cheerfully, "Let us cross over the river, and rest under the shade of the trees." [167]

[165] *McGuire*, 228.   [166] *McGuire*, 228.
[167] *McGuire*, 229. In this final quotation, McGuire's words are followed. The verb is "cross" over the river. Many of the early authorities insisted that the verb was "pass."

CHAPTER XXXVII

"HAVE NO FEAR WE SHALL NOT BEAT THEM!"

A WAIL WENT up everywhere in the South.[1] From the time the first news of the wounding of Jackson had reached the Confederate people, they had felt a concern that hopeful professional assurances had not relieved. "His extraordinary ability," the *Examiner* had said, "and the astonishing prestige which attends him everywhere, is a power of the republic, and the loss . . . would be ill replaced by the accession of 50,000 troops to our present force."[2] In a later article, the same paper had suggested that if Jackson were invalided, he should be made Governor: "This torn and suffering State needs now a great and good man for Chief."[3] The *Enquirer* had lamented: "We could better spare a Brigade or a Division. It would be grievous to think that his banner will never more flash out upon the Yankee rear. . . ."[4] That Jackson would not die, the *Whig* had assured its readers: "We need have no fears for Jackson. He is no accidental manifestation of the powers of faith and courage. He came not by chance in this day and to this generation. He was born for a purpose, and not until that purpose is fulfilled will his great soul take flight."[5]

Now that hope was disappointed and faith was challenged, there was an emotional outlet in such ceremonies as a battling people could provide. His body was shrouded by his staff officers. As his uniform was cut and blood-stained,[6] he was clad in civilian dress, but about him was wrapped a dark blue military overcoat.[7] The decision was to transport the body to Richmond and to send it thence to Lexington, instead of carrying it by the shortest route to its burial place.

To escort him, or, at the least, to file past the open coffin and

---

[1] Cf. *Richmond Enquirer*, May 12, 1863.

[2] *Richmond Examiner*, May 5, 1863.

[3] May 6, 1863. [4] May 8, 1863.

[5] May 9, 1863. [6] *Dabney*, 728.

[7] *Mrs. Jackson*. 458. Cooke, *op. cit.*, 447, was in error in saying that Jackson was buried in civilian clothes to preserve his uniform.

to attend his body to the railroad station, the Stonewall Brigade hoped to be designated. The inimitable Casler recorded: "The Brigade rigged up in the best they had, cleaned their arms and were anxious to go, and kept waiting impatiently until, finally, the order was countermanded and we did not get to see him. We all thought very hard of it, for we wished to show our respect for our beloved commander, and gaze on his face once more; but that small privilege was denied us. His only escort was some doctors and officials who never saw him in battle, while the men who had followed him from Harpers Ferry to Chancellorsville, had to lay idly in camp." [8]

Truth was, Lee apprehended a new move by the Federals and could not detach a large escort or even himself leave headquarters long enough to ride to Guiney's and to pay the tribute of his presence. "Jackson," he said to the officer who came to ask for the assignment of the Stonewall Brigade as escort, "never neglected a duty while living and he would not rest the easier in his grave if his old brigade had left the presence of the enemy to see him buried." [9] For this reason, the escort to Richmond consisted only of those who at some period had been the dead General's staff officers. Three of these—Pendleton, Smith and Lacy—went with Mrs. Jackson and her friends, [10] in a special car attached to the regular train Monday, May 11. [11]

In the suburbs of the Confederate capital, the train was stopped in order to spare Mrs. Jackson the ordeal of having to leave it before the eyes of a multitude downtown. Mrs. John Letcher, wife of the Governor, and other ladies met her and conveyed her by carriage and along quiet streets to the Governor's Mansion where mourning dress and veil were awaiting her. [12]

All the pomp the grieving city could command it displayed for the body of the fallen soldier. When the train was stopped at Fourth and Broad and the coffin was removed, the few church bells that had not been moulded into cannon were tolled. All business stopped. The city's natives and all the refugees and all the visitors thronged Broad Street. [13] As fortunate chance had it,

[8] *Casier*, 233.   [9] *Douglas*, 228.
[10] Mrs. Hoge and Mrs. Chandler.
[11] *Pendleton*, 270; *Douglas*, 229; *Mrs. Jackson*, 459.
[12] *Mrs. Jackson*, 459.
[13] *Richmond Dispatch, Richmond Sentinel*, May 12, 1863.

Arnold Elzey was in command of the Department of Richmond [14] and in that capacity served as Chief Marshal. A comfort it must have been to some of "Old Jack's" men to know that his body was in the keeping of one who gallantly had shared in the Valley Campaign. Elzey led the procession down Broad to Ninth, and through Ninth to the entrance to the Capitol Square. Thence between lines of troops at present arms, the casket was borne to the Governor's Mansion, where, for the night, it was placed in the center of the reception room. Over the coffin, by the President's order, a handsome new "national flag," the first of a modified white design, was draped.[15]

That night to the Mansion came the soldier whom Jackson most had wronged—Brig. Gen. "Dick" Garnett. From the time Jackson had put him under arrest for withdrawing the Stonewall Brigade at Kernstown, Garnett had never served under Jackson, but now, tearfully, he looked down on a face that had lost its fire. Then, taking "Sandie" Pendleton and Kyd Douglas by the arm, Garnett went to a window and spoke what was in his manful heart: "You know of the unfortunate breach between General Jackson and myself; I can never forget it, nor cease to regret it. But I wish here to assure you that no man can lament his death more sincerely than I do. I believe he did me great injustice, but I believe also he acted from the purest motives. He is dead. Who can fill his place!" [16]

The next day, in order that other tens of thousands might see, a new procession carried the body uptown.[17] This time Jackson was attended by four of his Generals. Besides Elzey, among the mourners was "Dick" Ewell, who almost had recovered from his Groveton wound. "Maryland" Steuart was by the hearse also; so was "Dick" Garnett. These and the other officers of the guard of honor brought the body back to the Capitol, where it was laid in state before the Speaker's Chair in the Confederate House of Representatives—the hall of the House of Delegates of Virginia, where the resolutions against the alien and sedition laws had been

14 This department had been established April 1, 1863. *O. R.*, 18, 953. See *supra*, p. 480.
15 It was while the body was in the Governor's Mansion that Frederick Volck took the death-mask reproduced in 2 *R. E. Lee*, opposite p. 562.
16 *Douglas*, 38.
17 The route was down Governor Street to Main, up Main to Second, North on Second to Grace, and down Grace to Capitol Square. W. A. Christian, *Richmond*, 242.

debated, and John Marshall had sat in cautious judgment on Aaron Burr, and the convention had voted secession in 1861, and a delegate had asked when a nomination was placed before the members, "Who is Major Jackson?"

To the hall now were admitted all who could file past during the day and a long evening. Many of those who came were sick or mutilated men of his own command. Some of them had seen the blaze of his blue eyes or had felt the lash of his denunciation of stragglers, and some had heard him say endlessly on the road, "Close up, press on, press on." [18] Like Ewell, perhaps, some of them in 1862 had thought him mad, but now as they gazed at him dead, they were proud of every mile they had marched under his orders.

On May 13, with added tributes, the body was placed aboard the Virginia Central train and was carried to Gordonsville, whence by the Orange & Alexandria it was transported to Lynchburg.[19] From that city, on a canal boat, it was sent to Lexington, which was reached on the evening of May 14.[20] Everywhere along the route there was repetition, more distressed, of the scenes on the road from Wilderness Old Tavern to Guiney's. Then it had been food and drink that had been brought out for him; now it was spring flowers.[21] Covered with these blossoms, the casket lay for the night of the 14th in Jackson's old class room.

On the 15th, Friday, after a funeral in the church of which he had been a deacon, the body was committed to the earth.[22] The escort was the V. M. I. cadet battalion, some convalescents and invalided veterans of his own Brigade, men from military hospitals and a squadron of cavalry, which chanced to ride into Lexington at the time of the funeral. The leading flag was that of the Liberty Hall Boys, a flag that had been used for some

[18] Christian, op. cit., 242–43, gives succinctly the essential facts. Richmond newspapers of May 12–14 are crowded with details.

[19] The Richmond Dispatch, May 13, 1863, editorially expressed regret that he was not buried in Hollywood Cemetery of that city, in a place of honor next to President Monroe; but the paper explained that his wishes concerning his place of burial had been fulfilled.

[20] The old "packet" Marshall, which remained for many years on the canal bank above Lynchburg, traditionally was the boat on which the body was moved to Lexington.

[21] Dabney, 751; Mrs. Jackson, 462 ff. A line of interest on personal hygiene of the day appears in Mrs. Jackson's maternally proud remark that the General's "child was often called for, and, on several occasions, was handed out of the car windows to be kissed" (op. cit., 463).

[22] For the ceremonies at V. M. I., see Richmond Sentinel, May 19, 1863.

time as the regimental standard of Jackson's Fourth Virginia.[23]

In all this five-day ceremonial, a few only of the millions who had admired Jackson had opportunity of paying tribute to him. With voice or with pen, those who could not march in processions or stand bareheaded on the street, sought to express what Jackson had meant to the Confederacy and to them. The President telegraphed General Lee: "A great national calamity has befallen us, and I sympathize with the sorrow you feel and the embarrassment you must experience." Lee himself, in general orders of May 11, spoke of "the daring, skill and energy of this great and good soldier," [24] and often besides, in referring to the dead General, he used those same simple adjectives, "great and good." [25] So deeply was Lee moved by the loss that he scarcely could speak of Jackson without tears, and, to the end of his days, he never mentioned his greatest lieutenant otherwise than with deep, affectionate admiration. "Such an executive officer," he said, "the sun never shone on." [26] Any disparagement of Jackson was an offense to him.

Officers of lesser grade and men in the ranks shared both the grief and the admiration voiced by the commanding General. Wrote Pender before Jackson died, "It is devoutly to be hoped he will be spared to his country." [27] Ham Chamberlayne found no other comfort than that "we can better spare [Jackson] now than we could have done before the battle of Kernstown." [28] In

23 See William Couper's *One Hundred Years at V. M. I.*, 2, 190–91, with references to the *Lexington Gazette* of May 20, 1863. Jackson's body lay undisturbed until June 25, 1891, when the casket was moved to a new vault nearby, over which a bronze monument was to be placed. Ostensibly for identification of the body, the casket was opened in the presence of a few witnesses. Bones and his clothing alone remained. By that time, it had been forgotten that he had been wrapped in a blue overcoat. The newspaper account stated: "The texture of the cloth was apparently well preserved, but it had turned in color from grey to blue" (*Rockbridge County News,* June 25, 1891).

24 *O. R.*, 25, pt. 2, p. 793.   25 *Ibid.*, 792, 812, 821.

26 2 *R. E. Lee*, 524; 3 *ibid.*, 1–2. In none of the published correspondence of Lee or of Davis is there any reference to the possibility that Jackson may have been under consideration, just prior to Chancellorsville, as commander of the Army of Tennessee; but Dr. J. William Jones, in 19 *S. H. S. P.*, 156, stated that from "an authentic source" he had been told of such a prospect. As Dr. Jones received many of Mr. Davis's confidences, late in the life of the ex-President, it is entirely possible that Davis related this to Jones.

27 To Mrs. Pender, MS, May 9, 1863—*Pender MSS.*

28 *Ham Chamberlayne*, 181. Wrote Wingfield, in his *Diary*: "Jackson's death has turned all Richmond into a city of mourning" (*Wingfield*, 25). At Chaffin's Bluff, the men of an artillery company forwarded $100 to the *Richmond Sentinel* to start a fund for a monument to the dead General. Said the Captain: "That renowned 'old Hero' served us all gallantly when living, and we desire to perpetuate his memory" (*Richmond Sentinel*, May 18, 1863). The paper commented in these words on this "gift by men who are receiving $11 a month": "A monument to such a man, built by contributions by such men—oh, this is fame indeed."

Winchester, with her usual discerning judgment, Mrs. McDonald wrote: "'The Mighty has fallen,' but he carries to his grave the hopes, and is followed by the bitter tears of the people in whose defence he lost his life, and who loved him with grateful devotion. No loss could be felt as his will be. In every great battle fought in Virginia, he has been a leader, and has never known defeat. Success crowned his every effort. . . ."[29] Pathetic, in its different emphasis, was the cry of Rev. Dr. W. S. White, Jackson's pastor: "Oh, sir, when Jackson fell I lost not only a warm personal friend, a consistent, active church member, but the best deacon I ever saw."[30]

In the press, lament was universal. The *Richmond Sentinel*[31] recalled the time when Jackson's Valley campaign "revived the sinking hopes and hearts of our people." Said the *Enquirer:* "We have gained no victory on the Rappahannock since this was to be its cost."[32] The *Whig* wrote: "What others did or attempted from impulses of ambition, patriotism, or sense of duty, he did from compulsion of conscience, and a reverential conviction of obligation to his Maker."[33] As the *Examiner* saw him: "There was the stuff of Cromwell in Jackson. Hannibal might have been proud of his campaign in the Valley, and the shades of the mightiest warriors should rise to welcome his stern ghost."[34]

Many a Southern versifier sought to reflect a people's grief. When Tucker De Leon later collected the war poetry of the South, he found forty-seven dirges on Jackson, and at that probably did not have access to scores besides.[35] Among all these poems, unhappily, one only rose above mediocrity—Henry Lyden Flash's "Stonewall Jackson."[36]

29 *Mrs. McDonald,* 162.   30 19 *S. H. S. P.,* 158.
31 May 13, 1863.   32 May 12, 1863.   33 May 12, 1863.
34 May 11, 1863. The *Charleston Mercury* reprinted on May 13 an editorial "Lee and Jackson" from the *Richmond Whig* of May 9, but the *Mercury* on the 14th apologized for doing this because the article in the Richmond paper had stated that Lee "reduced chaos after Donelson to form and order." Said the *Mercury:* "We like not superlatives. Exaggerated praises necessarily lead to apparent detraction. It is, indeed, an exceedingly awkward and ungracious task to seem even to diminish one so patriotic, so distinguished and so successful as General Robert E. Lee." The paper went on to insist that Lee was not above criticism and that Beauregard, not he, deserved credit for what had been done in the restoration of confidence after Donelson.
35 *De Leon,* 296.
36 The *Richmond Whig,* reprinting this poem May 18, 1863, credited it to the *Mobile Advertiser and Register.* It appears in Miss Emily Mason, *Southern Poems of the War,* 2d edition, 334, in H. M. Wharton, *War Songs and Poems,* and in various other collections. This fifth quatrain is the one most often quoted in Southern books:

> Oh, gracious God! Not gainless is our loss;
> A glorious sunbeam gilds the sternest frown;
> And while his country staggers with the cross—
> He rises with the crown!

Unpoetic, perhaps, but resolute was the petition to the War Department by the officers and men of Jackson's old Brigade that his wishes be fulfilled and that the command be styled officially the Stonewall Brigade. "In thus formally adopting a title which is inseparably connected with his name and fame," the resolution of the command promised, "we will strive to render ourselves more worthy of it by emulating his virtues, and, like him, devote all our energies to the great work before us of securing to our beloved country the blessings of peace and independence." This request the War Department granted. As of May 30, 1863, the First Brigade of Jackson's old Division became formally the "Stonewall Brigade," the only command larger than a Legion that had an official name on the Confederate roster.[37] Tragically the Brigade itself soon was little more than a name.

Most notable of all the tributes to Jackson, in correct presentation of the public's judgment, was Secretary James A. Seddon's long reference in his annual report. The whole passage was eloquent. Two sentences, midway, told the story of Jackson's rise and fame. "Without disparagement to others, it may be safely said he has become, in the estimation of the Confederacy, emphatically 'the hero of the war.' Around him clustered with peculiar warmth their gratitude, their affections, and their hopes." [38]

From the moment that the death of Jackson had seemed probable, the same questions had concluded every lament—Where was his successor to be found; what would be the effect on the Southern cause of a loss so dire? The *Richmond Whig* had said: "The leader who succeeds him, be he who he may, will be impelled, as by supernatural impulse, to emulate his matchless deeds. Jackson's men will demand to be led in 'Stonewall Jackson's way.' The leader who will not or cannot comply with that demand, must drop the baton quickly. Jackson's corps will be led forever by the memory of its great chieftain." [39] Less confident, mingling resignation and deep perplexity, were the words of the command-

---

[37] *O. R.*, 25, pt. 2, p. 840. "Laurel" Brigade, "Orphan" Brigade, "Light" Division and similar descriptive names, though generally used, had no official status.

[38] IV *O. R.*, 2, 994.

[39] *Richmond Whig*, May 9, 1863. Cf. *Richmond Dispatch*, May 12, 1863: "No doubt the puerile Yankees will be encouraged to believe that, now that Jackson is dead, the subjugation of the South is certain. Let them cross the Rappahannock again and the delusion will be dispelled. The veterans of Jackson's corps, the men whom he led and loved, will show at the first opportunity whether they are capable of avenging his death."

ing General: "I know not how to replace him. God's will be done. I trust He will raise up someone in his place . . ." [40]

Most often mentioned was "Dick" Ewell. It was widely reported that Jackson on his deathbed had expressed the wish that Ewell succeed him, [41] but this was denied vigorously by those who favored the advancement of Powell Hill. On that score, Dorsey Pender cautioned his wife: "Do not believe all you see about the last words of Jackson. Some designing person is trying to injure Gen. Hill by saying that he frequently said that he wanted Ewell to have his corps. After it became apparent that he would die, he was delirious most, if not all the time." [42] In the judgment of some, the sole question concerning Ewell was whether, after the loss of his leg at Groveton, he could be sufficiently active to exercise field command. [43]

Ewell's own attitude was flawlessly generous. He had been conscious that his slow recovery had embarrassed his chief and his subordinates, and he had been convinced that Early had earned command of the Division "Jube" had led during his long absence from the field. In March, Ewell had written Early: "When I am fit for duty, they may do what they please with me, but I think your claims to the Division, whether length of time or hard service be considered, are fully equal, if not superior, to mine. I don't presume they will interfere with you. What is very certain is that I won't ask for any particular duty or station, but let them do as they see proper with me." [44]

In that same spirit of self-effacement, Ewell wrote Beauregard during Jackson's illness that he hoped the Louisiana General would return to Virginia. [45] Steadfastly, Ewell's sentiment was that which he voiced in another paragraph of the letter to Early: "I was in hopes that the war might be brought to a close before the end of Spring but I have lost all hopes of that. I don't want to see the carnage and the shocking sights of another field of battle though I prefer being in the field to anywhere else as long as the war is going on . . ." [46]

By the date of Jackson's death, Ewell could walk readily on his

---

[40] R. E. Lee, Jr., 94.　　　　　　　　[41] Wingfield, 25.

[42] Letter of May 14, 1863—Pender MSS. None of those who attended Jackson recorded any mention by him of Ewell or of anyone else as a possible successor.

[43] Cf. Pendleton, 272.　　　　　　　　[44] Hamlin's Ewell, 118.

[45] Old Bald Head, 134–35.　　　　　　[46] Ibid., 134.

wooden leg with the help of a stick and, to everyone's amazement, he soon showed himself acrobat enough to mount his horse from the ground and to keep his seat when mounted.[47] It has been said of him, after Port Republic, "Never defeated, never surprised, always at the right place at the right time, he has earned and well merits the title of General." [48] Did his physique match his record? Would the President and General Lee conclude that he could endure the strains of long marches, of cold bivouacs, of far-spread battlefields?

Was Powell Hill better qualified? In the Autumn of 1862, Lee had esteemed him, after Longstreet and Jackson, the best commander then with the Army. Lee had intimated, even, that if a third Lieutenant General had been needed, Hill would have been qualified.[49] Nothing had happened after that time, despite Hill's quarrel with Jackson, to lower Lee's estimate of the ability of Hill. On the 6th of May, as soon as the enemy again was North of the Rappahannock, and Hill was sufficiently recovered from his bruises to ride, Lee had restored him to temporary command of the Second Corps and had returned Stuart to the direction of the cavalry.[50]

That bespoke confidence in Hill, some of whose lieutenants felt at the time that he deserved more credit for the victory at Chancellorsville than had been allotted him.[51] Said Pender: "It is strange what a jealousy exists towards A. P. Hill and this Division and for what cause I cannot see unless it is because he and it have been so successful. I hope to stick to him, for he sticks to me." [52] That was the attitude of most of Hill's Brigadiers. They did not think he had as strong a staff as he needed,[53] but they enjoyed his hospitality,[54] they admired him as a leader and they liked his fiery spirit—even when he threatened to burn Washington in reprisal for the mistreatment of women and children in Northern Virginia.[55] Outside his Division, feeling against Hill may have existed among a few of Jackson's more emotional

[47] *Pendleton*, 276.
[48] *Richmond Enquirer*, June 18, 1862, p. 1, col. 3.
[49] See *supra*, p. 247.   [50] *O. R.*, 25, pt. 2, p. 782.
[51] *Cf.* 12 *C. V.*, 492–94.
[52] Letter to Mrs. Pender, MS, May 14, 1863—*Pender MSS.*
[53] Pender to his wife, MS, Mch. 28, 1863—*Pender MSS.*
[54] Cf. *Conner*, 110.
[55] Pender to his wife, MS, April 9, 1863—*Pender MSS.*

friends. Happily, on the other side, there is no confirmation of the statement made later by Kyd Douglas that even after Jackson's death, Hill neither forgot nor forgave their quarrel.[56]

Officers who speculated on the choice of a successor to Jackson did not pit Hill against Ewell, but some of Hill's supporters were both jealous and suspicious of Stuart. The Chief of Cavalry is not known to have hoped for the command of the Second Corps, or even to have desired it. He may have advocated the course General Lee subsequently followed.[57] Although some of "Jeb's" admirers thought he should be Jackson's successor,[58] Stuart himself was more concerned to receive full credit for what he had accomplished May 3. In seeking that credit quickly, to increase his own glory and to confound his critics,[59] he brought on himself a mild reprimand from the commanding General. In answer to some complaint at lack of mention in dispatches, Lee wrote Stuart: "In the management of the difficult operations at Chancellorsville, which you so promptly undertook and creditably performed, I saw no error to correct, nor has there been a fitting opportunity to commend your conduct. I prefer your acts to speak for themselves, nor does your character or reputation require bolstering by out-of-place expression of opinions."[60] That was flattering and reassuring but it also was a tactful caution against vainglory and self-advertising.

Failure to receive prompt praise in dispatches was not Stuart's only distress after Chancellorsville. He mourned for Jackson, he mourned for Channing Price. The work of that invaluable staff officer Stuart entrusted, with uncommon discernment, to the former adjutant of the Third Virginia Cavalry, Henry B. McClellan. Fortunately for Stuart, he had invited McClellan to become a member of his staff in April; and when he lost his fine young

---

[56] Douglas, 196.

[57] Cf. Lee to Stuart, May 23, 1863. "I am obliged to you for your views as to the successor of the great and good Jackson. Unless God will raise us up one, I do not know what we shall do. I agree with you on the subject, and have so expressed myself. It is now in the hands of others" (O. R., 25, pt. 2, p. 821).

[58] Cf. Alexander, 360 and W. W. Blackford's MS Memoirs 297-98.

[59] Cf. W. H. C. Whiting, O. R., 18, 1048: " . . . what is Stuart doing, allowing that band [the Federal cavalry] to harry the country?" Cf. Pender to his wife, MS. May 22, 1863: "Stuart lost as much with the army as he gained in the fight, for all saw that he was so totally deficient in dignity that all his fighting could not overcome it."— Pender MSS.

[60] O. R., 25, pt. 2, p. 792; the letter is dated May 11.

cousin, he could lean almost from the start on McClellan, who was then Major and A.A.G.[61]

The much-loved Channing had a brother, Thomas Randolph Price, who had been studying philology in Europe from 1859 until almost the end of 1862. Then Tom ran the blockade homeward and, through the effort of Channing and of his cousin "Jeb," received a lieutenant's commission in the Provisional Engineers and an assignment to Stuart's headquarters. Contrast between a student's life in comfortable Berlin and a soldier's existence in the mud of a winter on the Rappahannock was more than Tom Price could endure with equanimity. In addition, the new lieutenant of engineers did not like the somewhat flamboyant style and the endless, noisy camp chatter of his kinsman. Outwardly, Thomas, who was then 24, bent himself to his duties; inwardly he raged. Not long before the actions in May, he was sent with another engineer to build a bridge above Chancellorsville[62] and, on his return, was heard to complain long and often that the advance of the enemy had forced him to abandon all his baggage. In particular, Price deplored the loss of his diary.

After the battle, the reason became apparent: "Jeb" received a Northern newspaper clipping that contained printed extracts from the diary, which had been picked up and had been read with amused zest by some Federal. Publication of this sort was not unusual in an army where many diaries were kept incautiously and were lost through carelessness or capture. The embarrassing fact was that in his diary, Tom Price had recorded not only his yearning for Berlin but also his overcandid opinions of his cousin and chief. "Oh, for Berlin," was duly entered and printed; so was "Gen. Stuart in his usual garrulous style explained," and on and on. The army laughed; Stuart reddened but probably said

61 *Cf.* Stuart to H. B. McClellan, MS, April 13, 1863. Almost in the language of a presidential commission, Stuart began: "Reposing special confidence in your patriotism, fidelity and ability, and desiring to award faithful and gallant service, I have determined, if agreeable to you, to ask that you be commissioned . . ." etc.—*McClellan MSS.* This faithful staff officer, a first cousin of Geo. B. McClellan, had three brothers in the Federal army. The *Munford MSS* include a letter from Col. Carswell McClellan, one of these brothers, to Gen. T. T. Munford, July 1, 1890. In this letter, Colonel McClellan described how, one night, he met Henry under flag of truce on the Rapidan: "As we parted in the gray dawn, I told him that, bitterly as I regretted his decision, I was prouder of him fighting on your side than I would be to have him with me hampered with any doubts as to the right involved."

62 See the MS memoirs of his brother officer, Lieut. Frank S. Robertson, *In the Saddle with Stuart.*

nothing; some of his staff waxed angry. William Blackford wrote later, half in wrath and half in amusement: "Whatever his peculiarities may have been, General Stuart had saved Price from being conscripted into the ranks as a private soldier, and this at least should have made him silent." [63] There was, of course, nothing for Thomas to do but to seek transfer from Stuart's staff.

If Stuart had been cherishing ambitions to be the successor of "Stonewall," this incident might have deepened the impression of frivolity and lack of dignity he already had created. Lee knew that these were superficial weaknesses and that Stuart was an intelligent, tireless and capable soldier; but some of Stuart's numerous enemies might not have conceded that much at a time when he was alleged to be seeking to prevent the choice of Powell Hill as commander of the Second Corps. One day, in the camp of Hill, it was rumored that Stuart had gone to Richmond in an effort to oust Hill from the Second Corps. Next day the whisper was that Stuart had resigned because he himself had not received the Corps command. [64]

Besides Ewell, Powell Hill and "Jeb" Stuart, no other officers of Lee's army appear to have been mentioned widely as immediate successor to Jackson. By seniority, Harvey Hill was next to Ewell among Lee's Major Generals; both Harvey Hill and Lafayette McLaws held older commissions at that grade than did the commander of the Light Division or the Chief of Cavalry. McLaws had ruled himself out of promotion by what he had not done at Maryland Heights and at Salem Church; Harvey Hill was at the moment engaged in another painful exchange of notes that led the commanding General to believe more firmly than ever that Hill would not assume responsibility. [65] If Harvey Hill

---

[63] *W. W. Blackford's MS Memoirs,* 300–01. Thomas R. Price subsequently became a scholar of high distinction. See *D. A. B.*

[64] Pender to his wife, MS, May 22, 23, 1863—*Pender MSS.*

[65] See *supra,* p. 275. In January, 1888, Early noted the complaint by Longstreet in the *Century Magazine,* reprinted in 3 *B. & L.,* 245, that D. H. Hill and McLaws were passed over because they were not Virginians. In a letter to Davis, 10 *Rowland's Davis,* 27, Early observed that Harvey Hill was not then with the Army of Northern Virginia. Hill had been relieved at his own request, "as I always understood it," Early wrote, "because he could not get along very well with General Jackson, though they were brothers-in-law." No confirmation is found elsewhere of what almost certainly was a lapse of memory on Early's part. Major Robert Stiles, who knew the North Carolinian well, remarked that Hill's "worship of Stonewall Jackson" held a place next after and close alongside Hill's religion. Cf. *Stiles,* 72, and in 21 *S. H. S. P.,* 25. Hill's orders to his command, announcing the death of Jackson, were among the most fervent and laudatory of all. *O. R.,* 18, 1073.

and Lafayette McLaws were not considered when perhaps they expected to be, two others who probably did not anticipate that honor so soon were regarded as of the stature of future Lieutenant Generals. These men were John B. Hood and "Dick" Anderson. They were rated "capital officers" by General Lee who added: "They are improving, too, and will make good corps commanders, if necessary."[66]

Around hundreds of mess tables, Stuart, Powell Hill and Ewell were discussed as the three among whom a choice would be made. Nothing was certain until May 23. Then, almost a fort-night after the death of Jackson, notice was sent to "Dick" Ewell in Richmond that he was promoted Lieutenant General. On the 25th, formal orders directed him to proceed without delay to Fredericksburg and to report to Lee for assignment to duty.[67]

Ewell received the news, so far as the records show, with no undue elation, and as he felt able to take the field, he prepared immediately to obey orders. Before he left Richmond he allowed himself time to fulfill, with proper consent, one ambition that he probably had cherished long: He married his widowed cousin, Lizinka Campbell Brown, daughter of George W. Campbell, for-mer Senator from Tennessee, Secretary of the Treasury and Min-ister to Russia.[68] She was an able, strong-minded woman of about 44 and she had the complete, unquestioning affection of her sol-dier cousin, whom she probably rated far higher as a soldier than he himself ever dreamed of doing.

Surrender had been unconditional. He who was regarded as incurably the bachelor had been a gallant suitor. Before the ope-ing of the Valley campaign he had written his lady in this wise concerning her son, Campbell Brown, who was on his staff: "I assure myself often that you are carried away in regard to myself by your anxiety for the safety of myself and Campbell and that your love for your son is reflected on me. Still in spite of this I cannot help hoping that the future has happiness in store for me. Your expression, 'In life or death we shall be united,' is to me fraught with promise. It has seemed to me were our union lim-

66 *O. R.*, 25, pt. 2, p. 811.
67 *O. R.*, 25, pt. 2, pp. 824–25. He was commissioned May 23, to rank as of that date. *Wright*, 16.
68 Judge Campbell, as he usually was called in Tennessee, spent a tragic two years in Russia, where Lizinka was born. Three of his four children died there within a week, of typhus.

ited to this world that it would be comparatively valueless. During my life I have looked to knowing you and loving you in another world and your letter supports the thought. You may think I am in my dotage but I cannot weigh my words. We are falling back and it is doubtful when I can write you again. . . ." [69] Now, in a wrathful world of reality, she was his; but not in his mind so completely his that he could introduce her as such. For a time she was, to bowing Generals, "my wife, Mrs. Brown." [70]

In part, the appointment of Ewell was made because of sentimental association of his name with Jackson, and in part because of admiration for his unique, picturesque and wholly lovable personality. Of his ability to lead a Corps nothing was known. Everything was a gamble. "Old Bald Head" had never handled more than a Division and he had served directly with Lee for less than a month. [71] In that brief period, Ewell probably had not seen the commanding General more than a dozen times, though Lee, of course, knew Ewell's stalwart reputation as Jackson's principal lieutenant. When Ewell was advanced to corps command, nothing was said of his brief connection with Lee. So closely was Ewell's name linked with Jackson's, and so justly popular was "Old Bald Head" for his gallant generosity that none questioned, apparently, either the appointment or his ability to fill it.

Perhaps Ewell's reserved commanding General should be excepted from this statement. Lee may have wished to divide risks at the same time that he recognized merit. On the morning of May 24, the day after Ewell was promoted, and perhaps before the news of his advancement reached the men on the Rappahannock, Powell Hill received a call to Army Headquarters. He was admitted to Lee's tent and in a few friendly sentences was told that the two existing Corps were unwieldy for operation in a wooded country, that the President had consented to the establishment of a Third Corps, that it would consist of Hill's old Division, of Anderson's transferred from Longstreet, and of a third Division still to be formed, and that this new Third Corps was to be commanded by . . . Ambrose Powell Hill, Lieutenant General, P.A.C.S. [72]

As in October Lee had recommended the promotion of both

---

[69] *Old Bald Head,* 78; for the marriage, see *Hamlin's Ewell,* 103.
[70] *Gordon,* 158.   [71] June 27–July 13; Aug. 15–24, 1862.
[72] *Lee's Dispatches,* 91.

Jackson and Longstreet, so now he had advocated to the President, who heartily approved, the elevation both of Ewell and of Powell Hill. Concerning Jackson's earlier lieutenant, Lee had told the President, Ewell "is an honest, brave soldier, who has always done his duty well." Hill had been recommended by Lee as "upon the whole . . . the best soldier of his grade with me." [73] Lee had justified in sound words the advancement of the two men: "Inasmuch as this army has done hard work, and there is still harder before it, I wish to take advantage of every circumstance to inspire and encourage them, and induce the officers and men to believe that their labors are appreciated, and when vacancies occur that they will receive the advantages of promotion if they deserve it. I believe the efficiency of the corps would be promoted by being commanded by lieutenant-generals, and I do not know where to get better men than those I have named." [74]

There was little open grumbling at these promotions. Longstreet in later years wrote that Ewell deserved promotion, but "Old Pete" pointed out that both Harvey Hill and McLaws were Powell Hill's seniors. The chief of the First Corps stated flatly that Harvey Hill "was the superior of General A. P. Hill in rank, skill, judgment, and distinguished services," and he intimated that McLaws, also, was entitled to consideration above A. P. Hill. Against Harvey Hill and McLaws, said Longstreet, "was the objection that they were not Virginians." [75] At the time the promotions were made, "Old Pete" voiced no objection and, except for his waning personal dislike of Powell Hill, probably felt none. If anyone complained, it may have been Lafayette McLaws, who could affirm that he was overslaughed by the advancement of Powell Hill; but if McLaws said anything, it simply was to inquire why he was passed over. [76]

Hill's elevation meant that some officer would be named to head the Light Division and probably would be made a Major

---

[73] O. R., 25, pt. 2, p. 810. This letter of Lee to Davis, May 20, contains also Lee's assertion that two Corps of 30,000 men "are more than one man can properly handle and keep under his eye in battle in the country that we have to operate in."

[74] Ibid. Richmond newspapers contained numerous approving articles. Cf. Examiner, May 25, p. 1, col. 1, May 28, p. 1, col. 1; Dispatch, May 25, p. 1, col. 6, June 1, 1863, p. 1, col. 2. With its usual admiration for Hill, the Examiner, May 22, 1863, p. 2, col. 2, spoke of Hill as "the Blücher of Sharpsburg, whose name rises like a star in the bulletin from every battlefield. . . ."

[75] 3 B & L., 245 and n. See the reply of Col. William Allan, ibid., 355.

[76] Ibid., 245 n.

General. Hill knew that his advancement had been expected by many brother officers even before the death of Jackson, and that Harry Heth and Dorsey Pender had been regarded as open, rival candidates to succeed him.

As soon as Hill left the commanding General's tent, on the day he was told of his promotion, he took the first opportunity of writing Lee a letter, which he delivered in person that afternoon.[77] The new chief of a Third Corps explained that he wished to claim no more for the Light Division than its due, but he asserted that it had "borne itself well and unitedly on every field from Mechanicsville to Chancellorsville." The letter continued: "I ascribe [the Division's] good conduct to its esprit de corps, to its pride in its *name,* and to its uniform 'shoulder to shoulder feeling,' and good feeling between the different Brigades. If a judicious appointment of Major General is not made, I fear that all this will be lost."

Concerning the two candidates, Hill went on: "Of Gen. Heth, I have but to say that I consider him a most excellent officer, and gallant soldier, and had he been with the Division through all its hardships, and acquired the confidence of the men, there is no man I had rather see promoted than he." There followed this fine tribute to the other aspirant: "On the other hand Gen. Pender has fought with the Division in every battle, has been four times wounded and *never* left the *field,* has risen by death and wounds from fifth Brigadier to be its senior, has the best drilled and disciplined Brigade in the Division, and more than all, possesses the unbounded confidence of the Division. At the battle of Chancellorsville, he seized the color, and on horseback led his Brigade *up to* and *in to* the Federal intrenchments."

Then Hill applied his point: "The effect of such examples of daring gallantry at critical moments is incalculable. I am very earnest in this matter, for I know that 10,000 men, led by a Commander whom they know, and have fought with, may turn the tide of battle, and I do not think the Confederacy can afford to have this Army defeated. Hence, as much as I admire and respect Gen. Heth, I am conscientiously of opinion that in the opening campaign, my Division under him, will not be *half* as effective as under Gen. Pender."

77 *Lee's Dispatches,* 91.

Wherefore, Hill suggested what Lee already had decided to recommend—that two Brigades of Hill's command be united with two other Brigades, so that, if Heth were promoted, he might have this command, while Pender became a Major General to head his own Brigade, McGowan's, Thomas's and Lane's.[78]

This plan was submitted to the President. Although Davis at first understood Lee to prefer Heth to Pender,[79] the Chief Executive quickly saw that Lee wanted both men promoted. Higher rank for Heth was put in some doubt by the fact that he had been nominated by the President in October, 1862, and had been refused confirmation by the Senate.[80] This had caused Lee to hesitate about suggesting the n⸝.ne a second time, but in view of the need of a qualified man for a new ninth Division, the commanding General and the President had decided to proceed.[81]

One other obstacle stood in the way—a third candidate for early promotion in the person of Robert Ransom, Jr., who came from the same State as Pender. Political ties might be twisted and friendships taxed by preferring one to the other. A choice between Ransom and Pender was avoided by the expedient of sending Samuel G. French to Mississippi and of advancing Ransom to take French's place and thereby of clearing the way for Pender.[82] This arrangement was outlined by Lee as concerned Heth and Pender, and by Davis as it involved Ransom; but the part of it that related to the Third Corps was handled in such a manner that it was made to appear to be the work of Hill.[83]

Heth had so many old friends and bound new acquaintances to him so readily by his social charm that few begrudged what manifestly he had desired. Ransom was pleased, his wife appeased. Pender's promotion was the most interesting of the three because it is the only one concerning which the sentiments of the gentlemen most immediately affected by the honor progressively are presented through candid letters. In March, writing of the elevation of his friend Brig. Gen. Stephen Lee to the next grade, Pen-

---

78 Hill to Lee, MS, May 24, 1863, *Wilkins MSS.* Hill's somewhat weird spelling has been corrected.

79 *Lee's Dispatches*, 91; *O. R.*, 51, pt. 2, p. 716.

80 *Wright*, 33.   81 Cf. *O. R.*, 25, pt. 2, p. 811.

82 *O. R.*, 18, 1077; Ransom was appointed May 27, 1863, to rank from May 26 and thereby to be Pender's senior by one day. *Wright*, 33, 34. For the correspondence leading to these promotions, see *Lee's Dispatches*, 91 ff, *O. R.*, 25, pt. 2, pp. 810–1ʳ 827; *O. R.*, 51, pt. 2, p. 716.

83 See Lee's letter that invited Hill's nomination, *O. R.*, 25, pt. 2, p. 827.

der had told his wife: "I think if claims were considered, I should be promoted too, but I have given up that idea. If the war can come to an early end I shall be content to get through with it. You will think me just as much a hero as if I were a full General and love me just as much, and what more need I care for?" [84] After Chancellorsville, though he minimized his wound and did not mention the fact that he led a charge with the flag in his hand, he confided to Mrs. Pender: "If not before, I won promotion last Sunday; and if it can be done, I think I shall get it." [85] Once he had the advancement he coveted, he became so much engrossed in the administration and discipline of his troops that he ceased to record his feelings. It was his nature to desire, to strive, to achieve and, having reached his goal, to minimize what he had gained.

Difficulty was faced in procuring the troops assigned Pender. Two of the four Brigades were in the Carolinas, whence the district commanders were loath to permit any troops to depart. Some unpleasantness with Harvey Hill and sharp misunderstanding occurred before an accord was reached. Such as it was, this bargain confirmed Lee's belief that Harvey Hill would not exercise discretionary powers and that, ipso facto, he was not suited to the type of command Lee exercised.[86] That was the end of Hill's place in Lee's esteem as a departmental commander, though the North Carolinian did not lose the personal good will of his chief. Nor did he lose then or thereafter his merited reputation as a superb combat officer.

Ransom would remain South of the James, but the new Major Generals, Harry Heth and Dorsey Pender, would take their places in the new Third Corps. Rodes would command the former Division of Harvey Hill. Together, these three promotions completed the divisional command because the fourth vacancy had been filled at the peak of the emergency that followed the wounding of Jackson and the discovery that Colston was unsuited to lead a Division. Scarcely had Trimble begun to conquer his osteomyelitis than he fell sick again.[87] As always, his spirit was free; his

84 Mch. 28, 1863—Pender MSS.

85 Ibid., May 7. It perhaps should be noted that Pender's unpunctuated sentences have been conformed to standard usage.

86 Cf. O. R., 25, pt. 2, p. 832; ibid., 51, pt. 2, p. 718; Lee's Dispatches, 99–100.

87 O. R., 25, pt. 2, pp. 801–02.

flesh held him captive. He could not take the Division that Jackson long had saved for him. In Trimble's stead, "Old Allegheny" Johnson, who had been slated for D. H. Hill's Division—now assigned Rodes—was called from Richmond on hurried orders. By May 8, he joined the Army of Northern Virginia.[88] Trimble, for his part, was given charge of the Valley District, which "Grumble" Jones had not directed to public satisfaction. Although the assignment was not one that a man of Trimble's fighting impulse[89] desired, it was accepted cheerfully and with a certain satisfaction because of Jackson's service on that famous battleground. Said Trimble: "I hesitate to incur so great a responsibility after the brilliant achievements of General Jackson in that district, but as I know the country well, having been in his command last year, I will hope, by diligence and zealous effort, and with the favor of Divine Providence, for success under such orders as I may receive."[90]

So much for the Major Generals, all of whom seemed competent. Cadmus Wilcox was deeply and not unreasonably disappointed that he was passed over.[91] If the selections were a bitter cup for anyone else, no taste of it lingers in the records. As for the Brigadiers, Paul Semmes was back; but the promotion of Rodes, of Heth and of Pender, the death of Paxton, the retirement of J. R. Jones, the absence of Lawton, the disabling of Francis Nicholls, and the relief of Colston from command necessitated the promotion of eight men to the grade of Brigadier General.

Was there sufficient qualified material from which to draw? One promotion was a matter of course. Difficult, for example, as Pender's place would be for any man to fill, Col. Alfred M. Scales of the Thirteenth North Carolina had led the Brigade several times and had demonstrated his capacity.[92] Similarly, John B.

88 *O. R.*, 25, pt. 2, pp. 774, 787; *ibid.*, 51, pt. 2, p. 703; 5 *Rowland's Davis*, 481.

89 Cf. *Douglas*, 212: "There was fight enough in old man Trimble to satisfy a herd of tigers."

90 *O. R.*, 25, pt. 2, p. 822. For the preliminary correspondence and the orders, see *ibid.*, pp. 774, 787, 801–02, 810, 812, 837, 840, 866–67, 879.

91 Cf. C. M. Wilcox to his sister, MS, May 16, 1863: "If I am not promoted now, I shall be really discouraged, for I know that no one could do more than I have done with the means at my command. Everyone is talking of the injustice done me and I am now really sick with disgust"—*Wilcox MSS.*

92 He will be mentioned frequently in the pages that follow. For his career, see 4 *C. M. H.*, 349. See also 1 *N. C. Regts.*, 669; *Wright*, 106; *O. R.*, 27, pt. 3, p. 909. He was commissioned as of June 15, 1863, and was assigned to succeed Pender five days later.

Gordon was fitted logically for transfer to the command of Rodes's old Brigade, with which he had distinguished himself, but a gratifying circumstance kept Gordon elsewhere. To assist Early, it will be remembered, Gordon had been assigned temporarily to Lawton's old Brigade of Early's, formerly Ewell's Division. So completely had Gordon won the hearts of his fellow-Georgians in the operations around Fredericksburg that the officers of Lawton's Brigade unanimously petitioned that Gordon remain their chief. Lee thought it wise to accede to this request.[93]

Aside from Scales and Gordon, trouble immediately was encountered in finding competent men. To spare the feelings of the affected soldiers, nothing was said publicly to indicate the seriousness of the shortage of higher officers, but the grim truth was, in six Brigades that lacked Generals, not one of the senior Colonels was ripe for promotion. Perhaps Lee was expecting more of Brigadier Generals and was setting higher standards for them, but for the first time, attrition at the level of brigade command was threatening dangerously the organization of the Army. Some of the most reliable, veteran regiments of the entire Army might be rendered ineffective because they would not be well led.

What was to be done? For a time, Rodes's Brigade could be left under Col. E. A. O'Neal of the Twenty-sixth Alabama. Again, though Col. J. M. Brockenbrough of the Fortieth Virginia was not suited for promotion to the command of Field's, later Heth's, Brigade, Brockenbrough could be counted upon to keep together a command sadly reduced in numbers.

This temporary arrangement would leave four brigade vacancies. All of them most unfortunately would be in the famous Jackson-Trimble-Colston-Johnson Division. Every one of its Brigades required a commanding General. Where were they to be found? Who could take the Stonewall Brigade? J. R. Jones's Brigade readily might have been given to Col. T. S. Garnett of the Forty-eighth Virginia, but Garnett had been killed on May 3. Trimble's old Brigade, of which Colston now was relieved—who was to handle it? Three of its regiments were from Virginia,

93 For the related correspondence, see O. R., 25, pt. 2, p. 810; O. R., 27, pt. 3, p. 865; 5 Rowland's Davis, 481; Lee's Dispatches, 94. Gordon, it will be recalled, had been appointed Brigadier in November, 1862, but had not been confirmed because there was no vacancy for him. He was reappointed May 11, 1863, to rank from May 7, 1863, and was confirmed Jan. 25, 1864. Wright, 95.

two from North Carolina. Unpleasant state rivalries had shown themselves: how were they to be resolved? Lastly, could anything be done with Nicholls's Louisiana Brigade that had lost its most promising chief? The surviving senior Colonel was absent and was not regarded as suited to command.[94] Was it to be admitted that this excellent Brigade could not be supplied with a qualified officer of appropriate rank?

That must not be! To support and assist a new divisional commander in the person of "Allegheny" Johnson, competent Brigadiers must be provided, but from what source? The answer given the interested troops and the expectant officers was itself evidence of the Army's strait. In the first place, it was decided that "Maryland" Steuart, who had recovered from his vexing wound,[95] could be utilized as an old regular Army man to take the Virginia-North Carolina Brigade of Colston. Experience with Archer's Brigade had indicated that where an officer well schooled in the "old army" took a Brigade that had regiments from more than one state, rivalries might be ended.[96]

Paxton's Brigade presented a second and more vexing problem. So famous a command deserved the best unattached Brigadier who could be found. That man, in the judgment of Lee, was Col. James A. Walker of the Thirteenth Virginia, Early's old Brigade. During the Maryland operations, Walker had been "loaned" to Trimble's Brigade, at the head of which he had done so well that he had been recommended in October for promotion.[97] He had not been advanced then, but he had been distinguished anew at Fredericksburg in December when he had been in charge of Early's Brigade.[98] Qualified Walker was. Although he had no connection with the Brigade or with the Division, he was made commander of the Stonewall Brigade.[99]

This was a choice doubly sensational because of previous relations between Walker and Jackson. In 1852, at the Virginia Mili-

94 *O. R.*, 25, pt. 2, p. 810. 95 *McKim*, 122.

96 Cf. *O. R.*, 25, pt. 2, p. 830. For references to Steuart subsequent to the last entry concerning him, see McKim, *loc. cit.*; *O. R.*, 19, pt. 2, p. 688; *O. R.*, 18, 1070; *O. R.*, 25, pt. 2, pp. 810, 817. Numerous disconnected references will be found in W. W. Goldsborough, *The Maryland Line in the Confederate Army.*

97 *O. R.*, 19, pt. 2, p. 684.

98 For Walker, see 3 *C. M. H.*, 676; *O. R.*, 25, pt. 2, p. 809; *Hamlin's Ewell*, 115–16; 9 *S. H. S. P.*, 561.

99 His appointment was dated May 16, with rank as of May 15, 1863 (*Wright*, 104–05).

tary Institute, Walker, who then was a senior, had professed himself insulted by some remark made to him by Professor Jackson. After a sharp exchange of words, the belligerent young Walker challenged the teacher to a duel. Jackson debated whether he should accept, but the question was decided for him by the court martial and dismissal of Walker from the Institute. The younger man had remained a bitter enemy of Jackson's until the war. Then, in time, each acquired respect for the other. Walker laid down his grievance; Jackson did what he could to advance Walker. Now the Colonel of the Thirteenth Virginia was to have the unusual honor of transfer to Jackson's Brigade, and of promotion over the heads of the senior officers of five of the most famous regiments of the Army.

A strident, echoing outcry was made by the field officers of the Stonewall Brigade. They were outraged. In protest against the appointment over them of a newly promoted man from another Division, they tendered their resignations. Moreover, as if to anticipate the question, Whom would you have preferred? they named three whom they said they would have accepted cheerfully. One of the trio was "Sandie" Pendleton, Jackson's A.A.G.[100] The resignations were declined so quietly and with so much tact that no trace of the incident appears in the official records.

For J. R. Jones's Brigade, as for Paxton's, choice of a new commander had to go beyond the Brigade and the Division. The man promoted was Lt. Col. John M. Jones, inspector general of Early's Division. Jones was a West Point graduate[101] of the class of 1841 and had served at the Academy for seven years as assistant instructor of infantry tactics. When he resigned to defend Virginia, Jones was a Captain of six years' standing in the Seventh Infantry. McLaws also had been a Captain; Cadmus Wilcox had been a First Lieutenant in the same regiment. While McLaws had risen to divisional command and Wilcox long had been a Brigadier, Jones had no more than the star of a Major on his collar. Why he had mounted no further was suggested vaguely in Lee's letter to Davis at the time of the appointment: "Should [Jones] fail in his duty, he will instantly resign."[102] If this meant that

---

100 *Pendleton*, 273. The other two are not mentioned in available records.
101 *Cullum*, No. 1097.   102 *O. R.*, 25, pt. 2, p. 810.

Jones's enemy was strong drink, the new Brigadier met and overcame that adversary.[103]

Steuart for Colston's Brigade, "Jim" Walker for Paxton's, John M. Jones for J. R. Jones's command—this left the Louisiana Brigade, but there, even when Lee looked through the other Divisions, a suitable man could not be found at once. There had been a suggestion that Col. J. B. Walton of the Washington Artillery might transfer to the infantry and head the Brigade. Longstreet did not think Walton would be willing to accept the command; Lee was doubtful whether the gallant old artillerist was suited to the post.[104] In the end, Nicholls's Brigade, as well as Rodes's and Heth's, had to be left without commanding officers of proper grade—an ominous admission that superior, developed material of high command had been exhausted temporarily. In addition, there was a prospect that "Extra Billy" Smith [105] soon might resign to become Governor of Virginia, an office for which he was an active and favored candidate. One diarist expressed the opinion that "Extra Billy" got a heavy vote in the Army because the Virginia soldiers wished to get rid of him as a commander.[106]

Such was the reorganization necessitated by the loss of Jackson, which the Army felt to be irreplaceable, and by the establishment of a Third Corps, which prudence, good organization and justice to Ewell and A. P. Hill demanded. How those two officers would handle their enlarged commands, it was impossible to foretell. The preliminaries of active campaigning were auspicious. When Ewell arrived with his bride, on the 29th of May, after an absence from the Army of nine months, his and Jackson's old Divisions met him at the cars and gave him a cheering salute.[107] After "Sandie" Pendleton saw the rejuvenated new Lieutenant General he wrote home: "All are pleased with [Ewell]. His health is pretty good now, and he seems quite pleased to get back into the field. He manages his leg very well, and walks only with his stick, and mounts his horse quite easily from the ground." [108]

103 Jones was appointed May 16, to rank from May 15, 1863, and was assigned to duty May 21 (Wright, 105; O. R., 25, pt. 2, p. 816).

104 O. R., 25, pt. 2, p. 810.

105 Appointed Brigadier General as of April 23, to rank from Jan. 21, 1863; assigned May 19 to Early's old Brigade (Wright, 103; O. R., 25, pt. 2, p. 809).

106 Wingfield, 26.

107 Jed. Hotchkiss' MS Diary, 197. For Ewell's orders, see O. R., 25, pt. 2, pp. 824–25, 840.

108 Pendleton, 276.

"Old Bald Head" was glad to take over Jackson's competent staff officers, some of whom had offered to seek other duty,[109] and he was overjoyed to be again with his troops. On June 1, 1863—a fateful date in the administrative history of the Army—Ewell assumed direction of a reconstituted Second Corps which, to repeat, was composed of his old Division under Early, Jackson's former Division under Edward Johnson, and Harvey Hill's under Rodes. Simultaneously, Ambrose Powell Hill became the first commander of a new Third Corps. Included in it were part of his own Division, with Dorsey Pender as its chief, Heth's Division, half of which had been Hill's own Division, and third, "Dick" Anderson's Brigades, which were transferred from the First Corps.[110]

The adjustment of the artillery to this organization of three Infantry Corps proved a matter of no difficulty. To each of the Corps, three battalions were assigned. Instead of a general reserve, provision was made for a reserve of two battalions for each Corps. That is to say, each Corps was to have five artillery battalions, the Army, fifteen. As the number of organized artillery battalions, fourteen, lacked one of sufficing for this organization, a fifteenth was created. At its head was placed Maj. William T. Poague, long-time Captain of Jackson's own Rockbridge Artillery and, more recently, second in command of McIntosh's Battalion.[111] This was a most merited distinction for Poague but it confirmed his separation from his old battery.[112]

These assignments of battalions to the various Corps chiefly were of interest in strengthening or dissolving old associations. Longstreet's artillery organization remained intact. That of the Second Corps was unchanged except that Nelson's Battalion, previously of the general reserve, became one of the reserve battalions of the Second Corps. Nelson's was an undistinguished battalion— that and neither less nor more. The new Third Corps was not

[109] Pendleton, 273, 276; Jed. Hotchkiss' MS Diary, 197.

[110] For the orders, see O. R., 25, pt. 2, p. 840; Hotchkiss' MS Diary, 199.

[111] Orders for the establishment of this battalion have not been found, but Poague did not have a battalion on April 16 (O. R., 25, pt. 2, p. 729) and did command one of unspecified units in the organization of June 2, 1863 (ibid., 850). At Gettysburg (O. R., 27, pt. 2, pp. 290, 673) he had Wyatt's, Joseph Graham's, Ward's and Brooke's batteries. The second-named of these did not join Poague until June 21 or later (ibid., 673).

[112] Which already had been assigned to J. Thompson Brown's Battalion. Cf. O. R., 25, pt. 2, p. 720.

stinted. Every one of the five battalions designated for it was good. Quick as Hill was to take offense at any alleged slight, he seems to have been entirely satisfied with the batteries allotted him.

Under this organization, Pendleton ceased to be Chief of the Reserve Artillery, for the reason that there no longer was any general reserve. He reverted to his one-time status as Chief of Artillery of the Army, though he remained Brigadier General.[113] His corps chiefs of artillery—who were they to be? As Colonel Walton did not wish to take on himself the responsibilities of infantry brigade command, he was the titular and undisputed chief of the First Corps' guns, as for months he had been. This was a proper assignment. Walton embodied the spirit of the Washington Artillery, but he was no longer young nor alertly active. Much as Longstreet admired and respected Walton, the commander of the First Corps soon was to look to the sober-faced and scientific Porter Alexander to handle the artillery in the field.

The Second Corps inevitably would suffer much from the absence of Stapleton Crutchfield during the long months he would require to adjust himself to the loss of a leg. He was continued, of course, in the post he had earned, but in his stead would serve the senior battalion commander assigned the Division—J. Thompson Brown, an able and conscientious soldier, patient and diligent in administration but not brilliant.

For the Third Corps, Powell Hill of course nominated and Lee approved [114] Col. R. Lindsay Walker. This officer, 36 years of age, and a Virginian of high connections, had been graduated from the Virginia Military Institute in 1845 and, after some years as a civil engineer, had been engaged in farming. On the outbreak of hostilities he had been commissioned Captain. First as commander of the Purcell Battery of Richmond and then as chief of artillery of Hill's Division, he had shared, and always with honor, the fortunes of Hill's men on nearly all their fields of battle after those of the Seven Days.[115] Walker was not the theatrical type whom soldiers cheer on the road and deride affectionately around the campfire, but he was the skillful leader that men are glad to have in battle. Careful and free of recklessness, he knew

113 Cf. O. R., 25, pt. 2, p. 851; O. R., 51, pt. 2, p. 720.
114 This was the procedure authorized June 2, 1863; see O. R., 25, pt. 2, pp. 850–51.
115 At that time he was incapacitated by illness. Cf. supra, Vol. I, p. 522.

when the artillerist can afford to be bold. Never backward when the order was "Forward," he had shown at Fredericksburg a stubborn skill on the defensive.[116]

Reorganization of the cavalry was another part of the endless task of promoting the worthy, of replacing the incompetent and of making good the losses due to attrition. Specifically, after Chancellorsville, the need was, first, to increase the mounted troops for offensive operations. In Southwest Virginia, under Brig. Gen. A. G. Jenkins was a force of three large regiments and five battalions of horse. These troops had not been well schooled in cavalry tactics or in hard fighting at close quarters. Some of Jenkins's men had the complex of home guards, and some preferred the life of a guerilla to that of a trooper, but many were good raw material. They were badly needed by Stuart.

After much diplomatic correspondence Lee procured three regiments and one battalion, but received polite assurance from Maj. Gen. Sam Jones that the remaining units could not be spared and would not be detached otherwise than on order of the Secretary of War.[117] With the force that reported to cavalry headquarters, Jenkins himself came, a man of oft proved daring and gallantry but of untested administrative qualities. Lee debated whether, in these circumstances, it might not be wise to give Jenkins at the outset a quiet post.[118]

Besides Jenkins's men, who had to be tried in the field by the side of veteran Brigades, there was a prospect of getting from North Carolina and Southern Virginia some of the curious Brigade of Beverly Robertson, who, it will be remembered, had quietly been transferred after Lee's Army had entered Maryland in September, 1862. Inasmuch as Harvey Hill in the North State had denounced Robertson's men in every tone of vehemence,[119] he could not object to ridding himself of them. Hill agreed to send Lee one of Robertson's regiments, then consented to the dispatch of a second.[120] Despite the smallness of this force, Robertson offered to return to Virginia with it.[121] He received assurance that this would be acceptable to Lee, who never had lost his good

---

[116] For Walker, see 3 C. M. H., 680–82. The assignment of batteries and the designation of corps chiefs of artillery are given in O. R., 25, pt. 2, pp. 580, 859.
[117] O. R., 27, pt. 3, pp. 858, 867–68.   [118] Cf. O. R., 25, pt. 2, p. 789.
[119] O. R., 18, 891, 1047, 1048, 1051, 1075; see supra, p. 470.
[120] O. R., 18, 1084, 1088; O. R., 25, pt. 2, pp. 782, 820–21.
[121] O. R., 27, pt. 3, p. 1007.

opinion of Robertson as an organizer and instructor.[122] Stuart's judgment is not recorded, but before the end of May, his roster included Robertson and the Fourth and Fifth North Carolina.[123] These troops and their commander at once were involved in plans that Lee and Stuart had been considering to increase and to equalize the size of the cavalry Brigades so that Tom Rosser and Williams C. Wickham might be made Brigadier Generals.[124] For the moment these plans failed. Lee declined to create new Brigades unless there were more troops.

Besides Robertson and his Brigade, W. E. Jones and his regiments that had been in the Shenandoah Valley were added to Stuart's immediate command. "Jeb" had been anxious not to have Jones with him again and had been active in trying to get "Grumble" transferred to the command of the Stonewall Brigade after Paxton's death. In this, "Jeb" had met with no encouragement from headquarters. Said Lee: "I am perfectly willing to transfer [Jones] to Paxton's Brigade if he desires it; but if he does not, I know of no act of his to justify my doing so. Do not let your judgment be warped." [125] That, of course, silenced "Jeb" but it did not satisfy him. The commanding General could make the two men work together. He could not make them like each other.

When the opportunity of another offensive came, or perhaps before that time, there was still another prospect of adding to the cavalry of the Army. John D. Imboden with some help from "Grumble" Jones had penetrated into Western Virginia, April 20–May 14. In weather as vile as that of Lee's unprosperous summer campaign of 1861, Imboden had driven the enemy out of several villages and across forbidding mountains. No great results had been achieved, but as Lee subsequently wrote, the expedition "rendered valuable service in the collection of stores and in making the enemy uneasy for his communications with the West." [126] Now that Imboden again was on the eastern face of the Alleghenies and had rested his men, the mounted units might assist Stuart temporarily, but whether they would help stoutly was another

122 Cf. O. R., 25, pt. 2, pp. 820–21.   123 Cf. O. R., 25, pt. 2, p. 826.
124 See O. R., 25, pt. 2, pp. 820–21, 828, 836.
125 O. R., 25, pt. 2, p. 789.
126 O. R., 25, pt. 1, p. 1035. Imboden's report immediately precedes this endorsement.

question. In Western Virginia, Imboden had lost by desertion 200 men from a single battalion after he had forbidden them to seize citizens' horses for private use.[127] A command that would do this scarcely would respond with the spur to Stuart's bugles, but undisciplined as were Imboden's rangers, they could ride, they could shoot, they could drive cattle, and they could guard a countryside. They must be employed.[128]

While this third major reorganization of the Army was being effected between May 7 and approximately June 6, the First Corps was reunited by the return of Longstreet from the Blackwater. The Corps did not seem quite itself without "Dick" Anderson's men, but its other Divisions had undergone no change in leadership and were little diminished in number.

Besides the strength of the returning veterans of the First Corps, the Army received during May three new Brigades. The first of these was Junius Daniel's large if raw North Carolina Brigade, which Harvey Hill had exchanged for Colquitt's depleted command.[129] Daniel was unknown to most officers of the Army of Northern Virginia and was unfamiliar with its methods, but he was of high standing in North Carolina. His Brigade was assigned to Rodes's Division, which Colquitt had left. The other accessions, which went to Heth's Division, were the North Carolina Brigade of Johnston Pettigrew and the Mississippi Brigade of Joseph R. Davis. These troops had been involved in long negotiations to which, severally, Lee, President Davis, Governor Zeb. Vance of North Carolina and Harvey Hill had been parties. The bargaining would have appeared more appropriate among jealously cautious allies than among the officials of a Confederacy engaged in a life-and-death revolution. In the end, Pettigrew and Davis were sent to Northern Virginia on condition that, temporarily, Micah Jenkins's and Robert Ransom's Brigades were to be left in Southern Virginia and in North Carolina.[130]

This exchange, like the one involving Junius Daniel, was not wholly acceptable, and for the same reason: In the place of tested

[127] O. R., 25, pt. 1, p. 102.
[128] Cf. Lee to Imboden, May 23, 1863, O. R., 25, pt. 2, p. 819. Cf. ibid., 852.
[129] O. R., 25, pt. 2, pp. 798, 813. A sketch of Daniel will be found in Vol. III.
[130] John R. Cooke was included for a time in the negotiations but soon was slated for return to Virginia (see O. R., 25, pt. 2, pp. 843, 848). For the correspondence over the troops that should and should not be sent to Lee, consult ibid., 18, 1057, 1061, 1066, 1074, 1077 ff; ibid., 25, pt. 2, pp. 798, 811, 813; Lee's Dispatches, 99.

veterans it gave the Army of Northern Virginia troops of little experience in combat, and some officers whom Lee tactfully styled "uninstructed," lest the antonym of the more familiar word "trained" stir sensitive spirits.[131]

A pleasant aspect of the coming of the new Brigades was the return to the Army of Johnston Pettigrew, who had the good will of many officers who had known him on the Peninsula in the spring of 1862.[132] Incidentally, in the event of accident to Heth, the command of the Division would fall to Pettigrew, because his commission antedated that of any other Brigadier in the Division.[133] Joseph R. Davis, who added another Mississippi Brigade to the Army of Northern Virginia,[134] was a nephew of the Confederate President, on whose staff he had served for some months.[135] As a brigade commander "Joe" Davis, at 38 years of age, was entirely without combat experience, though he had been with Longstreet in front of Suffolk.

While Daniel, Davis and Pettigrew took their places in the camps along the Rappahannock, the Army of Northern Virginia made ready to embark on the adventure of operating without "Stonewall" Jackson. The First Corps, though reduced to three Divisions, had its command well organized. Its divisional and brigade leadership was more uniform and seasoned than that of either of the other Corps. Ewell, it must be repeated, was himself the greatest question mark of the Second Corps. Under him, Early had able Brigade commanders with the possible exception of the valiant but unmilitary "Extra Billy" Smith. The famous Division of Jackson had a new chief in "Allegheny" Johnson [136] and four new Brigade leaders, three of whom were strangers to

131 O. R., 18, 1063.   132 See *supra*, Vol. I, p. 244.

133 Feb. 26, 1862; *Wright*, 71. Archer was appointed June 3, 1862. *Ibid.*, 84.

134 Davis had one North Carolina Regiment and three from his own State. The other Mississippi Brigades were Barksdale's and Posey's.

135 Joseph R. Davis was the son of Jefferson Davis's older brother, Isaac, who had married Susan Garthy. Singularly little concerning Joseph Davis appears in O. R. prior to December, 1862. His appointment as Brigadier General, according to Wright, 91, was made Oct. 8, 1862, but no assignment to command is in O. R. until his Brigade is mentioned in Gustavus Smith's field return of Dec. 10, 1862, O. R., 18, 793. Sundry references in *ibid.* show that J. R. Davis's Brigade for some time was stationed near Richmond.

136 Johnson had never fought under Lee, but some of his troops had. In Western Virginia, Johnson's old command had consisted of the Twenty-first, Twenty-fifth, Forty-fourth, Fifty-second and Fifty-eighth Virginia, and the Twelfth Georgia (O. R., 12, pt. 1, p. 487). The first three of these regiments now were with John M. Jones; the other Virginia units of Johnson's former command were with Smith of Early's Division; the Twelfth Georgia was in Doles's Brigade, Rodes's Division.

the men. The remaining Division of the Second Corps, Rodes's, was less sharply reorganized, and was under a man whose recent promotion had come after a clear demonstration of his capacity for command.

The weakness of Second Corps command could be stated explicitly: Of the seventeen corps positions that called for officers of rank from Brigadier to Lieutenant General, seven only were filled by men who, at the rank prescribed by the regulations, had led the same or corresponding units during the Chancellorsville-Salem Church operations.[137] If the comparison were pushed back to the Fredericksburg campaign, which had been fought less than seven months previously, this alarming fact would have been established: Of the seventeen general officers of the new Second Corps, three only, and those three Brigadiers, had been in regular command, Dec. 13, 1862, at the prescribed grade.[138]

In Hill's Third Corps, there was a new Lieutenant General, one Major General, Pender, whose insignia were fresh, and one, Heth, whose divisional experience was of the shortest. Of the thirteen Brigades of the Corps,[139] eight were under experienced general officers of appropriate rank, two were led by Brigadiers without combat experience at their grade, and three were in the care of senior Colonels.

To summarize the Army as a whole, as of June 6, two of the three Corps commanders, Ewell and Hill, had to prove their ability to handle the larger forces entrusted to them. Of the nine Divisional chiefs, four could be counted as definitely experienced —McLaws, Anderson, Hood and Early. Two were new in their posts, Johnson and Pender; two had been briefly in acting command of Divisions, Rodes and Heth; and one, Pickett, though administering a Division for some months, had never led it in combat. Among the thirty-seven Brigadier Generals of infantry, twenty-five had a measure of experience at their grade, though neither in experience nor in ability were they uniform. Six Brigades had new leaders; six others were in charge of Colonels. Even with these men of inexperience or doubtful capacity, it was an

---

[137] Namely, Generals Early, Hays, Gordon, Smith, Iverson, Ramseur and Doles.
[138] Viz., Hays, Iverson and Doles. In those operations, Early had commanded Ewell's Division but as senior Brigadier and not as a Major General.
[139] Anderson's Division had five, instead of the usual four Brigades.

army command of much prowess under a superlative General-in-Chief . . . but it lacked Jackson.

Men who missed Jackson, almost without exception, looked to Ewell as the leader who best embodied the distinctive spirit of the Second Corps, a spirit which they felt the Confederacy must keep alive. The impressions made immediately after Ewell's return to the army were, for the moment, confirmed. He showed sustained physical vigor at headquarters, but after a few weeks only of married life there may have been some indications that he had another commander besides General Lee.[140] The agility of "Old Bald Head" amused; his presence with the troops recalled Jackson. In elaborating what he previously had written, "Sandie" Pendleton said: "General Ewell is in fine health and fine spirits,—rides on horseback as well as any one needs to. The more I see of him the more I am pleased with him. In some traits of character he is very much like General Jackson, especially in his total disregard of his own comfort and safety, and his inflexibility of purpose. He is so thoroughly honest, too, and has only the one desire, to conquer the Yankees. I look for great things from him, and am glad to say that our troops have for him a good deal of the same feeling they had towards General Jackson." [141]

Troops were pleased not only with Ewell but also with the prospect of maneuver. They had enjoyed their weeks of rest after Chancellorsville—"a little bright island in a sea of strife," [142] and while the patriotic were troubled over the extent of desertion,[143] they believed themselves stronger than before battle.[144] That was not the consummation of their belief. They had defeated Hooker at his strongest when two of their Divisions under Longstreet were absent. Even though the fighting in the tangled Wilderness had cost them Jackson, they had added so spectacular a victory

---

140 Cf. *McKim*, 134: "We were of the opinion that Ewell was not the same soldier he had been when he was a whole man—and a single one." While this remark occurs in McKim's narrative of early June, 1863, it is possible he read those events in afterlight.

141 *Pendleton*, 277.   142 *Caldwell*, 88.

143 For this curious period of desertion, see *O. R.*, 18, 1052–53; *O. R.*, 25, pt. 2, pp. 787, 814–15; *O. R.*, 51, pt. 2, pp. 702, 706 ff, 709–10, 711, 712, 714–16, 717; 5 *Rowland's Davis*, 485–88. The question arises whether these desertions reflected a belief that the war was won or the same conviction that caused straggling in the Maryland expedition of 1862, the conviction that "invasion" was wrong.

144 1 *R. W. C. D.*, 326; Pender to his wife, MS, May 27, 1863: "Hood and Pickett are both within striking distance and also Pettigrew's Brigade, making us 10 to 15,000 stronger than before"—*Pender MSS.*

to so long a record of success that they now considered themselves invincible. Their commanding General, appreciative of valor but usually conservative, was of his soldiers' sanguine mind.

All the spring there had been talk of another offensive North of the Potomac [145] to feed the Army [146] and to wrest the initiative from the Federals. The strategical problem might seem as difficult as one young officer suggested when he told how he had heard Lee say, with a long look across the Potomac, "I wish I could get at those people over there." [147] Hooker could not be assailed on Stafford Heights, nor could his position easily be turned; but nearly all the Confederates were convinced that Lee would find a way of carrying the war into the enemy's country. Said the new Major General, Dorsey Pender: "All feel that something is brewing and that Gen. Lee is not going to wait all the time for them to come to him." [148]

The first days of June brought confirmation of all these predictions. Up the Rapidan the flank of the First Corps was extended; [149] Stuart was instructed to keep all his cavalry together; [150] efforts were being made to accumulate cattle to be moved with the Army; [151] on the morning of the 3d of June McLaws's Division quietly left its camps and started for Culpeper; that night, without explanation, Heth's men got orders to take the place of Rodes's pickets; by mid-morning of the 4th, Rodes's camps were deserted; then on the 5th, Early and Johnston started up the Rappahannock. [152] Soon the new Third Corps alone was left. Culpeper, men whispered, was the immediate objective, and after that—Maryland? Pennsylvania? A victory that would decide the war? Another and a worse Sharpsburg? Dorsey Pender answered for the Army—"Have no fear we shall not beat them . . . !"

[145] *Ham Chamberlayne*, 161, 162.
[146] Pender to his wife, MS, Apr. 17, 1863: "I see nothing left for us but to go. If we do not, our Army will be on short rations and discontented and we accomplish next to nothing here. . . . This is a very different army from the one we marched into Maryland last year and they have not as good a one to meet us. I am for going. . . ."—*Pender MSS.*
[147] *McKim*, 134.
[148] To his wife, MS, May 18, 1863—*Pender MSS.*
[149] *O. R.*, 25, pt. 2, p. 840.   [150] *Ibid.*, 844.
[151] *Ibid.*, 846–47.
[152] These movements and the reasons for them are described in detail in 3 *R. E. Lee*, 18 ff.

APPENDIX I

TRANSMISSION OF THE "LOST ORDER"

IN 2 *B. & L.*, 603, appears the best narrative of the finding of the "Lost Order" (S.O., 191, A. N. Va.), the text of which is printed in *O. R.*, 19, pt. 2, pp. 603–04. The copy that fell into Federal hands did not include the first and second paragraphs, which were of no importance to the Federals. McClellan's earliest account of the incident and of the interpretation he put on the order is presented in 1 *Com. Con. War*, 439–40.

D. H. Hill, in *Land We Love*, February, 1868, asserted that the only copy of the order received by him was the one from Jackson, but he must have realized that suspicion of negligence attached to his head-quarters. He accordingly procured from Maj. J. W. Ratchford an affidavit that no other copy than the one from Jackson reached the divisional A.A.G., and then, having exculpated himself and his staff, he maintained that the Army had gained, rather than suffered, because of the loss of the order.

His argument was to this effect: Because the order stated that Long-street would halt at Boonsborough, McClellan proceeded with much caution and great force against South Mountain. Had the Federal commander known how few were the defenders of the mountain, the blue Divisions would have stormed the pass, would have captured the Confederate wagon train and would have interposed fatally between Lee and Jackson. The whole question was reviewed in 12 *S.H.S.P.*, 519–20, 13 *ibid.*, 420, and 21 *ibid.*, 131 ff.

In 1892, when Col. William Allan's authoritative *Army* was pub-lished, he stated categorically that a citizen of Frederick who chanced to be present when the order was handed McClellan notified Stuart of that fact "after night." Allan, *op. cit.*, 345–46, said that "before day-light," Lee knew of the "Lost Order."

Colonel Allan's authority was respected by all writers on the war, but as Stuart and D. H. Hill did not state in their reports that they knew on the 13th–14th of the loss of the order, most studies of the campaign took the view that in this instance, even the careful Allan was misinformed. General Lee's own reference in his report to the find-ing by McClellan of the lost order was not regarded as confirmation of Allan's statement, because Lee prepared his official account after North-ern authorities had admitted in print how they had profited by the

"Lost Order." The present writer, in 2 *R. E. Lee,* 369, n. 72, took the view that the Confederate commander did not know on the 14th of September that McClellan had a copy of S.O. 191.

After the publication of that book, Dr. William Allan of Charlotte, N. C., son of Col. William Allan, courteously placed at the writer's disposal two highly interesting memoranda of conversations held on the same day, Feb. 15, 1868, with General Lee at Lexington. One memorandum was by Colonel Allan, then a Professor at Washington College, and the other by E. C. Gordon, at that time clerk of the institution and subsequently a minister of distinction. To both these gentlemen, General Lee spoke of the article by Hill that recently had appeared in *Land We Love.* Lee manifestly was somewhat irritated by some of Hill's assertions and was less disinclined than usual to discuss military events. Mr. Gordon was so impressed by what General Lee said that he hurried back to his office and wrote down as fully as he could remember it, all that Lee had revealed. Colonel Allan also made his memorandum early, though perhaps not so promptly as Gordon did.

The two documents are of sufficient importance to justify publication in full. Dr. Gordon's memorandum is preceded by a letter to Colonel Allan, dated Nov. 18, 1886.

Col. Wm. Allan
  McDonogh, Md.
My dear Colonel,

On my return from Richmond, after an absence of more than two weeks from home, I found Thom's letter of 2d Nov., enclosing yours to him of Oct. 27th.

I have concluded to send you the *Mem.* I made of my conversation with Gen. Lee. I have not time to copy it. You can have this done—or such parts of it as you may want. Moreover, I prefer that you should see it just as it is, with all the marks of age, and the eagerness with which it was penned. It has some verbal blunders; which, however, do not interfere with but testify to, the truthfulness of the essential points. I went directly from Gen. Lee's office to my own, and at once as rapidly as I could put down all that Gen. Lee had said respecting the "Lost Dispatch."

The conversation made a great impression on me. Then only did Gen. Lee ever talk to me particularly about the war. He was excited, and somewhat indignant with Gen. Hill, particularly with his strictures on General Jackson.

I did not enter in the *Mem.* the estimate he gave me of Gen. McClellan—the substance of which was that he was an able but timid commander; nor could I have entered upon the *Mem.* the flashing of his eyes when he said: "I went into Maryland to give battle, and could I have kept Gen. McClellan in ignorance of my position and plans a day or two longer, I would have fought and crushed him." This quotation is not in the *Mem.* but I have given, if not the *ipsissima verba* of the sentence, the substance of it with a fair amount of verbal accuracy. The distinct and emphatic impression made on me by the conversation was that Gen. Lee attributed without hesitation the loss of the campaign to the "Lost Dispatch."

When I had my recent conversation with Thom, I had not read the *Mem.* for several years. I doubtless misled him respecting the matter of the receipt of the Dispatch. You will observe that the *Mem.* does not state that Gen. Lee had, or had seen, Hill's personal receipt. Gen Lee's testimony is that the order got to Hill's headquarters and was not lost by a courier. In this respect my *Mem.* corresponds exactly with yours. I recollect distinctly that Gen. Lee said: "I do not know who lost the Dispatch—I knew it was lost and the losing of it with the fact that it fell into Gen. McClellan's hands enabled him to discover my whereabouts; revealed to him in part my plans, and caused him so to act as to force a battle on me before I was ready for it."

Several times I have been tempted to give this *Mem.* to the public. I have been restrained by the fact that it would arouse D. H. Hill's anger, and do Gen. Lee no good.

Thom seemed to think that the time had come when it might serve the purpose of defending Gen. Lee from the assaults of Longstreet and others. I have not seen these assaults, and consequently cannot judge about this matter. I do not wish to be involved in any controversy. I have no time for it; nor do I think it would be quite seemly in a man of my position. At the same time, if it can help you in defending Gen. Lee from any unjust and unworthy assaults, it is at your service.

When you are done with it, please return it to me.

With kind regards to Mrs. Allan, as well as to Lyle and yourself, I am

Very truly yours

E. C. Gordon

P.S. All the interlineations, erasures, pencil marks, etc., belong to the *Mem.* as at first prepared.

Interesting Memorandum of a conversation held with Genl. R. E. Lee [by E. C. Gordon] in Lexington, Va., on the 15th of February, 1868.

Going into the Genl's Room on business as usual, when about to leave I asked him if he had read Genl. D. H. Hill's article in the February (1868) No. of the "Land We Love," entitled "The Lost Dispatch." He replied that he had not read it all, but had noticed the principal points in it; that he had not read Mr. E. A. Pollard's book, and was not able to judge of the merits of the question at issue between him and Genl. Hill but that he was sure that Genl. Hill's account of the matter was not correct in several particulars. At some length Genl. Lee then described his movement across the Potomac, the capture of Harpers Ferry, and the operations preceding the battle of Sharpsburg. He stated that McClellan was up to the time of his finding the dispatch in complete ignorance of the whereabouts and intentions of the Southern army. That his, McClellan's, army, widely extended, with its left on the Potomac, was moving only a few miles every day, feeling its way with great caution. Stuart with his cavalry was close up to the enemy and doing everything possible to keep him in ignorance and to deceive him by false reports, which he industriously circulated. That he (Genl. Lee) proposed as soon as possible after the reduction of Harpers Ferry to collect his troops and deliver battle and although Harpers Ferry had not fallen so soon as he had hoped, still if McClellan could have been kept in ignorance but two or three days longer, he did not doubt then (nor has he changed his opinion since) that he could have crushed the army of McClellan, which was to a great extent disorganized and demoralized. That McClellan was informed of his movements, and the position of his troops by the Dispatch to Genl. Hill there could be no doubt. That he himself had gone to Hagerstown at which place there was a quantity of flour, and while there, he received dispatches almost simultaneously from Genl. Stuart and Genl. Hill stating that McClellan had changed his tactics and was endeavoring to drive back Genl. Hill who was near Boonsboro. That Genl. Hill *ought to have* had all his troops up at the mountain, while in fact part were back in Boonsboro. Soon after this intelligence reached him in regard to McClellan, another dispatch arrived from Stuart, stating that he (Stuart) had learned from a gentleman of Maryland who was in McClellan's headquarters when the dispatch from Gen. Lee to Genl. Hill was brought to McClellan, who after reading it, threw his hands up and exclaimed "now I know what to do"—and that he (Genl. Lee) had been much surprised at the sudden change in McClellan's tactics until he learned that he (McC) had thus found out his (Lee's) position, and in consequence he cannot agree with Genl. Hill that the losing of the dispatch was advantageous, but on the contrary a great misfortune. That according to Gen. Hill's account if another dispatch had been lost, the South would have been victorious!! That Genl. Hill is mistaken in his remark in regard to his not receiving orders from him (Genl. Lee) directly. That Genl. Hill had moved up from Richmond, and not being then regularly incorporated in a corps, had been ordered by him to cross the Potomac and had done so in advance of the army—that when Genl. Jackson afterward crossed he had taken command of all the troops then north of the Potomac and thus for a time Genl. Hill was immediately under his command, but that by the very order in question, Genl. Jackson moved with his three divisions together and Genl. Hill was left to bring up the rear and thus removed from Genl. Jackson. That he is confident the order was sent directly to Genl. Hill and that he supposed Genl. Jackson also sent a copy of the order to Genl. Hill—that he, Hill, might know through him that he was no longer under his command. That he cannot suppose the order was lost by a courier as couriers were always required to bring receipt to show that written orders were safely and surely delivered. That Genl. Hill is also mistaken in regard to Genl. Jackson's move to Harpers Ferry being contrary to or without orders. That even if he did not receive written orders to that effect, he remembers distinctly that in a private conversation with Genl. Jackson, the movements were agreed upon and that Genl. Jackson with his usual promptness executed them. Finally in regard to the point made by Hill that it is strange Genl. Lee did not have him cashiered for such great carelessness, Genl. Lee said that he did not know that Genl. Hill had himself lost the dispatch and in consequence he had no grounds upon which to act, but that Genl. Stuart and other officers in the army were very indignant about the matter.

E. C. Gordon

Col. Allan's comment on Mr. Gordon's letter and memorandum follows:

The foregoing was backed thus [by Mr. Gordon]:

Memorandum of a Conversation held with Genl. R. E. Lee at Washington College, Lexington, Va., 15 Feb. 1868—in regard to the operations of the So. Army in Maryland preceding the battle of Sharpsburg and the *"Lost Dispatch."*

(Mr. Gordon was at the time clerk to Gen. Lee and the Faculty of Washington College.)

By comparing dates this conversation with Gordon took place on the same day as that with me which is entered in the earlier part of the book. Gordon always went to see what the General wanted as soon as he (the Gen'l) came to his office, and his conversation no doubt preceded mine—I had lectures about 10 to 12 A.M. and usually went in to see the General before going to lecture. I no doubt saw him an hour or so after Gordon—His talk is substantially the same, as is evident. I knew nothing of his talks with Gordon or of Gordon's notes of it until this fall (Oct. 1886).

Colonel Allan's entry in his own scrapbook is to this effect:
Memoranda of a Conversation with
Gen. R. E. Lee, held Feb. 15, 1868

On going in to see the Gen'l, after talking on other matters, he asked me if I had seen a piece in D. H. Hill's magazine, entitled Lost Dispatch in reference to the first Md. Campaign (1862), and said that there were many mistakes in it. "Hill (the author) says the loss of the dispatch was advantageous to the C. S. cause, but he takes an entirely different view from me." The Gen'l then gave an outline of this campaign.

He said that after Chantilly (about Sept. 1) he found he could do nothing more against the Yankees, unless he attacked them in their fortifications around Washington, which he did not want to do, and he therefore determined to cross the river into Maryland, and thus effect two things—1st, to relieve Va. from both armies, as he thought such a movement would force Gen'l McClellan over the river—and 2nd to live for a time on the abundant supplies in Maryland. That in reference to this he talked to Gen. Jackson, who advised him to go up into the Valley and cross the Potomac at or above Harpers Ferry, cleaning out the forces at Winchester, etc. He (Lee) opposed this, because it took him too far from McClellan, and might not induce the latter to cross over, which was his main object, and he therefore ordered Jackson to take command in advance and cross in Loudon and move towards Frederick, destroying the canal, etc. He sent Stuart with him, and had just ordered D. H. Hill (who had just come up from Richmond), to White's Ferry in anticipation of this. He told Jackson to take Hill with him. He came on with remainder of the army as soon as he could. At Frederick he made Stuart divide his cavalry and threaten both Baltimore and Washington on both flanks of McClellan, giving out on each flank that he (Lee) was behind with his whole force. Stuart reported McClellan near Rockville, advancing very slowly, meanwhile covering Balt. & Washington, uneasy and uncertain. The Yankees still holding Harpers Ferry, etc. in the rear. He formed a plan to overwhelm them by sending three columns, Walker, McLaws and Jackson to center at Harpers Ferry and if possible catch them. Jackson was to take his own three divisions only. Lee kept D. H. Hill and Longstreet and Stuart with himself, Stuart still to demonstrate and deceive the enemy. He had the orders sent from his own headquarters to Hill, as the latter was now under his immediate command, and it was perfectly proper for Gen. Jackson to do so too, to inform Hill that he was no longer under his (Jackson's) orders. The orders named the points to be reached by the divisions concentrating at Harpers Ferry, and indicated the purpose, but this had all been fully *explained* to Jackson verbally, and no one could imagine that the order did not contemplate just what Jackson did. He then retired from Frederick as McClellan advanced, and held the Gap in the Mountain with Hill, keeping Stuart to watch and deceive the enemy. He then took Longstreet and went to Hagerstown, to capture flour and stores there which were being run off to Pa. Longstreet did not like marching, and said "Gen., I wish we could stand still and let the d——d Yankees come to us!" The night he was at Hagerstown he rec'd a dispatch from Stuart, saying that McClellan had taken the advance, and was pushing with his whole force, and that he (Stuart), was falling back. Later, an alarming dispatch was also received from Hill to same effect. Lee then wakened Longstreet and began to march back at daylight. Hot day and troops tired when they reached Boonesboro but gap was held. Stuart informed him of report of a Md. gentleman, who said he was at McClellan's H. Qrs. when Lost Dispatch was found and that he (McC.) openly expressed his delight. This night Lee found out that Cobb had been pressed back from Crampton's Gap, and this made it necessary to retire from Boonesboro Gap, which was done next morning and position at Sharpsburg taken. Message was sent to hurry up Jackson (who was a day later than expected), and battle was given at Sharpsburg with a tired and weakened force (about 35,000 men) and not all on the ground till late in the day. Had the Lost Dispatch not been lost, and had McClellan continued his cautious policy for two or three days longer, I (Lee) would have had all my troops reconcentrated on Md. side, stragglers up, men rested and *intended then to attack McClellan,* hoping the best results from state of my troops and those of enemy. Tho' it is impossible to say that victory would have certainly resulted, it is probable that the loss of the dispatch changed the character of the campaign. He spoke very highly of Jackson, said D. H. Hill had such a queer temperament he could never tell what to expect from him, and that he croaked. This was the case around Petersburg in 1864, when Beauregard complained of it to Gen. Lee....

(The rest of this conversation has to do with the origin of the turning movement at Chancellorsville.)

These memoranda show, first, that General Lee in the autumn of 1868 believed the finding of the "Lost Order" was a major reason for the failure of the Maryland Expedition. Lee was convinced, second, that the copy of the order signed by his A.A.G. reached Hill's headquarters. General Chilton was of the same opinion. In replying December 8, 1874, to some inquiry Mr. Davis had sent him, Chilton reminded the President that when important orders were dispatched, the courier was required to bring back the signed envelope or other evidence of delivery. Had a receipt not been returned by Hill's headquarters in a case so important, said Chilton, the omission almost certainly would have been noted. (7 *Rowland*, 412.)

The memoranda prove, also, that Lee received during the night of September 13–14, or on September 14 information that McClellan was said on credible authority to have a copy of S.O. 191. Lee's movements thereafter took into account the probability, if not the certainty, that McClellan knew the disposition and plans of the Confederates.

Left in doubt is one question only: When did Lee receive from Stuart the report of the statement made by the citizen of Frederick? Mr. Gordon's understanding was that Lee said Stuart sent him the bad news during the night of September 13–14. Colonel Allan's language in his memorandum might be interpreted to mean that Lee did not hear about the lost order until the afternoon of the 14th, but in 14 *S. H. S. P.*, issued in 1886, Colonel Allan said unequivocally that Lee received the information during the previous night.

The known factors for timing the receipt of the news of the "Lost Order" are: (1) Hill and Stuart sent dispatches to Lee after nightfall; (2) Lee told Gordon that information of the reported finding of the order was received by him "soon after" dispatches from D. H. Hill and Stuart; (3) Hill said that instructions from Lee were received about midnight. (See *supra*, p. 171.)

If these instructions were in answer to Hill's dispatch, as seems likely, then Lee heard from Hill before 10 o'clock, because an absolute minimum of two hours would have been required to send back to Boonsborough, even at a gallop and by changed horses, a reply that got there "about midnight." A dispatch from Stuart, then, anent the "Lost Order," might have reached Lee "soon after" 10 P.M. The time might have been an hour earlier, but scarcely before 9 P.M., if the messenger from Hill to Lee left Hill "after nightfall." Anyone with a knowledge of Stuart's promptness and regularity in forwarding reports to Lee will find it difficult to believe that, if Stuart had this important news on the night of the 13th–14th, he would have waited even half an hour in sending it off to headquarters.

Finally, were there no other evidence to confirm the statement that Lee said he got the news of the "Lost Order" during the night of September 13–14, this would have to be considered: After dawn, even a native might have found difficulty in crossing the guarded mountain passes, as Stuart's informant did.

For these reasons, the conclusion is warranted that the news reached Stuart early in the night of Sept. 13–14, passed swiftly to Lee, and almost certainly reached G.H.Q. the same night, though the hour cannot be determined.

There seems no justification for the statement in Fitzgerald Ross, *The Cities and Camps of the Confederate States*, 45–46, that: "Hill lost an equally important order before the seven days' fighting around Richmond, and it was found on a prisoner who was captured at Gaines's Mill. Unaware, perhaps, of its importance, he had not sent it to headquarters, or it would have done incalculable mischief." In this, Ross may have misdated and misplaced the finding at Hill's Point, N. C., of a note of Hill's. Concerning this, Hill wrote April 26, 1863: "The note . . . was not important, at least I think not." (*O. R.*, 18, 1023.) None of the detail of this is known.

Manuscripts listed here solely by the name of an individual are described briefly in Vol. I, p. 741 ff. The few collections mentioned in more detail are those that were not sufficiently used in Vol. I to justify inclusion there, but have been consulted in the preparation of this volume. In the manuscript section of the General Bibliography, Vol. III, will be found references to all the principal manuscript sources.

BRIG. GEN. E. P. ALEXANDER—A volume of his papers, chiefly souvenirs, is in the Library of Congress.

COL. WILLIAM ALLAN—A scrap book and various important memoirs of the Chief Ordnance Officer of the Second Corps are the property of his son, Dr. William Allan of Charlotte, N. C.

LT. GEN. RICHARD H. ANDERSON.

MAJ. W. N. BERKELEY.

LT. COL. W. W. BLACKFORD.

MAJ. J. K. BOSWELL.

COL. J. THOMPSON BROWN.

LUCY R. BUCK, Front Royal, Va.

MRS. ROBERT RANDOLPH CARTER of Shirley—Post bellum memoir of life at Shirley, Charles City County.

BRIG. GEN. R. H. CHILTON.

BRIG. GEN. P. ST. GEORGE COCKE.

BRIG. GEN. R. E. COLSTON.

BRIG. GEN. JOHN R. COOKE.

MAJ. JOHN ESTEN COOKE.

MAJ. R. L. DABNEY.

DECKER BROTHERS LETTERS—These letters, owned by Dr. Henry Decker, Richmond, Virginia, were written during the war by Walker John Decker and Marshall Elton Decker, who lived in the Wilderness, belonged to the Ninth Virginia Cavalry, and often acted as couriers for the principal officers.

LT. GEN. JUBAL A. EARLY—All of his surviving MSS, including many letters from other officers, are in the Library of Congress.

BRIG. GEN. N. G. EVANS.

LT. GEN. R. S. EWELL.

COL. J. W. FAIRFAX.

BRIG. GEN. RICHARD B. GARNETT—The papers in his defense at the court martial ordered by Jackson are in the Confederate Museum.

BRIG. GEN. R. S. GARNETT.

D. H. GORDON, Fredericksburg, Va.

MAJ. J. A. HARMAN.

COL. J. C. HASKELL.

MAJ. GEN. HENRY HETH.

LT. GEN. D. H. HILL.

MAJ. JED. HOTCHKISS.

LT. GEN. T. J. JACKSON.

GEN. JOSEPH E. JOHNSTON.

GEN. R. E. LEE.

BRIG. GEN. A. L. LONG—A memoir of his service prior to his appointment as Chief of Artillery.

MAJ. GEN. JOHN B. MAGRUDER.

MAJ. H. B. McCLELLAN.

MEDICAL DIRECTOR HUNTER McGUIRE.

MAJ. R. J. MOSES. His MS memoirs of the war are owned by his grandson, Lionel B. Moses, of Evanston, Ill.

BRIG. GEN. T. T. MUNFORD.

MAJ. GEN. W. DORSEY PENDER.

BRIG. GEN. W. N. PENDLETON.

MAJ. CHANNING PRICE.

MAJ. GEN. S. DODSON RAMSEUR.

MAJ. GEN. ROBERT RANSOM.

LT. FRANK ROBERTSON, Assistant Engineer, Cavalry Corps, Army Northern Virginia—A post bellum MS memoir, "In the Saddle with Stuart," which contains some unpublished incidents of the preliminaries of Chancellorsville and of the operations in Pennsylvania, June–July, 1863. This memoir belongs to Pres. F. R. Reade, Georgia State Woman's College, Valdosta, Ga.

MAJ. GEN. THOMAS L. ROSSER.

JOHN SPEAR SMITH—A collection of the papers of this distinguished Baltimorean includes his diary, that of his son, Louis, and various family manuscripts and letters from Confederate leaders. These papers are the property of Robert Hill Carter of Richmond and of Dr. Burr Noland Carter of Cincinnati.

MAJ. GEN. W. B. TALIAFERRO.

LT. COL. WALTER H. TAYLOR.

MAJ. GEN. I. R. TRIMBLE—His later wartime letters, rich in interest, are owned by his great-grandson, Dr. I. R. Trimble, of Baltimore, Md.

MAJ. GEN. CADMUS M. WILCOX—In addition to the memoirs, etc., mentioned in Vol. I, numerous of his wartime letters were found in 1942 by his niece, Mrs. Moncure Burke, Washington, D. C.

R. S. WILKINS—A distinguished collection of Confederate autograph letters is among the treasures of this Bostonian.

SHORT-TITLE INDEX

(Cumulative for Volumes I and II)

Alexander. E. P. ALEXANDER. Military Memoirs of a Confederate.
Allan's Army. WILLIAM ALLAN. The Army of Northern Virginia in 1862.
Allan, William. WILLIAM ALLAN. History of the Campaign of Gen. T. J.
  (Stonewall) Jackson in the Shenandoah Valley of Virginia.
Avirett. J. B. AVIRETT. The Memoirs of General Turner Ashby and his
  Compeers.
Beale. R. L. T. BEALE. History of the Ninth Virginia Cavalry.
Beale, G. W. G. W. BEALE. A Lieutenant of Cavalry in Lee's Army.
Beauregard. P. G. T. BEAUREGARD. Commentary on the Campaign and
  Battle of Manassas.
Bigelow. JOHN BIGELOW, JR. The Campaign of Chancellorsville.
B. & L. Battles and Leaders of the Civil War.
Brent. J. L. BRENT. Memoirs of the War Between the States.
Brock, Miss. "A Richmond Lady" [Sally Brock]. Richmond During the
  War.
Caldwell. J. F. J. CALDWELL. A History of a Brigade of South Caro-
  linians Known First as "Gregg's" . . .
Casler. JOHN O. CASLER. Four Years in the Stonewall Brigade.
Chamberlaine, W. W. W. W. CHAMBERLAINE. Memoirs of the Civil War.
Chamberlayne, Ham. C. G. CHAMBERLAYNE, ed. Ham Chamberlayne—
  Virginian.
Chesnut, Mrs. MARY BOYKIN CHESNUT. A Diary from Dixie.
Christian's Richmond. W. A. CHRISTIAN. Richmond, Her Past and Present.
C. M. H. CLEMENT A. EVANS, ed. Confederate Military History.
Com. Con. War. Report of the Committee [of the U. S. Congress] on the
  Conduct of the War.
Companions in Arms. "A Distinguished Southern Journalist" [E. A. POL-
  LARD]. The Early Life, Campaigns, and Public Services of Robert E.
  Lee, with a Record of the Campaigns and Heroic Deeds of his Com-
  panions in Arms.
Cooke's Jackson. J. E. COOKE. Stonewall Jackson, A Military Biography
  (edition of 1866).
Conner. MARY C. MOFFETT, ed. Letters of General James Conner.
Cullum. G. W. CULLUM. Biographical Register of Officers and Graduates
  of the U. S. Military Academy.
C. V. Confederate Veteran.
D. A. B. Dictionary of American Biography.
Dabney. R. L. DABNEY. Life and Campaigns of Lieut.-Gen. Thomas J.
  Jackson.
Daly, Mrs. LOUISE HASKELL DALY. Alexander Cheves Haskell.
Davis. JEFFERSON DAVIS. The Rise and Fall of the Confederate Govern-
  ment.

INDEX

Unless otherwise indicated or generally familiar, all place names in this index are for Virginia, which in 1861 included the present State of West Virginia. The rank credited to officers is the highest held in either Union or Confederate service, including brevets, at any time, and not merely during the period through May, 1863. In the case of men who held commission in the United States Army before secession and subsequently served as officers in the Southern Army, the Confederate rank only is given.